The
Faces of
REASON
AN ESSAY ON
PHILOSOPHY AND CULTURE
IN ENGLISH CANADA 1850-1950

LESLIE ARMOUR AND ELIZABETH TROTT

The Faces of Reason traces the history of philosophy in English Canada from 1850 to 1950, examining the major English-Canadian philosophers in detail and setting them in the context of the main currents of Canadian thought. The book concludes with a brief survey of the period after 1950.

What is distinctive in Canadian philosophy, say the authors, is the concept of reason and the uses to which it is put. Reason has interacted with experience in a new world and a cold climate to create a distinctive Canadian community. The diversity of political, geographic, social, and religious factors has fostered a particular kind of thinking, particular ways of reasoning and communicating. Rather than one grand, over-arching Canadian way of thinking, there are "many faces of reason," "a kind of philosophic federalism."

The book has two dimensions: "it is a continuous story which makes a point about the development of philosophical reason in the Canadian context. . . . it is a reference work which may be consulted by readers interested in particular figures, ideas, movements or periods."

Leslie Armour, who received the Ph.D. degree from the University of London, is Professor of Philosophy at the University of Ottawa. The major published works of this prolific author are Logic and Reality *and* The Concept of Truth.

Elizabeth Trott, who holds the Ph.D. degree from the University of Waterloo, has taught philosophy at several Canadian universities. She has written and presented many national radio programs for the CBC.

The Faces of REASON

AN ESSAY ON PHILOSOPHY AND CULTURE IN ENGLISH CANADA 1850-1950

LESLIE ARMOUR AND ELIZABETH TROTT

Wilfrid Laurier University Press

Canadian Cataloguing in Publication Data

Armour, Leslie, 1931-
    The faces of reason

Includes index.
ISBN 0-88920-107-2

1. Philosophy − Canada − History. I. Trott, Elizabeth
Anne. II. Title.

B981.A75   191   C81-094938-5

Designer: George W. Roth, AOCA MGDC

CONTENTS

PORTRAITS

by Kathryn Cole

WILLIAM LYALL
1811-1890
Dalhousie University

viii

GEORGE PAXTON YOUNG
1818-1889
Knox College   University College
University of Toronto

JOHN CLARK MURRAY
1836-1917
Queen's University
McGill University

JOHN WATSON
1847-1939
Queen's University

GEORGE JOHN BLEWETT
1873-1912
Victoria College
University of Toronto

GEORGE SIDNEY BRETT
1879-1944
University of Toronto

ACKNOWLEDGMENTS

S PECIAL THANKS ARE due to many people. Amongst them are
Clifford Williams who lent us his two theses and other research
material which proved indispensable; Roland Houde who gave
us full access to his as yet unpublished massive bibliography; Yvan
Lamonde who shared with us his work on French-Canadian thought;
Hilton Page who guided us through the work of some Maritime thinkers; the Reverend William Briggs who shared with us memories of
Rupert Lodge; Thomas Goudge who shared his extensive knowledge
on many issues; and the Reverend F. W. Waters who gave us notes on,
and shared his personal knowledge of, James Ten Broeke.

Sincere gratitude is extended to Constance Blewett who lent us
books of her father, George Blewett, and an unpublished biography of
him by William J. Rose; to Alice M. S. Lighthall who spoke with us
about her father, W. D. Lighthall, and lent us his books; to Molly Irving
who provided us with material about John Irving; and to Walter H.
Johns who arranged for us an interview with John Macdonald.

There are many others, too numerous to mention, from Canada,
who talked and corresponded with us and to whom we owe thanks.
During research travels to England and Scotland further insight was
gained into the traditions and backgrounds of the philosophers who
came to Canada in discussions with Robin Downie, Margaret Paton, Sir
T. M. Knox, and Richard S. Peters, and to them go special thanks.

Allison Johnson probably knows as much about philosophy in
English Canada as anyone alive and he willingly shared his knowledge
and his books. Michael Cross and George Grant shared with us historical perspectives, and Morton Paterson, who initiated the first work-
shop on Canadian philosophy, corresponded with us about Blewett.
Douglas Verney and Robin Mathews took a constant interest in our
project and urged us on. And the works and encouraging words of
Northrop Frye and George Grant helped us finish the task.

The sheer logistics of discovery were simplified enormously by
archivists across the country—in particular Sandra Guillaume, Charles

xv

Armour, and the entire archival staff at Queen's University. Special mention must also be made of librarians who went out of their way to give us extended loans of old books, and who dug out material "of interest"—in particular, Sharon Brown, Susan Johnston, and Lila Laasko.

Credit must be given to Cindy Bellinger who unpuzzled some of the manuscript from tapes and typed much of it; to Kathryn Cole for her perceptive art work; and to Jean Trott who did the final proofreading. The help of Diana Armour, Vern Trott, Joanne and Bruce Moyle was crucial to completing the task. And without the help of the Canada Council the task could scarcely have been begun, or finished. This book has been published with the help of a grant from the Canadian Federation for the Humanities, using funds provided by the Social Sciences and Humanities Research Council of Canada. We are grateful.

Finally, personal thanks go to Professor Harold Remus, Director of Wilfrid Laurier University Press, for so willingly putting the lengthy manuscript into print, and to Janet Kaethler, Copy Editor, for examining and checking every detail graciously and professionally. Her help was indispensable.

September 1980

L.A.
B.T.

NOTES FROM THE AUTHORS

PHILOSOPHY DOES and should, no doubt, arouse the passions as well as the intellect. But when it does, one is apt to be surprised. Philosophy is not really, however, composed of distant abstractions but of animating frameworks of ideas which give meaning to the structures they organize. To call attention to a body of philosophy which has its centre in a place and time is, therefore, very often at least, to evoke meanings which threaten the established understandings. To revive Canadian philosophy is, inevitably, to raise the possibility of the viability of a culture whose values in some respects clash with those of the cultures whose world views tend to dominate our affairs. Just because a different set of meanings is involved, such an intrusion may seem irrelevant and incomprehensible. But it may also seem threatening.

I first heard of the Canadian idealists (principally of John Watson) when I was an undergraduate at the University of British Columbia. But even then and there Canadians were a distinct minority and the books of Canadian philosophers were not easy to come by. When I arrived at the University of London as a graduate student in 1952, I discovered that Watson was not forgotten in England, though he was mainly remembered as a Kant scholar.

Over the years, I found and read some works of Watson, and learned more of Blewett, but other interests supervened until 1969 when I returned from a sabbatical leave in England. I found that my

My own personal involvement in doing research on Canadian philosophy was initiated during the course of my doctoral studies at the University of Waterloo. I had rejected an offer of a place as a doctoral student at the London School of Economics in order to do an extended study on theories of the Absolute under the direction of a Canadian scholar in my own country.

Professor Leslie Armour, my supervisor, first suggested to me that I might include some thoughts of Canadian philosophers in my thesis on "Experience and the Absolute." The idea was well-received by some members of my committee, but not by all. Nonetheless I did in-department chairman at the University of Waterloo had responded to the concerns expressed by Robin Mathews and Jim Steele about the "de-Canadianization" of Canadian universities with a memorandum announcing that "there *is* no Canadian philosophy" (he added "in the sense in which there is American philosophy"). That chairman was an American in a department dominantly American—the products of an educational system in which, for the most part, Canada is a blank space on the map populated mainly by hockey players without teeth. But such a reaction is not inconceivable amongst Canadians, either. It is no doubt compounded by the natural tendency—which one also finds amongst Englishmen in Paris or Frenchmen in New York—for men to band together with their countrymen and look with disdain at the natives. When one is abroad, the local culture is threatening even though the same idea may seem quite harmless from the safe perspective of home.

But the case for Canadian philosophy did have to be *made*. It was not to be found set out in a neat treatise, though the foundations for such a treatise had been laid by men like John Irving and Allison Johnson. I set out at once for the libraries in Montreal and Toronto. The result was a passionate controversy. The Canada Council provided money and many people provided help—above all Betty Trott, who proved indispensable, first as senior research assistant and then as co-author. But the atmosphere of controversy is not ideal for a task which requires a measure of detachment and critical judgment. Fortunately, the Cleveland State University was looking for a department chairman. They extended to me an invitation which resulted in

clude an assessment of the theories of two major philosophers, John Watson and George Blewett. It was during that period of my work and research that I came in contact with the works of several other notable Canadian philosophers, and I realized then that I had explored only a few of the available works of our early scholars. Much work needed to be done and with this book, Leslie and I have made but a modest beginning.

During the course of my research in Canada there were those who provided me with assistance, generous beyond my expectations. But I must add that I encountered more scepticism than I expected.

During the course of my research in the British Isles I met with enthusiastic responses from many persons knowledgeable about our Canadian philosophers. Memories of pleasant discourse during tea time with Sir Malcolm Knox in Scotland and Professor R. S. Peters in London helped obliterate some of the less enchanting moments I encountered amongst colleagues in my own country.

Professor Armour's constant enthusiasm and leadership have been vital to the project and I am grateful to him.

One fact became obvious to me as I was working on the book, and has become more so since its completion. Interest in Canadian scholarship, both past and present, is increasing yearly, particularly amongst graduate students. Many times I have encountered students in education, history, sociology, psychology, literature, and political science, as well as in philosophy, who pressed me for details of Canadian philosophical theories. I was happy to provide assistance. It is our hope that this book will be of use to future scholars, not only of six of the happiest years of my professional existence. This book is only part of the work I was able to complete in those years. I hope that it shows the results of an atmosphere of serious and critical understanding which my colleagues there provided, and that they will think that I used wisely the time which was so often available only because they generously shared in the day-to-day tasks of my life as a department chairman (and, in my final year, as Dean of Arts and Sciences).

It needs hardly be said that without the hard work and creative intelligence of Betty Trott, this book would not exist.

philosophy, but of all the humanities.

Geraldine Sherman, Executive Producer of the program *IDEAS*, CBC-FM Stereo, is also aware of the growing interest and approved the production of nine hours of programming in 1980 on "Early Canadian Philosophers." I am very grateful to her for giving me the opportunity to write and present them with Max Allen as Producer.

Of my parents, who have sacrificed enormously and worked willingly to see the project through, I am deeply appreciative.

Ottawa, Ontario
September 1980

Toronto, Ontario
September 1980

PREFACE

THIS IS A STUDY of the history of philosophy in a particular setting—a study of the connections between certain rather general and fundamental ideas and the circumstances in which they have been embodied. The ideas are those widely agreed to constitute "philosophy" in its academic sense and the circumstances are comprised of events and institutions which we know as English Canada. "Philosophy," "history," and even "Canada," are problematic terms. The enterprise involved in delineating their relation is itself a subject of legitimate concern.

There is little agreement about what philosophy is if one insists upon details. But it is certainly widely enough construed to include the theory of knowledge, the theory of value, the development of very general models of the nature of reality, and the art or science of inference. The theory of knowledge is what links the cognitive disciplines, and the theory of value is the link between the normative disciplines. Whether the theory of knowledge and the theory of value are, themselves, ultimately one subject is a matter of philosophical dispute. One who knows what knowledge is presumably knows what there is or might be to know. In some way one is involved with the question of what reality is like, or with what it is not like. One who is interested in these questions is surely concerned with the art or science of inference. One's ability to frame questions of such generality is a product of what one knows in the most general sense; the extent to which one or another thesis seems probable or palatable is related to one's beliefs or values. Thus, for example, one's ability to envisage the whole of nature as a mechanistic system must stem from one's ability to recognize some occasions or devices as being machine-like. One's resistance to such a notion is likely to depend upon whether or not one has certain beliefs about human beings and whether or not one values free action. Mechanistic determinism is more likely to be a view held in a society with a fair amount of scientific knowledge and in a highly organized, impersonal society composed mainly of atheists than in a society composed of persons with no scientific knowledge who lack much organization and who are polytheists. It seems natural that the philosophy of Thomas Hobbes should develop along with the first flush of modern science and after the breakdown of the general power of the Roman Catholic Church. That it should be associated with a highly organized society which seemed threatened with anarchy seems equally natural. But it is only when one has a substantial body of material to work from that one can establish such connections at all.

This book is not a compendium of everything written in Canada by anyone who might be considered a philosopher. It deals with those philosophers whose writing was extensive and covered a substantial variety of topics. Furthermore, it deals with them in their context. If one is dealing with a philosopher whose work proceeds, for instance, from a consideration of the ideas of Kant and Kant's followers, one must find out what distinguishes his thought from its model, how Kant could have been understood in a certain way, and what philosophical and cultural elements might have been involved. Critical analysis, the establishment of the philosophical background, and the location of the most general elements in the historical situation are all features of the task. In the case of Canadian philosophy, the necessary sorting could not have been done if nothing had been known: We were able to draw upon the pioneering work of John Irving, Roland Houde, and Clifford Williams.

The time span was fixed for us by events: The first professional philosophy produced in Canada seems to have been a book published by James Beaven in 1850 and that, as well, might reasonably be taken as the period, roughly, when the ideas which were to issue in Confederation were becoming quite firmly fixed and the notion of "Canada" as we now know it was becoming intelligible. There is a coherent development of Canadian philosophy up to a period which certainly ends a few years after World War II. After that, though some traditions remain, the deluge of fashionable ideas from abroad and the mass immigration of philosophers who embodied them complicate the story.

Spatial boundaries are drawn for reasons of political necessity or convenience. Culturally, Canada is dominantly a collection of French, Scottish, and Loyalist settlements—linked by the fact that these groups were relatively untouched by, or actively resisted, the European upsurge of enlightenment individualism—and of groups of people who settled around them and were influenced by their proximity in space and time. Geographically, however, Canada includes groups of people not very obviously influenced by that dominant culture—

Englishmen in British Columbia, Americans in Alberta, and many others—and significant numbers of native peoples who are culturally what they are, in part, because they *were* included in Canada but who still have an ambivalent relationship to that culture (which worries many of them and the more thoughtful of us).

The word English in the title is, perhaps, easy enough: We have confined ourselves to what was written in English on the assumption that Canada is a place, however arbitrary, but that English Canada is simply that part of the Canadian situation associated with the English language. Philosophers at McGill who worked in English form part of our concern while philosophers at the University of Ottawa who worked in French do not. The association of language with component sub-cultures is not, indeed, perfect but it is close enough to do for rough and ready purposes. And though there are very close relations between them, there are characteristic differences between philosophy in French Canada and in English Canada which warrant an initial separation. Hopefully, this is only a prelude to a study of the relations between them. A strong start on the study of philosophy in French Canada has been made by Yvan Lamonde and Roland Houde.[1]

Within English Canada we have had to make our choices as best we could. We have confined ourselves to philosophers who lived for long periods in Canada and who wrote their most important works while they were here. Some of the major figures we have written about were native Canadians but most were not, and we have not explored the technicalities of official nationality. (The notion of Canadian citizen as opposed to British subject is a very recent one in Canada.)

We are concerned with philosophy in its usually understood academic sense. But it would have seemed odd to have ignored Bucke and Lighthall even though many professional philosophers will find their deviation from the accepted canons sufficiently great to justify their omission.

We have been concerned to locate the philosophers in a culture. The sense of culture as the system of ideas which provides one's basic orientation in belief and value is itself critical and by no means easy to explicate. Indeed, it must be approached obliquely just because it is what is always there in the background but seldom made explicit.

The critical feature of a culture in the intended sense is the manner in which it assigns meanings to human actions and to public events. As a rule one knows there are two cultures when there are two

---

1   Yvan Lamonde, *Historiographie de la philosophie au Québec, 1853-1971* (Montreal: Hurtubise HMH [Les Cahiers du Québec, 9], 1972); Roland Houde, *Histoire et philosophie au Québec* (Trois-Rivières: Editions du Bien Public, 1979).

groups of people who, characteristically and repeatedly, assign different meanings to the same act or event. But cultures change and evolve. That must be particularly the case with "Canadian culture," young, open to the influences of the outside world, and subject to the changing composition of its population. The problem, therefore, is to identify the coherent base from which one starts and the process through which change takes place.

One of the most crucial features of any set of cultural determinants (or even cultural symptoms) is the working concept of reason. We employ reason to extend the reach of our culture, to change it by assigning new meanings, and to resist encroachments by others. A central concern of nearly all (perhaps all) philosophers has been with the nature and uses of reason. The concept of reason, therefore, seems to provide a useful starting point for inquiry. Our study does show characteristic notions of reason and it does show that notions have tended to change in ways which have parallelled the changes in other social phenomena—and so we have called it *The Faces of Reason*.

If philosophy is connected with reason and reason is connected with culture, then philosophy has unavoidable social implications. One may become free of one's presuppositions only by bringing them clearly to light and by understanding their force. In *La trahison des clercs*, Julien Benda deplored the sell-out of the intellectuals in our time.[2] Instead of keeping their minds on the true and the eternal, they have, he thought, become the lackeys of the state and served whatever political end is convenient for the moment. But he also noticed something else: Our time is one of cultural imperialism. Politicians seek to impose their vision of a culture on as much of the world as they can influence. The Romans valued and respected the Greek culture as Alexander had valued and respected the cultures of the world he conquered. But the great powers of our time seek cultural homogeneity. (Perhaps in an era dominated by mass communication when political power depends upon popular response and when the economics of mass production demand a mass taste, that is not surprising.) Most of what Benda said is surely true, and the creation of an understanding of one's culture is the intellectual's best defence against those who would obliterate it for political reasons, and his best chance of coming to terms with his own presuppositions so that he *can* seek the eternally true. (This book, at any rate, is a work by two metaphysicians whose professional lives have been devoted to what are, at least, persistent attempts to understand what it is to make claims about the nature

2   Julien Benda, *La trahison des clercs*, trans. Richard Aldington as *The Treason of the Intellectuals* (New York: W. W. Norton, 1969).

of truth, the character of the Absolute, and the ultimate structures of logic.)[3]

The project which originated at the University of Waterloo has taken not the two years we supposed, but nearly ten. A grant from the Canada Council helped us begin the task but the manuscript which we hoped to confine to 100,000 words grew into 300,000 words. The present version has been reduced by one-quarter at the request of the Canadian Federation for the Humanities. Financial assistance for publication depended on a shortened manuscript.

Our book has two dimensions. In one, it is a continuous story which makes a point about the development of philosophical reason in the Canadian context. In another, it is a reference work which may be consulted by readers interested in particular figures, ideas, movements or periods. For the former, it is important that there not be repetition; for the latter, chapters must be made as self-contained as possible. Where there is a conflict, limitations of space have made it inevitable that the former take precedence over the latter. In all, there was at least three times as much material as we expected. What we have achieved is only a beginning.

The principal casualty of the deletions was a final chapter which sought to trace the fate after 1950 of the movements described earlier. In fact, the idealist movement continues—though it has been given new shapes by intersection with other philosophical ideas. There are Canadian philosophers strongly influenced as well by movements as diverse as Oxford analysis and Husserlian phenomenology. What John Irving called the "Toronto school of intellectual history" flourishes still, as does Roman Catholic philosophy in a Thomist tradition. And there are signs of new activities in system building. These may be obscured by the imported ideological duststorms of the day, but they are there. The last chapter, however, had constantly to be updated as the work moved toward publication and it merits a separate (hopefully short!) book. Other deletions included important parts of the discussion of the British idealists—a discussion necessary to exhibit clearly the originality of Murray, Schurman, Watson, and Blewett. Much biographical material was sacrificed along with an extended discussion of Caldwell and his relation to Watson, a section which related Mur-

---

3   Leslie Armour, *The Rational and the Real* (The Hague: Martinus Nijhoff, 1962), *The Concept of Truth* (Assen: Van Gorcum, N.V.; New York: Humanities Press, 1969), *Logic and Reality* (Assen: Van Gorcum, N.V.; New York: Humanities Press, 1972); Leslie Armour and Edward T. Bartlett III, *The Conceptualization of the Inner Life* (Atlantic Highlands, New Jersey: Humanities Press, 1980); Elizabeth Trott, "Experience and the Absolute" (Ph.D. dissertation, University of Waterloo, 1971).

ray's psychology to some present-day trends, and a discussion of Watson's last fragmentary notes on psychology.

The authors regret the deletions but we will be glad to help any reader seeking additional information.

Ottawa and Toronto
February 2, 1981

ONE

BACKGROUNDS AND THEMES

P
HILOSOPHY, CONSIDERED as an academic discipline, came to English Canada in the middle of the nineteenth century. James Beaven published, in 1850, what was, in all likelihood, the first technical philosophical work written in English in Canada.[1]

Others had taught philosophy before him in a less formal way and others, inevitably, had included philosophical reflections in their writings. But the enterprise launched with Beaven's appointment in Toronto was deliberate and distinctive. Philosophy's time had come because a pluralistic community needed a common strand of reason and Beaven symbolized the appropriate response.

His major philosophical work seeks to show how reason may provide a common core which underlies a vast variety of religious belief and it reveals a man much changed from the narrowly oriented high-church Anglicanism with which he had arrived in Canada. Outwardly he remained the "dry old stick," in the words of a later president of the University of Toronto;[2] but his writings reveal a man sensitive to the situation in his adopted country: He remained an Anglican attached to his dogmas, but he understood the significance of the final abandonment of the dream of an "established church" in Canada. He remained an Englishman in manner and diction, but he understood that he lived in a country in which the English must accept the dominance of the Scots and the Irish. The new politics were more than he could readily accept, but one may guess that he understood that the upper middle class from which he came would no longer rule simply as a matter of course.

Philosophy, in its most general sense, is an attempt to use reason to establish what, without it, is most often established by emotion and intuition: a basic world view, a preference for one set of values over

1   James Beaven, *Elements of Natural Theology* (London: F. and J. Rivington, 1850).
2   *Dictionary of Canadian Biography, 1871-1880*, ed. Marc La Terreur, vol. 10 (Toronto: University of Toronto Press, 1972), p. 40.

another, and a set of criteria by which knowledge may be distinguished from unfounded belief. It tends, therefore, to come into its own in the lives of individuals when circumstances force a change in one of those ingredients and in the affairs of communities when circumstances either force such a change or compel men with different basic outlooks to make common cause. Philosophy, one may guess, came to James Beaven in much the way that it came to English Canada. Beaven had been a minor religious propagandist, a modestly successful preacher, and a scholar with a rather limited outlook. In Canada, his learning needed repair and his beliefs needed defence. Both facts may have come as a surprise to him. But the country was in the same condition. If we are to understand our subject we must first look at that condition.

People frequently change countries so that they will not have to make other changes which they regard as more fundamental or more important. For many highland Scots, Canada provided an alternative to moving to the towns, becoming paid employees, or subjecting themselves to social forces which threatened their tightly-knit communities. For many Irishmen, Canada offered an alternative to being on the losing side in economic, social, and religious conflict. For English dissenters and Scottish Baptists among others, Canada was large and open enough to provide them with an opportunity to continue their religious practices while escaping the handicaps which were associated with them. For the most part, they did not come with the intention of building a brave new world but with the intention of preserving whatever seemed important to them. Furthermore, they tended to come not one by one, but in groups and clusters, and then to scatter according to the various plans of land settlement agencies and companies. Thus, even now, across parts of Ontario there are patterns of alternating Catholic and Protestant villages—an arrangement which tends to promote the inward-looking homogeneity of one's own cross-roads but gives the surrounding world something of an air of hostility. Such a situation makes for a rather conservative outlook. Mixed with these arrivals had been a population which moved north on the premise that the American revolution was an unwarranted interference with Divine Providence and established wealth. These migrants did not, presumably, find the conservative outlook uncongenial.

One cannot, however, simply sit in one's cowshed and play the bagpipes. Somebody had to decide whether there was to be an established church, how the schools were to be run, whether the English could still rule by divine right, what relations ought to obtain with the French in Lower Canada, how the remaining land was to be divided and where the roads were to go.

The peculiarity of these questions in English Canada is part of the peculiarity which has influenced philosophy in English Canada. Presumably, if the British had cared enough they could have settled the answers to these questions in London and sent young men with Oxford educations to see that they were carried out. Presumably, they did not care that much, or everyone had had enough of contumacious settlers during the American revolution, or Mackenzie's little rebellion had frightened a lot of bureaucrats who knew well enough what it was to confront prickly Scots. Perhaps if the migrant communities had been less concerned to protect established values and more concerned to preach some new road to salvation, they would have produced leaders capable of uniting the region around some all-embracing set of principles from which answers to these various questions could have been deduced. But they did not. Finally, had they been richer, better organized, or closer to each other in a smaller country, the various communities might have settled their differences by violence. Admittedly, it was not unknown for boys from the Protestant villages to throw stones at the St. Patrick's Day parade in the next village or for boys from the Catholic villages to disrupt the Orangeman's Day parade by tying a mare in heat to the post office just before King Billy came by on his huge white stallion. But serious violence is expensive, requires organization, and usually demands a desire on the part of some to convert others to their point of view. One fears that, in English Canada, most of the settlers supposed that God had *intended* the others to hold whatever benighted views they held in order that He might not be confused about who it was who was saved.

Whatever the reason, the inhabitants of English Canada have generally regarded the English as effete and not worth listening to, have refused to produce anything like a "charismatic" politician (would anyone really claim Mitch Hepburn for that role?), and have carefully confined their violence to the lacrosse box and (more recently) the hockey rink.

The remaining solution seemed to be to reason with one another. The Scots, a sermonizing people for whom religion was frequently more a matter of doctrine than of emotion, brought the tradition of public reasoning with them. The Irish, used to a society in conflict in which the practice of explaining oneself to others was normal enough, came with much the same tradition. The United Empire Loyalists were more often Anglican, contemptuous of others, and from a social class not so used to having to explain itself. They turned out to have less influence on the development of the colleges and universities in general and on academic philosophy in particular than did the Scots, but

3

even they had been through a time of public debate and understood its techniques and tactics well enough.

The impact of such influences is not easy to trace. The concern with public education which the need for public reasoning was bound to feed was not in any way unique to English Canada. The creation of a federal system of government which made possible the retention of regional interests was almost inevitable. As a device, it was hardly new and it was at work and in plain view south of the border. Its Canadian form provided, it is true, a somewhat different balance of powers between the central and regional governments but that had a variety of complex explanations.

In the development of philosophy in Canada the relevant influences seem rather clearly apparent: Though we shall find that James Beaven's successors adopted a fair variety of philosophical positions and stances, the use of reason runs through a hundred years of their writings as a basic theme which constantly lies just below the surface. A philosopher, whether he is worrying about morals or about universals, pondering problems in logic or in the philosophy of science, is, most of the time, reasoning. The way in which he reasons thus figures as a topic linked to every other topic.

The single point which we would make if we could make only one point in this book would be this: Dominantly in English Canadian philosophy reason is used as a device to explore alternatives, to suggest ways of combining apparently contradictory ideas, to discover new ways of passing from one idea to another. Only rarely is it used as an intellectual substitute for force—as a device to defeat one's opponent, to show his ideas to be without foundation, or to discredit his claims to philosophical thought. There is, in short, a kind of philosophical federalism at work, a natural inclination to find out why one's neighbour thinks differently rather than to find out how to show him up as an idiot.

It is unlikely that there is a simple explanation for this. When it was decided in 1850 to create the first official "chair" of philosophy, it is improbable that the appointing committee went out to look for a man who would behave as James Beaven did or that their successors went out hunting for philosophers of Beaven's intellectual build. It is likely that the same forces which slowly shaped the new University of Toronto into a federal structure in which credal rivals could share a common home also made a certain notion of philosophy and of reason attractive. Men who responded to that intellectual climate would tend to stay and to thrive while others would tend to find the milieu unattractive.[3] And it was the need for a kind of philosophical federalism which forced institutions to make common cause, which created the federated university which we know well, and which has rendered almost (though not quite) extinct in Canada the university or college tied to a single denominational unit.

If we are to make this point, we must first clarify the concept of philosophy which is relevant and consider the various senses in which a philosophy might be said to be Canadian, or American or Greek or German or British or French. After that it should be possible to return to a more trenchant account of the special features of life and culture in English Canada, a more sophisticated account of the nature and use of philosophical reason, and then to sketch the ways in which philosophy in fact developed in English Canada. For just as there are those who doubt that there is such a thing as "Canadian philosophy," so there are those who doubt that "reason" is more than a cover word for thought processes of which one happens to approve. And it has never been particularly easy to put one's finger on the distinctive features of life and culture in English Canada.

No one has ever been very satisfied with any definition of philosophy. One can circumscribe it by saying that philosophers are concerned with the attempt to substitute reason for faith and intuition and that their concerns confront certain basic issues: What are the most general and pervasive features of reality? What features, if any, of the real, bear on the meaning of human life? What criteria should be applied to claims to knowledge? What things or states of affairs are valuable? How should one order the things or states of affairs which are valuable? Under what conditions can it be said that a conclusion follows from one or more premises? What are meanings and what makes sentences or propositions meaningful?

On most of these issues people have various opinions. For the most part, however, they do not differ on them in the most easily understandable ways. Two people who have regularly driven from Ottawa to North Bay will, usually, either give the same directions to a third person who wants to make the trip or will differ in their advice depending upon some difference in the experiences they have had. Their advice will,

3   It is not so obvious to us that this should be true. But, in 1850, there was scarcely a subject in the curriculum in which religion did not figure prominently. In the sciences, one's attitude to the conflict between science and theology was already crucial and would become more so. Even the teaching of classical languages provided an opportunity to muse on the contrast of pagan and Christian virtue. We are a little embarrassed at the controversies and report them in muted tones but some of the adventures come through in H. H. Walsh, *The Christian Church in Canada* (Toronto: Ryerson, 1956).

5

normally, differ from that of another person who has never made the trip in that it is more likely to be accurate enough to get one there. But it is not experience of the world which makes two people differ about metaphysical questions and it seems improbable that value questions depend upon exposure to events and to practice—though it is true that one will frequently come to value activities only after one has learned to do them well.

Again, what one believes about quantum mechanics depends mostly (though not wholly) on how much education one has had in physics. Two physicists are likely to disagree about the best interpretation of certain propositions and may well disagree about how knowledge in the relevant area is now to be extended. But they will share a common framework of belief and expectation within which they can carry on their discussion. There is not likely to be the same measure of agreement between two theologians about the nature and existence of God or about what that existence means to human beings.

Experience, education, skill at reasoning in a given area are frequent explanations for human disagreement but they generally do not explain the kinds of disagreements about which philosophers concern themselves. There seem to be two reasons for this.

One is that the kinds of questions which traditionally have interested philosophers—and, to a large extent, this goes for philosophers in the Indian as well as in the Western tradition—are of such a kind that, whether one wants to or not, one almost necessarily goes about with ready-made answers to them. One must expect *something* of the world—that tomorrow will be much like today, that objects thrown from high buildings will fall down and not up, that men will continue to die, that one's friends will recognize one next week, and so on. Thus one has some belief about certain very pervasive features of the universe. One goes about, what is more, *giving* meaning to one's life and to the events around one and one could hardly evade the mental hospital if one did not. In that process one must have a sense of what it is for something to be valuable and have ordered one's values into priorities. Indeed, questions of this sort generally fall within the rubric of Kant's notion of practical reason. Kant supposed that claims such as those about the existence of God and the immortality of the soul were essentially postulates of practical reason. His notion of practical reason is very complex and technical, but we may agree, in a general way, that such claims are apt to figure as beliefs which provide an order to one's affairs within which one may make the necessary decisions. Finally, one does, after all, devote a good part of one's life to reasoning. One may not be able to state the rules under which one decides what conclusions

6

follow from what premises but one is very likely to be able to make quite satisfactory inferences for oneself—assuming again that one is not in need of urgent attention from physicians or psychiatrists.

The second reason is that questions of this sort arouse strong feelings. We are now talking about beliefs about what matters most— one's loves and hates, the redemption (or otherwise) of one's soul, one's sense of how the line is drawn between illusion and reality. To change one's mind about any of these things is, to an important extent, to change oneself. If one makes enough such changes one becomes (in a fairly intelligible sense) someone else.

If one sees this, some issues about philosophy become clear. One *philosophical* position is that the proposed substitution of reason for faith and intuition just cannot be made. Another is that we have long since reached the limit of such substitutions. We have taken the spirits from the trees, discovered how chemistry differs from alchemy, gone beyond Newton, and distinguished physics clearly from theology. A third is that every question which is, itself, intelligible has answers upon which reason (in some sense) bears—and so on. One may call these second-order positions—positions which are about the extent (or manner) to which one can do philosophy at all.

In general, though, one cannot pursue them without some first-order philosophizing. Given some argument or arguments for the existence of God one may well begin to see not just why those arguments succeed or fail but why arguments of a whole general kind must succeed or fail. When one does that one is usually falling back on one's logic or one's general theory of knowledge and one finds that all arguments of a certain kind meet or fail to meet stated criteria. By altering one's logic one may create a new rule under which what formerly did not follow from a given premise does now. (Russell and Aristotle differed over the question of whether or not it follows from "All balls are red" that "Some [at least one] balls are red.") Or one may extend one's theory of knowledge in such a way that what formerly did not count as a valid claim does so now. (The debate between the supporters and discounters of miracles stems, *in part*, from the fact that they have rival theories of knowledge: The doubters tend to be people who think that every valid claim to knowledge can be stated as an instance of conformity to natural law.) At any rate, it usually requires a first-order claim like "God exists," "Everything real is a material object," "No promises are binding," "All life is valuable," for such debates to get going.

But it is then sometimes claimed that, after all, philosophical debates are characteristically those which have no possible outcome. For, if the

7

philosopher is the keeper of the rules of logic and the creator of theories of knowledge, he can always, one might suppose, adjust his stock in trade so as to have something in hand to validate (or invalidate) anything which is proposed to him. Inevitably, the answer to this objection is "yes" and "no."

Suppose (what is not always the case) that the philosopher is a serious man. He can then only change his logic and his theory of knowledge if he is prepared to live with the result. If he allows one inference to stand, he must allow all the others like it to stand. (It is sometimes said that the great scholastic systems of the high Middle Ages finally broke down in a welter of distinctions which no one, any longer, could manage. Indeed, the last of the very great philosophers in that tradition, Duns Scotus, gave the language, according to the Oxford English Dictionary, the word dunce, probably because his distinctions had become too subtle. It might well be that Christianity, as then understood, could not consistently be accommodated to any logic then available and the attempt to evade inconsistency by the manufacture of distinctions was a principal cause of the downfall of those systems.) Similarly, if x is good evidence in one case, x ought to be good evidence in the next. Essentially, the claim that the necessary substitutions of reason for faith and intuition cannot be made is the claim that there is no set of such substitutions with which one can satisfactorily live. Rarely, indeed, is it taken that the proposed substitutions are an all-or-nothing thing. Like Thomas Aquinas (but unlike Duns Scotus) most people and many philosophers seem to have wanted to draw a line beyond which the substitutions are not to be made and philosophers who have persisted in crossing the lines have been given the hemlock, the stake, and the jailhouse.

It is fair to notice, though, that the test probably *is* what one can live with consistently. Such a "life coherence" test, if applied honestly, rigorously, and continuously, is very likely the highest standard that we can expect human beings to live up to. Reason on such a view becomes not a device for rendering one's opponents prostrate or a device for excusing one's own sins but a constant prod to the exploration of new experience, the testing of new arguments. Philosophy becomes, then, a highly personal matter which no one can completely do for you— though many people might do it together. It becomes an activity rather than a body of doctrine and these are all further reasons which bear on the question of why issues in philosophy are not exactly like those in geography or in physics.

Even if we stop short of deciding whether all that is finally true or not, such a vista gives us some insight into the conditions under which philosophy is likely to arise and, therefore, some insight into the question of what it would be for there to be Canadian philosophy (or Greek philosophy or German philosophy). It will only be, for the most part, when established intuitions and items of faith are called into question in some way that one will, after all, expect philosophy to get going and only where there is a strongly felt need to examine such matters in concert with others is there likely to be philosophizing as a public activity.

Such conditions are likely to include challenges from other cultures, failures in established institutions, internal injustice and unrest, rapid social or technological change, or even highly traumatic individual occurrences. One might very easily think that no human being lives under conditions so stable and satisfactory as to render him immune from the temptation to philosophize. But that is probably false. For though there are widespread conditions which lead to the temptation to philosophize, the obvious alternative to philosophizing is a simple change in intuition or faith.

We must look for something less obvious, since philosophy, in the sense that we have been talking about it here, is not common. It has been a part of what we call Western civilization since about 500 B.C. Indian philosophy (if we confine our attention, again, to philosophy in the same sense) may well be a little older. Philosophy in China did not flourish in quite the same way and philosophy in Muslim civilization, derived from Greek philosophy, prospered for only a few hundred years. Even in Western civilization, there is a period (from the sixth to the ninth century) when relatively little that would be called philosophy seems to have appeared and it cannot be said that philosophy has prospered everywhere in the West at any time.

The likelihood seems to be that it is only when there are challenges of the sort suggested, and accompanied by conditions which make it desirable that some tolerable plurality be established, that philosophy is likely to be of widespread importance or interest. The Greeks, who had taken to trade, had acquired both riches and some taste for personal independence. A trader abroad is on his own and, when he returns, he does not fit easily into a social system which renders him anonymous again. Furthermore, Greeks abroad acquired new and strange ideas which had, somehow, to be accommodated. Much of Plato's concern is with the imposition of some kind of rational order on the chaos which these conditions brought about. Only reason could adjudicate (if anything could) the dispute amongst the partisans of many varied intuitions. But the superficial social order was only one of many concerns of the Greek philosophers. The pre-Socratics seem to have turned, first, to the larger cosmic order—seeking principles of unity with which to make sense of the plurality and confusion that confronted them. Greek philosophy was not a childish form of political philosophy or social economics but an urgent effort to come to grips with an underlying reality—for only by finding such a reality could one hope to unleash the power necessary to bring rational order to the chaos. That that power was not forthcoming is a fact which helps to explain the scepticism of the New Academy. And, should we wish to cast doubt on the enterprise, we might also ask what would have happened had the Greeks been gripped by a new faith or intuition. It seems all too likely that such an event would have provided the social cohesion which philosophy could not provide. Yet the Platonic vision continues to haunt us even though it does not compel us to action and the Aristotelean synthesis continues to be a live option for making sense of our world.

One might suggest, too, that philosophy in India arose out of the same needs: It belongs to a period of the adjustment between the Aryan peoples moving south through the sub-continent and the Dravidian peoples whom they encountered, but there the story is slightly different: Hinduism became a religion which recognized the insights of all the contending parties and it fell to philosophy to make rational sense of this acceptance. Indian philosophy, as a consequence, characteristically consists of large-scale systems which have a religious base and which seek to show that they, better than their rivals, impose order upon and make intelligible the vast array of common insights.

In the Moslem world, Greek philosophy took hold and was developed into new and imaginative systems at just the time when that civilization was spreading across the known world and its partisans had to contend with a wide variety of cultures. When the Arabs retreated from Europe and their leaders retreated into a religious fundamentalism, Arab philosophy collapsed, too. Even in the West, where we think we have a continuous tradition, philosophy fared ill in the immediate aftermath of the Roman Empire when Christianity reigned supreme and unquestioned. Is it an accident that philosophy returned to life in the Carolingian period when Europe was finally awake to the importance of Arab civilization and that it flourished best in the high Middle Ages when philosophers like Thomas Aquinas were addressing themselves directly across the boundaries of culture to the Arab intellectuals? After the thirteenth century there is, again, a gap.

What the college curriculum writers like to call "early modern" philosophy reaches its peak only in the seventeenth and eighteenth centuries when there is, within Europe, a powerful clash of intuitions and faiths. The Reformation and the new science both provided occasion for the philosopher to try to weave a commonality of reason against a conflict of outlooks and values which threatened to tear Europe to pieces. Descartes, Spinoza, and Leibniz were responding to a very real and pressing human crisis—a crisis which, we must guess, was strong enough to overcome the ordinary reluctance of most intellectuals to confront their own strongest feelings with cold reason. The incompleteness of their success led Locke, Berkeley, and Hume to moderate the claims of reason in a succession of strategic retreats. One cannot, really, make a simple distinction between the "continental rationalists" and the "British empiricists." But the British empiricists do represent a different sense of what has to be done and do represent, for the most part, a return to immediacy. The clash in values and outlooks was not nearly so threatening in Britain as on the continent and the need for a large scale philosophical synthesis was therefore substantially absent. Why venture into dangerous speculative worlds when one may live quite comfortably in one's own snug world? David Hume, a consistent High Tory, was to demonstrate clearly that philosophy might be used to defend one's beliefs from assault as well as to mediate value claims and, though he is often counted as a sceptic, he basked in the snug conviction that there never can be enough evidence to overturn our natural beliefs.

It is from this period in the eighteenth century that philosophy began to take on national colouring. It is probably fair to say that British philosophy took on distinctive characteristics first. Isolation, a fairly swift and complete transition to the new style in religion, and a measure of political stability following a quick transition to modern political forms all played some part.

By the end of the eighteenth and the beginning of the nineteenth century, massive system building had become associated with the Germanic style. Why should we find our Kants and Hegels on the fringe of European civilization and not in Paris, Rome, or London? No account of a social situation will explain the insight which led Kant to question the whole foundation of Christian Wolff's reconstruction of Leibniz. And no such account will explain just how it was that Hegel came to see a radically new and different meaning in Kant's antinomies. But it is not far-fetched to think that the whole concern with systematic construction had to do with the fact that Germany itself was a fragmented culture which was only forged into a country with the utmost difficulty. The German-speaking peoples were divided from one another by religion, by ethnic origin, and by geography which left them scattered amongst Czechs, Slovaks, Poles, and Frenchmen. The need to find a rational mediation for these conflicts is obvious and real and Leibniz, Kant, and Hegel all addressed themselves to the specific social and political questions at issue and each tried to show that he had a universal system which could effect as much rational mediation of conflicting values as was possible.

Almost simultaneously, one finds James and John Stuart Mill along with Jeremy Bentham at work reconciling the British conscience to its new place in the world. Officially, solemnity was the order of the day, and the world was to be conceived mainly as a set of hazards to be overcome on the way to heaven. In practice the beginnings of the industrial revolution combined with some success at empire building had made the middle class British quite rich and worldly. Bentham and the Mills set out to show that pleasure was not merely acceptable but bound up with duty. No one, perhaps, would accept the notion that it was a duty to pursue pleasure for oneself. But if I can show that it is my duty to see that your life is pleasurable and yours to see that mine is pleasurable, we have arrived at a state of affairs in which I can solemnly take credit for a dutiful life of self-enjoyment. The British were, however, interrupted in this blissful orgy of self-justification by the arrival of a crisis of a different sort.

· Scientific belief very likely responds to change in a way which is quite different from those changes which come upon the beliefs we have been calling philosophical. These differences of response and of believability form part of the subject matter of the theory of knowledge. Industrial progress in Britain and elsewhere in Europe created wealth which could be used either in the disinterested pursuit of knowledge or in the pursuit of specific information which would, in its turn, create more wealth. In the nature of things, something of each took place and scientific knowledge not only increased rather rapidly, it also acquired a large measure of general acceptance. In part, the machine-monster theory of the world favoured by nineteenth-century physics and made plausible by the visible expansion of machine technology was responsible for the clash with traditional belief. A government-financed biological survey led, however, to a trip around the world for the young Charles Darwin and that led—as he began to assemble his notes on living creatures old and new—to the theory of evolution and to the final assimilation, in popular theory, of man to nature.

The century was to be largely preoccupied with a plurality of beliefs and practices which seemed unlikely to come together as a unified whole. But this kind of conflict is one of those in which philosophy seems a natural activity. John Stuart Mill responded by

12

investigating the nature of reality, the existence of God, and the future of man. He concluded, not unreasonably, that reality consisted of permanent possibilities for sensation, that it was slightly more likely than not that God existed, and that man, now in control of his own destiny, had an unlimited future. These bulletins from the philosophical front were, however, rather brief and the demand for a larger system remained unabated.

German system building, which had been largely out of fashion in Britain since the eighteenth century, came back. Hegelianism arrived at Oxford and at the Scottish universities in the last third of the century. Green, Bradley, Bosanquet, and the Cairds were to dominate British philosophy until well after the turn of the century. Its original attraction was that it set out to take history seriously—to explain why we are where we are in the order of human events—to reconcile religion and science and to give a sense and direction to political reform. Bradley largely disposed of Hegel's historical pretensions (to his own satisfaction and, momentarily at least, to that of most British philosophers). He also pared down the religious dimensions of Hegelianism to a rather straightforward faith in the efficacy of reason. Green used Hegelian ideas effectively as a weapon of political reform though Bosanquet gave Hegelianism a significantly more conservative twist. All in all, its subtleties and difficulties tended to get passed over and Hegelianism emerged rather different and very British—decent and reasonable and without the rumbling Wagnerian overtones which come with Hegel's oracular utterances. What was at issue was how one might accept the findings of science without having to suffer the loss of self-image which comes with thinking that one is a machine. The complex religious and political struggles which animated Hegel and his compatriots had no immediate counterparts in Oxford or Edinburgh.

The same period saw the genesis of a distinctively American philosophy in much the same way. The same crisis of belief led to something of an upsurge of Hegelianism (which reached its strongest domestic influence in Josiah Royce), but the dark complexities of such systems seemed not altogether relevant to a straightforward prosperous society which had such faith in itself that not even the Civil War seems to have diminished its self-confidence. It could be argued that American society is best celebrated in Royce's theory of community and that Royce and not James (the son of a Swedenborgian minister, brother of an exiled Anglophile, himself more at home in Paris than in Omaha) represents a truly American philosophy.[4]

4   Royce's Absolute may well be a cosmic version of the uniform and orderly society
      imagined by the Boston Brahmins amongst whom Royce spent much of his adult

Popular wisdom insists that pragmatism, with its emphasis on practicality and success, its Deweyite jargon which sounds like social science, and its faith in individual response is the "truly" American philosophy. The word pragmatism has to do with the notion that truth is related to the experience of the utterer of propositions—perhaps the notion, ascribed by Plato to Protagoras, that man is the measure of all things. But in fact it is not subjectivist or individualist in its implications as they are developed by the American trinity, James, Peirce, and Dewey. For they all claimed that, in the long run, what was confirmable by many would come to triumph over what was merely confirmable by a single agent and that a community might be defined by its collective and converging responses to experience and values. They thus established a priority of public over private values. And though they did insist that one must grasp the outcome of one's beliefs if they are to have any meaning at all, they were not insisting on a crass valuation of the practical as superior, somehow, to the theoretical, but rather trying to give a meaning to the theoretical. They intended to champion theory against unreflective practice and to insist on what James called "the long run" as the test of truth. Peirce traced his philosophical lineage to Duns Scotus, perhaps the least "practical" of philosophers.

Philosophies are very often responses to what one thinks the world needs rather than reflections of the way in which it is. Though they are likely to reveal to others assumptions of which the philosopher himself is not aware and which tell us something about the philosopher's place, time, and condition, they also tell us what he has diagnosed as wrong in his society. Many of the American pragmatists were social reformers. They feared rampant individualism and a crass and unquestioning respect for technology and simple success.

Thus James devoted much of his life to calling attention to the possibilities which remained for meaningful religious experience; Peirce laboured to find an adequate theory of community; and Dewey sought a theory of education which would be an antidote to selfishness. At the same time all of them *did* build into their systems common assumptions of their culture: They all supposed that societies could be created by men by deliberate choice; that evil was an accident of ignorance and bad organization; that experience, though it needs to be coordinated, is essentially individual in its orientation; that morality is in some measure separable from religious or metaphysical belief.

life. A rather more open-ended version of Hegelian doctrine is found in the writings of men like Peter Kauffman and J. B. Stallo and offers a more authentic American vision.

Out of such mixtures of uncritical assumption and critical reconstruction, philosophies develop and come to have distinctive national characteristics. They are not mirrors of the national mind: Americans are not pragmatists by nature and birth. The British are not all philosophical analysts and the Germans are not necessarily system builders on the pattern of Kant and Hegel. But philosophy does often grow in response to some need—or, perhaps, the philosophies that attract attention are, not surprisingly, those which are responsive to some felt need. Would the followers of Sartre and Heidegger in France and Germany have responded to these dark oracles if social conditions had been different? The *angst* and ambivalence they celebrated in their very different ways surely stemmed from the collapse of public values in the years before World War II. The acceptance of these claims to ultimate irrationality suggests that Europeans then and later had quite frequently given up on reason. Or is that merely how *we* see or saw them? Why did we not decide that Louis Lavelle (who succeeded Henri Bergson in the chair of philosophy at the Collège de France) was the great French philosopher? Was it *we* who thought that, if the French were not celebrating the limits of reason, then they ought to have been? But surely Sartre has a wider and more persistent following than Lavelle. And, though Martin Foss *may* be a greater philosopher than Martin Heidegger, it is true that Heidegger had a far greater impact on a place and time. The places and times may not so much make philosophers as pick them up.

Thus the logical positivists of the Vienna Circle made their mark on and left their disciples in the English-speaking world. That might have been true even if they had not, for the most part, migrated under pressure from the Nazi authorities. Faced with the uncertainties of the world of the 1930s, one response was that of the existentialists and of the more romantic and less orthodox phenomenologists: to celebrate one's *angst*, one's estrangement from being or whatever. The other was to return to the classical tradition of empiricism and insist that certainty is to be found in immediate experience and that to stray beyond certainty is to indulge in Romantic nonsense. The latter position was that of the positivists. It had appeal in the English-speaking world where the educated élite in the universities had suffered little from the depression and felt itself fairly well protected against the physical intrusion of the political horrors of continental Europe.

Logical positivism proved a more drastic purgative than had been imagined and seemed, eventually, to threaten not merely the metaphysical superstitions of the heedless system builders but the foundations of science as well. It never did, therefore, make inroads in continental Europe and gradually faded from sight in the English-speaking world as well. In England, and later in the United States, it was replaced by the ordinary language philosophy which stemmed from the work of men like Gilbert Ryle at Oxford as well as from the work of the later Wittgenstein. In its most popular form, ordinary language philosophy proposed not to solve all the galling puzzles of traditional philosophy, but to dissolve them. It was claimed that they stemmed from the misuse of language and that no one, in full knowledge of the workings of the language, would really ask whether only ideas are real or whether men have free will. The ordinary language—as philosophers like Peter Strawson realized—contains its own picture of the world. One who musters a defence against the new words and uses of words proposed by philosophers therefore defends that world picture against assault. It may not be far-fetched to think that the defence of that cosy, orderly world against the anxieties expressed by the continental philosophers was a natural enough result of the relief Englishmen and Americans felt at having survived the war with their institutions and values intact. Marxists might suggest a darker explanation: The ordinary language philosophers were expressly defending the language (including the language of evaluation) used by a prosperous, élite middle class against the inroads and incursions of philosophers who, whatever their class, were apt to call middle class values into question. Again, however, one should bear in mind that not all the philosophers in England and the United States were influenced by logical positivism or by the ordinary language analysts. Somewhere in the English-speaking world one could (and can still) find philosophers of almost any reasonable persuasion. It is sometimes not the work itself which is determined by the social conditions of a place and time but the relative popularity of that work.

With those examples in mind, we can continue our basic quest. It now seems clear enough what one could mean by saying that there is or is not "Canadian philosophy" and what it would be rash to pretend. It is not as if all Greeks or all Germans held the same philosophical position—so that idealism might be "the German philosophy" and materialism "the Greek philosophy." There are British idealists, German idealists, Greek idealists, and French idealists of various periods. What is likely to be influenced by their place and time is the kind of system created and the questions a given system sets out to answer. Thus, though John Locke and Jonathan Edwards were both philosophical theists, the influence of their respective places and times does not show in that fact. It shows in the fact that Locke was mainly concerned with God's intentions with respect to the distribution of property, while Edwards was mainly concerned with predestination

16

and the redemption of sinners. Locke is reacting to a struggle between the landed nobility and the rising middle class. Edwards is coping with people who, having founded a community for allegedly religious reasons, were increasingly interested in cod fishing.

Nor is it always or usually the case that social situations influence philosophy by making of philosophers champions of whatever beliefs happen to be superficially popular at the moment. Few German philosophers supported Hitler. Many however, took part in convincing the intellectual public of the vacuousness of reason and, thereby, may have made it easier for Hitler's opinions to seem acceptable.[5]

It is also not the case that particular places and times can really claim the rights of origin to a given philosophical stance. If there are empiricists, there will sooner or later be rationalists, and if there are materialists, there will sooner or later be idealists. The Greeks can claim, for the most part, to have originated all such rather standard positions. But it does not really mean much, apart from the details, to say that someone is an idealist or a rationalist. Of what idea or ideal is his reality composed? What notion of reason undergirds his claims that reason is the source of knowledge?

Finally, for a given place and time to have its "philosophy" is not at all the same as for such a place and time to have originated a great philosopher. Spinoza belongs, in a general way, to a certain sort of post-Reformation rationalism with which one may readily associate Descartes and Leibniz as well. But though he was a Jew of Spanish origin resident in the Netherlands, it would be absurd to call his philosophy Dutch, Spanish, or Jewish. It is not that he pre-dated a period in which more parochial distinctions became appropriate. If he did, he barely did. But he formed a cultural anomaly. His insight satisfactorily resists any such classification. If a great philosopher made for a national philosophy, there would have to be a Dutch philosophy with Spinoza at its head. (There may be a Dutch philosophy but, if so, it is perhaps a special kind of post-Husserlian phenomenology.) Descartes is very likely a greater philosopher than Bergson or Sartre but Bergson and

5   The celebrated argument over Martin Heidegger's association with the Nazis raises intriguing points. Surely Hitler was unlikely to derive strength from philosophical support for his position. Indeed, a philosophical analysis of it would very likely have made it less believable even if the analysis were done by a philosopher who set out to offer his support. Thus Heidegger's flirtation with Nazi doctrine is almost certainly, historically, less important than the tendency of his philosophy (like that of the logical positivists) to cast doubt on the efficacy of reason. Once absolved from the obligation to reason about political matters, one may sit back and enjoy the emotional impact of Nazi rhetoric. But whether this is blameworthy or not depends upon whether or not there *is* a connection between reason and morality.

Sartre represent different strands of French philosophy in a way in which Descartes does not. Descartes remains a major—perhaps *the* major—source from which French philosophy descends, but what is special about French philosophy is very likely the *way* in which it descends from Descartes. Every other modern philosophy is influenced by Descartes as well. (French philosophy, perhaps, is substantially characterized by a special emphasis on the importance of immediate personal experience, one strand of many in the Cartesian complex.)

What we are looking for, then, is probably something subtle and special: the particular way in which reason develops as it comes to be substituted for insight and intuition in order that certain kinds of conflicts might be overcome in a reasonable way. It is for that reason that this book is called "The Faces of Reason." The reader must not expect to find some surprising new doctrine called "the Canadian theory" or some great figure called "the Canadian philosopher."

On the contrary, he will find many doctrines, a variety of figures of more or less weight—frequently disagreeing with one another and showing their associations with their places and times in complex ways. The themes we shall find have to do with the ways in which reason has shown itself in this milieu. But to make sense of the notion that there are such themes, we shall have to hazard some guess as to what, at least, some of the crucial features of the milieu really are.

Popular wisdom tends to focus on ethnic diversity and on geography. We do have rather a lot of both in common with the Soviet Union though no one—on that ground anyway—would expect us to have a closely related philosphical past. (Admittedly, what little evidence there is suggests that the Russians find it easier than the Americans to accept the fact that we *do* have a philosophy, as the Soviet *Istoria Filosofii* suggests in volume five, 1961.)

There are many cases of ethnic and cultural diversity, many cases of thinly settled (or selectively settled) areas which open onto wide horizons. And, though the attempt of people like Donald Creighton to associate some important features of our history with the way in which the St. Lawrence system opens into the continent represents a reasonable use of the impact of geography on culture, it invites comparisons with the impact of the Tigris and the Euphrates as well as with the Congo—all of which have the effect of opening central continental regions to trade and commerce.[6] Such comparisons are apt to make the head spin.

6   Creighton's emphasis on the special features of Canadian geography is, indeed, more relevant to the distinction between Canadian history and the history of our

18

The artifacts of the Canadian situation may be more important than the crude facts of transplanted cultures and wide open spaces. Language is amongst the most potent of human artifacts and the location of French speakers between two bodies of English-speaking peoples undoubtedly had a profound effect on, at least, the post-Confederation formation of ideas: We needed ideas which were capable of spanning spaces and which could link sub-cultures which, because of their distribution, tended to grow in significantly different ways. It takes a moderately high level of generalization to find something which unites Ontarian with Maritimer, and such a level of generalization must provide for the integration of values which tend, on a lower level, to compete with one another: Thus the Ontario manufacturer is at once at odds with the wholesaler of codfish in Nova Scotia. The latter lives at the mercy of the world price for fish while the former can surround himself with protective tariffs. The fish dealer must, consequently, be persuaded that some substantial and worthy scheme for the enhancement of life or the protection of dignity is involved if he is to be induced to take part in a political scheme which will make Canada possible. Such a scheme may really amount to no more than the protection of his own parochial culture against the incursions of Americans; but it must still involve a vision of the human condition.

The railroad and, later, the highway have also had a real function within the delineation of a Canadian culture and one much easier to pin down than the need to surmount a language enclave: Settlers brought with them a great variety of religious and social practices and, in the new communities, the church tended to be the centre of both. The railroad spread a thin settlement across a vast space. One could not accommodate all the possible sects in the same tank town. The lines between different species of Protestants became harder to trace as Baptists made common cause with Congregationalists and Presbyterians with Methodists. And the lines between Protestants in general and Roman Catholics (themselves assembled from many backgrounds) became firmer. Both provided material for the philosopher—the one because there was an increasing need to look for a common basis of

neighbours whose geography is different and hardly constitutes an attempt to apply a geographical theory about the bases of historical processes in general. (See his *Empire of the St. Lawrence*, 2nd ed. [Toronto: University of Toronto Press, 1956].) The book contains a better balanced account of the theory than any summary by its critics. There is a good account of its relations to other relevant theories offered by Canadian historians in Carl Berger, *The Writing of Canadian History* (Toronto: Oxford University Press, 1976). The point is merely that emphasis on geography differentiates without providing anything like a final explanation.

belief and the other because it had to make the same traditional message clear to peoples of diverse backgrounds. Their co-existence—often through parallel school systems and in societies in which many individuals did not cross the lines between the camps in their ordinary social lives—posed the question of why either of them should tolerate the organized wrong-headedness of the other.

We have vast prairies and high mountains. Very likely it is not the space itself but the artifacts and the culture which were brought to bear upon it which have had telling results. The organization of the grain farm separated farmer from farmer and created a society quite different from that of northern Europe. The plow turned some of the prairie eventually into dustbowl and the railroad brought cattle ranges in areas which could not otherwise have supported such an industry. The closeness of the western culture to its American counterpart stems from the fact that much the same technology and social organization was brought to bear on much the same landscape. The differences between the two had something to do with the ideas which each was given for support: The wild west was an American west, almost an enactment of the Hobbesian world in which there is a war of all against all. The Canadian west was, by comparison, tame. The difference is often attributed to the North West Mounted Police and to the fact that the men of that force were recruited from bodies such as the London Metropolitan Police. But that does not wholly explain the fact that the law was welcomed in western Canada and won acceptance by showing itself superior to the bad men in many adjacent parts of the United States. Given the conditions of life in the nineteenth-century west, one might see men as mutually dependent and as suffering from the lack of a traditional society which would give them security of place and function, or one might see them as essentially self-sufficient individuals for whom their independence and their isolation were conditions of virtue.

Though the French and the British who settled the Canadian west differed in much that mattered, and finally collided in the tragedy of the Riel rebellions, they had in common that they came from societies which had escaped the full force of the dissolution of traditional societies in Europe. The French were in Canada before the revolution; the British managed to maintain a kind of continuity which differed vastly from the persistent strands in post-revolutionary America and France. They thus saw community as natural and individuals as attaining merit in the context of some communal good. Not only was there no wild west on the prairie: In the Fraser River gold rush, Judge Begbie, to the astonishment of Americans lately arrived from California, managed, almost single-handedly, to keep law and order. Law and order were assumed goods on both sides of the mountains.

In the furthest west, the effect of the mountains was mainly created by social design: The preference of an essentially British population to join Canada rather than to forge links with the adjacent parts of the United States gave the mountains a significance they might not otherwise have had. The railroad was promised as a condition of Confederation and became a kind of symbolic umbilical cord—a sign and portent that someone cared on the other side. Its magical and not very economical ability to traverse territory through which a man and a horse might never survive was also a token of human mastery of nature, creating a culture in other ways more American and less like the more completely transplanted societies of the Maritimes. Yet that sense of mastery was invariably muted by the realization that the great mass of nature remained wholly untamed.

We might summarize these features of the culture like this:

The great diversity of places produced a variety of sub-cultures and fed the notion that society must be held together by aims of great generality and of fundamental importance. One may imagine all the Swiss, despite their cultural differences, rallying around the notion that they ought all to get rich. But one cannot imagine Canadians answering the same rallying cry. The reason is not that Canadians are less crass. It is that what will make an Ontario manufacturer rich will probably cause a disaster for a prairie farmer or a Nova Scotia fisherman. Nearly all the Germans *might* get together to exercise their lust for power (conventional wisdom has it that they did so on one or more occasions). But can one readily imagine Canadians doing that? Surely not. Had we all gotten together in Montreal to make bombs, we might have been able to frighten Vermont. But, spread out across the continent in a thin line (our noses half frozen and our hands in mitts) we frighten no one and are, indeed, terribly vulnerable. The Canadian population is bigger than the United States Marine Corps, but not much bigger. For us, there is no Belgium into which we might march. Indeed, unlike the Americans, we cannot even frighten each other into a continuing union.

What is there that could hold us together? First of all there are religious notions of the sources of human obligation. Canadians were able to imagine that Timothy Eaton might be saved by (and cared about by) the same God who cared about a remittance man in British Columbia and, in fact, our political reform movements from the CCF-NDP on the left to the Social Credit movement on the right have had a strong religious base. Then there are general welfare concerns—the interests of the sick, the feeble-minded, the blind are much the same in British Columbia or Ontario and the possibility of unifying disparate parts of the population by appealing to these common needs has not been lost on politicians. The need for information was the earliest and has remained the most persistent of such concerns and has developed, by a natural extension, into the cultural concerns connected with broadcasting and the spread of the arts. Radio was a godsend (first capitalized on, indeed, by politician-preachers like William Aberhart) and ultimately television proved even more so: The need to communicate across great distances could be turned into a virtue. The authorities dreamed of a new and national culture as an instrument of benevolent government. So much has it become assumed that government ought to (even if it does not really) operate on this elevated level of general principle that a recent Liberal prime minister was able to tell prairie farmers that it was not his job to sell wheat and a recent Conservative minister of works was able to refuse altogether to honour the ancient custom of granting contracts to party supporters: We remain too diverse to be gripped firmly by the most obvious kinds of crassness. It is at any rate clear that our various single intuitions would not suffice to unite us. Good or bad, we need a general theory.

Then, too, we have been forced to come together in ways which have produced new institutions (like the United Church of Canada and the Canadian Broadcasting Corporation) and to develop still other institutions (of which the federated University of Toronto is a good example) which allow groups of people fairly unlike one another to exist, nonetheless, in conditions of reasonable amity. Protestants and Catholics can work in the same federated university even if not in the same church. These notions, too, have made us dig for something very general and acceptably basic: There must be something everyone would want in a university or that all sensible people would want to hear on the radio. The result need not be exalted: Newman's uncompromising ideal Catholic university might have been a better one than any which came into existence on a federal plan in Canada. The output of the Canadian Broadcasting Corporation is sometimes as bland and uninspiring as tapioca pudding. We can all too easily agree on a nationally subsidized theatre which produces Shakespeare and a national orchestra which plays Mozart when we ought to have something which demands more of our imaginations and minds. One must shudder at the thought of a novel which would appeal to an Eskimo seal hunter, a Saskatchewan potash digger, and the president of the British Columbia Sugar Refining Company, but we can safely bet that some Toronto publisher is even now trying to have it written.

22

Ideas may become general by becoming vague and bland. They may also become general by becoming comprehensive and fundamental. Our culture is apt to favour one as much as the other.

The blandness which is often complained about in Canadian life has, no doubt, many explanations, but it is worth noticing that all the components of the cultural and geographical milieu about which we have been talking tend toward a pattern of orderly and tranquil social change and this fact in itself has been an influence on the pattern of problems to be confronted. A strong communitarian tendency implies that social change must take a community with it as a unity. Such a situation is apt to put strong pressure on individuals to conform and to leave them rootless and forlorn if they break with the community. A plurality of such communities spread out in space and, because of successive waves of immigration, representing, in time, a series of adjustments to the new environment, provided a response. In Canada, the individual has usually been able to evade the pressure to conform by merging with another community and to avoid the feeling of rootlessness by casting his lot with his new choice. The effect of a multiplicity of essentially original communities which simply could not be dissolved made more feasible the continuation of still more communities. Ukrainian communities in Alberta changed and so did Scottish communities in Ontario and no doubt they became more like one another, though they did not change in exactly the same ways or in exactly the same directions. No one thought it very strange, however, if an Albertan of Ukrainian descent took up curling, whiskey, and the United Church of Canada and eventually, perhaps, acquired his own kilt and tam-o-shanter.[7] The demand for rapid and violent change is generally the result of a failure in some striking way of one's society to meet one's expectations. The dustbowls and the depression of the nineteen-thirties destroyed the expectations of tens of thousands of Canadians and, indeed, the riots in Regina and Vancouver had in them the potential for revolutionary violence. That may have been the closest we have come to large-scale social disruptions (though there were moments during World War I and World War II which had more potential for destruction than we usually credit them with). Generally, the individuals have been able to identify themselves with some con-

7 The influence of the Scots on our language, accents, ideas, ambitions, drinking habits, religion, and dress is very great and this book will attempt to explain some features of that. It is worth noticing, though, that the Scots, though dominant in Canadian business, education, and general culture have usually managed to maintain their native posture as underdogs to the arrogant, effete, and slippery English and thus to retain the affection of the real underdogs. Even in Quebec, a Scotsman is not (quite) *anglais*.

tinuing community which meets their most immediate needs and which consists of a group with whom they propose to change, if at all, in concert.

This sense that the development of society is continuous and is not made by one man or a dozen sitting down and drafting a plan on paper, even if they do so to the cheers of a thousand others standing outside, has been one of the distinctions between Canada and the United States. The attempts to paint our Fathers of Confederation and make them look like the signers of the Declaration of Independence has generally provoked laughter even from generations of school children. We have not seen them as very important because we have not thought, for the most part, that *anyone* could have the kind of importance which Americans assigned to their historic figures.

For the same reason, presumably, we have not done much by way of creating heroic leaders. We have not minded that our first prime minister drank too much, that the prime minister who lasted longest in office did so with the help of his ouija board, or that memorizing the list of the holders of that office makes little more sense than memorizing the telephone directory. The comings and goings of such men have seemed a mere surface activity: Communities, unless they were deliberately created by men in the first place, are likely to have their own directions, patterns of change, and prospects. A clever politician may make things a little better, a stupid one a little worse.

Canadians have not always been inhospitable to those who have claimed to be able to effect sudden and miraculous change. "Bible Bill Aberhart" (whose doings—as we shall see—attracted the attention of a Toronto philosopher)[8] won an election in Alberta by a vote which still takes the breath away. But whether the voters believed that he could solve all their ills or whether they were just annoyed with the United Farmer government (some of those members were up to shenanigans not welcome amongst United Churchmen) or whether they had simply despaired of dust and depression no one really knows. At any rate, when Aberhart did not do anything very significant the voters did not turn on him. They kept his Social Credit Party in power for a generation and appeared quite pleased when the party abandoned, item by item, all its original pretensions. Similarly, "socialists" in the guise of CCF and NDP—parties theoretically committed to the notion that social planning can foster human decency—have been elected to office in provinces from Manitoba westward. But their claims have usually been very modest. They have been social tinkerers rather than large-

---

8 John Irving, *The Social Credit Movement in Alberta* (Toronto: University of Toronto Press, 1959).

scale social engineers, and they have usually moderated their claims while in office. The history of the party from the Regina Manifesto onwards is that of a group of men and women who have moved from the notion that they know what the good society is to the notion that they have a good insight into the cutting edge of desirable social change and can, therefore, rightly claim to speed that change and to make it less painful. Irritating as it may be, they have moved from a strictly ideological organization on the European plan to a peculiarly Canadian stance.

It has often been remarked, that, at times (part of the Bennett years, the Bracken period, the Diefenbaker time) the Conservative Party (officially and splendidly *Progressive* Conservative) has held to policies not far from those of their "socialist" rivals. Hardly anyone was surprised when a philosopher like George Grant moved from one to the other. Both after all preached social responsibility, the containment of the most virulent kinds of individualism, orderly social change. The Red Toryism of popular legend (at least amongst intellectuals) is related to a traditionalist communitarianism—a position which comes naturally once one accepts a certain view of social change.

If one were to look for counter examples, one ought to look, seemingly, to the Liberal Party—an organization which in origin was the champion of individualism (the small "l" liberalism of the Manchester partisans of *laissez-faire*). Surely there one must find men who think or thought that social change was the outcome of individual effort and that the political surface took precedence over the social sub-structure. Mackenzie King *sometimes* thought of himself as the businessman's friend. But he also thought of himself as the worker's friend. It is true that he took legal action after 1935 to undo much social reform and to return more nearly to a competitive individualist society. But in fact that was a momentary aberration, quickly reversed, and the Liberal Party has shown itself the champion of communitarian virtues.

The differences between political parties in Canada have, for the most part, been small-scale and technical: The roaring issues have been free trade, comprehensive versus special-purpose welfare schemes, national intervention in health care, the railroads, control of foreign corporations and investments. One can take *any* position on these questions consistently with any ultimate goal and it cannot be said that politics in Canada has been devoted much to debates about ultimate goals—the ultimate goals have tended to be widely understood and accepted—and so once again we have all the excitement of tapioca pudding.

25

Associated with these circumstances is something, as we have suggested, much more important: a certain sense of the use and powers of reason. Philosophically, reason has been thought of in many different ways: (1) as a formal foundation out of which knowledge may be spun; (2) as a kind of force for determining and showing what ought to be taken seriously and what derided; (3) as a device, arbitrary in its nature, by which one may generate rules of one's own making for one's own pleasure; or (4) as something revealed in the natural order of things. The first and third of these notions figure in American history in a large and perhaps decisive way: Reason, as original foundation, is the basis of the natural law theory which animated the Jeffersonian concept of constitutionalism; reason as arbitrary rule of one's own making lies behind the individualist notion in modern theories which hold that the rules are what the winners of certain competitions say they are. The second notion of reason lies behind a common kind of British constitutionalism and of Oxford "ordinary language" philosophy. Those who have been properly educated (i.e., at a decent public school and Oxford or Cambridge) simply see that events, policies, and human conditions fall into kinds and sorts. To have reason on one's side is to grasp what the sensible fellows grasp and to reject what they reject. When one has discovered which is which, one devises a logic (formal or informal) which absolutely guarantees the result that one intends and, thereby, shows that one's opponents are idiots. The fourth, which has its roots in Plato and Aristotle, maintains that reason is primarily a function through which one may seek to expand one's experiences, to reconcile conflicting values and claims. It develops historically through a society with continuity and enables one, progressively but imperfectly, to see, as the facts accumulate, something of the real underlying structure. One may never quite demolish another's position (for he may show how his view follows by another logic) but one may claim a small measure of increasing clarity.

The whole thrust of a communitarian, pluralistic society which has, for the most part, escaped violent change tends to favour this fourth use of reason. Canada in the hundred years which figure in this book confronted the changes and problems of the rest of the world from that background. Many Englishmen, many Americans, and a good many Canadians saw the growing conflict of science and religion in the nineteenth century as a conflict which would naturally and properly be resolved in favour of one or the other. Dr. White, the second president of Cornell University, wrote a massive two-volume work detailing the "warfare" of science and theology.[9] It was not widely

9   Andrew D. White, *A History of the Warfare of Science with Theology* (New York: D. Appleton, 1896).

thought that there was anything odd in posing this confrontation. For the most part, however, philosophers in Canada saw the conflict as one to be resolved. Surely there were different principles which must be accorded different status, different experiences which must be accounted for differently.

Again, the growing availability of wealth throughout the nineteenth century brought, everywhere, continuous and persistent demands for a new mode of social justice. It was the gulf between availability and delivery which made Marx think that society must ultimately be conceived through the class war. In England, the middle class finally took the part of the working class in order to end the powers of the upper class. If, in the United States, armed conflict between slave holders and northern industrialists had not exhausted the nation and made peace seem unusually attractive, the theoretical conflict between capitalist and worker might have broken through to the surface. In Canada the tendency to put distance between competitors—a possibility even more available north of the international boundary than south of it—partly prevented confrontations, and the absence, over large tracts of the west and of southwestern Ontario, of great variances of affluence diminished the motive for hostility. Official Conservative as well as Reformist doctrine had it that the rich were, in any case, responsible to the poor though it was rumoured that in Montreal wealthy Presbyterians could arrange not to have sermons preached on the matter of the camel and the eye of the needle. Philosophers like Paxton Young began the practice of carefully delineating issues of value conflict, and the social theories of Watson and Murray were careful efforts to balance the rival interests—though Murray, to a degree, admired both Marx and Henry George.

In Europe, for the most part, the war between science and religion seemed to have been won by science and the war between the classes seemed to be a stand-off awaiting some dramatic new event, when World War I altered the whole climate of ideas. Such a massive upsurge of irrationality cast doubt on human ability to understand and, therefore, on all theorizing. It also cast doubt on the future availability of wealth (so much destruction made everything uncertain) and on the likelihood of a society stable enough to achieve the kind of social justice which had been demanded.

In Europe and America, a variety of philosophical movements developed in response: The existentialists and some of the phenomenologists diagnosed the sickness as something which stemmed from the core of human nature. The positivists of the Vienna Circle advocated reliance only on the immediacy of sense-certainty and decried the slipshod tricks of reason which seemed to lead beyond the surface of the obvious. In two new and strange versions, in fact, the war between religion and science had erupted anew. The depression brought demands for different forms of social organization. The results included Mussolini and Hitler—somehow backed by the philosophical retreat from reason. Marxism became embroiled in the desperate adventure of human repression when it became evident that, left to themselves, pig-headed and selfish men might never achieve a classless society.

In Canada, the development of philosophy was only partially interrupted by these events. The attempt to understand the range of human experience and value as a coherent system had resulted finally in the systems of Blewett and Watson. Blewett's life had been cut short, not by the war, but by a swimming accident. Watson lived until the onset of World War II. The revival of religion went on through the work of these philosophers whose systems form the intellectual background for the creation of the United Church of Canada.

The upsurge of new philosophical responses did lead to reassessments by philosophers like Rupert Lodge and George Brett. But they were of a character which had no obvious counterpart in Europe. Lodge doubted whether human reason could settle on a final system but claimed that philosophers could determine the range of feasible systems and we might learn, yet, how to live with one another's preferences. Brett determined to return to the history of ideas as an antidote to foolish, hasty, and implausible theorizing. He saw ideas as developing slowly but in a comprehensible way and our place in history as something which we might overcome only by understanding it. Both these were exercises in caution. Lodge and Brett were both powerful men who exercised influence on the choice of young men who were to lead the next generation in Canadian philosophy. But there is no evidence that they were suppressing underground movements toward positivism, existentialism, instrumentalism or any of the philosophies generally in vogue in universities in England, continental Europe, or the United States. Indeed, there seems every likelihood that they reflected the mood of their time and place—a mood of retrenchment, but a comprehensible response in terms of the Canadian environment.

Thus the great system builders—Murray, Watson, Blewett, and (perhaps) Schurman—had for the moment no successors, but the popular philosophies of the day outside Canada had no foothold either. Within Canada, orthodoxy was enforced by the arrival from outside of men like Etienne Gilson and Jacques Maritain who came from France to share in a milieu in which Catholic thought retained both its vitality and its openness to enlarged understandings.

The coming of another world war seems not to have changed the mood appreciably, at least so far as the written record goes. It is difficult to establish that very much of great significance was written during World War II—as if, perhaps, the writing (or publishing) of philosophical work was altogether too frivolous an activity. There is, however, some evidence that reflection on a world at war brought some modest change in philosophical activity or outlook. The urge to look at the inner workings of human society was certainly aroused, if only because the sight of such organized irrationality was followed by the realization that the war had also brought us the possibility of the total destruction of human beings. Thus one finds a philosopher like John Irving trying to find a new mixture of theory and practice in his studies of the Social Credit movement, or a social scientist like Harold Innis turning to philosophy (or at least writing philosophically) in a search for new and more basic human understandings.

There was no one following in the footsteps, still, of Watson and Blewett, but the influence of Lodge and Brett continued after the war. As an academic enterprise, and that is the concern of this book, philosophy seemed stagnant. The universities were growing rapidly, but though there was a large concentration of philosophers at the University of Toronto and a modest gathering at McGill, they were more often scattered across the rest of the country in pairs than found in flocks. New ideas were in demand but it was thought that they would be forthcoming from the great American centres of social science and not from philosophers, domestic or foreign. For what people wanted to change was the scope and wealth of their country. (They wanted to sell more wheat to more places, improve the steel industry, multiply the population with family allowances and easy immigration laws.) Their values had lately been rescued intact from Adolph Hitler and they had no desire to change them. (Admittedly, they desired to change the ideas of troublemakers—criminals, madmen, communists. But American psychiatry and sociology should take care of the first two and the family allowance of the third.) The fear of total destruction brought with it a measure of complacency—a desire to hang on tight to what they had. Thus they wanted more engineers, doctors, lawyers, and "good-guy" social scientists, not philosophers.

Philosophy had occasionally prospered in Canada outside the academy (we shall talk about Bucke and Lighthall as examples) but, originally, the forces which built the universities built the philosophy departments and no other institution or social region provided the same or similar impulses. In the post-war world, the forces which built the universities were no longer building philosophy departments. The impulse, after all, had been a measure of social division and a confrontation of human dilemmas which required the cunning of reason as a condition of tolerability.

There was not much left of the war between religion and science. Science had won. Most intellectuals thought there was only mopping up to do. (Some fifteen years later, when a body of Baptists attempted to assert their authority over their own foundation, Acadia University, they were widely thought not so much wrong as mad.) The community had reached its own mode of stability and seemed, as we have said, to require tinkering by social scientists and little else. The traditional Canadian insistence that the natural environment is to be regarded neither as sacred nor as something to be played with at will—an insistence emphasized very strongly by George Blewett, for instance—had mainly been forgotten and the (then) American view that nature is what you make of it was as common on one side of the border as on the other.

A later realization that a new view of man's relation to nature is a desperate urgency, that continuity of community is, after all, not something one can take for granted or easily live without, and that the apparent conflict of human values is not a passing fancy, have all played a part in creating a new surge of nationalism. But this book is intended neither as inspiration for that movement, nor merely as record. It is an assessment of what we have achieved and a clue to what we might still need to achieve.

Some possible misconceptions need to be dispelled. The reader will find that a good many of the philosophers who are dealt with at length in this book—Young, Murray, Watson, Blewett, Schurman, Stewart, amongst others—were strongly influenced by various strands of British, German, and American idealism. There is nothing surprising about that—philosophers in the United States, Germany, Britain, France, and Italy were, for the most part, influenced by the same thought forms in the same period. The interest, therefore, is in the special features, the particular arguments, the unusual attitudes discernible in such thinkers.[10] The idealism of Hegel and his followers

10 Charles W. Hendel, an American-born historian of philosophy, denied the existence of a "Canadian national philosophy." (Charles W. Hendel, "The Character of Philosophy in Canada," in *Philosophy in Canada—A Symposium* [Toronto: University of Toronto Press, 1952], p. 27.) In a Soviet appraisal of philosophy in Canada the author challenges Hendel: "But the specific feature of Canadian philosophy, as determined by the country's historical conditions of development, lies precisely in its adaptation to local conditions, with a corresponding unique refraction of the

had, after all, many strands: It set out to be a synthesis of Western philosophy in the special sense that it was designed to explain the course of philosophy from the pre-Socratics to Kant and to chart its course thereafter. One might find in it most anything. Philosophers did. What is interesting in Canada is the way, for the most part, that it was used as the instrument of a kind of philosophical federalism—but even that is too general, easy, and smug a notion.

We shall also deal with a significant (though smaller) number of philosophers whose views, on the surface at least, put them in opposition to all the idealist schemes and plans. But the selection has nothing to do with these doctrines. We have simply chosen all those thinkers who could reasonably be called philosophers in the traditional (largely but not wholly academic) sense and who met certain obvious conditions: They must have lived in Canada for a substantial period of time and done their significant work here. And they must have produced sufficient work so that an extended analysis is possible. Short papers—even if numerous—are usually not enough if one is to search out underlying assumptions and to show the ways in which a cast of mind emerges. We have tried to be straightforward and to avoid far-fetched inferences. The kinds of generalizations which have tended to fill this chapter occur only at intervals and we have kept them well away from the detailed analysis of the philosophical theories so that there is, so far as possible, never a confusion between what the philosopher is saying and the use to which we are putting him.

The reader will understand the limitations on the whole enterprise: Little has been written about most of the philosophers here. Eventually, if the history of philosophy is any guide, many of our understandings will surely be revised. Similarly, the social and intellectual history of Canada is still imperfectly explored and this work will look different when, in due course, the rest of the context in which it belongs becomes available.

philosophical and sociological ideas borrowed from abroad." (See V. V. Mshve-nieradze, "Early Canadian Philosophers: A Soviet View," *Marxist Quarterly* [Spring 1962], p. 65n.)

31

TWO

REASON AND AUTHORITY

James Beaven and Natural Theology

B EAVEN'S *Elements of Natural Theology*[1] was published in London in 1850, a year after King's College, Toronto, in which he had been Professor of Divinity, was officially closed and prior to his appointment as Professor of Metaphysics and Ethics at the University of Toronto. Fittingly enough—though probably accidentally—it marks both Beaven's personal transition from professional theologian to professional philosopher and the transition of academic philosophy in English Canada from a fiefdom of religion to an independent concern.

The moment was an interesting and crucial one in the development of what was to become Canada. Thirteen years after Mackenzie's rebellion and seventeen years before Confederation sectarianism was the crucial issue. In what was to become Ontario, Methodists and Anglicans, led respectively by Egerton Ryerson and John Strachan, struggled for social, political, and educational power. Presbyterians, Baptists, and a host of other sects were only slightly less obvious in the struggle. The two "Canadas" had been brought into uneasy union as an aftermath of Lord Durham's conviction that the colonists could hardly govern themselves worse than the British did and that the French in "Lower Canada" (now to be "Canada East") ought to be assimilated into a general culture. Protestant and Catholic now faced one another as two dominant blocks in a union—a situation which exacerbated the concerns of Catholics in English Canada.

Ironically, Egerton Ryerson, who had been appointed Assistant Superintendent of Schools of Upper Canada (Ontario) in 1844, was sent abroad to look for solutions to the sectarian struggles and chose Ireland as a model. (He had inspected the Prussian model, too, but, not surprisingly, concluded that Prussian education would go down badly amongst his constituents.) Ireland, however, was still an undivided

---

1 James Beaven, *Elements of Natural Theology* (London: F. and J. Rivington, 1850). Hereafter referred to as *Elements*.

island and had faced a problem not unlike the Canadian one. Ryerson recommended to the United Legislature of the Canadas that the newly developed "national" Irish textbooks be adopted in Canada and hired Thomas Robertson, a Chief Inspector of Schools in Ireland, as principal of the new Toronto Normal School. He was partly disappointed by the fact that the School Act of 1846 made special provision for the separate education of Catholics and Protestants in Canada East. In the end, the same division was to come in part (eventually in the primary but not the secondary schools) in what was to be Ontario.

Nonetheless, Ryerson became Superintendent in 1846 and was to be a dominant force in education in English Canada for a long time. The hunt for a rational agreement around which men of different sects could unite was on. It was not just that both politics and social life required an understanding—the simple facts of economics forced it as well.

English Canada was still a string of small towns carved out of an encroaching wilderness. The areas of substantial settlement by the 1850s were not so different from the present ones—a concentration around the western end of Lake Ontario, a thin line of settlement along the lake to Kingston, and a considerable band extending through what is now southwestern Ontario. The "Queen's bush"—the areas which are now Grey and Bruce Counties— was opened to settlement in 1847 and settlers did come but the population never became dense. The total population remained minute and the cost of indefinitely many school systems was prohibitive. (In Quebec, the cost of the new act of 1846 led to the burning of schools in protest. In Ontario, it led only to grumbling.)

In higher education the same problem had to be solved. Colleges which were to become universities had been founded in what, given the population, amounted to profusion: Presbyterians, Baptists, and Methodists had founded colleges in the Maritimes. Ontario was to have not one but two Presbyterian institutions. It was also to have, immediately, Anglican and Methodist institutions. Baptists and Catholics would not be far behind.

The solution—though it was not to prove an exclusive solution—was the new University of Toronto to which Beaven was appointed the first professor of philosophy. Shortly thereafter, it was organized into colleges with a "secular" University College and a cluster of denominational colleges. Beaven went to University College though his denomination is now represented in Trinity College.

No doubt Beaven wrote his *Elements* because he was interested in the rational foundations of natural theology and not as a tract with which to enter the political arena. Still, the fact that he was interested is surely not unrelated to the fact that, in his own life as well as in the community in which he lived, the problem of a solution to the wars of the sects was urgent. If one examines the situation within his own denomination and his own position within it, it becomes obvious that the need must have been even more pressing.

James Beaven was born in 1801 in Wiltshire and educated at Oxford. The first forty years of his life seem to have passed uneventfully. By 1843 when he came to King's College, Toronto, he was a conservative high churchman in religion and a conservative monarchist in politics. (In a published lecture which he gave at Oxford, he defended King Charles against Parliament with such verve that one would have thought that Cromwell must have been in the audience and that the parliamentarians must have committed their regicide yesterday.)

Canadian Anglicanism was hardly of that stripe. Though Anglicans tended to form the social "upper crust," the Church in England had some difficulty in getting clergymen to move to Canada and the church here was largely staffed by men from the "Celtic fringe" who had friends or relations amongst the Scots, Irish, and Welsh settlers. (Despite his Welsh name, Beaven himself seems to have been unmistakably an Englishman.) Beaven's habits of preaching in the college chapel in a surplice and intoning the service produced what the author of his entry in the *Dictionary of Canadian Biography*[2] discreetly calls "ripples" amongst his colleagues. The plainest appearance and the plainest service were the order of the day in Canada.

Beaven thus found himself involved in the controversies which animated every sect. It is plain that he did not like it though he changed nothing of his outward manner and demeanour. Daniel Wilson, a president of the University of Toronto, was eventually to call him "a stupid dry old stick that we would be well rid of."[3] Ernest Hawkins, a secretary of the Society for the Propagation of the Gospel, wrote him off in 1849, saying "the worthy Dr. B. rather bored me."[4]

But all this is unfair. Evidently, neither Wilson nor Hawkins managed to catch Beaven in the mood in which he wrote *Recreations of a Long Vacation.*[5] A little book of great charm and shrewd practicality, it

2   *Dictionary of Canadian Biography, 1871-1880*, ed. Marc La Terreur, vol. 10 (Toronto: University of Toronto Press, 1972). Hereafter referred to as *Dictionary*.
3   Ibid., p. 40.
4   Ibid., p. 40 (from Hawkins' personal journal, August 24, 1849).
5   James Beaven, *Recreations of a Long Vacation* (Toronto: H. and W. Rowsell, 1846). Hereafter referred to as *Recreations*.

emerged in 1846, the product of a visit Beaven made to the Indian missions of his church.

Educated clergymen were not easy to find in the 1840s, at least amongst the Anglicans. In England, the industrial revolution was rapidly leaving the Church of England behind and it was becoming not the national church it claimed to be but the church of a waning aristocracy, a rising professional class, and a group of rich farmers. Increasingly, prosperous merchants and industrialists were becoming what the English call "Nonconformists" (the making of words seems always to have been the work of those who attended the "established church"). Their workmen, if they did not stay home on Sunday, went to the Nonconformist chapel and not to the church.

The result was that the clergy of the English established church were not so often men who would be attracted to an Indian mission. Beaven was appealed to for help in recruiting staff for the missions and he was by no means sure that they justified the use of scarce talent.

His natural reaction was to make a tour of the missions. The tour took him across peninsular Ontario to Brantford on the Grand River, down to Lake Erie, around the peninsula to Lake Huron, and by boat to the Sault—the meeting-place of Lake Huron and Lake Superior.

He made meticulous notes on buildings, fences, scenery, and men. He knew how to build a fence, he calculated the optimum size for windows and churches to obtain the most warmth in winter and the least warmth in summer. Nor did the ability of the sturdy little Indian horses to manoeuvre the carriages over near-impassable roads escape his attention.

> In short, it must be evident that English horses would have been down a dozen times in the course of an hour; but our little Indians went through it all most patiently, and were perfectly ready for a merry trot when we came to a bit of plank. Indeed, Canadian horses in general are remarkably sure-footed, and a broken knee I have not yet noticed.[6]

Beaven's knowledge of road building was extensive and he devoted an entire chapter to a most detailed description of roads in Canada, after which there are several pages on types of carriages suitable for travelling them.

The beauties of nature never eluded him, nor the brutality of the land with its bogs, stones, and occasionally ferocious weather. He also saw the bugs. He does not dwell on the disadvantages of the land or lapse into Wordsworthian raptures. Nature, to him, is a fact, to be enjoyed, worked with, treated with caution. One can survive in it, but

6   Ibid., p. 58.

one had best measure, calculate, and stay watchful. Beaven was becoming a Canadian.

His attitude to the Indians, however—that and his cool, unthinking élitism—are of most interest to us. The journey shows a change in him. The Indians, before he set out, seemed to him just "objects of interest and curiosity."[7] Perhaps he first felt a twinge of fellow-feeling for them when he began thinking about the complex affairs of the New England Company.

The Company had been formed for the simple purpose of providing missions for Indians in the American colonies. The American Revolution undid its work: The Indians to whom it ministered were loyal to the British crown and fled to Canada. The Company could not order its missionaries to follow them, as Beaven drily puts it, into a hostile country. Its funds, however, were committed by the trust deeds of its incorporation to the welfare of just *those* Indians. In the end, it used its money to support what were now Canadian Indians. Beaven clearly approved of those Indians if for no other reason than that they, "savages" though they might be, felt loyalty to the Crown.

A growing sympathy for the Indians was accompanied by concern at the way in which his countrymen remained English despite everything. "Everything English is most valued,"[8] he noted, carefully inventorying the contents of a mission house, and expressed his disappointment at the lack of Indian curiosities.

Finally, he concludes that the Indians really *are* worth the time of a hard-to-find Anglican priest. They are "*capable* of cultivation, as the children of our own peasantry: but not a whit higher in any respect. Their moral character likewise is pretty much on a par with that of Englishmen in country districts; in chastity, no doubt, much higher."[9] (Beaven knew his English country life, all right.) He catches himself quickly, though, lest he go *too* far and notes that the Indians are rather child-like, "requiring constant supervision and discipline."[10] (One feels that the savages might, with a little wrong advice, easily fall into the hands of Baptists and Methodists.)

In other ways, too, Beaven was changing. If Torontonians found his high churchmanship a little lavish, he found the church he visited while he was detained in Detroit "revolting."[11] He deplored lined and cushioned pews "stuffed in a style we should be ashamed of in England. The contrast between the luxury of the worshippers, and the slighting treatment of the holy table, and the want of a fitting position for the

7   Ibid., p. 2.
8   Ibid., p. 31.
9   Ibid., p. 55.

10   Ibid., p. 88.
11   Ibid., p. 95.

bishop, was most revolting to my feelings."[12] (Changing, yes, but not all that much—the lack of a fitting place for the bishop bothers him still.)

His visits to the American shore provided an opportunity for Beaven to work off some of his pent-up wrath at American democracy. He was pleasantly surprised to find that his American acquaintances cheerfully admitted the "corruption"[13] which ran through their public life. One senses that he was a little disappointed that his opportunities to tell them how much he disapproved of their way of life were truncated by their own admissions.

His emotions vented, Beaven settled down to a short lecture on the theory of government. On this occasion he does not revert to the divine right of kings. Democracy, we are told, really fails because "the complicated relations which wealth engenders are inconsistent with the permanent maintenance of the theory, that government is or should be so simple that every one can understand it,—which is the theory of democracy."[14] Such a complicated society, he argues, "must pass through aristocracy or oligarchy into monarchy or tyranny."[15] Monarchy he regards not as a species of tyranny but as a settled tradition in which it is the function of the monarch to govern not in his own interest but in the interest of all his subjects.

Surprise that some of the Americans who support democracy are, in fact, high churchmen prompts him to reflect on his own convictions. In the end, he confesses, there is no "real inconsistency"[16] between high church convictions and the conviction that "republicanism is the best form of civil government."[17] Nonetheless, it rankles. "I could never yet understand how a person whose mind was formed by the Scriptures could be anything else but a lover of monarchy in the abstract, however much he might feel it his duty to acquiesce in that form of civil polity under which Divine Providence had cast his lot."[18] And then we do come back to the divine right of kings. "I must always think that form of civil, as well as ecclesiastical polity, to be best, which most directly tends to train the mind to reverence and submit to the one universal *monarchy* of the Supreme Being, and the limited *monarchy* which he has ordained in every family."[19]

It was not to be long in Canadian philosophy before John Clark Murray began to champion the cause of the liberated woman, but there is none of that for Beaven. He castigates the Americans for allowing liberty and licence to creep into family life.

12 Ibid., p. 95.
13 Ibid., p. 105.
14 Ibid., p. 100.
15 Ibid., p. 101.
16 Ibid.
17 Ibid.
18 Ibid., pp. 101-102.
19 Ibid., pp. 102-103.

When he reached the Sault it seemed to him that the Indians who lived there, too close to the Americans, suffered for it. So, indeed, did those Indians who fell into the hands of the followers of John Wesley and those whose bad luck (or Divine Providence?) it was to be converted by Catholic missionaries. Here, he is a little less hopeful about Indians in general and repeats his warnings that they need constant tutelage. (Perhaps his views about Indians should be matched against his views about Irishmen. He solemnly records that much of the problem of American democracy can be traced to Irish immigrants. Indians, one feels, were regarded as distinctly an improvement over Irishmen.)

Beaven was quite capable of being persuaded to take Indians seriously as human beings, just as he was quite capable of admitting that a man might hold republican political views without falling into eternal damnation. He can distinguish, almost always, between a good argument and his own bias. In short, he was neither blockhead nor bigot.

All of this is stage setting for his philosophical views. The *Elements of Natural Theology* was not his only philosophical work though it is to it that we shall devote our attention. In addition, he wrote a volume on the life and works of St. Irenaeus.[20] Irenaeus was Bishop of Lyons—a rather lonely post in southern Gaul—around 180 A.D. He had, however, rather a lot in common with the Alexandrian Platonists—being one of the sources of the strand of neo-Platonism which runs quickly into early Christianity. He was likely born at Smyrna in Asia Minor and his native language was certainly Greek. His most important work was a tract against the Gnostics, a colourful sect given to magic and mysticism and a focal centre for assault for philosophers from Plotinus to Augustine. A champion of strict orthodoxy against an array of hair-splitting heresies, Irenaeus was exactly Beaven's cup of tea.

Beaven's book on Irenaeus is like much of his minor theological writing from the period before he came to Canada. (That work includes a number of small handbooks for the clergy—*A Manual for Visiting the Sick, Questions Upon Scripture History, The Doctrine of Holy Scripture*, and *On Intercourse with the Eastern Churches*.) Though more scholarly than the minor works, it is written in the same dry style, emanating a self-assured smugness characteristic of those who write books like *A Help to Catechising* (another of the minor works). It turns out, if one follows the book through to its final chapter, that Beaven is mainly interested in Irenaeus because Irenaeus fought a long and hard

20 James Beaven, *An Account of the Life and Writings of S. Irenaeus* (London: J. G. F. and J. Rivington, 1841). Hereafter referred to as *S. Irenaeus*.

battle against the Gnostics. Beaven finds that Gnosticism is kindred to many of the "errors"[21] he thinks characteristic both of Roman Catholics and of "those Protestants who have rejected the Apostolical succession"[22]—characteristic, that is, of everyone except those who subscribe to the doctrines of the Church of England. He finds that, like the Roman Catholics, Gnostics questioned the truth of scripture and pointed out inconsistencies in its texts. Like the non-Anglican Protestants, the Gnostics ran to many special heresies ranging from predestinarianism to incorrect estimates of Satan.

Though the book is a scholarly and accurate account of the life and thought of Irenaeus himself, Beaven accepts quite uncritically all that Irenaeus has to say about the Gnostics—a procedure much like taking the description by the leader of the opposition as the gospel truth about the prime minister.

Beaven puts great emphasis—as Irenaeus did—on the alleged sexual irregularities of the Gnostics. He recounts with relish Irenaeus' stories of the part which sexual licentiousness played in their religious beliefs. If Beaven did not know of the long tradition of ascribing such peculiarities to one's religious opponents, he was more naïve than seems likely. Yet the most amazing accounts of Gnostic mass seductions seem not to raise a doubt in his mind.

Whether the book was successful or not we do not know. It started its career, however, with the advance subscriptions of a distinguished list of patrons—including Adelaide, the Queen Dowager, and the future Cardinal Newman.

All this was in 1841. Beaven was to abandon the hack work of clerical guide-book writing and the minor scholarship represented by the S. Irenaeus book. When he began to think for himself, his style relaxed and his mind proved undeniably fitted for greater tasks.

Beyond that, Beaven wrote a dozen other short works (mostly lectures and sermons) which do not greatly concern us here, and translated a volume of selections from Cicero. Hardly prolific, but not lazy, he was an accomplished classical scholar as well as a man with a firm grasp on the history of philosophy.

It may be surprising that he should feel impelled to write at all in the circumstances in which he found himself. Still, English Canada in that period, although isolated, was by no means a desert of the mind. William Lyon Mackenzie quoted Hume, Reid, and other Scottish philosophers in his newspaper as though their names would at least evoke recognition. The Scottish settlers brought with them clergymen

21   Ibid., p. xiii.
22   Ibid., p. xiv.

for whom it was second nature to pack an argument into a sermon. Not for them simple pious homilies.

Beaven's *Elements* is the most obviously philosophical work in a growing tradition of works bordering on religion and philosophy. While there is no evidence that Beaven read or paid attention to many (or any) of these works, the fact that writing (and even publishing) them was part of the normal practice of the community must have made it seem a natural thing to do. He was contributing to what was already a community tradition.

Before we come to assess his *Elements*, therefore, it is appropriate to sketch some of this background: In the late seventeenth century Quebec already had seminaries. In 1789 King's College was founded in the Maritimes. (The situation in the Maritimes will emerge more in Chapter Three.) These institutions were under strong church control. Although William Lyall, the earliest noteworthy Maritime philosopher, published his major work *Intellect, The Emotions, and The Moral Nature*, in 1855, philosophy did not become a subject of independent study at Dalhousie University until 1863 and only then because of the persistence of Thomas McCulloch.

In the two decades prior to 1860, no less than a dozen independent universities began active operation in Canada, all of which have survived in one form or another to the present day. Many of the colleges in that region opened between 1840 and 1850. McGill was thirteen years old when Queen's and Victoria opened in 1842.

The fact that the population represented a variety of religious and political viewpoints, often put forth by aggressive and antagonistic groups, accounts for the existence of the several university foundations amongst a population of less than two million.

Certainly at the non-Catholic institutions the major concern of philosophers and theologians centred on the doctrines of the Scottish "common sense" philosophers and the "moral intuitionism" of Paley and Butler. There was little interest in social concerns, though the economic doctrines of the Manchester School (Adam Smith, David Ricardo, W. S. Gill) found their place on some curricula. (No one seems to have attempted an explanation of the relationship between the political economy of the Manchester School and Scottish intuitionist ethics.) The situation is not surprising since nearly all early Canadian universities were staffed with theologians and intellectuals from the Scottish universities. Well schooled in other fields of science and mathematics, with a belief in the central importance of God, they had what amounted to reverence for moral responsibility and the importance of sound mental faculties necessary to gain insight into the dictates of God and conscience. And they taught and fostered an energetic involvement in religious dispute. It would be a mistake to think that early philosophical teaching in Canada was mere theological oratory of a deadening kind. The powers of reason were always emphasized and encouraged as a means to theological and moral truths. By means of reason these truths would be revealed to all men. Intuitionism insisted that the knowledge of such truths was right and morally good. Man's conscience confirmed his rational arguments. Of course, if he were mistaken in his reasoning he had sinned. No one simply could close his eyes and see the way. Consequently parishioners were not converted through faith, but convinced through reason.

Added to this emphasis on rational argument was the belief that all men, women, and children were entitled to an education. No one, whether rich or poor, was barred from Scottish universities if they had the proper schooling, and such schooling was made available to the poorest rural areas. In England it was only the rich and the upper class that received sufficient schooling and it was assumed that universities were for the élite alone.

Consequently, the import of Scottish teachers meant that church preaching was much more intellectual, and encouragement to learn and read and discuss things reached far into the sparse population.

It is interesting to note that during the forties and fifties in Canada when the beginning of the transition from religious argument to philosophical argument found its roots in the universities, the social conditions were such that religion was a relevant factor in the need for law and order among the people. Prohibitionism was strong (although patent medicine sales increased) in a very pious society.

This religious involvement proved detrimental to political unity and religious disputes meant a fragmented society. The people themselves paid little attention to government, having survived several changes of political status, and it was only with the emergence of major efforts at expanding and uniting (with the building of railways) that the religious fervour began to subside.

In such an atmosphere of theological rhetoric mixed with intellectualism, philosophy began to make headway. Canadian academics were profoundly aware that the scriptures and moral philosophy do not deal with precisely the same aspects of morality and one may be a necessary supplement to the other. Philosophy began as the servant of theology but soon established its own domain. Its first task was to reveal the psychological features of the mind to show that moral and religious beliefs of the scriptures could easily be acquired. The struggle between philosophy and theology became more obvious as the universities matured. The de-emphasis of church doctrines and the gradual escape from church power allowed the split to widen sufficiently that people such as Watson and Murray could no longer ignore it.

Against such a background Beaven's work was inspired and, as we shall see, philosophy and theology were to receive an equal share of the credit in his thoughts.

His main predecessors are worth noting. Because philosophy enjoyed a long tradition in Scotland and was compulsory for all degrees, these theologians usually came well equipped to assume university positions as professors of moral and mental philosophy. The difficulty in finding financing for the expanding universities contributed to their gradual secularization. (As the churches could no longer carry the burden, other sources needed to be tapped.) The universities did not, however, dip much into the secular pools of thought lest they contaminate Christian goals. Only when it became "safe" did Kant and Hegel and other idealists become worthy of study.

Knox College, at Toronto, seems to be the earliest institution to have made the distinction between philosophy and theology when it rejected the "auld kirk" policies of the church of Scotland and formed the "Free Kirk" in 1844. Its leading worker was John Bayne, minister of St. Andrews in Galt. Bayne adhered strongly to religious supremacy and believed that the ethical and religious convictions of the church could override any political mandates based on secular principles.[23] He was a firm proponent of moral intuitionism and was prepared to advocate the supremacy of the individual's moral principles even at the expense of social harmony and the "good of all."

Bayne offered a three-part theory of action: Reason and feeling play a part but the will is independent of them. Reason offers propositions, the feelings provide approval or disapproval, but the will acts. There is thus no ultimate excuse for bad behaviour. With such a rigorous stand the plausibility of Bayne's argument depends on the view that the same moral and religious truths are available to everyone. Had Bayne seriously considered the various conflicting beliefs surrounding him he would probably have had some misgivings about the dogmatic nature of his opinions. He stands firm, however, suggesting that the knowledge of right and wrong is immediate, and shortcomings in one's belief in moral truths are accompanied by corruptions in one's nature. Indeed the perception of right and wrong is due to the com-

---

23 John Bayne, *Is Man Responsible For His Belief? A lecture delivered before the members of the Hamilton Mercantile Library Association, on the evening of the 18th of February, 1851* (Galt: James Ainslie, 1851). We are indebted to Clifford Williams who kindly shared with us his research on Bayne and other figures of the period.

bined effort of intellectual insights and moral "feelings." Bayne's rigid adherence to doctrines of revealed truth prompted him to attribute the corruption of human nature to God's arbitrary gifts of divine grace to some, but not to others. Thus he concludes that man in the unregenerate state sustains a moral nature "opposed to the truth of God revealed in the Gospel."[24] This seemingly contradicts his previous position that moral truth is publicly accessible and that man has responsibility for his beliefs, but, like most dogmatists who are often found to advance untenable doctrines, Bayne was unruffled by his inconsistent viewpoints.

What we see in Bayne is the combination of philosophical argument and questions with the religious orthodoxy of the church. Beaven had begun, hesitantly, to loosen the ecclesiastical confines. Bayne, along with his contemporaries, remained unshaken by the philosophical arguments of their English and European predecessors.

An even more obvious case of the struggle to maintain church supremacy over political dogma is found in the writings of Henry Esson, Professor of Mental and Moral Philosophy, at Knox from 1844 to 1853. In a phamphlet entitled *A Plain and Popular Exposition of the Principles of Voluntaryism*[25] Esson suggested, rather obliquely, the appropriate relation between religious groups and the government. What he advocated was a complete separation of church and state. The authority of the individual conscience was a sufficient ground. In Esson's opinion, no human law can supersede private conscience. Government and the laws of man are quite remote from religious belief and moral conscience; they are to ensure and maintain freedom of thought, belief, speech, and worship for each person. Esson is defending the democratic belief that the state should not dictate moral belief. The proper function of law is protecting the moral convictions of the citizens, and not forcing on them the moral opinions of government legislators and other external authorities. Esson was concerned to maintain as much reasoned status for the church as he could summon. As a supporter of the Free Church he recognized the political power in the established churches of England and Scotland. Consequently, he supported strongly the leanings toward democratic equality which the establishment regarded as a threat to its legislative influence. Individual religious autonomy would mean that the government could not "support" any one church and its doctrines in exchange for support of government policies or land deals.

24 Ibid., p. 31. (Bayne continued, "... and till a change be wrought in the heart, there can therefore be no true belief," p. 32.)

25 Henry Esson, *A Plain and Popular Exposition of the Principles of Voluntaryism* (Galt: P. Jaffray & Son, 1851).

In 1848 during a feud at Knox College between Esson and his colleague Robert Burns, Professor of Theology, it became clear that Esson regarded philosophy not as a means of justifying religious principles, but as a subject independent of theology and interesting in its own right.[26] Esson stated that he had been greatly influenced by the Scottish philosophers Reid, Stewart, and Beattie, and by Joseph Butler's moral philosophy. Esson was reluctant to have idealism attributed to his beliefs, however. There was a certain suspicion of idealism prevalent at the time and the belief that it led to dangerous speculation and moral degradation was common. He did believe that inculcating a sound moral philosophy was the goal of philosophic pursuits and the only way to arrive at moral truths was to begin with an analysis of the psychological process of knowing. Mental philosophy and moral philosophy were to him inseparable—the former preceding. As we shall see, Canadian adherents of the Scottish school most frequently begin their moral philosophy by way of an analysis of the nature of the human mind, its structure, the sources and limits of knowledge, and criteria of justified beliefs.

In Esson's time, the struggle between religious and political bodies, and the urgency of religious and moral autonomy, meant that the validation of moral and religious beliefs was an important task. Esson continued his post until his death in 1853. He seems to have been the first person in British North America to be designated "Professor of Philosophy," and he upheld the autonomy of that discipline against criticisms of his theological counterparts.

It was in this upheaval that Beaven took root. He had been appointed to teach theology at King's College, Toronto, but with its secularization into the University of Toronto, he found himself (much to his concern, in a "godless institution") Professor of Metaphysics and Ethics.

There were two other figures of interest. William Turnbull Leach's career at McGill coincided with Beaven's at Toronto. Leach arrived in Canada, an ordained Presbyterian minister with an M.A. from Edinburgh, in 1835. He was confronted by the struggle between the Reform Party and the Family Compact. Being a member of the "established church," he opposed any Reformist tendencies to democracy and suggested that maintaining "the pious and profane, the wise and the foolish, the base and the honorable" to be equally capable of governmental tasks—that is, supporting a government of egalitarian bent—was not only foolish but also contradictory to the orders of

26 Henry Esson, *Statement Relative to the Educational System of Knox's College, Toronto, with suggestions for its extension and improvement* (Toronto: J. Cleland, 1848).

Providence and decrees of God.[27] Leach believed that the majority in every community were wicked and only "kept civil" by law. Since the wicked were most numerous, then if all had a vote, wickedness would increase. The state could only be preserved from anarchy by having its "best elements" dictate the laws in keeping with the proper—religiously based—morality.

Leach's authoritarianism did not go well with his colleagues, who had growing liberal sentiments, and in 1842 he was expelled from his church. He went to Montreal, became minister of the Anglican Communion Church, and then Professor of Classics at McGill in 1845. Later, he held the position of Professor of Logic and Moral Philosophy until 1872 when he was succeeded by John Clark Murray. At 67, he became a dean and Professor of English Literature. He retired in 1881. With Leach's highly religious interests, speculative philosophy was probably greatly undernourished until Murray assumed his post. Leach did teach Sottish common sense philosophy and in 1867 Albert Schwegler's *History of Philosophy* was introduced in the curriculum. Questions on Kant appeared on examinations. For all his reactionary tendencies, it seems that Leach was in touch with the developing philosophical trends in North America.

The Church of Scotland controlled Queen's, Ontario's first university, and so it was natural that a prominent clergyman was invited to become Professor of Mental and Moral Philosophy. James George left his church in Scarborough, near Toronto, and joined Queen's in 1853. A graduate of Glasgow, he was not well trained in philosophy.

As acting principal of Queen's he opened each year with an address. In his 1855 discourse we find George exploring the relationship between piety and intellectual labour.[28] His main emphasis is on religion. Atheism, he said, is conducive neither to being a poet, nor to doing scientific research. Furthermore, he did not believe that outside religion there could be a valid account of the nature of the moral world. He also attacked industrialism as "decivilizing" and degrading morally, in a little book, *What is Civilization?*, published in Kingston in 1859.[29] What caught his attention was not the advance of technology but the plight of the people left in its wake.

27 William Turnbull Leach, *A discourse delivered in St. Andrew's Church, Toronto, on the fourteenth day of December, 1838, being a day of public fasting and humiliation, appointed by authority, British Colonist* (Toronto, 1839).
28 James George, *The Relation Between Piety and Intellectual Labor: An address delivered at the opening of the 14th session of Queen's College* (Kingston: Daily News Office, 1855).
29 James George, *What is Civilization?* (Kingston: James M. Creighton, Book & Job Printer, 1859).

The factory system in England has been the means of acquiring great wealth for individuals, as well as for the country . . . yet, who is so ignorant as not to know that as it has been generally carried on, it has tended to reduce masses of the working classes physically, as well as mentally, to great degradation. . . . The accumulation of wealth, then, among a people—especially when accumulated in few hands—is not necessarily a civilizing agency, and in fact, may be a great enemy to true civilization.[30]

What is of most interest to us in George's works is the emergence of an emphasis on reason. An enlightened conscience, not "business know-how," marks the truly civilized man and this, according to George, requires the cultivation of reason. Only reason can grasp moral truths. George is the first to break from the traditional intuitionist position on ethics. For him, reason, quite separate from the sentiments or the will, is the source of moral motives and assists us in both intent and action. This is the first tinge of an emphasis on rationality which was to dominate philosophical positions for the next fifty years. George does not make a clean break, however, and claims that only reasoned religion, not philosophy, produces good men. George seemed outraged at attempts to give morality a non-religious basis and at the growing trend towards secularization in other areas. Still, it was a beginning.

George's most complete statement of social life was a sermon "On the Duties of Subjects to Their Rulers" which he preached in 1838 after the rebellions in Upper and Lower Canada. It was later published in a book containing a collection of sermons called *Thoughts on High Themes* in Toronto, 1874.[31] George views the distinct separation between those who govern and those who are governed as an important dichotomy to maintain. Those who govern have their powers ordained by God, they are keepers of the common good, to which all men must subordinate their individuality. The chief political duty of subjects is obedience, not just to laws, but to men. The main guidelines were to be found in the British constitution under which the colonies were directly subsumed. Nationalism, "national pride" as he calls it, is merely the "arrogant estimate of a people as to their own superior worth, with a foolish and insolent contempt for others."[32] It did not occur to George that maintaining control over colonies was a direct way of not only filling the pockets of England, but also sustaining at home the inflated national pride which accompanies one's "exploratory" successes. National pride, he claimed, leads to national ruin.

30 Ibid., pp. 5-6.
31 James George, *Thoughts on High Themes: Being a Collection of Sermons* (Toronto: James Campbell & Son, 1874).
32 Ibid., p. 248.

George, Beaven, and Leach clung tightly to their paternalistic conceptions of government in the new land, but they were outdated long before their works were published, for the union of the Canadas, the growth of the railways, and the cry of the unions were all mounting forces within which monarchical paternalism was rapidly floundering.

The emphasis on reason as a useful tool of moral development and understanding was George's most significant contribution. His obituary in the October issue, 1870, of *The Presbyterian* described him as a "prince among reasoners. His powers of analysis were specially acute and searching."[33] His great powers of oratory seemed to convince the most doubtful man. George himself was extraordinarily handsome with a white mane of wavy hair—"which in his youth might have stood for Milton's picture of Adam's."[34] Indeed, the square chest and broad face may have contributed to George's uncomely departure from Queen's on the crest of a lingering scandal (which his obituary politely ignores)—having been accused of fathering an illegitimate child to the sister of a faculty member. The accusation plagued George through various letters and court appearances for eleven years. (A lengthy poem of abuse was published against him in 1865.)[35] George fought the case (maintaining his innocence) and held his job but the pressure mounted time and time again until the clergyman finally retreated. In 1866 he left Queen's and returned to take up his parish in Stratford, Ontario.

Two other books by George, *The Poetic Element in the Scottish Mind*, and *Fireside Sermons* for parents and their children, while elegant in script, do not warrant our attention here.

Among the Baptists in Canada there was growing concern about the continuing hold the American colleges had over them. Their origins were in the United States and they depended on American colleges to train their ministers. John Strachan had pointed out, in 1825, that not enough devotion to the mother country was being encouraged and soon the population would be deluged with opinions unfavourable to England.[36] (Americanization of attitudes and life styles, it would seem, is not a new threat and was seen as a very real

33 Quoted from the obituary of James George in *The Presbyterian*, 24 vols., 1848-1875 (October 1870), vol. 23, p. 242.
34 Ibid., p. 239.
35 A poem found in transcripts of the examination of James George in Court, Kingston, September 21, 1864, entitled "The No-Conscience Theory in Practice—A New and Startling Discovery by the Most Profound of Modern Philosophers" (Toronto: The Globe Steam Job Press, 26 & 28 King Street East, 1865).
36 James Edward Wells, *Life and Labours of Robert Alexander Fyfe, founder and for many years principal of the Canadian Literary Institute, now Woodstock College* (Toronto: Gage, undated).

threat over one hundred years ago.) Freedom of dependence upon American seminaries and colleges helped motivate the founding of Canadian Methodist, Baptist, and some Presbyterian institutions. In 1857 Robert Alexander Fyfe, Canadian-born, helped to found the Canadian Literary Institute at Woodstock which later became McMaster University and, as principal, lectured on moral philosophy for the next seventeen years. Fyfe studied in the United States with Henry J. Ripley, Ezra Chase, and Francis Wayland and, like his fellow philosophers in Canada, was a follower of Scottish moral intuitionism.

Although the separation of philosophy from religious doctrine was minimal, philosophy was recognized as an independent discipline, and as the scholars in Canada pulled farther from the reins of the "established churches" their philosophic endeavours began to assume more speculative forms. Without exception these early scholars were clergymen and most were educated soundly at the Scottish universities. They were intensely interested in religion and this fervour was behind the numerous educational institutions founded in which to air and debate their views. The theological doctrines which divided men one hundred years ago fathered the academic institutions of today.

Beaven's *Elements* is a work in a long tradition. Like Thomas Aquinas, he seeks to separate that part of theological knowledge which may be obtained on the basis of reason alone from that part which may only be obtained through divine revelation. It is his view that one can, by natural reason, substantiate a metaphysic which will assure one of the existence of God and of the immortality of the soul. It is also his view that one can, by philosophical investigation, settle some crucial issues about the ultimate nature of reality. He is careful neither to deride the natural sciences nor to belittle their place in the scheme of knowledge. If we try to conjecture about the questions he is trying to answer we will come to this kind of conclusion: His concern is less with the question, How can it be that the Christian message is a true one?— for he has no real doubts about that—than with the question, If what we know from experience and science is the truth about the world, how are we to understand the ultimate nature of a world which gives rise to these experiences? Behind this lies the question we have suggested, Are there any basic truths around which all men can unite no matter what their special claims to revealed truth? Bound up with all of these is the further question: In the light of what demonstrable truths are we to interpret the Christian message?

Beaven is simply arguing for two propositions which had been argued for—in one way or another—over a span of more than two thousand years. One of them is that certain doctrines crucial to but not

48

exclusive to Christianity, in particular the existence of God and the immortality of the soul, can be demonstrated without appeal to special revelation. The other is that reason and faith do not contradict but rather complement one another.

The tradition contained, in fact, at least four basic kinds of arguments for the existence of God. One of them is the cluster usually called "cosmological" arguments. The essence of them is that the patterns of causal explanations for things and states of affairs in the world are such as to create a set of dependence relations which hold either between things and states of affairs themselves or between actual and possible states of affairs. That situation might be construed in many ways but, crudely, the argument is that this complex is rather like a file of mountaineers roped together. If they are simply tied to each other, they will all fall off the mountain. At least one of them must be tied to something outside the system—in their case, someone must have his axe in the mountain. In the case of the world, there must be a link to something outside it.

The second cluster contains the so-called "ontological arguments." The point of them is that God, as a matter of logic, simply cannot fail to exist. The idea of God is not the idea of a possible thing or state of affairs but the idea of a necessary thing or state of affairs. For nothing could bring God into existence or remove Him from it. If He ever existed, He must always have existed. His existence is either impossible or necessary.

The third cluster is made up of arguments which derive in a special and peculiar way from experience. It contains the "design" arguments—the arguments which proceed from the proposition that the order and arrangement of the universe suggest a purposeful design to the proposition that there must, therefore, be a designer.

The final cluster consists of "moral" arguments, the most common forms of which are the doctrine that we need God to sustain the proposition (which we know independently to be true) that we are reasonably entitled to expect men to obey the moral law, and the doctrine that the knowledge we have of high-order values can only be explained if those values are actually instantiated. Their instantiation can occur only in the being of God.

All of these argument clusters, in fact, go back to antiquity though they tend to be associated with philosophers who developed them in the forms around which debates have most commonly centred. Thus the cosmological arguments are associated with Aristotle and Aquinas, the ontological arguments with Anselm, Descartes, and Leibniz, the design arguments with Aquinas, Paley, and Newton, one form of the moral argument with Kant, and the other with a long Platonic and neo-Platonic tradition.

Arguments for the immortality of the soul have been many and various though two kinds of them stand out. One, associated with Plato, hinges on the indivisibility of mind—the apparent impossibility of splitting minds in parts and distributing them in space and time. The other stems from a certain reading of Aristotle associated strongly with Aquinas, amongst others, and is usually represented as an inference from the proposition that the mind, since it is capable of knowing things which are not spatial and temporal in kind must itself transcend space and time.

The view that faith and reason are independent but mutually complementary is, above all, a Thomistic doctrine and derives from the debate between Thomas and the followers of St. Bonaventure who maintained, on the contrary, that faith and reason are inseparable and both are required at every step in knowledge. (The practical relevance of this issue should be obvious. The view of Bonaventure leads directly to the demand for separate schools. The argument is that there is no knowledge which does not need to be informed by faith. The theoretical relevance of the issue is more complex. One view depends on the doctrine that there are many kinds of things to be known in the world and that, therefore, there will be different routes to different kinds of objects which we want to know. The other entails that there is one kind of thing to be known and the different modes of knowledge merely reveal different aspects of it.)

Beaven confronts these traditions from the stance of a man in the middle of the nineteenth century who faces certain kinds of preferences for modes of knowledge and who is looking for arguments which will persuade his readers in the face of beliefs which he has no serious hope of altering and, indeed, as a man who, despite a certain aloofness from the spirit of the times, really has no desire to change the central core of public belief. We must look to see what this amounts to.

Beaven mentions some forms of the cosmological argument with approval, but he does not think they are likely to be persuasive, because they are abstract. The Kantian form of the moral argument receives a nod, but he does not think it bears much weight. The ontological arguments—which in recent years, have again attracted philosophical attention—he does not even mention. The weight of his book rests on the design arguments but he laces his long discussion together with a theme which, in part, is his own. He is not so much impressed by the usual features of the design argument—by Paley's view that the world is a mechanism which works together for an end as if its parts were the parts of a watch, by Newton's view that we ought to be surprised at the regularity and lawfulness of nature, or by Thomas' view that the world is well designed for the saving of human souls. Some of these features, as we shall see, he casts substantial doubt upon. What impresses him is a certain view about the relations between mind and matter.

In order to understand this, we must examine some of the background views. He is clearly writing for men for whom the scientific revolution of the sixteenth and seventeenth centuries has become the commonplace of nineteenth-century technology. Furthermore, he is surprisingly aware of the extent to which nineteenth-century geology and biology have already trampled on some sensitive areas of theology and he confidently—and rightly—assumes that it will not stop there.

His book was published nine years before Darwin's *Origin of Species* and he was no doubt working on it for some time before it was published. Yet he accepts Lamarck's "facts" as "undeniable." He knows that geology has established the age of the earth as very great and he is aware of the evidence of fossil remains. Doubts come to his mind about the mechanism of evolution and the origin of life. He remarks that it has not been shown that life can develop out of the liquids which covered the earth in its early stages and that the development of species shows gaps. Both these remain, to some extent, problems even now. He did not have available a detailed mutation theory of evolutionary development and we must remember that theories about the development of protein molecules date from only the last few years. But there remain problems about biological "missing links," and the natural development of molecular structures out of which life could develop is an issue which continues to merit scrutiny. Beaven simply states his doubts. He does not build on them any argument beyond the argument that not everything in nature is obviously capable of a simple natural explanation.

He expects his audience to take such things seriously and there is no hint in the book that religious men might find a theory of evolution outrageous. He could not have known just what stir the publication of Darwin's book would create but he was not far from the mark if he expected to address an audience in Canada: Eighty years later it would be possible to have a "monkey trial" in Tennessee but the response was generally quieter in Canada. There were opponents of evolution in Canada but they were fewer and many of them were on the lunatic fringe.

The question, then, is, given that the earth is very old, that species have developed over time and were not created as they are now, that the process has been very wasteful, how is one to make out a case for the design of the world by a benevolent deity? The classical objection to all design arguments has been that there is a great deal of waste and a substantial amount of evil in the world. What God would create a world so full of pain and do it so inefficiently? Why should it take God so long and why should He not, at least, prevent the very worst evils and make a show of reasonable tidiness in the process? The "problem of evil" cuts at the very heart of Christian theology. A bad world and a good God who has unlimited power seem utterly incompatible.

There are ways of weaseling out of the problem—but Beaven will have none of them. He admits frankly that he does not know what to say about the amount of evil in the world. He is willing to accept some of the excuses traditional to Christian apologists. Men make much of the evil themselves. Pain sometimes has good results—it warns men of danger and it forces them to face up to their actual condition in the universe. But he refuses to see this as an adequate excuse.

What, then, is the counter-argument? Beaven first introduces it briefly in his quick look at the cosmological arguments: What is true, he says, is that matter is not capable of arranging itself. (We can imagine it this way: There are physical laws like the law of gravitation which determine the distribution of material objects once one has them in the world. But there is nothing in the nature of the objects—nothing in their descriptive properties—which guarantees this arrangement. It is just a fact that it happens. Since it does happen, we can make the necessary observations which lead us to postulate the laws. But though gravitation explains the distribution of some objects, what explains gravitation? There may, of course, be other physical explanations. There may be particles speculatively called "gravitons" [about which Beaven could not have known] but one could still ask why *they* behave the way they do. The answer to that cannot be in "physics." It is either by chance or by design that they behave as they do.)

Throughout the book he takes this position. Life requires the working together of a variety of natural laws on a matter which is susceptible to the final result. Is it design or chance? Beaven argues that it is only minds which can produce innovative design. Matter is what it is; the laws of nature are what they are. But neither of them are capable of changing their natures or of entering into purposive enterprises. We do know that we are capable of innovative enterprise and that we have minds. If nature shows signs of such enterprises and they involve the manipulation of large blocks of the universe which are quite beyond our control, are we not entitled to make a similar inference?

There are several threads to this which require some unravelling. That can be done, in some measure, by considering an objection to all design arguments which Beaven does not seem to tackle head-on though one must surmise that it is at the back of his mind. An obvious objection to Paley's watch and watchmaker analogy is that we can compare the watch to the rest of nature. If a man discovered a watch in the middle of the British Columbia desert, he would notice that, in many respects, it was unlike the rest of the world around it. Its parts worked together; one could, by observing it, guess its functions. It would stand out in ways which would justify us in inferring that it had a maker. But the design argument is intended to be about the whole world. We cannot compare the whole universe to anything else. How, then, do we know what kind of world would count as evidence for "design" and what kind of world would count as evidence for chance? We can find designs *in* the world, but that does not by itself make a *designed world*.

Beaven, we must suppose, deliberately takes his stand within the world and looks for threads of design running through it. The signs of those threads, if any, will be the signs of mind. What will count as such signs?

Laws, in Beaven's view, will, *as such*, be clues from which we may arrive at the view that there are such signs. For matter will not be self-arranging. There is a lack of clarity about what he actually thinks matter *is* and we can only infer the views which would be compatible with his theory. From what he does say, however, it seems fairly obvious that he thinks matter is whatever it is that comes to be arranged in the various patterns which form the subject matter of such sciences as physics, chemistry, geology, and biology. These sciences are, evidently, about the patterns in which matter is arranged and not, literally, about matter itself. Otherwise there would not be several such sciences (as Beaven clearly thinks there are) but only one. Now if the same subject matter yields several sciences because there are different characteristic patterns, the patterns must be independent of the material they organize in the sense that that material might or might not have been organized that way.

In essence this is the fairly standard view that the principal outcome of scientific investigation is the discovery of laws. For laws refer specifically to the patterns. (A physical cosmology, for instance, traces the successive arrangements of certain matter-patterns over a time span. A biological analysis of a specific life form seeks to detail the process by which a succession of material arrangements succeed one another.)

If the laws (and patterns on which they depend) are independent of the material which is instantiated in them, they require a separate explanation. The sciences do not generally try to explain how a certain law came to hold—it is simply assumed that the law of gravitation always applied, or that Boyle's law has been true wherever there have been gases. The explanation for the "occurrence" of laws, therefore, is not itself a part of science but some other kind of inquiry.

To repeat, if matter itself simply gave rise to the laws (and if "matter" were one kind of thing) one would expect there to be only one set of laws and one science. This is the basis of Beaven's doubt that the occurrence of "life" is self-explanatory. It is not his claim that there is something mysterious which is "more" than matter, and added to the process, and it is not his theory that matter cannot give rise to "life." Rather it is his theory that a new kind of pattern requires a new kind of explanation. This is buttressed with the more fundamental claim that *any* demonstrable law will require a special explanation and the real claim seems *not* to be that the creation of "life" would require divine intervention but that the plurality of law forms is evidence that matter is not simply self-organizing—for then it would have a preferred arrangement.

But what about chance? Beaven's answer is not perfectly clear. In one place he argues that any law requires an explanation other than chance, presumably because the very occurrence of a law implies a continuous non-random distribution, but the general tenor of the long argument seems to suggest that he puts weight on the fact that the world generally has a direction in which stability and complexity continue to grow. There may be chance elements in the world but we find in it substantial stability and distributions which have a strong likelihood of persisting.

The force of these contentions may depend upon just what theory of matter Beaven holds and how well it could be substantiated. If matter always requires some other agency in order for its distributions to make intelligible patterns of the kind which are susceptible of scientific investigation, then the contention is a strong one. If, however, matter has an intelligible order and structure of its own, the contentions are weak. Beaven seems to prefer the suggestion that, since matter is clearly susceptible of various patterns, it has no preferred pattern of its own.

There are passages in which there is an idealist undertone—passages in which Beaven compares the workings of nature to the workings of our own minds. Presumably, whatever it is that we grasp when we imagine and dream is somehow "there" to be organized but only becomes intelligible and available to us when we organize it in thought. Matter may have that relation to the mind of God and Beaven sometimes suggests that it does. Equally, a theory in some ways like Artistotle's would do as well for him. A theory, that is, in which matter is simply, in itself, potentiality on which forms can be impressed, would serve his purposes just as well. A theory which held that matter consists of its own structures—that one is investigating not a particular form of matter but matter itself when one does, say, molecular chemistry or atomic physics—would be incompatible with his theory.

If Beaven's underlying contention is correct, then even the ultimate reduction of biology to physics would not weaken his case for we would still have to explain how, given the many possibilities, matter came to have one regular form rather than another. If one could show that the pattern and the nature of matter were identical, this first leg of his argument would collapse under him.

The reader would guess, however, that this argument about laws as such is only a clue to the real case. What impresses Beaven most is the array of laws which must function together in order to produce a phenomenon like life. It is there, he thinks, that a high-order intelligence begins to appear in the world. And here the point about comparisons inside the world begins to tell. We can see that there are many pattern kinds and within each pattern many laws. They must function as a unity in order to get a phenomenon like life. To get the individual laws, the universe needs to manifest only an array of quite mediocre intelligences—perhaps even nothing more dramatic than a set of tendencies to order, which we might or might not choose to dignify with the title "intelligence." But to get them all to function together, he thinks, would require more than this.

It seems to Beaven beyond the limits of the reasonable to suppose that such a thing just happened. Life, in itself, is purposive. Every living creature manifests a direction of activity which is closely related to its structure. Could all this purposiveness be the result of a random concatenation of laws within which there is no purpose?

Once again, we need to notice the basis of this argument. It is rather more subtle than the ones which commonly animate strains of the design argument. If the laws themselves required no animating intelligence, the argument would not be very strong. But if intelligence is required for the laws themselves then more intelligence is required for the particular arrangement of them which gives rise to so complex and strongly purposive an activity as that manifested by a living organism. And that intelligence must be unified.

This, of course, leads Beaven to the conclusion that there is one intelligence behind the universe and that it is appropriate to call it God.

The strength of this argument is, ultimately, not easy to assess. Assessment would require a complete metaphysical system and one can only draw upon the hints which Beaven gives us. The task of sustaining the argument may be one which would be reasonable to attempt. Indeed, those who would draw upon the design argument could well do worse than to go back to Beaven.

It should be noticed that what Beaven thinks he is doing is establishing a reasonable presumption in favour of his case. He is quick to point out some of the problems and to admit them openly—the problem of evil, for instance. He closes without treading on ground which might well have led him into considerable unorthodoxy. The feeling he leaves is that his God is rather like a British monarch. He has a constitutional framework which simply represents the possibilities of nature. He can and must work within it to the best of His capacity. Though, like the British monarch, He has unlimited theoretical power, His real power is constricted. Men could not work as moral agents or as rational builders of their own world in a nature which was constantly subject to change without notice. Any way of organizing the world, perhaps, would lead to waste and evil for what God can do is to organize the laws of nature. To correct the process would require new laws with equally universal application and heaven knows how much new waste and disaster. (In these respects he sounds a little like Berkeley and, indeed, much that he says would fit quite neatly into Berkeley's system, though were he to adopt Berkeley's system, the route to God would be more direct, and we must suppose that Beaven thought Berkeley unlikely to commend himself to his audience.)

We shall shortly examine Beaven's view of the relations between natural theology and religion. Before we come to that, however, we must examine his arguments for the immortality of the soul.

Interestingly—but not surprisingly, given his manner of arguing for the existence of God—he rejects the arguments which, traditionally, are most common. The Platonic arguments, including the one which is based upon the indivisibility of mind, he rejects specifically. "It is disappointing to observe how little of solid argument there is in these reasonings; in fact, there is not one of them which is not based upon some false or doubtful assumption."[37] The argument developed out of Aristotle and used extensively by Thomas Aquinas—the argument based upon the power of the mind to know things which are not material in kind—is not mentioned specifically by Beaven, though it might be argued that a version of it is implied in the arguments he does use.

37 Beaven, *Elements*, p. 195.

Characteristically, he wants to get his hands on something one can grasp in a concrete way. He finds two lines of argument appealing. One is that it would seem in this life that we are being prepared for something. We go on developing, especially in our moral life, and our life, as he says, is "progressive." The argument is not that we go on getting better and better like some character out of Horatio Alger or Samuel Smiles. Beaven is arguing that we go on developing our moral capacities and, though we may, in fact, get better or worse, our moral abilities grow. One would not call a small child either good or wicked in the sense that one believed it actually capable of understanding the nature of moral judgments. It takes both intellectual capacity and substantial experience to make the issues intelligible. Indeed, it is only well into adulthood that the human animal is able to grasp the sense of a thread to his life which is capable of judgment as a unity. One sees, learns, meets people, interacts with them, and so on and then, at some point, it becomes sensible to ask about the meaning of one's life and to judge it.

Yet even then it remains incomplete. One has, inevitably, only done some of the things which lie within one's capacity, one has only begun to act out the meaning which one has discovered in one's life. This seems, at any rate to Beaven, somehow lacking in sense.

> . . . all knowledge of moral excellence renders us capable of higher moral action; and all improvement in moral action gives us both ideas of something morally higher, and power to realize them in ourselves. Our nature, then, is progressive; its tendency is to unlimited advancement; and the only way in which that tendency can be carried out, is by affording us an unlimited existence.[38]

It is this argument which we described as a nod in the direction of Kant's moral argument. It would take both God and immortality to provide the basis for this program.

The best one can do with such an argument is to point out that, since we are creatures who choose and do so constantly, values of some kind do enter into our lives. Since we live under the limitations of our biology and the limitations imposed upon us by society, we do find that our ability to act on our values is severely restricted. We constantly live with this clash—without it art and literature would be substantially bereft of major themes. There is a strong suggestion that we are training ourselves for a part in a play which will never be staged—we are constantly refining our values and the gulf between them and the domain of action open to us widens throughout life. If our lives are "progressive," they are also apt to be frustrating.

38 Ibid., p. 192.

Now what is the meaning of this? How does it come that we are not simply creatures of instinct and conditioned reflex, content to act on built-in possibilities and happy to take our pleasures where we find them? A modern critic of the situation would turn to a psychological explanation.

A follower of B. F. Skinner[39] would urge that we are simply conditioned inefficiently. As a result, our conditioning breeds conflict, guilt feelings, and irrational and ineffective action. A Freudian[40] would argue that the conflict is the result of our attempts to adapt to civilization by suppressing our basic drives and that the result is a sick subconscious mind which generates endless conflict. A Jungian[41] might argue that we have lost effective contact with the collective unconscious, and so on.

Notice, however, that the problem is still with us. Where today one might seek a psychological solution, Beaven seeks a metaphysical solution. The conflict, he argues, is caused by the fact that we are not designed only for this life. We are designed for something more. The practical upshot of this difference is very great: It is the difference between developing the conflict in a controlled and rational way and trying to see what one can learn from it, and trying to get rid of it by conditioning, psychotherapy, or—if one would be even more modern—escape into the dream world of drugs.

Beaven is aware that, even for his audience, this part of the argument would not be enough. He adds to it essentially by drawing upon the material of his earlier argument about God. The argument is not that God, if He exists, would surely have made us immortal. Beaven has already confessed that we do not know enough about God to be sure about that. We cannot, finally, dispose of the argument about evil, for instance. But what we do know, he says, is that we have minds which must be like the Divine mind in important respects. Though he cites Cicero (he is fond of Cicero and quotes him constantly) in support of this proposition, he doesn't really tell us much about it. We are expected to recall the earlier argument and to realize that he (like Cicero) says, "it is by analogy from the human mind that we reason to the Divine."[42]

39 B. F. Skinner, *The Behavior of Organisms: An Experimental Analysis* (New York: Appleton-Century-Crofts, 1938).

40 Sigmund Freud, *Abstracts of the Standard Edition of the Complete Psychological Works*, ed. Carrie Lee Rothgeb (New York: International Universities Press, 1973).

41 Carl Jung, *The Undiscovered Self*, trans. R. F. C. Hull (London: Routledge & Kegan Paul, 1958).

42 Beaven, *Elements*, p. 192.

The point is just this: We have been able to argue for the existence of God because we have been able (he thinks) to discern the work of mind in the pattern of nature. Now the argument seemed to be that matter could not be the explanation of its own patterns, structures, and laws. We know by inspecting our own minds that we, ourselves, order events and our own lives. We know that we render things intelligible by bringing them to the patterned state which enables consciousness to work on them. Mind itself is independent of nature.

Ultimately, Beaven is brought to retract a little of his own assault on Plato's argument from the unity and indivisibility of mind to the immortality of the soul and even to the argument that the soul "gives life to the body."[43] "Both the last," he grudgingly admits, "are sound and correct arguments, if properly put...."[44] What he means by "if properly put" is that the arguments are reasonable if what one understands by them is simply the ordering of matter by mind—the choice of possible forms by the imposition of intelligence. Mind, then, is not the sort of thing that Plato's way of putting it might imply (though Plato is obscure and there are many ways of interpreting him). Rather mind is the intelligence which manifests itself through the patterning of nature. It is not something added, it is something which appears *in* the pattern of nature. As such it can appear in any pattern and is not bound to any. If that is true, it, in one sense, transcends all those patterns and its immortality is a natural feature of it.

Once again, the assessment of this argument must depend upon the production of a more comprehensive metaphysic than Beaven gives us. But it is not a ridiculous argument and there is an element about it which is Beaven's own.

Thus we come at length to the final point of the book: the distinction between rational theology and revealed religion. Earlier Beaven has referred to all the usual claims of authority and rejected them as useless whenever "the fundamental doctrines of all religion are assailed."[45] The point is that once one has a basis to go on, one can make sense of claims to revelation. If one knew there was a God and that men were immortal, one might be able to assess claims about the incarnation of God in the person of Jesus, the resurrection, and the likelihood that popes have special guidance from God. If one has no such basis, then conflicting claims have no adjudication.

Reason in Beaven's view comes, logically, first. It informs all men who can think and it provides the ground upon which one can look at

43 Ibid., p. 197.
44 Ibid.
45 Ibid., p. 6.

one's religious claims. More than that, it unites all men, not in the sense that all men will necessarily be persuaded by the same arguments, but in the sense that all men can take part in the give and take of the reasoning process. It is the basis of a rational community.

Furthermore, it will not be true that revealed religion will influence all claims to knowledge. Reason in that sense is independent. Science stands on its own grounds and, apparently, can proceed without the final necessity of a satisfactory metaphysic though it will take that metaphysic to make it intelligible in the larger sense. The philosopher, if he is wise, it would seem, attends to the scientific facts and uses reason to arbitrate more basic claims. Out of that he gains the foothold which will allow reason to umpire the disputes between those who claim special revelation.

THREE

REASON AND INTUITION

William Lyall and Philosophy in the Maritimes

W ILLIAM LYALL WAS born only ten years later than James
Beaven, and Paisley is only a few hundred miles north of
Beaven's Wiltshire. But in intellectual outlook the two men
were worlds apart. The hushed certainties of Beaven's Anglicanism
contrast sharply with the fierce debates which surrounded Lyall's Free
Church Presbyterianism. The neat, reasoned progression through
which Beaven moves from first principles and gentlemanly science to a
well-ordered system is, equally, unlike Lyall's attempt to build a
philosophy from a patchwork of insights gleaned from twenty centuries. Though in the end both Beaven and Lyall are willing to concede
that there are unanswered questions, Beaven's concession is the even-
tempered acceptance of a High Church Anglican who knows that, in
the end, all is right with the world, while Lyall's acceptance is clearly
that of a man whose philosophy is still in the making and who thinks
that a new piece of the jigsaw puzzle may turn up at any moment.

In background and original religious outlook, Lyall is almost a
twin of George Paxton Young whom we shall meet in the next chapter.
But there the resemblance ends. Young went to Toronto, became the
champion of free thought, and broke with his church. In the process,
he became an embodiment of the intellectual development of English
Canada. Lyall went to Halifax, worked almost alone, quietly assembled
his own philosophy in a way that was to prove unique, and remained
the loyal and unpretentious servant of his church.

Beaven and Paxton Young, in their different ways, present one
pattern quite common in the lives of Canadian philosophers. Thrown
into a small community, they tended to become its intellectual leaders.
With few philosophers to talk to, they became, quite naturally, involved
in a variety of intellectual concerns and helped to give those concerns
form and direction. In turn, those concerns influenced their
philosophies. William Lyall represents another quite natural pattern.
Left to himself, he turned inward. As the *Dalhousie Gazette* put it after

his death, "He loved the seclusion of his study and the society of the mighty dead."[1] The result was a philosophical system which, while it brought him an honorary doctorate from McGill and a charter membership in the Royal Society of Canada, attracted little attention. Indeed, he published his massive work *Intellect, The Emotions, and The Moral Nature*[2] when he was forty-four and, though he lived to be nearly eighty, he wrote little else of significance. One must surmise that he had little encouragement to write more.

He had been educated first at the University of Glasgow and then at Edinburgh, where he encountered the thought of Thomas Brown which was to leave a lasting mark on his philosophy. For a time he served as a clergyman in Scotland and took the part of the Free Church in the Great Disruption of 1843. He had a church in Linlithgow when, in 1848, he came to Ontario as a tutor at Knox College. Two years later, Paxton Young replaced him at Knox when he decided to accept a chair at the new Free Church College in Halifax. The Free Church College of Halifax had a staff of two: Lyall, who served officially as Professor of Mental and Moral Philosophy and Classical Literature, and Andrew King, who was Professor of Theology. In fact, Lyall taught all of the arts subjects. The classes cannot have been large. For the academic year 1852-53 the enrolment was twenty-three—two from New Brunswick, one from Prince Edward Island, and twenty from surrounding parts of Nova Scotia. Still, Lyall had to teach half a dozen subjects.

He continued that regimen for a decade until the Free Church and the United Presbyterians joined forces to open a college at Truro. He served three years at Truro and then went back to Halifax to accept the Chair of Logic and Psychology at Dalhousie University where he remained for the rest of his career. After 1860, his duties were probably lighter, but still exhausting by contemporary standards.

To grasp what Lyall faced, one must look at some of the complexities of the development of higher education and of philosophy. The story involves a tangled welter of institutions which have their explanation in the rivalry between religious sects and in the rivalry between, on the one hand, all of the sects and, on the other, those who, like Lord Dalhousie, foresaw the inevitable need to pool resources and to create secular institutions.

The earliest universities in English Canada were located in the Maritime Provinces. King's College was founded in 1789. Their predecessors, in turn, were theological seminaries. The needs of a young

1 *Dalhousie Gazette*, January 30, 1890.
2 William Lyall, *Intellect, The Emotions, and The Moral Nature* (Edinburgh: Thomas Constable; London: Hamilton Adams, 1855). Hereafter referred to as *Intellect*.

society for educated men manifested themselves primarily in the demand for school teachers and for clergymen. School teachers were scarcely thought to need more education than would be required in a secondary school. They could, therefore, be taken care of in the very institutions in which they were to work. (By the 1850s, this attitude had changed but, even then, something less than the university was usually thought sufficient for a teacher.) Clergymen, however, presented a special problem. They were not only thought to need sufficient education to expound the esoteric doctrines of the religious bodies to which they were affiliated, they needed also to be equipped to do battle with their sectarian rivals. Thus, in the scattered communities along the Atlantic coast there grew, very quickly, a variety of institutions. Acadia, Dalhousie, the University of New Brunswick, and Mount Allison were among the earliest of them. In general, philosophy was regarded simply as an adjunct to religion. Dalhousie where, given the secular convictions of its founder, philosophy might well first have taken root, did not really begin to flourish until 1863. Elsewhere, in general, philosophy did not establish itself as a significantly independent undertaking until the late 1840s and 1850s.

While philosophy in the Maritimes owed much to men like Thomas McCulloch, who were slightly earlier, no Maritime philosopher before Lyall produced important work which was strictly philosophical.

The development of philosophy in the Maritimes really takes place at much the same time as the development of philosophy in Ontario despite the rather earlier start which the Maritime universities had.

In both settings the independence of philosophy had much to do with the Scottish attitude to religion. The Scottish sermon was never simply an emotional plea. Nor was it a pontification which played upon the fear of hell and the promise of heaven. Rather, it took the form of an argument in which a series of statements and counter-statements were developed until a final position was presented as the balance of reason. Such a technique had always required education. By the fifteenth century, Scotland had four universities while England had only two.

Scotland had developed a tradition that every man, however poor, was entitled to an education and the inhabitants of Edinburgh had long been familiar with the sight of students arriving from the countryside bearing their sacks of oats to see them through the cold winter.

This tradition was imported into Canada, especially to those regions, such as the Maritime Provinces and eastern Ontario, which had very large Scottish populations. The only way that a church could cope with an educated population was to produce a philosophy. If it was to be a reasoned philosophy, the issues had to be considered on their own merits.

The work of men like McCulloch and Lyall thus developed naturally in the surroundings. So did the work of Paxton Young in Ontario. Equally natural, however, was the splintering of effort and the consequent founding of a great many institutions in a way which was bound to produce massive workloads and a good deal of isolation.

Thomas McCulloch, for example, almost single-handedly built Pictou Academical Institution and fought its long and losing battle to achieve degree-granting status. The splintering had other results as well. McCulloch was ever engaged in religious struggles. Somehow, he found time to write two books attacking popery, and one defending Calvinism.[3] Most of his expressed philosophy is to be found in two lectures on the nature of liberal education[4] and between the lines of the Stepsure Letters—the work on which his fame chiefly rests.[5]

The Stepsure Letters, written for *The Acadian Recorder* and published originally in 1821 and 1822, recount the imaginary life and times of Mephibosheth Stepsure in a Nova Scotian village at the beginning of the nineteenth century. They evidently contain a thesis and a clear perspective. The thesis is that men flourish so long as they stay close to nature in general and to the land in particular and occupy their minds with serious reflection on the human condition.

From this idyllic state, they are frequently led astray by opportunities in trade and occasionally by charismatic religion and sex. But, being Scots, they are most vulnerable to trade.

McCulloch's thesis is really that the creation of social institutions which lead men away from the natural and necessary trades and into

3 Thomas McCulloch, *Popery Condemned* (Edinburgh: Pillans, 1808); *Popery Again Condemned* (Edinburgh: A. Neill, 1810); *Calvinism* (Glasgow and London: William Collins, n.d. [The date is often given as 1849, but the copies in Knox College, Toronto, The National Library, Ottawa , and the Dalhousie University Library are undated. The copy in the National Library bears a handwritten inscription dated 1847.]).

4 Thomas McCulloch, *A Lecture Delivered at the Opening of the Building Erected for the Accommodation of the Class of the Pictou Academical Institution* (Halifax: A. H. Holland for the trustees of the Pictou Academical Institution, 1819); and "A Lecture Delivered at the Opening of the First Theological Class in the Pictou Academy" *The Christian Recorder* (Glasgow), May 1821.

5 Thomas McCulloch, *The Letters of Mephibosheth Stepsure* (Toronto: McClelland & Stewart, 1960). The "Letters" originally appeared in *The Acadian Recorder*, for December 22, 1821, and in sixteen subsequent issues ending on May 11, 1822. The McClelland & Stewart edition is taken from the 1862 edition (Halifax: Hugh Blackadar).

retailing, the manipulation of money, and the search for the softer kinds of bodily satisfaction end in personal disaster and, but for the good sense of the community, would lead to communal disaster as well. It seems evident that he is offering, in effect, a critique of capitalism.

In fact, however, his characters, though endearing, are also incompetent and perhaps the creation of a school of retail management would have been more to the point in the situation as he actually describes it than a critique of capitalism. Though he has a wonderful time lampooning charismatic religion, the orthodox kind is not, surprisingly, more reassuring. The damage done to religion by Parson Drone, as McCulloch describes him, must have equalled that of several saloons.

Indeed, the problem one has in trying to extract McCulloch's philosophy from the book is that he enjoys himself far too much and is much too good an observer of human nature to confine himself to philosophical examples and caricatures. For much the same reason, his defence of Calvinism is not easy to pin down. McCulloch not only loved religious debate, he had clearly been raised on standards of fairness as well. There is, for instance, a long chapter attacking universalism, the (to McCulloch) outrageous doctrine that everyone will ultimately go to heaven. But in fact, McCulloch meticulously locates every scriptural passage which *favours* the doctrine he is attacking. By the time he has made the universalist case, his own position seems feeble by contrast.

In the same spirit, his two essays on a liberal education urge that it is not enough to raise the young on the scriptures and the classics: His proposals are always those of a philosopher urging a philosopher's education and when, finally, in 1838 after twenty-two years at the Pictou Academical Institution, he was called to Dalhousie, the future of philosophy was in some sense established, though it did not really become secure until William Lyall took up the chair in 1863.

We may imagine Lyall, then, fresh from the religious controversies of Scotland, two years in Ontario behind him, and the task of sustaining a very tiny, struggling college in front of him. Halifax was, and would long remain, a small garrison town. The gray stone of its public works blends, imperceptibly, into the gray rock of its long, winding harbour. Only the deeper chill of its winter and the small proliferation of frame buildings would have distinguished it from his native Scotland. There, surrounded by his books, he settled down to put coherence into the rich collection of philosophical ideas which had been forming in his mind.

From an examination of his findings, we can form an idea of his method. Though his work develops against the background of the

Scottish common sense philosophers of the time, it does not do so in a straightforward and obvious way. (It will be more convenient to discuss that background in the next chapter when we trace the development of Paxton Young's thought.) From them, however, he gleaned the doctrine that there are basic certainties which are simply given to us. The problem of reason, as Lyall apparently sees it, is to give meaning to those intuitions. That means finding a way to make them fit together coherently. It also means developing concepts which will render them intelligible, and developing new intuitions by exploring the ways in which the concepts one develops conflict with each other.

Lyall worked his way through a great variety of philosophers. He writes at length about Descartes, Locke, Kant, Fichte, Cousin, and his immediate predecessors in Scotland such as Reid, Chalmers, and Thomas Brown. These philosophers provide the background for his development of the problems of knowledge, mind, and matter. But, surprisingly perhaps, there is a strong influence of St. Augustine upon him. In the end, it seems to be the Augustinian streak which, worked into his own philosophical framework, provides a unique strand in Lyall.

He begins, in the tradition which dominated philosophy from Descartes to Hegel, with the problems of mind and matter and their correlates, problems of knowledge of the self and of the world.

It is here that his method shows itself. Descartes' problem, essentially, was to find an original certainty on which to build. If nothing is known for certain, there are no standards by which we can compare claims to knowledge. Descartes thought, as St. Augustine had, that our strongest certainty was the certainty of our own existence. He argued that one could not deny that certainty, because in order to deny or to doubt, one must exist.

One of the historical problems has always turned on the question of whether Descartes intended "I think, therefore I am" to be an argument or whether he thought it an original insight or a basic intuition. Obviously, if it is an argument, then one can ask whether the premise, by itself, is certain and whether there is not a degree of doubt about any attempt to move from the premise "I think" to the conclusion "I exist." Lyall agreed with Cousin that it could not be an argument. "I exist" is a proposition independent of all argument. It is not a judgment but a natural truth which, as Cousin had said, strikes the understanding at once and irresistibly.

Reading it this way, Lyall is able to resist the movement and argument from the certainty of one's own existence to what has been called the egocentric predicament. That problem arises because, if I am more certain of my own existence than of anything else, then I have one *kind* of knowledge of my own existence and my own internal states and another *kind* of knowledge of the rest of the world. The problem becomes to determine how I can pass from knowledge of myself to knowledge of anything else.

Lyall urges that Descartes could not have moved in *argument* from "I think" to "I exist". He says:

> Consciousness is a simple feeling, and its testimony to self, or to a being in which that consciousness resides, is no more direct than its testimony to what is not self: the feeling in either case is but a feeling, and the ground of a conviction. The question as to the existence of an external world depends altogether upon the constitution of that mind which, as being ultimate in the question, is thought to deny the existence of an external world, or at least to render it impossible that we can ever attain to the knowledge of its existence.[6]

He is alleging that consciousness, in and of itself, is not more directly related to one kind of object of knowledge than to another. It is not that consciousness guarantees the existence of something. We are guaranteed our own existence by an original insight which we would only give up in case we were faced with a counter-claim which made its case by providing a greater intelligibility. However, there can be no such counter-claim. I may be wrong about what I am but not wrong in believing *that* I am. A counter-claim could only take the form of asserting—curiously—that I was deceived about my own existence. In that case, someone else would exist. And all that would mean was that I was confused about the correct description of the entity involved. That seems to be what Lyall means by claiming that the certainty about my own existence is an original "intellectual" proposition.

If one takes this position, then one can work as easily to knowledge about the external world as to knowledge about oneself in the sense that one's original starting point does not presuppose the priority of one over the other. This analysis is an example of the way in which an original intuition or insight comes to be intelligible by considering the alternatives. In the process, if Lyall is right, we have learned how to construe the insight which was Descartes' but the insight itself stands unless there is some effective counter-claim.

Once the insight has been clarified, we can work first to the idea of externality, then to the idea of an external world, and, finally, to the idea of mind. The idea of externality arises, Lyall thinks, partly (as Brown had urged) from the feeling of resistance which consciousness encounters in its relations to the objects of knowledge. The

6   Lyall, *Intellect*, pp. 19-20.

idea of externality becomes the idea of space when that feeling is made concrete through the sense of touch. But that is not the whole explanation. It requires, equally, another original intuition which is brought to consciousness in this process. For none of the situations which philosophers have invented to explain the sense of externality would, by themselves, give rise to this conviction. Any sensation may be the result of an external world or may be the result of the inner workings of our own minds. Once again, the belief that there *is* an external world has to be taken as an original claim and accepted unless an effective counter-claim is forthcoming. But our experience becomes more intelligible and our conceptual patterns fit together more successfully on the hypothesis that there is an external world. The sceptic is wrong to believe that this conviction should be discarded merely on the ground that it cannot be proved. For the sceptic is assuming some superior principle. Superior principles are only the results of effective challenge of original insights and of a kind of clarification which would bring about new insights.

The idea of externality is, then, immune in the sense that it stands as an insight which all men have and which nothing succeeds in challenging. The idea of an external world is beyond this. It is the idea, first, that there is space and this we derive, objectively, from the development of our sense of touch.

Is it the case that, if we put the original insight and the inference from factual sensation together, the compound is subject to successful challenge? Lyall says it is not. As usual, he tries to consider what the counter-claim would amount to. He discusses Kant's view that space is simply the "form of sensibility."[7] Kant had argued that space and time, alike, are not objectively existing features of the world. They are rather the forms in which our experience is cast. We cannot imagine experience without space and time. But, Kant urged, if we consider space and time apart from our experience we simply end in the set of paradoxes we know as the antinomies. Thus it would appear that the two are inseparably linked and that we have no ground for saying anything specific about the world apart from our experience of it.

Lyall replies that we have no idea of a form of sensibility any more than we have an idea of space without experience. Kant's counter-claim is no more intelligible than the original claim that there is an objective space. If that is true, it is not a ground for giving up our original intuition. In short, Lyall would turn Kant's arguments back on himself. If it cannot be shown, independently, that space and time have an existence apart from experience, it equally cannot be shown that they

7   Ibid., p. 54. Lyall thinks this is the essence of Kant's view of space.

do not have such an existence. There is, then, nothing to choose between the two hypotheses except that one squares with our original intuition and insight and provides us with an effective model in terms of which we can talk about the world, and the other, in the name of intellectual clarity, introduces unintelligible notions.

This ties in with Lyall's earlier line of argument—a line of argument associated, in part, with Brown. Lyall wants to attack the whole suggestion that our experience in the form of our consciousness is somehow more closely tied to events in our own minds than to events which are independent of them. Descartes, by arguing that we have more effective and immediate knowledge of our own inner states than of anything else, created a model which led to the view that all of us, somehow, are locked up inside our own heads. Consciousness, on this view, always has for its object—at least, when that object is a direct object—events in our own minds. Lyall sees no reason to accept this and, if our interpretation of him is correct, he appears to be arguing that we are not locked up inside our own heads but that we are, rather, where our experiences seem to be. This means that consciousness can be as well associated with "external" objects as with "internal" ones.

Lyall admits that the case of time is different and considerably more complicated. He discusses Locke and Cousin at length but he rejects the view that the notion of time arises from the succession of ideas. In part, he says, it does arise from repeated occurrences of the idea of self which produces the notion of duration. But the idea of time is not the idea of succession. Succession *measures* time and in order to apply a measure one must know, already, what it is that one is measuring. We cannot imagine a situation which would be correctly described as the situation before there was any time or a situation which would be correctly described as the situation after the end of time. Kant, it would seem, is correct in associating time and experience. Yet, Lyall thinks, Kant is wrong in supposing that we render the situation more intelligible by regarding time simply as the form of our experience. Indeed, Kant is wrong altogether in putting the issue that way. For if that were the correct analysis, then time would be the succession of ideas. If that is all there were to it, we would understand what it was for there to be no time—namely what it was for ideas to remain fixed and stable. Yet we should say of fixed and stable ideas that they endured for a long time.

Once again, it seems to be a matter of an original intuition which we subject to analysis by inspecting the kinds of experiences which go along with it. But there seems to be nothing which Lyall can find which associates time with an objective construction. Space is associated with an objective construction through our tactual sensations and a sense of resistance which the world offers to us. Time, we become aware of through our memories of ourselves, through the interplay of our successive ideas, and through the development of our own sense of self-identity. All these lead back naturally to an analysis of time as an internal and subjective construction. Lyall resists this move simply by urging that the internal states involved are only measures of time and that time must be something else—something which can neither be associated specifically with the external and objective world nor specifically with the internal world.

It is simply that the best way to cope with our intuitions about space and time is to regard them much as common sense does. Lyall finally says, "We cannot explain time, as we cannot explain space. But we can understand it if we do not seek an explanation."[8]

He has, however, one more line of approach. He argues that it is because we have the contrasting ideas of an external world and of space and time that we are able to understand the notion of mind and how mind is, finally, radically different from the objects in the external world. He argues that it is in intellection and morality that we finally make a distinction. He appears to use the term "matter" as a word of convenience to designate whatever it is that occupies the objective external world. That world has a causal order within its space-time framework. He can associate many things with the causal order and admits that, if we analyze our experience, we cannot tell for sure when a sensation ceases to reflect the material world and when it comes to reflect the internal worlds of our own minds. But he says we can draw the line between sensation and intellection. We can tell when we have mental states that have no association with the material world. Thinking and sensing are two different things and we cannot locate thinking in the material world.

Lyall means that to think of material objects as thinking about each other is to think of them as something quite other than material objects. To think that two plus two equals four is not to think of a collection of material objects but to think of an association of principles. We cannot locate such principles in space and time nor can we literally locate our thoughts in space and time. Thus, he urges many times over that "mind cannot be *an organic result*."[9] If we were only creatures of sensation, the situation might be otherwise, for what we take to be a sensation may be part of a material object or it may be caused by an immaterial object.

8   Ibid., p. 65.
9   Ibid., p. 92.

But no combination of material objects can make us think that two plus two equals four.

The point seems to be this: Imagine a calculating machine. Let us suppose that it processes electrical impulses and ultimately prints out the solution to a problem of arithmetic on a piece of paper. Now the sensations which you have when you see that piece of paper are themselves, no doubt, caused by material objects—interaction of light rays with your optical apparatus and your neural system—and what you see Lyall would describe, in common-sense terms, as a material object in space. Similarly we might attach to that calculating machine another machine which picked up light rays reflected from that piece of paper and interpreted them. It might even interpret the print-out of the first machine by abstracting the general arithmetical principles evident in the first machine's production. But all of this, we might say, occurs at the level of sensation. Neither machine would properly be said to "think." For the print-outs of both machines are simply sets of physical objects—heaps of ink on pieces of paper. Thinking takes place when we understand and give a meaning to what is going on. Meanings are assigned and described and do not simply consist of the rearrangements of material objects.

Lyall draws upon the significance of his earlier argument.

> It is not too much, surely, to say, that we can mark a mental state as distinct from one of sensation. Is it too much to affirm that we mark a total disparity between a sensation and an idea—that we can at once discern the difference? Does not the simplest idea testify to its purely mental or spiritual origin? Is not our very first idea—that of *self*—separate from even the consciousness which begets it?[10]

If consciousness were tied to our ideas in the way that that quotation denies, then the argument for the existence of a material world could not have been set in train. For then we would have been locked into the position that consciousness has a primary association with our own mental states. Once more, Lyall's method is visibly at work. He tries to sort and clarify intuitions and then to integrate them into a coherent pattern. At that point, he re-examines the situation to see what new intuitions come to light. In this case the new intuition is the immediate distinction between idea and sensation which leads to the ultimate distinction between mind and matter.

He finds two other grounds for the distinction. One of them is in the idea of morality. If mind and matter were not separate, how could

10   Ibid., pp. 92-93.

71

the idea of morality arise? The idea of morality, for Lyall, is the idea of a rule or principle which ought to govern our affairs. Nothing in the physical world could give rise to such an idea as distinct from ideas about what it is practical, prudent, or pleasant to do. The mere fact that we can raise the suggestion that perhaps one ought not to do what is practical, prudent, and pleasant, suggests another origin of our ideas. Eventually, he will try to derive his notions of morality from the concept of love and its association with being itself and God. This is the Augustinian streak in Lyall and we will come to it later. Here he is merely concerned with the idea of morality as part of the obvious distinction between mind and matter.

The third component which, in his mind, reinforces the distinction is the human desire for immortality. Because man is involved with thought—in Lyall's term, with intellection—he transcends the immediacies of space and time. He can even raise questions about the reality of material things and about the ultimacy of space and time themselves. This is not, for Lyall, evidence that space and time might be "unreal"; rather it is evidence that the mind of man is not simply the outcome of the material world. We are driven, in our analysis of time, to the idea of eternity because we cannot conceive of the beginning and end of time. But eternity manifests itself to us most clearly in our immediate grasp of eternal ideas. We also seem to have an affinity for this eternal realm. We are constantly seeking knowledge which transcends space and time. When we examine our concept of the self, we can see that it is not, itself, immediately tied to the gross realities of space and time. More importantly, it is not immediately tied to our transitory consciousness either. Thus we have a sense of ourselves as beings who belong to another domain.

The more we refine our accounts of the ways in which ideas develop psychologically and the more we refine our accounts of our relation to those ideas, the clearer it becomes to us that man is not simply an "organic result." If this is so, then the distinction between mind and matter must hold.

Lyall admits that there are serious difficulties about the interaction of mind and matter. If they are quite different in the sense of having nothing whatever in common, how does one influence the other? We know that our experiences are associated with our brains, our entire nervous system, and our physiology. Once we have accepted the reality of space and time, we have no ground for doubting that this relation, ultimately, is real. Yet we cannot explain it. Lyall seems to think that this is associated with the fact that we cannot explain space and time themselves though we can in some sense understand them. It is only on the hypothesis that there is a God who has created the world that it seems possible that these two systems should be brought into line. Lyall thus falls back on a hypothesis which goes back to Malebranche in the face of a difficulty which is intractable in his system.

Perhaps he found it reassuring that at some point in his philosophical system, one simply had to call upon God to explain the mysteries. Such a tactic, however, is less reassuring to the reader who is well aware that philosophers had consistently and habitually used God as a device to get them out of conundrums of their own making. Surely, if there is a God, He has better things to do than fill in the holes in the systems created by men like Malebranche and Lyall.

The interaction problem is, indeed, serious and it is one of the reasons for the gradual breakdown of dualistic philosophies of the kind which Lyall was inclined to champion.

It is worthwhile, therefore, to inquire as to how Lyall arrived at this position and as to whether or not there is some way out of it which is consistent with the rest of what he has to say. It appears that what essentially belongs to the material world, in his system, is identified mainly by certain kinds of causal relations and by location in space and time. The term "matter" seems to be, in that system, largely a term of convenience. It corresponds to common-sense usage and it gives a sense of ordinary obviousness to his position. It is not, however, clearly explicated and Lyall may have made complications needlessly for himself.

In his system it seems to be simply the case that space and time are objective orders in which things appear. As objective orders, they are real enough but so is the order represented by the number system or the order represented by Euclidean geometry.

If our knowledge is really as objective as Lyall claims, it would seem to follow that this is only possible if things can appear in a variety of orders. One would think that, for such knowledge to be possible, the same thing would have to appear in the order of objective space and time, in the order of our perceptions, in the order of our memories, and, one supposes, if Lyall's God exists, it also appears in the order of the eternal perceptions of God. It is an essential part of his case to maintain that there are these various orders, that they are independent of one another, and that they are all sustained by our basic intuitions about what the world is like. But it equally seems to be a basic part of his case to maintain that things in different orders are not different kinds of things. If that were the case, then our perceptions would be internal states created by our own nervous systems and only tenuously related to the external world. Yet he argues continuously that we have real and direct knowledge of things in the external world and that this knowledge comes to us through our perceptions.

It seems simply natural for him to urge that the same thing can appear in several orders. If that is true, then the problem is not the interaction problem created by the fact that there are different kinds of things which have no properties in common. Indeed, the things in our minds may be the same things which appear in the external world. They are simply differently ordered. They will seem to have one set of relations to each other as things "in the mind" and another set of relations to each other as things "in the world." This does not in any way preclude there being some special things—in particular the objects of intellection which so concern Lyall—which have only one order— the order of natural reason. Thus it might be the case that if one attends to the "material" world successively as we do in our direct perceptions, the order which they have gives rise to the notion of causal connection. If we look at them as we do in our memories, the connection between them is the connection which we give to them by that particular mode of attention. If God looks at them, He no doubt sees them as an eternal co-existing set. These properties are not incompatible with each other and it would not seem to require the specific and continuous intervention of God to make the connection between them hold effectively.

Lyall does not exploit such notions because it is part of his program to stay in the domain of common sense. But not to exploit these notions is to undermine the theory of knowledge which he wants to champion. One would suppose that his system could, in this respect, be tidied.

There may be another reason for urging such a tidying. One of the issues which most concerns Lyall is the problem of "free will." In one sense, he has no problem about free will because the mind, in its imaginative function, in its intellective function, and in its moral function is simply not part of the ordinary physical world. But this is a rather Pyrrhic victory. For men certainly, on Lyall's view, have bodies and bodies are certainly part of the physical world whose very defining characteristic is a set of causal relations. If men's minds are free but their bodies are bound by the laws of physics, then their freedom does not seem to amount to much.

If, however, there is not a fundamental distinction between kinds of things but only a distinction between the ways in which things can be ordered, the problem largely disappears. For the orders are represented simply by different kinds of experience—perception, intellection, or whatever is the right description of the divine program of eternal co-inspection. Things grasped through perception will have and seem to have causal connections. But that is only one aspect of them. Grasped in another way they have different connections and they can be changed in different ways. It will emerge, as we go along, that Lyall's ultimate Augustinian program would seem to require him to re-examine the sort of ways in which he states his ontological position. The Augustinian tendency only becomes apparent late in the book after other issues have apparently been settled. It is quite conceivable that his thought was developing as he wrote.

We must now pass to Lyall's moral theory and return briefly to the present discussion when we have completed that investigation. His moral philosophy is compounded of two elements—a theory about the nature of moral rules and a theory about the relation of morality to emotion. We have already noticed the first of these and it is as well to begin with an account of his theory of emotion. An emotion, he describes as a movement of the mind consequent upon some appropriate cause. The will, he thinks, is the only active principle of the mind—emotions are not actions.

An emotion literally is distinct from an affection. An emotion proper is the first or sudden excitement of the mind in response to some situation, while an affection is the continued exhibition of that state of affairs.

In general, for Lyall, emotions are directed and have two sorts of objects. One of these is a direct object. Thus, one hates somebody, is angry at something, feels relief in the presence of something, and so on. The other is an indirect object. The indirect objects are the states of mind which the emotion produces or the outcomes of the actions stimulated by the emotions.

There are two kinds of exceptions to this rule. One is represented by the kinds of emotions, like cheerfulness, which represent the states of mind themselves and are not associated with external objects. The other is the most important component of Lyall's analysis of emotion—love. A thing loved is loved for its own sake. Since its ultimate sustaining object must be something which can be loved for its own sake and not for the sake of an indirect object, love, combined with intellectual understanding, must lead on to the only thing actually capable of sustaining love for its own sake. That, in Lyall's view, is *being* itself.

This analysis needs to be examined carefully for it contains the basis not only of Lyall's account of the mainsprings and wellsprings of human action but, equally, his account of the ultimate nature of morality and of being. The emotions, first of all, are what connect us to objects in the world. The purely intellectual aspect of thought is wholly unlike and unrelated to the objects of the physical world. Emotion provides a bridge because emotions, initially, are directed to objects in the world and, by reason of their connection to the secondary objects which are states of mind, they provide the background for the intellect. He describes emotion as the "atmosphere of the mind; it is its vital breath."[11] But emotion is also something more than that. Emotion provides us with the initial impetus to action. Emotion stimulates desire and opens the way for choice simply because it provides an open ambiguity and because it tends to have both a direct and an indirect object. In this psychological context it is possible, on Lyall's view, to talk about the will. He argues that though objects stimulate emotions and emotions stimulate desires, we cannot claim that desires are the "causes" of actions in the way that one event in the physical world can be said to be the cause of another. Rather, emotions give the intellect something to work on and the intellect, along with the emotions, structures the will. Literally, insofar as the present authors can tell, he is saying that the cause-effect relationship involved here is not like the cause-effect relationship in the physical world because there is not a one-to-one relationship between cause and effect. On the one side there is a complexity involving a plurality of objects while on the other side there is a single act which is said to be "caused." Does one act because one is stimulated by an object and desires the outcome of the act in the physical world or because one is stimulated by a prospective state of mind and desires that? (One might state the case in terms of the classical conundrum: Does the missionary go to the leper colony because he wants to heal the lepers or because he desires the state of mind which goes with having the satisfaction of a life devoted to self-sacrifice? He cannot tell because both elements will normally be present and either one might be said to be the "cause" of the outcome. Since the emotional situation is, itself, one of ambivalence we cannot talk about causes and effects in quite the ordinary way. Rather, we can say that the missionary decided in the light of these considerations or that his will was structured by them.)

The analysis becomes more plausible in the light of Lyall's other contentions. One of them is that there is a basic moral emotion. A moral emotion, however, is inextricably bound up with an intellectual element and is not a pure emotion. The other contention is that we are motivated by the special emotion of love.

Moral emotion inclines us toward some things and away from others and is normally a component of the situation which precedes and accompanies action. Its intellectual element takes the form of impressing on us the need for regularity of principle. It structures the

11 Ibid., p. 284.

will by demanding coherence of action. In this respect, Lyall admires the formal aspect of Kant's moral theory. But this formal element is not, in his view, sufficient to account for morality. For we need to be impelled toward specific acts and outcomes. One can be determined to act coherently only if one is determined to act at all. And one must enjoy, amongst possible actions, the choice already guaranteed by the open-textured ambiguity of the stimulus-response situation created by the nature of our emotions, our demands, and the impetus to action.

Thus, a rule like Kant's categorical imperative—"act only on a maxim through which you can at the same time will that it should become a universal law"[12]—is not sufficient. The gap, in part, is filled by the original moral emotion which appears to us as a moral intuition. The world contains many good things and not all of them are compatible with one another. Thus the desire—if you want to press the analysis, a third-order desire—to act morally might only end in frustration if all we had was the intellectual element of morality combined with the moral emotions stimulated by specific, given objects or states of affairs. To complete the moral analysis, something else is needed. This Lyall finds to be given in love. When love is stimulated by an object, we value that object in and for itself. When it is absent altogether we feel a profound lack, a lack which is felt partly because of the very power of the emotion and partly because, without it, we are missing a final principle of action.

If we combine the emotion of love with the intellectual analysis of morality, we eventually get to the outcome which solves the moral riddle. For the intellect is capable of analyzing the object of love, determining its limitations, and urging us on beyond it to something without limits. It is not Lyall's view that the immediate objects of love are irrational and are to be discarded but, rather, that the intellect shows us the background of being within which they have their meaning and significance and urges us to direct our love to this larger context.

We can thus see, on Lyall's view, how right action is ultimately possible but, how, with all this help, is wrong action possible? Wrong action seems to proceed from many kinds of mistake. One can mistake other emotions for the moral emotions—one could mistake the desire for possession for the desire for something inherently good. One can become lost in the ambiguities of direct and indirect objects and in the ambiguities of first-order desires (desires for objective states of affairs or outcomes), second-order desires (desires for specific states of mind),

12   This is a literal translation; cf. the Prussian Academy edition of Kant's *Werke*, vol. 4, pp. 420-21.

and third-order desires (desires for a morally good state of mind and a morally good objective state of affairs). Finally, the power of the emotion of love could, itself, lead us astray by obliterating from our consciousness the clear awareness of the context in which limited objects, objects which are neither being nor God, derive their value. (The terminology here—the expressions about the orders of desire, for example—is not Lyall's. It is added in the hope of increasing the likelihood that Lyall's very complex analysis will be intelligible in summary.)

This examination of the ways in which wrong action becomes possible should help, also, to clarify our understanding of his point about causation and the will. One can now see that the will is structured in many ways. It is structured by emotion, by the orders of desire, by the intellectual understanding which is aroused by the moral emotions, and by the demands of love and our intellectual reflection upon it. But all of these structures operate in such a way as not to have a unique necessary outcome in action. The intellect is capable of reflecting all of these structures just for the reason that the nature of the emotions and the situation bring the intellect into play. This reflection, in its turn, provides yet a further structure. One can always go on indefinitely and, from the perspective of reflection, a variety of actions will always be possible in any situation which *is* reflected upon.

In one sense, it is the intellect which is free. For it is the intellect which is wholly divorced from the physical world. But the intellect must have something to reflect upon and therefore, itself, becomes structured. Action is free because it cannot be associated with a real determining cause. We thus talk of "free will." But it would seem to be Lyall's view that we must do so in a way which actually takes account of what goes on. To talk of the will is to talk of a principle of action. One cannot talk of a principle of action without providing a structure for it. The will is not a mysterious faculty which has no origin. It does indeed have a structure. In fact, it has a very elaborate structure. To talk of the way in which it becomes structured is, indeed, to talk of limitations on the will. It could not choose without a principle of action. It could not choose without an impetus to action. It could not choose without the very elaborate structure of kinds of object and orders of desire. Yet all these fall short of the final determination which we would ordinarily describe as "causality." They do so because of the way in which they are arranged. Reflection can always make a difference and reflection involves deliberation and deliberateness—things which we associate with the world. It is not just that the descriptive situation does not enable us to tell which of the kinds of object or levels of desire is the "cause" of the action but that none of them, by themselves, *could* be "the cause" of the action and they cannot be added together so as to make a cause of action, for the levels are separated from one another by reflection and thus do not have a cumulative effect.

Now this is a very complex description of the situation compounded, in part, of the Scottish "moral sense" theories, Kant's intellectual analysis of morality, and Augustine's philosophy of love on the one side, and an elaborate, if rather traditional, psychology on the other. All of the elements which Lyall, in his reflections in his study and in the classroom, found attractive come to have their place in the patchwork quilt. He is, indeed, an eclectic.

Some features, however, deserve special attention. One of them is Lyall's whole attitude to emotion.

The notion that emotion is essentially a hindrance to rationality and something which would be eschewed and eradicated in the name of calm, deliberate action has had its defenders at least in the popular wisdom. But Lyall waxes lyrical for page after page in speaking of emotion. Without emotion, in his view, the mind is empty, incapable of action, and—odd as it may seem—morally uninformed. Emotion is not merely to be welcomed in its pale form as moral emotion, the sentiment of benevolence, or whatever. It is to be welcomed in all its richness, and the hazards it presents by way of the stimulation of rash acts are to be faced cheerfully and without regret. Indeed, without emotion we would have no connection with the objective world.

The other aspect of Lyall's philosophy which deserves special attention is his view of love. To be sure, he says some very odd things in the course of his text. Sentences like "The love between man and the other sex is altogether peculiar," "*It is love*, though love of a special and peculiar kind," "Let it be considered that love in itself *is absolute* . . . ," and "Love may be contemplated as an absolute emotion existing even apart from an object to exercise it or call it forth"[13] require some unpuzzling in the absence of any detailed explanation.

Essentially he is echoing St. Augustine. Augustine found it necessary to add to his intellectual refutation of the philosophical sceptics the simple fact that he felt love and that he loved being. It was this along with his certainty of his own existence which suggested to him that knowledge and morality were possible. Lyall is calling attention to the remarkable fact that we do have the emotion of love. He refuses to analyze it out as self-interest. He refuses to try to explain it away as something which we value because of the state of mind in ourselves. For he insists that it is absolute. He insists that one who loves, values the

13 Lyall, *Intellect*, p. 405.

object of his love for its own sake. He is not here talking of the "romantic love" which associates its desires with its own idealized object. For he is aware that one may love an object whose imperfections one knows and, knowing them, may love it nonetheless for all that. One may be driven beyond it to love the being which gives it its special value but even that does not detract from it. When he says it is possible to conceive love existing even apart from an object to exercise it or call it forth, he is apparently simply calling attention to the fact that we see at once and know intrinsically that love, as such, is inherently valuable. It is this, perhaps, which remains most strongly in Lyall as the residue of the "moral intuition" theory. He is reckoning with a brute fact but he is also trying to give it its place in the intellectual understanding of things.

Since love is absolute and nothing else is, it appears to follow on his theory that it is our awareness of love which suggests to us that we ought to respond to our moral emotions. Since, by themselves, they are relative—relative to the ability of the intellect to order them in a coherent way and relative to the other demands of desire upon us—we might, if we had only them, be able to justify ourselves in ignoring any one of them and, perhaps, any set of them.

But there is more to this. If his argument is correct and love leads us from its immediate objects, surrounded as they are by conditions and limitations, to what is ultimately worthy of absolute value, then we have a link between thought and feeling—a link which leads from both of those to Lyall's ultimate theological convictions. For only what is wholly unlimited can justify, finally, absolute allegiance. Suppose X loves Y. If X really does so, he does so unconditionally and without reservation. But, as he reflects on his situation, the limitations of Y must, in the end, become clear to him. As limitations, they suggest that there are occasions on which he should not give his unconditional allegiance to Y, but this conflicts with his love. In the end, he can only justify the combination of the two kinds of awareness if there is an ultimate being which is inherently valuable and without limitation in itself and within which there is a special and unique place to be occupied by Y. In that case, the limitations of Y are simply part of what makes it possible for Y to occupy that place in being. But that is only comprehensible in the case that *being* itself does measure up to the conditions.

An ideal man who understood his love would love each thing for what it is and for the potentialities it has to play its special role in the totality. Individual men, in reality, are not given that degree of omniscience or that range of emotion. But they *do* have their loves. We are, therefore, left with two options: We can explain their loves as illusions, as misplaced sentiments of self-interest, as psychological traumas which bind them irrationally to particular objects. Lyall seems to be arguing, that is exactly what they are not. We all know what those emotions which have both first- and second-order objects are like. We all know what self-interest is. We all know what desire is. Love works to counter all of these. To explain it in terms of them is to deny a distinction which every man can make for himself. The other alternative is to suggest that there is something which really does give rise to this emotion, namely *being* itself, and to hold that that being is capable of giving rise to it and, thus, to put our faith in that being.

Suppose love could be conceived without reference to being itself. Then if it needed an object it would become relative to the occurrence of that object. But if it did not need an object, then it would not motivate us to seek the good. It would be a simple abstraction. But love is not in that way relative and it does motivate us. Therefore, we are not wholly without justification in supposing that we can go beyond particular things to being itself. Lyall, however, is well aware of the pitfalls. Being is itself very abstract. He is well aware of the need to grasp such clues as he can. Thus his strange remark about the peculiar nature of man's love for the other sex. It is there that we find a response from the objects that we love and it is in that response that we begin to see the potentiality for regarding love as, finally, objective. But it takes an act of faith to believe that our love will ultimately be reciprocated.

The easiest way to see the inherent difficulties in Lyall's philosophy is to notice the variety of models of world-pictures which appear in it. To some extent, this is obscured from us by Lyall's honest preoccupation with detail.

One way of classifying the world-pictures which philosophers habitually have used is by reference to the kinds of causal relations which predominate in them. In the Greek atomists—Democritus and Leucippus—and later, in Epicurus and Lucretius, various versions of a particle and space model of causal relations were developed. This picture of the world, characterized by the view that the world consists of bits of matter distributed in space and time and that the relationships between them are in some ways like the relationships between pool balls on a table, had obvious attractions, though its champions, apart from the Stoics, were quite rare in ancient times and rarer still through the Middle Ages. Still, it survived into modern philosophy to appear as a component in the philosophy of Descartes, as the dominant feature in the philosophy of Hobbes, and as a principal motif of the "scientific" philosophies of the nineteenth century. One of its ancient rivals was the natural teleology of Aristotle. Aristotle, like the atomists, was inclined to see the world as a collection of bits and pieces. Though he was disinclined to see the bits and pieces as all of the same kind, it did seem to him correct to urge that the world formed a unified causal order. If one has a world composed of different kinds of things, causal relations conceived from the model of the push and the pull of mechanical devices cease to provide an overall general explanation. Thus, while Aristotle cheerfully accepted "efficient causes"—causes which do work by the push and pull of mechanics—as an ingredient in individual situations, he urged that the world must be held in a unity in a different way. In Aristotle's universe there is imposed on the heterogeneous array of things in the world a set of purposes which he calls final causes. For everything in the world, there is a natural state and a natural place, and things tend to find that state and place. Aristotle's theory faded from view for a time in the ancient world as it lost ground to its Platonic and neo-Platonic rivals, but emerged again in Arab philosophy and came to dominate the later Middle Ages. Thereafter, it slowly faded once more.

The ancient rival of both these views was the essentially logical model which developed out of Plato and his neo-Platonic successors. On that view, the world is a system held together by relations of logical necessity. Neo-Platonists argued that the various components of the world were simply unintelligible without each other and required one another for their very existence. On such a view, the world comes to be, in reality, a unity. It does not consist of bits and pieces of things but of various aspects which can be discerned. Things which seem to us bits and pieces do so because they lack intelligibility. Lacking intelligibility, they lack, also, on this view, some measure of reality.

In Plato's view, the ultimate reality is an all-embracing order. Unreality is chaos. As human beings, we live at an intermediate point on this scale, partly real through our participation in the ultimate order, partly immersed in chaos. We are free, in a sense, because we are participants in both being and non-being. Augustine's world-picture came in its turn to be a rival of this kind of Platonism because it replaced the sense of order and connection as logical necessity with the notion of order and connection as the manifestations of various kinds of love. Things move and are moved, for Augustine, by their natural affinities. The love which is the nature of material things brings them together. "My weight is my love," he once said. Gravitation, if you like, is a form of love—a form appropriate to physical things. But love, for Augustine, takes on a series of ascending forms. Man is part physical creature, and part rational creature. The love that is appropriate to him is the love of reason and truth. Truth, since it is eternal and not bound in space and time, draws man out of his habitat in the physical world. God, says Augustine, is the final truth. In short, the mechanics of the atomists, the natural teleology of Aristotle, and the natural necessities of Plato would not do for Augustine, the Christian. He, therefore, seized upon a reconstruction already to some degree latent in Plotinus and substituted one kind of causal relationship for another. Platonism, neo-Platonism, and its Augustinian variants had, thereafter, a checkered career. They dominated Christian philosophy until the high Middle Ages when Aristoteleanism finally triumphed. They appeared again a few hundred years later in the Cambridge Platonists, again in a new variation in Hegel, and, in our time, important elements of those systems survive in the systems of men like Whitehead.

These various models have had many variants and philosophers have frequently tried to combine them. Descartes employed a mechanical model for the whole of the natural world apart from God and man. (Even animals, he thought, were mechanical devices.) But the attributes of mind in man he defined negatively. Mind lacks extension and so does not figure in the material world. He was less successful in adapting the other models to fit the part of the world composed of God and man, and less successful still in satisfying his critics that he was able to cope with the interaction between two worlds. Spinoza adopted a logical model, but modified it to allow for attributes and modes within which mechanism might seem to operate. Once again, a world so fragmented, however sophisticated the manner of explication, becomes difficult to cope with.

If we return to Lyall, we will see that he uses various of these models as the occasion demands. He is a mechanist about the physical world. His preliminary analysis of first-order objects and emotions suggests a contemporary mechanical stimulus-response model. But somewhere, on his view, mechanism stops short. He is a Platonist about the intellect. Intellect represents order, eternal principle, and the transcendence of the shadow world of space and time. But these two worlds are separated by a gulf which he realizes must be bridged, at least at the level of descriptive psychology. The austere and otherworldly intellect must be brought into contact with the mechanical world. It is here that the secondary objects of emotions, that emotion as the background of the intellect and the object of its attention, come into play. But what causal relations ultimately hold here? Lyall draws upon the Augustinian model. Causation here is in terms of objects sought and avoided, a feeling of benevolence, and the feelings of self-satisfaction. But all this cannot simply be a chaos of conflicting poles, for action does result. Thus, he introduces the Augustinian notion of love as the final formulation of direction.

83

He realizes that this makes sense only if *being* itself and the Augustinian love are interrelated. Thus he pursues the notion of love through its logical analysis to an account of the goal which will ultimately sustain and justify our belief in its reality.

The difficulty is obvious. Is this being whose nature it is to express itself in love the ultimate reality? If so, how are we to construe the mechanical world which we met in the early parts of the book? How are we to cope with the thinly disguised Platonism which seems so clearly implied in his analysis of the intellect? Are these only appearances? Are they stage-props for the play in which the ultimate being expresses its love?

The more one looks at Lyall, however, the more one comes to feel that the Augustinian streak in him represented his most powerful personal conviction. He was cautious and canny enough not to let this run away with him and he sought diligently, in an heroic examination of the details of descriptive psychology, to find the basis of a compromise which would reconcile this conviction with a more acceptable view of the world.

Similarly, it seems clear that, in Lyall's morality, love takes precedence over rule and regulation. Though that has always been, no doubt, an article of Christian orthodoxy, it collided rather forcefully with Victorian morality and Presbyterian common sense. Thus, Lyall would like to give Kant his due, to find a place for the insights of the Scottish philosophers of common sense, and to locate the place and function of more mundane and pedestrian moral sentiments.

FOUR

REASON AND MORALITY

George Paxton Young and the Foundations of Ethics

P AXTON YOUNG's career is a reflection of the intellectual tensions and changes which troubled and strengthened English Canada from the 1850s onwards. He was just seventeen years younger than James Beaven and both of them joined the tiny academic community in Toronto at about the same time. Young became a professor at Knox College in 1851. The difference between their intellectual outlooks is the difference between a man who made minor adjustments to a body of traditional beliefs and a man who introduced new and radical ideas.

Young holds a remarkable place in the history of Canadian philosophy. He was the first of the long and influential line of Canadian idealists and the first to mark a firm line between religion and philosophy—a line which caused him, briefly, to give up his livelihood. Though his writings are mostly fragmentary and frequently known to us mainly through notes of his students, enough survives to make him an object of continuing interest.

Young was born in Scotland in 1818 (a few sources give 1819), went to Edinburgh High School and on to the University of Edinburgh. He faced the schism in the Church of Scotland ("the great disruption") and chose to study divinity at the Free Church Hall. He served as a clergyman in Paisley and in London and then—for reasons which seem now lost—resolved to come to Canada. It did not take him long to obtain a church in Hamilton and he quickly made a reputation as a preacher.

A volume of his sermons from that period reveals little which would suggest his later career—unless one reads between the lines. The schisms which wracked the church in Scotland had exact parallels amongst Presbyterians in Canada and Young wrestled with the problems that posed. Perhaps that is the meaning of his sermon which urges that "making peace" is the first duty of a Christian, though on the surface it is concerned, innocuously enough, with the proposition that it is the business of religion to bring peace and harmony to the soul. One of the sermons is devoted to relations between employers and employees, but it seems a little too even-handed when one reflects that, though employers probably did need to be instructed in their duties to employees, most employees of the time had little opportunity to be remiss in their duties to their employers.[1] On the surface, Young was rocking few boats and his flock apparently found him both intelligent and intelligible—easy enough to listen to and, so far as one can tell, little disturbing.

Young was appointed to the Chair of "Logic, Mental and Moral Philosophy," and the "Evidences of Natural and Revealed Religion," at Knox College. The satisfaction of noticing that most things of importance in a theological establishment had been put in his hands must have been somewhat tempered by thoughts of the immensity of the task. His obituary writer in the Knox College Monthly remarked long after that "nothing but the poverty of a college can justify the laying of so much work upon one teacher."[2] Actually, he found time to work at mathematics and oriental languages as well.

For eleven years he laboured at Knox and we can only speculate about what went on in his mind. We know that by 1870 he had reached the philosophical position expounded in his pamphlet *Freedom and Necessity*.[3] Much of the rest of our knowledge comes from shorthand notes edited and published by James Gibson Hume in 1911.[4]

In 1864 he decided that he could not subscribe to the terms of the Confession which his church had adopted. He resigned from Knox College and then from his official status as a Presbyterian clergyman. He did not formally abandon his church membership but he subsequently refused to serve in elected church offices or take part in any of the teaching activities of the church. In 1878, he made a kind of truce. In May of that year he wrote to the minister in charge of St. Andrew's Church, saying " 'If you and your Session will allow me to come to the Lord's Table, putting my own construction on the act, I shall be glad to profess in this way my purpose to live soberly, righteously and godly.' "[5] They were, notice, hard terms: He was not about

1   George Paxton Young, *Miscellaneous Discourses and Expositions of Scripture* (Edinburgh: Johnstone & Hunter, 1854).

2   Obituary, *Knox College Monthly and Presbyterian Magazine*, vol. 9, no. 5 (March 1889), pp. 265-66.

3   George Paxton Young, *Freedom and Necessity* (Toronto: Adam, Stevenson, 1870).

4   George Paxton Young, *The Ethics of Freedom: Notes Selected, Translated and Arranged by his Pupil, James Gibson Hume* (Toronto: University Press, 1911). Hereafter referred to as *Ethics*.

5   Daniel James Macdonnell, *Death Abolished: A Sermon Preached in St. Andrew's Church, Toronto, March 3, 1889* (Toronto: Toronto Mail Job Print, 1889), p. 10.

to profess his belief in anything—only his determination to live in a certain way. But he was accepted and continued to attend St. Andrew's regularly until just before his death. He never relented to the extent of holding any church office though he was once elected to one by a large majority.

No doubt this was the most traumatic episode of his life—a life for the most part tranquil and surrounded by admirers—but we know almost nothing about it. He made no public statements. Many of his friends wrote memorial notes after his death, but none suggested that he had been privy to the details of Young's decision. It seems clear that he was not about to make a public attack on an institution whose sincerity was not in doubt and that he did not think that a public statement of his conclusions would create a real understanding of the situation. His philosophy was known to anyone who cared to listen to him teach.

His growing commitment to reason and to an ideal of self-realization suggested the grounds for this stance. A man, in his view, could only grasp what reason opened to him; and at each stage of human development, historically and in the life of the individual, what must seem fitting and believable depends upon the state of self-development one has reached. The ultimate truth and the ultimate development of the human mind—insofar as such things can be envisaged—must go together. As things are now, what one man can grasp may elude the mind of another and both may be the victims of misperception. One invites others to follow one's reasons but one ought not to try to compel others to one's conclusions or even, in the absence of argument, to announce one's conclusions.

Later, we shall come to grips with the details of Young's philosophical position. But it is fair to notice the aspects of it which may well have influenced his break with Knox and his decision to forego his ministry. We cannot be sure just when he came to various views, but it is likely that two all-embracing positions were settling firmly in his mind: the conclusion that men are free and, in an important sense, make their own fates, and the conclusion that reason and only reason provides an adequate basis for belief and action.

One might think that the collision would have been the obvious one: The historic connection between Presbyterianism and the Calvinist doctrines of predestination and justification by faith suggest that Young must have always been in the wrong church. But the conflict was most likely much more subtle than that. It is difficult to know how widespread such Calvinist beliefs were amongst Presbyterians in Canada in the middle of the nineteenth century; but discussions of them had probably worn thin with time and the immediate situation thrust other matters into the foreground. H. H. Walsh's *The Christian Church in Canada*[6] barely mentions them, though Young does receive passing attention.

More likely, the collision had to do with the whole situation which arose out of "the great disruption." When, in 1843, Dr. Thomas Chalmers led his followers out of the Church of Scotland and into a new Free Church, the issue was mainly over relations between church and state and over the failure of the church to respond to the needs of the new industrial working class. Young's inherent liberalism led him to follow Chalmers.

At first, the reaction was to try to patch things up. In general, Presbyterian churches in Canada announced that they would welcome Free Church ministers into their fold. The hope was that, where the issues of church and state were quite different, the schism would make little difference. Remote areas, hard-pressed for staff, seemed unlikely to care much whether their minister was on one side or another of a little understood dispute in Scotland.

This reaction did not, however, last. Bitter disputes arose in various Presbyterian churches in Montreal and elsewhere and "disrupting" became a frequent occurrence in individual churches as well as in church-governing bodies.

Gradually, attempts at re-unification came to be successful but they tended, also, to be associated with attempts at doctrinal uniformity. People became concerned about what the man in the next pew actually believed and about whether or not he was likely to become a "disrupter" in one cause or another. There is little doubt that Young became increasingly frustrated with a situation in which one's choice seemed to be between subscribing to a doctrinal conformity and creating a new fragmentation.

From his behaviour and his few remarks on the subject, indeed, it would be reasonable to infer that he wanted to avoid both these choices. He refused to subscribe to the specified articles of faith and he refused, equally, to challenge them with a new set of his own.

What he finally demanded—and got—from his church in 1878 was a declaration of tolerance, an open agreement to accept him on his own terms. When he refused to hold church offices, his ground was that his church refused to make such tolerance a public policy applicable to everyone.

While such an approach had obvious practical overtones, it is equally obvious that it stemmed from the central core of his

6   H. H. Walsh, *The Christian Church in Canada* (Toronto: Ryerson, 1956).

philosophy: Men are responsible for themselves and conviction stems from reason, not from some set of dogmas agreed upon at a church meeting.

Most of his friends firmly believed that he remained, in some basic sense, a Christian throughout his life and that his disputes with the Presbyterian church in no way altered those convictions. There is probably no real dispute about that, though whether what he considered Christianity would have been accepted by anyone else as something which ought to go under that name is another issue and one on which we can only throw a little light. Hegel sometimes maintained that he was a good Lutheran but we may surmise that, if he was, he was the only one. Young's case may well be less extreme, but it is open to doubt. When we discuss the details of his philosophy we shall see how far we can resolve that doubt.

Young left Knox and the ministry and became, from 1864 to 1868, Inspector of Grammar Schools for what was to be the Province of Ontario. He played there a major role in establishing the Ontario High School system and in working out a system of education which played a vital part in making possible the growth of universities with real standards. It is said that his annual reports formed, for years afterwards, one of the bases of educational policy.

Whatever challenge that job offered him, he apparently wanted to get back to his studies and to his students. Knox College, too, realized the loss it had suffered. In 1868 the college invited him back on the clear understanding that he was Professor of Philosophy and had no duties whatever with respect to religion or theology.

Sectarianism still wasn't attractive to him, and three years later he became Professor of Mental and Moral Philosophy at the non-sectarian University College. Though he gave some lectures at Knox in the year 1871-72, he finally severed his connections there and remained at University College for the final eighteen years of his career.

The years of his church disputes were crucial years in Canadian history. Confederation came as the formalization of structures which were already accepted and it brought the acceptance of the idea of a nation which had been gradually forming. But it also marked in large the issues which the development of Young's mind represents in microcosm.

Young, like so many of his countrymen, had come to Canada fresh from the excitement of sectarian dispute and fired with enthusiasm for new causes. In Canada, these causes took on another aspect. A Presbyterian in Canada was surrounded by a great variety of faiths. A first reaction, as the history of Presbyterianism in Canada strongly suggests, was to carry on the controversies as if one were at home. In a new country one first notices one's own kind. But it quickly became obvious that the real situation was radically different.

That meant having institutions of all kinds which were adapted to a pluralistic society. Young's vision of a church is just that. He sees the reasonable requirement of a church as the requirement that its members jointly undertake to live lives which are consistent with public morals and a genuine attempt to understand the truth. Sobriety and righteousness ring a little sanctimoniously in the modern ear but Young, probably, did not mean sobriety in the sense the word came to have during the temperance controversies, and "righteously," no doubt, only meant according to the rules of right action. Within those bounds people might believe as reason directed them.

Young found himself in a setting in which the developing University of Toronto had to become a federation of colleges representing differing fundamental points of view. The denominations were not about to give up all interest in an institution which must have, as one of its principal functions, the training of clergymen. Equally, no denomination could easily "go it alone." (Some could and did "go it alone" for a long time, but the task was never easy.) However, a university in the provincial capital of Ontario was too important for any major denomination to be excluded. In general, the denominations came to terms in Toronto.

Young started out in this atmosphere but grew increasingly uncomfortable with the simple notion of a federation of denominations. Like his ideal church, his ideal university was a place in which every man might find a home if his intellect justified it and he was prepared to live by reason. The secular University College had a powerful attraction for him and for men like him. For that reason if for no other, it came, finally, to form the major part of the university.

There Young was at home as few men ever have been. His death in 1889 was marked by a large issue of the student newspaper *Varsity* with tribute after tribute in terms which few academics would expect to receive today. The *Varsity's* interest was no sudden upsurge of post-mortem enthusiasm. For years it had marked his birthday with special tributes and reported his words with awe. Students took down his lectures in verbatim notes and circulated them amongst themselves. (Luckily, some still survive in the university library.)

It is not easy to be certain that one has put together an adequate account of Paxton Young's philosophy. The largest single surviving fragment is the volume edited by his pupil, James Gibson Hume, and published in 1911. It is just seventy-six pages long and those pages include a brief biography written by Hume and some notes on Young's philosophy by Sir Daniel Wilson. Some of it consists of a lecture entitled "Freedom and Necessity" which was originally published as a pamphlet in April, 1870, and some notes on free will, conscience, and moral theory. The notes were transcribed from a special shorthand which Young frequently used. Other existing fragments include essays on Sir William Hamilton, a lecture on natural religion, and an essay on Ferrier's *Institutes of Metaphysics*. There is also a fairly extensive review of an edition of the works of Reid. For the rest, there are notes left by his friends and the lecture notes taken by students to which we referred earlier.

The discussion of his philosophy seems naturally to fall into three parts: the development of his metaphysical idealism, his doctrine of free will, and his moral theory. All three are certainly closely related and, to an important extent, we can deepen our understanding of his philosophical position by seeing how they fit together.

In *The Ethics of Freedom* Gibson Hume remarks that "it would seem that at first he was drawn somewhat to the teaching of Sir William Hamilton. To the last he was opposed to the views of David Hume . . . ."[7] It would be natural for him to be well versed in if not convinced by the philosophy of Sir William Hamilton, which may well have been a dominant force at the University of Edinburgh when he was a student. Even then, however, revolution was in the air. Hegelian idealism was coming to Scotland and we do not know just when Young got wind of it. We do know that by 1856 he had certainly abandoned the Hamiltonian doctrine and the associated versions of the Scottish philosophy of "common sense."

Gibson Hume suggests that his conversion from Hamiltonian doctrine was associated with his belief that Scottish philosophers of "common sense" were all too closely tied to theological mistakes of the Presbyterian church. Whether that is so or not, the evidence is clear that he quickly developed philosophical arguments which led him to adopt a form of the new idealism.

One of his early arguments may have had a theological basis though it had nothing to do with the Presbyterian church. It may be as well to begin with that, for that will show us not only something of his criticism of Sir William Hamilton but also something of the route he took from theology to philosophy.

In 1856, in two essays—one concerned with Hamilton and the other with Ferrier—Young attacked the subject-object dichotomy. What seemed to provoke him in the Ferrier article to doubt the ultimate pervasiveness of subject and object in all possible experience was

7   Young, *Ethics*, p. 5.

his concept of God. The supreme being, he argued, could not have that kind of relativity in experience. For what that "relativity" means is that there is always something of one's own subjective activity in the structure of one's experience and so there is always an irreducible element of the object—conceived as that which is simply "given"—in one's experience too. If that were true, even God could not know all there was to know for He could not tell, any more than we can, to what extent His own activity altered the data.

One might think of this problem as a theological worry. To take that view of all possible knowledge is to deny the reality of the traditional "supreme being." But, as Young puts it, it is obviously much more than that. What he is questioning is the whole model used by people like Hamilton and extended in parts of the work of Ferrier. He is questioning the model because there is nothing absolutely necessary about it. Surely one can conceive of a being whose experience does not have this duality and that must provoke one to ask what the experience of such a being would be like and whether there is not another model which might, indeed, throw more light on our own experience.

In the essay on Hamilton, he makes clear that he thinks there is such a model. He argues against Hamilton that subject and object or ego and non-ego are not two different things which somehow become involved with one another in a mysterious process of experience. They are, he urges, two aspects or two sides of the *same* thing. In this, he is evidently going back to a problem faced but left unsolved by David Hume.

Hume had argued that when we come to examine our experience we find only, as we remarked earlier, the "bundle" of impressions and ideas. If you try to think about yourself, you will find, according to Hume, that you cannot. For there is no special component of your experience which you could identify as the "self." Hume had urged in one passage that there seems to be a "theatre of the mind." There seems to be a stage on which the action of our experience is played out. Yet no matter how hard one tries, one cannot identify that theatre as a component of one's experience. In another passage, Hume had urged that the arena of our experience is a kind of commonwealth. There are many components which work together and seem somehow to make a whole but that whole cannot be identified as another thing of which we are aware. It seems likely that Hume thought that the theatre image called attention to the fact that our experience seems, continuously, to have a unity and a coherence about it, while he thought the commonwealth image called our attention to the problem of continuity of experience. In the main body of his *Treatise* Hume leaves the problem there. His view is that, so far as we can tell on *his* principles of knowledge, there is no real "self" of which we can have effective knowledge. In an addendum, however, he confesses that he is in no way satisfied with his analysis and that the problem is a vexed and muddled one.

Now what Young seems to be claiming is that there is an alternative model which would enable us to see what this problem was. He does not in these essays mention Hume, but we know, from all the reports, that he was frequently preoccupied with trying to overcome the problems left by Hume and that he regarded Hume's theory as a disaster. If it is the case that subject and object are not two things but two aspects of the same thing, as Young maintains, we can easily see why the problem should have proved vexing to Hume. For it will not be the case that one can ever identify the self as a component in what is "given" in experience. When one analyzes things as objectively given, one simply gets a set of determinate objects of knowledge. These may well, on such an analysis, seem to resemble Hume's impressions and ideas. When one analyzes things from the stance of the subject, one finds that the meaning of all of one's experiences is in the relation of them to oneself. One finds oneself in the structure and in the organization of one's experiences.

This is the basis of Young's idealism. He argues that one comes to see that there is nothing in experience which cannot be associated with the structure of a self and that all possible experience can be analyzed in terms of such structures. On the other hand, there is nothing in experience which cannot be analyzed, equally, as part of an objective system and rendered into a structure of objective knowledge. There is nothing left over which is of necessity purely "subjective," just as there is nothing left over which is purely "objective."

Any systematized scheme of knowledge can be regarded as the manifestation of mind and intelligence. For the factor which converts the subjective to the objective is the rational system by which one organizes the data. Without this, everything is, as Hume would have argued, simply a brute, given, irrational surd. The whole of the objective system of the world is not something which we can regard as the manifestation of "our minds." But, so far as it is orderly and rational, it is evidence of the activity of mind. We could regard this as the "supreme being" of which Young speaks in the essay on Ferrier. That conclusion, as one must suppose that Young would have admitted, is not literally necessitated. For all we know of the larger order of the world is that it is an order and that it is rational. If one supposes that Young, despite his break with organized religion, continued to hold a theistic hypothesis throughout his life, one will see that, to an important extent, this account of the nature of self and knowledge would do much to make such a position seem reasonable to a man of Young's temperament.

The idealism which he began to develop was very close to the idealism of T. H. Green. Gibson Hume argues that Young put forward such positions long before Green's *Prolegomena to Ethics* was published. From Young's early essays, in which one can readily discern this line of thought, one must suppose that that is, indeed, true. Green's *Prolegomena* was published only after Green's death and Green, like Young, had been dealing with these ideas in the classroom for a long time. There is not the slightest evidence that Young and Green exchanged ideas or that there were any third parties who might have carried ideas from one to the other. It is quite natural that Young, faced with Sir William Hamilton, should have developed such notions. Green, in his turn, had spent many years studying Hume and was concerned to combat the moral doctrines of John Stuart Mill. In the course of his reading of Mill, Green would certainly have been thoroughly familiar with Mill's criticism of Hamilton. Thus it is likely that Young and Green came independently to the same ideas. In later life, Young came to read Green and developed a warm admiration for him. If he was disappointed that Green should become famous for the expression of ideas which he had first, he never expressed that disappointment.

If we turn to Young's involvement in the "free will" controversy, we can see how the main line of his thought is strengthened and deepened. He begins his discussion of free will in a very traditional way, insisting that each of us is immediately conscious of the fact that each of us is a free agent. Elsewhere he has cast continuous doubt on the belief that there are immediate data of experience which can be understood apart from the rational structures which give them meaning. Though he dislikes the notion of the "common sense" philosophers that our immediate experience and our basic beliefs constitute a set of initial presumptions which have to be rebutted by philosophical argument, he nonetheless insists that our "consciousness of freedom" is both immediate and significant. It is immediate, apparently, because it is part of the whole pervasive character of our awareness. This consciousness is important because there is not a simple "datum" which could be seen as having a different significance if put in a different context and, therefore, we cannot simply transfer it to some physical system in which it would have an explanation. As we understand him, at any rate, his point is that the consciousness of freedom is something which arises from the total context of our awareness at any moment.

Against this, philosophers have argued that the choice is between determinism and indeterminism. Though determinism—the doctrine that for each and every event, including the events which comprise our own lives, there is an objective cause—flies in the face of our immediate consciousness, its alternative, indeterminism, is absurd. For what we mean by "free will" is surely not the proposition that events "just happen."

Young canvasses a number of philosophical opinions including those of Jonathan Edwards, John Stuart Mill, and John Locke. He finds them all to be a tissue of confusion.

> The arguments, on both sides, were directed largely, and, in this respect, to good purpose, against unreal conceptions, which had been associated with the reality held by both parties in common. Wishing to extend their knowledge beyond the facts which exist to be known, and by this means to provide a support for convictions that could have stood well enough on their own behalf, the philosophers, whom I have been venturing to criticize, evoked Chimaeras from the abyss of inconceivability, and thrust these forward in front of the simple truth, as its main stay and hope; here, the Chimaera of Strongest Motives; there, the Chimaera of Liberty of Indifference; phantoms, which were regarded, the one by the combatants on the one side, and the other by the combatants on the other, as inconsistent with the very life of the truth they had been summoned to defend; and which certainly,as only darkening and defacing the truth by the smoke which they threw around it, behooved by all means to be driven from the field.[8]

We shall not follow him through all these philosophical horrors but, rather, seek to clarify the issues as he apparently understood them. Views which have to be contended with include these: We might argue, for instance, that everyone, ultimately, acts on what Young, drawing on one of the strands of the philosophical argument, calls his "strongest motive." One does what one seemingly wants to, but that is because one is impelled or compelled by motives which are in one's nature or character. It might well be put equally strongly as the doctrine that one acts, finally, on one's strongest desire. If one did not desire it, the circumstances being what they are, one would do something else. These are versions of psychological determinism. They rest on the manner in which one determines to use words. If one decides that words like "strongest motive" and "desire" are to be used in such a way that one can always identify a "strongest motive" or a "desire" with every act, then the doctrine follows by definition. But Young urges that this is a misunderstanding. It relates motives and acts as though they

8   Ibid., p. 32.

were in one sense separate and intelligible and in another sense unintelligible without one another. If one denies their separation, motives cannot literally be the causes of acts. But if one really insists on their separation so that they can be intelligible apart from one another, then it does not follow that everyone always acts on his strongest motive or desire. (In that case there is no necessary connection between motive, desire, and act.) Another of the views Young calls the liberty of indifference theory. On this view, one is free provided one's psychological impulses are in balance so that the "will" is free to act. But, against this, Mill had argued that it really makes nonsense of our immediate consciousness of freedom. For it surmises that one is free when one is not aware of anything which would determine one's act. But the will cannot determine, surely, what it is not aware of and this, in Young's view as well, leads one into a mare's nest. Another view Young derives from Locke's sentence in which it is said that liberty is "the power in any agent to do or forbear any particular action according to the determination or thought of the mind, whereby either of them is preferred to the other."[9] Young describes this as a "miserable view of freedom."[10] For this view involves the notion that freedom is simply bound up with what we can do and implies that we feel ourselves to be free when we will acts which happen. Not only does this, as Young says, seem to deny what we are immediately conscious of—"ourselves, as true agents to be responsible for what we do"[11]—it also seems not to touch the real issues. For we might feel ourselves to be free only on account of the fact that our desires and what we attain happen to coincide. It does not explain how freedom could be possible.

The first and third of these theories are either determinist themselves or compatible with determinism. The second tries to drive a wedge in the causal order through a "principle of indifference." All of them, in Young's view, are uninformative, baffling, and inherently misleading.

But Young, to be sure, wants no part of what is called "indeterminism." For if it is just a case that our acts are not determined by anything, then one must ascribe them to chance. This, at most, would be a form of the principle of indifference. At worst, it simply has nothing to do with the problem. For there is no obvious connection between what happens by chance—even assuming that anything happens by chance—and our immediate consciousness of freedom. It is this immediate consciousness of freedom which is an issue. It is this which Young thinks we must explain.

9   Ibid., p. 20.
10 Ibid.
11 Ibid., p. 22.

The solution is simply an application of the general principle by which he developed his idealism as a solution to the problems left by Hamilton and the problems exposed by Ferrier. Young argues that the relation of the acting subject to the act is not like the relation of two mechanical entities interacting with each other so that one can be said to be the cause of events which form part of the history of the other. The agent, in exercising his free will, is not a kind of engine driver pulling levers. He is not a mechanical cause at all.

The relation can be understood simply as the relation of two aspects of the same event. To describe it as the free act of the agent is to describe it from its inner perspective. To describe it as an event in the causal order is to describe it from its outer or objective perspective.

The act is given a rational structure by our own reasoning in exercising our free will. Insofar as it has a rational structure it can be related to the other events in the world. From the inside this can be conceived as our reason structuring the events. The order which is put on these events can be seen, from another side, as part of the total rational order of the universe. Perhaps this is clearer if we draw upon Young's remark that motive and act, for instance, are *not* separate. To have a certain motive *is* to act in a certain way. It is to be the kind of person who puts a certain structure on the events of his life. The motive does not cause these acts. Rather, it becomes clear and intelligible in the course of them. To say that we always act from our "strongest motive" is to say nothing. What we mean by our "strongest motive" is the motive which does appear as part of the order of our affairs in the world.

Either way, this makes all the causes in reality "volitional," for to say that there is a causal relation turns out to be saying that there is a rational order in things, and to say that there is a rational order in things is to say that something manifests itself intelligibly. We could, therefore, think of the world as a system in which Young's God or Hegel's Absolute manifest themselves as a concrete rational order. They do so amongst a set of other "agents" whose existence is evidenced by the kinds of rational order which we can find in the world. We know that some events are ascribable to human motives. The order reflects those motives which manifest themselves in the world. On that view, we are all perfectly free from our inner perspectives, but we are free, in the context of the world, to effect those actions which the greater rational order permits. Whether one chooses to give a name like God or the Absolute to that greater rational order is, no doubt, a matter which depends upon other decisions.

From another perspective, however, the world is simply a single rational order in which all explanations consist of delineating the appropriate kinds of reason and in showing the appropriate kinds of order. Young does not explore these further questions in his essay on free will. He is content, there, to try to dissolve the traditional conundrums by applying a general principle which functions elsewhere in his philosophy. This will be more intelligible when we have completed our investigation of Young's moral theory.

Let us then place these vexed issues aside for a moment and look at the way in which Young develops his moral theory. As usual, he develops his position out of the criticism of other theories. In this case, it is the utilitarian theory of John Stuart Mill and a rationalist theory which he ascribed to Calderwood which arouse his ire.

We might summarize the version of Mill's theory which Young wants to attack this way: What men desire and what is desirable are the same: happiness. Happiness consists of pleasurable sensations rightly distributed. Happiness, conceived this way, is itself good. But no man has more claim to the good than any other. Right action consists of that behaviour which brings about the good. It therefore follows that what one ought to do is to choose those acts which will produce the greatest happiness for the greatest number of men.

The theory may be described as "hedonist" in that it urges that it is happiness in the sense of pleasurable sensation which is the good and the aim of all reasonable men. It may be described as "utilitarian" in that it is a consequentialist theory. Mill, in writing his essay *On Utilitarianism*, did not specifically distinguish the two elements and the expression "utilitarianism" now is sometimes used to designate Mill's theory in which the consequences to be desired consist of a certain distribution of happiness and sometimes used to designate any consequentialist theory. It is important, however, to make the distinction.

Young attacks utilitarianism on the ground that it involves "a denial of disinterested action,"[12] on the ground that "the moral ideal or end of life cannot be simply the (product) of pleasure,"[13] and on the ground that it gives quite a wrong portrayal of reason and conscience.

Consequentialism, he thinks, involves the abhorrent doctrine that it simply does not matter what one intended to do as long as things come out all right. In short, by attending to consequences, Mill, in Young's view, undercuts the whole notion of moral responsibility. For one can only be responsible for what one intended to do. Young's theory of freedom entails that motive and act, intention and outcome, are all related in a simple indivisible whole. Mill, in constructing his moral theory, separates them, and this is one of the reasons that Young

12 Ibid., p. 50.
13 Ibid., p. 55. (The parentheses are in the original text.)

thinks Mill is unable to solve the free will problem. If one were to construct the situation as Mill's theory demands, one could not account for free will. Furthermore, it seems to Young simply outrageous that one might intend evil acts and receive moral credit for good acts.

The second criticism—the one about the denial of disinterested action—also stems from what Young thinks to be a massive conceptual muddle perpetrated by Mill. He concedes that Mill did not intend to deny disinterested action, but he argues that, in Bain's words, "the disinterestedness evaporates in the analysis."[14] For the whole theory is based on the optimization of pleasure. The pleasure to be optimized is my own and everyone else's. I cannot ever, therefore, escape from encountering my own interests in the calculation.

But this, he alleges, is a special kind of nonsense. He refers to the case of the good Samaritan. He says: ". . . if the good Samaritan had not been a man of such a character as to love his neighbor disinterestedly, he would have felt no pleasure in seeing the good he was able to do to his neighbor."[15] Some pleasures, in other words, can only occur because disinterestedness does occur. If I must always calculate my own pleasures first, I cannot develop this disinterestedness and thus not only are some moral occasions impossible but also even the things which Mill wants to champion—pleasures—become restricted by the process.

The relation of pleasure, happiness, and the good also seems to Young to have been sorely muddled by Mill.

> Take the pursuit of knowledge. The Utilitarian asks, would a man pursue knowledge if it did not give him pleasure? The reply is: a man would certainly not pursue knowledge if it did not meet some want of his rational nature.
>
> But this is an entirely different thing from saying that knowledge would not be pursued if it did not yield pleasure. To identify these two statements, would be to assume what cannot be conceded, that pleasure is the form of satisfaction sought in the pursuit of knowledge.
>
> But it is argued, the acquiring of knowledge gives a man pleasure. A glow of agreeable feeling is experienced as new truths unfold themselves. Granted. But, because agreeable feeling *results* from the attainment of an object of desire, it does not follow, that this agreeable feeling was the thing desired.
>
> If a man did not possess a nature in virtue of which knowledge is loved by him for itself alone, and without any reference to the pleasure to be found in the attainment of knowledge, the attainment would not yield him pleasure.[16]

14 Ibid., p. 50.
15 Ibid., p. 52.
16 Ibid., pp. 51-52.

The argument here, again, is that there must be ends beyond pleasure. But, if that is so, then what is "the good for man"?

It is here that Young's own philosophy begins to intrude and to develop. He says:

This can be answered only partially. The true good or Summum Bonum of a rational being becomes apparent only as his nature rises to fuller and fuller development. But the question though admitting only of a partial answer, can be answered sufficiently for the purpose in hand. We can point to many things distinct from pleasure, in which men of ordinary moral character seek satisfaction, and in which as a matter of fact, they find more satisfaction than any amount of pleasure could give. For instance, the pursuit of knowledge, self-sacrifice for the good of others, and the habitual, constant performance of what a man regards as his duty.[17]

Amongst other things, Young is arguing here that one cannot simply lay down what is good in a single proposition valid for all men at all times. The good depends upon the extent and development of one's reason. No good is possible without some rational development. For to say that an action is good is to say that it is morally right. To say that it is morally right is to imply that someone is responsible for it. Given Young's analysis of freedom, that is possibe only within the context and confines of rational development. Thus the good and reason are inextricably intermixed, but the one does not follow from the other by any simple definition, as we shall see in considering Young's analysis of Calderwood and his critical notes on Kant.

Young's last major criticism of Mill derives from his notes on conscience. It amounts to a criticism of Mill's whole manner of getting his ethical theory going. It is a commonplace to complain that Mill simply confused what is desirable in the sense of being good with what is desirable in the sense of being a possible object of human desire. Young does not use this somewhat simple-minded if classic objection. Rather, from his essay on conscience, one may derive another thesis which seems clearly directed at Mill—though Mill is not there mentioned by name. The point seems to be that, whatever one thinks of such notions as desire and desirability, there must be some way of getting one's moral theory going. What is it that can tell one whether one ought to respond to one's desire for pleasure in general or one's desire for some particular pleasure? The traditional answer is that one appeals to one's conscience. But if one's conscience is actually a reference point capable of yielding an honest moral decision and not merely

17   Ibid., p. 51.

a storehouse of one's existing preconceptions, it must be a manifestation of reason. For all deliberation involves reason.

We cannot, however—as we will see from Young's criticisms of other philosophers—simply proceed from an idea of reason to ideas of the moral law. He says:

> The Reason is the source of the ideas of right and wrong. It is the source of these ideas however not in a purely abstract form, but in connection with particular courses of conduct, which are thought as right or wrong. In the thought of particular courses of conduct as right or wrong, a rule for action is provided, though the rule may not be (absolutely proved.) Conscience in a man is simply Reason (considered) as providing such a rule, according to the degree of the *development* of Reason as it may be more or less in agreement with the absolutely desirable or morally good.
>
> It may be said; is not this to represent Reason, as self-contradictory? If conscience in one man, or the reason as developed in him, pronounces a certain course of conduct to be right, while conscience in another man, or the reason as developed in him, pronounces the same course of conduct to be wrong, is not Reason at variance with itself?
>
> No, unless development be self-contradictory.[18]

What he is alleging here is that reason does not occur in a vacuum. It occurs, as Young has always argued, in the context of forming and informing the structure of experience. Reason in any given man, therefore, can only be developed within the context of experiences which he is granted. Only so far can he tell what is right or wrong. Thus right conduct may not be the same for all men though two men who share the same community will, by sharing the same community, begin to share a common experience and out of this may develop a common rational order.

To pursue this line of thought at the moment, however, is somewhat premature. To see its real effect and final outcome, we must notice Young's analysis of the work of Calderwood.

Calderwood[19] had claimed there was a single moral principle—"one supreme principle"—which urges "it is right to use our powers for rational ends." From this, Calderwood had attempted to derive a great many moral principles such as "Honesty is right" and "Purity is right."[20]

But Young argues that, without some concrete content, Calderwood's enterprise degenerates into nonsense.

18   Ibid., pp. 59-60. (The parentheses are in the original text.)
19   Henry Calderwood, *Handbook of Moral Philosophy* (London: Macmillan, 1890).
20   Young, *Ethics*, p. 64. (Ascribed by Young to Calderwood.)

... the alleged supreme principle is too indefinite to serve as the starting point of any such deduction as Dr. Calderwood attempts. When it is said to be right to use our powers for their rational ends, or for their natural ends, what is meant by rational or natural ends?

If the meaning be, those ends to which our powers *ought* to be directed, then the proposition; it is right to use our powers for rational ends, or for their natural ends, is reduced to this, it is right to use our powers for the ends for which it is right to use them.

If the phrase "rational" or "natural ends" means anything else than the ends to which our powers ought to be directed, one would need to be informed of what *is* meant; before he can make any use of Dr. Calderwood's supreme principle or deduce any subordinate principle from it. No such information, however, is given by Dr. Calderwood.[21]

Calderwood had seemed to think that one simply "intuited" such basic moral principles. But Young thinks that this does not help at all.

If moral principles were intuitively apprehended they would be valid absolutely and without exception. But there are at least some of the ordinarily accepted moral principles that seem to admit of exceptions in extreme cases.

If moral principles were intuitively apprehended they would be universally accepted. As a matter of fact, there is scarcely one moral principle that is universally accepted. . . .

Not a few of the ordinarily accepted moral principles depend on conceptions of such a character as to show that the principles are not ultimate.[22]

Once again, Young is drawing attention to the fact that reason only works in the concrete. But what is it that reason is working toward? Young is fairly clear about this. Reason must work toward the completion of the structure of individual experience as a rational order. This is a form of what one might call a "self-realization" theory. But one needs to notice the basis of Green's theory and the qualification which that entails. He says:

Kant and Green practically identify the moral law with the command "Be ye perfect."

What constitutes perfection of personal character? This will appear more and more as reason develops and unfolds itself. Though we do not know in full we know in part so that the thought of perfection is not a vain imagination. You may obey in so far as you have definite ideas about what is required to constitute perfection.[23]

21 Ibid., pp. 65-66.
22 Ibid., p. 67.
23 Ibid., p. 72.

Thus, again, what it is you want to do is dependent in part upon your own experiences and what your own reason dictates in those circumstances. But it is the nature of reason to make a general rational order. Kant was right about that, but he surmised that the reason somehow provided an independent authority which imposed the same law on everyone at all times whereas, for Green, reason can only work within each of us and on the basis of one's own experience.

But will not this run him into a head-on collision with the principle which he asserted in his criticism of Mill—the principle that disinterested action is both possible and good? Young apparently thinks not. For one of the things one learns in the condition of one's own perfection is that disinterested action is necessary and good. It is necessary that one should perform disinterested actions in order that one might establish relations with other people which enable one to make rational decisions. It is simply not rational to act always in one's own interest or even always to consider one's own interest. For though rationality does not demand the same actions of all men at all times, rationality does not, of itself, place any man in a special and privileged position.

Here he thinks even Green, one of his heroes usually, is muddled.

Green says the good will differs from the bad will in virtue of the objects willed. The good will aims at one thing e.g. the good of your neighbor, the bad will aims at something different, injury to your neighbor. What is called Kant's "purism" insists that in each moral act there must be a conscious explicit intention to fulfil the law by that act. He seems to assert a duty apart altogether from the circumstances and quite irrespectively of the consideration of the superiority of one end over another. I do not see how this can be maintained. The very fact of the good Samaritan seeking one end intrinsically higher than another constitutes the rightness of his action.[24]

Now the point seems to be that while, as Young has asserted earlier, Green is right in asserting against Kant that the object willed makes a difference to the case, Green is not quite right in asserting that the good will differs from the bad will in *virtue* of the objects willed. For the willing and the object are not entirely separate. They both occur in the circumstances of the rational order created by the individual. Thus the objects concerned *are* important, and there is "a measure of truth"[25] in Kant's view that "duty always requires us to sacrifice inclination."[26] The morality of the situation emerges as one reasons about it

24 Ibid., p. 73.
25 Ibid., p. 74.
26 Ibid., p. 73.

and one's inclinations become subordinate to the rational order one develops. Still, the rational order one develops is always relative to one's circumstances.

There is no doubt that this moral theory coincides exactly with Young's life-long attitude to such institutions as the Presbyterian church and his life-long attempt to create a community in which individual conscience will be supreme. It also suggests very strongly a philosophy for an essentially pluralist society—the society which Canada was becoming at the time of Confederation.

The reader may find it easier to arrive at a critical assessment of theories such as Young's after we have examined theories like Watson's. Here, one can at least notice that what is crucial is the developing theory of reason in Young's philosophy. Reason is no longer the impartial arbiter which appears in Beaven's philosophy or the device for setting together the bits and pieces of experience and knowledge which we saw in the philosophy of Lyall.

Reason, instead, is the development of the inner structure of man. It is not, in Young's view, a device which can be used as a kind of substitute for force in an attempt to compel assent. It must be developed within each of us in the context of our own experience. There is not an ultimate separation of reason and experience. Furthermore, reason is neither our master nor our slave. We are not compelled by distant abstract principles but, on the other hand, we cannot use reason simply as a device to rationalize and to justify whatever it is we want justified. There is a real order. There is an idea of perfection whose details we do not know but which can, nonetheless, serve as a goal as we make our own experience, our own lives, and our own communities more coherent.

Young's philosophy, fragmentary as it is in its written form, still provides the possibility of numerous lines of development and, on analysis, it turns out to be, in itself, remarkably coherent.

FIVE

REASON, AUTHORITY, AND THE STRUCTURE OF EXPERIENCE

John Clark Murray

IF ONE HAD TO choose only one Canadian philosopher to be rescued from oblivion, one could make an excellent case for John Clark Murray. Whatever one's taste in speculation and controversy, there is something to be found in Murray. If one's taste is for metaphysical speculation, one finds in Murray the first signs of a systematic foundation to the idealist traditions in Canada. If one's taste is for theories of truth and knowledge, Murray's unusual activist version of the coherence theory of truth still requires study. If one's taste is for descriptive psychology, his two books still contain worthwhile insights. His *Introduction to Ethics*[1] remains a useful place to take one's puzzles about moral theory for review.

But Murray was much more than a philosophical theoretician. His concern about women's rights nearly cost him his job at McGill and his manuscript on the rights of workers and the diseases of industrial capitalism might still raise eyebrows. His forceful articles in *The Open Court* on Canadian independence and free trade took Canadian concerns about our relations with the United States to the home address of the American audience.[2] His nose for controversy and his sharp appreciation of the likely future are hardly excelled.

Murray was born in Scotland at Thread and Tannahill just outside Paisley on March 19, 1836. He was not quite a generation younger than Paxton Young and a little more than a generation younger than James Beaven. That generation made a difference. Though he professed himself always an ardent admirer of Sir William Hamilton, the end of the Scottish philosophy of common sense was already in sight when he was a student. Indeed, we have an unpublished essay dating from the end of his days as a student at Edinburgh in which, though he subjects

1   John Clark Murray, *An Introduction to Ethics* (London: Alexander Gardner, 1891).
2   See, for example, Professor J. Clark Murray, "Can Canada be Coerced into the Union? (A Canadian View)," published in *The Open Court* (Chicago, Illinois: Publisher, E. C. Hegeler, Editor, Paul Carus, 324 Dearborn Street, 1895), no. 411, p. 4561.

the work of Ferrier to extensive criticism, it is already obvious that he is fascinated by the new and more systematic idealism.

His father, David Murray, was Provost of Paisley and Murray had the means to study. He used it at once, after his graduation from Edinburgh, to explore German idealism at Heidelberg and Göttingen. If new ideas were to be found, Murray was not the man to ignore them.

Then, too, the Canada to which he came was already unlike the country which Beaven and Paxton Young found. Murray arrived at Queen's in Kingston five years before Confederation. Though the university was scarcely more than a building in a clearing near the old garrison town, Canada was already beginning to take obvious shape. When he moved to Montreal ten years later to become Professor both of Logic and of Mental and Moral Philosophy at McGill, he found a substantial, thriving, and cosmopolitan city. He was to remain there until his death in 1917, and, though he married a Scots girl in 1865, he became increasingly Canadian in his concerns and he developed a strong interest in the integrity and unity of the country as a whole.

The intellectual life of Montreal was quite sufficient for a civilized and scholarly man and, with its growth and industrialization, it was to exhibit the host of problems characteristic of modern industrial societies. There he could observe the problems of industrial workers, the problems of a society divided by class, by race, and by cultural outlook. There, too, he could and did meet firsthand the realities of moral issues which seem, all too often, disguised from philosophers whose fate it is to live out their lives in more traditional and bucolic academic surroundings.

Murray was to live through the Boer war with its destructive fragmentation of Canadian loyalties and through the long, slow build-up toward the inevitability of World War I. He saw what was happening, saw its meaning, and bitterly denounced the armaments race and the corruption of industrial society by unbridled capitalism. He witnessed the growing demand for the education of women and the attempt by those in authority to fob them off with the second-rate. The process angered him and led him into a long and bitter battle with Principal Dawson at McGill. He saw the growth of an industrial pro-letariat and noticed, in the life of the working man, the alternation of poverty, misery, and occasional bursts of colourless vice. That angered him too, and he denounced it in measured terms in a fine, copper-plate hand—words now being published. (His wife, Margaret, was a founder of the Imperial Order of Daughters of the Empire and one cannot help feeling that anyone who played a part in the origins of that august, but hardly revolutionary, organization must sometimes have been in-trigued with Murray's views about education and the organization of industrial society. [How many of the founders of that organization can have been married to men who described Karl Marx as "rigidly scientific"?][3])

He believed in free trade because he believed that free trade was necessary to eradicate the poverty of the world, but he was in other ways no continentalist. He warned those who might doubt it that Canadians valued their independence and that they had both the resources and the determined skill to make it stick. Murray was, evidently, a man of several characters. Urbane, witty, and gentle in arguments, his books have the authority which comes from thinking long and coherently about what one writes. But in controversy he could be determined and acid. Beneath all that, there remained a streak of Scots piety. He thought that Christianity was, quite simply, true. He never failed to say so when the opportunity arose. But his belief, at the same time, seems never to have dissuaded him from any inquiry whatsoever. In his manuscript on the state of industrial society, he makes the necessary bow to the truth of Christianity. He remarks, however, that Christian principles are scarcely precise enough to provide us with all we need to know, and gets on with the business at hand.

His loyalty to Christianity was matched by his loyalty to men and institutions who had influenced him. Though Murray left Queen's in 1872, he continued for many years to return to Kingston to give special lectures—especially on Sunday afternoons. He also acknowledged his debt to Sir William Hamilton. His book, *Outline of Sir William Hamilton's Philosophy*,[4] he explained, was intended to acquaint the reader, in as simple form as possible, with Hamilton's thought. He has been unfairly accused of not being aware of the criticism of Hamilton but a perusal of his books on psychology makes it clear that this is a mistake. He quite straightforwardly intended to discharge his debt to Hamilton, and did so.

In tracing the development of Murray's thought we shall move from the concrete to the abstract, and begin with his social and political philosophy as it appears in his unpublished work. We shall then proceed to discuss his moral theory and then his theory of knowledge as it appears in his books on psychology and, finally, as best we can with the rather limited materials he left, his most general metaphysical views.

Murray's social and political philosophy is best expressed in the manuscript which he entitled "The Industrial Kingdom of God." In its

3 John Clark Murray, "The Industrial Kingdom of God," handwritten manuscript, Acc. No. 611/75, McGill University Archives, Montreal, p. 121. Hereafter referred to as "Industrial Kingdom."

4 John Clark Murray, *Outline of Sir William Hamilton's Philosophy* (Boston: Gould & Lincoln, 1870).

some 320 pages, Murray, despite its title, is not obsessed with religion and seems, in general, to derive his moral theory from a combination of general principles and experience. It is divided into two parts, called Labour and Property. It confines itself to a discussion of social relations in an industrial society and a discussion of the relation between morality and economic theory, but one can infer from it a reasonably general account of Murray's theories and attitudes about public morality.

He begins with a discussion of labour. Much of his argument is devoted to denying the proposition that labour is, in the ordinary sense, a commodity. He draws attention to the traditional distinction between rights which can be transferred and those which are inalienable. Rights in property, ordinarily, can be transferred from one person to another but no one, in Murray's view, can alienate his personal rights. A man cannot sell himself into slavery. It is unthinkable that the person who makes the purchase could acquire, thereby, an actual moral right to govern the person who sells himself.

The essence of this distinction, Murray thinks, lies in an understanding of the nature of persons as such. Persons are not things. They do not acquire a value which can be transferred; rather, they are the sources of value. Anything which can properly and legitimately be bought and sold is, in the ordinary sense, a commodity. It has a fixed and determinate value in relation to some social situation in which the transaction takes place. It is thus possible to contrive for it the notion of a fair price, a just contract, or a reasonable exchange.

A person is simply not like that. His value is not relative to a social situation with its intricate set of ends and means, his life does not hold a fixed and determinate worth, he is not literally limited in value by his history, his prospects, or his utility. Rather, to be a person is to transcend those limitations by reason of being that which gives things their value. Murray would reinforce this analysis of the logic of the situation with the religious notion that man is of infinite worth and created in the image of God. Though, in that context, he would no doubt accept the proposition that persons are not the ultimate source of their own value, they are, nevertheless, the source of values in the social situation.

As a consequence, there are basic personal rights. In the economic situation of the capitalist world personal relations develop in a context in which there are labourers and employers of labour. The employers are inclined to see labour simply as a commodity and the system in which they work reinforces that notion. Labour is a cost of production—a cost, like any other cost, to be minimized in the interest of economic survival and profit. But the thing which the labourer is selling is himself. It is reasonable for men to sell their services but unreasonable for men to sell themselves.

The problem, as Murray sees it, is to determine how to make and sustain this distinction. As a person, the labourer retains his inalienable rights. If his services are, in the social context, the part of himself which occurs in the social process then the labourer continues to be entitled to the result of his labour. To hold that he has a title only to part of that result is to hold that he can alienate a part of himself. Morally, this is both reprehensible and a simple, straighforward misunderstanding of the value situation.

One apparent outcome of this is that it appears as though one should adopt a form of the labour theory of value. What there is in the world consists of natural resources transformed by someone's labour into marketable commodities. Can one settle the issue simply by tracing the products back to their source in the labour of individuals and rewarding those individuals in a way which is proportionate to their efforts?

Murray has evident sympathy for this theory—a theory widely held and supported in various forms by, among many others, John Locke and Thomas Aquinas. But it is difficult to assess effort, given the complex kinds of tasks and the great variety of social situations in which production takes place. It also tempts one, by adopting one definition of labour rather than another, to construct theories which end by favouring one part of the productive community against another.

The main thing, he thinks, is to find a way to preserve the personal rights of labour. These personal rights extend to a sufficient return on one's labour to maintain oneself as a person and to maintain one's functions as a citizen. In the end, he suggests a social organization in which there are arbitration courts which will determine the minimal conditions for employment of labour and also determine, given the complexity and shape of a specific industrial process, what really is the fair share of the labourer.

In a chapter entitled "Disadvantages of Labour," he divides the worker's problems, in his usual systematic way, into extrinsic and intrinsic disadvantages. Extrinsically, the labourer suffers from a lack of resources and from the weakness of a single individual who must often face very large organizations. Murray is well aware of the tendency to monopoly and of the destructive social effects of monopoly but, even short of that, the worker cannot be expected to bargain effectively with powerful groups having vast resources. Workers can organize themselves into a trade union but, though organization of trade unions was becoming easier, as Murray points out, it remained a very difficult undertaking indeed—fraught with legal harrassment, outright violence, and overt social pressure.

Even if he succeeds in forming a trade union, the labourer is relatively unlikely to achieve anything like a full measure of justice. The trade union is apt to be relatively inefficient. It may be wealthy in comparison to the individual worker; it is not likely to be wealthy in comparison to a combination of industrialists. Though it may have at its disposal a good deal of talent, talent will be relatively difficult for it to obtain and maintain. Even such a much more obvious latter-day phenomenon as the likelihood of corruption in trade unions was noticed by Murray. It stems, in part, from the relative powerlessness of the individual union member.

Suppose that the industrial worker organizes successfully and does bargain effectively with his employer. What happens? His employer raises the price of the commodity which he produces. He does not necessarily, in the process, pay his labour a fair and just share. Beyond that, the effect of such activities may be to the detriment of workers in other industries. A competition between workers is likely to be established and in such a way that there is no guarantee of a satisfactory net return to any one of them.

Murray then begins to probe into the basic workings of the economic structure. He calls attention to Henry George and Karl Marx. George had put forward the theory that all wealth, ultimately, derives from property.[5] The effect of labour is always to make property more valuable and the owner of the property controls the wealth. Hence George proposed a system of property tax to restore the social balance and proposed a society which would, in that way, control the creation and distribution of wealth. Murray admits that there is much to be said for this proposition, but he feels that it somehow evades the point. Logically, it must be true that all wealth results from the transformation of resources. Yet the effect of George's theory is to distract attention from the essential features of the social process.

Murray described Marx as rigidly scientific; he conceives that there is much to be said for Marx's view that the root of the problem can be seen in the organization of the capitalist system and, as Murray reads Marx, in the existence of capital itself. The possession of capital becomes a device for the exercise of social control. Yet capital, in itself, is accumulated by a system which makes it inevitable that a proportion of the effort of the worker accrues to someone else. Capital is thus the fundamental kind of injustice. As such, in its attempt to maintain itself, it spreads injustice throughout the system in which it works.

5   Henry George, *The Land Question* (New York: Robert Schalkenbach Foundation, 1945; first published in 1895).

In logic, this is a theory much like that of Henry George. It simply structures the evidence in another way. Murray thinks that the examination of such systems is by no means unenlightening and certainly not irrelevant to our understanding of the situation. Still, Marx's theory, like George's theory, seems—in Murray's view—a special kind of evasion.

It is an evasion of the moral issue because it fails to distinguish between the undesirability of the state of affairs in itself—the undesirability of there being ownership of real property in George's theory or the undesirability of there being capital as such in Marx's theory—and the moral outrages which result, in actuality, from a lack of regulation. Though capital, unregulated, represents an injustice and spreads that injustice through a whole society, it does not seem to be Murray's view that the injustice results from the phenomenon but rather that it results from its lack of effective regulation and from its occurrence in a society which lacks adequate social structures to deal with it intelligently.

The accumulation of capital makes possible enterprises which may or may not be to the public benefit, Murray says in Section 2 of Part IV. Unregulated, they are apt not to be to the public benefit. Given a society which lacks an appropriate social structure, its undesirable result is likely to be a virtual necessity—a kind of necessity which Marx discerned with his scientific approach.

It can, for that matter, pollute a whole society. Murray notices the armaments manufacturers. With their capital, they are able to make money out of what amounts to wickedness; they are able, with their power, to create a situation in which workers are really unable to choose whether to work for them or not. Society not only permits this, it positively encourages it. What, then, is the answer? Murray expresses great sympathy with the co-operative movement which had grown up in England and spread to North America, but he remarks that great successes of consumer co-operatives in England were not matched by attempts to set up co-operative forms of industrial production. (To a large extent, what Murray says remains true. The success of producer co-operatives seems to have been largely confined to agriculture.) He sees hope in a theory which was officially adopted only about 1950 by the Liberal party in England—what has come to be called "co-ownership." On this view, the duty of capitalists extends to taking their employees into the business as partners, distributing shares, profits, and important features of the decision-making process.

Evidently, however, such schemes, unless backed with stringent legislation, are simply naïve. Murray had not missed the lessons to be learned from reading Marx and Henry George. The industrial forces to be contended with are simply too great for us to expect that we will overcome them by some program of voluntary action.

Murray states his own conclusion. So long as the present system of remunerating labour prevails, he says,

> ... it is impossible to see how the workers of the world are ever to get a fair share of the wealth they co-operate in producing. The only way in which this end can be attained is by adopting a different system of remunerating labour,—a system which will regulate the reward of the labourer by some proportion to the product of his labour. A perfectly equitable system cannot of course be introduced all at once. Every thorough and permanent reform is a slow growth, and the ideal system of industrial organisation must grow out of the present. The capitalist therefore cannot be expected to vanish at once; in the interest of the great mass of the labouring classes it is extremely undesirable that he should vanish. Without the leadership of organising capitalists most of the industrial work of the world at present would be so disorganised that scarcely any labourers would know what to do. It may therefore be assumed that the relation of employer and employee will continue for some time to come. As long as it does continue, workingmen must simply make the best use of it they can to secure a just proportion of the wealth they help to produce under it. Probably the most ready advance towards a perfectly fair system of remuneration, without abolishing the relation of employer and employee, is the adoption, wherever possible, of payment by piecework.... The market price of a commodity can often be told with exactness. It is often possible also to tell the exact cost of production, less the workman's wages. In such cases it is known what value the workman's labour contributes to the commodity and it is not unfair that he should claim the full value of his labour.[6]

Such a program, Murray thought, could be enforced by courts of arbitration. But even that would only be an approximate beginning.

> ... in many cases difficulties are connected with the adoption of payment by piecework; and even when the system is adopted, it is often impossible to determine with any exactness the value of the labour bestowed upon an article, for the unfortunate reason that the employer cannot tell beforehand the price which he will obtain for his commodities when they are thrown upon the market. The fluctuations of prices are so great, that the manufacturer and merchant are often left to mere guesswork in forming their calculations; and the misfortunes of business life prove that the most intelligent men may make ruinous miscalculations at times. Even payment by piecework therefore may in some cases give but a petty share of the whole

6   Murray, "Industrial Kingdom," pp. 222-24.

value of a commodity to the workman, while in other cases it may turn out that the workman has in his pay received far more than the whole value which the commodity realised.[7]

Thus, Murray urges that this system be extended using its principle as the basis of a "system of copartnership [which] may be carried out with many variations in detail" in such a way as to involve "no violent revolution of present arrangements, which might be fraught with danger and distress both to labourers and capitalists."[8] Of course Murray's proposal does involve severe curtailment of what were then thought to be quite basic rights of private property. But this does not worry him unduly. He insists that we must learn "to distribute the wealth, whose methods of production we understand, so as to avoid the appalling inequalities of the present system,—the answer to this question will form the crowning achievement at once of Christian philanthropy and of social philosophy."[9] He remarks that, "the present system" has, with variations, been in use for so long that men "are apt to believe it has its foundations in the very nature of things."[10] He notes the contrary:

. . . the profoundest researches into the origin of social institutions seem to be disclosing the fact, that the system of private or individual property arose out of an earlier system of common property, traces of which are yet to be found in many parts of the civilised world, especially in the interesting survival of village communities. Under this system of common property, or communism, as it is usually styled in our day, the wealth produced in any community, instead of being allowed to fall into the uncontrolled possession of private individuals, is retained as the common property of the whole, and then distributed among the individual members. All the schemes, that have ever been proposed for the distribution of wealth follow one or other of these two general types, though of course the types admit of an indefinite variety of forms in detail.

It is not wonderful, therefore, that reflective minds in all ages have refused to recognise the system of private property as having its foundation in any irreversible law of nature. It is not wonderful that small communities of men, inspired with a common enthusiasm which recoiled from the selfishness engendered by private property, should, like the early Christians, have adopted a communistic division of their possessions. Nor is it wonderful that many of the labouring classes, under the increased intelligence which the spread of popular education has given them in recent times,

7   Ibid., pp. 224-25.
8   Ibid., p. 225.
9   Ibid., pp. 244-45.
10 Ibid., p. 245.

are beginning to claim, in language which the privileged classes can no longer mistake, either an entire re-organisation of society in the direction of communism, or such an alteration of the laws which govern the distribution of private property as shall enable them to enjoy a larger and more certain share of the wealth they help to produce than under present regulations can ever fall to their lot. The privileged classes, therefore, who own the larger part of the world's wealth, are urgently called to look with earnest eyes at the present situation of affairs, and to consider, with dispassionate impartiality, what is the real nature of the right they claim over their private property.[11]

Now Murray admits that, given the facts of the case, it may turn out that private property can be justified but that will only be so if a just distribution can be obtained. He remarks that nowhere in the civilized world does the law really allow a man to dispose of his property as he wishes. The question is not whether there should be some restrictions on the use of private property but whether we can derive a set of restrictions which will end injustice.

It will, in Murray's view, require substantial legislation. The legislation will have to direct itself not just to the immediate equitable reward of labourers but to the restraints of capital in general.

. . . the injury done to society by the niggardly spirit of many a wealthy churl is not confined to this comparatively passive resistance to measures of social advantage. It sometimes take a more aggressive form of active hostility. Such are, for example, the efforts, unhappily too often successful, sometimes on the part of a single capitalist, but more frequently on the part of a combination, to enhance the price of commodities in general use, it may be even, of some necessary of life, by buying up and thus controlling the entire supply. It is evident that conspiracies of this kind practically assume a power which ought to be accorded only to the supreme authority in every state,—the power of taxing the people by levying an impost upon articles of daily consumption. It is further evident that a conspiracy of this sort strikes at the very foundation of popular or constitutional government. For it is a commonplace of political science, that the indispensable safeguard of every popular constitution is the power of the people to control taxation; and if that power can be usurped by irresponsible persons, it does not matter whether these are a party of private conspirators or the rapacious agents of a despot, the people are equally the victims of a tyrannical extortion that is incompatible with the essential conditions of freedom. The great capitalistic conspirators of our day are in fact simply a survival, under altered conditions, of the great predatory chiefs of a ruder social state, who levied blackmail on all who accepted their rough and uncertain protection, while they plundered unrelentingly all who refused to submit to this capricious and oppressive tax. The capitalists may perhaps plead in defence that their

11   Ibid., pp. 245-47.

action is not prohibited by law, while the depredations of the old freebooters were always suppressed by the legal government wherever it was strong enough to enforce its authority. But this is a very imperfect account of the facts.[12]

(At this point in his manuscript Murray recounts the history of that "outlaw" he described in the Border Ballads[13] who is finally brought to book by James V. Though Murray hardly admires his ancestor, one suspects that he thinks him a substantial improvement over the capitalist freebooters of modern Montreal.) Fired with this view, Murray goes on for some time castigating capitalists for an assortment of offences. But even this does not move him to accept revolution. For he still believes that the theories of people like Marx and Henry George essentially evade the issue and that the solution is better law, better education, more stringent control, and the enactment of economic principles into legislative prescriptions. To understand some of this more clearly, we must introduce into the discussion Murray's account of the obligations as opposed to the rights of those who labour in society and of the essential handicaps which they face in trying to carry out those obligations. Murray is still enough of the old moralizing Presbyterian to resist quite firmly the doctrine that any set of conditions entirely justifies one in a lapse from morality. He calls attention to drink, gambling, and prostitution (the last he refers to with Victorian obliqueness as "the vice which is shameful to name").[14] He points out that, despite the enormous pressures of capitalism, not all of the working class becomes degenerate. Indeed, that is part of its problem. He notices that those who seek education, resist despair, and do not fall into clutches of vice are apt to be utilized by employers and become foremen. He thinks that it is the duty of every citizen to seek education, to show willingness to work, and to make the best use of his talents. Admittedly, there are plenty of excuses for failure to do so and they excite Murray's sympathy and not his contempt.

Marx had envisaged the happy collapse of capitalism and had imagined that society would then be taken over by the surviving working class. Marxists have thought that, naturally, the working class would be able to seize the means of production, organize it efficiently,

12 Ibid., pp. 264-66.
13 Murray, *The Ballads and Songs of Scotland* (London: MacMillan, 1874), mentioned in "Industrial Kingdom," p. 267.
14 This prudery is not really typical of Murray. It is worth mentioning only because the manuscript of the "Industrial Kingdom" shows occasional signs of having undergone various transformations from a simpler intention to its ultimate more scholarly one.

and work its way toward that delightful day when the state would wither into oblivion.

Murray thinks that this simply would not happen. For people are not made particularly kindly, humane, or efficient by the depredations of capitalism. To abolish the capitalist in a revolution is to expect that labour would be able, then, to carry out its social obligations. Murray simply doubts this.

Murray, a moralist by nature and philosophical conviction, cannot bring himself to accept the Marxist view that the legal and political process is essentially a super-structure which is really dependent on the economic sub-structure. He thinks, on the contrary, that the economic sub-structure is essentially bad because of lack of moral and legal restriction. As always, he is far from naïve and he realizes the severe restrictions which one must place on one's hopes for his courts of arbitration. Indeed, he prefaces his proposal with a long account of the known past failures and likely future failures of such devices. It is best to state his measured conclusion in his own words:

> ... if a special Court of Arbitration is desired, the utmost it should be expected to do at present is to express an opinion on the question at issue after hearing the representations of both parties. But we must not underestimate the force of such an opinion on the part of competent men, especially if selected voluntarily by the contending parties on account of their technical knowledge and trustworthy character. Public opinion would probably make it impossible for either party to act in defiance of the verdict of such referees. Something like an aspect of legality might be given to courts of this kind by the law simply recognising them as legitimate means of settling trade disputes. . . .[15]

It may be thought that the practical application of Murray's theories would expose the extent to which Murray is hardly typical of people in general. Throughout his life there is little evidence that he ever put his own self-interest ahead of causes which he frequently pursued to his own peril. But will everyone be amenable to the kind of moral suasion which he suggests?

To urge this is to take what is probably a rather shallow and simple-minded view of Murray's philosophy of law. Only a little of that philosophy comes to the surface in his published works, but what there is suggests a view rather like the following: We may think of the law as a set of devices which compel and control, ultimately, because the sanction of force lies behind them. A little reflection will show that this view is quite utterly false.

15 Murray, "Industrial Kingdom," pp. 221-22.

It is true that the law is effective, to some reasonable degree, against bank robbers but that is because relatively few people have a high opinion of bank robbery. Force is effective against quite small minorities. If everyone wanted to rob banks, force would scarcely do any good.

Law exists as a set of beliefs expressed in action by the great body of men in a given society. Its control mechanisms work, at most, against deviant minorities.

When, therefore, we seek new legislation to correct existing social abuses, we must be very careful. Murray points out that many past attempts to establish the just price and the fair share through courts of arbitration turned out to favour the wealthy over the poor, the capitalist over his labourer, the influential over the obscure. But that is because there was a lack of clear public conviction. In Murray's time as in ours, most people had few articulated convictions about the rights of labour and about just distribution. In such a period, the educated part of the most intelligent sub-groups in a given society are most likely men who are already in power, and when one seeks to find men to staff one's courts of arbitration—men with a knowledge of economics, law, industrial relations, and moral and political philosophy—one will most frequently find oneself face to face with a powerful élite.

Murray, therefore, urges against immediate unlimited powers of regulation as opposed to powers to make strong recommendations. He looks forward to the day when his courts of arbitration can have real and effective power. Meanwhile, he insists that such courts should not be appointed. Election, rather, is the right procedure and one must first identify the range of interests and each natural interest group should elect its own representatives.

The real difficulty, perhaps, and Murray well knows this, is the problem of urgency. How long can we expect existing social arrangements to last? As it has turned out, we had more time than even Murray might have thought. But frequently his writing conveys a sense of the urgency of the situation. Without action, one cannot resist the arguments of the followers of Marx. Without action, the poor may become desperate. Without more effective education the system will play ever more effectively upon the ignorance and prejudice of the masses.

Yet his proposals are of such a kind that carrying them out must necessarily be a very long-term arrangement. On the other side, he sees hope and he notes that, however ineffective they might be for various purposes, the organization of trade unions has become easier and more and more workers are organized each day. (In our own time, industrial organization seems to have reached a plateau at least partly because, as Murray would insist, there are still limits to the effectiveness of such organizations.)

Even in the kind of society we have, he notices, education can lift a man from one social position to another. The development of valuable talents, especially rare ones, is an effective way of beating the system.

(If this now seems less obvious, it may be because another of Murray's favourite themes has caught up with us. He frequently notes the harsh and bitter effects of the "law" of supply and demand. We may, finally, have reached the point at which the supply of educated men has made it virtually impossible to develop special skills which would guarantee one a secure place in our society. At any rate, the range of such opportunities seems to have narrowed.)

Here and there in his book Murray reverts to a religious theme. Might not poverty be good for us as a means of getting to the kingdom of heaven? Humility, Murray admits, is desirable. Poverty does keep one from a chained preoccupation with material goods. But Murray does not think much of it as an educational force. Being hungry does not improve one's thoughts and, like nearly all the Scots philosophers, Murray is inclined to the view that one must *think* one's way into the kingdom of heaven. Anyhow, the brutalizing effect of poverty creates men who may well seek brutalizing activities—drink, gambling, and prostitution. In general, Murray thinks that questionable promises of an eschatological solution are a feeble excuse for maintaining hell on earth.

Perhaps the oddity of Murray's book is the contrast between the frequent violence of his denunciation of capitalist free-booters and the reasoned gentleness of his solutions.

To understand this, one must go back, once more, to the basis of his social philosophy. The basis of it is the fundamental distinction between persons and things.

It is worthwhile, as we move to the close of this part of our discussion, to see this through Murray's own words.

The personal rights of men . . . are involved in the very fact of their being men. A clear and full understanding of these rights implies a recognition of the essential difference between a *person* and a *thing*. There is no distinction in human thought profounder than this. A certain school of speculation indeed has, in ancient as well as in modern times, endeavoured to escape from the recognition of this distinction as absolutely essential by reducing persons, in the last scientific analysis, to things. At the present day this school maintains that unintelligent things, and not any intelligence, were the first of existences, and that, in the form of atoms or some similar shapes, they have

118

kept arranging and rearranging themselves, till they reached at last a highly complicated combination which we call man.[16]

Murray responds to this out of his idealistic convictions. He urges that the theory that men can be reduced to unintelligent things would destroy the basis of science itself. For science requires thought and unintelligent things by definition cannot think.

Murray points out the real difference between men and things:

A thing, having its entire nature and life determined by the agencies of its environment, is merely a means to the accomplishment of ends outside of itself; it has in fact no self to form an end for anything. But a person, moulding his nature and life by his own consciousness of what he is doing, is no mere instrument of outside purposes; he is an end to himself. This it is that gives for each man an infinite value to himself, making him feel that the true worth of his life is to be found not in anything external . . . that in fact he might possess the whole world of external things, and yet it would profit him nothing if he were not also master of his own self.[17]

All that Murray is saying in his critique of industrial capitalism stems from this premise: Men are the sources of value insofar as they are the only things in this world which are ends in themselves. They may derive their value from a greater being, but they are the givers of value in this world because it is they who form the ends around which the means must be determined. If capitalist industrialists use men as means to private ends, at the cost of the degradation of their workers—the cost, perhaps, of the creation of an uninhabitable world—they deny all this. It is really from the notion of the inalienability of the personal rights of man rather than from the notion of the labour theory of value that Murray, finally, determines his doctrine of the just reward and the fair price.

But it is this, as well, which requires the gentleness of his solution. Men are infinitely valuable but also, as the facts show, infinitely fragile. They cannot suddenly be expected to create a new social system. They must be led and not compelled if they are to maintain their status as moral agents. All of this requires time, stability, and social organization.

Reason may have to take concrete form in law. But even law, for Murray, is ultimately a species of rational persuasion.

Reason is always a device for co-ordinating experience, for opening new alternatives, for overcoming prejudice but never, in itself, a

16 Ibid., pp. 38-39.
17 Ibid., p. 40.

substitute for force, a kind of compulsion. It does not justify the kind of compulsion which wholly goes beyond the limits of rational persuasion. It may take the form of law which becomes binding in practice but we are reminded, by numerous and various examples, that law, itself, does not work except in a suitable climate of opinion.

Murray's view of reason in his social and political philosophy runs perfectly parallel to his use of reason in his metaphysics, his theory of knowledge, and his descriptive psychology. His political philosophy, while it may be surprising, given his background, his friends, and his position, is not different from the rest of his philosophy. Indeed, as we shall see, the whole of his philosophy forms an integrated structure.

One cannot, for example, easily understand Murray's political philosophy independently of the moral theories which he put forth in his *Introduction to Ethics*[18] and *Handbook of Christian Ethics*.[19] They are both judicious and careful books. In them, Murray appears more as the judge summing up for the jury of his readers than as an advocate of a cause. Still, as so often when judges summarize for juries, one can discern his opinions and attitudes.

An Introduction to Ethics begins with some points which were, even then, commonplaces and some others which are now commonplaces but were not so then. He reminds us that one's moral theory must depend to a large extent on one's background view about the nature and prospects of man but he argues, too, that in the last analysis only an apprehension of value itself will serve to sustain a moral theory. One cannot derive "ought" from "is." He criticizes some of the Scottish philosophers of "moral sense" on the ground that they were sloppy about this distinction.

This presents something of a conundrum. On the one hand, he urges that we must know something about the nature of man, something, that is, about the natural facts of the situation, in order to have a moral theory. But, on the other hand, he urges (and later philosophers have generally agreed) that one cannot simply derive one's moral theory from these facts. If "ought" cannot be derived from "is," how is it that the natural facts of the situation bear upon moral theories at all?

Essentially, in Murray's view the connection is this: If we were simply a part of physical nature, moral rules could hardly be binding upon us and the apprehension of values could hardly be expected to lead to action. Furthermore, as would emerge from an analysis of his critique of moral theorizing, reason must, in his view, bear upon the

18   John Clark Murray, *An Introduction to Ethics* (London: Alexander Gardner, 1891).
19   John Clark Murray, *A Handbook of Christian Ethics* (Edinburgh: T. and T. Clark, 1908).

outcome of moral deliberation. But, if we were merely parts of physical
nature, our reason could only be a feature of that nature, and so,
value-neutral. It has been argued that, even if we were simply mechanical creatures, moral judgment would still have its place if right moral
judgments, however mechanically, produced right actions. But it does
not seem to be quite this position that Murray is concerned with or that
he is arguing against.

He is concerned with freedom as a condition for the apprehension
of value and with our separateness from the physical world as a feature
of *this* process. We could not, in other words, understand moral judgment if we were not beings with a dimension of freedom to our natures.

Indeed, the mere fact that we can develop this understanding is,
for Murray, apparently, evidence for the position which he wants to
take about human freedom. He argues that, in morality as in much
else, action precedes theory. It is because we can and do act morally that
we can consider moral theories and can try to regulate our conduct
coherently according to such theories. It is not because we have such
theories that we are able, initially, to act morally. Rather, we find
ourselves faced with a problem. If we were merely part of physical
nature, how could the question ever arise? Suppose that we are always
wrong in our moral judgments. Still the possibility of being wrong
about anything would seem to indicate the possibility of cognizing
objects which are not, simply, features of nature. (This argument is
inexplicit and runs through the background of what Murray says. It
seems to be a notion which may have derived from his early interest in
Ferrier.) But we do have to face the problem of morality because we do
act in ways which bring values to our attention.

Ultimately, Murray's position is even more subtle. For he would
argue that reason itself does not bear mechanically on action. He says:
"... the legislative function of the moral reason ... enjoins, not so
much particular rules of conduct, as rather a general spirit for the
government of life in particular cases. And therefore, further, the
obligations which moral reason imposes are not to be conceived merely
as restrictions of human freedom."[20]

The application of the rule to the particular case is, in part, an act
of invention. It, itself, involves freedom. Once again, we could not
understand morality without freedom. So he says: "And consequently,
so far from restricting my freedom, it rather posits freedom as a reality
in my life, because it frees me as a rational being from the tyranny of
those non-rational forces which are organized in my individual human
nature."[21]

20 Murray, *An Introduction to Ethics*, p. 234.
21 Ibid.

And thus he argues that man is not a simple feature of the physical world, that the relation of cause and effect in moral reasoning is not like the analogous relation in reasoning about the physical world.

But how are we to get at the essential nature and business of ethical theory? Murray takes, importantly, the same tack as Hegel. He does not mention Hegel by name but it is likely that this way of looking at the problem developed from ideas which he met during his studies in Germany.

He notices that one can, to an important degree, divide moral theories into two kinds which he calls the Epicurean and the Stoic. Basically, Epicurean theories—which run from Epicurus to Mill—are those which locate the good in reference to some inner state, characteristically pleasure. Stoic theories are those which locate the good by reference to reason. The Epicurean theories are in general utilitarian in that they suppose that one evaluates acts in terms of their results. Stoic theories are, in the terminology most frequently used now, deontological. They are theories which seek to determine those acts which are good in themselves or fundamental duties and seek to do so by identifying adequate moral rules.

Murray argues against the Epicurean theories, though he knows that from their beginning in the work of Epicurus himself, they have not really fallen into the trap of recommending gross pleasure as an end in itself. They nonetheless fail because they fail to do justice to the moral situation. Not only do we not always seek pleasure, but we discern that acts are frequently right independently of their consequences. Every worthwhile cause, as Murray says, has had its martyrs. The Stoic theories, on the other hand, fail insofar as they misguidedly seek to reduce morality to mechanical obedience or to preordained rules.

The truth, rather, is that we do grasp, by way of reason, general principles which are able to guide us. We do grasp, as Murray pointed out in his political philosophy, that men are entitled to be treated as ends in themselves. Reason, reflecting on the nature of value and its relation to man and nature, is capable, as Murray argued, of demonstrating this. We do grasp such principles as that a man is entitled to the fruits of his labour and to a position in society which is consistent with the dignity of man. But, if we were simply to confine this to a formal principle—as Kant may *seem* to have done—the situation would become incomprehensible. It is because we are able to grasp the intrinsic desirability of the ends and states of mind which the Epicurean moral philosophy brings to our attention that we are able to give concrete meaning to the moral rules which reason suggests.

It is crucially important to Murray, therefore, that we should bear clearly and continuously in mind that the rules must be applied to the concrete situation. They give guidance, but the life which they animate in giving guidance is derived from our immediate consciousness of particular ends.

Thus the two rival kinds of theory seem to be, in Murray's view, not real rivals at all. Each illumines an aspect of the moral situation. Each becomes an unbelievable travesty of the moral life if it is exaggerated and pursued in isolation. Murray therefore devotes the last 150 pages of the 398 page *Introduction to Ethics* to the exploration of particular moral issues. In our time, with the elaborate division of substantive ethics from meta-ethics, this last part of Murray's book would be regarded as "casuistry" and, all too likely, written off as not a fit pursuit for a philosopher. In Murray's moral theory, however, there is no substitute for this and there is ultimately no separation of ethics and meta-ethics.

It is important to notice another basic tenet of Murray's theory: He denies the view of human society which makes of it a simple aggregate of atomic individuals. Equally, however, he denies that view of human society which makes our society a kind of organism whose parts, individual persons, are related to it in the way in which cells are related to the human or animal body. He admits:

> It is quite true that the individuals composing such a society are not to be treated as isolated atoms that have no interdependence. On the contrary, each individual becomes in a very real way an organ with a specific function to perform for the good of the whole.[22]

Still, that is not the whole truth.

> In mere organization the members have no function except as organs, as *means* to the *ends* of the whole organism. In society the members are indeed, in one aspect, organs serving as means to promote the ends of the whole community; but there is a profounder aspect in which the social organism is merely a means to promote the ends of its individual members. For every member, as an intelligent moral being, is an end to himself.[23]

Thus the point that Murray is trying to make is that individuality, itself, is a social function.

22   Ibid., p. 260.
23   Ibid., p. 261.

But, so far from being opposed, the two are in reality one and the same principle looked at from opposite points of view. The freedom of the individual is an empty abstraction apart from the social order by which it is maintained, and social order is properly the realization of individual freedom.[24]

What Murray seems to be describing—though he certainly does *not* use the word—is a dialectical relationship. He accepts that individualization is a desirable goal; the promotion of individuality and, hence, our individual freedom, is a social obligation. But it would appear that he rejects the doctrine that we start out as perfectly individualized social atoms. There is, then, an overriding obligation to promote the interests of the community because it is only if one has a community which is appropriately organized that one can develop individuals. Individuality is the result of a relation between a man and his community.

A further consequence of this, logically, is that, at any given time, the moral rules which we can apply in a society are relative to the degree of individuality attained in that community. This is an important reason for the stand which Murray takes in his applied moral philosophy. We know, at present, that the worker is being cheated. We know that we can improve this situation by legal exhortation and by making people more clearly aware of their obligations to one another. For, in our society, we have reached just that level of individualization at which the elaborate division of labour on which our society depends can be developed. On the other hand, though Murray would accept—in his social philosophy, in the occasional references to religious doctrine in the *Introduction to Ethics*, and in the *Handbook of Christian Ethics*—that the Christian exhortation to love one another represents a valid underlying moral rule, he would not urge that we can always, at present, be blamed for not acting on it. For we are not, given our present social arrangements, able to be sufficiently clearly aware of one another to grasp the infinite value of each man as an individual, and we are not ourselves sufficiently well individualized to be capable of the requisite action. More mundanely, Murray urges that, in our present situation, it would be quite foolish simply to demolish the whole of an existing society and to imagine, like Marx, that out of the debris, the working class would simply arise ready-made and able to govern justly. Murray, no doubt, would have agreed with F. H. Bradley that it is quite difficult, if not impossible, to be a good man in a bad society, though one can surely strive to be and succeed in being a fairly good man in a fairly bad society.

24   Ibid., p. 262.

From this, too, arises Murray's concern that we must first see and understand our acts and discern the value in them before we can formulate the rules that are appropriate to our various existing occasions. In his discussion of suicide, for instance, Murray calls attention to the fact that though it is not true that suicide was invariably looked upon as acceptable in ancient cultures, it was true that the attitude to suicide was very different from that which has gradually come to obtain in those cultures where the influence of Christianity has been strong. He notices that this has been a slow effect of Christian thought, deriving more from a change in attitude to human suffering and from the growth of generalized respect for persons than from any specific moral rule. Indeed, there is, Murray says, no specific prohibition on suicide in the New Testament. It requires a climate of ideas and a situation favourable to grasping the implications of appropriate moral rules for morality to take effect.

All this is not to say that Murray is some kind of historical relativist. Indeed he is not. It is not that the soundness of moral precepts changes; it is rather that what we can expect of men with respect to discerning those precepts changes. The Christian, Murray thinks, avoids suicide because he thinks there is a divine plan and that he would be wrong not to co-operate with it. The ancient intellectual of classical times frequently saw himself in the grip of a wholly impersonal fate. In that circumstance, suicide is an act of courage and a declaration of one's own value in the face of that fact. The situation of the man who believes in the Christian ethic is, evidently, different. For him to commit suicide would be for him to behave like a spoiled child.

Whatever is right or wrong about these background world views, it should be obvious that one must do more than simply announce a new moral precept if one wants to create conditions under which it is sensible and reasonable to expect a change in behaviour.

Murray's views, however, cut deeper than this. His discussion of suicide takes place in the context of what he calls, in general, duties to the body. We have a general duty to maintain our bodies in some reasonably appropriate condition. For if we fail to do so we may well not be in a position to act morally. We may fail to be in the required position simply because our bodies are not capable of the action required or, more subtly, we may not be able to act because of physical conditions which have influenced our minds in such a way that we face constant distraction—we cannot think clearly and habitually misperceive the world. This much is simply a commonplace. But what Murray draws from it is more than that. It is, again, that there are conditions for right action and we cannot expect that, in every case, men will meet them equally. Men who live in societies in which starvation is a frequent occurrence, disease the normal condition, and physical debilitation a commonplace should be regarded differently from those who have different opportunities.

This leads naturally into a topic which Murray very frequently discusses: habit. Like Aristotle, he sees morality as bound in habit. For we cannot make moral decisions instantly unless we make them habitually and we cannot always deliberate. It follows, therefore, that one must develop what Murray calls a conscience by laying the basis for habitual action. This, like the problem of bodily conditions, influences what we can expect of men. What has been their habitual circumstance? What opportunities have they had to restore moral situations? What opportunity does the situation permit for moral deliberation and reflection? All these are issues which make it simply impossible to indulge in a mechanical application of moral rules.

In their turn, these issues lead us to demand different orders of moral rules. It is not enough to draw up a code of ethics and tell men what to do! One must first produce the appropriate society: One must produce the conditions for free inquiry, and one must produce the conditions which will make it possible for men to be, reasonably often at least, in good physical condition. When one can estimate the chances of these outcomes being successful, then one can begin to develop appropriate rules and to use those as one of the devices for changing the basic situation.

All this is more obvious than its logical entailments. For its logical entailments include the proposition that we face a serious theoretical problem in determining how moral knowledge is possible. With all of the restrictions upon us, we can probably only discern the moral situation dimly and our attempts to specify our moral discernments in the form of effective moral rules are, surely, likely to be even more feeble.

Thus Murray entitles one of his chapters "Uncertainty of Speculative Moral Theories"[25] and, though this chapter contains well-known criticisms of standard moral theories, the point of it, in part, is to call our attention to the basic uncertainty about the moral situation. What we can do, in fact, is to notice values, to determine rules for the actualization of those values, and to strive to erect what we have learned into a logically coherent system which will be a basis for actual action.

This system will, however, grow. Every piece of knowledge about the nature of the world, about the nature of man, and about what people do will influence it in one way or another. Every change in the

25　Ibid., p. 235.

structure of communities, every change in one's personal relations, and every change in one's religious awareness will add to the material to be systematized and may well lead to the disclosure of new values.

It is not easy to summarize Murray's final moral view but the essence of it seems to be this: There are two sources of value—the discernment of the ultimate worth of the individual person; and the value of rational inquiry and the attempt to put coherence on one's life and thought. We receive, as it were, basic moral data in the form of our personal and interpersonal relations and we discern the unalterable necessity of rationality. As our situations change, the balance of data and system is constantly changing as well. We can see, perhaps, that the final end is something like Kant's kingdom of ends but we cannot lay that down in concrete form. We can only work our way toward it.

There are two strands of thought in Murray's moral philosophy which, occasionally, threaten to dominate the complex. One of them is a kind of Kantian formalism and the other is the kind of self-realization theory which was fairly characteristic of most of the post-Hegelian idealists. Further, there are occasional statements which might lead one to think that one or other of these strands is about, finally, to take over. Invariably, however, he cuts himself short and introduces the necessary caveats.

The Kantian strand becomes clear in the section on "The Ethical Ideal" in the *Handbook of Psychology*. Murray says:

> The same imperious necessity, which demands of the intelligent being, that his conduct shall be intelligent, refuses to let him rest content with any rule which is of limited application to himself or to others. It is not in accordance with the claims of intelligence, it is not reasonable, that any one moment, or any one person, should alone be considered in acting. The intelligent agent, therefore, finds satisfaction only in a rule of conduct which is of universal application,—a rule giving him an aim for one moment which is not discordant with the aims of any other,—an aim for himself which does not conflict with the aims of other persons. This is that absolutely harmonious end,— that realisation of universal law in the particular act,—which constitutes the ethical ideal.[26]

But he at once pulls back from that straightforward Kantianism.

> The preceding remarks are not, of course, to be taken as an exhaustive analysis of the ethical consciousness. This mental stage always involves an element of feeling, which is not only often predominant, but even at times completely submerges the intellectual factor.[27]

26 John Clark Murray, *A Handbook of Psychology* (London: Alexander Gardner, 1885; Montreal: Dawson Brothers, 1885), p. 236.
27 Ibid.

A few sentences later he strengthens his caveat:

> But this is a mere form, to which specific contents must be supplied. For we are not told what end is that which can be universally prescribed for human conduct. Is it pleasure or perfection, is it respect for self or respect for others, is it the will of the Infinite Being, or the laws of nature, or the conditions of success in the struggle for existence? These are questions which need not be discussed here; they carry us beyond psychology into the domain of ethics.[28]

The tendency toward a self-realization theory is well illustrated in a passage from the *Handbook of Christian Ethics*: "virtue is identical with self-love in the most reasonable sense of the term, that is, with a love which seeks the true good of the lover himself."[29] Murray insists that self-love means the individual's regard for his own real good. "The selfish man, therefore, in general is one who allows himself indulgences which imply no regard for his own interests any more than for the interests of other persons."[30]

But he quickly modifies this policy with a substantial dose of Kantianism by insisting, of course, that a proper regard for one's own real good and one's own real interest involves regulating one's conduct by rationality and that, in turn, requires rules.

One might expect that a man who wrote a book called *A Handbook of Christian Ethics* would have a moral theory which depended strongly on his religious convictions. This, however, is obviously untrue. Though it is the case, as we suggested earlier, that Murray simply regarded Christianity as true, his reason for subscribing to Christian moral theory is simply that Christian moral theory accords well with what he is able to determine, independently of it, by his own moral theory.

Christianity, to him, is part of the development of human thought—a crucial phase in which certain elements of human consciousness and conscience emerge. He regards it as an amalgam of Judaism, Greek metaphysics, and the later philosophy of the Stoics. Perhaps his only eccentricity is the weight which he is inclined to place on Stoicism.

To Murray, it appears that Christianity represented an important human advance at two crucial points. One of them has to do with the emergence of Christianity as a general religion and the significance which that has for the possibility of a moral consciousness which will

28 Ibid., p. 237.
29 Murray, *A Handbook of Christian Ethics*, p. 115.
30 Ibid., p. 116.

extend to all men. He sees this as being of transcendent importance and on page 42 of the *Handbook of Christian Ethics* he elaborates.

> The partition-walls of nationality itself, as well as of other divisions among men, must be borne down before the advance of moral intelligence. Human beings must at last become conscious of a moral relation with one another on the simple ground of their common humanity, without regard to any of the distinctions, whether natural or conventional, by which they happen to be separated.

The other breakthrough he sees as the emergence of a goal, an ultimate end, postulated by Christianity as love. The essential point of this is that Christianity postulates an ultimate end for men which transcends all arrangements of mere advantage. "For love is no mercenary barter in which both parties bargain for an equivalent in kind. Real love goes forth freely to do good without thought of compensation."[31]

These ideas and ideals, however, require a vehicle to make them intelligible and convincing. That vehicle, essentially, is to be found in elements of classical Greek metaphysics. By postulating a rational universe, the Greeks were able to portray a world in which it would become intelligible that all men were bound together by the common reason which forms a common strand in their basic humanity. It also made it possible to conceive of a real nature beneath the twists and turns of surface differences between men and made it possible for men to envisage a world beyond the mundane simplicities of everyday life.

Murray seems to think, however, that this, by itself, would have not been quite enough. To complete the picture, it required the orderly outlook on nature and systematization and the respect for universal law which went with Stoicism.

It is this notion of natural system combined with the demand for a general humanitarianism which Murray finds to be the contribution of Stoicism to the development of Christianity. Without this addition, Christianity, we might agree, could have been as muddled an eclecticism as Gnosticism for, though the necessary ideas of system and generality are no doubt in the Greek philosophy of an earlier period, Gnosticism, too, was able to assimilate many of the dominating ideas of Stoicism. Murray is very likely reasonable in insisting on the role of Stoicism in the historical context—a context in which Christianity, to survive, had to compete, ultimately, for the allegiance of the intellectual population.

31   Ibid., p. 99.

His attitude to Canada, like most of his articulated views, was complex and must suffer, somewhat at least, in any attempt at summary. He believed ardently in the desirability of Canada's survival as an independent country but he believed, equally ardently, in free trade and in a morality which must transcend nationality.

He watched with little pleasure the development of government after Confederation. Some of this, perhaps, stemmed from his own rather special convictions. "The Industrial Kingdom of God" contains some strong words about strong drink and Murray knew as well as we do the habits of Sir John A. Macdonald. He knew a great deal, too, about the railroad scandals. He made shrewd estimates, in general, of the amount of bribery, corruption, self-seeking, and the blatant pursuit of party interests which were so characteristic of the first years of the new dominion.

It seems likely that if Murray could now read the controversies between the supporters of the Whig theory of Canadian history and the supporters of Donald Creighton's Laurentian theory, he would surely have been surprised.[32]

He would not have seen, in Canadian history, the slow unfolding of liberal principles. Nor does it seem very likely that he would have seen in the development of Canada the thrust to build a commercial empire leading into the heartland of the continent which so fascinates Professor Creighton. He saw a series of immediate political problems to be solved and a development which went on after Confederation much as it had gone on before Confederation—a series of responses to problems in Canada and in Britain each of which was coped with in terms of the demands of the moment and, usually, without much thought about how successive solutions to successive problems might fit together. At any rate, Murray's casual writings about the political and economic situation—frequently in the *Open Court*—show relatively little conviction of a unifying thread.

The situation in Canada seemed to him ready-made for politicians to exploit. If you create the country on a promise to build a railroad, you are able to justify all kinds of profitable activities in order to get the railroad built quickly. If you have a highly pluralistic community with many interests to be balanced, there will emerge politicians looking for profitable ways of balancing those interests.

It seems reasonable to think that his interest in the independence of Canada is closely related to his view that societies in the West were changing very rapidly. As a consequence, he regularly recommends a

32 For a good account of such theories—and of doubts about them—see Carl Berger, *The Writing of Canadian History* (Toronto: Oxford University Press, 1976).

very flexible approach to political and constitutional matters. His proposals for economic reform are a combination of basic principles and fairly tentative suggestions as to how those principles might best be applied. Canada, with its constitutional openness, its real but imperfectly formulated communitarian bias, and its immense resources, provided perhaps the ideal basis for the possibility of the kind of reform which Murray had in mind.

American constitutionalism with its ringing set of eternal truths and its individualist bias must have seemed inherently less flexible. In addition there must have been a continuing element of nostalgia for British constitutional practice which Canada could meet and the United States could not.

One might also speculate that Murray's interest in a morality which ultimately would transcend nationality and provide a basis for the uniform accommodation of a great variety of cultures would find a natural home in the Canadian context.

It hardly needs to be said that Murray was no conventional nationalist in the sense in which that expression would have been understood in Europe. He clearly did not mean ever to assert that there were "natural nations" which would persist through the whole of the human adventure. Such a view would surely have run counter to all his principles. Yet his whole approach to morality and to religion suggests that it is most unlikely that the whole of the truth would be instantiated in any one time in any one community, or that the whole of the truth can be understood in any one time through the single perspective of any set of beliefs. It therefore becomes very important that the world should be so organized as to provide a variety of alternatives in our political and moral life. There is little doubt that he saw Canada as one of those alternatives which deserved preservation. It deserved to be preserved not because it had a natural and final superiority over any other community but simply because it provided a desirable and functional vehicle for the development of a set of alternatives which Murray thought to be important.

Would Murray have developed in just the same way had he remained in Scotland? It seems fairly certain that the answer to that question is "No." The successors of Sir William Hamilton in Scotland—and had Murray remained there he would surely have ranked amongst them—were either people who made minor adjustments in the Hamiltonian philosophy or people who made a clean break and became systematic idealists in the Hegelian tradition.

Murray fits neither of these categories. He seems at no time to have been, in the literal sense, a disciple of Sir William Hamilton or a tinkerer with the Hamiltonian system. The earliest essay which we have, an unpublished essay on Ferrier in the McGill Archives, shows a good deal of sympathy for Ferrier despite its criticisms and despite its reassuring protestations of the greatness of Sir William Hamilton. Murray's short book on Hamilton is, indeed, a simple summary of Hamilton's philosophy. The *Handbook of Psychology*, on the other hand, shows a clear grasp of the criticisms one might make of Hamilton.

Equally, however, Murray worked his way rather slowly toward a systematic idealism and the extent to which he can be said to have joined that philosophical school is something we will examine later. Throughout, he remains his own man.

The combination of his writings in political philosophy and his casual political writings suggests reasons for this. He believed that political principles arise out of empirical attempts to solve particular problems. General principles, themselves, develop out of a history of consciousness and conscience. This theme occurs in the *Introduction to Ethics*, the *Handbook of Christian Ethics*, and his two (nearly identical) works on psychology, the *Handbook of Psychology* and the *Introduction to Psychology*.

Thus Murray did not think that anyone was in a position to lay down a final system now or at any foreseeable time in the future. His passion for order and system led him to applaud both Sir William Hamilton and his idealist successors, but his immediate experiences led him to be quite cautious about these things and to separate, as clearly as he could, as we shall see a little later, the notion that there is an underlying structure to truth and knowledge which one can know from the notion that one can know the flesh and bones which fill out that structure.

The experience of living in a society which had the curious property of being both a new creation and the continuation of a set of very old traditions must have reinforced these notions. He was surely impressed by the fact that one cannot simply create an ideal society overnight. He could see both what had happened in Canada in the early years after Confederation and what had happened in the United States in the century which had elapsed since the revolution. Both perspectives convinced him that one had to work piece-meal. At the same time, his own Scottish background and his own experience of the intersecting traditions that made up Canada impressed him with the fact that there is a direction of social development and led him to believe in the real prospect for progress.

On the whole, philosophers who remained in Scotland were less interested in history, perhaps because they were not in the midst of an

132

intersection of historical traditions. (Oddly enough, Hegel's passionate interest in the philosophy of history did not carry over to his British emulators either in Scotland or in England. It was not until Collingwood that the philosophy of history became an important activity amongst British idealists. F. H. Bradley, it is true, had written an essay on the philosophy of history, but it is not an essay which would encourage historians.) At the same time, the philosophers who remained in Scotland seemed more inclined to pin their faith on their ability to develop finished systems, and it would not be extremely rash to suggest that there is a relation between this fact and the fact that they lived in societies which did not give so strong a sense of newness and of the possibility of immediate innovation.

Perhaps the fairest conclusion is that Canada's influence on Murray was real though moderate, just as Murray's influence on Canada was real though moderate.

The place in which his influence on Canadian society was strongest was the organization of higher education itself. In particular, though, the point of influential intersection turned out to be over the issue of education of women.

Murray fought for equal rights and the status of women. Both in the senate of McGill and the public forum of the university, he spoke out for effective co-education and he worried senior officials with his addresses to the students. Such previously unheard-of outbursts disturbed the peaceful atmosphere of conservative McGill, and the suggestion of women in the same classes and courses as men made Murray an object of scorn in the eyes of his peers and colleagues. Indeed, their displeasure brought senatorial threats to his job and Murray tried to reassure them several times that he did not intend to upset the paternal traditions. Yet that was his exact intention and his crusade was held in check, each time, only until the pressure relaxed. But his fight was long and often bitter.

His case for women was well thought out, and fragments of it in handwritten notes remain in the McGill archives. Some of them are in printed form, apparently printer's proofs. In his notes, he says that although the day has long gone when a woman could be compelled to marry without her formal consent, "when any force could be brought to bear upon her other than that force of circumstances which is capable of subduing natural inclinations,"[33] there is much in the posi-

33 John Clark Murray, notes on "Rights of Women," Acc. No. 611/81, McGill University Archives, Montreal, p. 1. Hereafter referred to as "Rights of Women." (Many of Murray's ideas can also be found in "The Higher Education of Woman," an address delivered at the opening of Queen's College, Kingston, 1871.)

tion of women which makes marriage not altogether a matter of choice. The contrast between a savage state and a civilized one can be seen in the relative positions of women. In uncivilized states one sex exists for the sake of the other, whereas in civilized ones members of both sexes are treated as persons. There is no better gauge of the state of civilization in a society, Murray observes, than the position which it assigns to women. Clearly he believed that there was room for improvement at McGill.

Murray argues against those who suggest that Christian teachings have encouraged the belief that men ought to keep women in a state of subjection, with a series of quotations from the New Testament, and with the charge that they have not read the spirit of Christian teaching, only the letter. He maintains that Christian spirit requires that social institutions draw no distinctions between the sexes.

Murray decides to limit his evaluation of the positions of men and women to the educational advantages enjoyed by each. Is it not surprising, he asks, that all the great public schools, colleges, and universities of the world, with very few exceptions, are run on the obvious supposition that their educational advantages shall be enjoyed by the male sex alone? Although some women had gained access to classrooms in some colleges, Murray laments the fact that they were ignored. The assumption is, of course, that legislators never thought that women would need much more than elementary education, because their role was to marry and raise children. That women would have to support themselves was not an important concern. He claims that women have been discouraged from elevating the mind because it was not necessary for their societal roles. Such limitations on possible occupations violate the natural rights of every human being. Furthermore, he adds, even in that limited range a superior education is *not unnecessary.* Murray suggests that restricting women to their confined social roles is without foundation in natural justice, and hence exclusion from education is unjustified. To oppose women's claims to equal rights is to oppose all progress. Along with the relation of capital and labour, Murray classes the position of women in society, and refers to them as the two great social problems of our time.

Among the fundamental rights of humanity is the right to physical existence and therefore the right to the means by which that existence is maintained. And here we shall find a glaring discrepancy between this right and the position assigned to women. This right implies that no one shall in effect be barred from earning a living as long as his occupation does not conflict with the rights of others. Now men are brought up with this view in mind, and certain classes of women from poorer families who cannot support them learn to earn a living. But the girl whose father can support her until she marries or perhaps as long as she lives is scrupulously prevented from developing her own abilities even to the extent that she could support herself. So she is forced into marriage under the guise of unfeeling love, or must choose a life of unrewarding and unremunerative labour, because she lacks the training for higher things. One cause of this predicament of women, Murray suggests, rests in the gallantry of men, and the other rests in the unconscious tendencies of their selfishness.

A poor man labours for his daily bread. A rich man's labour will support him more than one day. So a very wealthy man enjoys the freedom from perpetual toil. Consequently he desires that his wife and daughters be free from the dreariness of labour. But that, as a general principle, should be applied to women of the labouring (industrial) classes as well and the difficulty of supporting all women, married or not, is obvious. Murray concludes that women have only three courses open to them—to get married, to live with a relative, or to seek work in the very few, poorly paid occupations open to women. The first is unjust in that it forces women to regard marriage as a natural means of support, whether or not they consider it desirable. They must either marry, or starve. Perhaps the sacred ends of marriage would be better preserved if there were freedom with both parties to choose.

The second alternative leaves women with a depressing sense of dependence. The third, Murray assumes, needs no comment. The selfishness of men can be seen in the attitudes of the wealthy who keep their women idle as showpieces of their wealth—the status of a man's wife is a "sort of stalking horse for the display of his own riches."[34] This concern for display of wealth can extend so far that men become ashamed of only possessing that wealth which they have earned themselves. Their ideal is not to be contaminated with industry and trade at all. If, in this situation, women work, they cannot be flaunted as a display of wealth. And women themselves feel that working would lose them their social position.

Murray says it is to be hoped that society will change so that the woman who wastes her time will have a less respectable societal rank than the factory girl. He does not suggest that women are suitable for all jobs, or should necessarily be preferred to men. "The principles of free trade, moreover, if carried out, would soon distinguish the employments at which women could be most profitably occupied from those which it would be a greater economy to reserve for men."[35] But it

34 Ibid., p. 9.
35 Ibid., p. 10.

is entirely wrong that a woman should be excluded from particular occupations purely on the grounds that she is a woman.

Such an extension of women's roles in society would clearly necessitate a change in the style of their education, most of which he considers to be trivial in its aim. Either existing institutions should be opened to women, or their own colleges be upgraded considerably in quality. And the social roles of women must be definitely changed. Excluding women from paying jobs is clearly unjust. Indeed that right to higher education should be recognized even if there is no change in their role. At this point, Murray seeks to counteract the claim that advocates of women's rights are inadvertently suggesting that women neglect their family duties. This is a mistaken claim and its strongest opponents would be the advocates of women's rights. What they want, says Murray, is genuine recognition of women's duties: "they claim, for every women, high and low, matron and maiden, a right to be something more than a mere ornament of human life,—a right to have, like every man, specific duties in the industrial arrangements of society."[36] No one, Murray suggests, has denounced more strongly than the proponents of women's rights, the idleness of ladies of wealth who can pay others to do housework. The housewife is performing an industrial occupation upon which the comfort and existence of society depends. Seldom does she obtain sufficient pay for the economic function she performs. Domestic functions are held by Murray in high esteem.

There is no reason other than its superfluousness for domestic duties that higher education should be unavailable to women, and such a reason, Murray contends, is rubbish. Men do not have to prove the necessity of a higher education, before they can enter university, nor even its occupational advantage. Neither should women be denied an education purely for its own sake. And although the duties of the house can be performed without a university education, there is no reason why their performance would not be enhanced by literary or scientific training. Even keeping a house organized and tidy requires a good deal of mental and physical agility. He observes that the efforts of men to keep house have been the subject of much journalistic humour.

> The fact is, that a man breaks down on undertaking the peculiar work of a woman, not simply from being unaccustomed to it, but as frequently from the fact that the routine of his own occupation has not cultivated that rapidity and originality of mental action which are developed by the efficient management of a household.... I know none of the ordinary industrial

36   Ibid., p. 12.

136

occupations of men, which affords scope for the exercise of a more varied intellectual power, of a finer aesthetic culture, and of greater moral tact, than may be displayed by the wife and mother.[37]

Such talents deserve as high a training as their worth.

The fitness for a life-companionship, which must be of infinite moment to all concerned, the care of children through those years which influence, perhaps more powerfully than any others, their permanent physical, mental, and moral character, the ingenuity of providing for the ever-varying emergencies in the daily life of a family—these things give opportunities for the display of an intellectual vigour and quickness, as well as of a moral culture, for which no training can be considered too high.[38]

In fact, Murray's views about the education of women are a microcosm of his views about applied moral philosophy generally. For this is the situation in which just the relation between theory and practice which seems continuously to have interested Murray emerges with some clarity.

His opponents believed that women should be given a special and separate education because, obviously, they were special and different. To give them the same education as men, they argued, would be both inappropriate and foolish. Inappropriate, because it would assume that women were, in the requisite ways, just like men. Foolish, because, by ignoring the difference between men and women, it would either lead to inefficiency or lead to a generation of women who sought to imitate men and would, inevitably, fail in the process.

But this is an example, in Murray's view, of just the way in which existing social and political theories in fact influence and structure the societies to which they are applied in a way which makes them come to seem truisms when, on deeper reflection, one might well conclude that they were not only false but outrageous as well. Women may well have been and may well be "different." But, in significant ways, this is a function of the roles which they are assigned in society as, obviously, are the ways in which they are educated. By applying such theories one creates a situation in which it seems natural to go on treating women as significantly "different." If, however, one moves to the level of theory, one can see that some mistake has been made. If one analyzes the prospects of education from the viewpoint of the "speculative ideal" which Murray outlines in his two books on psychology, one sees that knowledge, as such, cannot be "different" for men and women. For the

37 Ibid., pp. 14-15.
38 Ibid., p. 15.

properties associated with knowledge are perfectly general and differences of physiology, or even of emotional response, are simply not relevant to them.

Similarly, there is nothing in Murray's moral theory which would lead one to think that there are or ought to be one set of rules for men and another set of rules for women. Nor is there anything in Murray's notion of economic justice which would lead one to make a separation.

This would be the obvious mistake because it would make no allowance for the situation as it existed in society. Likely, neither men nor women could adjust instantly to a social situation in which the same physical, legal, and moral expectations were put upon them. No doubt for this reason as much as because of the fact that he was there and able to be immediately influential, Murray devoted his efforts to the problem of the education of women. At that level no justification could be made for withholding from women facilities equal to those granted to men. Long before the Supreme Court of the United States grasped the point, Murray realized that in educational matters the attempt to provide facilities which were separate but equal was doomed to failure. One cannot get an "equal" education unless one is allowed to participate in exactly the same process as those with whom one desires equality. Given that students, after all, educate one another more than they receive education from teachers, would it be likely that segregated facilities would provide equality? Given that the best minds are, anyhow, few, would it assist the process to divide them into two groups? Murray's answer was an obvious and resounding "No" to these questions.

From education, the movement for women's rights was bound to spread. It would spread on an established basis; men would see from the educational process that women were, after all, their equals in the things that counted. Education would provide access to new social functions and roles and, in the process, the prevailing models and reactions were bound to change.

This continuous interchange between theory and fact constitutes, if you like, a kind of dialectic, though Murray seldom if ever uses the word.

The nearest that he comes to it is in the section on the speculative ideal in the two books on psychology. This section is also the best introduction to his more abstract philosophy—his theory of knowledge and his metaphysics. It is, furthermore, the bridge—a bridge deliberately built—between his moral and political philosophy on one side and his epistemology and his metaphysics on the other. Its deliberateness can be seen, at least, from the fact that in the same section of both books on psychology, he relates the speculative ideal, the ethical ideal, the religious ideal, and the aesthetic ideal by spelling them out successively and in parallel ways.

What Murray is doing under the heading "The Speculative Ideal" is laying down his theory of truth. At the time Murray was writing, the common theories were the "correspondence theory," the "coherence theory," and, newer and more localized, the "pragmatic theory." At just that moment of time, the traditional "correspondence theory" had yielded pride of place to the post-Hegelian forms of the "coherence theory." It was only beginning to be effectively jostled by the American pragmatists.

Murray, however, really rejects them all in the name of a theory which only came to be articulated widely later, indeed, not effectively until the philosophy of R. G. Collingwood. Even that articulation is not identical with Murray's.

It is worthwhile, therefore, to sketch just briefly the rival theories in order that the significance of Murray's own theory can become comprehensible. The "correspondence theory," which some people believe goes back to Aristotle, would appear to be the ordinary "common sense" account of truth. According to that theory, the proposition expressed by a sentence is true if and only if it corresponds to the state of affairs alleged. Simply, the sentence "The cat is on the mat" is said to be true if and only if the cat *is* on the mat. This theory seems so obvious at first glance that few people besides professional philosophers are able to grasp why anyone would question it.

The difficulties in it, however, are fairly clear if one gives a little thought to the matter. Some sentences express propositions about the past and others express propositions about the future. To what, then, do such propositions "correspond"? The past is usually supposed to be gone and the future is not yet. It may well be said that such propositions correspond to the "facts" about the past and about the future. But what are facts? Are they a special and new kind of metaphysical entity, which remains a feature of the world after the things they are about have gone and, more puzzlingly even, do they exist before the things they are about come into being? Even greater difficulties are caused in the context of a theory of knowledge. Somehow, truth and knowledge must go together, for one cannot know that a proposition is true unless one knows the thing that it is about.

But it should be noticed that, in fact, we compare one proposition to another in determining knowledge. We do not—because we cannot—compare a proposition, literally, to a state of affairs. If we are uncertain about whether or not the object in the next room is an

139

elephant, we assemble some elephant experts and we compare what we say to what they say. Furthermore, what satisfies us that some allegation is true is, in general, its coherence and not some mysterious comparison between a proposition and a state of affairs. Consider: Suppose you are looking at a set of railway tracks and they appear to meet in the distance. They don't, of course, but how do you know that they don't? Insofar as you can relate the proposition you are uttering to a state of affairs, the sequence of events goes like this: You start with the proposition that railway tracks are made in parallel. You compare that proposition to the proposition you are tempted to believe when you look at the tracks. That, perhaps, *is* the proposition expressed by the sentence "The tracks meet in the distance." What makes you reject that proposition is not some set of "facts" which you happen to know "independently" of the situation, but rather the incoherence which would result from accepting the new proposition. You have some beliefs about railway trains. One of these beliefs, very likely, is the belief that the wheels are fixed to the axles in such a way that they will not slide toward the centre of the axle. Another belief, quite likely, is the belief that, if the wheels did slide toward the centre of the axle, the train would be very likely to tip. A train moving on tracks which grew progressively closer to each other, then, would surely be wrecked. But you believe that trains pass along this track every day without coming to harm. It is not easy to believe that innumerable train wrecks have somehow been covered up and that we simply have not heard about them. All your beliefs about trains, in short, form a coherent pattern which would be destroyed by the introduction of the new proposition. You tend, therefore, to reject it. Your tendency becomes stronger when you walk down the tracks and discover that, though the tracks still seem to meet in the distance, the point at which they begin to converge is always some distance away from you. Ultimately, like everyone else, you will form the view that the tendency for tracks to seem to meet in the distance is an "optical illusion." This belief, in its turn, is surely strengthened by what we happen to know about physics or optics, the workings of the human brain, and a variety of other things.

What impresses you, in short, is that, as you work your way through these problems, you are able to build up a coherent body of beliefs which renders your experience intelligible and which can be generalized to cover the whole range of that experience. Experience, in short, gives rise to the temptation to utter various propositions but does not, itself, arbitrate between them. It will strengthen or weaken your commitment to various propositions because, after all, it is the succes-

140

sion of experiences which gives rise to the tendency to utter the sentences which express just the variety of propositions which you want to integrate into your finished system. But the role of experience—and this is the role which we most customarily equate with the "role of facts"—must be understood in its proper place.

These and other considerations gave rise to what came to be called the "coherence theory" of truth. According to that theory, a sentence succeeds in expressing a true proposition if and only if the proposition it expresses would have a place in the most general of all systems to which one might be committed. This system, if one is to be committed to it, will have to be coherent. For one cannot be committed to a contradiction. There is no way of explicating a commitment to "P and not-P." Just what this coherence consists of is another matter. The post-Hegelian idealists were generally committed to dismantling the dichotomy between reason and experience and the coherence they had in mind has properties in common with the suggestion made above: A system is coherent if its parts do not collide with one another in a logical way and if it enables one to integrate things one wants to say in the light of one's experience. One's experience is influenced by one's conceptual apparatus and by the propositions one already believes. The logical relations of coherence, therefore, tend to take the primary place as such systems develop and, in this sense, most of the post-Hegelian idealists were rationalists. (This kind of "rationalism" must be distinguished quite sharply from the older rationalism. The older rationalism attempted to proceed from "self-evident" propositions which were, if you like, eternal truths, by a process of formal deduction to a finished system. The idealists who came after Hegel were inclined to dismiss this elaborate pyramid system and to maintain that there were not simple, self-evident propositions. Rather, experience gives rise to belief, belief when structured conceptually alters experience, and the process goes on in a dialectical way producing a system of ever-widening circles like ripples produced by a pebble in a pool of water.)

It was, however, increasingly difficult to specify the logical nature of the coherence involved and the issues became progressively more technical and cumulatively more difficult. Would not the coherent system of all propositions turn out to be, after all, eternal and fixed? Are there not problems when the dichotomies between reason and experience, language and referent, possibility and existence have been dissolved? It might be argued, moreover, that this theory left an unexplored element—the involvement of the truth-seeker in the process—and made truth merely another feature of the natural world. Somehow, such an outcome would be a mistake, for if truth is simply part of the world, then we still need to know the "truth about truth" and we have simply moved the problem without solving it.

Considerations such as these and reflection upon the possibility that there might, in the end, turn out to be more than one coherent body of propositions provided part of the motive of the exploration and development of the pragmatic theory. Truth as finished, fixed, and immutable seemed somehow, to men like William James, a new kind of philosopher's nightmare.

William James urged that truth must be what "satisfies," but he urged that it must be what satisfies "in the long run" and he added his belief that what must satisfy in the long run will turn out to be what is empirically verifiable. Charles S. Peirce (from whose writings the contemporary use of the expression "pragmatism" seems to derive) was inclined to take a more complex and, apparently, tougher view: He urged that the truth, in the end, would be what the community of scientists was "fated" to believe. John Dewey later, was to modify a version of the pragmatic theory and to turn it into what became known as "instrumentalism." Dewey thought that the purpose of thinking was to solve problems and that propositions were, in reality, truths or instruments which one used for this purpose. They were good or bad depending upon how well they worked. The goal, he thought, was an unimpeded experience structure, a pattern of experience free of frustrations, blockages, and inner conflict. Dewey tended, however, to back away from the traditional word "truth" and to substitute for it "warranted assertability."

All of these theories present, if one examines the writings of their orginators with some care, a somewhat uneasy mixture of literally "pragmatic" theories (theories which make of truth a certain relation between a proposition and the state of mind of one who believes it) and "ideal observer" theories (theories which present truth as what an observer who was placed in the position of best advantage and reflected to optimum effect would say). James's introduction of the notion of "the long run" and his insistence on the importance of empirical verification tend to convert his original pragmatic theory into an ideal observer theory. The truth, for James, is what you would believe were you to survive through the long run while doing, fairly constantly, the right things. Peirce's community of scientists instantiate, collectively, the ideal observer. Even Dewey seems, most often, to have in mind an idealized kind of experience whose ideal nature one would grasp were one well placed. The theories are all, it turns out, enormously complicated.

It would appear to be at this point in the debate that Murray enters. He introduces the topic in the chapter on "Idealisation" in his two books on psychology. He says:

> The term, Idealisation, is here employed to designate the latest and fullest outgrowth of intellectual life, in which the earlier and simpler activities culminate.
>
> . . . Idealisation is, literally, the formation of an ideal. Now, an ideal is an object which receives its determinate character from an idea, as this term is understood in its earlier and higher signification. But in this signification idea means the general concept which, in the Platonic philosophy especially, was supposed to constitute the real essence of every individual. . . . An ideal is, therefore, an object which is thought as an embodiment, not of particular accidents, but of universal principles.
>
> . . . The general concept is the end which the intelligence seeks to realise in determining the ideal object. But the object thus aimed at is various, and it varies in accordance with the various activities of intelligence, of which it is the end. These activities may be purely speculative, concerned merely in the exercise of the intellect. . . . The ideal of the first activity is truth absolute, that is, an absolutely harmonious system of thought. . . .[39]

It would appear, here, that Murray is working toward a coherence theory. As usual, however, he quickly backs away and introduces qualifications: "But truth, as its etymology implies, is an activity of mind; it is what a mind troweth."[40] (He says, in a footnote, that "troweth" is an early spelling of truth.)

What he is denying, provisionally, is the doctrine which might seem to be implied in coherence theories that truth is simply another component of the world. His problem, then, is to relate the activity associated with truth to the coherence standards which he thinks define the speculative ideal.

He does this by examining the basis of cognition itself.

> A perception, even in the simplest form, is a consciousness of resemblance between a past and a present sensation,—a *re*cognition of a past sensation in the present. Generalisation is a consciousness of resemblance between different phenomena, which are on that ground thought under one category or class. And reasoning was shown to be a consciousness of resemblance between relations. All cognitions are thus reducible to a consciousness of relations, which increase in complexity with the development of intellectual life.

39 Murray, *A Handbook of Psychology*, pp. 220-21.
40 Ibid., p. 222.

But all consciousness of relation is not cognition. To make it cognition, the relation must be not merely an accidental coexistence in an individual consciousness; it must be independent on the accidents of an individual's mental life; it must be valid for universal intelligence. In a word, it must be, not a subjective association, but an objective connection. Such a consciousness is truth, knowledge, science.[41]

The suggestion, here, is that the formal and ultimate idea of truth is described by the coherence theory. But what the coherence theory really describes is what a perfectly developed intelligence would arrive at were it to work for an optimum time under optimum conditions. The attempt to arrive at truth on our part is, therefore, an attempt to approximate to this standard. We claim that a proposition is true insofar as we think we have achieved this standard.

The standard, however, is neither correspondence with a state of affairs in the world, nor individual satisfaction. The standard is the model of the ideal cognizer.

In reality, however, the standard is also not simply formal coherence. Formal coherence is the form which the structure of the ideal takes. It must be filled in and we cannot grasp, in advance, the ultimate form which it will take. Once again, it seems clear that Murray has in mind a dialectical relation between experience and conceptual structure. The further the process goes, to be sure, the tighter the logical constraints become:

Accordingly, the endeavour after truth is an effort to bring all our consciousnesses—all our trowings—not only into harmonious relation, but into such connection, that they shall all be thought as dependent on, necessitated by, each other. All scientific research sets out with the assumption, that every truth is in thinkable unison with every other; and scientific effort would be at once paralysed by the suspicion, that there is any factor of knowledge which, in the last analysis, may be a surd quantity, incapable of being brought into intelligible relation with the general system of thought. The labours of science, therefore, aim at discovering to consciousness this reciprocal connection of different truths; and the intellectual ideal is thus a system of thought, in which all cognitions, that is, all truths, all objective connections, are conceived as component factors of one self-consciousness. Such a system is absolute truth.[42]

Shortly, we shall have to inquire as to what such expressions as "one self-consciousness" and "absolute truth" mean and consider the

41 Ibid.
42 Ibid., pp. 222-23.

extent to which Murray is developing a metaphysics along with his theory of truth. First, however, our immediate priority in the discussion seems to be to try to disentangle the implied elision or confusion between knowledge and truth in the passages that we have been citing from *A Handbook of Psychology*.

Such expressions as all cognitions, that is, all truths, and the paragraph in which cognition is defined as a mode of consciousness and consciousness, in this form, is said to *be* "truth," suggest that Murray is either opposed to making the distinction or that he is allowing it to go unmade for some special reason. Indeed, when he says such a consciousness is truth, knowledge, science, he seems to be making the elision quite flatly.

In general, the distinction between *theories* of truth and *theories* of knowledge is this: Theories of truth specify a standard to be met. Correspondence theories specify that the standard is a certain relation between a proposition and a state of affairs or a set of facts. Coherence theories specify that the standard is a certain relation. Pragmatic theories specify that the standard is a certain relation between a proposition and the state of mind of one who believes it, and ideal observer theories specify that the standard, ultimately, lies in a comparison of claims to truth with what the ideal observer would report. Theories of knowledge, on the other hand, generally specify a methodology. Rationalism is the doctrine that knowledge is acquired by the perspicacious use of reason and empiricism is the doctrine that knowledge results from appropriate attention to sensory data. In these terms, Murray is supposing both a theory of truth and a theory of knowledge. His theory of truth specifies a certain standard which appears to be a combination of standards recommended by those who would subscribe to the coherence theory and standards recommended by those who would subscribe to some form of the ideal observer theory. His theory of knowledge recommends, again, a certain methodology—a series of reasoned reflections on experience leading to the ultimate discovery of a genuinely coherent experience.

It is the fact that Murray wants to introduce, apparently, coherence both as a standard for truth and as a feature of experience that leads him to relate his theory of knowledge and his theory of truth in such a way as to produce an elision.

Suppose, however, one asks what *is* truth and what *is* knowledge: The consequence of Murray's way of putting his two theories together is that both turn out to be a certain state of consciousness. This may produce a minor confusion and, no doubt, it might have been better for Murray to expound his standard, his methodology, and his account of the nature of truth and knowledge in a way which kept the issues separate. But, to an extent, the issues he is raising here are an aside in his description of the nature of psychology. After his remark about the "system" which "is absolute truth," he adds, "Here it would be out of place to sketch such a system, even in general outline. This is the work of philosophy, in the strict sense of the term."[43] Unfortunately, no such "strictly philosophical" work of Murray's, so far as we know, exists.

A real issue which is raised here, however, comes out clearly when one notices that, for Murray, both truth and knowledge are states of consciousness. They fit together in such a way as to make his doctrine, on that level, coherent. But one should notice the implications of this view. For it is here that it becomes quite clear that Murray *is* an idealist.

One can only hold that truth and knowledge are states of consciousness and also hold that the correspondence theory of truth is false if one holds that reality itself is, finally, a "state of consciousness." For, otherwise, truth and knowledge only are truth and knowledge because that state of consciousness corresponds to something else.

Murray obviously is prepared to assert (as quoted earlier) that "all truths, all objective connections, are conceived as component factors of one self-consciousness."

They seem not to be, but this is because common sense follows the simplicities of correspondence theories and fails to realize that the distinctions that we make are *within* our experience and not between our experience and something else. We cannot get outside, not because there is some special limit to human knowledge or because the human mind is deficient for its task, but because, after all, there is no "outside." To put it this way still makes it sound as though we are caught in a prison. In Murray's view we are not. Experience and knowledge can go on expanding so long as there are questions to be asked and something which counts as the answer.

To dig deeper we must cope with Murray's metaphysics. Its most elaborate statement occurs in the long section of the two works on psychology which is devoted to what Murray calls the "General Nature of Knowledge."[44] It is here, in the discussion of space, time, substance, and cause that Murray's idealism is stated quite categorically.

Some stage-setting is required for this discussion. Strictly speaking, the discussion is epistemological and Murray is raising, primarily, questions about how we can have the kinds of knowledge which fall

43 Ibid., p. 223.
44 Ibid., p. 274. See also John Clark Murray, *An Introduction to Psychology* (Boston: Little, Brown, 1904), chap. 6, p. 328.

under these headings. For the most part, the discussion is about how we pass from an awareness of our own sensations to an understanding of the structural features of the world. He starts with what might be taken to be two sets of premises. One of them is subjectivist and, in a general way, Humean. The other set is not unlike the one adopted by the "common sense" philosophers in the Scottish tradition.

The first set takes it as obvious that, if one distinguishes what one thinks one knows from what one is aware of, one will conclude that immediate awareness is composed only of sensations. I may think I see a tree, but if I ask what data are given to me, the data will turn out to consist of my awareness of green and brown coloured patches. Under normal circumstances, and with appropriate repetitions, I come to accept the object of awareness as a tree. This acceptance involves an inference which, given the premises, can never really be justified. For I may be quite wrong about it. Sometimes, after all, there is no tree there. I may be watching a movie or a clever trick done with three-dimensional projection machines, or I may be experiencing an hallucination. For all any of us *really* know, we may all be disembodied brains in vats of nutrient solutions who are fed electrical signals by some more powerful idiot.

More than this, none of us knows for sure that his sensations correspond to those of other people or even that there are any other people. Worse still, none of us knows, in these terms, whether we ourselves exist as continuing entities whose careers and real knowledge extend beyond the simple awareness of the moment. It is true that you *say* that you see what I see when I say I see a tree, but how do I know that you are using language in the same way I do? Suppose you were born with a peculiar kind of colour blindness such that when other people saw red things, you saw green things and vice versa. You would, to be sure, have learned to say "red" when you saw things which the rest of us saw as red. You would have said "green" when you saw the things that the rest of us saw as green. For your mother would have said "red" and "green" on the appropriate occasions. But you would have been "seeing" (what we call) green things when you were saying red and red things when you were saying green. We do not know, by any possible device, that this does not actually happen. Then, again, my knowledge of you is, on this view, nothing but my awareness of a set of sensations. Whether somebody lurks behind those sensations or not is an open question. You may be a robot wired for radio control and run from Venus. Or, so far as you know, everybody else may be a figment of your imagination. Finally, you do not know much or anything about your personal continuity. You only know what you are aware of at the moment. As Bertrand Russell once put it, you may have been created five minutes ago along with all the rest of the world complete with all the bits of awareness which you call your "memory." Hume suggested that, when you search for your real "self," for the "theatre of the mind," that stage on which the events of your world seem to take place, you do not really find anything. You find only a "bundle" of sensations which, for some reason or other, you regard as representative of a deeper self which you never grasped as an entity occurring in direct cognition.

Now, as far as it goes, Murray accepts all this. But he also accepts another set of premises. While the first or "subjectivist" set of premises forms a well-known and standard philosophical position, the second set of premises Murray puts in a way which is more nearly his own.

It derives, in some measure, from the Scottish philosophers of common sense. What those philosophers were saying was that the subjectivist position in its Humean form failed to take account of other things which we know. We know, for instance, that we are successful in carrying on our daily lives and in identifying large ranges of objects of cognition. We do sometimes mistake phantoms for physical objects, mirror images for adjacent rooms, and strange, creepy sounds for burglars in the night.

Still, the point is that we are aware of all these things; we do not very frequently make the kinds of mistakes which one would think might occur with great frequency if the Humean form of the subjectivist position were, in fact, all that there was to say. Hume himself had suggested that, in addition to the sensations which composed immediate awareness, there were other factors to be taken into consideration. For one thing, in addition to these sensations—which he called "impressions"—there were what he called "ideas." Ideas, for Hume, were all compounded from impressions but tended to give us a stable psychological life as a result of a process of association by which similar impressions came to be compounded into a single idea. Beyond that, there were our "natural beliefs." These "natural beliefs" could neither be substantiated by the flow of impressions nor yet rebutted by that flow. If nothing logically justified the inferences we made from sensations then, similarly, nothing logically could rebut them. They were thus secure. (Hume, by politics, was a "High Tory" and there is an obvious link here between his general epistemological position and his political views. In politics, a High Tory is precisely one who believes that there is never enough evidence to upset our natural beliefs.)

These concessions the common sense philosophers thought to be insufficient for the purpose. Any literal law of association might combine like sensations into any number of patterns. It cannot explain how

148

we get a stable, coherent, and intelligible world rather than a world which is patterned some other way. It can only explain how it happens that our world is patterned at all. Furthermore, the strength of our "natural beliefs" about the world is very surprising on this account. One would think that when one saw that one's natural beliefs had, after all, no logical foundation, they would come to seem unsubstantial and, ultimately, merely arbitrary whims of our imagination.

The common sense philosophers, therefore, were inclined to turn the logic of the case in upon itself. They were inclined to urge that what is at stake is not the manner in which we infer the existence of an objective world which is independent of us from our sensations, but rather, how we might come to challenge the existence of that world. Given our success in dealing with the world, in short, they thought the onus of proof for its dubiousness must lie with the challenger and that, apart from a somewhat doubtful psychological theory which analyzes all experience into sensations or impressions, there was not much of a challenge forthcoming.

Murray, evidently, does not think that the challenge is to be put or met in quite this way. He accepts that it is fair to ask "what is it that we are really immediately aware of?" Much of a sensationalist analysis follows. But he accepts from the other side the premise that he has, *somehow*, additional knowledge. It is this which must be explained.

He puts it this way:

> To sum up, there is thus evolved to our consciousness a world of *objects*, placed over against *ourselves*, extending throughout an immeasurable *space*, and undergoing alterations during a limitless *time*—alterations which are produced in the objects by each other in consequence of their *reciprocal causality*. There are, therefore, certain supreme categories, under which the intelligible world is thought, and which are indicated in the terms italicised in the preceding sentence. These being the universal categories of the intelligible world, their interpretation involves the interpretation of the general nature of knowledge. Consequently, we find that the problem of the ultimate generalisations of psychology gathers round these categories and their implications.[45]

The conclusion to which Murray comes is that sensationalism combined with associationism is simply not enough to account for the existence of these general categories. He distinguishes between the philosophical attempt to establish the ultimate validity of these categories and the psychological demand for "scientific explanation"

45 Ibid., pp. 274-75.

of them and allows that only the second is his concern here. In pursuing it, he pronounces on at least the first crucial aspect of the philosophical issue.

He begins by attacking "associationism."

> ... the problem before us reduces itself to the question whether every phenomenon in consciousness, however complicated it may be, appears on analysis to be simply a sum of sensations. It can scarcely be denied that in many cases such an analysis seems obviously impossible. The relations existing between sensations are something quite distinct from the sensations related. No mere repetition of a sensation, even in infinitely varying associations, could ever give me the consciousness that it resembles, or differs from, another sensation. Resemblance and difference are facts which cannot be seen or heard, cannot be tasted or touched, or felt by any other form of physical sensibility.[46]

The point which Murray is making here is a logical one. To form ideas and even general categories for the association of sensations, one would have to know how one sensation fitted together with another. But the fact that one sensation resembles another is not a fact about the two sensations. It is something which can only be discovered by putting the two together and applying a standard to them. Part of this argument is probably as old as Plato but what Murray is working toward is not a formal logical argument for the reality of universals but an effective distinction between the receipt of sensations—a passive process, and the formation of ideas—an active process.

He goes on to notice that some associationists in the early nineteenth century sought to develop a kind of "mental chemistry"—a science of psychology in which it would be possible to relate the process of association to the models of classical mechanics. One would then explain the "production" of ideas out of sensations much as one explains the formation of complex physical compounds out of elemental molecular entities. After all, as Murray notices, in chemistry we do find that one apparent substance is readily replaced by another in the appropriate circumstances. We can combine oxygen and hydrogen in an appropriate way and get water. Surely, this is no more puzzling intrinsically than the amalgamation of sensations into an idea which is quite different from them. Murray notices, however, that even the scientific explanation is incomplete and somewhat puzzling. "Attempts to formulate the procedure as nothing more than a peculiar collocation or a peculiar movement of the atoms of oxygen and hydrogen"[47] are

46 Murray, *An Introduction to Psychology*, pp. 332-33.
47 Ibid., p. 334.

"only an inexactness of thought."[48] What Murray has in mind is that the scientific explanation tells us the conditions under which water can be compounded out of oxygen and hydrogen, but it still remains a fact that something new has emerged which cannot be described simply by amalgamating the descriptions of oxygen and hydrogen.

Murray would argue that the analogy between chemistry and mental chemistry breaks down in the face of the facts.

> In a case of chemical combination it is true that in a certain sense the combining elements disappear; but in another sense they do not. For their continued presence in the combination can always be made evident by methods of analysis at the disposal of the chemist,—methods so exact as to establish the general law that there is no loss of quantity either in the composition or in the decomposition, that even in the chemical changes of the material world its elementary constituents are completely conserved. But nothing analogous to this can be evinced in the so-called mental chemistry. There, by hypothesis, the atoms of mental life—the elementary sensations—disappear; but there is no psychological process, like that of chemical analysis, by which the associated sensations can be recovered, and their contributions to the complex mental state made evident.[49]

Thus associationism cannot be rescued by appeal to mechanical analogy. Murray, however, wants to make a larger point than this. If we could explain our mental life in terms of the physical world, one could make a kind of case for an escape from subjectivism into materialism. For, though it does not logically follow that any inference from subjective sensation to the independent reality of a material world would be valid if mechanism could explain the mental life, it would, nonetheless, be anything but unreasonable to hold that materialism was a likely hypothesis if such a fit obtained. Suppose that we were to find that there was a kind of "mental chemistry" which parallelled physical chemistry and that, furthermore, every event in one of these systems had an exact counterpart in the other system. Logically, one could still hold that this was merely a fortuitous fact. Practically, however, one would find such a position very difficult to maintain. Furthermore, in that case, the materialist hypothesis would explain much of our attachment to general propositions which cannot be substantiated by a simple appeal to sensation.

Murray is thus building a case by elimination. Faced with the subjectivists' claims, there have seemed to most philosophers, traditionally, to be only three alternatives.

48 Ibid.
49 Ibid., pp. 334-35.

One of them is to accept the scepticism which goes with the subjectivist claim about sensations. Such a scepticism comes in many forms—from the "mitigated" scepticism of Hume with its reliance on natural beliefs to the classical withholding of belief which dates from Pyrrho. The second alternative is to try to vindicate our claims to knowledge by reference to the models which we currently use in developing our theories about nature—especially those theories which are fundamental to the physical sciences. If this program could be extended to psychology, it could even be used to account for the array of appearances which gives rise to the subjectivist position and to the scepticism which follows from it. Ideally, one could show that the sceptic is merely, in his mental states, one more outcome of the total physical person. For if that program were successful, it would follow that there is a physical explanation for the panoply of appearance itself. In general, such a program would lead to materialism. The third alternative is to try to show that reason stands on its own ground and that there is a rational and intelligible order in the universe which exhibits the properties of mind. If reason does stand on its own ground, then there is a species of objective knowledge and a natural intelligibility in things. On this view, science itself makes sense because it is part of that total pattern of intelligibility. This task leads to what is commonly called "objective idealism"—the doctrine that the ultimate reality is the rational and intelligible order in things. This kind of idealism is to be distinguished from the subjective idealism which is simply one of the interpretations of the subjectivist, sensationalist scepticism about which we have been talking.

Murray has rejected subjective idealism along with its fundamental basis in this sensationalist case by claiming it can, in no way, account for the simple facts of our mental life. In the previous passage which we have been discussing, he rejects materialism on the ground that no mechanical model will suffice to explain our mental life either.

The point that he makes is that the categories by which we structure our experience and the general ideas which govern the basic features of our lives must have their own origins. Neither sensations themselves nor some hidden mechanism which might lie behind sensations are capable of explaining the simple fact that we have the ideas that we do. Neither of them is capable of explaining the fact that we find a world to be intelligible—that knowledge, after all, *is* possible.

Murray does not merely rely upon the logical argument to show that general ideas cannot be compounded from sensation merely by association, or upon the assertion that the parallel between chemistry and the mental life is logically incomplete. As the argument develops, he tries to centre it on the basic fact of intelligibility at every moment of our waking life.

> If our mental life be merely a succession of feelings, if the consciousness of each moment absolutely vanishes as that moment passes away, there can be no principle in consciousness to connect the different moments by a comparison which goes beyond each and cognises its relation of priority or posteriority to others. For this there must be some permanent factor of consciousness,—a factor that is out of the succession which it observes. That factor is self-consciousness; and without self-consciousness the consciousness of time is thus seen to be impossible.[50]

We should notice the force of this argument. Both the sceptical subjectivist and the mechanical materialist hold that reflection on our conscious states is a preliminary to diagnosing situations. But reflection—whether it takes the form of doubting, the form of assessing evidence, or the form of constructing models and general hypotheses—invariably involves time. To carry out an argument, I must persist through a span of time. I must know, at the end of the argument, what the premises originally meant. If I were locked into a simple consciousness at the present moment, I could not do any of these things. But if all I had to go upon by way of original and fundamental knowledge consisted of my immediate sensations, I could know nothing of the distinction between past, present, and future. Everything would seem to be a present. For sensations do not come with labels like "past" and "present" pasted on them. They simply come. Something else is required to explain the consciousness of time. This something else cannot be a simple mechanism either. Suppose that we were able to translate our descriptions of experienced memory into descriptions of brain states and to explain brain states straightforwardly in terms of physics and chemistry. This would be useful enough in its way—and, quite likely, we shall be able to do it one day—but it still would not explain the consciousness of time. For the point about the consciousness of time is that it requires an awareness of something other than the present. The electro-chemical processes which go on in our brains and are associated with memories, of course, all take place in the present. How is it, then, that we are aware of the past at all?

It can only be, Murray thinks, because we are able to cognize "some permanent factor of consciousness,—a factor that is out of the succession which it observes."[51]

50   Murray, *A Handbook of Psychology*, p. 289.
51   Ibid.

What this means is that for knowledge to be possible at all there must be something which is outside time and that something must be a portion of our personal self-awareness, a feature of our continuing cognition. Murray is not here calling attention to some strange or occult phenomenon. He is simply calling our attention to something which goes on at every moment of our experience. We are always aware of the distinction between the past, the present, and the future.

The argument, ultimately, is that no experience would be possible at all if there were not this fundamental basis for it.

Murray drops this discussion rather quickly and, when he adds, "Thus also memory is explained,"[52] the uncharacteristic smugness seems hardly justified even in the face of another paragraph about memory itself. To have identified one of the necessary conditions for a phenomenon is not, after all, to have explained it. Nevertheless, Murray has hold of a very forceful argument against the classical empiricist who seeks to ground all knowledge in sensation.

The sensationalist cannot simply reply that our ostensible cognitions of time are simply illusory. For in the context of Murray's psychological investigations, the question is not about the veridical nature of our cognitions of time but, rather, about our simple ability to think about time at all. The mere association of sensation will not, in itself, give rise to a concept of time.

If we can experience events in a directional order, we are acquiring knowledge about time. It might well be that this knowledge about time is, itself, still subjective—for the order in which I perceive events may not be the order in which you or anyone else perceives events and, even if we all perceive events in the same order, we may not perceive them in a preferred order which we would want to call "objective." Even then, our cognitions of ourselves as extra-temporal entities seem still to be guaranteed by Murray's argument.

Actually, the position which Murray wants to take does seem to guarantee, in a sense, an objective time. For, in the context of Murray's objective idealism, an objective time requires, principally, that there should be an *order* of events which is ultimately intelligible. "Objective time," in this sense, is simply the order of events within which the events become intelligible and, in a scientific context, the order of events within which they can be seen to exhibit law-like patterns which we call explanation. Winston Churchill's accession to power makes sense in the context of certain events in World War II. In experiments in thermodynamics, we expect the thermometer to rise after we have

52 Ibid.

depressed the piston in the adiabatic enclosure. The preferred order of events is established by a certain coherence between them.

Murray pursues this theme in his discussion of substance. He introduces this discussion by noting, "The cosmos, that is unfolded to self-conscious intelligence, is a world of *things, objects, substances*."[53]

He says:

> The empirical theory on the notion of substance has not advanced since the time of Locke. A number of simple ideas, Locke explains, are found to occur together; in more modern language we should say, that a number of sensations are uniformly associated in our experience.[54]

Here we have, once again, the sensationalist theory of classical empiricism. Locke urged, in the end, that substance is an "uncertain supposition of we know not what"[55] for he could not find any way to explain how it was that sensations came to be associated in this way.

Murray says:

> It is a striking proof of the impossibility of eliciting this idea from sensations, that Hume, on the empirical principles of Locke, denies not only the objective validity of the idea, but even its very existence, on the ground that there is no sensation, from which it could be derived. The empiricists of the present day generally accept Hume's doctrine, but proceed in defiance of it by starting from an object outside of consciousness,—a substance or force,—as the generator of consciousness itself.[56]

These "empiricists of the present day" were the materialists of Murray's time. A later generation of empiricists—a generation which became influential in philosophy twenty years or so after Murray's death—tended to return to Hume's original position if for no better reason than that it had become clear that the starting point of those to whom Murray objected was inconsistent with their premises.

Yet, even if we do not all have a coherent idea of "substance," even if, as still more recent philosophers would urge perhaps, we do not have any ordinary use for the expression "substance" itself, it still remains true that, as Murray urges, we do find that the world "unrolls itself before conscious intelligence"[57] in a way which involves things

53 Ibid., p. 295.
54 Ibid.
55 John Locke, *An Essay Concerning Human Understanding*, abridged and edited by John Yolton in two volumes (London: J. M. Dent & Sons, 1965; first published in 1690), vol. 1, p. 53.
56 Murray, *A Handbook of Psychology*, p. 296.
57 Ibid., p. 297.

and objects. And we do not have any better way than Locke had to explain the association of sensations to make objects. Why do we not perceive the world as a simple collection of sense data? Perhaps by some conscious "reduction" of the kind which Husserl suggested (though it would not be exactly Husserl's reduction) we could experience things in that way and cease to regard them as clustered. (People can be quite easily shaken from the rut of their ordinary perception by psychological demonstrations which show them how much of themselves they put into ordinary perceptions and which show them the extent to which all perception is conditioned by one's state of mind, one's attention, and one's preferences. Imbued with such caution, one *might* come to perceive the world as a set of atomic sensations.)

The difficulty is that, in order to get an intelligible world, one has to have a world which contains continuance and preferred customs. One always explains the changes in something by postulating something else which remains unchanged through that process or operation. We explain certain kinds of chemical changes by supposing an identity of molecules in different combinations and we explain more fundamental physical changes by supposing a continuation of basic atomic structures through a variety of changes. There always, in short, have to be reference points on which our explanations can catch hold.

Murray asks, therefore:

How comes it that the world shapes itself thus to intelligence? It arises from the fact, that otherwise there would be no intelligible world at all; it is therefore the form of the world, that is implied in the very nature of intelligence. For to be intelligent is to be self-conscious; and to be conscious of self is to be conscious of notself. Consequently, the very act of intelligence, by which we are conscious of sensations, projects these into an objective sphere, transmuting them into qualities of objects, and thus forming out of them a world that is not ourselves.

Accordingly, in their psychological aspect at least, qualities are simply the form in which self-conscious intelligence construes sensations. By a similar construction is formed the notion of substance as that unity by which qualities are essentially connected, and which remains unaltered amid their changes. For the variable elements—the qualities—of things in the world of consciousness can be conceived, even as variable, only by relation to that which is permanent. The very conditions, under which alone an intelligible universe can be conceived, render necessary the notion of substances as enduring while their qualities change.[58]

Murray's position is quite strongly Kantian. Like Kant, he supposes that the human mind arranges things in such a way as to make an

58 Ibid.

intelligible world. But, unlike Kant, he does not surmise from this that there must be a world which is independent of consciousness and which is close to us by reason of the very fact that our minds arrange things in their own peculiar pattern.

It is here that Murray develops most clearly the kind of objective idealism to which he seems consistently committed.

> The fundamental idea involved in thing, substance, or object is the idea of *existence, reality, being*. Reality, in fact, is simply the Latin for *thinghood*.... It has often been pointed out that there is a significance in the common German word for existence. It means simply *being there* (*Dasein*). Anything that is simply *there*, simply before my consciousness at any moment, exists for me during the moment of its presence. But it may have no existence beyond, or independent of, my conscious life. If so, then it has merely a *subjective existence*....
>
> But in its stricter sense existence or reality refers to something independent on the capricious conditions of any individual consciousness, something that *is* for other intelligences besides myself. In contrast with such *objective existence* anything that exists merely within the sphere of my subjective experience is characterised as a mere *appearance*. Accordingly existence or reality, in the very highest sense of the term, is predicable of that which exists or is a reality for all intelligence. Such existence is *absolute*.[59]

What Murray is saying is this: If we ask if something or other exists, we are entitled to answer "Yes" if that thing enters into anyone's experience in such a way as to be identifiable and intelligible. But this answer, initially, is ambiguous. Suppose I say "God exists" and someone asks me why I say that. My reason might be that God exists in the consciousness of the believer, that he is able to identify those occasions when he is aware of God and distinguish them from other occasions, and that he is unable to give me a coherent and intelligible account of this object of cognition. If I am challenged I shall have to admit that, for all I know and the believer knows on this ground alone, God exists only relatively. God exists, that is, in *relation to* the consciousness of the believer. What people generally want to know is whether, to use the term in Murray's way, God exists *absolutely*. God would exist absolutely if and only if He existed, as Murray puts it, "for all intelligence" and this condition would be met if one needed to postulate the existence of God in order adequately to explain the possibility of experience itself or, at least, in order to explain the possibility of the kinds of experience which everyone has.

59 Murray, *An Introduction to Psychology*, pp. 364-65.

The issue, in this sense, between the subjectivist and the objectivist is *not* in Murray's terms an issue about whether the object exists only *in* the consciousness of individuals or whether it exists independently of the consciousness of all individuals.

The condition of existence, whether relative *or* absolute, is that the thing said to exist should be *there*. For it to be there it must be identifiable and intelligible. It must have within it that minimum of rational order which constitutes the basis of the claim that it is there. Thus the question is not its independence of consciousness. Independence seems to imply exemption from the demands of intelligibility. If we were to imagine things independent in *that* sense, we would simply be playing into the hands of the sceptic, the subjectivist, or the sensationalist. For then, there would be no line of inference which would take us from any experience which we had to the proposition that the thing itself was there. We are not entitled to abandon the world to the sceptic, the subjectivist, or the sensationalist, in Murray's view, because our experience does involve us with ideas which transcend those limitations.

He explains his position in this way:

> It is evident that all science, all genuine knowledge, endeavours to penetrate beyond appearance, beyond the fleeting phenomena of individual conssciousness. And why? Because otherwise knowledge would be impossible. If consciousness could grasp nothing but vanishing sensations, or vanishing groups of sensations, it would be impossible to know anything; for the moment we became conscious of anything, it would have vanished, leaving nothing to be known. The very possibility of knowledge, therefore, implies that there is a certain permanence in the facts which make up our conscious experience; and it is this permanent factor amid all changes that forms substance in the world of our knowledge.
>
> And here perhaps we find also the source of those two supreme forms under which the objective world is conceived,—the world of objects coexisting in space, and undergoing successive modifications in time. For the world takes its intelligible form from its being posited by intelligence that is conscious of self, as something that is notself.[60]

The point is that neither subjective self-consciousness nor the objective world—what he calls the "notself"—is absolute in itself. Both, therefore, are only relatively real. "The notself cannot be thought as an absolute identity. It is the opposite of the identical factor of consciousness; it is a construction of factors which are necessarily thought as varying, i.e., as in time."[61] The conclusion is inevitably that reality is a

60 Ibid., p. 365.
61 Murray, *A Handbook of Psychology*, p. 298.

union of subject and object. Neither can exist without the other. Neither is the cause of the other. Both, ultimately, are aspects of the same unity rather than sharply differentiated entities.

This does not mean that the "external world" is a fantasy spun by our private intellects. It means that, insofar as we can have knowledge of it, the external world is an intelligible order which is the concrete manifestation of reason. It thus cannot be thought of without thinking, as well, of the intellect which embodies it. To think about nature is to think about the intelligible order which derives, not from any particular mind, but from the notion of rationality itself. Equally, the self as consciousness is not conceivable apart from the external world. To have a consciousness is to have an object of cognition. Murray avoids the technical language of a position which seems to owe much to Fichte and Hegel but the process which he is describing seems to be inherently dialectical. To think of the subject is to think of the nature within which it is embodied. To think of nature is to think of the subject which is involved in its intelligibility.

Murray goes on to notice that we can avoid some of the traditional puzzles about space and time—in particular those raised by Kant in the discussion of the antinomies of the *Critique of Pure Reason*.

> Space and time would thus appear to be forms in which the world must necessarily be conceived in order to be intelligible—in order to be an object to self-conscious intelligence. This view of these forms takes away the ground from the puzzles which have been often built upon them since the time of the Eleatic Zeno. It has been often maintained, even in recent times, that human intelligence is the helpless victim of a mysterious antinomy or contradiction in applying the notions of space and time; and from this alleged fact various metaphysical inferences have been drawn with regard to the intrinsic impotence and limitation of our intelligence.[62]

Evidently, it *is* Kant to whom this quotation is directed and the *Critique* is mentioned in the footnote to the following page along with works of Mansel and Spencer. But Murray says:

> Notwithstanding the high authority under which these perplexities have been propounded, it does seem that they imply a misapprehension regarding the nature of the notions upon which they play. It is quite true that we cannot think an absolute limit to space or time, while we are equally unable to think of them as absolutely unlimited. But the reason of this is to be sought in no mysterious impotence, which restricts in a special manner the finite intellect of man. The impotence arises from the fundamental condition of all

62   Ibid.

thinking—the law which prevents thought from contradicting, and thereby removing, its own positions. For space and time are, as we have seen, forms of relation; and to ask us to conceive them under those modes, which the doctrine in question pronounces inconceivable, would be to require the conception of a relative which is not related to anything.[63]

He spells this out by noticing what would happen if one thought that time had a beginning: ". . . time means a relation to a before and an after. An absolute limit to the past, therefore, would be a time with no before; an absolute limit to the future, a time with no after. But either limit would be a time that is not a time."[64]

Murray argues, similarly, that one cannot conceive of a finite space. He says that space is "a relation of mutual outness; the very idea of space implies that every space has something outside of it."[65] In other words, one would simply fail to have a spatial relation if one came to the end of space.

He wants to argue that the notion of an infinite space or an infinite time is inconceivable. In this case, his reason is not so clear. What he says is this:

An infinite space or time, as the writers on the subject explain, is a conception that could be formed only by the infinite addition in thought of finite spaces and times; in other words, the conception implies an endless process. But when I am asked to form the conception now, I am asked to think a contradiction; I am asked to end a process of thought which by hypothesis is endless.[66]

This is obscure for two reasons. One of them is that it is not clear that one could only conceive of infinite space or time by the addition of successive finite components. The other is that, whereas the argument against a finite space or time is based on an analysis of the intrinsic nature of spatial and temporal relations, the argument against infinite spaces and times appears to be based mainly on a limitation of the imagination. The first argument would substantiate Murray's point that we are not to follow Kant in supposing that the difficulties about space and time should lead us to believe that, whatever reality is like, it is, in itself or as what Kant would call a noumenon, quite distinct from the world of our experience. In contrast, the second argument—the argument about infinite spaces and times—would seem to substantiate

63 Ibid., pp. 299-300.
64 Ibid., p. 300.
65 Ibid.
66 Ibid.

Kant's thesis. Taken together, they would have a stronger tendency to substantiate Kant's thesis. For one might argue that, on logical grounds, space and time could not be finite. On psychological grounds, one can see, if Murray's argument is correct, that we cannot conceive of infinite spaces and times. Therefore, one might easily conclude that real space and real time have properties which imagination can grasp and that they simply lie outside the realm of human cognition. Such a conclusion would certainly be fatal to Murray's objective idealism.

One must surmise, in this situation, that Murray did not succeed in his discussion of infinite space and time in expressing what he wanted to express. For he could hardly have imagined himself to have substantiated a position which he had just explicitly rejected. One could, luckily for Murray, conceive of a better argument about infinite space and infinite time—one which would follow the pattern of his argument about finite space and finite time. For one might argue, given the assumptions Murray is working from about the relation of nature to space, that space *is* exactly a set of relations which obtain between a collection of points or regions. These relations establish an order. Time is a set of relations—if time is relational at all—which obtain between a collection of events and establish an order for those events. Murray's whole notion of there being an objective space and an objective time depends upon the existence of these ordering relations and upon the fact that the ordering relation actually succeeds in establishing an intelligible order. But now suppose we have an infinite space and an infinite time. Some points or regions in an infinite space will be related to one another such that, whatever one takes to be the measure of distance, it will not be possible to specify the distance between them. For one cannot, by definition, traverse an infinite series. No finite number of such units would be the expression of distance between at least two such points or regions. In fact, if the space *is* infinite there will be infinitely many such points and regions which lack that relation to one another. Furthermore, there will be many points or regions which lie at an identical distance—namely an infinite distance—from a given point or region and yet those points and regions will not be identical with one another. The difficulty with this situation lies in the fact that, if one starts from the perspective of two of these points or regions which are infinitely removed from a given point, they will turn out to be at varying distances from a third point which is intermediate between them and the original point. This would be intelligible if they were arranged like points on the circumference of a circle all of which are equidistant from the centre and stand in different relations to various intermediate points on the radii. But, since this space is infinite and

161

thus extends indefinitely in all directions, it will turn out that two different points on the *same* radius will be the same distance from the centre—namely an infinite distance—but will fail to be identical with one another. A similar argument can be made about time.

In an infinite time, there is some point in the distant past which is infinitely removed from the present. If there is such an event in past time and past time is infinite, there are many, indeed infinitely many, such events. But though all we can say about any one of them is that it is infinitely removed from the present (we cannot assign a determinate number of years to it for that would make it only finitely removed), it will still turn out that various events which are infinitely removed from the present are related to one another by finite periods of time. It will turn out, that is, that there are events in past time which both are and are not well ordered with respect to the present. This is what happens with infinite spaces as well. There are points or regions in them which both are and are not well ordered in relation to a given point or region. This seems to make Murray's point: Finite space and finite time fail to meet the requirements of spatial and temporal relations. Infinite space and infinite time also fail to meet the requirements of the relations specified. To be sure, a thorough approach to and analysis of these problems would require a much more elaborate statement of the nature of the relations than Murray has provided and the argument we have offered to make Murray's position consistent would, as well, require considerable elaboration.

Still, one can see what Murray is concerned about. He wants to show both that space and time are not purely objective entities in themselves and he wants to show that this is no reason for adopting the Kantian distinction between the phenomenal and the noumenal worlds—the distinction between the world of experience and the world as it really is. What he wants to urge is that space and time are relations and that they require the activity of a cognizing intelligence. Space and time appear to be infinite because there is no limit to the number of ordering operations which could be undertaken sequentially. They seem to be finite because one cannot imagine this order coming to an end. But this is just what one would expect if they were the creations of an ordering intelligence.

Murray's intentions become even clearer in his discussion of cause. For the most part, Murray simply carries out the implications of his earlier discussion in undermining both the sceptical subjectivist position and closing the loopholes which might lead to materialism. As usual, he accepts some of the original premises of the sceptical subjectivist. In particular, in this case he accepts Hume's analysis of the concept of cause.[67]

Hume had pointed out that to say that X is the cause of Y is, in general, to call attention to a combination of experiential and non-experiential elements. Some of the basic criteria which we use for identifying causes—regularity, temporal succession, and contiguity—derive from situations which have a high experiential content. (They are not, as Murray's analysis earlier pointed out, wholly experiential. Both regularity and succession require the notion of time which is not given in experience if experience, in its primary form, consists of sensations. The same thing is ultimately true of contiguity if, as Murray suggests, spatial relations themselves derive from an operation which is not simply the passive receipt of sensations. Nevertheless, given the spatial-temporal framework, it is in experience that we notice the things which give rise to these components of the causal relation.) Hume urged that these empirical or quasi-empirical notions were not enough to sustain the concept of cause. There must also be what Hume called "necessary connexion." For, when we say that X is the cause of Y, we mean that, but for X, there would be no Y. The world is full of examples of regularity, succession, and contiguity which we would not regard as examples of causal connections. There is a regular connection between the weekly reports of freight car loadings and the state of the economy. Furthermore, it is usually the case that changes in the economy generally are preceded by falling or rising levels of freight car loadings. The relation of contiguity is usually maintained. For the economy which goes into decline is the economy in which the freight cars are located and not some other. But an economist who claimed that the cause of the depression was the low level of freight car loadings would be saying something much like Calvin Coolidge's assertion that the cause of unemployment was "too many people out of work." If one wants to generalize, the happenings of each day are always preceded by and are continuous with the light from the rising sun, but we do not claim that the sunrise is the cause of these events. The reason is that we expect to find something like Hume's "necessary connexion" between events before we are willing to ascribe the word "cause" to the relation.

Murray accepts all this and takes a rather strong position about the proper philosophical analysis. He says:

67 David Hume, *A Treatise of Human Nature*, reprinted from the original edition (1739) in three volumes and edited by L. A. Selby-Bigge (Oxford: Clarendon Press, 1964). Hume's discussion of cause as requiring a perceived "necessary connexion" can be found in Book I, Part III, Sections 2 and 12.

. . . the thought that the two [the event we called the cause and the event we called the effect] are essentially connected, so that the one cannot appear without the other—this is a new thought, wholly different from either or both of the terms in the sequence.

This thought, again, is the thought of a relation or connection, and cannot therefore be identified with sensation. It implies a consciousness which goes beyond transient sensations, and connects them with each other by a comparing act. This act is rendered possible by the presence in consciousness of a permanent factor that is not itself merely one of the phenomena which flow in unceasing variation. It is this factor by which, as we have seen, a plurality of co-existent qualities are connected into the unity of a substance. The same factor connects the successive moments in the world that rolls before consciousness.[68]

Now the doctrine that "the thought of a relation or connection" is something which "cannot be identified with sensation" is strong meat. There is an old and rather fundamental puzzle which comes to readers of Hume about "relations of impressions" and "impressions of relations." (You will remember that what we generally call—and Murray always calls—sensations, Hume calls impressions.) In general, Murray appears not to have taken quite this position in the earlier argument. In his discussion of space, for example, there appears the following passage: ". . . space is not a feeling; it is not a subjective state, or an association of subjective states. It is a relation of objects; and, as a relation, it can be known only by comparison."[69] Whether this is meant to suggest that there are not "impressions of relations" or only that, as it suggests, you would have to have two comparable sensations in order to have a direct cognition of a relation, is disputable. When Murray first raised the question, the issue was about what Hume called impressions and ideas. Murray had argued that you cannot derive ideas (essentially concepts with application to more than one instance) from sensations (essentially given atomic data). Here the issue was not that the relation was not given in experience but that the comprehension of it as applying to more than one possible instance cannot be given in experience and that the "assembly" could not, therefore, be purely a matter of association. In the discussion of time, Murray was dealing with a particular relation which derives from a relational property which, in its turn, cannot readily be conceived as given in experience. If X is past while Y is present, X has the relational property of pastness with respect to any observation which is simultaneous with Y. But this pastness is simply not one of its sensible properties. Yet the concept of

68 Murray, *A Handbook of Psychology*, pp. 301-302.
69 Ibid., p. 294.

time depends on our ability to identify things as having that and other similar relational properties. Now, on some views of relations it follows, pretty much without argument, that relations are not given in sensation. Some of these views of relations seem intrinsically commonsensical if the matter is put in certain ways. If I say "The shovel is in the hole" and invite you to look for the sensory experiences which confirm that proposition, you will be able to "see" the shovel and the hole but not the "in." What is suggested, here, though, is that relations are rather like bits of string which hold things together.

It may be that Murray had some such view in mind for he apparently thinks that what he is saying is obvious enough. That it is not altogether obvious may be seen if we look at some examples which are put somewhat differently. Suppose X has the relational property of being far away from me. I might well say that it "looks far away." Indeed, that may be my evidence for thinking that it *is* far away. Things do, after all, have a characteristic look when they are far away. They look small and vague in a way which is quite different from that of things which *are* small and rather ill-defined but are close up to us. (Compare the appearance of a ship on the horizon and the appearance of a small orange blob on a red canvas so painted that it seems to fade into the red around it.) More simply, things feel lumpy, sound discordant, and look fragmentary. All of these are relational properties and anyone who knows that some X has one of these properties, knows some relation. Is it really true that none of these properties is "given" in sensation? Bear in mind, that an alternative view of relations is that relational properties are primary and that the basic statements which express relations are translations of statements which express relational properties.

This is not the place to go into a substantial discussion of the theory of relation. Even this much discussion is included only for the reason that Murray seems to have extended his earlier theories when he comes to cause and to have committed himself to a view which might be difficult to defend. It is, therefore, important to see whether Murray needs this particular position in order to substantiate his discussion of causality.

Our contention is that he does not, but this requires some explication. The issue really is about what *kind* of a relation "causality" is. Murray in fact suggests that it is not a relation which could hold between discrete entities. So long as X and Y are two distinct things with nothing in common, it is not possible to establish that X is the cause of Y. This becomes clear if one looks at even the simplest mechanical models of causal relations. Suppose that X and Y are two billiard balls on a billiard table. If X is moving and collides with Y, we would, naturally, urge that the movement of X is the cause of the subsequent movement of Y. But this is because X and Y are components of the same space and because, at the very least, we assume that two things—constituted in the way that billiard balls are—cannot occupy the same space. Even more than this, as our explanation becomes more sophisticated we search for laws which will explain the relation of proportionality which holds between the mass and velocity of X and the subsequent movement of Y. We come to conceive of X and Y as features of the same energy system. In short, to make our point we have to establish that the elements in our causal explanations are components of a single system which has some set of unifying properties.

We must, now, step back and remember the context in which Murray is raising the question. He has assumed, throughout the discussion, that we start with a set of sensations each of which, taken by itself, is atomic in the sense supposed by Hume—namely in the sense that the occurrence of any one sensation does not entail the occurrence of any other sensation. They are not related in the way that components of the number system are related so that it follows, logically, that if there is a number 17 there is also a number 99. Each sensation simply is what it is. Now Murray wants to know why we develop a successful notion of causality. After all, we not only do deploy the notion of cause, but we are also, quite often, sufficiently successful at the enterprise in that we are entitled to believe that we have identified causes. On the associationist view, the most that can be said is what Hume says: Like sensations naturally become associated with one another in a way that establishes a pattern of regularity. But, though the regularity thesis has frequently been accepted even by philosophers of science, it does not seem to do justice to our common-sense view of causality and we would not, except in very specialized circumstances, be tempted to associate patterns of regularity, temporal succession, and contiguity with causal connections. One alternative is to adopt a model in which we regard the sensations concerned as representing states of affairs in some interconnected system such as physical space-time. Murray's concern with philosophical psychology is to raise the question, How are we able to construct such models?

He gives the same answer which he gave to problems about the continuity of the self.

It [causality] implies a consciousness which goes beyond transient sensations, and connects them with each other by a comparing act. This act is rendered possible by the presence in consciousness of a permanent factor that is not itself merely one of the phenomena which flow in unceasing variation.[70]

Without this, Murray argues, it would not be possible to have an effective concept of causality.

To put it another way, when we construct models of physical space-time and come to regard sensations as representing interconnected parts of them, we are representing not so much the physical world as a property of our own direct cognitions. We are aware of this "presence in consciousness of a permanent factor." We are aware, that is, of the continuity of our own existence. The attack is really on the theory of awareness put forward by the associationist sensationalists. Hume, to be fair, was not unsympathetic to this view. In the passage of the *Treatise of Human Nature* in which he talks about our feeling that "the mind is a kind of theatre,"[71] a stage on which the events of our lives take place, Hume seems more puzzled by his inability to explain the sense of personal continuity in the context of his own theory than certain that he has produced an argument against the proposition that we do know that there is a personal continuity. In an appendix to the work, he said:

> I had entertain'd some hopes, that however deficient our theory of the intellectual world might be, it wou'd be free from those contradictions, and absurdities, which seem to attend every explication, that human reason can give of the material world. But upon a more strict review of the section concerning *personal identity*, I find myself involv'd in such a labyrinth, that, I must confess, I neither know how to correct my former opinions, nor how to render them consistent. If this be not a good *general* reason for scepticism, 'tis at least a sufficient one (if I were not already abundantly supplied) for me to entertain a diffidence and modesty in all my decisions. I shall propose the arguments on both sides, beginning with those that induc'd me to deny the strict and proper identity and simplicity of a self or thinking being.[72]

He then repeats some of his original argument. He remarks that "Every idea is deriv'd from preceding impressions; and we have no impression of self or substance, as something simple and individual."[73] He elaborates this at some length, but then he says:

> So far I seem to be attended with sufficient evidence. But having thus loosen'd all our particular perceptions, when I proceed to explain the

70 Ibid., p. 302.
71 Hume, *A Treatise of Human Nature*, p. 253.
72 Ibid., p. 633.
73 Ibid.

principle of connexion,which binds them together, and makes us attribute to them a real simplicity and identity; I am sensible, that my account is very defective, and that nothing but the seeming evidence of the precedent reasonings cou'd have induc'd me to receive it. If perceptions are distinct existences, they form a whole only by being connected together. But no connexions among distinct existences are ever discoverable by human understanding. We only feel a connexion or determination of the thought, to pass from one object to another. It follows, therefore, that the thought alone finds personal identity, when reflecting on the train of past perceptions, that compose a mind, the ideas of them are felt to be connected together, and naturally introduce each other. However extraordinary this conclusion may seem, it need not surprize us. Most philosophers seem inclin'd to think, that personal identity *arises* from consciousness; and consciousness is nothing but a reflected thought or perception. The present philosophy, therefore, has so far a promising aspect. But all my hopes vanish, when I come to explain the principles, that unite our successive perceptions in our thought or consciousness. I cannot discover any theory, which gives me satisfaction on this head.[74]

The weakness of this section of Murray's *Introduction to Psychology* seems to be that the conclusions he is coming to should force him to a basic reconstruction of the whole theory of experience. But the line of argument which he chooses begins with two sets of basic assumptions—one borrowed from Hume and his successors and one borrowed from the common sense philosophers. The argument is designed to show the inadequacy of the first set taken by itself and the need to do justice to the second set. Murray is thus working critically and negatively and appears to be, for the most part, satisfied to get the conclusions that he wants without working out the whole of a new and radical theory of experience. As argument, with a few amendments, it comes off not too badly. As a piece of original philosophy, it seems to demand more work.

The position which he seems to adopt is a position which passes from criticism of subjectivist sensationalism, to a kind of Kantian structuralism and then proceeds to show that we do not need the bifurcation of the world which Kant's system demanded. He is thus opting for a kind of critical objective idealism which goes beyond Kant but does not quite extend to the radical reconstruction envisaged by Hegel.

Murray thinks, always, that there is a real and objective world—that there is a real space, a real time, and that it is filled with real objects. But he thinks that the nature of this real world is that it is the objectification of rational intelligence and that one can no more think of the

74   Ibid., pp. 635-36.

object without the subject—or as he puts it, the notself without the self—than one can think of colour without space or change without time. They are simply interrelated concepts. The implication is that there is a kind of dialectical relationship between self and the notself but this Murray does not explore at length. Essentially, he thinks that this is a piece of philosophical psychology, that what he is explaining is how we come to have the kinds of knowledge we do, how we are able to create the concepts involved in that knowledge, and, ultimately, how we should go about conceiving of ourselves as related to the appearance of nature and to the ultimate reality. What needs to be explained, Murray thinks, is the knowledge we do have, not the knowledge we don't have. The knowledge we do have is consistent with this kind of objective idealism. To go beyond that and suppose an objective "notself" wholly independent of intelligence or of the thinking self would be to demand an explanation for knowledge we don't have. For none of the knowledge we do have is fully independent of ourselves or, since it consists of an intelligible order, of intelligence itself. But neither does he think that the world is spun out of our own heads. Rather, the possibility of our having heads to spin derives from the fact that there is a basic and fundamental intelligence in the world.

We must remember that the context in which Murray chose to state his views was determined, in large measure, by the necessary form of the two works in which he set them up. The *Handbook* of 1885 went through several editions after its first publication in London and Montreal. In its preface he simply says it is "designed primarily to introduce students to the science of psychology; and to this design every other purpose, which the book may serve, has been made subordinate."[75] When the *Introduction* was published in Boston in 1904 he said that "as this design has been maintained in the present work, the new title is even more appropriate than the old."[76] The two works parallel one another very closely, though "many parts came to be so completely rewritten."[77] Both titles, perhaps, suggest something which is not quite the case. A book, now, which employed those words in its title might be expected to be either a neutral summary of rival views or a compendium of accepted assumptions, "truths," and generally accepted conceptual structures. Murray's books contain, in fact, his own views and the outcomes of his own inquiries and scarcely purport to summarize all the known material.

75 Murray, *A Handbook of Psychology*, preface.
76 Murray, *An Introduction to Psychology*, preface.
77 Ibid.

He did make a distinction between those issues which he thought pertained to psychology and those which he claimed belonged to "more general" philosophical inquiries. We have tried to give *some* emphasis to that distinction though we must admit that it is not absolutely clear. This issue is of some interest because it forms a continuing sub-theme of Canadian philosophy almost from the beginning to near-contemporary writers like George Brett, whose massive history of psychology will be discussed in a later chapter.

What then is the "psychology" with which the philosophers we are discussing were so involved and how does it differ from the "science" of psychology which has grown up since the real or alleged separation of philosophy and psychology? Should we now abandon as simply outdated philosophical speculations which transgress on "psychology" or other problems which were and are really philosophical but which, nonetheless, impinge on psychology?

It all depends, as C. E. M. Joad used to say, on what you mean. But it seems undeniably true that many of the problems which philosophers like Murray wanted to discuss remain philosophical, remain alive, and have something to do with psychology. Murray, for example, raises basic questions about what we might now call the explanatory models which are appropriate to psychology. Some of the questions involved are simply matters of descriptive facts and these, to a large extent, are the proper subject matter of a "scientific psychology" which can and does proceed in a way which is substantially independent of philosophy. Others of them are inherently logical and depend for their outcome on an appropriate philosophical examination of the situation.

What Murray suggests in the last chapter of *An Introduction to Psychology* is that the problem of volition—the problem, if you like, of "free will"—is a central feature which links all of these issues. He also urges that it can only be understood through a combination of philosophical analysis and an examination of the psychological facts. He is, thus, essentially denying the possibility of a final division of philosophy and psychology. This problem is a quite real one in our own time. Indeed, it may be one of the crucial issues in our faltering search for an understanding of the human predicament. It is worthwhile to examine it in some detail.

At the beginning of his last chapter Murray says:

> The problem . . . is essentially identical with those ultimate problems regarding the general nature of knowledge which were discussed in the sixth chapter of the first Part of this Book, and therefore little remains to be done

but to explain the bearing upon this problem of the principles involved in the previous discussion.[78]

What he is going to suggest is that an understanding of the free will problem depends, primarily, upon the attainment of an adequate theory about the general nature of knowledge, its structure, and its objects.

The clue, he gives in these words:

As we have seen in the previous discussion on self-consciousness, it is this distinction of self from the whole universe of notselves that alone renders intelligible the cognition of that universe. It is also the independence of self on the universe of notselves that alone renders intelligible its voluntary action on that universe. For a volition is not an act to which I am impelled by the forces of external nature beating upon my sensitive nature; it is an act in which I consciously set before myself an end, and determine myself towards its attainment. The very nature of volition, therefore, would be contradicted by a description of it in terms which brought it under the category of causality.

This freedom of the self from determination by the world of objects is the fact which alone explains, without explaining away, the consciousness that there is within us a centre of intelligent activity which is, in the last resort, impregnable by any assaults of mere force.[79]

This, however, is the conclusion of an argument that requires a fair bit of explication. Murray starts by trying to clarify the notion and scope of psychological determination.

He suggests that one must accept the obvious facts:

... it may be admitted that the majority of actions—all the actions which make up the routine of daily life—are of the mechanical type, even though they may be the result of habits voluntarily formed, and may therefore continue subject to voluntary restraint. Man is encircled by the systems of natural law, limited by them in his original constitution.[80]

Furthermore Murray urges:

... we may throw aside as a meaningless fiction, that sort of freedom which has been called the "liberty of indifference,"—that is, a power to act free from the influence of any motive whatever. Whether such a freedom can be claimed for man or not, it is not worth claiming; for a motiveless act cannot

78 Ibid., p. 505.
79 Ibid., p. 509.
80 Ibid., pp. 505-506.

171

be an intelligent act, since it implies no intelligence of the end which the act is designed to accomplish.[81]

Earlier, as well, Murray has traced at great length and with some care the range of human sensations and emotions and their relation to action. He would certainly conceive that we always act against the background of emotion and that that background establishes the effective limits of action. Part of this, what Murray calls "the chronic, probably organic, condition which forms in personal character a predominant tendency to certain forms of emotional excitement,"[82] is so much a part of us that it becomes difficult even for us to bring it to consciousness. Rather, we notice it in the overall pattern of our lives in what he calls "*temperament* or *disposition*."[83] As well, there is a "temporary condition which creates a predominant emotional tendency for a limited time"[84] and this Murray calls mood. Action frequently takes place in context of "the ephemeral explosion" of "the feeling, of the moment."[85] Furthermore, this background is itself "evolved from the raw materials of sensation."[86] It is thus Murray's view that there is a real possibility of discovering psychological laws, that the usual techniques of analysis through stimulus and response—through the observation of behaviour and its manipulation in experiment—has a great chance of success. Indeed, there are two very general direct laws which he mentions. One of them he calls "The Law of Similarity" and this law asserts: "States of mind, identical in nature, though differing in the time of their occurrence, are capable of suggesting each other."[87] The other he calls "The Law of Contiguity" and that law asserts: "States of mind, though differing in nature, if identical in the time of their occurrence, are capable of suggesting each other."[88] These are really, as Murray would concede, the basis of the "associationist" position and, though he has subjected it to severe criticism in its ability to explain certain very fundamental notions, he would admit that it has very wide scope.

Murray would not only concede that there can be and ought to be a "scientific psychology," he would also concede that any reasonable understanding of volition or free will must take account of this fact. This fact does seem to buttress theories of those whom Murray calls "Necessitarians."[89] But what they seem to do, Murray says, is simply to

81   Ibid., p. 506.
82   Ibid., p. 371-72.
83   Ibid., p. 372.
84   Ibid.
85   Ibid.

86   Ibid., p. 371.
87   Ibid., p. 84.
88   Ibid.
89   Ibid., p. 507.

assimilate man's consciousness into the general domain of natural phenomena. They urge that "consciousness therefore stands related to other phenomena precisely as these are related to each other, each being acted upon by the rest and reacting upon them, so that all are absolutely determined by this reciprocity of action."[90] The difficulty with this stems from the fact that:

> On this view man's self is not a real unity, forming by its unifying power, out of an unintelligible multiplicity of sensations, an intelligible cosmos; it is a mere name for a factitious aggregate of associated mental states. The only actual self is the sum of feelings of which we are conscious at any moment; and the actual self therefore differs with the variation of our feelings. Such a self evidently offers no intelligible source of any activity that is not absolutely determined by natural causation.[91]

In effect, this theory turns in upon itself. If there is no self—only what Hume called a "bundle" of impressions and ideas—then how is it that we understand anything? Do sensations make reports about each other? Do impressions and ideas stand there making comparisons to each other? Murray's claim is really that association does not, by itself, explain enough for us even to understand our claims to knowledge, let alone the fact that we really have knowledge. Something more than that, something which Murray, throughout his book, calls "comparison," is required. It is because we must compare sensations, ideas, feelings, and so on to each other in order to have any intelligibility that we must prove that there is a self which is a unity and which stands, somehow, apart from the mere arena of sensations and feelings.

Indeed, it is *because* there is a possibility of a scientific psychology that one needs to postulate free will. We only grasp the origin of our feelings and sensations, the explanation of our acts in psychological laws, and the relation of our subjective impressions to an objective reality because we are, obviously, able to stand back, compare, and reflect. As Murray puts it: "The notselves that make up the objective world have no real point of unity, no selfhood; so that from themselves nothing can originate. But the self is a real self, a real centre of unity, from which radiate all the unifying functions of intelligence that form into intelligible order the world of sense."[92]

It is, therefore, when the psychologist begins to reflect on the possibility of the knowledge that he claims that he is forced, if Murray is

90 Ibid.
91 Ibid., pp. 507-508.
92 Ibid., p. 508.

right, to retreat from his straightforwardly mechanical model. But how does this reflect on the actual practice of psychology?

This question probably cannot be answered very satisfactorily on the basis of the text which Murray has left us. It is worth posing because it forces us to ask ourselves how we are to interpret what he says. There are at least two different interpretations. On one of them, Murray is alleging that, over and above the "facts" which belong to a "scientific" psychology which seeks orderly laws, like those which are implied in the classical physics of mechanics, there are other facts which are simply not available to the psychologist who studies what his subjects do and say. These other facts come to us when we reflect on the workings of our own minds and when we reflect on the nature of knowledge itself. To the outward observer, what seems capable of explanation is mechanical and law-like. To the inner eye it is different. On the other interpretation, Murray is not alleging that there are additional facts but that there are different perspectives on the same facts and that one of these perspectives has a logical priority over the other. Within the system which the "scientific" psychologist constructs, everything appears to have its place in a law-like sequence of events. But when the psychologist reflects upon his practice, he comes to grasp the other perspective. He realizes that he, himself, must be outside the system he constructs just for the reason that he could not, otherwise, construct it. He also realizes that he is not able to represent himself within the system. For the system consists of individual psychological events linked to one another by the appropriate laws. These psychological events are perceptions, emotions, actions, and reactions. But he himself is not simply a collection of these events. If he were, he would not have the continuity of existence which enables him to perform the acts of comparison and identification which make the construction of any system of knowledge possible.

There is a tension between the two views both of which, quite probably, can be found in Murray's writings. On one view, public behaviour is primary and the right rational order is the order which gives the right emphasis, in claims to knowledge, to each particular piece of public experience. On the alternative view, experience itself is structured by the way in which we use reason and reason, itself, is the primary objective knowledge. There are hints in Murray that he wants to follow Hegel to the extent of holding a dialectical position about the relation between the two. For instance, in his discussion of the self and the "notself," the suggestion seems to be that the self is the creature of reason but can only know itself through the content which appears in experience. This view, ultimately, tends to make reason primary and experience something which is to be explained by the workings of reason. Despite occasional wholly "rationalist" passages, Murray does not want to seem to go further than Hegel in this position and revert to a traditional rationalism—the kind of position sometimes associated with (though not altogether fairly) Spinoza and Leibniz. On that view reason, itself, is the final object of knowledge and experience is, in some ways, a hindrance which misleads us. It is characteristic of such views that they tend to view reason as a fixed object of cognition, something there to be discovered, something which is wholly immune to change. Murray generally associates reason with intelligibility. As such, reason is capable of development. What seems to us now as irrational is capable of becoming intelligible as the interplay of reason and experience develops. Apart from some basic moral propositions which seem to Murray immune to change because they simply derive from that fundamental aspect of human nature which makes of us free beings who transcend the limitations of the space and time of experience, Murray seems never to want to traffic in finalities. The intelligible always derives from some standard which, itself, is subject to development. Thus Murray never besieges his reader in a way which would suggest that he construes reason as a substitute for force and thinks that he can compel a conclusion. His effort, rather, is always to direct the reader to the structure and pattern of his own experience and to urge him to draw his conclusion there.

SIX

REASON, CULTURE, AND POWER

Jacob Gould Schurman, The Philosopher as Office-holder

PLATO THOUGHT THAT things would go badly with the world until philosophers became kings or kings philosophers. The record, however, has not been promising. Plato retreated speedily from his own attempt to help the tyrant of Syracuse mix philosophy and politics. The emperor of Rome quickly snuffed the—perhaps half-hearted—attempt of Plotinus to establish Platonopolis. St. Augustine's city of God is still some distance from Hippo. Boethius' diplomatic success ended with his execution. After the Middle Ages philosophers expanded their worldly pretensions but mostly they had little to show for them. Leibniz meddled in European politics, but he was left at home when his master became king of England. Hobbes frightened both the roundheads and the cavaliers in the English revolution. Locke eventually found it prudent to live in Holland. Hume held minor offices but he found them scarcely profitable and not very edifying. Hegel trifled in constitution-making without much success. In our own time, the record is even less promising: Alfred Rosenberg may not have been a philosopher at all, but he was hanged for being a bad one. Gentile seems, in incredible innocence, to have become Mussolini's minister of education—an office he resigned two years later. Heidegger recoiled from his political friends—but not soon enough.

Philosophers, of course, *have* been successful in influencing the course of events. The American constitution might almost have been written by John Locke. Marx and Engels share the praise and blame for much that goes on in the world though they are frequently damned for what they themselves would have praised and praised for what must have been distant from their minds. Here and there the philosopher as king has almost emerged. It is only convention that prevents Thomas Jefferson from being wholly accepted as a philosopher. Nicholas of Cusa, while recognized as a philosopher, was an efficient and powerful church diplomat. Mostly, however, these philosophers who have come close to power have struck sorry figures. Against the background of such a record, modest success is worth studying.

Jacob Gould Schurman could at least claim that. A Maritimer, Schurman went to the United States in his early thirties. He quickly became President of Cornell University and went on, after the Spanish-American War, to become President of the Philippine Commission. Still later, he became an important figure in the New York Republican Party, and United States Ambassador to Greece and Macedonia, China and Germany. The eighty-eight years of his life span a period beginning during the reign of Queen Victoria and ending during World War II. He was in the Philippines when Americans first began to wrestle with the problem of imperialism. He was in the Balkans to watch the façade cracking on Pax Britannica. He dined with Hitler and learned to detest him at first hand. He was influenced by the main course of American thought and he exercised, in his turn, a perceptible influence on American policy.

Schurman was born in Prince Edward Island in 1854. He studied first at Prince of Wales College and then moved to the mainland to Acadia University. Upon graduation, he went to England to the University of London where he stood first in the examinations for the B.A. degree in 1877 and then went on to a Master's degree in 1878. He won a fellowship which enabled him to travel for two years and he spent the time in London, Paris, and Edinburgh. When it ended, he was offered a teaching post at Acadia. Two years later he was offered the Chair of English and Philosophy at Dalhousie.

While he was at Acadia he had published his first book, *Kantian Ethics and the Ethics of Evolution*.[1] It attracted some attention and Andrew White, the first president of Cornell, sought him out. Schurman met with White and Ezra Cornell's son, Alonzo, in New York and was offered the Chair of Philosophy at Cornell in 1885.

His scholarly reputation seemed to be secured with the publication, in 1887, of his second book, *The Ethical Import of Darwinism*.[2] William James, Martineau, and McCosh wrote to him praising it.

When the presidency of Cornell fell vacant in 1892, Schurman was the unanimous choice of the trustees. He held the office for twenty-eight years and even then, his resignation, as a fat file of letters testifies, produced almost consternation. Though it would hardly seem unusual for a man to retire as his sixty-fifth birthday was approaching, Schurman, in fact, resigned the presidency of Cornell only because his political and diplomatic career demanded it.

1   Jacob Gould Schurman, *Kantian Ethics and the Ethics of Evolution* (London: Williams & Norgate for the Hibbert Trustees, 1881).
2   Jacob Gould Schurman, *The Ethical Import of Darwinism* (New York: Charles Scribner's Sons, 1887).

His friendship with the Cornell family introduced him to the larger world of politics, especially Republican politics. When, in 1899, the United States faced the problem of determining a future for the Philippines, Schurman was appointed president of the commission established by the President to make recommendations about that future. The task was to lead to a thirty-year involvement in the affairs of the Philippines and in the frequently significant quarrel between those Americans who had developed imperial ambitions and those who believed, as Schurman himself did, that American involvement in other peoples' affairs should be as brief as possible.

He remained, however, mainly on the Cornell campus for another decade until he was appointed U.S. Ambassador to Greece and Macedonia. World War I saw him back in Cornell again, but scarcely out of political life. In 1917, he was Vice-President of the New York State Constitutional Commission.

By the end of the war, he had decided to give up the presidency of Cornell and he did so on what seemed the first feasible occasion. Through the twenties and early thirties he pursued his diplomatic career as Ambassador to China and Germany and as a frequent advisor to Presidents and to the State Department.

He was nearly eighty when, in some more serious sense, he retired—but he retired to live in Washington where his voice continued to be heard almost until his death in 1942 at the age of eighty-eight.

The early years in Canada and in England and the beginning of his career at Cornell were wholly devoted to scholarship. In philosophy, he was, like Murray, edging his way toward a kind of idealism. He could not accept the evolutionists' attempt to reduce morality to the conditions for survival. He continued to insist that the basis of value did not lie in the realm of scientific fact. But he was impressed by the metaphysical implications—as he thought of them—of the theory of evolution, and he became increasingly concerned with the necessity for construing reality as a developing process which had a place in it for novelty. Even more strongly, he was convinced that the implied new view of the universe had serious consequences for theology.

In Schurman's philosophical writings there is a strong sense of the conflict of ideas—an urge to hang on to much that was traditional in moral theory, in metaphysics, and in theology combined with the feeling that these ideas were being challenged, and that they required development as a result, at least, of the new perspectives which the biological sciences were providing.

Schurman does not doubt that a synthesis of the new and traditional views is possible but he is clear that there is a challenge to which he must respond. He does not have the detached certainty with which Beaven responded to the first flurry of interest in the theory of evolution. He is not, like Lyall, a man whose intellectual problems were created from within the history of philosophy and could be met by the creation of an effective synthesis of ideas already available. Nor is he, like Paxton Young, a man whose insights were illumined by clashes within his own culture. Finally, he lacks Murray's supreme self-confidence. The arguments in Schurman's books are, invariably, tortuous and laboured. He is a man facing what he knows to be a difficult set of problems.

It is useful to remind ourselves of some of the background of Schurman's problems. The particular shock which the theory of evolution created in its impact on current belief stemmed from the notion that men are the product of a long natural process by which, in Darwin's view, the forms of living organisms were created by a process of natural selection and adaptation to the environment. Until the nineteenth century most thoughtful religious believers took it for granted that the world disclosed by scientific investigation could be accommodated to the design argument for the existence of God. Though nature might seem impersonal, distant, mechanical, and capable of sustaining itself without divine intervention, it could all be regarded as an elaborate set of stage props for the celestial drama. But, for that drama to make sense, it had to be accepted that God produced man as a special creation—that he put man on the stage in order to fulfill his own purposes.

To an important extent, the development of classical mechanics from the fifteenth century onwards, tended to support this view. For, just by the manner in which physics and astronomy developed, the distinction between the inanimate world and the world of living things was accentuated. Everything in inanimate nature was neat, tidy, and susceptible of an immediate explanation. It was all consistent with the activity of a deity who had thought it out with care, implemented his plan with precision, and created exactly the stage he wanted for his drama. By contrast, living things appeared inexplicable by simple mechanical means, were capable of independent and arbitrary action, and were somehow set apart from the rest of nature. To be sure, important writers, including Hobbes, had suggested that mechanical explanation could be extended to include the domain of living things and even to include man himself. But this remained unconvincing as an abstract theory. At a very immediate level, human physiology appeared to resist effective scientific inquiry and medicine remained remarkably primitive well into the nineteenth century. The biological sciences remained, for the most part, mere exercises in description and classification. If anything, these elaborate classifications (classifications which continued to dominate structural biology well into the twentieth century) only increased the impression of divine activity. For, as the forms of life came to be explored and classified, they seemed to represent something like the great chain of being, an array of properties ordered so as to achieve in the world the instantiation of the divine attributes.

The theory of evolution struck a serious blow to the body of traditional belief. It struck two vital organs. Man could no longer be thought of as a deliberate creation of God. Moral belief must find a new base.

The first issue can best be put this way: If the appearance of man on earth was left to the chance of natural selection, if man was the product of animal forces competing violently for regions of the environment, if man could be explained merely by the occurrence of the amoeba together with the natural environment, then it would appear, at best, that God had chosen a tortuous route to the attainment of his aims. Surely such a sloppy inefficiency was inconsistent with the very existence of God. Even worse, if there were a God who had arranged things this way, then there would have been no reason to believe that man was the apex of natural attainment. God might well have in mind the production of a superior species and might regard man only as a way-stage on his route. If evolution had been going on for millions of years, surely there was no reason to think that it would stop now.

Such a view also cast grave doubts on the claims of human beings to be able to know and understand their universe. So long as it was supposed that man was the special and deliberate creation of God, it could be supposed, with equal likelihood, that God would have created man with a mind capable of understanding the universe—capable, at least, of understanding enough of the universe so as to be able to manage his own affairs, discover the divine will, and attend to the matters necessary for his own salvation. But, suppose that man was not a deliberate and special creation. Then, it might well be the case that our minds, themselves merely the product of biological evolution, would fail disastrously outside the realm of what was necessary for their own biological survival. Not only might many things be closed to us just as much of the world is, presumably, closed to the amoeba, but we might distort reality in our attempts to know it simply because we had wholly inadequate and inferior equipment. Thus, our concepts of God, our notions of salvation, our dreams of the eternal status of men, might all be simply part of our evolutionary adaptation to our environment. The species which came to replace us might regard us with as little concern as we regard the mosquito. Indeed, even if there were a God, such a God might feel no more concern for us than we feel for the ants we accidentally tread upon at a picnic.

In short, the whole of man's image of himself along with the whole of his certainty and satisfaction in his religious belief was, somehow, at stake. Christianity, at least, became very much less plausible when one came to see the significance of the theory of evolution. The challenge was real and serious.

But that wasn't all. The thing that men in their most reflective moments had prided themselves most upon was moral theory. No other creature appears to moralize. Tigers behave like tigers and are not praised or blamed. Wolves are much more charming creatures than mythology would have us believe, but it is not because they have well-developed moral theories but because they have well-developed inherited and instinctual patterns of behaviour. Only men are expected to hold their natural inclinations in check, to behave well not because it is profitable but because it is good, and to act coherently from principle rather than from instinct.

So long as it was possible to maintain a satisfactory schism between life and inanimate nature, the question of whether one should act with or against nature simply did not arise. Nature was the neutral stage on which the play took place. That separation was the work of modern science and, perhaps, the conceit of modern technology. But, in earlier times, at least throughout the Christian era, the unity of man and nature was conceived as a unity of intelligible purpose. Man and nature in the cosmology of St. Augustine, for example, were thought to be equally animated by the natural love of God. Men might set their hearts and minds against that force, but nature was part of the providential conspiracy to bring them back to the light. The situation posed by the theory of evolution had its counterparts in ancient times, of course, but even then, the challenges were not quite the same. The Greek atomists, Democritus and Leucippus, imagined the world as composed of material atoms in a void. Democritus apparently envisaged the movement of the atoms as entirely random. His best advice to men, the victims of an illusion which made them think that they were more than momentary concatenations of material particles, was "Be cheerful." Epicurus embellished this theory (without improving it much) and it lasted into classical times in the poetic hexameters of Lucretius. But these were theories, tied loosely to prevailing outlooks on the world, and often in a context in which there were many options. They expressed one version of the quite central Greek feeling that men were the victims of fate and became tragic heroes or comic figures when they rebelled against their fate.

By late in the nineteenth century, the theory of evolution was offered in a context which was part and parcel of the prevailing scientific outlook. In the name of science, men claimed to *know* that man was merely a by-product of nature. More than that, the details of the story and the structure of the Darwinian explanation tended not only to reinforce the point but also to leave the strong suggestion that nature, itself, could not be regarded as an orderly and planned structure.

The notion fired the imaginations of various thinkers and some of them, to be sure, attempted to put it to use in finding deeper, grander, and ever more providential plots in the history of the world. Some people were tempted to see the evolutionary process, in these terms, as a linear series of events which moved from primitive and undeveloped forms of life to the ultimate achievement in adaptability: man. But the gradually unfolding facts did not quite suggest that. In those terms, it turned out, there was regress as well as progress and there was colossal waste in the form of very highly developed species. For the optimists forgot that there were at least two dimensions involved. One can survive by having elaborate strategies and great adaptability, but one can also survive by having so simple a mechanism as to be suitable to almost any environment and by having the ability to fill the available space with great rapidity. The successful, in short, include the virus as well as man. Indeed, where man survives through an ability to convert hostile environments into friendly ones—by being able to clothe himself, heat his houses, use other animals to turn nondigestible food stuffs into digestible ones, and even take oxygen tanks to the tops of high mountains—some very simple organisms survive by having a structure to which hardly any environment is fatally hostile. They may even be able to survive freezing, boiling, ejection into outer space, and long immersion in beer-vats. The more complex organism can readily be the victim of a very slight miscalculation. It can think its way into booby traps as well as out of hostility. The simple organism need only rely on the low probability of obliteration. Furthermore, complex organisms compete with each other and even try, as we all know, to contrive environments in which other organisms of the same kind must necessarily perish. Men radiate each other, burn each other alive with jellied gasoline, defoliate one another's forests, and grow rich by polluting the air which similar organisms must breathe. The virus is content to occupy its own bit of the environment.

Does anyone now doubt that it is quite likely that the virus will survive man? And does anyone doubt that that likelihood is higher than the likelihood that man, himself, will be replaced by a still cleverer and more complex organism?

Now Schurman came into this story, as it were, when the news was still fairly fresh from the front. The word was out that man had been dethroned from his pedestal. If one could laugh at Hobbes's view that man was "matter in motion," one could not laugh so easily at the new reports. The optimists who sought to put the new news to clever uses which would still preserve the more basic notions of human dignity were, most often, simply made to look silly. It was genuinely hard to imagine that God contrived a world in this curious and complex way and designed it so as to have such a low probability of any desirable outcome.

Faced with this situation Schurman attempts to understand the accumulated facts in terms of a larger framework which will render them intelligible. His philosophical books were all published within a span of fifteen years from 1881 to 1896. They gradually reveal and give structure to his response.

His concern in the first two of these books was, largely, to free moral inquiry from the constraints of misunderstandings about the significance of the facts of evolution and, at the same time, to give appropriate scope to the notion that one cannot regard either man or morality as having been created instantly and all of one piece.

Throughout, Schurman is addressing himself to an audience which has, in his mind at least, quite precise characteristics. It consists of people troubled by Darwin, likely to have been worried by Spencer, and educated in a way which made Kant the central focus of modern philosophy.

In a way, this is curious. It is not surprising that large segments of Maritime society should find Kantian morality and the Kantian mixture of rationalism and attention to experience attractive, though the evidence we have does not suggest very strongly that Kant played anything like a dominant role in college curricula of the period. More surprising is the suggestion in Schurman, and after him in Watson, that Herbert Spencer is the most significant intellectual opponent of the hour. Neither man had a high opinion of Spencer as a thinker, though both treated him with a measure of respect and took seriously his attempts to integrate the findings of evolutionary thought into a philosophical schema. In Canada, so far as we can tell, Spencerians were very few and far between. In the United States, "social Darwinism"—a set of doctrines which certainly derived strength from

Spencer—had a vogue, but it was an on-and-off thing not unlike the flurry of rather sceptical attention that, in recent years, attended the writings of Marshall McLuhan. In England, Spencer served as a centre of debate rather than as a master to be followed.

It certainly must have been true that Spencer had his followers in Canada. One of the present authors attended a school in British Columbia named after him—though it seems doubtful that those who named it had thought out and worked through carefully the Spencerian conclusion on the education of the poor and the weak. (It was, after all, a school provided through public taxes.)

The nearest thing to a Spencerian amongst serious thinkers in Canada seems to have been W. D. LeSueur. LeSueur was a civil servant—long the secretary of the Post Office Department in Ottawa—as well as an historian, literary critic, and President of the Royal Society of Canada. His works included biographies of Frontenac and Mackenzie.

LeSueur was a sceptical, careful, and civilized man. Born in Quebec in 1840, educated first in Montreal and then at the University of Toronto, he remained a rather charming example of bi-culturalism at its best and became, philosophically, something of a disciple of Auguste Comte and, in literature, an expert on Ste. Beuve.

He would have nothing of Spencer's metaphysics of the "unknowable" but he was equally sceptical about materialism and idealism. The former he doubted as a metaphysics because it went beyond the evidence of immediate experience. The latter he doubted because it tidied the world in a way which made him dubious and because he thought it likely to enlist reason in the service of fiction. He understood the kind of idealism—represented in most of the Canadian idealists—which sought not to make the world an internal feature of our own experience but, rather, to dissolve the subject-object distinction. He simply believed that the evidence would not sustain such notions. Materialism seemed to him, as well, to have moral defects—its narrowed focus created a perspective which might well lead to bad moral decision making. All this he stated with care and precision in a paper called "Materialism and Positivism" published in 1882 in *Popular Science Monthly*.

Spencer's ethics, however, in the form in which it appeared in *The Data of Ethics* seemed to him more defensible, at least in part. In a paper published in *Rose-Belford's Canadian Monthly* in 1880 and reprinted the same year in *Popular Science Monthly*, he takes on Spencer's critics. The original and neutral title "Mr. Spencer and His Critics" became "A Vindication of Scientific Ethics" in *Popular Science Monthly*—a small sign, perhaps, of the difference between Canadian and American culture. In it, LeSueur makes a number of simple points: Ethics has a history; moral beliefs change and they change in response to other factors and not independently of everything else. He seems to hold that we can create moral theories, but not moral beliefs. Moral beliefs can be clarified and re-enforced but it would be foolish to attempt to create them without the appropriate social conditions. We can also see that the history of moral beliefs reveals something of what it is that allows societies to survive. In this sense, there can be a "scientific ethics" and that science, one may hope, will devote itself to two tasks: the delineation of the history of morality and the discovery of the principles which both bring about changes in moral outlook and determine what moral beliefs are efficacious for civilization.

LeSueur will, however, evidently have nothing to do with the individualism which characterized Spencer in at least some of his moods. True freedom, LeSueur argues, is the rational subjection of the individual to law. Excessive individualism makes decision making impossible. Only co-operation in an organic society can bring about survival and sustain civilization.

He admits that it can be argued that no one will accept a morality for which the only reasons that can be given are reasons deriving from an evolutionary story. But he urges that the revelations of scientific ethics work on belief "in a different way" than do those of traditional theories. Scientific ethics appeal to reason and prudence. Buried and unexpressed in his essay, however, is the notion that there is a direction to moral development and that some societies are better than others. The best ideas sustain the existence of what we (not LeSueur) called "civilization" in the paragraph above. And this suggests a different basis for values.

LeSueur never wrote a major philosophical work. His few philosophical essays, consequently, remain a source both of interest and frustration. They continue to fascinate because they show a good, questioning, ultimately sceptical, mind at work. But they are frustrating because we do not know how he would have elaborated his position or answered the obvious questions.

Would he have chosen a metaphysics on moral grounds—the grounds on which he rejects materialism? Or would he have remained a positivist? (His essay on positivism is always couched in the third person; he never really commits *himself*.) Would he have found additional "sources" for the validation of value judgments? We simply do not know.

Perhaps, however, it is fair to think of Schurman as having some-one not too unlike LeSueur for his intended audience—someone who accepted part of Spencer, questioned the rest, was open-minded but needed hard and firm arguments. Let us see how Schurman fares.

Schurman begins, essentially, by trying to establish the autonomy of ethics. He argues, in what is now a thoroughly familiar mode, that one cannot finally derive ethical conclusions from premises which have no ethical component. It does not follow, in short, that because evolution has proceeded by the selection of the fittest in a natural competition, that the "fittest" in the sense implied are those who deserve to survive. Thus one cannot conclude, as Herbert Spencer seems to have concluded, that it would somehow be wrong to impede this process. (Spencer, at least at times, really believed that social processes deliberately designed to protect the weak were in fact wrong because they inhibited the selection of the fittest. Spencer even opposed public libraries.) There is nothing in the facts which would compel us to the opinion that later and more involved species, or later and more involved civilizations, were really "better" than their predecessors. Schurman thought that all such views were essentially pernicious and, though he is not entirely immune from the common Victorian feeling that man was "progressing" inevitably and was destined for some wholly desirable end, he is concerned to undermine the smug self-satisfaction which went along with that view.

Somehow, he claims, one must have the basic knowledge of the good in its own right if one is to come to any conclusions about morality and right conduct in general. Otherwise one is merely expressing one's preferences for one state of affairs rather than another.

He begins by seeking this conclusion in the writings of Kant. Those writings are the natural place to begin such an argument, for the *Fundamentals of the Metaphysics of Morals*[3] is the classical source of one version of the doctrine of the autonomy of morals. Kant begins his inquiry by asking what sorts of things might be called good in an unqualified sense. His answer is that none of the usual things that men at once think of are good in that sense. Power is only good—if it is ever good at all—in the hands of good men. Money is evil in the hands of villains. Intelligence is a thing we would like to have but a thing we would prefer bank robbers to be without. Even happiness is only good in its appropriate context. It is not good, after all, to be happy while watching one's best friend incinerated. The only thing, he says, which is good in itself and without qualification is the good will. The good will is

3   Immanuel Kant, *Fundamentals of the Metaphysics of Morals*, trans. Otto Mantney-Zorn (New York: D. Appleton-Century, 1938; first published in 1785).

not just that intention (with which, it is said, the road to hell is paved). Rather, it is that fixed determination which results in action.

But what constitutes the good will? Kant gives various answers all of which are related to each other. His first and most famous character-ization of the answer is the rule that the formula of the good will is "Always act on that maxim, the universality of which you can also will to be that of the law."[4] His second and more illuminating answer is that the good will is exhibited in the acts of those who act always so as to treat themselves and all other rational beings as ends in themselves and never merely as means. He elaborates this notion of a "kindgom of ends"—a society of men each of whom is an end in himself and is treated as such. Kant's final formulation, therefore, urges that good will is exhibited in the acts of those who act always in a manner which is appropriate to membership in the kingdom of ends.

What Kant is saying is this: Men differ from one another in very many ways. Some are intelligent and others stupid, some are strong and others weak, some have amazing and surprising talents and others appear quite unable to do anything out of the ordinary. But, if the only thing which is good in itself, and without qualification, is the good will, then, when we consider them as moral agents, men do not differ from one another. The will, the source of morality, is the same for all men. Hence, whatever moral rules there are, they are perfectly general. If I authorize myself to perform some act, I must authorize all other men to do so equally. It is this which gives rise to the "universalization" princi-ple. Equally, all men stand together as the source of morality. There is, therefore, no excuse for one person's using another as a *mere* means to his own ends. (Of course we all, all of the time, must use other people as means to our own ends. The prohibition is not against that but against using them "merely" as means. Whenever I use another person as a means, I must, at the same time, seek to advance his own ends.)

Now, in a sense, these are purely formal requirements. They state, as it were, the logic of morality. Schurman, like most philosophers, read and understood Kant's ethical views mainly in terms of the *Fun-damentals* and understood the *Fundamentals* itself mainly in the light of the statements which appeared at the beginning of that work. It seemed to him, therefore, that, though Kant had done yeoman work in establishing the autonomy of morals, and to a degree, the logic of morality, he had failed to complete the task because purely formal considerations are not enough. This becomes fairly obvious if one tries to apply the rules. If I ask which acts I can will to become "universal laws," I at once run into the problem of the level of generalization.

4   Ibid., p. 55.

Suppose, as someone once suggested to Kant, I am accosted by a madman bent on murder who asks whether I have a knife. If I say "no," how do I describe the act? If I describe it as "telling a lie," then it is clearly wrong for I cannot will a proposition of the form "all men always ought to tell lies." For such a rule would make communication among men impossible and undermine all of the conditions for morality. When Kant was asked if lying is ever right, he replied that lying is never right. But that left unanswered the more interesting question: Should I describe the act concerned as telling a lie? That is not, at any rate, its *complete* description. For I am also engaged, presumably, in trying to cope with a lunatic in some humane way. To tell him that I do have a knife might be an act which I would describe as "leading a lunatic on to murder." It is, surely, equally obvious that leading lunatics on to murder is wrong and Kant would have said that too. The problem is that, if one chooses the very abstract level of description, there are many descriptions available. If one chooses a very concrete description, it may be difficult to relate the act to any general moral principle at all.

There are other difficulties, too, which interested Schurman and men like him, when they came to re-examine Kant in the light of the new crisis. For instance, I can only will those acts of which I can conceive and what is conceivable varies from time to time, culture to culture, and from person to person depending upon the state of his knowledge and mental development. In the most obvious way, a professional military strategist, faced with a difficult situation, might well be able to contrive a way out of it which would result in no loss of life while an ordinary citizen, suddenly faced with the same decision, might only be able to conceive of solutions which were extremely bloody. Yet, if morality is the same for all men and the right act for me is the right act for you, should we fault the citizen if he chooses the best solution he can conceive of? In writing history, we are apt to fault the Greeks for not conceiving of effective notions of a unified alliance of city-states. Yet, given their background and the range of current ideas, it was almost beyond practicality to conceive of a single constitutional practice which would be fit to govern both Spartans and Athenians.

Now it may well be that all such criticisms of Kant represent serious misunderstandings. What Schurman does, in fact, is to apply Kant's doctrines from the *Critique of Pure Reason* to Kant's ethical writings and accuse him of having failed to grasp the extended significance of his own point. In the *Critique of Pure Reason*, Kant distinguished between the structural features of experience—the framework of space and time and the categories of organization and explanation—which, he thought, were the necessary foundation of human thought and the same for all men, and the content of experience (what he called intuition) which is particular. He argued that one could not derive an account of the structure of reality merely from an account of the structural features of experience and that these structures were not, themselves, really genuine objects of knowledge at all.

Schurman claims that, by parity of reasoning, the formal structure of moral theory does not yield any specific knowledge of moral practice. It must be combined with experience in order to give it force. He argues, indeed, at one point, that such experiences would have to be of a very specific kind in order to give the appropriate force to the outcome: ". . . if speculation in the guise of moral philosophy takes up the problem, it will find that the domestic virtues have the same warrant as justice or benevolence—that warrant being, in a last analysis, an inexpugnable consciousness of their right to us and authority over us."[5]

What Schurman seems to be suggesting is that there are experiences which might well count as direct cognitions of moral particulars. The examples may be somewhat difficult to cope with. The "domestic virtues" about which he is talking in this chapter are those associated with the maintenance of the family and of marital relations in what is essentially a Christian tradition. They are particular ways of organizing a special class of interpersonal relations. Justice, traditionally, is a relation of proportion which has to do with values in distribution and the appropriateness of responses to acts which exhibit merit or the lack of it. Benevolence is a sentiment which entails a disposition to act generously toward others. The quoted passage, therefore, involves a number of issues which lie on different levels not all of which seem equally appropriate to a consciousness of right.

A little thought, however, seems to indicate fairly clearly what Schurman has in mind. If you find fault with someone because he fails to perform some specific duty such as paying his income tax, you would expect, if challenged, to offer reasons for your judgment. The reasons might well be "Kantian" in kind: You might argue that paying one's income tax is necessarily a universal obligation and that, unless one held the absurd position that no community was worth maintaining, he could not consistently will that everyone should always fail to pay his income tax. (One might will that at some particular time—for instance when one's community is engaged in a wicked war—it would be desirable if everyone failed to pay his income tax. But one could not argue that it ought to be a universal rule.) This argument would not suffice to make that case against any specific instance in which someone refused

5   Schurman, *The Ethical Import of Darwinism*, p. 264.

to pay his income tax. At least one other premise would be required. That other premise might be that the society in question was sufficiently benevolent to justify its continuance. But suppose one offered that other premise and met the surprising rejoinder: What makes you think that benevolence is good? At this point one could only urge that no one would ask that question except in the context of the kind of philosophical debate which consists of the picking of nits. It is simply characteristic of moral experience that we know perfectly well that benevolence is good and desirable and anyone who sets out, deliberately, not to be benevolent must be morally blind.

It seems simply to be Schurman's view that, whenever one gets into a moral argument, the argument will involve at least one premise of this kind. It is not clear, of course, that the situation would work equally well for the other examples which Schurman cites. One who says "Justice is bad" is, surely, at least as perverse as one who says "Benevolence is bad." But the situation is not the same. Justice is a property of rather large-scale systems. If I am charged with making a just distribution of the community's supply of fish, and you come by and see that I am giving Smith two ounces of fish, you can't tell from inspecting that act whether I am actually making a just distribution or not. Whether or not two ounces is a just portion will depend upon how much fish we have, how much preference we have to give to the active and hardworking members of the community in order to keep them supplied with sufficient protein to insure the survival of all of us, what arrangements we have for storing fish to meet future emergencies and so on. Furthermore, in order to give any concrete meaning to justice, one will have had to determine whether principles of the form "equal shares for all" are more or less just than principles of the form "equal pay for equal work." The explication of justice may well involve exactly the giving and taking of reasons of just the sort which comprise the Kantian ethic. It may well still be the case that the explication of justice will ultimately involve reference to some principle which can only be seen to be right as the result of a direct moral cognition. But it does not seem that all of the problems associated with justice consist of the kinds of issues which might be settled by the direct cognition of moral particulars.

Justice differs from benevolence in that one would certainly expect to give reasons for a particular delineation or explication of the concept of justice in a way that would not be appropriate in defence of the view that benevolence is good. Perhaps, however, one should notice that the case about benevolence is not *entirely* open and shut either. Part of the difficulty is that benevolence is associated with goodness in such a way that it would be difficult to hold that benevolence was bad without landing in the logical contradiction which faces one who says that goodness is bad. Of course, goodness is good. The question is: What does it consist of? Similarly, benevolence is good but the question remains: How do we tell which acts are benevolent? Those acts are benevolent which are motivated by thoughtful concern for others and an overall disposition to generosity. Suppose I am a brain surgeon and I think you have a tumour of the left parietal lobe. I want to excise it. But you prefer to remain as you are. I come along while you are asleep, inject you with an anaesthetic, and go ahead with the operation. Is my act benevolent? It is surely motivated by the appropriate concern for others and by some generosity on my part. For I can hardly expect that you will later pay your bill. On the other hand, it shows very little concern for your fundamental human rights, your dignity as an individual, and your own expressed desires.

Perhaps this example simply shows the desirability of combining appeals to direct moral experience with appeals to a Kantian rationality. The act is benevolent but bad. Yet that does not make benevolence bad. It means that benevolence must be combined with the demands of the categorical imperative. Or so, at any rate, it seems that Schurman would have argued.

We might go on for some time exploring the hypothetical details of a moral system which Schurman really sketched only in outline. But we have pursued the matter far enough to be able to return, with some semblance of rational understanding, to the issue in the context in which Schurman himself wanted to raise it. Schurman's problem, after all, was to show that morality had its own foundations. That meant that he wanted to show first of all that moral claims were not merely arbitrary; secondly that they did not derive from purely scientific contentions; and, most importantly, that the truth of the theory of evolution did not influence them directly. For these purposes, a straightforwardly Kantian rationality would have sufficed. But Schurman was also grappling with the historical consciousness which had been growing consistently and continuously throughout the nineteenth century. The theory of evolution only added force to a view which had been growing long before Darwin, the view that human nature is not internally fixed and static and that human beings do change over time. Since they change over time, it does not follow, in every sense, that morality will remain constant throughout time. This change, whatever it amounts to, is inconsistent with a pure Kantian rationalism.

It seems that what Schurman wanted to come to grips with, therefore, was essentially this question: Given that, in a substantial sense, moral truth is constant, how can we account for the fact that a given act is not always right or wrong at every place and every time? Had he been willing to abandon his objectivist moral convictions and the whole of Kantian rationality, he might, as many philosophers in the nineteenth century did, have succumbed to another equally simple view—historicist relativism. But this, too, seemed to him to fly in the face of the facts. facts.

In terms of our elaboration of the examples Schurman used, we can see how he works his way out. First of all, there is more than one source of morality. Reason gives us the formal properties of morality. It tells us that moral rules are general and bind one man as well as the next. But this does not tell us what to do. Experience gives us a direct acquaintance with certain moral properties. We know, for instance, that benevolence is good. But this does not tell us what to do either. For the fact that an act is a benevolent act does not necessarily make it, as we have seen, a good act. Benevolent acts must be brought under the formal rubrics of a rational morality.

If we put these requirements together, we get, at least, a more complete theory. Reason tells us what to look for. But experience may not yet have revealed to us all of the value properties of the world, or it may be that our social, our political, and our aesthetic situations leave us blind to some states of affairs. Thus, while the basic values need no justification—if they were in need of justification they would not be basic—it remains true that knowledge of them, by themselves, will not always tell us how to act. A value system, in short, can grow through the interplay of reason and experience. We may be able to grasp the difference, as well, between two acts which instantiate the same fundamental value without, thereby, both becoming good. Imposing brain surgery on one who is not able to make clear his own desires may well be a benevolent act which is also good. Imposing brain surgery on one who is both rational and conscious and has expressed his opposition to it, may be benevolent but bad. The difference has to do with Kant's principle that rational beings should be treated as ends in themselves. In the larger sense, we may be able to distinguish between acts which are acceptable in a highly individualistic society but not acceptable in a highly communitarian one. In the former the act of making a profit at the expense of others may not be reprehensible, since the system may operate on the assumption that such acts are a motive for increasing productivity and may have made provision for the amelioration of the worst consequences of such acts. In a highly communitarian society, on the other hand, such an act might amount to taking unfair advantage of others and might have disastrous social consequences. If such a case were made, it would seem, on Schurman's view, that the distinction amounted to different appreciations of basic values in the two societies and a different context created by the relative unawareness of each of the values of the other. With time, experience might well change the reaction in each of these societies. As this change took place, acts formally regarded as acceptable might well come to be seen as wrong.

Schurman, however, is not invariably clear about this situation. His remarks in defence of the essentially Christian notion of the family and marriage suggest that it is simply and always wrong to conduct one's personal relations with the opposite sex on any basis other than the one which conventional Christian morality prescribes. Such views are ambiguous. If we go back to our previous example, we can see what this ambiguity consists of. Imagine, again, our two societies, the one individualist and the other communitarian—one consistently aware of the values of individual self-realization and the other consistently aware of the values of the community considered as an entity in itself. And let us imagine that our individualists come to understand the value of community and, thereby, set limits to the range of individual action which are somewhat narrower than those which they established before. (They begin, for instance, to pass legislation governing the exploitation of the environment, to pass anti-trust laws to regulate private and corporate profits, and so on. At the same time, our communitarian society becomes rather more aware of the importance of the individuals. It provides public support for artistic enterprises which do not represent the most popular taste, it provides more options in education, and it adopts many standards for judging private acts which do not depend, solely, on considerations about the good of the community.) In each community, as the awareness of additional values grows, it will come to be seen that acts which were formerly thought to be acceptable are, in fact, wrong. In one obvious sense, the acts which now seem to be wrong were always wrong. That is simply the sense in which the values might be said to be discovered and not simply invented. In another sense, it would be foolish for historians in the latter days of each of these societies to describe the acts which took place earlier as "wrong acts." For, without whatever experience it was which brought the new values to the attention of the members of those societies, they could not possibly, on Schurman's view, have known the acts in question to be wrong. For his view is that pure reason will not, by itself, tell us what is right or wrong. The Kantian rationality must necessarily be supplemented by moral experience of the kind which gives us direct acquaintance with values. Thus, if we have now learned the virtue of the Christian notion of marriage, we are entitled to urge that it was always the case that Christian marriage represented the most virtuous situation. But this would not entitle us to believe that the marital arrangements of assorted Melanesian Islanders were wrong. In order to be able to pass any judgment upon their practices, we would have to bring to their attention whatever experiences are relevant, unless the case was one of those which followed simply from the formal properties of moral arrangements as such.

In *Kantian Ethics and the Ethics of Evolution*, Schurman develops the outlines of a theory of the state which is intended to help with this understanding. Moral propositions involve a frame of reference—a community to which they may be supposed to be relevant. Thus a man in a right-wing despotism may have to tell lies about the whereabouts of his Communist friends though he knows that truth telling is a required moral activity. What this tells him is that his community is in need of reform—the principle holds but cannot be applied in his society. Later in his work as a diplomat and in his historical investigations, Schurman was to encounter, again, the need to develop this theory of the state—in order to assess the claims of nationalism in the Philippines, in the Balkans, and in Europe after World War I and in order to cope with the moral problems of the unfolding twentieth century. A theory can be pieced together, though it is a task beyond the scope of this book, but he was never able to find the time to put it together himself in the form of a philosophical study.

In *Agnosticism and Religion* he shows no doubt about the function of philosophy. He speaks of its "divine mission" and that divine mission is to "redeem us" from "immersion in sense and matter."[6] The question which it poses for him is how this redemption is to take place. Schurman's strategy is to examine, first, the nature of knowledge. What he wants to show, actually, is that knowledge itself cannot be understood in terms of the mechanical behaviour of matter or in terms of the immediacy of sensation. He thus wants to attack at once two positions which are both inimical to his project and which are, seemingly, supported by the theorizings of nineteenth-century biologists and physicists. Classical, mechanical materialism would seem to receive substantial support from nineteenth-century physics which sought to explain every phenomenon in terms of perfectly regular physical laws which operate upon material particles. The theory of evolution seems to

6   Jacob Gould Schurman, *Agnosticism and Religion* (New York: Charles Scribner's Sons, 1896), p. 90. Schurman's most important point is made on p. 107: "The consciousness of God is the logical *prius* of the consciousness of self. . . ." He repeatedly exploits the notion of a *divine prius*.

strengthen this position by making it possible to hold that life, itself, had developed, over time, from inert material states. The "sensationalist" position represented an alternative to this materialist scheme, one equally consistent with the evidence and equally inconsistent with Schurman's position. On the sensationalist view, we are only aware of our own sensations. We infer the "material world" from those sensations. The laws of physics, on this view, can be regarded as simply statistical correlations between sensation components which figure in the observations of those who propose the laws. Again, nineteenth-century physics generally purported to be empirical. It purported to derive its theoretical conclusions from actual observations. Insofar as it could be regarded as successful in this, it lent as much support to the sensationalist position as to the materialist position. If biological theories such as the theories of evolution could be integrated with the appropriate theories in physics, then they, too, could be regarded as lending support to the same thesis. Neither of these theories seemed satisfactory to Schurman. Nor did any possible combination of them. For neither lent any support to the existence of God or to the traditional religious verities and both tended to cast doubt on the kind of moral theory which Schurman wanted to support. (If the world consists only of material objects or only of sensations or of some combination of the two, it is difficult to see how the world can have room for God. Even Berkeley's God is, like us, a spiritual substance and not a mere conglomerate of sensations. It hardly needs to be said that it is somehow absurd to think of God as an accumulation of material objects.)

Schurman's first attack is on the notion that knowledge is, itself, mechanical. While we may obtain information from machines which record and organize data, knowing does not take place in the machine but in us. The dials on the machine can be read but they must be understood and assigned meanings before we count the outcome as knowledge. If knowledge merely consisted of the rearrangement of material particles, whether in machines or in our brains, it would simply be another state of affairs in the world—an object of knowledge rather than knowledge itself.

Equally, knowledge demands that we go beyond sensation. For knowledge requires classification and classification demands something more than sensation. For sensation to yield knowledge it must be seen as organized, but sensations do not carry with them their own organizing principles and labels. (Schurman's argument, here, bears some resemblance to arguments used by John Clark Murray.) These classifications might, of course, be arbitrary. But then they are simply something which we do to sensations for our own convenience. But in that case, we would not count the outcome as knowledge. Schurman is not inclined to the view that, ultimately, we do not have any knowledge. Even on the pragmatist view in which one would regard knowledge as simply what is "useful," one would have to ask: What is it useful for? To know what is genuinely useful to us, we have to know something about ourselves, our position and prospects in the universe, and something about the organization of things.

If we have knowledge it is because we know something about the ultimate organization of things and this something cannot be derived simply from the examination of material objects or the examination and analysis of our own sensations. With respect to knowledge in general, as with respect to moral theory, Schurman is insistent that knowledge is necessarily the outcome of a long developmental process in which experience and principle are played off against one another. It cannot be had merely by the exercise of our own rationality any more than it can be had merely by the analysis of our own sensations.

Reason might tell us the necessary framework within which things in the world might occur but, by itself, it could not tell us what does occur. Schurman is generally faithful to that part of the Kantian doctrine which asserts that pure reason, by itself, is impotent to determine the state of the world but his attack on "sensationalism" is in no sense a declaration of the insignificance of experience.

But, if both reason and experience are necessary and if they must be played off against one another in knowledge in general, much as turned out to be the case in the special instance of moral knowledge, what is the principle in terms of which this synthesis is to be achieved? Just as, in moral theory, the principle turns out to be the ultimate coherence of the pattern of our lives against the background of what we can see about the nature of human beings, so, in knowledge in general, Schurman's position is that what we are looking for is an ultimate unity of coherent explanation.

This ultimate unity goes far beyond anything which could be described in terms of matter and sensation. If it is, in itself, real, then it must be characterized.

This ultimate unity is both the test of reality and the explanation of it. It is a test because it is when experience and reason are seen to form a coherent system that we are inclined to say we have discovered or encountered the real. What we mean by such expressions as hallucination, illusion, and misperception is a situation in which we are confronted by isolated and incoherent sensations. If they are substantially divorced from reality, we call the situation hallucinatory. If they are related to a real object but not quite in the way in which we immediately think, we call the situation illusory. If they are approximations which can be corrected by further observations, we call the situation a misperception. It is coherent and rational order which gives to sensation the character of the real. Similarly, what we mean by mistake, invalid inference, contradiction, irrational belief, and so on is that cluster of situations which represent the incoherences of reason. But reason, by itself, is a system which is empty in the sense that mathematics is empty. It is about everything and therefore about nothing. It requires concrete content before we can claim that it approaches reality. Both experience and reason must, therefore, be arranged in a coherent order and must bear upon one another in a coherent way before we are content to claim contact with reality. But this ultimate coherent unity is also the explanation of things. We say we have explained the formation of oil when we have located the events which result in its production at the right place in the order of things. Hence we associate the life, evolution, and decay of appropriate organisms with changes in the surface and the climate of the earth and, when all the pieces are locked together like a well-formed jigsaw puzzle, we say we have "explained" the occurrence of oil. But these explanations are only possible if there is a final, coherent order of things. If there is not such an order, if, for instance, there is more than one way in which the parts of the jigsaw puzzle will fit together, then our claim to have "explained" is baseless. But what could provide the basis for such an assurance?

Schurman believed that such an assurance could only be forthcoming if the ultimate unity which was the test and the explanation of things had additional properties of the kind usually associated with the nature of God. For unity must extend to the future as well as to the past, must encompass all possibilities, all likelihoods however remote, and all the events which could be conceived of, not merely by us but by any mind which might conceive. But how are we justified in making this leap from the nature of knowledge, the test for reality and the preferred way of explaining things, and our own *belief* that knowledge is possible to the proposition that knowledge is actual and God or the logical "prius" is really a feature of reality?

Furthermore, if we were to make this leap, would we not actually end in conflict with those components of the mainstream of nineteenth-century thought which Schurman himself was inclined to accept? For will it not turn out that the ultimate unity must itself be timeless and incapable of change? How could anything be a logically complete order encompassing all actuality and possibility and still be

197

subject to change? The God of tradition does not change but the God of tradition was thought to be, in some important sense, quite separate from the world. Schurman's God or logical "prius" is clearly tied to the world in important ways which we shall come to see.

In choosing the expression "prius," a word which the *Oxford English Dictionary* records as first used in English in 1891 by H. Jones in his book *Browning*, and a little later by Edward Caird in his *Essays Literary and Philosophical*, Schurman was trying to combine the notions of logical priority and primacy of principle with the notion of something which was ultimately real but whose reality was expressed through the system in which it had a part.

The principle, in short, must be the kind of principle which, though complete in itself, can only exhibit itself through a system in time.

His first approach to this is to link the notions of knowledge and reality. Knowledge, as he had pointed out, cannot consist merely of the arrangements of material particles or of sensations. It must transcend them. But knowledge has two other important properties. To be knowledge it must be knowledge of the real or knowledge consistent with the real and, to be knowledge, it must exhibit the properties of a mind. Furthermore, Schurman argued that to know something is to become what you know. This notion, which goes back, after all, to Aristotle, is a source of perpetual puzzle to philosophers. To remain apart from the thing which one knows is always to be in the position of the sceptic. To become the thing which one knows, in the literal sense, would be to be absorbed by that thing so as no longer to count as a knower. The solution has to be to conceive of reality as the kind of thing which is revealed in the transformation of knowledge.

Schurman, therefore, wants to conceive of the world itself as the developing structure of knowledge. But, so far, he has only linked the notion of knowledge, the notion of the ultimate unity of explanation, and the beginning of an idea of God. He has not shown that that knowledge is possible. In the middle parts of *Belief in God: Its Origin, Nature, and Basis*,[7] he outlined his basic argument. We shall try to indicate the main stages of this argument and to illustrate them, in the best way we can, with our own interpretations. All philosophical arguments suffer from attempts to compress them and this damage can be overcome, if at all, only by substituting interpretations which maintain the coherence of the argument. This argument was of great impor-

---

7   Jacob Gould Schurman, *Belief in God: Its Origin, Nature, and Basis* (New York: Charles Scribner's Sons, 1890), pp. 129-69. Hereafter referred to as *Belief in God*.

tance to Schurman and, for that if for no other reason, caution is necessary.

He begins by attempting to show that two of the basic alternatives with which one might start are unintelligible. One of them is the notion of creation out of nothing; the other is the notion of what he calls an "eternity of a chaos of atoms."[8] The first is unintelligible in the basic sense because it postulates a fundamental break in the system of explanation. To say that the world is created out of nothing is to utter the proposition that, ultimately, there is no explanation. But this is inconsistent with the possibility of knowledge and one who has a belief about the world, any belief about the world including the belief that it was created out of nothing, is claiming to have knowledge about the world. The idea of an eternal chaos of atoms, by which Schurman seems to mean a notion of a random universe, is unintelligible on the same grounds. Randomness, literally, is the absence of order and the absence of order is the impossibility of explanation. In fact, any approximation to randomness is only an alternative order and to claim that an order is random is, essentially, to say that it is not an order which follows necessarily from any principle. But that must, also, mean that it is unintelligible. In any case, only an eternal order is intelligible. For such an order has a correspondence with the internal order of reason. But that is what one would mean by rational order in the context of a philosophical position like the one Schurman is putting forward.

If a universe created by arbitrary fiat is unintelligible and a random universe is unintelligible then only a universe through which causal connections run *is* intelligible. The argument seems to be that there are only these possibilities. We can eliminate two of them and we are entitled, therefore, to opt for the third. If a causally connected universe is an ordered universe then it is true that the universe is either ordered or it is not. And if the two logically possible kinds of order are causal and volitional order, then, if volitional order—the notion that the universe is created by fiat—is unintelligible, that leaves, indeed, only the causal possibility.

Of course, this is much too simple and Schurman knows it. It is much too simple in the sense that there are many arrangements which might well be called "causal orders." He therefore turns his attention to the construction of a satisfactory notion of causality. The crucial phase in this construction is his analysis of the notion of causality as a necessarily internal relation. Though there has been long debate about the notion of "internal relations"—A. C. Ewing distinguishes some sixteen

8   Ibid., p. 154.

possible meanings in his book *Idealism: A Critical Survey*[9]—we can assign a fairly straightforward meaning to Schurman's use of the expression without doing his argument particular violence. In this sense, an internal relation is one which makes a difference to its terms while an external relation is one which does not. Two events, X and Y, in short, are externally related in the case that X and Y would be the same if their relation was different, and internally related in the case that they would be different if their relation was different. In this sense, Schurman's argument is simple. Suppose that X is the cause of Y. Now suppose that we believe that X and Y are externally related. Then Y might have been exactly as it is without having the relation of being caused by X. This means, apparently, that Y could have existed without X. But if X is the cause of Y, this is nonsense.[10] Similarly, if X and Y are externally related then X might occur even though Y did not occur. But if X occurred and Y did not occur then X is not the cause of Y. Therefore the assertion that X is the cause of Y combined with the assertion that the relation between X and Y is an external relation is, again, nonsense.

What follows from this, in Schurman's view, is that, if the universe represents a causal order, then its components are internally related. This means that none of them would be what they are if any other members of the causal system were different. This leaves two possibilities. The universe might consist of several independent causal orders or it might consist of a single causal order. If it represents several distinct causal orders, however, there is an element of randomness in it—namely that randomness expressed in the proposition that there are several causal orders. But randomness anywhere tends to affect the whole system of explanation. A random event is an event which might occur anywhere at any time. If some events in the universe are caused and others are random, we could not tell, in effect, which was which. For, whatever the causal explanation, it is true as likely as not that the event just occurred randomly. In any case, it is Schurman's point that randomness is not, in itself, an intelligible notion.

He concludes, therefore, that the universe is a single, unified, intelligible order. No part of that universe could be what it is unless every other part were what it is because, if it were not a single, unified,

9   Alfred Cyril Ewing, *Idealism: A Critical Survey* (London: Methuen, 1934).
10   One must, indeed, suppose that X and Y are events and one is *the* cause of the other. If X and Y are properties of events, one can well imagine that they are externally related as one can, indeed, if X and Y are "things." But if X and Y are events and if events are unique in the sense that one and only one event is the occupant of any moment of time at any designated place the claim may be true by definition and its denial, therefore, "nonsense."

intelligible order, some events in that universe would be externally related to one another or some events would be random or some events would have a merely volitional unity.

Now Schurman wants to maintain that such a unity represents what Hegel called being-for-itself. This is an important and not altogether easy notion.

While Schurman is clearly borrowing ideas from Hegel, it is equally clear that he does not mean exactly what Hegel meant by the expression "being-for-self." Hegel introduces the notion first in chapter three of his *Science of Logic*.[11] It arises out of his consideration of determinate being. Determinate being is distinguished from pure being by reason of the fact that determinate being consists of distinguishable elements each of which has a quality and a quantity. Pure being is whatever it is that everything which *is* has in common, and it is not, in Hegel's view, an intelligible notion if considered merely by itself. The concept of pure being collapses into the concept of nothing simply by reason of the fact that it is what *is* but, at the same time, what is not anything determinate. As such it is the absence of all determinations which constitute quantity and quality. And that turns out to be nothing. Thus we are driven from the notions of pure being and nothing to the notion of determinate being because we can neither dispose of the notion of pure being nor yet formulate it in an adequate way. To dispose of it would be, literally, to regard it as "nothing." Yet there is a world. The minimum condition for any world, therefore, is that it should include determinateness. Determinateness is given if one assigns some quality and if one assigns that quality to anything, something, everything—in short, to some quantity. This, in its turn, yields problems and this is how we get to the issue of being-for-self.

Once we parcel out, as it were, being into quantities and qualities, the components of being become dependent upon one another. One distinguishes two things by assigning some quality to one of them and withholding it from the other. Thus both things become determinate by reference to one another and only by reference to one another. We first think of these entities as *"absolutely determined being"*[12] but we realize that they are not absolutely determined but relatively determined. Each one is a unity in and for itself, what Hegel calls "immediately *a* being-for-self—the One."[13] But "the One passes into a

11 G. F. Hegel, *Science of Logic*, trans. A. V. Miller (London: George Allen and Unwin; New York: Humanities Press, 1969; first published in German, 1812-1816; first published in English, 1929), p. 157.
12 Ibid.
13 Ibid.

plurality of ones—repulsion—and this otherness of ones is sublated in their ideality."[14] It is this which gives the real notion of "quantity" so that "quality, which in being-for-self reached its climax, passes over into *quantity*."[15] In being-for-self, proper, we really have only quality for, if we consider the thing in itself, it simply *is* its properties.

Thus, for Hegel, being-for-self is a transitory moment in the dialectic as it is originally introduced. What Schurman has in mind, however, is what one might call real being-for-self—the condition in which there is something ultimately real which is genuinely self-contained and has being not relatively but absolutely. It is not Hegel's Absolute that he is seeking, for the absolute in the Hegelian system is not a transcendent unity but something which is immanent in the world and comes into being in the literal sense through the dialectical development of the world. Schurman is seeking the God who will function as a divine prius. Thus what he needs is not the immanent unity which will become the developed reality of the world but something which has, literally, being-for-self and exists now. For it must be quite real in and of itself and yet it must be the guiding explanatory principle of the world. It is, in effect, the ontologized unity of principle which makes explanation possible. It is not just the occurrence of that principle for that would merely be a structural feature of the world. It is that unity of principle regarded as a real thing.

Now Schurman's reason for asserting the reality of this being-for-self, the logical prius, is simply that we do find that we do have knowledge but we also find that the world is not, in itself, complete and unchanging at the present moment. If there were no real underlying unity of principle we could not have knowledge. If that unity were simply the structural principle which will be developed as the world unfolds, knowledge would be possible in the future but not in the present.

So far, one might still be tempted to raise the objection that all of this lies in the domain of the hypothetical. Surely, one may say, if we have knowledge *then* we might be tempted by Schurman's argument. But who is to say that we have knowledge? Schurman does not conceive the argument as running in quite this way. The main line of argument which we have just outlined he would regard as moving us, essentially, from the domain of the hypothetical to the domain of the actual. For what we saw originally was that those states of the world which would sustain an essentially sceptical position are, in fact, unintelligible. The random universe makes no sense. A universe composed of material

14 Ibid.
15 Ibid.

objects makes no sense. A universe composed of sensations makes no sense. That far, indeed, one is still in the realm of the hypothetical. That far, one may say: If we have knowledge, then atomistic materialism, pure sensationalism, and so on are false. But, what Schurman thinks he has shown by his argument for the intelligibility of the notion of the divine prius, is that an alternative model of the universe *is* intelligible. This is quite different, for now we not only know what some of the conditions for intelligibility are but that something *is intelligible*. What is intelligible, of course, is the notion of a universe whose components are related by internal relations and which contains as one of its members a proper being-for-self—the logical prius.

Can one now speculate that the real world fails to instantiate what, by the original elimination, constituted the one possibility for an intelligible world? One might suggest that we could even doubt that there is a world at all. But this would be a curious kind of doubt quite unlike any others that we have entertained and it is not one that Schurman is prepared to entertain. If we understand him correctly, then what he is saying is something like this: Suppose you admit that there is a world. Then you admit that you have understood the most general conditions under which such a world would be intelligible. If you deny any of the conditions, unintelligibility results. But you cannot both say that there is a world and that that world is unintelligible. For that would be a contradiction. One who says that the world *is*, is making a pronouncement which must, itself, be intelligible. In an unintelligible world, one cannot even say that. We might want to raise a variety of further issues and to distinguish, for instance, between the proposition that the world is intelligible and the proposition that intelligible discourse is possible in the world. Schurman does not pursue his dialectic to this level.

But one who finds his dance of the dialectic not very satisfying might reflect that Schurman is supposing that much of what we take for knowledge is, indeed, genuine knowledge. He does not seriously doubt that the advances of nineteenth-century physics and biology are substantial and that, though they will no doubt be amended, they will not be totally overturned. The world has proved intelligible enough to yield to us some important insights into its structure. One who denies these things is, in any case, hardly a party to the debate that Schurman is participating in.

We must constantly remember that the whole of his effort takes place against the background of his desire to salvage important parts of traditional belief in the face of an honest and quite general acceptance of the scientific "progress" of his time. We ought, therefore, to ask ourselves how his attempt fares against the background in which he is most consistently and persistently working.

That background included a substantial challenge to religious belief on the ground of evolutionary theory. Most importantly, it raised questions about whether we ought not to regard our most basic beliefs as merely provisional on the ground that creatures further evolved than we are might be in a better position to grasp the ultimate nature of the universe. It could be suggested, after all, that our present predilections to believe are simply biologically conditioned. We get such information about the universe as our biological structures permit. Perhaps, then, we distort the incoming information and come to entirely wrong conclusions about the world.

Now what Schurman wants to insist upon is that, indeed, the world does change. Hence his God is not the final unity of the universe but the divine prius, the general principle through which the world exhibits itself and the general principle conceived as an existing being. Thus his universe can accommodate change and any kind of development which is consistent with the requirement in principle that reality is, finally, a unity which does exhibit a principle. But what about the argument that we may not be able to think well about the universe, that we may not be in receipt of good data about the universe, that our whole intellective process may well be simply a biological device to insure our survival? As such, it might so filter all of the information as to make it quite literally impossible for us to come to rational conclusions. What Schurman is arguing is that our knowledge of the fundamental principle does not depend upon other features of the state of our knowledge. When he urges that some states of affairs are not intelligible, he does not mean intelligible to us but intelligible per se. A formal contradiction, for instance, is not the kind of thing which might be overcome by having a better mind. If to urge that the components of reality are externally related to one another and that they form a causal unity is to utter a contradiction, then no amount of further evolution will enable us to overcome that contradiction. Such a state of affairs is not unintelligible because we lack some better apparatus by which we might grasp its nature, but because it simply cannot be grasped. Even God cannot think contradictions, not because he lacks some power which he might have had, but because, literally, nothing *counts* as thinking a contradiction.

What may be more worrying is the way in which he assembles the components of this notion. His logical prius is what makes sense of the ultimate underlying unity of reality. But it is not simply that unity. It is the being which instantiates the principle of unity and thus guarantees that unity will ultimately be exhibited in nature. It is the guarantee of meaning and structure in the universe. But this means that the universe, considered by itself, without the logical prius, is, in fact, unintelligible. It is only intelligible given that the logical prius does function and that the divine plan is carried out. This is a little bit puzzling because, as Schurman admits, it makes of God a being with will—a volitional being. And a volitional being might choose not to carry out the plan. In that event the universe would be unintelligible and, on what appeared to be Schurman's premises, could not exist. Thus it would seem that God could cause the universe never to have existed. No doubt Schurman would argue that this is a profound misunderstanding. The will of God is the guarantee of the intelligibility of the universe. God, presumably, is not free in the sense that you and I are but free in the sense that His will corresponds to reality. He could not change His mind and cause the universe never to have existed, because to do so would be actually inconsistent with His own volition.

These questions and answers are, of course, reminiscent of Leibniz and we raise them speculatively and speculate about Schurman's answers simply to suggest that, no doubt, there is a good deal of the traditional rationalist in Schurman.

He tries to overcome the sense of an elaborate, but probably tricky, logical apparatus by casting a wider net. He says:

> The question really is whether for the sake of completely realizing the scientific ideal of explaining everything by determinable mechanical processes, the self in whom and for whom and through whom all this scientific knowledge exists should itself be brought down to the level of the categories through which it explains the world of objects; so that whatever spiritual content resisted such reduction should be declared illusory surplusage even though it included the beautiful and the good, the belief in freedom, and the hope of immortality. It is from its notion of the self, the inevitable centre of everybody's world, that every system of philosophy takes its origin and tone. And the mechanical philosophy will always be found irrefragable by the man who, as Schelling somewhere says, is himself able to realize it in practice; that is, who does not find unendurable the thought of working away at his own annihilation, surrendering the freedom of the will, and being merely the modification of a blind object in whose infinitude he finds sooner or later his own ethical destruction.[16]

Mostly, he is echoing Hegel—though, as usual, with his own special emphasis. Just a little later, Schurman says that Hegel is right to insist "that identity and difference are both necessary to the being of

16 Schurman, *Belief in God*, pp. 221-22.

the infinite spirit."[17] In the passage just quoted, what Schurman is doing is going back to the section of the *Phenomenology* in which Hegel,[18] talking about the material world envisaged by the Stoics, suggests that if one conceives of a world of material things, one can no longer locate oneself in that world. Self, which, after all, was a necessary ingredient in the construction of theory, turns out to have constructed itself out of the world. But Schurman wants to cut deeper than that particular passage in Hegel would suggest. He wants to argue that, in a mechanical, material world, the self would indeed disappear. But he wants to urge that the contradiction is not just that the self has constructed a theory in which it no longer finds a place for itself, but that the theory itself entails the reality of something which transcends the domain which it describes. For such a theory paints the world as an organized causal unity, not as a merely random concatenation of particles. The world of nineteenth-century physics like the world of the Stoics, was, after all, quite different from the world of the Greek atomists in that, precisely, the early atomist notion of the random movement of particles in a void is gone. But it is Schurman's argument that such a unity is not possible unless it proceeds from a more fundamental principle. He also wants to call attention to the fact that we are aware of ourselves as thinking beings and that we must account, oddly enough, for the possibility of an intellectualizing self which, somehow, can conceive of possibilities far beyond the limits of the mere material world. However much we may cheerfully admit that our ability to think at all depends on our being creatures in that world, we must, somehow, find room for more than there is in that world.

He admits that "even this belief in God is anthropic as well as cosmic in its character."[19] But he does not find this an objection.

> For if the universe as a whole supplies the facts for the explanation of which this hypothesis was needed, it is from man alone we borrow the content of the hypothesis. The self-conscious essence that is at home with us in the human microcosm we see to be the interpretative principle of the all-embracing macrocosm.[20]

No doubt, all of this raises the additional issues with which Schurman would finally have to cope. He not only faces some of the classic

17 Ibid., p. 227.
18 G. F. Hegel, *The Phenomenology of Mind*, trans. James Baillie (London: George Allen and Unwin, 1931; first published in German in 1807; first published in English in Great Britain in 1910), pp. 242-46.
19 Schurman, *Belief in God*, p. 219.
20 Ibid.

Leibnizian conundrums which we mentioned, he also faces problems associated with the relation of human free will to a divine prius which knows where it is going and seems to go there to spite us. But his divine prius may be an infinitely imaginative builder of jigsaw puzzles. It may be able to weave into the final picture a suitable place for whatever acts we, in fact, perform. And perhaps even the nature of time changes as the universe nears its natural completion.

Though *Belief in God* dates from his early Cornell days, it is part and parcel of his original philosophical work and outlook. No doubt, the book was the development of ideas which remained in his mind for many years.

If we are to understand the next phase of his career, we must return to the choice which he made in 1885 to leave his post at Dalhousie in order to take the Chair of Philosophy at Cornell. His two years at Acadia were followed by only three at Dalhousie. There is at least some evidence that while he was at Dalhousie he became increasingly preoccupied with the form which higher education had taken in the Maritimes. He set about writing a history of Dalhousie which he never finished, but some of the notes which he left are very revealing. The intention of Lord Dalhousie—what Schurman calls the "broad minded and far seeing policy of the noble Earl"[21]—had been to found a university at which all men of whatever faith might find an education. This was immediately frustrated by a controversy in 1838. Technically, it centred around the rejection of a proposal that a certain Dr. Crawley be appointed to the Chair of Classics. In fact, the battle raged around Thomas McCulloch who figured earlier in our discussion. McCulloch's appointment to Dalhousie—in effect his transfer from the principalship of Pictou Academy—stemmed from religious grounds and Crawley was explicitly rejected on those grounds.

In effect, this decision amounted to the adoption of the policy that all Dalhousie professors would be members of the Church of Scotland. Schurman described the situation this way:

> The peoples' College [it is not clear who gave it that tag] hitherto vainly struggling to get born, had, as we have seen, in 1836 narrowly escaped being suffocated ere it drew its first breath.... The idea of a peoples' College escaped annihilation only to fall a prey to sectarian jealousy, which, though forcing it into life charged it also with the germs (principally) of death. This ill-fated Institution which had the exclusiveness of its governors, whose names were on its trust but whose hearts were in this exclusive Establishment at Windsor, had allowed to remain for nearly a score of years a silent

21 Jacob Gould Schurman, manuscript notes regarding the establishment of Dalhousie as a "peoples' College," Dalhousie University Archives, Halifax, p. 17.

mockery, instead of an active testimonial of the broad minded and far seeing policy of the noble Earl whose name it bears became next a sanctuary of discord, in which were propagated, on a large scale and with issue then undreamed of, the direful feuds that had kept the Pictovian temple of Janus open uninterruptedly since 1836.[22]

He also maintained an interest in Canada, if we are to judge from *The Forum* magazine for March, 1889. In his article "The Manifest Destiny of Canada," he sought to explain to Americans why the proposals made by Senator Edmunds and Senator Sherman which suggested eventual political union between the United States and Canada rested on a misunderstanding. He referred to the Louisiana Purchase of 1803, and the acquisition of Florida from Spain in 1819, of Texas from Mexico in 1853, and of Alaska from Russia in 1858. But he added:

> ... the case of Canada is different, infinitely different, from that of all the territories ceded during the nineteenth century. There you annexed unpeopled lands, by purchase or conquest. Here, on the contrary, you have to do with five million human wills, to be followed in the next generation by twice that number. The destiny of Canada will be settled by the people of Canada. For them there is no manifest destiny but what they themselves decree. The question is, What is this likely to be?[23]

He had no doubts that the decision of Canadians would be to remain Canadians. He was, indeed, boastful. He claimed that peoples of northern Europe had produced the "... races that succeeded Rome in bearing, as they still largely bear, the civilization of the world. And analogy suggests that under the bracing climate of Canada, in centuries yet to be, civilization may in the New World find its sturdiest supporters."[24] Americans, he remarked, might think of Canada as too cold for civilization.

> But Canada has an advantage over the States in its lower altitude, and altitude has almost as much to do with temperature as latitude. And apart from this, the January isothermals in Canada are more favorable for the maintenance of an energetic white race than the July isothermals in the southern States.[25]

22 Ibid., pp. 16-17. The *Dalhousie Gazette*, in reprinting Schurman's notes, changed the final 1836—probably an error in script—to 1826. Other minor changes were noticed.
23 Jacob Gould Schurman, "The Manifest Destiny of Canada," *The Forum* (March 1889), p. 2.
24 Ibid., p. 3.
25 Ibid.

In the same article he attacked the position taken by Goldwin Smith—the same Goldwin Smith who was later to become his friend.[26] Smith had urged that the slow settlement of Canada and the fact that the English had failed to assimilate the French provided a good argument for the political union of Canada and the United States. But Schurman was disdainful:

> ... in spite of Mr. Smith's great knowledge and experience of the New World, and his sympathy with democracy, this is surely the voice of the insular Englishman, with his prejudices against the Celt, and his inability to understand that government in modern times, or at least since the successful application of the federal principle, does not require an assimilation of provincial laws, races, religions, or languages. Of course the French-speaking population of Canada live under federal laws and institutions which are essentially English. And if the Province of Quebec is governed in accordance with local laws and customs, it is no concern, as it is no disadvantage, to the rest of the Dominion.[27]

When Schurman goes on to say, "There is no conflict of races in Canada,"[28] even the most ardent nationalist will have to admit that he somewhat overstepped the bounds of reality.

But the argument which he generally makes is reasonable. He urges that Canadians have an elaborate and complex government which is, in fact, well suited to their diversity and to their particular needs. Indeed, it is the very ability of Canada to unite a multiplicity of peoples under a federal scheme without trampling on individual cultures and rights which is the strength of Confederation.

> The Canadian Constitution, lacking the prior sanction of history and experience, will in the future probably require alterations and amendments. But the machinery for this purpose is easily set in motion. Canada may be trusted to make the instrument as good as possible. And it admits, in theory at least, of a perfection not attainable by any other. For though a written constitution, it is not, like the American, rigid, but retains, in proper degree, the flexibility of their common English original. It blends happily the essential features of both. It combines with the federal principle the system of parliamentary and responsible government, the lack of which in the legislature of the United States, eminent critics, American and British, have deplored as a calamity. It is with good reason, therefore, that Canadians prefer their own political institutions to those of their neighbors.[29]

26 Goldwin Smith was a British educational reformer who became Professor of Constitutional History at Cornell in 1868, but moved to Canada in 1870.
27 Ibid., p. 6.
28 Ibid.
29 Ibid., p. 10.

He was to change his mind somewhat a little later, but there is no doubt that he left Canada a convinced Canadian.

There is nothing to indicate that Schurman, when he went to Cornell in 1885, had any hope of an administrative career. But a mere seven years later, when the president who had succeeded White retired, Schurman was the unanimous choice of the trustees and, apparently, of the faculty as well. At thirty-eight, he must have thought that he had reached the climax of his career, but it was to prove only the beginning of a surprising life.

He was not a man to look back. The year that he became President of Cornell, he became a United States citizen.

He devoted himself vigorously to the development of the university. He founded the first research professorships and he did regular battle on behalf of the faculty.

An extract from his report of 1911 is typical of views which he had held continuously. In it he compares American universities to those in England and Germany and remarks, as so many scholars have after him, that the tendency to run a university as if it were a business corporation is ultimately disastrous: ". . . the ideal of a business corporation engaging professors as employees and controlling them by means of authority which is exercised either directly by 'busybody trustees' or indirectly through delegation of usurpation by a 'presidential boss,' . . ."[30] could only obstruct the university ideal. He suggested that a president, even in his kindliest moods, could not think the "Board of Trustees" representative of the university. Professors, he thought, ought to be represented on the board—a demand only now coming widely into acceptance.

Like John Clark Murray at McGill, he campaigned, as well, for women's rights and, later, was to campaign for women's suffrage. Sometimes he had difficulty keeping his own convictions clear in the context of the presidential rhetoric. For one of his first addresses to the student body at Cornell in September of 1893, he had written a note to himself as a reminder that, now that Cornell had women students, he should refer to "both sexes." He did so, but later in the text of the speech he slipped and urged all the students to "Let Cornell manliness become celebrated."[31]

He did not feel himself much bound by Cornell's conviction that universities ought to be essentially practical in outlook and action. He continued to urge that everyone ought to learn Latin and Greek and

30 President's Report, Cornell University, 1911-12, p. 5.
31 Notes and typescript in the Archives of Cornell University.

that "an educated man now as always will find in the humanities the most important subjects of education."[32]

The compromise which he struck was of a pattern which was to become a crucial determinant of American higher education. At Cornell one could, indeed, study anything—but one could only do it in a framework which provided for a liberal education. Schurman worried about the tendency for such programs to become spread so thin as to be insignificant. But he met this challenge by trying to keep in his own mind and before his faculty a clear view of that which was most basic and most important and by trying, constantly, to make the point that fundamental humanitarian studies are not impractical. Rather, they provide an enlargement of the mind which makes practical innovation possible because it is that enlargement of the mind which enables one to see new possibilities in old settings.

Schurman, then, was clearly nobody's man. He had his own view about higher education. He stood his ground in the face of his trustees and he urged his faculty on to the kinds of fundamental achievement which make for an important university. Yet he seems to have remained beloved by them all. No doubt it was easier then than it is now for a president to survive an office for twenty-five years but, even then, Schurman's was no mean achievement.

Inevitably, he became involved in politics. Alonzo Cornell introduced him into the Republican Party, and, a few years later, he was vice-chairman of the New York State constitutional convention. He was brought to national prominence, however, at the turn of the century when, after the confusion which followed on the Spanish-American War, the United States in effect took over the Philippines and Schurman became the president of the Philippine Commission. The situation was a curious one which was to have a profound effect on American thought in politics.

Spain had governed the Philippines for nearly four hundred years but corruption, the use of forced labour, and internal bitterness between rival groups had rendered the Philippines almost ungovernable. The secret societies which fought guerilla actions against the Spanish authorities had been operating quite effectively since 1892. Widespread armed hostility had broken out in 1896. The rebellion was finally broken in 1897, but the Spanish were compelled to sign a pact guaranteeing a variety of reforms within a three-year period. Into this situation, on May 1, 1898, Commodore George Dewey arrived with the

32 Jacob Gould Schurman, "The Adaptation of University Work to the Common Life of the People," 46th Annual Convocation of the University of the State of New York, October 22-24, 1908, and New York State Education Bulletin, no. 443, March 15, 1909.

American fleet. In the battle of Manila Bay, the Spanish fleet was totally destroyed. The United States actually acquired the islands, however, under the terms of the Treaty of Paris in exchange for twenty million dollars cash. The inhabitants of the islands were not entirely pleased with the result. Though they expected more from the Americans than they had from the Spaniards, most of them, evidently, hoped that Americans would go away quickly. Americans, in turn, also expected that the United States would leave quickly. Indeed, the public mostly saw the acquisition of the Philippines as a device to end the corrupt Spanish rule and to make democracy possible.

The situation, in reality, was not to be solved so simply. For one thing there was no obvious agreement amongst the Filipinos themselves as to how they should be governed and by whom. For another, the country was a patchwork quilt of peoples, interests, and creeds, and the component patches were not well stitched together by any effective communication system. The term "Filipino" originally denoted a person of Spanish descent who was born on the islands but most of the people were, in fact, Malays, and they themselves were divided into several ethnic and linguistic sub-groups. In *their* turn, the Malays regarded themselves as being quite different from the indigenous peoples of the islands.

The situation required some organization. The question was, what kind? Schurman, as President of the Philippine Commission, fought a long and, essentially, a losing battle. Details of his exchanges with John Hay, who was the Secretary of State during the negotiations, did not become public until thirty years later and the extent to which Schurman represented an embattled minority, often a minority of one on the Commission, is perhaps even now little known. He favoured a constitution which would have given the islanders almost immediate effective self-government subject only to some reserve power. What they got was really government by the United States with the promise of eventual self-government when the islands had developed to the point at which self-sufficiency would be feasible. Inevitably, despite years of campaigning by Schurman and many others across the United States, the time never quite seemed to come for that final step. It was only in the depression of the 1930s, when Americans became fearful of cheap labour and cheap goods imported into the United States under the existing arrangements, that it became politically feasible to grant the Philippines real independence. Even then, final independence was not to come until after World War II.

Schurman's developing position was a little ambivalent, but not unusual for the time. He saw no fundamental objection to the notion that the developed countries ought to govern undeveloped countries

212

provided they did so genuinely in the interests of the latter. He retained the nineteenth-century conviction that the civilization of western Europe was destined, in any case, to spread around the world. His quarrel was not with Americans interfering in the internal affairs of the Philippines, but with the undue prolongation of that interference and with the possibility of its perversion into government in the interest of the United States. While this position may well have been defensible—especially in the case of a country like the Philippines which had been brutally exploited and left, perhaps, genuinely unable to draw upon any effective tradition for its own self-government—it left Schurman and his friends in a relatively weak position and without much powerful support. For they had conceded that the islanders had no absolute right to govern themselves and it could always be argued, whatever the conditions for self-government were, that they had not yet quite been met.

Even in 1932, when Congress finally passed an act which would give final independence in 1944, the act was vetoed by Herbert Hoover. Luckily, Franklin Roosevelt came to power immediately and the matter was settled.

Schurman's views, meanwhile, seemed to be becoming increasingly conservative on many topics. He did not approve of Theodore Roosevelt's "New Nationalism" essentially because it seemed to have increased the powers of central government unnecessarily and because it seemed to him that it immediately fostered undesirable interference in business and would lead to even more undesirable interference. He attacked attempts by the government to regulate the shipping industry and the railroads. He attacked anti-trust legislation. The continuous sympathy which he held for everyone whose civil liberties were interfered with—whether they were Communists harassed by the federal government or the New York Legislature or women who were not allowed to vote—was, of course, in no way incompatible with this kind of conservatism. Schurman had simply become convinced of the desirability of American capitalism and convinced, in fact, that attempts to regulate it or interfere with it would, in the end, lead to a disastrous loss of individual liberty.

He was not, however, a man to hang onto his views in the face of clear evidence of their unsatisfactoriness. By the time Franklin Roosevelt came to power and the effects of the depression were obvious, he had changed many of them. He wrote to Roosevelt expressing at least a measure of support and agreeing that the American people had fallen on terrible times indeed.[33]

33 Letter to Franklin D. Roosevelt, Cornell University Archives.

Throughout this period, there is no doubt that substantial tensions existed in Schurman's thought. The brave new world of education opened up by Ezra Cornell, the obvious growth, prosperity, and genuine individual liberty which Schurman found in the United States moved him to a rather temporary but quite real belief in at least important facets of the traditional American individualist doctrine. But the experience of the Philippines, the later experience as Ambassador to Greece, his experiences as Ambassador to China in the 1920s and, certainly, World War I itself provided a constant counterpoint to these views.

Even in 1916, in a Lincoln Day address to the Republican Club in Utica, he was driven to remark that: "A nation is not merely an economic organism, still less it is a military machine. A nation is more than a physical entity. A nation is at the same time a moral personality."[34] In his deliberations on the Philippines, he called attention to the Canadian solution to analogous political problems and he was frequently stirred to remark that nations tend to have a life of their own and are more than a simple aggregate of individuals.

The Hegelian streak in him never died and the sense of real communitarian values never died in him either. He consistently tried to make the point that Cornell University was more than a business organization, more than a random collection of individuals organized for some specialized kind of production.

His developing political theories never came to be expressed in philosophical form. When he retired from Cornell it was to devote the rest of his life—through the 1920s and 1930s—to diplomacy.

When he returned to Germany, to the source of many of the ideas which had animated him throughout his life, it was as American Ambassador and it was to face a Germany which had moved from economic and social collapse to a dictatorship which he found as incomprehensible as it was reprehensible. The country which had produced the noblest of human ideas had fallen into the most despicable of dictatorships. The reason, he thought, surely must be the organization of world politics—the imposition of de-humanizing systems, of irrational economic forces which could not be understood well enough to be controlled, and the inability of those ideals to withstand assault by irrational forces. He never became convinced that it was the ideas or ideals themselves which were at fault or that there was a fatal flaw in human nature. Rather, he saw that men lose faith in rationality in the face of the incomprehensible. The solution, he thought, could only be

34 Address to the Lincoln Dinner of the Republican Club of Utica, February 12, 1916. Typescript in Cornell University Archives.

achieved by patient understanding—especially at the diplomatic level. The irrational forces could be controlled but only by co-operation and understanding.

It therefore seemed to him of much more crucial importance to attend directly to these issues than to return to his study for philosophical contemplation. He remained physically more vigorous at seventy-five than most men are at forty.

But even when he finally returned to the United States to a well-earned retirement, it was not to be spent in Ithaca writing but in Washington consulting. He seems never to have become discouraged. He wrote charming and sometimes picturesque letters which, if they infrequently show much humour, also never display any overt bitterness or despair.

He died in 1942 still full of energy—still believing that the divine prius would, in the end, take care of the world. The one thing which seems never to have occurred to him is that he might return to Prince Edward Island or, indeed, to Canada. Though he had been for forty years a major figure in American diplomacy and for longer than that a major world figure in education, there is nothing in the files to suggest that anyone every invited him to return to Canada. References to Canada became fewer in his letters and virtually non-existent in his public statements after his years as President of the Philippine Commission.

SEVEN

REASON AS SOCIAL UNDERSTANDING

John Watson—Part I

W
HEN JOHN WATSON came to Queen's in 1872, he was twenty-five years old. Queen's (only six years older than Watson) was a clearing in the woods by the lake. Watson remarked that its builders had taken seriously Aristotle's definition of a building—four walls and a roof. But Queen's had already had one remarkable philosopher, John Clark Murray, on its staff and a number of highly entertaining ones as well.

The fulsome praise which Edward Caird had lavished on the young Watson in his letters of recommendation must have aroused a certain amount of scepticism in Kingston. But Caird's estimates turned out to be true. Watson was to go on to become a Gifford lecturer (even now, the highest honour which can befall a philosopher in the English-speaking world) and was eventually to be matched against Josiah Royce in a famous series of lectures at Berkeley. Caird never changed his mind either. "Watson," he wrote later "is perhaps a man of the 'driest light' that I know. I do not know anyone who sees his way more clearly through any philosophical entanglements."[1]

Canada, in its contemporary form, was, of course, still younger than Watson and Queen's. Watson was to exercise an important influence on the country. Young men went out from Queen's to man the growing civil service, Presbyterian churches across the country, and the newer universities in the west. For more than fifty years, Watson was a dominant—sometimes *the* dominant influence—at Queen's. He played a significant role in the intellectual background and even in some of the practical negotiations which led to the United Church of Canada. His pupils seem to have carried with them an echo of that dry voice and its persistent demand for reasonableness and it often stayed with them for life.

1   Robert Charles Wallace, ed., *Some Great Men of Queen's* (Toronto: Ryerson Press, 1941), p. 24.

Canada also influenced Watson. Though, as we shall see, he was and remained a devotee of a particular kind of philosophical idealism, the form which it took was significantly different from the form it had found in Germany, in England, in Scotland, and in the United States. His book, *The State in Peace and War*,[2] seems to be a plea for the application of the British North America Act to the government of the world. His view of the history of philosophy was much influenced by the notion of a traditionalist society. His view of politics as a slow development of the interplay of reason and experience—something not subject to simple, immediate, final solutions but, nonetheless, subject continuously to the application of reason—is the basis of a kind of pluralist federalism which has obvious roots in the Canadian experience. His constant communitarian outlook, again, has evident connections with the Canadian situation. His rational religion almost became the creed of the United Church.

In short, the themes which we have found to run through the developing pieces of Canadian philosophy come together to form a coherent unity in Watson. One should not misunderstand this. The interplay of the man and the society in which he found himself is obvious enough. That society, to some small degree, had, no doubt, been influenced by his philosophical predecessors. But there is comparatively little reason to think that—apart from his contact with John Clark Murray—Watson was directly influenced in a significant way by earlier philosophy in Canada.

Apart from a few entanglements in financial disasters, there was little excitement in Watson's personal life. He remained at Queen's, fought the usual battles of academic politics, held administrative posts at times, raised a family, played billiards, and wrote plays. His life, for the most part, was the life of the mind.

He produced a number of introductory surveys, major commentaries on Kant, briefer historical analyses of Comte, Mill, and Spencer, a book on political philosophy, and several works—one of them running to two volumes—on rational religion. He wrote constantly, and at the time of his death, in 1939, left unfinished work in philosophical psychology. Beyond all that, the archives at Queen's are bulging with his notes and letters.

The philosophical tradition which Watson inherited had its roots in Kant and Hegel but it came through Edward Caird who, in turn, had been a close friend of Thomas Hill Green.

Green had been strongly influenced by Hegel's outlook on metaphysics, morals, and politics. But he found Hegel obscure and his

2   John Watson, *The State in Peace and War* (Glasgow: James Maclehose & Sons, 1919).

arguments frequently less than compelling when he subjected them to the best analysis he could. He was forced, therefore, to work out the problems largely on his own and, though British idealism is frequently described as "Hegelian," the expression refers more to a general outlook than to any specific line of argument. In particular, no British philosopher, in fact, undertook to reconstruct either the elaborate formal dialectic of Hegel's *Science of Logic* or the elaborate dialectic of experience as it appears in Hegel's *Phenomenology of Mind*.

Green, to begin with, had strong interests in education and in political reform. He was appalled by the class bias in British education and by the underlying rampant individualism which he saw as the basis of a society which seemed largely incapable of taking a satisfactory view of itself as a single community. He saw in philosophers like John Stuart Mill the combination of this individualism with the essentially self-referring ethic of pleasure. For all the protestations of Bentham and Mill about "the greatest happiness of the greatest number,"[3] Green, and after him Bradley and Bosanquet, saw in this the notion of an aggregation which could never be satisfactorily carried out. First of all, it seemed to them that the notion of self-realization as the acquisition of pleasure (and Mill had defined happiness in terms of pleasure) was a gross perversion of human nature. Secondly, it seemed to them that this doctrine obscured the bonds between man and man. To overcome this, Green was looking for a different view of selfhood. At a deeper level it seemed to Green that the problem went back to Hume who had conceived of the self as a "bundle"[4] of impressions and ideas all of which had their origins in sensations.

Green was aware of Kant's solution. But Kant's attempt to link the self, the orderliness of the world, and even the schema of space and time to the structure of experience did not tempt him. For, though this meets the objection of those who would hold that we are acquainted only with the contents of experience, it results in a distinction between experience and the remainder of reality—Kant's distinction between the phenomenal and the noumenal worlds. In this way, reason is prevented from bearing on experience in the understanding of morality. For experience yields only ordered facts for Kant, just as, for Hume, it yields only atomic particulars. Pure practical reason, in Kant's view, does yield moral rules but, like the nature of reason itself, they are

3   For a discussion of the utility principle in Mill and Bentham see *Mill's Utilitarianism*, ed. James M. Smith and Ernest Sosa (Belmont, California: Wadsworth Publishing, 1969). *Utilitarianism* was published in three parts in 1861 and first published in its entirety in 1863.

4   David Hume, *A Treatise of Human Nature*, ed. L. A. Selby-Bigge (Oxford: Clarendon Press, 1964; first published in 1739), p. 252.

entirely universal. As such, they do not grip the particular demands of the situation. Hegel's proposal, in effect, to abandon the noumenal and to exhibit reason and experience as dialectically related aspects of a single situation was, therefore, appealing to Green.

Green's other major concern was with the problem of freedom. Mill had conceived freedom essentially negatively. *On Liberty*[5] is a work which describes the conditions under which men are to be immune from interference by the apparatus of the state. Its suggestion seems to be that men are ready-made individuals and need only be protected from this kind of interference in order to be free. In nineteenth-century England, this seemed to Green a travesty of the facts. Millions of people, usually badly housed, badly educated, and badly fed, seemed to him hardly free beings at all. They could exercise their freedom to escape through strong drink and they could exercise their freedom, at intervals, to choose between rival sets of candidates for parliament most of whom had been educated at the best schools and the best universities. Surely, freedom required more than this—it required the power to do something, the power to realize one's own capacities, the power not to choose between well-educated men, but to be oneself.

Hegel had espoused the notion of positive freedom, but Hegel's notion was difficult to grasp and, what is more, entangled with Hegel's philosophy of history—a philosophy of history which seemed to entail that the course of human events was, at least in the larger sense, determined by the nature of things. Green was little interested in that notion, but he did pay serious attention to Hegel's view that, para-doxically enough, it is the structure of law which does give freedom. Men are free not just because laws obstruct interference with their acts but, much more seriously, because the framework of law provides positive opportunity not merely for those activities which form a part of "civil society" (the domain of public institutions, contracts, corpora-tions, and so on) but, ultimately, for the kind of self-identity which derives from having a place in society and the opportunity for self-development to fill that place.

The crucial development in Green's philosophical programme came, however, when he returned to the study of Hume in search of the source of Hume's error. In the course of preparing a definitive edition of Hume's work and writing a volume of introduction to it, Green came to the conclusion that the source of Hume's error lay in the problem of relations. He noticed that, in Hume's account of experience as an atom-

5   John Stuart Mill, *On Liberty*, ed. Albury Castell (New York: Appleton-Century-Crofts, 1947; first published in 1859).

ic collection of impressions and ideas, the problem of relations proved exceptionally vexing. We can point it out with a crude example. Suppose you see a shovel in a hole. You can see the shovel and the hole. But what about the "in"? The "in" is not given as a separate datum. Yet all our statements about the world involve relations between the given data. Hume was not unaware of the problem and, for that matter, devoted a good part of his *Treatise* to a discussion of problems about relations, including an account of the basic kinds of relations. Green thought, however, that Hume gave up the ghost when he came to discuss the problem of space. He did not want to identify space with colour—the obvious available "impression." In attempting to account for the structure of space, he implies that space is a relation. Green says: "It is a relation, and not even one of those relations, such as resemblance, which in Hume's language, 'depending on the nature of the impressions related,' may plausibly be reckoned to be themselves impressions."[6] If Green is right, Hume is in a serious difficulty. For he cannot deny that we have knowledge of spatial properties. He cannot correlate space simply with colours and with sensations of touch. He cannot admit that there is a separate "impression" of space for no one would claim to have that impression. This situation, in Green's view, becomes even worse when Hume tries to explain our idea of the continuous identity of objects in the face of the flux of sensations. For we ought to have, on Hume's view, no proper idea of such an identity and it is difficult to know how even a "fictitious" idea of such an entity could be constructed out of relations which were that special kind, like resemblance, of which one might almost claim there are impressions.

Green's conclusion is that Hume's philosophy at this point breaks down. It will not do, however, to simply reinstitute Locke's "something I know not what"—the underlying substance—to hold the bits and pieces of experience together. Nor is it really the case, on Green's view, that Hume is fundamentally wrong in his account of immediate experience.

The alternative, as Green suggests in a long discussion in his *Prolegomena to Ethics*,[7] is to regard relations in some way which will not entail their being things.

6   Thomas Hill Green, *Hume and Locke*, with an Introduction by Ramon M. Lemos (New York: Thomas Y. Crowell, 1968), p. 208. Green's Introductions to Hume's *Treatise of Human Nature* were first published in 1874.

7   Thomas Hill Green, *Prolegomena to Ethics*, ed. A. C. Bradley with an Introduction by Ramon M. Lemos (New York: Thomas Y. Crowell, 1969; first published in 1883, ed. A. C. Bradley, brother of F. H. Bradley). See especially p. 16 for the formal example of the engineer and the train signals.

The solution which he suggests is that it is mind which does the relating. We relate things. Relation is an activity and not another kind of thing. This does not mean that we, ourselves, make up the world to our own specifications. But when we spot a mistake, it is, nonetheless, essentially a mistake in relation. Green cites the case of an engine driver who causes a train wreck by misperceiving a signal. It is not that he perceived what was not there. And it is not that he failed to perceive what was there. His problem was that he related what was there in the wrong way and so perceived the signal in the wrong position. Knowledge, for Green, is a matter of ordering experience correctly. The normal standard for this is the coherence which leads to a rational order. We reject the perceptual order which makes railway tracks seem to meet in the distance because we realize that, on that basis, we cannot get a coherent pattern for all our experiences. We regard the bugs seen by a victim of delirium tremens in a different light than we regard the bugs seen by the entomologist. But that is because we can get coherence in our experience by regarding one of the perceptions as something special to the person concerned and the other as part of the "order of nature."[8]

A number of important conclusions follow from this. It is the basis of Green's view that reality itself is the exhibition of an ultimate consciousness. While this conclusion was comforting to someone who, like Watson, with his Free Church upbringing, was looking for a liberal and rational religion, there are more dramatic implications for our view of the human self and the human condition in the immediate world.

Essentially, Green's theory involves the notion that the human self is something which develops over time as, in the process of becoming conscious of its relations to sensations, it gradually frees itself from the dominance of those sensations and, as it gradually understands its relation to its own desires, is capable of freeing itself from those desires. Green says:

> Every step in the definition of the wanted object implies a further action of the same subject, in the way of comparing various wants that arise in the process of life, along with the incidents of their satisfaction, as they only can be compared by a subject which is other than the process, not itself a stage or series of stages in the succession which it observes.[9]

The self thus comes to recognize itself. Its freedom is something which grows upon it in a process. This guarantees that freedom cannot be

8 Ibid., p. 19.
9 Ibid., p. 91.

obtained merely by removing occasions of interference. Freedom must, rather, be the outcome of a deliberate process of growth.

This theory runs dramatically into conflict with each element of the theories of philosophers like Mill. Self-realization is not a matter of accumulating pleasures. It is a matter of developing an inner coherence in the course of matching the rational order of the world. No one is perfectly individuated. Everyone draws upon a common universal consciousness. And freedom is the outcome of self-realization.

These views were developed but not substantially changed in the philosophy of Edward Caird to which Watson was directly exposed. In England, idealist doctrine underwent considerable development in the philosophy of Bernard Bosanquet. And it underwent a dramatic transformation in the hands of F. H. Bradley. For the cautious balance of reason and experience developed by Green, Bradley substituted an all-out attack on the experienced world in the name of reason. He argued for an underlying unity of mind by means of an attack on the notion of relation itself. While Green had substituted, apparently, relating as an activity for relations as things, Bradley simply announced that the concept of relation was not itself intelligible. But a world without relations must be a unity and that, in Bradley's view, becomes intelligible only as the notion of an ultimate mind which becomes fragmented in our experience of it.

Politically, in England, the theory moved from the reformist doctrines of Green to the rather more conservative position of Bosanquet and what amounts to the studied indifference to politics exhibited by Bradley.

In Scotland, the idealist theorists remained reformists. Some of them, like D. G. Ritchie, became, in effect, socialists. But it was in its reformist mood that Watson met the theory and, against his Free Church background, found it attractive.

It was to change in Watson's hands, too, but not at all in the way it changed in the philosophies of Bradley and Bosanquet. Like all the British idealists, Watson believed that morals, politics, and metaphysics were intimately related. But he was compelled to work out his own metaphysics in a way which turns out to be significantly different from that of any of them. The best single brief example of Watson's own point of view in this context can be found on page 185 of his *Outline of Philosophy*: Here we find him discussing a position which is utterly antithetical to the positions of Bradley and Bosanquet, a position which he ascribes to Spencer. He quotes Spencer as saying, "My real self is 'one and indivisible,' different selves are 'absolutely and for ever exclusive.' "[10] He then goes on to say:

Now, in one point of view, this assertion of individuality deserves the strongest commendation. In maintaining that all forms of existence are individual, it brings into prominence an aspect of reality that is lost sight of when all concrete forms of being are resolved into an inscrutable and unintelligible Power. And in particular, it emphasizes the distinction between beings that are self-conscious, and beings that are not self-conscious, implying that in the strict sense of the term the only true individual is the self-conscious subject, which, in all the changes through which it passes, is aware of itself as identical.

But, while it is an important truth, that individuality can properly be affirmed only of a being that is self-conscious, it by no means follows that to be self-conscious is to be aware of oneself as a separate individual, having no relation to any other existence. It may easily be shown that the consciousness of individuality is on this supposition impossible. If we suppose that in being conscious of himself, the subject is conscious of nothing else, it is manifest that such a being would have no consciousness even of himself. For all reality would for him be limited to determinations of himself, and therefore he would never contrast with these determinations the determinations of other forms of existence. To be conscious of myself implies that I am conscious of myself as possessing a character which distinguishes me from other modes of being. My individuality is for me the consciousness of what I feel, know, and will. But if I have no consciousness of what is felt, known, and willed by others, I must be incapable of distinguishing between myself and other selves. It is therefore only in relation and contrast to other selves that I become conscious of what I as an individual am. Assume, therefore, that I am absolutely limited to the consciousness of my own feelings and thoughts and volitions, and obviously I should be unaware that others have different feelings, thoughts and volitions, and therefore unaware of my own peculiar individuality. The consciousness of self is therefore relative to the consciousness of other selves.

It may be said, however, that while I am no doubt conscious of other selves as having feelings, thoughts, and volitions, yet I am capable of distinguishing these from the feelings, thoughts, and volitions which are peculiarly my own, and that the consciousness of what is mine constitutes my particular individuality. And this is true; what I feel, think, and will belongs to me in a sense that nothing else does; it is mine because it implies a peculiar self-activity on my part. It is the distinguishing characteristic of self-conscious beings that they are self-determined. But self-determination is not the same thing as the determination of an exclusive and separate self that has no relation to anything else. This may be shown by a consideration of the two main forms in which self-determination is exhibited, viz., knowledge and action.[11]

10 John Watson, *An Outline of Philosophy*, 4th ed. (Glasgow: James Maclehose & Sons, 1908), p. 185. Hereafter referred to as *Outline*.
11 Ibid., pp. 185-87.

You will notice, here, that there is no sense of F. H. Bradley's view that apparent selfhood is a kind of illusion. Neither is there any sense of Bernard Bosanquet's view that there is a final primacy to the community. Rather, the two are seen as evenly balanced. Furthermore, the argument is not the rather all-embracing one which Green uses about relations—an argument which always colours his most specialized and detailed accounts of phenomena in general—but rather it depends upon the close inspection of the particular facts of the particular situations. He does not doubt that individuals have feelings, knowledge, and volitions. He can tell this from the analysis of our own affairs. But we can see that one could not have these if there were not other individuals with whom we could contrast ourselves. To know what I feel is one thing. To know, simply, that there is a feeling, would be another. To say that *I* feel something or other is to imply that there is a relation between myself and that feeling which does not hold for anyone else. If I were the only individual in the world, that notion would make no sense. I must come to have *this* kind of self-identity through the gradual individuation of myself against the background of a society. But this involves a complex series of influences and involves me in the continuous belief that there is a rational order to a world in which I live and have my being. If there were not, none of these distinctions, in Watson's view, would have any meaning.

What this suggests to Watson is the gradual development of a community which takes its meaning precisely from the differentiation of its members into individuals. It simply would not suffice if all of us turned out to be the same—for then, again, there would be no point in talking about *my* feelings, *my* knowledge, *my* volitions. A rational order must, therefore, be *created* on two levels and *found* on a third.

We must create, within ourselves, a rational and coherent order which enables us to identify ourselves as individuals. We must create, on the level of the community, a rational order whose meaning is to be found in the specific differentiations of the individuals who compose it. But we must also find a rational order in nature for, without that, the actions on which we depend for our differentiations will be, themselves, meaningless. The fact that I can see that I *am* an individual and that my individuality depends upon the community and upon nature is, for Watson, a powerful reason for believing that a rational order does run through nature. We shall see more of this as we proceed through the discussion of Watson's metaphysics. For the moment, however, we should notice how this view leads to a conclusion about morals and politics which is not identical with the views of any of the British idealists. Experience depends on reason for its articulation, but

224

it is not illusory. Its differentiations which lead to morality are not, therefore, as Bradley thought, the by-products of a logical blunder. The community's life is important but its meaning lies not in itself but in individuation. Thus the importance of the community is to be found in the individual, and the community is to be, as much as possible, shaped by rational deliberation.

On the other side, it is not so much the problem of relations which leads to the notion of a universal consciousness as it is, in Watson's view, a demand for reason. It is those relations which are inherently rational which sustain the view which Watson came to call Speculative Idealism. There is in knowledge an important element of discovery as well as an element of creation and this is more clearly stated in Watson than in Green. Furthermore, on Watson's view, the nature of reality forces us to the kind of view which we might call rational federalism. This rational federalism is simply a by-product of the fact that the community must, if it is to develop at all, develop itself in a set of variegated individuals. The demand for uniformity of behaviour in persons or uniformity of character outlook in persons is, on Watson's view, fundamentally misguided if it means more than whatever uniformity is required for individuals to fit effectively into a community.

This is one side of the background of Watson's development. Another part of the background relates to the specific controversies of the time. In particular, Watson was compelled to face up to the controversy between religion and science. His Free Church associations lent themselves naturally to a liberal outlook on religion and his conviction that all the facts must be faced allowed him no room for evasion. He did think that some aspects of the theory of evolution, if they were wrongly interpreted, would lead to a head-on collision with propositions which he wanted to maintain. This included the fundamental proposition that knowledge is possible and the proposition that men are free.

On one side, since he believes that what he calls "the three great . . . spheres"—nature, mind, and God—are ultimately "related,"[12] he cannot finally isolate a universal consciousness or something like Schurman's divine prius from the process of the world. On the other side, he must try to set limits to the interpretation of the theory of evolution so as to permit knowledge and objective values.

These major tasks began with the first public lecture[13] he gave at Queen's and continued to interest him to the end of his writings. Let us,

12   Watson, *Outline*, p. 20.
13   John Watson, *The Relation of Philosophy to Science*, Inaugural Lecture, October 16, 1872 (Kingston: William Bailie, 1872).

briefly, follow him through at least one statement of these concerns. In his *Outline of Philosophy* he says:

> Now, I think there can be no doubt that the tendency of Darwin's theory of the nature of man is to abolish the distinction between intelligence and non-intelligence, though it is rather certain of his followers than Darwin himself who hold that the mental and moral qualities of man may be explained on the principle of natural evolution alone.[14]

He says he thinks that "this extreme view may readily be shown to be untenable."[15] But he carefully draws the consequence of the proposition first.

> There is on this view no more room for any free activity in knowledge on the part of man than on the part of an unconscious thing. Hydrogen exhibits by its natural constitution an affinity for oxygen, but it would be regarded as a pure fiction to endow the hydrogen with any capacity of freely selecting the oxygen as its mate. For, it would be said, hydrogen cannot *refuse* to unite with oxygen under certain conditions: the union is absolutely determined by the natural characteristics of both. In the same way it must be denied that in man there is any freedom in knowledge; he can know only that which his inherited disposition fits him to know: to suppose that he could have a different disposition, or react differently under the conditions, is incompatible with the principle of natural evolution.[16]

Obviously, if there is no freedom in knowledge, there is, in the serious or theoretical sense, no knowledge at all. For if one is simply determined to believe what one does believe, all one's claims to objectivity and seriousness evaporate.

Watson is equally clear that freedom of action would be ruled out on such a theory.

> Primitive man inherited certain tendencies from his animal ancestors. Thus, like them, he has a selfish tendency and a social tendency. Which of these shall be predominant will be determined by the interaction between the organism and the environment. The moral sense is developed by the conditions under which man is placed. In virtue of his love of approbation and his fear of punishment—both inherited peculiarities—the savage comes to have a feeling of pain when he follows the selfish desire for his own pleasure. Right and wrong are therefore names for the pleasure of approbation and the pain of disapprobation respectively. But the individual man can no more

14 Watson, *Outline*, p. 131.
15 Ibid.
16 Ibid., pp. 132-33.

determine which of these shall predominate than he can alter his bodily stature or endow himself with new senses. We must suppose that in the majority of men the love of social approbation is stronger than the love of individual pleasure; because, otherwise, the extension and development of the social bond would be impossible. But this only shows that the inherited disposition and the environment tend on the whole to the evolution of higher sociality: it does not show that in the individual there is any free activity.

Thus the theory of natural evolution, when it is employed to account for the mental and moral qualities of man, leads to the conclusion that there is no freedom either of knowledge or of action.[17]

He assaults the position about knowledge in a closely reasoned argument. First of all, men have such mental characteristics as curiosity, wonder, and memory. It will have to be explained, if the form of the theory of evolution he has just been expounding is true, how these characteristics came to be. Curiosity implies

... an *interest* in some object, and a concentration of *attention* upon it for the purpose of discovering what are its properties. It is further implied in curiosity that the subject believes in the intelligibility of the object. Now interest, attention, belief in the intelligibility of the object, all involve the faculty of distinguishing one object from another by an apprehension of the properties of each; and this again implies that the apprehending subject is capable of separating between himself and the immediate impression that he has from moment to moment.[18]

The theory holds its ground well enough so long as what is involved is simply something like the flow of sensations. For, however difficult it may be to relate sensations and brain-states, we can at least conclude that the flow of sensation is simply a natural process (though it may be a process which is far from simple). But when we begin to explain phenomena like curiosity, we begin to drive a wedge in that natural process. The point is not that we might not explain curiosity on evolutionary grounds by seeking to show that curiosity increased the likelihood of survival under whatever circumstances there were for the development of men. Rather, the question is about the kind of process exhibited in curiosity. Can you design a mechanical object which is curious? Could developing cells in an evolutionary process become curious? Watson apparently believes not and his reason, evidently, is that to sustain curiosity one must begin to make fundamental hypotheses about the universe.

17   Ibid., pp. 133-34.
18   Ibid., p. 135.

THE FACES OF REASON

He [man] had . . . to free himself from the first impressions of the nature of things, by attention, comparison, and discrimination; that is, he had to separate between his impression of things and their actual nature. Such a faculty of distinguishing between the apparent and the real is the pre-requisite of all knowledge; and it implies that man was not the sport of the fleeting impression of the moment, but was in some sense its master.[19]

Watson is here raising a crucial point: the distinction between awareness of actuality and awareness of possibility. The process of the natural order can make one aware of any actuality. To be aware of potentiality is logically beyond its scope. Yet such notions as curiosity, simple notions which we cannot very well deny to have application, force us to make use of this distinction. And this distinction is the basis of the claims we want to make about knowledge. Evidently, knowledge includes whatever knowledge it is which justifies us in asserting the truth and theory of evolution.

Watson was equally determined to resist the encroachment of evolutionary theory upon the basic domains of freedom and value. He says: ". . . I have tried to show that knowledge implies freedom because it lifts man above the flux of immediate impressions and so liberates him from the tyranny of the sensible. Similarly, it may be shown that in his action, as properly understood, man is free because he is not under the dominion of immediate impulses."[20]

Equally, evolution does not explain morality. Watson says: ". . . selfishness is not the way to obtain the satisfaction of the individual."[21] Man, in his view, "is by his very nature social, and forms part of an organism in which the good of each is bound up with the good of all."[22] He notes:

. . . the feeling of dissatisfaction experienced by the individual when he acts contrary to the common opinion rests upon the very same consciousness of a self higher than his merely individual self. It is because he has the same consciousness of a social self as is embodied in common opinion that the individual man is dissatisfied with himself when he has sought for the satisfaction of his own separate self at the expense of others.[23]

He is continually seeking to relate experience to his rational framework. Thus, he calls attention to curiosity, but what interests him

19 Ibid., p. 136.
20 Ibid., p. 145.
21 Ibid., p. 148.
22 Ibid., pp. 148-49.
23 Ibid., p. 149.

is not so much the experience of being curious as the order which must hold between experiences if curiosity is to be possible. He is certainly interested in the social nature of man but, for him, the primary fascination of this notion lies in the kind of structure which experience must have if it is possible for a man to be aware that he has a social nature. What interests him about knowledge is that knowledge arises in a situation of contrast. So long as one lives only with the immediacies of experience, one cannot be said to have knowledge. One is aware. One reacts. Events take place. None of this is knowledge until it is ordered in a framework which goes beyond these immediacies. Merely being confronted, say, with a red patch does not give me knowledge. I am said to know when I have located the ostensible patch in an appropriate order. When I grasp that it is part of the surface of a fire engine and it belongs to the natural world or when I grasp that it is simply a part of the order of my imagination, I may be said to have knowledge.

The knowledge consists not of the action of classifying—a machine might do that and machines do order things—but, rather, of the understanding that what I am confronted with belongs to the order to which I have assigned it.

In this way, knowledge is very intimately intertwined with the availability of alternatives. It is the availability of possible orders which makes knowledge possible and it is that availability which poses the problem of knowledge. The problem of knowledge, on this view is essentially the problem of developing the criteria by which one assigns what one is confronted with to one order or another.

Now if the organic world described in evolutionary theories is wholly determined, there is no way of explaining how the consciousness of alternatives might arise. Existence simply has no alternatives within it. It is therefore not a system which could explain knowledge. On this conclusion, Watson and Schurman agree. But Schurman's solution is to explain the possibility of knowledge by going outside all the given orders which appear within the structure of experience. Watson's solution is to perform a close analysis of those orders and to try to show how the solution arises within them. As a consequence, for Watson, reason is much more intimately bound up with every aspect of the world and, in the end, Watson's God becomes not another thing outside the order but a structural feature of that order itself. Equally, what knowledge finally depends upon is reason, for the criteria for orders will turn out to be the criteria for the intelligible structuring of the confrontations of experience. Thus it is reason which is at the basis of reality and distinguishes reality from appearance.

Reason, for Watson, is never something added from outside the system by divine intervention, or merely a kind of arbitrary measuring device. Reason, rather, is built into the very nature of reality. It would not be going too far to say that for Watson reason *is* reality. We can now see, in principle, what Watson's solution to the problem posed by the theory of evolution is: It is that the theory of evolution is about the development of the data within the framework of the ultimate rational order. Evolution does not explain that order. Evolution, consequently, cannot explain our consciousness of that order. It merely explains the content through which the order is made manifest. Now it seems probable that no biologist, then or now, who understood the import of this doctrine would actually want to deny it. The evolutionary hypothesis in general and what one might call structural genetics in particular may well explain every detail of human physiology and may be able to relate each of these details to the gradual development of structures from original unicellular creatures or even from precellular molecular components.

But when it comes to explaining how it is that some of these developed structures are conscious in a way that does not merely involve reaction to the immediately given but involves the kind of action which leads to knowledge, the biologist would not, in general, claim to have anything to say. Perhaps the point is clear if one considers this situation: Suppose we were not the creatures that we are but rather creatures with an entirely different physical makeup. Suppose that like Professor Hoyle's "black cloud" we were essentially gaseous beings whose information interchange had an entirely different basis. Then suppose we came across molecular structures like the human brain and were able to analyze them and describe them completely. Could we *infer* from our description of the molecules, that these molecular assemblies were conscious and had knowledge?

This is not to say that we have "minds" in the Cartesian sense which are substantially quite different from our bodies or from the natural world. Watson thinks Cartesianism literally inconceivable.

Suppose the mind to be absolutely separated from all objects, and it has no conceivable nature. If we try to think of such a mind, we can only describe it by negations: we can say, that it is *not* extended or movable or ponderable: in short, that it has none of the predicates by which we may describe the material world. . . .

In this difficulty Descartes falls back upon the view that there are certain conceptions which the mind has by its very nature,—such conceptions as that of God.[24]

24   Ibid., pp. 138-39.

This "falling back" is, Watson thinks, entirely useless to Descartes. The solution lies in making the necessary distinction between the development of the data and the rational order which they manifest in the course of their development. It is this rational order to which Watson constantly refers.

Thus Watson does not want to try to defeat the evolutionists by falling back on some kind of neo-Vitalism. That was a popular solution at the end of the nineteenth century and one given popular support in the writings of Samuel Butler. It is interesting that this view seems to have had no major champion among Canadian philosophers. Whether that is the result of the impact of post-Hegelian idealism or whether it had something to do, as we shall see in our discussion of Blewett, with the kind of relation between man and nature which the Canadian environment made rather obvious, is a matter which cannot be settled. Watson wants no part of any escape through the medium of a "pure mind," a "vital force," or indeed of anything of a factual kind which would lie outside the domain of scientific investigation. It is just that scientific investigation, since it concerns itself with the objects of knowledge, concerns itself with the presentation of the data through which the ultimate order is made manifest. Philosophy, since it starts, most crucially, with problems about the nature of knowledge and value, is concerned with that order itself. The two inquiries are aspects of the same general investigation. One of these aspects cannot be reduced to the other. If we try to perform such a reduction, we destroy the whole knowledge-finding enterprise.

We can see this argument from a different point of view by looking at Watson on freedom and value. Freedom is not, for Watson, mere indeterminateness. That would involve some breach of the order of the natural world. Rather, freedom is the kind of thing which we find in knowledge when we discover that we have available to us alternative orders. We can act in the world because we can reflect and move from one order to another. A world in development, a world in which the data are presented in a way which manifests part but not the whole of the rational order is a world which is open to development not because it is indeterminate but because what it determines is a range of orders between which one may choose. Knowledge is not possible in any other circumstance. In the end, to grasp this, as we shall see when we meet Watson's general metaphysical theory directly, one must cease to regard the world as consisting of a set of essentially unyielding fixed things. Rather, it is a world of orders and alternative orders—a world of rational structures which appear through the medium of the data with which we are confronted.

The problem of value opens the issue from yet another perspective. Mind, conceived of as the rational order in things, is, in itself, perfectly general. It belongs not to you or to me but to everyone. We individuate ourselves within it. It is for this reason that we have a natural social nature. Whenever someone individuates himself, he does so by contrast to others. The phenomenon which Watson calls selfishness arises "only when the individual is conscious of the object of appetite, and when setting that object before his consciousness he seeks to realize it irrespective of the claims of others."[25] Selfishness is a kind of myopia. It arises from being blinded by the short-range demands of immediate desire and sensation. One cannot explain either the social consciousness or selfishness on the basis of biological evolution alone. It is all very well to say that the individual seeks his self-preservation and that, in the interplay of biological forces, those who seek their self-preservation must effectively survive best and reproduce their kind. But one needs to explain how selfish action arises in the first place. For one needs to explain how one gets a self in consciousness and not merely how one gets an individual biological organism out of the process. Evolutionary theory may well explain how one gets individuated organisms. It does not explain how one gets the individuation of consciousness. Bear in mind, again, that Watson does not think that the particular instantiations of consciousness are individual Cartesian mind-substances each of which is assigned by some mysterious process, one to a body. Rather, consciousness is the awareness of the order in things, and, as such, it is a common property which we all share. It comes to be individuated because what one is conscious of is not merely the rational order but the data through which that order manifests itself. One cannot have one without the other. There is, therefore, always a tension in human affairs, a basic instability in the relation of individual to community.

Were this not so morality would not only not arise, it would be an unintelligible notion. Morality is essentially the process of finding out not what is good for me or good for you but what is good in general. Morality represents the claim of the ultimate consciousness.

It is not a claim which is to be championed by the obliteration of the individual. The rational order of things must be made manifest through the individual. That order is entirely empty otherwise. In effect, Watson is accepting the demands of a Kantian morality but he is pointing out that it arises in a dialectical situation. The solution will have to be the accommodation of the individual in a way that does instantiate the claims of the ultimate rationality.

25 Ibid., p. 147.

We can see, once again, that Watson is simply making the point that some elements in our knowledge belong to the order or frame in which we move and others to the data which we encounter. He is drawing the line in front of the evolutionist not by denying the soundness and logic of his theory but by calling attention to its subject matter. The basis of morality is not the survival of the fittest. One who thinks that is merely the victim of the data of the moment. If one could understand the situation, the basis of morality becomes clear: "Learning that his true nature can be realized only by self-identification with the common weal, the individual man is not externally acted upon by a foreign influence. In submitting himself to the law of reason he is submitting himself to his true self, and such submission is true freedom."[26]

The special flavour of Watson's own thought is best brought out in his moral and political writings. It is, as one would expect, in those that the conditions of his place and time most clearly had their effect. Once we grasp his particular thrust in the areas of values, we can come to his metaphysical and epistemological theories with a better sense of what is particularly important for the study of Canadian philosophy.

The remainder of this chapter, then, will be addressed, in turn, to political and moral theory. A separate chapter will then begin with metaphysics and illustrate that position with a detailed discussion of rational religion. In that chapter, too, we shall be able to discuss Watson's relations to other philosophers of his most productive period, including William Caldwell, who sought to make peace between the idealists and pragmatists, and Jacob Gould Schurman's protégé, James Edwin Creighton.

The continuous theme of Watson's political theory is that the individual and his society are related to one another in a way which makes for mutual interdependence. Watson takes this with the utmost seriousness and, for him, there is no question of the possible supremacy of the individual over society or of society in any of its guises (including the state) being able to claim supremacy over the individual.

Society exhibits itself through the functioning differentiation of individuals. Individuals are developed in relation to one another and to society. Thus, though every genuine individual is essential to the society which exhibits itself through him, this metaphysical equality of importance does not entail the legitimacy of claims to precisely equal position and treatment. The importance of the individual stems from the fact that, in the total relation, he is different from every other individual and that his value is his own. The duty of society is to treat

26 Ibid., p. 149.

him in such a way as to make possible the development of his appropriate individuation.

> In order to realise the good will a system of Rights is necessary. As the ultimate object of society is the development of the best life, each individual must recognise the rights of his neighbour to as free development as that which he claims for himself. The justification of this claim is not any fictitious "right of nature," but the just claim that without freedom to live his own life under recognised external conditions, he is not capable of contributing his share to the common good. A man has rights which are recognised by society, but they are not made right by legislation, as Bentham held, but are recognised because they are essential to the development of the common good. The possession of rights and their recognition by society are not two different things, but the same thing; for, as the individual claims rights in virtue of his being an organ of the common good, so the State recognises his rights on the ground that they are required for the realisation of the highest good of all. The State, we may say, is under obligation to secure to the individual his rights, and any State which fails to do so ceases to fulfil its essential function.[27]

This theme Watson continues in his discussion of the relation of one state to another. Just as the state must not seek to make all individuals identical—for that is to undo the purpose of having a society—so it is not desirable that all states should be identical. Rather, the community of states exists to guarantee the possibility of the appropriate individual development of each. Its duty is to guarantee those rights and, ultimately, they require a level of government beyond the state. Watson is clear about this. "Now, it is certainly true that the proposed Federation or League would lead to a very decided transformation of that form of loyalty to one's country which is embalmed in the phrase, 'my country right or wrong'; but it is fair to ask whether this form of patriotism is worthy of a reasonable being."[28]

At every level Watson set himself against views which prevailed amongst philosophers and ordinary men then and now. He opposed the individualism of Mill and Spencer, he set himself against the contractualism of Rousseau and Kant, and the theory of state supremacy which appears both overtly and latently in Plato's writings. He opposed those who thought that the solution to the problems of the world was a world government which would guarantee that every society would be much like every other, and those who held that individual states must have their way. He spoke against those who argued that men owed loyalty to no government and as fiercely against those who held that men owed an unswerving loyalty to one government.

27 Watson, *The State in Peace and War*, p. 222.
28 Ibid., p. 260.

Though his book is entitled *The State in Peace and War*, and was occasioned by the massive reappraisal which World War I imposed upon all thinking men, it is not merely about the state, for he must distinguish, to make his point, between the state and society. The state, inevitably, is only one way of instantiating the complexities of society. It represents society if it is a good state but it is not that society.

Watson's theory, as always, is predicated on his theory of reason. But, again, it is his view that reason shows itself in the development of experience.

His basic approach to the problem is seen both in the historical organization of the book and in the specific ways in which he uses the historical material. The book begins with Pericles and goes on to a long discussion of Plato and Aristotle, the Stoics and Epicureans, and the political philosophers of the Middle Ages. Watson's discussion of the modern period begins with Machiavelli and Grotius and his discussion includes Hobbes, Spinoza, and Locke. Rousseau, Kant, and Hegel get a chapter to themselves as, not surprisingly, do Bentham, Mill, and Spencer. More surprisingly, before going on to expound his own theory, Watson devotes a chapter to Nietzsche, Haeckel, and the now forgotten but infamous Treitschke—the nearest thing to a real author who held the doctrines officially ascribed to the German militarists of 1914. In general, the point from Plato to Treitschke is that the limitations on the availability of reason at a given historical time are substantially the restrictions which limit the availability of experience in general. Thus Plato was not merely unable to see beyond the limits of the Greek city-state, he was also genuinely unable, in Watson's view, to envisage a society in which reason at its highest was instantiated in more than a small fraction of the citizens. Treitschke is given less generous explanations for his curious and damnable theories. Watson's remarks, nonetheless, lead one to associate some of his views with the peculiar economic circumstances of a Germany, which was a late-comer in the race amongst the European powers for colonies, with the "pedantic Frederick William the Third" who kept "the mass of the people" from "even moderate rights for many years,"[29] and with the historic tendency to disunion in Germany.

The moral is not that whatever is happening now is right because we could hardly have done anything else. The moral is that we must not expect to be able to solve all our social, political, and constitutional problems instantly because we may or may not have developed the regions of experience which would provide the basis for the discovery of the rational order which we require for a solution. This is not an

29 Ibid., p. 169.

excuse for doing nothing. It does signify the need to make certain that the power in society is not concentrated in any one institution— even the state. It justifies concentrating on those matters which we are able to understand clearly and it justifies the creation of constitutional devices which are designed to see to it that the governing mechanisms in a given society are responsive to new kinds of experience and to the development of reason over wider areas. Finally, it reminds us that our political institutions must always look to the future and that we must be suspicious of whatever collection of ideas happens to be available to us now. The closest thing to certainty which we can obtain is, as Watson implies in the preface, to be had from a study of the history of political philosophy. For he says:

> The development of political theory from the fundamental idea of Plato and Aristotle that the State exists for the production of the best life, through the long and troubled period of the Roman Empire and the Middle Ages, is a continuous development, in which one element after another obtains prominence, until we reach the period of the modern Nation-State, in which the ideas of check and balance, of a law of nature, of absolute sovereignty, of contract and utility, form stepping stones to the clear and simple conception of the State as existing for the establishment of the external conditions under which the highest human life may be carried on.[30]

We ought to be able to see, if Watson is right, that there is a pattern to the development of political theory, that new elements in the theory develop as new experiences develop, and that in the end, the whole makes sense when we allow for the special limitations surrounding those who propounded each theory. As usual, Watson thinks that few developed philosophical theories are simply false. Even Treitschke notices things which are important even though he distorts them. Each theory is correct insofar as it contains elements of rationality and incorrect insofar as it generalizes these elements to cover kinds of order for which those elements of rationality do not hold.

In the preface, Watson acknowledges his debt to T. H. Green and Bernard Bosanquet, but his theory, as usual, is not simply a recapitulation of those. One significant difference is in the use which he makes of the history of political theory, but a more profound difference from Green lies in the specifically dialectical account which Watson gives of the relation between the individual and society. He differs from Bosanquet in being substantially less conservative.

It is useful to follow Watson through his historical analyses in order to get a better perspective on his position. The words which he

30   Ibid., pp. vii-viii.

236

quotes from the famous funeral oration of Pericles immediately establish the region of his interest.

Pericles (in the translation from Jowett's *Thucydides*) says:

> Our form of Government does not enter into rivalry with the institutions of others. We do not copy our neighbours, but we are an example to them. It is true that we are called a democracy, for the administration is in the hands of the many and not of the few. But while the law secures equal justice to all alike in their private disputes, the claim of excellence is also recognized.[31]

The essential problem of political theory which Watson calls "the problem of uniting public authority with individual freedom"[32] is there perfectly expressed by Pericles. Plato grasped the problem firmly enough and proposed a solution to it which was, in fact, as good as circumstances permitted. He insisted that all men were equally entitled to a share of the good, that justice is the correct apportioning of deserts, that force and private gain were to be subordinated to the public good.

The deficiency of Plato's theory is, in Watson's view, first of all that there is an absence of reference to rights in his account of justice. The two higher classes in Plato's scheme have no individual rights. Their acts are all determined by their public duties. Differentiation is obtained in Plato's system by a scheme of class distinction but, within the classes, there is no further differentiation.

Furthermore, Plato conceives of reason as something which must be grasped by the few and applied to the many. Reason thus pervades the concrete structure of Plato's ideal republic but it is present only in the external ordering of that republic. For most of its citizens, there is no inner counterpart to the outward order. They are rational, if you like, despite themselves. Plato cannot conceive of a community in which all of the citizens collectively make decisions for the common good—a society in which each of the members is, in a fuller sense, a citizen. Hence his scheme ultimately fails.

> ... Plato's attempt to convert the individual into a pure organ of the whole is doomed to failure because it takes away that intense consciousness of personality which is the condition of the higher life. He who has no self cannot be unselfish. The good of the whole can only be secured by means of subordinate organisations. It is true that men must learn to rise above the separate individuality of the single life, but this advance can only be made by means of the moralisation which is afforded by the family, and by trade and commerce as implying individual rights of property.[33]

31 Ibid., p. 1.
32 Ibid., pp. 2-3.
33 Ibid., p. 30.

Nor does Watson think that a satisfactory society can be shaped by rigidly determining everyone's place in a hierarchy.

> ... Plato's whole conception presupposes a fundamental distinction between the working class and the governing class which can only result in degrading both. The workers are shut out from the training given by active participation in the government, and the rulers lose the valuable insight acquired by participating in active life.[34]

Finally, Plato makes what Watson generally thinks to be the greatest blunder of political theorists.

> Plato forgets, or does not realise, that the State cannot be stereotyped for all time, but must necessarily grow with the growth of men's insight. The citizen must be certain that any change proposed is really an advance, and this is only possible in a community where the whole people participate in the government and learn by experience what lines of action do not lead to its complete organisation.[35]

Aristotle provides important correctives in Plato's theory. Aristotle understands that man is basically a political animal, that politics is something to be understood in itself and not merely on the model of the household, and that the problem of politics is really to bind men together in a "free and orderly community."[36] Aristotle well expressed the Greek view that firstly man "should govern himself, and secondly, that he should govern himself under obedience to law."[37]

Nevertheless, Aristotle can only progress a short way towards the explication of this ideal.

> ... [His] speculations ... were based upon the experience of political life which he as a Greek enjoyed, and the interpretation of it that he gave was inevitably coloured by the presuppositions of the Greek mind. All that he could do was to attempt a rehabilitation of the City-State, by reference to its ideal as he conceived it. The interpretation of the State by Aristotle thus throws the clearest light upon the forces at work in it. The fundamental idea of Greek political philosophy was that the development of man's intellectual, artistic and moral nature is only possible by the concentrated activity of various minds all working towards a common end.[38]

It is this notion of the general, rational law, binding on all men, which Watson sees as the basis of Stoic political theory. Stoicism is the

34 Ibid., pp. 30-31.
35 Ibid., p. 31.
36 Ibid., p. 46.

37 Ibid.
38 Ibid., p. 47.

theory behind the Roman law. The Stoics were first to generalize effectively the political process from the confines of the city-state to the world as a whole. What is reasonable for one man is reasonable for all men. The law which binds one must, therefore, bind all.

But this Stoic concept of the world-state was too vague. It proved "powerless to serve as a permanent ideal of mankind."[39] For it lacks relevance to immediate pressing problems. Watson says:

> We can only have a true World-State when we have developed to their utmost the possibilities of each Nation-State, just as we cannot have a true Nation-State without the institution of the family and of private property, with the various industrial and commercial relations which they imply, and without that free play of individuality which gives rise to decentralised forms of association. A World-State based upon the combination of variously differentiated Nation-States is a possible ideal; a World-State which abolishes all the differences of race and nationality and individuality is an empty ideal. The fundamental mistake of the Stoics is seen in their doctrine that the highest good of man is in no way dependent upon the interests of the social life. This drives the individual back upon himself, and makes him indifferent to the ties of kindred and friendship, family and nation. The Stoics were weak where Plato and Aristotle were strong, namely, in not seeing that the consciousness of self as a spiritual being cannot be separated from the consciousness of self as a member of society.[40]

The paragraph we have just quoted expresses many of Watson's most basic convictions. The Stoics understood reason in the guise of what Hegel would have called the "abstract universal." But this is never enough. Reason is compelling only when it attaches us to the concrete situation. Moreover, a world-state is either one of two things: It can be the forcing of all men into faceless uniformity or it can be the kind of organic whole which is viable because it really does provide for the completest range of human potential which is consistent with the experience of the moment. A true world-state must be a federation of independent wholes. If it is not, it is doomed. For the possibilities of human nature which it excludes will intrude upon it as demands which it cannot meet and it will fragment and disintegrate.

This is also the model for Watson's answer to Plato's complaints about democracy. Just as a world-state which sought to impose an even uniformity would fail because it could not meet the demands of all of its members, so a democracy in which it is conceived that men will make rules which impose an even uniformity on all men must end in a

39 Ibid., p. 55.
40 Ibid., pp. 55-56.

struggle of factions or power groups. Plato conceived that the strongest group would, in the end, prevail and stamp out the others. But this is true only in the case where it is not the aim of the whole society to develop the range of potential which can be found spread through its individual members.

> It is true that the manifold relations of the individual life have only a relative value, and that no single interest must be allowed to absorb the whole self; but to say that man is greater than any individual interest is not to say that he is complete in himself apart from all individual interests. It is not true that man should be indifferent to all special interests because he must not allow himself to be completely immersed in any one. It is not true that the good of man can be realised in a merely internal state of the soul which excludes the family, the State and the various social relations into which men enter with each other. The progress of man consists, in one of its aspects, just in the multiplication of forms of association subordinate to the State.[41]

The limits of the process of individuation in the world-state are imposed by the fact that some modes of development are simply incompatible with the good of all. The Fascist State, the state which seeks to impose by force a narrow religion, a state which devotes itself to mere brutalizing pleasure, all of these have no place in the total federation. Similarly, the development of individual potential is limited by the necessity of preventing those developments which would destroy the whole. The state can tolerate many things, but not intolerance. The world-state can tolerate many species of society, but not those which would destroy other states or those which would destroy the individuals who are their basis.

These limits, Watson keeps telling us, we learn through time and experience.

> The ideal State cannot be antagonistic to the actual State; it can only be realised by the gradual expansion of actual States, an expansion which implies at the same time the internal development of each particular State. When the internal organisation has reached a fair degree of perfection, and has been purged of its narrow vision and its concentration on its own selfish interests, the way has been prepared for a wider form of organisation.[42]

Indeed, the distinction between the life of the individual and the ultimate governing law of the state merely paves the way for the development of ideas like those of Machiavelli. For the state comes to

41 Ibid., p. 56.
42 Ibid.

seem something other than its concrete embodiment and it seems to be the case that statesmen may do what the individual may not. It is not, Watson thinks, that there is *no* distinction.

> Machiavelli is no doubt right in maintaining that there is a distinction between public and private morality, and that a patriotic statesman may do many things which in a private individual would call for severe reprobation. But it is one thing to say that a nation, responsible for the whole life and prosperity of the subjects, cannot be judged in the same way as we judge an individual in his comparatively limited sphere of action, and another thing to say that it is absolved from all moral law and may employ fraud, deceit, treachery and violence under all circumstances and as a regular principle of action.[43]

It seems clear that Watson believes that the state is not a kind of super person and that, therefore, it is not enough simply to extend the rules from individuals to the state. But this is not to say that moral judgment is not to be brought to bear upon the state. Indeed, he says: "It cannot be admitted that statesmanship consists in the endeavour to secure special advantages for one's own people at the expense of other peoples—as if the real interest of one nation were necessarily in antagonism to the interests of all other nations."[44]

An essentially "constructionist" view of the difference between states and individuals leads, naturally, to the social contract theories which one finds in Hobbes and Rousseau. Such theories, after all, stem from the view that one starts with ready-made individuals combined with the view that what is at issue is the reconciliation of the interests of those individuals.

Watson's opposition to such theories derives from his metaphysics, from his moral theory, and, as usual, from some quite careful internal analysis of the theories themselves. He is in no position to support a "social contract" theory, if only because he does not accept the proposition that individuals ultimately exist in an intelligible mode apart from the community.

More importantly, the political issues have a moral aspect precisely because there is a universality of interest represented by the community—a universality of interest which compels rational men to view the world from a standpoint which is not that of their own personal interest. The individualist theory which leads to a social contract analysis, in the end, is not merely wrong; it is also for Watson, immoral.

Apart from these considerations of principle, Watson does not think the internal logic of such theories will stand close analysis. Rous-

43 Ibid., pp. 86-87.
44 Ibid., p. 87.

seau is committed to a theory of the general will in order to give some account of the way in which decisions are to be made. But the basis of a social contract theory precludes the possibility that there is a general will. Hobbes recognizes the problem and assigns absolute powers to his hypothetical monarch once that monarch has met the terms of the original social contract. In no other way, Hobbes thinks, can one get a resolution of the conflicting individual interests. The incoherence of both these theories stems from the fact that, on the one hand, they insist on the primacy of individuality but, on the other hand, they insist on providing some process whereby decisions can be made which are binding on everyone. If this analysis is pushed, it must in the end lead to a contradiction.

Even Kant falls under this dangerous illusion and his political theory ends in delusion. "The original error of making the State merely the result of Contract is further shown in Kant's attempt to assimilate the family and the State to a voluntary association."[45] Kant is forced, in violation of the idea of a contract, to maintain that it is right to force men to enter into society and to respect its laws.

Kant, in Watson's view, is pushed into even further incoherence. Watson sympathizes with Hegel's view of Kant's problem, a view which Watson summarizes as centring around the "opposition of morality and individual rights."[46] Kant's "conception of freedom is due to his opposition of morality and individual rights, leading to a purely subjective view of the former and a negative and abstract view of the latter."[47] On Kant's view of morality, morality ultimately becomes subjective despite his insistence on an objective general rule because the individual must decide which aspects of his moral acts ought to be generalized and which of the possible duties he is to act upon.

Clearly such a theory cannot solve the problem of providing a basis or a political programme which will be both moral and genuinely binding. Morality, in Watson's view, cannot be something imposed upon one from without in an arbitrary way. It must be something which stems from one's rational consciousness of one's own nature. The solution has to be a genuine theory of community.

Watson illustrates this point further in his analysis on Bentham and Mill. His analysis need not detain us because it parallels the analysis of hedonism and utilitarianism which will occupy us extensively in our discussion of Watson's moral theory. In *The State in Peace and War* Watson pays tribute to Mill's perception of the limitations of *state*

45 Ibid., p. 119.
46 Ibid., p. 128.
47 Ibid.

interference: "... his general idea is undoubtedly right, namely, that much which is best in human nature lies beyond the province both of social and of legal sanction."[48] But, again, Watson insists that the transition from the subjective pursuit of pleasure to the consideration of the general good cannot be made on theories like Bentham's and Mill's.

Throughout the long period of modern analysis and statecraft which spans the years between Hobbes and Mill, the tension between the individualist presuppositions of the great social theorists and the demands of a civilized society tended to be covered by gentlemanly understandings which, if they had in the end no rational basis, nevertheless showed an acute moral perception. Even Hobbes grasps the importance of peace and prudence. Spinoza insists upon an outcome to the political process which, if it could be achieved, would be not only morally acceptable but almost utopian. Rousseau respects the dignity and moral integrity of men. Kant was able to envisage the ultimate kingdom of ends. But this gentlemanly understanding was destined to break down as the realities of life exploited the logic of the situation.

The state with no rational ground is dependent on power and power itself is apt, in the end, to become a goal. Watson says:

> The aggressive and ambitious spirit which since 1870 has characterised the German people has been intensified by the writings of NIETZSCHE. In his later years, it is true, he spoke of nationalism with contempt, advocating a united Europe, and calling for men of rigid austerity and self-discipline; but his worship of power has been eagerly caught up by the new Germany which came to self-consciousness after 1870.[49]

Watson quotes Nietzsche as saying that the mission of Germany is to "carry heroism into knowledge and to wage war for the sake of ideas."[50] Watson continues: "It is therefore only natural that General von BERNHARDI should endorse the saying that 'without war inferior or demoralised races should only too easily swamp the healthy and vital ones, and a general decadence would be the result. War is one of the essential factors in morality.'"[51]

What Watson is arguing here is that the state, cut loose from reason, becomes an uncontrollable end in itself. Moreover, this tendency is latent in the individualist social contract theories which preceded the writings of men like Nietzsche. If it is true that, in Kant's

48 Ibid., p. 157.
49 Ibid., p. 171.
50 Ibid.
51 Ibid.

theory, one gets what turns out to be a subjective morality against an abstract theory of the state, then these too are in conflict and the conflict is one which can only be settled by commitment and emotion. The consequences in Germany seem to Watson particularly disastrous—as well they might in the midst of World War I.

> These are the ideas that TREITSCHKE instilled into the mind of young Germany year after year until they have now become all but universal there. Of his ardent patriotism there is no manner of doubt, but it can hardly be called the patriotism of a well-balanced mind. He adopts the doctrine of Bismarck that "even one's good name must be sacrificed to the Fatherland." In his *Lectures on Politics* his [Treitschke's] contrast to Hegel was shown with startling clearness. The State according to Hegel is based upon Will, "its binding cord being not force but the deep-seated feeling of order which is possessed by all." In criticising von Haller, the Treitschke of his day, he [Hegel] says: "It is not the power of the right that Haller means, but the power of the vulture which tears in pieces the innocent lamb." This opposition of Will and Force is obliterated in the writings of Treitschke, and it is from a confusion between them that his theory gets its plausibility.[52]

One must beware the state culture, but since men have common acts and recognize an infinity of interest and belief which requires a measure of common priority, they will recognize some authority of the state as the instantiation of that domain of common reason. In addition, they are aware of both their individuality as a feature of this situation and, if they are sensible, equally aware that there are severe limitations on the ability of any man or group of men to infer clearly the real bonds of reason and mutual dependence which link them. They will thus surround the state with other social institutions which effectively limit its power. They will not allow the state to be the sole and ultimate master of the university, the church, the arts, or, for that matter, the organization of the family. The church, for instance, is the concrete actualization of the common religious consciousness. It is not the whole of that consciousness and it exists to reflect rather than to regulate the common belief. But, in so doing, it will make its own demands on its members and on society and will act as an ameliorating influence on the state.

> Civilisation is necessarily a slow and gradual process, because it implies the response of those upon whom it is attempted to be imposed. Unless they respond, all that is secured is an external conformity, which is very different from a real assimilation of the new spirit, and is sure to be accompanied by hypocrisy and other evils.[53]

52 Ibid., pp. 171-72.
53 Ibid., p. 181.

Nationalism is in itself good so long, and only so long as it is recognized that no nation has a monopoly on merit and no nation is the final instantiation of the potentialities of the human being. Watson thinks that "even granting that one nation possesses all the highest qualities—a preposterous supposition—it would still be true that it has no right to impose its culture on other nations by force."[54] Equally, it *has* the right to defend itself against such impositions. Furthermore, it has a duty to assist in the development of its own culture. "Each nation has its own special task, but this task is perfectly compatible with the exercise of even-handed justice to other nations."[55]

How is it that "each nation has its own task"? There seem to be two reasons for this view on Watson's theory, one theoretical and the other practical. The theoretical reason is that each way of structuring a society necessarily opens some of the possibilities for the development of human reason but closes others. In consequence, insofar as they are rational they are complementary and not antagonistic. In reality, societies are certainly not perfectly rational and it does not follow that each state carries off its task, much less that it would be possible, at all times, to specify exactly what that task is. Practical reason demands that we regard each society at a given point in time as an assembly of states of affairs from which certain courses of action would be optimal for the instantiation of human reason. For no two societies will ever be identical. Furthermore, given the understanding available in any given society, only some programmes, amongst those which are desirable, can be carried out. For instance, it might be desirable at the present moment to nationalize the steel and oil industries in the United States, but it is doubtful whether that task is within the capacity of Americans given their present set of convictions and interests. The expression "task" here simply reflects the fact that there are a different set of problems to be solved in each society. It is sensible to devote much private and public energy in the United States to solving the race problem because the problem is a major feature of the social and political situation. It would be foolish to invest the same amount of private and public energy in such a project in Canada given that the problem simply does not form the larger part of the landscape. In Canada, it is crucial to find acceptable social solutions to the problems posed by a substantial plurality of languages. But, even though there are many people in the United States who do not speak English, it would be foolish to make a major social investment in the solution of that problem there.

In a larger sense, it is part of the general duty of societies to maintain their cultural structures insofar as they are rational struc-

54   Ibid.
55   Ibid., p. 261.

tures. For insofar as they have that property, each of them will perform a special function for men in general. It is not merely that the maintenance of alternatives provides a place to live for the man who finds a given society intolerable and must move. More than that, the differences of culture will make possible a variety of insights which should have a significant issue in philosophy, in art, in music, and in the common human task of understanding human conditions.

To get deeper into Watson's theory, we need to look at his analysis of the problem of property—both because it is a matter of some intrinsic interest and because within it the competing strands of Watson's theory come out, at least in a way which allows them to be dealt with. He says:

> Property, which is based on the abstract idea of personality, is essential to the free realisation of the higher life, being the external instrument for the realisation of that life. The actual distribution of property must depend upon the general social arrangements of the community. It may, however, be said generally that no arrangements which make it virtually impossible for a large section of the community to own property can be defended. Admitting the existence of private property, we cannot fairly object to the accumulation of property in the form of capital, which is used for the production of commodities. Inequality of property is in harmony with the common good, and in any case it is hard to see how it can be prevented in any community which allows freedom of competition. The idea of the older Socialists that men should be assigned advantages according to their capacities would be fatal to the development of the higher literary, scientific and philosophical purcuits. At the same time the legislation should be conducted with a view to providing for the possible acquirement of property by everyone; for without property, as Hegel says, a man cannot be a complete man. Hence the State has the right to interfere with anything that prevents a large number of the citizens from acquiring property. It may, indeed, be doubted if the present system of landed property in England does justice to the working class. Land is unlike capital in this respect, that it cannot be possessed by one person without others being deprived of it, whereas capital benefits both its possessor and those who labour under its superintendence. The system of landed property which has led to a class of landless men requires some readjustment and the State ought therefore to exerise some control over rights of property in land.[56]

What Watson seems to be saying is that there are some general principles which must be adhered to by any society which lays claim to the right to govern itself. Primarily, these have to do with providing the conditions under which there is a reasonable chance for the best

56   Ibid., pp. 234-35.

human capacities to develop. (Watson is serious enough about this and even lays down the conditions for a possible revolution; to justify a revolution, the rebels must show that their "conscience" is "really better than that which is embodied in the existing State";[57] they must show that all constitutional means have been tried and have failed or that they have been denied access to them; and they must show, finally, that "the evils from which we are suffering are so great as to entitle us to risk disorder and bloodshed."[58])

These principles, which apply alike to every society, include the right of *access* to property. This is a general principle in Watson's system because, like Hegel, he takes the view that property is necessary for the development of personality. (This does not have a very mysterious meaning: It seems to mean that one cannot be a brain surgeon unless one has a scalpel, one cannot be a scholar without books, one cannot exert a concrete influence on one's fellow men unless one is allowed to possess the tools of some important trade.) It is not, he thinks, that everyone is entitled to possess a certain amount or a certain kind of property. A man may value his liberty and leisure more than a given possession, and may not seek access to that possession. He is arguing for what is commonly called "equality of opportunity," but that is not all; he is arguing that the community must actually provide the means which a citizen can use to acquire property. The means might sometimes be education since education enables one to provide service for which others will trade property (Watson places the right to an education "upon the same basis as the right to life and liberty"[59]), but even education is not enough. Access will also require the maintenance of conditions of industry and commerce in which the individual has a positive power to participate. Hence, when the distribution of some commodities is like that of land, and because what is possessed by one cannot be possessed by another, the system becomes an entrenched class structure, and the state must openly intervene. Watson, in this passage, is chiding the British for their failure to provide what was provided naturally in Canada—free land. He would certainly have admitted that the situation was not as easy to deal with in England as in Canada, since most land in England had long been occupied but presumably, he would urge that there is nothing to prevent the state from buying up land from generation to generation and making it available to new claimants. A society which has wealth in manufacture and in the provision of banking services is in a good position to trade valuable intangibles for land and can do so at will.

57 Ibid., pp. 232-33.
58 Ibid., p. 233.
59 Ibid.

Beyond this, Watson thinks, what one will do will depend upon the general social arrangements of the community. In highly complex industrial societies, he does not think that socialism, as he understood it, will work. For he does not think that there is any way of determining whether what one may have is exactly equal to or equivalent to what another man has, and he does not see how the traditional slogan "From each according to his abilities, to each according to his needs"[60] can be cashed in such a society. Needs are relative to one's social conditioning and expectations. Abilities are virtually impossible to assess. Watson's remark about socialism and its relations to literature, science, and philosophy seems to derive from this concern. He believes that it is by no means impossible for the state to suppose that John Watson had as much ability to work on the production line at the tractor factory as to produce philosophy and, given the option of imposing work "according to one's abilities," it might choose to convert him into a tractor-maker. This seems a healthy enough fear if only because all societies have their quota of powerful Philistines.[61]

Obviously he does not think that the poor can be left to their poverty—he supports all those kinds of public services which are likely to make possible a genuine sense of community. The emphasis which he would put on public education—including the education of women—is forcefully ahead of its time. On the other side, he has an abiding distrust of power, a real fear of institutions which, though they can only represent one facet of the community, develop pretentious claims about their ability to represent the whole. He retains the Scots Presbyterian conviction that hard work is good for people and ought to be encouraged. (He objects to great wealth, apparently, only insofar as it implies great power.) He recommends as much openness as possible.

He realizes that there are limits to this openness, but he would like to establish them as broadly as possible. He says:

> We must make it clear what we mean by liberty. There can be no right simply to be allowed to do anything that one would like to do, irrespective of what it is we purpose doing. Liberty is good or bad according as the things which can be done are good or bad. The proper sense of liberty, therefore, is that every well-regulated society ought to secure to all its members, as far as possible, the opportunity of developing their natural gifts and powers so far as they can do so without detriment to one another or to the well-being of the community as a whole. . . . Liberty is the essence of opportunity, for self-

60 Karl Marx, *Capital and Other Writings*, ed. Max Eastman (New York: Modern Library, 1932), p. 7.
61 But Watson himself does not very seriously address the problem of matching social needs to individual desires in the context of a labour market.

development is the creation of law, and not something which could exist apart from the action of the State.[62]

To an important extent, the uncertainties of Watson's political theories derive from the structure of his ethical theory and his ethical theory is, in an important sense, more fundamental: Not all political problems can be readily solved on Watson's view because, after all, their solution involves a delicate trade-off between issues about individual rights and values, and social rights and values. And his theory, as we know, is one in which the two sets of rights are inextricably bound up with one another.

In discussing the historical background to Watson's work, we suggested that the idealist metaphysic which Watson developed had its origins in a pattern of thought which derived, originally, from T. H. Green's fundamental concerns about the understanding of human personality and the basic social and political situation which confronted Englishmen in the last half of the nineteenth century. In trying to get at the roots of these issues, Green came to question fundamental assumptions about the nature of the world. Watson pursued the assumptions in a way which made it even clearer that, for him, the nature of human personality was inevitably communitarian. Persons are not discrete substances—whether material or spiritual—but rather individuations of a common system. In this way, Watson had a ready-made grounding for the notion of obligation. If we derive our personalities from one another, it is ludicrous for us to suppose that we can, in the end, profit at one another's expense. For me to develop my personality at the expense of yours is for me to undermine the very basis of my own personality and so to nullify any gain which I might make. As it stands, however, to say this is not to say enough. It suggests that the argument for a moral theory is really a prudential argument. It suggests that I ought to behave well because there is, ultimately, no advantage in behaving badly. Someone might argue that it is required by morality that one act imprudently. He might argue that even if morality must fail, one ought to try it anyway. Someone with the temperament of Watson's old enemy Herbert Spencer or the temperament of Nietzsche might be willing to argue that it is the duty of great men to act in opposition to the community even if that means the destruction of the community because, whatever the metaphysical basis of personality might be, it is still necessary to take whatever risk might be needed in order to instantiate the highest-order values.

Watson must, therefore, take on these arguments—by implication even if not overtly—in order to ground his system. In essence, he must

---

62 Watson, *The State in Peace and War*, pp. 231-32.

find a basis for ethics which is not, *simply*, an extension of his metaphysics. For there is, really, a sense in which one must face ethical questions in their own right. Watson wrote no major work on ethics as such. Moreover, he regarded his philosophical system as a single unity and he would not have been willing to admit that any philosophical subject matter existed which could not be integrated into that system. He did, however, tackle ethics on its own ground and he did so in a way which made clear the manner in which ethical questions are to be treated in their own right, while still remaining a perfectly integrated part of his philosophical system. His best account of this situation is in a paper which he published in the *Journal of Speculative Philosophy*.[63] Watson was then not quite thirty but there is no reason to believe that in the remaining sixty years of his life he changed his opinion significantly. The paper was entitled "Hedonism and Utilitarianism" but, though much of it, certainly, is taken up with an attack on the theories of Bentham, Mill, and Sidgwick, it is by no means restricted to the topic of the title. Rather, Watson attacks the utilitarians in the course of developing his own theory.

The paper is fascinating for a number of reasons. One of them is that Watson gives a much more subtle and interesting account of the theories actually espoused by Mill and Sidgwick than one usually finds in the literature. Another is that it explains the fact that Watson attached great importance to hedonism itself. He went so far as to write a book on the history of hedonism because he thought such theories were major contenders for human allegiance.

At its simplest, hedonism is simply the theory that the good consists of pleasure. Traditionally, it came in two forms, egoistic hedonism and ethical hedonism. Egoistic hedonism is the doctrine that what one ought to do is to maximize one's own pleasures. Ethical hedonism is the doctrine that what one ought to do is maximize either the pleasures of all men or the pleasures of some intrinsically deserving group of men. The English hedonists of the nineteenth century—Bentham, Mill, and Sidgwick—all insisted upon some form of "ethical" hedonism. It should be obvious that any form of ethical hedonism requires the addition of some principle other than the simple "pleasure principle" and it is this which led to the development of quite complex and subtle theories.

Utilitarianism is the doctrine that acts are to be judged by their consequences. The alternatives to this view are frequently badly specified, but one of them, at least, is the doctrine that acts should be judged

63 John Watson, "Hedonism and Utilitarianism," *Journal of Speculative Philosophy*, vol. 10, no. 3 (1876).

simply as acts and determined to be right or wrong independently of their consequences. Another is the view that acts are to be judged by their intentions and a third alternative is that one ought to judge the motives of the act. Hedonism and utilitarianism seem naturally to go together, so much so that Mill simply entitled his major theoretical statement *On Utilitarianism*. It seems obvious enough that hedonism will generally entail utilitarianism. For pleasure is most naturally thought of as the outcome of an act rather than as a property attaching to the act itself, but, even if that were not true, to urge someone to seek pleasure would surely be to urge him to weigh most carefully the consequences of his acts, for almost any act will have an effect on one's future as well as one's present pleasure. It is not so obvious that utilitarianism entails hedonism and, indeed, that relation would frequently be denied. If one sets out to judge acts by their consequences, one must face up to the question: What are the morally relevant consequences of any act? Though Mill's equation of what is desired and what is, in the moral sense, desirable has almost always been regarded by philosophers as a simple equivocation, one is forced to ask oneself if anything can be desired if its *ultimate* outcome is not a preponderance of pleasure over pain. Even Kant felt compelled to concede that it would be difficult to justify the imposition of an obligation on anyone if the universe did not guarantee that, in the end, those who behaved well would be granted a state of affairs containing a preponderance of personal happiness. One might argue that if anything is evil, pain is evil and, if consequences are to be judged, one ought to judge the likelihood that it will be absent. It would take a Draconian masochist to urge that a desirable consequence of any act would be one in which there were many high-order values but all men were wracked with pain.

One should notice the point here: If one judges that a certain act—say the telling of a lie—is bad, just considered as an act, many considerations come into play. The maxim favouring the act, as Kant says, is not universalizable. For it is, in some sense, logically absurd if universalized. The statement "Lying is good" seems to express a preference which is at odds with itself. If it is good and if I ought to do what is good, then I ought now to be telling a lie and I ought, therefore, to say "Lying is bad." At least, one cannot say "Lying is everyone's duty" for then my obligation would be to tell the lie expressed by the sentence "Lying is not everyone's duty." Lying is also self-defeating, not in its consequences, but in itself, for the point of making factual statements is to encourage their dissemination and belief. But if lying were very general, lying would have no such point. This is not a proposition about the consequences of lying—for those may be highly particular in any given case—but about the logic of the situation. One might also urge that one who tells lies is pitching himself headlong against values which he must, simultaneously, hold and that by telling lies he has committed himself to a kind of schizophrenic life. But suppose we were to set out simply to test the consequences of a given lie. If that were all there were to it, we might argue, very plausibly, that the lie would be justified if it greatly increased pleasure or even slightly decreased pain. For that is, indeed, how men generally do argue when telling lies. To a man who has just had a heart attack, we may think it justified to tell lies about his health on the ground that, if badly upset, he might actually die and on the ground that his worsened health might cause substantial pain to others. Insofar as consequences are relevant, these seem to be the very consequences which count. If we begin to name values other than pleasures and pains, the case seems to grow increasingly absurd. It would be odd to argue that telling lies was justified because it would help men to save their souls, or because it would lead to progress in science or the literary arts, or even because it would lead to good and orderly government. All these values may be extremely important but, considered as *consequences*, they seem to be beside the point. The reason, evidently, is that they all involve values which are closely connected with the proposition that one ought to value *acts* as such. If a man's soul is to be saved, it will, presumably, be through faith or right action and the notion of convenient short cuts to heaven is somehow unpleasant. The progress of science and the literary arts depends so obviously upon honesty and upon being in a community in which men act well that consequentialism generally appears irrelevant to such considerations. The same is true, *a fortiori*, of good government. The best governments do not always have the best consequences. Rather, they are composed of men who act well in a society in which right action is possible. We do not argue that, at the time of Munich, the Czechs would have been well advised to cloak themselves in a pseudo-Nazi government. Far better to perish as oneself than to succeed while pretending to be a Nazi.

At any rate, historically, hedonism and utilitarianism tended to go together and Watson confronted them, primarily, in the theories of Mill and Sidgwick. Only one other qualification needs to be made in order to get the theory quite straight. Mill most frequently talked about happiness, but he made no secret of the fact that he meant by happiness "pleasure and freedom from pain." This is important because, in the history of Western philosophy, there have been two clusters of theories about happiness. One group of theorists urged that happiness consists of a preponderance of certain feelings. Theorists in the other group have generally insisted that happiness is essentially a matter of rational balance. In the theories he is discussing, Watson is at pains to point out that "'Happiness,' in the mouth of the Utilitarian, does not of course mean a conceived end of action, pursued from its adequacy to satisfy the rational nature of man; it is simply a synonyme [sic] for a sum of feelings. . . ."[64] Again, it is only happiness in this sense which can be regarded essentially as consequential. In the other sense, happiness is very closely tied to the nature of our acts themselves.

Now Mill, on his own view and Watson's, ran into immediate difficulties with two aspects of this theory. The first was the notion of the *quantitative* aggregation of pleasure. There were two aspects to this, to one of which Bentham had responded clearly enough but without realizing its implications, and one of which Bentham and Mill's father, James, had refused to countenance. The first has to do simply with distribution. Bentham had urged that what should be sought was the general happiness of men in a community. In so doing, he was really introducing another principle. For he was saying that what counted was not simply the amount of happiness produced by an act but the amount of happiness together with its distribution. To make Smith very happy and everyone else very miserable would not do even if, in amount, Smith's happiness outweighed the vague and faint misery of all others. The other issue has to do with the question of whether pleasures are simply pleasures, as Bentham, on the whole, was inclined to think or whether, as seemed obvious to Mill, some pleasures were intrinsically more desirable than others.

The second difficulty is that, somehow, we must associate our moral judgments with our judgments of the persons who perform acts. Watson quotes Mill as saying: "The morality of an action depends entirely upon the *intention*—that is upon what the agent *wills* to do,"[65] and remarks that Bentham held the same view about this problem. This introduces an obvious confusion into the situation, for here "morality" is used in reference to the judgment which we impose upon the man who does the deed. The act, in other words, is good or bad depending upon its propensity to produce pleasure or pain and, in the case that it produces pleasure and diminishes pain, upon the appropriate distribution. But the man who does the thing is a good man or a bad man if he is related to the act by an intention. This introduces yet another principle of morality. It suggests a justification of that special class of moral propositions which distribute praise or blame. Mill wants to do this and to eliminate the consideration of motives. He says: "But

64 Ibid., p. 274.
65 Ibid., p. 281.

the motive, that is the feeling which makes him will so to do, when it makes no difference in the act makes none in the morality."[66] The reason is that judging motives would undermine the propriety of the notion that one is primarily to judge consequences. The difficulty, as Watson points out, is that, if you eliminate the motive, you no longer have a description of the act which will enable anyone to associate it, in the strict sense, with the man who did the deed. This arises from the simple fact that it is hard to know what the description of the act then ought to be. An example, perhaps, will serve to straighten this out. (Watson's paper is regrettably lacking in examples, so we must contrive our own.) Suppose that one description of a given act is that it is the discharging of a revolver in such a way as to blow out Smith's brains. It is not enough to establish that Jones intended to pull the trigger if we want to characterize the act so as to make possible a moral judgment. If what he wanted to do was to frighten away a pack of savage dogs which was molesting a small child, that is one thing. The death of Smith, then, may be anything from a regrettable accident to a case of man-slaughter—depending upon how careful or negligent the operator was. If what he intended to do was to eliminate Smith so that he could run away with Smith's wife, the act is murder. The difference between the two is not precisely, as Watson suggests, one of "motive." It is more nearly one of what is called, in the law, *mens rea*. It all depends, that is, on the state of the gunman's mind and a crucial ingredient in that state of mind may well be his motives. We can see from this that even such questions as whether he simply intended to pull the trigger and nothing more or whether he intended to perform a socially valuable act or an act of murder cannot really be settled without recourse to a variety of other considerations. Watson's point is generally valid: Mill must admit more than *simple* intention in order to get any account of intention itself and, in so doing, he will doubtless create other objects of judgment which will interfere with his general utilitarian position.

We can now quite easily summarize what seems to be worrisome about hedonism and about utilitarianism or about any reasonable combination of them. They start out with the simple propositions about certain sensations and about the desirability of weighing consequences. They end by having to introduce considerations which have little to do with sensations of pleasure and which force one away from the simple-minded notion that one should simply judge consequences. What Watson wants to show is that, in every case, one must import considerations about the nature of reason. Only when we have succeeded in doing this, can we even estimate the relative soundness of the

66 Ibid.

kinds of propositions which philosophers from Bentham to Sidgwick have wanted to announce.

The first phase of Watson's theory, therefore, is developed by trying to show, in detail, just how reason must be brought to bear on this situation even if all one wants to say is precisely what Mill wanted to say.

At the beginning of the paper we are told that we will be shown what a "theory of conduct is, or ought to be," and how it is "the exact counterpart and reflection of a theory of knowledge."[67]

The first phase really amounts to this: We can see, from an examination of Mill's theory, that, even within the domain of considerations about pleasure and pain, we need a principle of distribution, a principle of selection, and a principle of judgment which is not purely consequentialist. Watson does not (at least so far as we are aware) ever consider the possibility that these principles, themselves, might be selected on hedonistic grounds. It would appear to be logically possible for a hedonistic utilitarian to hold, at least with respect to the first two required principles, that while one cannot *generate* the principles from a simple consideration of the data of pleasure or pain, one might nevertheless make one's choice between competing principles by asking oneself about their propensity to generate pleasure or pain. If one is faced with a choice between the view that what counts is my pleasure and the view that what counts is the best distribution of pleasure generally, one might apparently ask oneself which of these principles gave one the most pleasure. Similarly, if one must choose between pleasures on some ground other than a simply quantitative ground, one might ask oneself whether one was better pleased by, say, the theory that one should always choose intellectual over carnal pleasures or by the theory that carnal pleasures are always preferable. It is even conceivable that one might ask oneself whether one was better pleased by judging consequences always or by sometimes judging acts, though this third issue seems to present obvious logical difficulties which stem from the fact that one who was better pleased by judging acts than by judging consequences would be committed to the view that one should sometimes judge on some basis other than the propensity to produce pleasure. One might think of positions of this kind as being the most drastic form of what, in recent literature, has come to be called "rule" utilitarianism. (Essentially "rule" utilitarianism is the doctrine that one should ask whether acting on certain rules tends to optimize pleasure—or whatever other goal the utilitarian has in mind—and avoid asking whether specific acts are to be judged favourably on this

67 Ibid., p. 271.

ground or not. It would seem that "rule" utilitarianism will not work in that general form because one ends by judging a class of acts the members of which may vary enormously in their capacity to produce pleasures and pains. The rule could only be judged by summing these acts and attempting to strike a balance. Such a sum probably cannot be undertaken. In the form suggested above, however, the situation changes, for one is not judging the propensity of some distribution rule or some selection rule to produce a preponderance of pleasure over pain. One is rather asking whether maintaining that rule as one's principle of action would itself tend to please one or not.)

Watson does not consider this possibility for what, we would surmise, is a perfectly good reason. It would seem to lead to an infinite regress. Suppose I determine that Bentham's principle of distribution pleases me more than the principle adopted by the egoist. I ought then to ask whether this method of selecting principles pleases me better than an alternative principle—say a rationalist principle. But that will not entirely settle the case either. I ought then to ask whether decision making is pleasing, whether moral theorizing is pleasing, whether philosophizing is pleasing and so on. It is not merely that there seems to be no end to these questions in principle. It is also that, though committed to answering an endless array of questions, the hedonist who took this view would be committed, always, to answering them the same way. And he will fall into difficulty if it turns out, for instance, that playing pool is more pleasurable than moral theorizing. For, if it is, he ought not to bother, on this view, with moral theorizing at all.

At this point we can see something of what is wrong with the whole hedonist utilitarian system. It is very important to the hedonist, if he is right, that people should pay attention to him—whether they derive great pleasures from reading books by John Stuart Mill or Henry Sidgwick or not. For what he is purporting to do is to tell us what is "good" or what is "right conduct." One surely cannot offer as an excuse for behaving badly the proposition that it did not please one to study moral theory and it seems doubtful that Bentham, Mill, or Sidgwick would have thought so. It would also seem absurd to enter into an indefinite array of question answering when one had already determined exactly what all the answers must be.

It seems to us that this is essentially Watson's position: At some point in the determination of these questions one must leave the pleasure principle and fall back on reason. The issues are: the limitations of Mill's distribution principle, the limitations of the principle of selection, and the limitations of consequentialism. Let us look at the three issues in turn.

Watson devotes considerable space to dealing with Mill's attempt to show that our unease at the distribution principle which he adopts is consistent with the general belief in the desirability of justice. This raises, really, two questions: Is Mill's form of hedonistic utilitarianism actually consistent with the principles of general justice? If it is, can his principle be derived without departing from hedonism? Watson's answer to both questions is "No." It is worth quoting here at some length his response to each of these questions.

Of the first, he says:

The application of the Greatest Happiness principle to the sphere of subjective morality does not at once do violence to the convictions of mankind. There is one sphere, however, where the contradiction inherent in Utilitarianism, comes clearly to the surface. The absoluteness of the moral obligation to respect the rights of others has so strongly impressed itself on the human mind, that a shock is felt the moment it is hinted that the conception of Justice is resolvable ultimately into a desire for the general happiness. It is usually assumed that those acts classed as just differ in essential nature from those that are only expedient; being right in their own nature, quite irrespective of any consequences they may have. A contrast so decided the Utilitarian cannot admit, without giving up the derivation of morality from a calculus of pleasurable feelings; and hence the necessity of a special explanation of the conception of justice. Mr. Mill devotes a whole chapter to this topic; attempting to reconcile the apparent infinity of the claims of justice with the asserted origin of it in the desire of general happiness. His efforts are directed to the end of showing that the supposed difference in kind between acts of expediency and acts of justice is really a difference of degree, subjective necessity being confused by the influence of well-known laws of association with objective validity. That which constitutes the specific difference between justice and other obligations of morality is the fact that the former implies a correlative *right* in some person or persons. No one has a moral right to our generosity or beneficence, because although these are virtues, we are under no obligation to practice them towards any definite person, nor at any prescribed time. Justice, on the other hand, implies that there is something which it is not only right to do, and wrong not to do, but which some individual person may claim from us as a moral right. This being the distinctive character of the idea of justice, we can explain how the sentiment or feeling accompanying it has grown up. The essential ingredients in the feeling are, the knowledge that there is some definite individual or individuals, to whom harm has been done, and the desire to punish the person who has done the harm. This desire is the spontaneous outgrowth of two natural feelings, the animal impulse of self-defence, and the feeling of sympathy with those closely connected with us; both of which either are or resemble instincts. These impulses men possess in common with the animals. The superiority of man lies in the capacity he has of enlarging his sympathy beyond those to whom it is naturally directed, so as to embrace all human and even all sentient beings; and in his more developed intelligence, which enables him to perceive that the interest of others is also his own interest. The peculiar energy of the feeling of justice arises from the animal element of retaliation implied in it; its apparent necessity from the supreme importance of the interest it guards—security, the very condition of human happiness. This account of the origin of justice implicitly explains why there is a moral obligation to practice it. The feeling of retaliation in itself has nothing moral in it; it only becomes moral when exclusively subordinated to the social sympathies, i.e., to a desire for the general happiness. The moral obligation, then, to respect the rights of others lies in the fact that in no other way can the same amount of pleasure be produced, while every violation of justice strikes at the very basis of those interests which are the very condition of human happiness.

It must be at once apparent to any one who has got the clue to the *equivoque* latent in Utilitarianism that this account of the origin and binding force of the sentiment of justice involves, from first to last, a confusion between pleasurable feelings and objects that reason alone can constitute. It endeavours to explain in the first place, the origin of the feeling that accompanies the idea of justice; and, secondly, the moral obligation to observe rules of justice. The rights of others ought to be respected (to take the last point first) because a violation of them tends to diminish the ideal sum of pleasures the community is entitled to. The feeling of retaliation has nothing moral in it, but the same feeling when universalized so as to include an aggregate of individuals, takes on a moral hue and becomes a duty. Mr. Mill is in doubt as to whether this feeling is an instinct or only something resembling an instinct. If it is an instinct, it cannot in the first instance be a desire for pleasure, since pleasure must be experienced before it can be imagined as desirable. It may, however, be said that although it is at first blindly thrown out at an indefinite object, it afterwards takes the form of an imagination of pleasure. This assumption must be made, if the sentiment of justice partly derived from it is to be explained as a generalization of pleasure. The desire for one's own pleasure, we are to suppose, shows itself negatively in resentment against the person who, by harming us, decreases the amount of satisfaction we should otherwise have had. This natural desire for individual pleasure becomes moral when it is widened so as to include the pleasure of the "greatest number." But if there is nothing moral in the desire of the greatest amount of pleasure one may secure for himself, how does the mere fact that the desire is for a maximum of pleasure, to be distributed among an aggregate number of individuals, alter the essential nature of the feeling? The mere diminution of pleasure admittedly does not constitute injustice, for it is held to be right to lessen the pleasure of the wrong-doer.[68]

68   Ibid., pp. 285-87.

Mill's answer to the first question does not work for the obvious and simple reason that Mill has given up the construction of a moral theory and fallen back on a piece of descriptive psychology which fails to describe anything which remotely amounts to a duty. Furthermore, he has in the process made a damaging admission—the admission that the diminution of pleasure is not itself necessarily even to be regretted. He must of course make that admission for, whatever some of the sterner Victorian moralists may have thought, Mill was neither a fool nor an advocate of viciousness. Whenever, in fact, issues of general justice are introduced, it appears that a straightforward hedonism is inconsistent with a resolution of them. It will simply turn out, very often, that the appropriate aggregation of pleasures leads to actual injustice.

This obviously casts doubt on any attempt by Mill to sustain his principle of distribution at all. Watson wisely turns, at this point in his argument, to the position adopted by Henry Sidgwick. "If, as Mr. Sidgwick says, the mere fact that 'I am I' does not make my pleasure of more importance than that of others, neither does the mere fact that 'they are they' introduce any new element into the calculation, unless it can be shown that the good of the community is of more importance than the experience of pleasure by the individual."[69] But Sidgwick thinks that the desire for one's own happiness involves the admission that the desire for the general happiness *ought* to be the end of action and he appears to think that this follows from what might well be called a principle of indifference. Watson calls this "a conclusion that will not conclude."[70] It is, again, a confusion between experiential principles and principles of reason. Whatever goodness or merit attaches to any pleasure does so independently of any issue about who has that pleasure. There appear to be two queries here and, although Watson seems to have noticed only one of them, there is little doubt that his answer is fundamentally right. One of the questions arises from the fact that every sensible person would surely admit that the pleasure is not better or worse because of its relation to its possessor. Thus the pleasure of a simple peasant is surely as good as the pleasure of the wisest sage. And this might well lead us to the view that one of them has as good a claim as the other to any given pleasure. In one sense, this is certainly true. The fact that a man is a wise sage—if any one is—in no sense entitles him to collect all the pleasures in the world to himself. The fact that a man is a simple peasant offers no justification for the view that he ought to have only few and simple pleasures. Thus we might think that

69 Ibid., p. 287.
70 Ibid.

we were under a general obligation to provide pleasures in equal amount for each. Probably, we are under such an obligation, but the obligation does not follow from anything about pleasure. It follows from something about human beings. If we just consider pleasures, they are as good if one person has all of them as if they are world distributed. It is only when we consider human beings that this distinction arises. Watson does not in this passage cope with that question, but he is nevertheless right in believing that one cannot derive any such principle from a mere examination of pleasures.

The other question is this: If we are under an obligation to provide pleasure for anyone, that obligation presumably extends to everyone. But we cannot derive this notion from Sidgwick's principle of indifference. The principle may entail, as we have said, that pleasures do not acquire more or less merit as a result of their association with individuals who may be in one way or another more or less meritorious. But one cannot tell from hedonist principles that one is under an *obligation* to produce pleasure for anyone. We *do* seek pleasures. It seems absurd to imagine that we are *obliged* to. There is a great difference between holding, even, that I am justified in pursuing my own pleasures and holding that I am *obliged* to provide pleasure for myself. It would be very queer to attack one who chose the monastic life on the ground that he admitted that his life was not well filled with pleasure. Why should he seek pleasure if he doesn't want to? And if he does not seek pleasure for himself, why should he seek it for others? All of these questions simply suggest that one cannot after all derive a principle of distribution from an analysis of pleasure. Some non-hedonistic principle is an essential ingredient in any system which purports to be able to justify such a principle.

Watson wants to make two points about this. One is that it is only by an appeal to reason that one can justify the distribution principle to which Bentham, Mill, and Sidgwick all subscribe. The other is that once the distribution principle is grasped, it is not pleasure which turns out to be the good to be distributed but "that 'blessedness' which springs from the realization of reason by a being who in his essential nature is rational."[71]

Reason enters this way: "Except as a relation between persons, rendered possible by the substantial unity of their nature, the social feelings cannot be shown to be more praiseworthy than the purely self-regarding desires."[72] It is the appearance of reason as an orderly

71 Ibid., p. 289.
72 Ibid.

structure in experience that leads us, in any case, to construct the notion of the self which links the various pleasures and pains to which we are subject. We notice the unity in our experience but we also notice that that unity cannot be derived from an account of our immediate sensations. Rather, what Watson seems to want to say is that the unity in our experience is grasped in and through our attempts to make sense of that experience. Pleasures and pains are meaningful when, like other sensations, they are linked together to form an intelligible pattern. When we reflect on this pattern we see, however, that it goes beyond the rational construction of any individual sentient being. The very distinction between my self and the world makes sense only within a rational framework which gives a place to others. Otherwise, I might regard the whole world as my imaginary creation. I do not do this because it does not make sense of my life. I must regard part of the world as composed of others who have desires and the capacity to reason as well. It is when I come to see that my own claim is not, *rationally*, different from that of anyone else that I can proceed from self-interest to morality. Morality for Watson seems, in the end, to be the acceptance of the commitment to reason which goes into the process of making sense of my own life.

Reason in this way decrees that I shall not exploit my self-interest at the expense of others. Reason decrees that I shall take this position because, if I do not, reason will fail me and my attempt to make sense of my own life or of any other. This sense of reason, as something revealed through the development of experience as an orderly organizing pattern in that experience is, as we have seen, crucial to the whole of Watson's philosophy.

The conundrum which faces the hedonist with respect to the second issue—the principle of selection—turns out to be an analogue of the difficulty he faces in trying to find a principle of distribution. The selection problem arises for him in two ways. First of all, he must determine how to restrict the domain of consequences. For he cannot weigh infinitely many consequences which might accrue from any act. Secondly, he must be in a position, even if he has his distribution principle, to make a selection amongst what may well be an infinite class of possible acts many members of which might produce equally many pleasures or suppress equal amounts of pain.

Mill, as we have seen, had certainly noticed these difficulties and had proposed to introduce notions about the *quality* of pleasure as a way of delimiting the sphere and producing a selection principle. Watson concedes that this "alternative is openly or tacitly adopted by all Utilitarians; and indeed it is impossible to see how universalistic, can otherwise be distinguished from egoistic Hedonism."[73] Watson agrees with Mill that it would be "absurd" to do otherwise but he denies Mill's view that this principle is really compatible with hedonism as such. For one is then not judging pleasures but some other characteristic. He is inclined to drop the discussion of this issue there and simply point out, again, that reason must be employed to solve the problem. He might have pointed out that Mill's principle would not, in any case, have actually solved the problem. It is worthwhile to explore this notion a little because further exploration of it helps to make clear the grounds for Watson's own solution to the problem.

The indefiniteness of the situation is partly the result of attending to pleasure as such in isolation from the person who has the pleasure and, most importantly, from the community within which the judgment is to be made. An underlying theme of Watson's explication of the situation is always that what is at stake is a person in a community, that both exhibit the development of reason, and that both have their satisfaction in the fulfillment of a rational order. I am an individual and what is important to me is not simple aggregation of pleasures but the development of a life which has a satisfactory and satisfying meaning to it. I live in a community composed of other individuals who also want to give meanings to their lives and who hope to do so by developing a community which, itself, has a meaning to it. The sphere of moral inquiry is thus at once universalized and particularized. It is universalized because it goes beyond me to persons in general and all persons are to be taken account of. It is particularized because I am an actual person and I live in an actual community and the decisions that I make have relevance here and now. The best decisions are those that reasonable persons would all, alike, make if they were in the same position. But they are not abstract decisions and they are always relative to what I can do and know how to do.

If we bear this in mind, then, even if our concern is only about pleasure, we can achieve some semblance of an answer to the problem. Those pleasures which may be very intense now but which, if pursued, will render my life incoherent or even actually meaningless ought to be eschewed. Those pleasures which will help to render my life meaningful ought to be preferred. Similarly, those pleasures which I might have now at the expense of damaging the community are to be avoided while those pleasures which can be shared by everyone and which will help to maintain at least a minimum level of communal coherence are to be preferred.

73   Ibid., p. 274.

Mill would not, in all likelihood, disagree with this kind of outcome. Nor, indeed, would Sidgwick. What they would insist upon is the proposition that one can reach principles of selection without departing from the hedonistic ground. But Watson wants to stop them at every step.

> ... the Utilitarian is not entitled to suppose that pleasurable feelings differ in their "intrinsic nature." It is only by investing feeling with relations of thought incompatible with its transiency—by covertly bringing back the conditions of it which are ostensibly excluded—that generic differences can be predicated of one feeling as compared with another. To say that one feeling differs from another in kind, is to employ language the self-contradictory character of which is concealed because pleasure as a momentary feeling is confused with a determinate object, conceived as fitted to satisfy a rational being. The assertion that intellectual pleasures are higher than bodily pleasures, carries conviction with it only because the one class is regarded as more compatible with the higher nature of man than the other. The man, it is implied, who seeks to satisfy himself with the pleasures of sense, is either ignorant of, or willfully ignores the higher gratification he might obtain through the exercise of his intellectual faculties. But here the data from which a generic difference is inferred, are not mere feelings of pleasure, but pleasure as related to a being who "looks before and after," and whose rational nature will not be cheated by an object utterly inadequate to it.[74]

This then leaves us with the third issue faced by the hedonistic utilitarian, the difficulty which derives from his consequentialist convictions. The point that Watson has persistently been making seems to be simply that, as we saw earlier, the utilitarian will have to move from a purely consequentialist standpoint to a position which involves judging more than consequences. That follows simply as a corollary to any possible solution to the problem of finding a principle of distribution and the problem of finding a principle of selection. If we interpret Watson as we have been throughout the preceding discussion, this position can be put very simply. The aim is to get a rational plan for one's life and a rational plan for one's community and the two are not to be separated from each other. If this entails the attempt to impose meaning, then it is the meaningfulness of the act itself as well as, and indeed, much more than the consequences of the act which are to be judged. It might well turn out to be the case that, simply by acting randomly, one would turn out to produce more pleasures and fewer pains than one could by any specific programme of rational action. But there would be something wrong with this. To choose, again, one of

74   Ibid., pp. 275-76.

our own examples (since Watson supplies none), we do not normally praise the would-be bank robber whose shot goes astray and knocks the knife out of the hand of a man who, unknown to him, is about to stab the bank manager. Such fortuitous acts may have excellent consequences. They have nothing to do with morality. One must suppose that Watson would have an easy explanation for this example. No one thinks that our hypothetical bank robber with the bad aim is a good man because no one thinks that the accidental production of consequences is itself good. The act is to be judged for the meaning it has in the life of the man who does it and the meaning it creates for the lives of those on whom it impinges as a meaningful human relation. (Once again we do not judge extremely remote consequences morally because they do not impinge upon us as meaningful human relations. Even if I could show that some of my present problems are caused by the acts of Julius Caesar I would not blame *him*. For no human relation of a meaningful kind is created between the two of us by the causal connection.) Mill, on the other hand, would have serious difficulty coping with this example. He does, as we saw, concede that there are two kinds of questions to be answered and that one of them is not simply about goodness or badness of the outcome but about the extent to which responsibility for it should be assigned to the person who performs the act. He concedes that intentions are the link but he denies that motives are to be counted. We saw that his difficulty was essentially to get a description of the act while employing intentions and denying motives, or so, at any rate, Watson argued.

But we can see now that there is a larger problem which faces Mill. He must explain how and why consequences are relevant at all. Since his theory is conceived in terms of pleasure, consequences must be relevant. Since, however, it is virtually impossible to link the occurrence of pleasure to the goodness of the pleasure in a way that gives a coherent notion of responsibility, how can we cope with it at all? If Mill cannot cope with it at all, then his entire theory collapses.

It is essentially Watson's view that Mill, as usual, tacitly assumes more than his theory will allow him. In particular, he tacitly assumes that pleasures take place within the context of a developing human being, and as his theory progresses he appears to move more and more toward what might be called an "ideal observer" theory. (Mill does, at one point, urge that when choosing between rival pleasures one should value the judgment of those with a wide experience of different pleasures and he comes to put more and more reliance on what seems to be the judgment of the cultivated man.) But Watson has a deeper objection than this:

The only way in which feelings can be comprehended in one sum is by being related to a permanent subject of them, and so related, they are transmuted by the alchemy of reason and come forth as universalized feelings, i.e., as a conceived object, with which a rational being may be supposed without contradiction to identify himself. A particular feeling cannot be judged of without ceasing to be particular; and it is only by the unwarrantable confusion of pleasure as a mere feeling with an object that gives satisfaction because it is, rightly or wrongly, conceived as calculated to satisfy one's spiritual nature, that Utilitarianism seems at first sight so convincing, but is really so inconclusive.[75]

Watson goes on from this passage to attack Mill's latent ideal observer theory. But the point that he really wants to make, evidently, is that judging pleasures is quite different from responding to them. If one is going to have a moral theory and not merely a theory which describes how, as a matter of fact, people do respond to pleasures, one would have to have recourse to reflection on something other than pleasure. This is Watson's return to reason, but the issue must not be misunderstood. He explains part of the issue this way:

The choice is not, as it is usually represented to be, between the derivation of moral conceptions from Experience, or their foundation in Intuition; on the contrary, it may easily be shown that these rival methods, however they may pretend to differ, are at bottom beset by essentially the same imperfection. Both alike deny to Reason any share in the constitution of objects; for although Utilitarianism affects to obtain all moral distinctions from experience, while Intuition claims that right and wrong are given in an immediate judgment, still the former resolves experience into a series of feelings, and latter has no test to apply save the variable convictions of individuals. To make good its right to exist, Utilitarianism must be able to show, not merely that moral conceptions have grown up in time, and that the virtuous man adopts as his rule of life the good of his kind, but that an ethical system may be raised upon a purely Hedonistic basis. It has to be proved that, in the words of Bentham, "pleasure is in itself a good; nay, even setting aside immunity from pain, the only good; pain is in itself an evil, and indeed, without exception, the only evil;" and that, consistently with this fundamental postulate, legal, moral and social relations can be accounted for.[76]

Yet Watson does not think that the issue is a simple one in which, as it were, one might put experience (including intuition) on one side and reason on the other. Rather, as usual, he thinks that reason is brought into play in the context of experience.

75 Ibid., p. 277.
76 Ibid., pp. 273-74.

In the moral sphere, reason comes into play because we do have such experiences as those to which the utilitarians call attention. But we have these experiences in a context in which there are choices to be made. We must decide how to distribute pleasure. We must decide which pleasures deserve our attention. We must decide how to balance the consequences against the nature of the act. All of this forces upon our attention the fact that the desires, goals, and so on which attract our attention are located in the context of a community of persons. We come to understand that the choices make sense within this community, and in the course of this making sense we come to understand the rational principles which give intelligibility to the process. Thus reason is not an abstraction. Reason has, Watson implies, a "share in the constitution of objects."[77] The ultimate reality is not, on the one hand, a collection of sensations and it is not, on the other hand, an abstract structure of rational principle. The ultimate reality is the intelligible. It is the retreat to abstraction, whether that abstraction is a misguided kind of sensationalism or a misguided kind of rationalism—which imposes insoluble problems on the situation.

It seems quite clear that Watson's basic moral point, therefore, is this: In searching for a rule to guide us, we must search for what is intelligible in itself. Our lives are unsuccessful, unsatisfying, and meaningless just in proportion to the extent to which we cannot finally make sense of what goes on. Indeed, the worst human disasters are usually described by outsiders, if not by the immediate participants, as "senseless." War is senseless because no possible outcome of it can help to make sense of the lives of the participants. Murder is atrocious because the life of the victim becomes devoid of meaning in the act and the life of the murderer ceases to be capable of taking on a rational pattern. Armed robbery offers no clue to the reasonable distribution of goods in a way that will add meaning to men's lives.

The end of any rational human conduct must, as we read Watson, be a community in which the life of each participant contributes to the meaning of the life of every other participant. What finally pleases will not necessarily be pleasure in the sense of a sensation contrasted with pain. It may be pleasure if one thinks of pleasure, as does Watson, as the social attitude—a community of meaning to which one can respond favourably with reason.

The goal must be a community because the individual, apart from the community, is a meaningless notion. He is not, then, an individuation of anything. It must be a co-operative community because no act of mine ultimately makes sense if it consists of my achieving my ends at

77   Ibid., p. 273.

the expense of another. It fails to make sense because I am simply denying the development of another in a way which makes it impossible for me to make sense of my own life. I depend on those others for my identity; to trample them is in part to destroy myself. Like Donne, Watson thinks it blindingly obvious that no man is an island.

We may ask, however, if Watson will not end in the difficulty which he ascribes to the utilitarians. Is he not saying "Reason is good"? Is he not saying "The sense of community is good"? Is he not saying "Making sense of one's life is good"? And if he is saying one or more of these must he not prove it to be so, just as he demands that Jeremy Bentham must prove that pleasure is good?

The answer, in Watson's mind, is surely "No." One might complain of Kant—always one of Watson's heroes—that Kant, as Bradley said, was urging us to do our duty for its own sake. Or one might complain of Kant that Kant was making of rational principle an end in itself. And one should surely prove, if that is one's position, that these things are good. One would surely, also, expect to find a logical as well as a factual problem involved in such a programme. For the programme involves the logical elision of duty, or universalized rationality, or whatever it ultimately is, with goodness itself. And there seems no way in which that can be achieved. It would have to be a necessary truth that these things were good—necessary in the logical sense. Yet, as Moore would have said, it seems that that cannot be the case because one can always ask "Is it good to do one's duty?" "Is it good to be rational?" "Is it good to act on universal principles?"

Watson's position is different. He is, to be sure, impressed by Kant's insistence on rationality, by Kant's insistence that moral principles are as binding on one man as on another, and, above all, by Kant's ultimate notion of a "kingdom of ends." But he insists that one must move beyond this level of abstraction, that reason, as reality, emerges in the context of experience. *In the context*, the question is one of how one can answer certain questions which are, in fact, pressing. One seeks to avoid pain. One seeks, as Bentham, Mill, and Sidgwick thought, pleasure. One seeks the realization of oneself. One cannot avoid doing these things—to do so is to fly in the face of one's nature—but one can ask what it is to do them *morally* and *well*. One answer is that a minimum condition of doing them morally and well is that one should not act in such a way as to undo what one has set out to do. One should not act in such a way as to frustrate the whole process. Another answer is that one must, whatever one's theory is, be able to make sense of one's act. These things are good in the special sense that they constitute a necessary basis of anything which would count as acting on a moral theory as opposed to acting on one's whims, acting on one's immediate desire, acting on one's calculated self-interest, acting prudently, and so on. If there is such a thing as morality, it is to be distinguished from all of these and it is to be distinguished as a species of acting on rational principle in the context of the given experience.

To prove that the end one has specified as "good" really is good, is to show that if one's acts are guided by it one is, in effect, acting first from moral principle and secondly moving toward something which could actually count as "an end."

EIGHT

REASON AS CONSTITUTIVE OF KNOWLEDGE AND REALITY

John Watson—Part II

TWO THEMES ARE seldom absent from Watson's writings. One of them has to do with scepticism, its challenge to conventional understandings of reason, and the need to show that it can be refuted. The other has to do with the relation of reason and experience as constitutive of the nature of reality.

Beyond these two themes lies the controversy of science and religion, and the attempt to excuse human failure and feebleness as the natural outcome of a world in which certainty is impossible.

In this chapter, we shall try to bring them together—to show how Watson's account of reality grows out of his consideration of the sceptic's case, how he thought new understandings of reason could reconcile experience and rationality and make religion reasonable.

Along the way, we shall encounter William Caldwell, the McGill philosopher who sought to mediate between the Canadian idealists and the American pragmatists, and James Edwin Creighton, who was editor of the *Philosophical Review*.

From the beginning to the end of his career, Watson invariably insisted that he was a "speculative idealist." We have already seen something of the background and development of this view. Its motives lie in Watson's long wrestling match with scepticism. He believes that knowledge *is* possible, but only if reality meets certain criteria. He believes he has a reason to think that reality does meet those criteria and those reasons are his reasons for being a speculative idealist.

Idealism, however, is, on the whole, somewhat out of fashion. To be sure, there are great contemporary idealists—Blanshard and Errol Harris amongst them. But even they are just a little uneasy about the word itself and, when someone like Watson announces that he is an idealist, it becomes crucially important to try to be precise and to specify just what this does and, more importantly, does *not* mean.

Watson is sometimes prepared to speak quite bluntly. In the *Outline of Philosophy*, he says: ". . . matter properly understood, is a manifestation of mind."[1] But we must not jump to conclusions—we first have to know what Watson means by matter and what he means by mind.

There is no short way about this task. At various times in the history of philosophy, "matter" has meant different things: a fundamental, unchanging, eternal structure, like the atoms of Leucippus and Democritus, a potentiality to acquire form, as in Aristotle, and a certain set of probability relations with respect to mass-energy transformations, as, perhaps, in contemporay physics. Mind has sometimes meant the capacity to exhibit intelligent behaviour, sometimes the status of a spiritual substance, sometimes the latent *anima*—the thing which animates the creature—and, sometimes, simply, the rational or intelligible order in things. The first of these notions created the shift from the original Greek word for "breath" to the modern "psyche" which lives on in the name "psychology." The second of these had a variety of ancient lives, was reborn with the Renaissance, and had a good run for its money in, at least, philosophies of Descartes, Berkeley, and in our own time, philosophers from McTaggart onwards. The third is the "anima" of Aristotle's *De Anima* or the mind-soul of Thomas Aquinas. The final view has roots even in Plato but is, essentially, a neo-Platonist and Hegelian view. None of these views remains unaltered by the particular philosophical context in which we find it and every actual view is vastly more subtle and complex than one can convey in a short summary sentence.

When someone like Watson says, therefore, matter properly understood is a manifestation of mind, we are little wiser than we were before we heard the saying.

Some features of Watson's position are clear enough. At no time does he countenance "subjective idealism," the doctrine that what is ultimately real is my immediate awareness and the immediate awareness of others like me. He will not countenance subjective idealism for an obvious reason. It leads naturally to solipsism. Solipsism, the doctrine that all I can really know to exist is my own immediate awareness, is, he thinks, self-contradictory. For if I *only* know my immediate awareness, I do not really know *that* either. I do not know that I exist as an individual unless I can relate myself to something else. If I knew nothing but my own awareness, I could not tell if I was co-extensive with the world or not. I could not form any notion of "myself" because

1   John Watson, *An Outline of Philosophy*, 4th ed. (Glasgow: James Maclehose & Sons, 1908; first published under the title of *Comte, Mill and Spencer: An Outline of Philosophy*, 1895), p. 183. Hereafter referred to as *Outline*.

there would be nothing to contrast it with. Indeed, subjective idealism does lead to solipsism in many ways. If my knowledge is confined to my own awareness, all of the evidence *may* be evidence about my own imagination, dreams, or even hallucinations.

We also know that Watson does not hold any form of the "spiritual substance" theory. If there were a spiritual substance which was the essence of me, only I could know it. For, by definition, anything which was apparent to others would count as part of what we ordinarily think of as the "material world." In fact, one who was both an idealist and a subscriber to the "spiritual substance" theory would have to be a subjective idealist. For if reality is of the nature of idea or mind and mind is of the nature of the spiritual substance, then it is only by direct subjective inspection that I can know reality.

Nonetheless, though Watson does mean by mind whatever it is that exhibits intelligent behaviour, he does not mean merely this. For one thing, it would be absurd to hold that everything in the world exhibits "intelligent behaviour." For another, he holds that that position is intelligible only within the confines of what he calls speculative idealism.

Nor will he concede that mind is simply whatever it is that "animates" the body. That position is scarcely consistent with the possibility of idealism at all. And, in modern terms, that position turns out to involve what used to be called in biology "vitalism." Watson wants nothing to do with the notion that there are unusual "psychic" forces which animate living things. Living things, indeed, are, for him, an integral part of a reality which forms a single system.

In general, everything that he says is consistent with the view that what he means by mind is the notion of a rational order or, rather, a series of rational orders which interlock and intersect with one another. It is perhaps unfortunate that he chose to retain the word "mind." But he is relying, after all, on a very old tradition and he is writing for an audience which consists either of his own students (most frequently his writing consists of works which he intended to use and did use as textbooks) or for an audience of other professional philosophers. While it is, alas, no longer true that every professional philosopher will understand clearly what he says, it certainly was true, at the time that he was writing, that he could expect to be widely and generally understood.

What is less clear in Watson is his theory of matter. The word appears often in the text, but not in the index of topics which he appended to his *Outline of Philosophy*. Customarily, an idealist is supposed to be someone who holds that matter is, in the end, "unreal." But

Watson is not a subjective idealist. He does not think that what is ultimately real consists of sets of sensations, impressions, or states of immediate awareness. Nor would he, as G. E. Moore seemed to think the idealist philosophers of the period did, want to deny the existence of matter.[2] He *would* want to say that material objects do not, as a class, form the deepest level of ultimate reality. Yet, what does this mean? It does not mean, in Watson's writings, that material objects are hallucinations like the crawling black things which sufferers from delirium tremens are said to see. Material objects are not even visual illusions of the sort that one gets by drawing a smaller box inside a larger box and connecting the four corners of each with diagonal lines. He simply means to assert that material objects depend, for their existence, on something more ultimate.

We have to get some notion of what his theory is and the best way is to follow one of his particular arguments in which talk about matter figures prominently. The most useful one is to be found in *An Outline of Philosophy*. The argument is important because here Watson promises to attend to the very matter we have in hand. "I shall try to show that instead of thus reducing mind to matter, we must hold that matter is a form of mind."[3] Nothing could be clearer. Nothing could be a more forthright declaration of the idealist position, a more straightforward challenge to the materialist and to the mind-matter dualist. He says:

> Inorganic existence, it is said, existed prior to life and consciousness, and therefore life and consciousness are the product of inorganic existence. The assumption here is, that consciousness is related to matter as effect to cause. Before we can admit the validity of this assumption, we must be certain that the relation between consciousness and matter can be conceived as a relation of effect and cause. Now, it is easy to show that the conception of causality here made use of is, at any rate, not the conception that is employed in scientific inquiries. When a scientific man asks what is the cause of the motion of a material body, his aim is to find out the particular conditions which account for this particular event, and the answer that he gives consists in stating those particular conditions. He points out the circumstances that have to take place before the particular event in question can happen. In all cases the circumstances are some form of motion, because in external things change always takes the form of motion. But when the particular mode of motion assigned as the cause of a particular change has been discovered, nothing has been determined in regard to the nature of existence as a whole; all that has been done is to point out the special relation between two events.

2   George Edward Moore, "The Refutation of Idealism," in *Philosophical Studies* (London: Kegan Paul, Trench & Trubner, 1922).
3   Watson, *Outline*, p. 177.

The idea of cause and effect, in other words, has a perfectly intelligible meaning when it is employed in explanation of particular events, but it does not follow that it has an intelligible meaning when it is employed to explain existence as a whole. When we pass from the one point of view to the other, we must ask whether we have not changed our conception.

Now, if it is said that matter is the cause of life and consciousness, it is plain that by matter cannot here be meant any particular form of material existence. There never is in an effect something essentially different from what is found in the cause. A material body can be called a cause only in this sense, that its motion is the condition of a motion in another body. The reason for distinguishing a material body from a living or a conscious being is, that while the changes in the former are all modes of motion, the changes in the latter are not modes of motion, but modes of life and consciousness. Now, if a material body, or any number of material bodies, is called the cause of life and consciousness, it is assumed that life and consciousness can be explained simply as modes of motion. If, however, the latter are modes of motion, there is no production of life and consciousness by matter, because there is no life or consciousness to be produced. The contradiction, therefore, to which the conception of matter as the cause of life and consciousness leads is this: If life and consciousness are distinct from matter, they cannot be its effects; and, if they are effects of matter, there is no distinction between them and matter. The ordinary conception of cause and effect thus breaks down when we try to explain by it the relation between matter on the one hand, and life and consciousness on the other. If we hold that matter has a real existence independently of life and consciousness, we cannot at the same time hold that it is the cause of these.[4]

This is the first leg of the argument which is going to prove that "matter . . . is a manifestation of mind."[5] Our immediate interest in it is in the view of matter which it puts forth. Matter, here, is a certain kind of structure. It is no longer the potentiality to acquire form as it was in, say, Aristotle or Thomas Aquinas. Rather, Watson is describing a species of the "structure" theory which seems to have gone along with the rise of modern science and the early development of modern philosophy.

His theory of matter seems, here, to be less Hegelian than his theory of mind. He wants it to correspond to the theory which he believes is endemic to modern science. His version of this view seems to go like this: The most basic of the sciences is physics. Physics is concerned with successive distributions of material structures. The change represented in these structures between any two moments of time is called motion. If we are to explain "cause," we shall have to take it as

4   Ibid., pp. 177-79.
5   Ibid., p. 183.

meaning, if anything, simply the application of certain very general laws in such a way that the difference of structure at different moments of time is intelligible.

Suppose, then, that we try to transfer this theory to the explanation of states of consciousness. We shall find that we face a difficult choice. Insofar as we could explain these states in the way that we cope with quite basic scientific issues, there would be nothing left over which one would properly call consciousness or even, if you like, life.

To the physicist, each successive arrangement of particles represents nothing more than a state of affairs which enters in to the formulation of the appropriate physical laws. Suppose, then, that "life" is one such physical arrangement and "consciousness" is another such arrangement. The names "life" and "consciousness" are, then, just so much excess verbal baggage.

Watson, as we have seen, has no doubt that there is such a thing as life and consciousness and that they are not mere excess verbal baggage. He asks us to suppose that we *do* have knowledge. Naturally, if we had no knowledge, we would not have the kind of knowledge which we call physics. But material objects cannot be said to "know" one another. Even if it is true that every state of knowledge is accompanied by a correlated state of some material system, the two cannot be equated. When there is knowledge, there is, actually or potentially, an accompanying state of consciousness. Every attempt to reduce one to the other simply produces a situation which we saw above: Part of the description becomes mere excess verbal baggage.

The choice, then, is between denying the proposition that material states of affairs can cause states of conscious awareness or holding that there are no states of conscious awareness. Even beyond the inconsistency, the latter position is simply not intelligible.

Watson says, ". . . the lesson to be learned from this is, that the conception of cause and effect as it is employed in scientific investigation is not adequate as a conception of the relation between existence as a whole and its various modes."[6]

He means by this that we cannot take material reality as the fundamental structure of existence and attempt to explain, by it, all of the modes of existence. When we do so, we lapse into unintelligibility. There seem to be two basic points involved here. One is that the conception of "matter" which Watson ultimately rejects is the conception of matter as a succession of ways of occupying space. In this conception, succession is construed as a species of motion and the ways of occupying space come to be conceptualized, primarily, as particles.

6   Ibid., p. 179.

Such structures represent a system of a certain kind. It is intelligible not primarily through primitive notions of a kind of collision between billiard ball-like bits of matter but rather as a structure which becomes intelligible through its expression in law-like forms. The notion of cause in some of its traditional forms thus becomes, quite literally, redundant. Either the notion of cause must be abandoned or it must be re-interpreted in some sophisticated way.

This helps to make more readily understandable Watson's second and—to him—much more important point. Such a "system" cannot accommodate consciousness and life, presumably, because if they are a part of it, they are uninteresting and the concepts which we use to express them succeed in expressing nothing.

The view which Watson takes of matter could, no doubt, be extended to account for later developments in physics. The notion of material particle which seems to be imbedded in his account is not in any sense fundamental. It is merely one of the forms which the application of appropriate physical laws might take. Nor is it very likely that any physicist would lament the passing of the concept of "cause" in the sense which Watson has in mind. "Cause" becomes merely a synonym for a certain kind of explanation. Since the explanation is one which applies within physical systems, it would surprise no one that it could not be carried over into an account of systems of another sort. Watson goes on to say:

> We may, if we please, still use the term "cause" to express the relation, but we must give to it a new meaning. Let us see what that meaning is.
>
> Prior to the existence of living beings, there existed inorganic things. Did these inorganic things exist as separate individuals, or were they only distinguishable aspects of the one systematic unity? The latter, as we have seen, is the true conception. We have therefore to conceive of existence prior to the appearance of life, as one single organic whole. But this organic whole had manifested itself only as that which passed through mechanical, physical, and chemical changes. Now, these changes were not related to the whole as effect to cause; they were simply the distinguishable aspects in which the one universe presented itself. These aspects can be viewed as related to one another in the way of cause and effect, but the universe as a whole is not a cause of which all these aspects are effects; or, at least, if we call it a cause, we mean simply that it is a principle of unity manifesting itself in all change. So conceived, cause must now be regarded as self-cause. That is to say, there is nothing outside of the one unity which explains or accounts for it, since beyond it there is nothing: the only cause to which we can assign it is itself. All forms of existence are therefore explained by this unity, but the unity itself is not explained by anything else.[7]

7   Ibid., pp. 179-80.

He is saying that if one wants to have an explanation of the universe in toto, one must meet certain conditions. That unity must, somehow, be self-explanatory. Now if one is going to explain things, as one really does in the sciences, by deploying a rational order to explain a succession of states of affairs, the rational order will be primary and the states of affairs will be derivative. Furthermore, such a universe will be, necessarily, intelligible. One cannot have a universe which has an explanation in this sense if it fails in intelligibility. One cannot, therefore, start with a universe which is lacking in the fundamental requirements for intelligibility and expect to derive from it an account of later states which are intelligible. The rational order must have been there always and must be primary. Without that rational order, we could not explain how there is "matter" in the sense of something which exhibits itself as having an intelligible explanation.

Watson pursues his argument in this way: "At a certain period [in the history of the universe] life makes its appearance. Whence did this life proceed? It proceeded, the scientific evolutionist tells us, from inorganic nature."[8] He quotes Tyndall:[9] "Were not man's origin implicated, we should accept without a murmur the derivation of animal life from what we call inorganic nature."[10] But he denies that this is ultimately intelligible.

This language suggests that life is the product or effect of that which is without life, i.e., that all the particular living beings which first appeared on the earth were originated by particular inorganic things. The radical imperfection of this view has already been pointed out. *No individual thing originates anything*; for every individual is what it is only by reference to the whole system of the universe.[11]

If explanations derive from systematic intelligible structures, then the intelligibility of particulars is derivative from the intelligibility of systems. Hence, he says:

What is implied in the origination of life is not that inorganic nature produced life, but that a new form of existence presented itself at a certain period of time in the history of the earth. But this life, although it has for the first time presented itself is not something that has come into being by a power belonging to inorganic things. And no one would be so absurd as to say that it originated from itself. Its origination can be explained only on the

8   Ibid., p. 180.
9   John Tyndall was a nineteenth-century British natural philosopher, physicist, and Superintendent of the Royal Institute.
10 Watson, *Outline*, p. 180.
11 Ibid., pp. 180-81.

supposition that it was implicit in the nature of existence *as a whole*. Outside of the unity that comprehends all possible existence there is nothing; and therefore life, when it appears, merely manifests in an explicit form what was already wrapped up in the one single existence that is manifested in all modes of existence. But, if this one all-inclusive unity is now seen to involve within itself organic as well as inorganic existence, its nature cannot be comprehended by looking at either apart from the other. It is neither inorganic nor organic, but both. Further, organic existence is of this nature that, while it contains all that is implied in inorganic nature, it also manifests characteristics that are peculiar to itself.[12]

The point is not mysterious. It is simply that, if the system manifests the property P at a certain time T, then the explanation of P is always in the nature of the system S which produces P. S is, therefore, the fundamental notion. P, whatever P may be, must be shown to be derivative from S or must be admitted to remain unintelligible.

Watson adds, a little confusingly, "The true nature of existence must therefore be defined as organic rather than inorganic; and it is therefore more correct to say, that organic existence has produced inorganic, than that inorganic has produced organic."[13] He admits that "both forms of expression are inadequate."[14] The position, as he first states it, would imply that one feature of the system *did* produce another—in contrast to the position which he had taken earlier. He is aware of this difficulty and he says, "... as no mode of existence originates any other, what we must say is, that in organic existence we have a fuller and truer expression of the nature of existence as a whole than we have in inorganic existence."[15] Even this does not quite straighten up the verbal tangle. What he needs to say is that, where S is the system concerned, S must have a set of properties which transcends any particular subset which might be said to be the manifestation of S at a given time T. The properties of S must account for any P at any time. Watson says, "... what is posterior in time is prior in nature: the first is last and the last first."[16]

He is clearer when he comes to make the same point about consciousness.

Consciousness appeared later than life. Granted; but the consciousness which thus appeared could not arise either from the particular forms of existence prior to it, or from itself: its explanation must be found in this, that

12   Ibid., p. 181.
13   Ibid.
14   Ibid.
15   Ibid., pp. 181-82.
16   Ibid., p. 182.

existence as a whole contained within itself, prior to its manifestation as consciousness, all that so manifested itself. There can be no absolute origination in the case of existence as a whole, since outside of that whole there is no reality and no possibility. What is shown by the appearance in the world of conscious beings is not a new existence, but a higher manifestation of the one existence that always was and is and shall be.[17]

This suggests that we are to understand consciousness as a manifestation of the pre-existing system and not that we are to say that reality always was "conscious." No doubt, in this quotation, Watson outruns the limits of prudence. It is doubtful that he really means to say "always was and is and shall be." But his choice of words does raise questions about some fundamentals of his metaphysical system and these deserve exploration here.

The problem of time in Watson's philosophy is a peculiar one. He claims flatly that to believe "the order of time as identical with the order of nature" is "to fall into the old mistake."[18] The "old mistake," of course, is the mistake made by those who fail to understand that what is ultimately real is the rational order in nature. But, for Watson, that order is, indeed, the order *in* nature. It is not a platonic universe somehow divorced from the appearances which ordinary men encounter. Rather, it is the very order which appears *in* experience.

Certainly, a rational order, as such, is not temporal. But Watson cannot take a position like Bradley's—the position, say, that reality is a trans-relational unity which simply surpasses the divided nature of all experience. Order, for Watson, is always an order *of* something; though it is possible to have a structured, substantive order which is inherently non-temporal, a-temporal, or trans-temporal. Bradley's supra-relational unity is, in the literal sense, non-temporal. It simply has nothing to do with time, for time is a relation. Plato's forms which participate in things are a-temporal, at least if they are conceived in a neo-Platonic form. They are not themselves in time. But they can order the world which is in time. They are indifferent, in themselves, to time but, at least a crucial subset of Plato's forms takes its meaning from its ability to organize things which are in time. McTaggart's universe of timeless loving spirits is evidently trans-temporal. It forms, in McTaggart's view, a series which differs from the time series we ordinarily think of ourselves as perceiving in being an inclusion series as opposed to an exclusion series. (Time as ordinarily conceived is an "exclusion" series because moments of time, by their nature, exclude one another. It cannot now both be two o'clock and four o'clock in the

17 Ibid., pp. 182-83.
18 Ibid., p. 182.

afternoon. The series McTaggart envisages has an order like the order of time except that its members do not exclude one another so that one may, eventually, come to perceive all "real" time as a simultaneous but still ordered series. This series is trans-temporal because it obviously transforms time. It includes what we ordinarily think of as time but renders it as something else.) But can Watson hold any of these positions?

His solution to the problem of the order of nature entails doing some violence to ordinary concepts of time. If he wants to hold that the material world is really a by-product of a non-material world, then he has to hold that time is not a fundamental feature of the world. That world appears to be temporal only because it shows some but not all features of the ultimate rational order. But Watson's continuous point is that the rational order is real because it is that order which gives significance and meaning to the world. We know that that order is logically prior to the apparent temporal order of the physical universe simply because we understand the physical universe only by discovering meaning and intelligibility in it. We are persuaded by physics because physics is intelligible. We would not be persuaded by physics if physics seemed to us a tissue of nonsense. But the process of giving and assigning meanings is itself temporal. Intelligibility results from conceptual schemes which give an order to regions of space and time. If we take this view—a view which, after all, is not identical with the views of Plato, Bradley, or McTaggart—time seems to become a crucial ingredient. It appears to take time for meaning in rational order to develop. It therefore seems not at all clear that to regard the order of time as the order of nature is the "old mistake." To get at Watson's serious view of the nature and problem of time, we must turn to the detailed discussions he offers in his Gifford Lectures, *The Interpretation of Religious Experience*. The issue about time first arises in his discussion of St. Augustine.[19] In the first volume of the lectures, Watson denies Augustine's neo-Platonist contention that the ultimately real is not in time but creates the appearance of time. But the objection is largely a theological one, the objection that Augustine has created a distinction, thereby, between the inner nature of God and the persons of the Trinity. This theological objection, however, is an obvious parallel to a philosophical one which is germane to Watson's whole metaphysical

19 John Watson, *The Interpretation of Religious Experience: The Gifford Lectures, Delivered in the University of Glasgow in the Years 1910-12*, 2 vols.: Part First, *Historical*; Part Second, *Constructive* (Glasgow: Maclehose, 1895). Hereafter referred to in the footnotes as *Religious Experience* and in the text as the first and second volumes of the Gifford Lectures. For the discussion of St. Augustine see Part First, *Historical* [vol. 1], pp. 82-83.

279

system. For it is the equivalent of urging that the ultimate rational order is abstracted from or separate from the order of the intelligible world. Thus far, Watson has obvious sympathy with the difficulties we have been raising. In the second volume of the Gifford Lectures, he reminds us of Kant's view that "to deny space and time to be conditions of our experience is to abandon the attempt even to explain the illusion of experience."[20] But he then goes on to develop what amounts to his own account of the transformation of time.

> To think of time at all we must think of it as a unity of homogeneous differences all of which are successive. There is no need to ask how we can experience a whole of time, for the simple reason that we have already experienced it. To repeat the unification of homogeneous successive differences will add nothing to our knowledge of time, because a repetition of the same thought is objectively the same thought.[21]

The point is that in each and every individual thought we transform and transcend time. For a single thought is a unity of intelligible meaning. If one merely heard the words of the sentence successively and could not unify them, one would never grasp the meaning.

The principle of such transformations is the same for every case. Thus we do not need to worry about Kant's problem, that time is in itself unintelligible because we cannot grasp, in thought, the ultimate unity of an infinite series of particulars. "Hence, it is at once impossible and superfluous to seek for a whole of time by any accumulation of differences. . . ."[22]

But though this notion of the transformation of time offers a clue to the problem of time in Watson's metaphysics, it is complicated by his flat assertion:

> . . . I am unable to see that space and time can from any point of view be eliminated, unless we are prepared to say that we have no knowledge whatever. For, with the elimination of space and time, as we must remember, there also vanish permanence, motion and change; and as without these all our sciences, whether physical or mental, disappear, nothing is left but the fiction of a reality that we can only define as that which is indefinable.[23]

(Despite Watson's frequent defences of Bradley, this last remark is clearly a jibe at Bradley's[24] notion that the ultimate reality is un-

20 Watson, *Religious Experience*, Part Second, *Constructive* [vol. 2], p. 214.
21 Ibid., p. 215.
22 Ibid.
23 Ibid., p. 216.
24 Francis Herbert Bradley, *Appearance and Reality* (London: Oxford University Press, 1969; 1st ed., 1893). Bradley's final observations about Reality are in Chapter 27. He

speakable.) He goes on to ram home the point. "Knowledge is never *a priori* in the sense that it is derivable from pure conceptions, but neither is it ever *a posteriori* in the sense of being based upon mere particulars; it is always, and in all its forms, the comprehension of particulars as embraced within a unity of some kind, even if it is only the unity of a single space and time."[25] Knowledge is gained through process that involves time. He gives us one more clue about thirty pages later. He says:

> Looking at man as in idea he is, it is no exaggeration to say that he contains in himself an element that is infinite. For, while he is "part of this partial world," on the other hand he is capable of comprehending the nature of God and seeking to realize that which in idea he is; and this power of comprehension and self-identification with God implies that, finite as in one aspect he is, in another aspect he is infinite. Thus he is capable of transcending in idea all limits of space and time, and grasping the principle from which all that is has proceeded. If man were not thus capable of transcending the limits of his finite existence, he would never become conscious of his finitude. In the simplest knowledge, as we have seen, there is involved that comprehension of something not ourselves which develops into the explicit consciousness of God. All our experience moves within the framework of an absolute unity, and no degree of progress ever carries us beyond it. The simplest discrimination of the difference between "this" and "that" is possible only because consciousness is a universal capacity for distinction and unification. And in the moral life the implicit infinity of the human spirit reveals itself in the unceasing effort after perfection.[26]

Watson is once again talking about the transformation of time. The argument he is offering is that we could not be conscious of our finitude, of our limitations, unless we could understand what it was not to be limited. This understanding is not a special revelation which comes from God, or a special insight of theologians, but, simply enough, a grasping of the fact that, in every thought, we escape from the immediacy of given, successive experience into the notion of a forged and created unity. This unity is an escape from time as a mere succession and, since we can see that any amount of knowledge whatever can be synthesized, we can understand how this process can be generalized so as to embrace infinity. Our sense of our own limitations is the sense that this is possible but not yet complete.

calls Reality "inscrutable" (p. 488), "nothing at all apart from appearances" (pp. 488-89), and finally states "It is in the end nonsense to talk of realities" (p. 489).

25 Watson, *Religious Experience*, Part Second, *Constructive* [vol. 2], p. 216.
26 Ibid., p. 245.

Time, then, is constantly being overcome. To return to more mundane examples, every piece of knowledge is, in some sense, an abstraction of events from their space-time context and the creation of a domain of meaning which is not spatio-temporal. The Roman Empire is long since gone, but we can still grasp it in knowledge and give meaning to it. As knowledge, it is safe from the trammels of time.

This may be easier to understand if one reflects for a moment on the nature of knowledge in general. Once something is known, it is, in a sense, isolated from time. Caesar crossed the Rubicon only once on his journey to take power in Rome. But once it is *known*, that event can be recalled at any time. And *sometimes* what is recalled is—in *some* sense—the actual event, Caesar's crossing of the Rubicon and not some other event. That means that there may be a knowable element which has a measure of independence from its place in time.

It requires a twist of thought to see how this programme can be made to dissolve the apparent difficulties in Watson's metaphysical system. He is admitting, cheerfully, that the finding of knowledge requires time. So does the creation of meaning. But these activities transform time. Time transformed is no longer in the same sense time. The world must always present itself as temporal. The temporal element in experience must never be forgotten. But this is a mode of presentation. The reality so presented need not be temporal.

Such a reality would be essentially composed of transformed time—time originally transformed in the mind of God in a way quite unlike ours. But it is presented to us for our transformation. The meaning of our affairs is in the transformation of time. The world, to us, will therefore appear as having a long and complex history. That history is real in the sense that it is the history of the presentation of events. The geologist who talks of millennia unknown to man does not lie. The astronomer who talks of spans of time far vaster than that also tells the truth. But we discover the truth in the process of transforming time and thus, we discover the reality which always was and will be.

This still makes for puzzles, of course. What is Watson's God up to? Why is the world presented to us as temporal? Is it some kind of play which we are obliged to present for the amusement of the deity? We shall face more of these questions later, but, for now, the answer seems to be that Watson envisages a very complex dialectic. In transforming time, we may come to be like gods—a thing which could not happen in any other way. For our lives can only acquire meaning in the process of confrontation with untransformed time. Only untransformed time makes possible knowledge. In a sense this is, in itself, the basis of the moral situation and the conflict with evil. For to be like God we must have knowledge and to have knowledge we must face untransformed time. "The conflict with evil is the struggle towards that unity with oneself which is inseparable from unity with God."[27] But there is more to it than that. God, in turn, is only complete and perfect against the background of the completed and perfect community of selves of which we are potentially a part. "Though the spiritual life of man must ever be progressive, it yet is in principle one with the life of God."[28] Watson wants to make a good deal of this.

He uses it as an argument for the proposition that "appearance and reality" must never be "separated." It is only because, in principle, men are perfectible that God is perfect.

How, then, does this finally bear on the question of time in Watson's metaphysics? It appears that time is a way in which reality appears. The appearance is not unreal, it is a *mode* of the real. Thus time, untransformed, is an essential feature of the world but it is an essential feature which is intelligible only if it is conceived as transformable and ultimately transformed. Truth is in the transformation of time and not in the immediacy of experience. It is in this sense that Watson is ultimately a rationalist and not an empiricist.

This leads us to other considerations about his metaphysical system which we must face, at least briefly, before going on to his rational religion. We have now seen in just what sense mind is prior to matter. It is prior in the sense that our concept of matter is only intelligible because rational order runs through it. But we have been led, on the one hand, to deny the ultimate and independent reality of time and, on the other hand, to regard reality as something which develops. Even God depends upon development.

Is it possible to reconcile these notions or is there, finally, a radical incoherence in Watson's system? If we can settle that, we must, then, ask about the extent to which Watson's system might break down into a radical scepticism simply because of the plethora of potentially rational systems by and through which we might grasp reality.

These two questions are related in the following way. If Watson holds that there is only one, ultimate, rational system, then development cannot really have any place in the system. But, if development has no place in the system, the rational order loses its unique connection with the particular structure of experience—for that structure, then, is only a surface appearance, something to be overcome in the transformation of time. This would seem to leave us with the choice between indefinitely many complete, coherent, rational systems which

27   Ibid.
28   Ibid., p. 246.

are imaginable. If, on the other hand, development is real, we cannot actually know what the final complete system will be like. In that case, again, we have indefinitely many potentially completed systems to choose from and we seem to arrive at a sceptical position via another route.

Now there is no doubt that Watson is constantly wrestling with the difficulties inherent in a coherence theory of truth. He believes that, by overcoming these, he can rid himself of the nagging sceptic. His critical analysis of the epistemology of Lotze is intended to achieve this by the development of a quite particular ground for rejecting Lotze's account of the relation between ideas and reality.[29] Lotze had adopted the view that each human being has access, really, only to the contents of his own mind and these contents consist of a set of ideas which should be contrasted with the ordinary concept of things.

Watson admitted that, in some sense, Lotze's premise was true: Whatever it is one thinks, it is one's own ideas that one thinks. But to get to Lotze's conclusion, one has to adopt the further premise that the distinction between subject and object is ultimate and irreducible.

Watson's rejoinder is that the distinction between subject and object arises only because of the imperfections of the immediate perspective and the limitations of the immediate knowledge of the subject. What is in my mind is, somehow, not "reality" only because it is limited and imperfect. But it is not so in principle. If it were limited and imperfect in principle the notion of knowledge would itself make no sense and the sceptic would win the prize by default. The fact of the matter is that even the sceptic states his position by calling attention to inadequacies and imperfections in the actuality of experience. He is a sceptic because he thinks there is some deficiency in our immediate situation and that this deficiency is, itself, intelligible. He says, in effect, if only you had such-and-such you would have knowledge, but you don't. Therefore your claim to knowledge is unsound. If he could not say this, there would be no ground for imposing standards which our immediate claims do not meet. But if he does say this, then he has to admit that we know what it is that we would need in order to have knowledge.

If we know what it is, we can, in principle, have it. For it would not be intelligible to us if it were not at least a potential kind of knowledge. The rational position, Watson thinks, therefore, is that what is incomplete is simply the range of our experience and our discernment of the rational order latent in it. He puts this in a number of ways.

29 Ibid., pp. 112-14.

What Speculative Idealism maintains is that, while the 'world' is a 'cosmos of experience,' and therefore exists for each thinking subject only in experience, it is a 'cosmos' just because the thinking subject is capable of grasping the permanent or essential nature of reality. There is no object apart from a subject, and yet it is only as the subject is capable of grasping the universal or necessary constitution of reality that there is for him 'a world of things.' This implies that, while in each subject there is a process of intelligent activity, through which alone his experience of a world of things originates, he yet is able to comprehend the true nature of the world because there is in him the principle which is involved in the actual nature of reality. The supposition that a world assumed to lie beyond intelligent experience is identical with what it is within intelligent experience is manifestly absurd, since it implies that the whole process in which the 'cosmos of experience' is gradually formed through the exercise of intelligence is superfluous.[30]

Watson is urging that what links the inner world and the outer world is, indeed, a common principle of rational unity. Later, he states this thesis as the thesis that truth and validity are not separate. Validity is usually thought of as a logical notion, a formal account of coherence. If, as Watson says, the two are identical, then truth amounts to coherence of a certain kind.

As a rule, the coherence theory of truth is attacked precisely on the ground that, as Bertrand Russell suggests, there may well be many equally coherent rational orders.[31] On Watson's view this is simply not true because the rational order and the order of experience are not separable. An order must be an order of something. It must have a content. We know which order we belong to because we do have some experience and the experience does contain within it the general principles from which the rest of the order may be inferred.

Watson, then, means to accept the option which involves the continuous and indissoluble link between the content of experience and its order. But we can look at this position, in its turn, as involving two further options.

On one of them, reality is already formed. It is simply that various percipients, amongst whom we number ourselves, happen to perceive it only partially and incompletely. Since there is an incoherence in the experience of each individual created by the difference between his partial perception and the true experience which represents the final rational order, experience seems to be in time. To overcome the incoherence, we are constantly shifting the ground and content of our experience.

30 Watson, *Outline*, p. 439.
31 Bertrand Russell, *The Problems of Philosophy* (Oxford: University Press, 1970; first published in 1912), pp. 70-71.

On the other option, part of the rational order in experience is the order of time and the development of the universe is an actual feature of it. The first of these seems most natural as the solution to Watson's problem except that, of course, if the temporal element in our experience is actually misleading, then when that misleading element is removed, there are many ways in which we can conceive the rational order which is to replace it. If it contains a falsifying principle, it apparently does not contain the principle necessary to infer the true rational order.

The second of these has within it the problem that we have already noticed: The universe in development seems open to many final plans each of which will have its own rational order. Either way, Russell's objection seemingly holds.

But it is, undoubtedly, the second of these that Watson *does* want to accept. In the second volume of his Gifford Lectures he appears quite conclusively to deny the model of the universe which would make of it a completed and absolute experience. He says:

> Nor can we accept the solution of Absolutism, which maintains that in the Absolute pain and evil disappear, being absorbed in a higher unity. From this point of view pessimism and optimism are alike indifferent; for whether we say that the world of our experience is the worst or the best of all possible worlds, it will remain true that these predicates have a meaning only from the relative or phenomenal point of view of our ordinary consciousness, whereas from the point of view of the Absolute there is no good or evil, but all is transmuted and glorified.[32]

Obviously, the completed universe of one of our hypotheses is the world of the Absolute in which nothing ever happens and good and evil are indifferent.

This passage from the Gifford Lectures makes exactly the point. The solution, if there is one, to the problems of Watson's metaphysics involves a value judgment. The end toward which the process tends must be not merely rational, but also good. If there is only one unique good state of affairs, then there is only one unique outcome to the rational development of the universe. This does not mean that reality must necessarily reach that stage. It only means that, insofar as it does not, what reality there is is tinged with unreality. It is tinged with incoherence, incompleteness, and irrationality. It will then continue as the process of experience. For experience is a process just because it does have, in Watson's view, an internal incoherence. There is a time to be transformed so long as there is incompleteness. The universe will

32 Watson, *Religious Experience*, Part Second, *Constructive* [vol. 2], p. 258.

go on forever unless it reaches completeness. But it always tends towards this goal for it is the lack of this goal which animates it.

If the premises involved in this argument can be substantiated completely they will, no doubt, overcome Watson's difficulty. However, they involve us in a set of new questions. Is goodness a unique state? Or are there many good states just as there are many rational orders? Are fact and value inextricably bound up or has Watson introduced an extraneous consideration into his metaphysics? Is he clearly aware of what he is doing or are these various passages from which we have been quoting *ad hoc* solutions to problems which he develops simply as he meets them? All of these issues deserve at least our brief attention. For Watson must address himself to them if his metaphysics is ultimately to prove acceptable. He comes closest to a solution in the twelfth lecture of the second volume which is headed "Evil and Atonement."

First of all, he argues that evil is a state of affairs, one inseparable from the developing process of the human condition, and one intelligible only by contrast to other states of affairs. It exists within the individual and within society.

> From what has been said, it is obvious that moral evil is in no sense something that can be imposed upon the individual from without: it exists only in so far as the phase of morality embodied in society is accepted by its members and conceived to be an expression of their true life. We may therefore say that every stage of society is good, in the sense that it expresses the highest ideal reached at the time. It is only by reference to a more developed standard that it can be called evil.[33]

The meaning of this passage for Watson's metaphysical system is reinforced when he says: "Man cannot be said to have been created either as good or evil, because morality exists only as willed by a rational subject."[34] A little earlier he has explained:

> The spiritual development of man is a process which is as inevitably determined by his spiritual nature as the process of the physical world by the laws operative in it. Therefore, evil is inseparable from the development of society. To suppose that absolute good could be attained at any given stage in the evolution is to suppose that the human spirit could overleap its limits, and anticipate the gradual process by which it learns to understand the world and so to understand itself.[35]

33 Ibid., pp. 280-81.
34 Ibid., p. 281.
35 Ibid.

And he goes on to say:

> ... what we must say is, that the spiritual nature of man is the product of a
> gradual process of evolution, each phase of which is a fresh conquest of the
> good as compared with that from which it has emerged; while from the point
> of view of a more advanced stage it is evil. Evil is therefore not the abstract
> opposite of good, but a lower stage of good.[36]

The more carefully he thinks about the matter, the more Watson becomes convinced that process is an inevitable and inseparable part of reality.

Rationality is itself a creation and this, though ambiguous, adds an important dimension to Watson's thought—a dimension within which the solution to the problems we have been sketching may lie. To say that rationality is something which develops is ambiguous because one may either mean "rationality" in the sense of the mental process by which we ideally make decisions and the mental processes within which we come to discern such notions of goodness, or one may mean rationality in the sense of the ultimate order in things. In general, Watson really refuses to distinguish between the two. For, if he did, there would be a simple "objective" world independent of us and another world which represented all possible conceptualizations of things. In that case, his theory of knowledge would develop the kind of impossible dualism which he frequently chides in others. But, if they develop together, in the sense that, for there to be a genuine rational order in nature is also for there to be the possibility of its identical twin in thought, then the two senses of rational are the same. More than that, the two are not "identical twins" except conceptually. We can easily distinguish between the concept of the order in nature and the concept of the rational order in our own thoughts. But, if knowledge in Watson's sense is possible, the two are simply aspects of one another. They seem to be identical twins when they are really one identical structure.

Suppose we regard the passages we have just quoted in this light. Then, it follows that truth *changes*. For, the imperfect rational order which nature represented before there were human minds is quite different from the more perfect rational order which is represented by a state in nature in which there are minds capable of representing it. This surprising conclusion does not seem to have occurred to Watson in these terms. But it is not, in itself, necessarily objectionable.

What it means is that the truth about the universe at a certain time is not necessarily the truth about the universe at a later time. This is not

36 Ibid.

just so in the trivial sense that there is more to the universe at a later time. It is true in the sense that, at earlier times, the relatively simple and undifferentiated structure of reality is capable of being represented by a comparatively large range of coherent structures. As it becomes more detailed, more clearly differentiated, more definitely structured, the truth about its earlier stages changes by becoming precise. For only those coherent systems which are capable of explaining its later states then have a claim to "truth."

If he is allowed this position, he can work his way out of the conundrums in which we found him. He need not worry about Russell's[37] objection that there may be many coherent systems which equally have a claim to be the truth because they are equally coherent and equally comprehensive. As the universe develops, and more of its potential becomes actual, the range of coherent systems which will adequately describe it will diminish proportionately. In the ideal case, they will diminish to one. But this ideal case might not ever come about. As the universe comes to have in it creatures in whom the rational order is instantiated in the way that we call "having a mind," a part of it becomes the ideas which are contained within those minds. Now *one* element in the problem involves what happens within those minds. They will have a range of freedoms and that range will have several dimensions. One dimension is defined by the extent to which the universe itself, at that time, is precisely determinate. Another dimension of that freedom is the range of potential errors. Now, if they use their "rational will" wisely, they will come to reflect, to an even larger degree, structures which are in the rational order. If they use them unwisely, they will come to reflect domains of error and these domains will become a region of the actual. They may assist or impede the orderly development of the universe.

Thus the range of systems qualifying as "true" may be larger or smaller depending upon what happens and depending on what the "feedback" effect of the activities of minds is on the environment itself. We *might* approach the state at which there is a single rational order. But evidently, we might not.

Thus truth becomes a goal toward which we work. Some passages in Watson's Gifford Lectures suggest that God, Himself, is a part of this development. Others suggest some uncertainty on this point. If this reading were given to Watson, however, he would have to accept the proposition that God is involved in the process of development and does not Himself become finally actual until the process is complete. For, at some stages of the universe, coherent systems excluding God

---

37 See footnote 31 above.

will be true, and in other stages, systems including God will take precedence over those excluding Him.

In short, scepticism is not overcome, really, if this is the correct reading of Watson, by reference to anything in the present but by reference to the ideal prospects of the universe. The extent to which this is a sensible reading of Watson will depend somewhat on our investigation of Watson's "rational religion." It also depends somewhat on the reading one gives to particular passages.

Watson may cheerfully accept a certain kind of relativity about truth. He may cheerfully accept that there are alternative rational descriptions of the universe at any time short of the time—if it ever comes about—at which the ideal state of affairs develops. The ideal state of affairs will be inferable from what we do know of the rational order, but we will not be able to assert that it is actualized. Truth, like goodness itself, will then become an ideal—something to be attained and not something pre-existing. This requires some dramatic change in the concept of truth that remains consistent with Watson's view of knowledge as the working out of rationality. On this view, as the ideal state is approached, the truth about the past of the universe will, itself, undergo modification. Mind becomes primary in the universe and central to truth. It comes, logically, to precede matter in the sense that, the more precise our accounts of matter become, the more precise, correspondingly, our minds become. The rational order in the one is simply unthinkable without the rational order in the other. The universe which could be correctly described as a set of material states—but also correctly described in a number of other ways—is transformed into a universe which simply cannot be described without the minds which contain the knowledge. It is the very occurrence of those minds which make the knowledge possible and the condition of the possibility of the knowledge is identical with the condition of the possibility of the detailed theory which is being described. That theory, consequently, depends for its truth upon the existence of the mind.

Throughout this process, time becomes transmuted as knowledge grows. It loses significance as there develop minds capable of moving freely throughout time and, as it loses significance, the truth changes.

Only this theory seems to be wholly consistent with everything which he says. But it does not seem to exist as a fully worked-out theory in his writings. Rather, his writings show a marked tension between the view forced upon him by his philosophical analyses that some kind of idealism is true and the view imposed upon him by the study of nineteenth-century science, the view that time is important, that the universe has a history, that men, minds, and perhaps God, develop in the universe.

It seems altogether possible that the theory which is most consistent with everything that he says would, nonetheless, have deeply shocked him. It seems unlikely that he would have welcomed this kind of relativity though he is often not far from the notion that truth is an ideal state and, as we saw, that notion, too, was clearly discernible in the work of John Clark Murray, who not only preceded Watson at Queen's but was, subsequently, a frequent visitor there.

No doubt Watson's entire metaphysics was, throughout his life, determined in part by his interest in Kant and Hegel, especially his interest in Hegel; in part by his determination to complete the work of Descartes and once and for all dispose of the sceptic; and in part by the tension between the two modes of thought with which he was most familiar.

It is certainly clear that Watson's form of idealism is complex and does not yield at once to immediate surface analyses. The prospective reader should be warned. He will certainly stumble on paragraphs which, taken in isolation, seem to be decisive. Even those, however, if read carefully and subjected to a word-by-word analysis frequently turn out to be capable of absorption into more than one interpretive scheme. We have tried to indicate the difficulties and to quote passages which exhibit Watson in one mood and another. The reader will do well to keep his own counsel.

Watson's metaphysical and epistemological position will become somewhat clearer if we relate it to some of the characteristically similar and contrasting positions of the time. His thinking was, in many ways, close to that of James Edwin Creighton, a protégé of Jacob Gould Schurman and long-time editor of the *Philosophical Review* in which many of Watson's papers were published. Obviously, the most significant contrast of the time was with the American pragmatists and instrumentalists and, while we have relatively little by way of direct and serious analysis of their work by Watson, we do have Watson's comments on William Caldwell. Caldwell sought to bring together the insights of the pragmatists and the idealists of the time—an undertaking which was far from foolish in the light of Dewey's obvious and acknowledged debt to Hegelianism. Watson thought little of Caldwell's effort but revealed something of himself in the process of responding to it.

Creighton was born April 8, 1861 in Pictou, Nova Scotia, studied at Dalhousie, and followed Schurman to Cornell where he was first graduate student and then faculty member until his death in 1924. He translated Bacon's *Novum Organum*, wrote *An Introductory Logic*, a text, in 1898 (by 1922 it had gone through four editions),[38] translated

38 James Edwin Creighton, *An Introductory Logic*, 4th ed. (New York: Macmillan, 1921).

Paulsen's life of Kant, and published more than a score of papers (fourteen of which are reprinted in a volume edited by Harold Smart).[39] He began as co-editor of the *Philosophical Review* (then, as now, something of a Cornell house organ) with Schurman. After 1903, he edited it largely alone although James Seth was an official collaborator. It was as editor of that journal that he mainly made his name.

Creighton's work is dominated by two ideas: The history of philosophy is an essential part of philosophy itself, and philosophy is a social not an individual process. He seems to mean by the first proposition that one could not understand, say, the philosophy of the nineteenth century if one did not understand something of what went before: The questions raised make sense in a sequence which must reflect something of the development of the human intellect itself. In this respect, he undoubtedly helped strengthen Watson's convictions and Watson moved closer to such a view as his work went on. By the second proposition, Creighton means to extend the first to include its natural analogue: If philosophy grows by an historical process of the interchange of views and is intelligible only in a context, then one might well suppose that, at any moment in time, it is also true that philosophy will make sense only in a social context. One man alone has little occasion to philosophize: It is only when he has inherited a set of challenges and finds a variety of positions in his immediate life that he must philosophize. The direct and immediate intuitions of a single life will seem self-sufficient when that life succeeds and will not seem readily capable of replacement when that life fails.

Thus his role as teacher, editor, and friend of active philosophers seemed to Creighton a natural and proper one—one that fitted neatly his procedural view of what philosophy was.

His substantive philosophical view centred around the proposition that the most important post-Kantian philosophical artifact was the concrete universal, the perfected individual through which the generalizations which enable us to theorize about the world become intelligible. He saw the task of the philosopher as mainly that of clarifying the universal. In a sense, he and Watson would have agreed about that, though Watson thought that the philosopher's task was mainly to respond to the details of various sceptical attacks and Creighton thought that that task was more positive: It was to work out the details of the concrete universal, to show how something can both be real (and so individual) and also amenable to reason (and so compounded of universals from which generalizations can be made). His essays frequently specify the task though they seldom purport to carry it out.

39 James Edwin Creighton, *Studies in Speculative Philosophy*, ed. with a bibliography by Harold R. Smart (New York: Macmillan, 1925).

This view, however, demanded a radical account of the unity of reason and feeling and a generalization of the thesis that rationality extends everywhere and is not bounded by a brute given. Frank Thilly describes his position, stating: "Feeling is part and parcel of thought, of reason, not an isolated event that remains the same, but interrelated with all the functions of the mind: . . . It is not mere subjectivity but an index of the form and order of thought."[40] One cannot, thus separate the given from the theoretical structure which we build about it. The only ultimate test is the completeness and the systematic nature of the structure that we build with reason. Watson used such ideas but he was more concerned with the details of the hard questions which his sceptical opponents might raise.

Creighton was prepared to allow—as perhaps Watson was not—for the development of individual sciences which might win their independence from the demand that they have a place in a finally integrated human knowledge. Thus he claimed that psychology was no longer a philosophy of mind, but "under the influence of experimental methods, has differentiated itself almost entirely from philosophy."[41] Those experimental methods, however, entailed an effective separation of the given from the theory—of immediate sensation or feeling from reason. Otherwise no experiment could confirm or deny any theory. The problem thus posed was a crucial one for the way in which Watson and Creighton viewed knowledge.

Creighton was content to leave it that psychology might go its own way. Watson understood that one could surrender that territory only at the cost of surrendering one's philosophical position. There is little doubt, however, that Creighton helped to provoke Watson to the thought processes which occupied the latter years of his life.

Watson did not often indulge in philosophical polemics with his contemporaries. The opponents with whom he skirmished mostly belonged to history. His concern with them was not so much predicated on the thought that they were safely dead as on the thought that philosophy includes its history as part of itself. Ideas, Watson thought, were only intelligible in the context of their development and of their alternatives. To get at the roots of an idea in a way which will enable one to come genuinely to grips with it, one must have seen it at work through twists and turns of time. Watson so firmly believed this that he even went to the length of writing a history of one of the theories he liked the least, a history which became a book entitled *Hedonistic*

40 Frank Thilly, "The Philosophy of James Edwin Creighton," *The Philosophical Review*, vol. 34, no. 3 (May 1925), p. 221.
41 Creighton, *An Introductory Logic*, Preface, p. v.

Theories from Aristippus to Spencer.[42] But usually his interest in opposing theories wanes markedly at about the period of the development of his own ideas. Thus, we find him interested continuously in men like Mill and Spencer but less vitally concerned with his contemporaries.

There are, however, exceptions. For the *Queen's Quarterly* he wrote a series of dialogues entitled "The Conflict of Idealism and Realism"[43] in which characters from Samuel Alexander and Bernard Bosanquet to Socrates amused themselves exchanging bon mots. They are amusing but not too informative. In the same year, 1924, Watson wrote a short paper for the *Philosophical Review* called "The Conflict of Absolutism and Realism"[44] which, though not amusing at all, also contains little that is new. Five years before his death, he wrote a paper on Whitehead's philosophy of nature which was read at the Eighth International Congress of Philosophy in Prague by one of his daughters.[45] He manages to be sympathetic to Whitehead while retaining his own position.

Of these relatively rare sorties to the contemporary front lines, the most interesting are certainly a paper in the *Queen's Quarterly* called "Some Remarks on Radical Empiricism"[46] and his assault, in the same journal, on William Caldwell.[47] (The Caldwell paper appeared in 1914, just after the appearance of Caldwell's book *Pragmatism and Idealism*.)[48] In both these papers, Watson stands his ground firmly. Indeed, here and elsewhere, he is suspicious even of the compromises admitted by Bernard Bosanquet in *The Meeting of Extremes in Contemporary Philosophy*.[49] Both of them are interesting, however, for the light they throw on Watson's own position and for the possibility they offer of clarifying Watson's relation to the work of other thinkers.

42 John Watson, *Hedonistic Theories from Aristippus to Spencer* (Glasgow: J. Maclehose & Sons, 1895).
43 John Watson, "The Conflict of Idealism and Realism," *Queen's Quarterly*, vol. 32, no. 1 (July-September 1924).
44 John Watson, "The Conflict of Absolutism and Realism," *Philosophical Review*, vol. 32, no. 2 (October-December 1924).
45 John Watson, "A Discussion of Dr. Whitehead's Philosophy of Nature with Special Reference to his Work, Concept of Nature," in *Actes du Huitième Congrès International de Philosophie à Prague, 1934* (Prague: Comité d'Organisation du Congrès, 1936).
46 John Watson, "Some Remarks on Radical Empiricism," *Queen's Quarterly*, vol. 18, no. 2 (October-December 1910). Hereafter referred to as "Radical Empiricism."
47 John Watson, "Pragmatism and Idealism," *Queen's Quarterly*, vol. 21, no. 4 (April-June 1914).
48 William Caldwell, *Pragmatism and Idealism* (London: Adam and Charles Black, 1913).
49 Bernard Bosanquet, *The Meeting of Extremes in Contemporary Philosophy* (London: Macmillan, 1921).

In approaching James and "radical empiricism,"[50] Watson remarks:

It is not good for any system to have things all its own way. The experience of man does not go round like a mill-horse in the same monotonous circle, but mounts ever higher by a sort of spiral process; and if our philosophy is to be living and to adapt itself to the form and pressure of life, it must change, or rather develop, taking up unto itself new material, and assimilating and transforming it.[51]

He adds, however, that "There is no danger in these days of any philosophy being raised to the 'bad pre-eminence' of undisputed sovereignty. Absolute Idealism is threatened not only by Radical Empiricism, but by the New Realism and by Personal Idealism."[52] He notes wryly that: "All alike claim to be based upon 'experience,' all in their own view are in close contact with life and fact, and all are perfectly certain that the others are divorced from reality and living in a region of abstraction."[53]

Though he is concerned to protect theology against James's forays into its domain, Watson's main concern in this paper is with the Jamesian account of experience. James accuses the absolute idealists in general of falling victim to the illicit reification of attractive abstractions. James saw the process of finding order in experience as the basis of the reason in reality which the post-Hegelian idealists, in one way or another, were inclined to capitalize upon. In James's view they extracted this order, projected it to an absolute completion, and called this reality. James did not doubt that there was order in experience. Indeed, he was inclined to think that "in the long run" what constituted utility in belief would be the result of acting on orderly convictions which experience would confirm and which could be used as the basis of a functioning natural science. But he thought that the order in experience might take many forms, that reality was not an effective unity or, at least, that such a unity could not be the exclusive basis of effective belief, and that experience must continue to surprise us.

Watson seems to read James, rather unfairly, as being himself the victim of an abstraction. For he sees James as making a separation between experience and order. In fact, James is not attacking Watson but a stereotype of monistic idealism which, as Watson seems to imply,

---

50 William James, *A Pluralistic Universe*, The Hibbert Lectures, Manchester College (New York: Longmans, Green, 1909).
51 Watson, "Radical Empiricism," p. 111.
52 Ibid.
53 Ibid.

may not have been held by anyone. But James has in mind, at least, F. H. Bradley and he is on safe ground with respect to the first half of Bradley's *Appearance and Reality*.[54] For there Bradley does take the view that we can mark off much of experience as only appearance on the ground that its description fails to measure up to appropriate logical criteria. Oddly enough, no one has been as critical as Bradley was in his *Logic*[55] of the tendency to take logical order for granted and the tendency to leave many of its relations unexplored and unexplicated.

But the real issue between James and Watson is surely not over "radical empiricism." Watson, unlike Bradley, would urge that we do find the order in experience, that we shall not know the final form of the order until our experience has developed to its limit and that, especially in matters of politics, we have to develop our view of logic along with our explorations of the order in reality. The difference between them is really over two questions, one of which Watson mentions but does not develop at length and the other of which seems to arouse such strong feelings that it is not clear what form a more seasoned answer would take.

The first of these issues is the one which James puts, in words quoted by Watson, as "the habit of explaining wholes by parts."[56] James thinks that what one must do is to collect, as it were, samples of the universe (or as it may well turn out, of the various "universes") and generalize from them. He is well aware that this entails the traditional problem of "induction" and that such generalizations have no formal validity. It is for this reason, perhaps, more than any other that James believes that all we can accumulate are useful beliefs and that he is, in the end, inclined to equate truth and utility. If we are confined to samples of the universe, then none of our generalizations will carry us beyond those samples and, one would think, none of them would actually sustain our conviction that we had acquired useful beliefs.

Now what Watson invariably holds is that one explains parts by wholes. One asks what overall rational scheme could give rise to this particular manifestation with which we are acquainted. To be sure, one's view of this rational ultimate whole may well change as one encounters more manifestations. Now this procedure is logically unobjectionable. One can reason from the whole to the part. The challenge which James is presenting is the challenge to explain how one came to be convinced that there was an ultimate rational whole. Watson's general defence is that, if one does not hold this belief, one falls into a self-contradictory scepticism.

54 F. H. Bradley, *Appearance and Reality* (London: Oxford University Press, 1893).
55 F. H. Bradley, *The Principles of Logic* (London: Kegan Paul, 1883).
56 Watson, "Radical Empiricism," p. 111.

For if the whole is not a rational order, why should the part be? And anyone who supposes that he can begin by explaining some immediate fragment of experience can only suppose that he is able to ascribe a rational order to that fragment. Yet this belief is as unsound as any other if the whole does not manifest rationality.

More particularly, Watson wants to urge that, in the occasions of experience which rise from our transactions of the world, we are constantly faced with features which go beyond their immediacy. His best case would be founded on the phenomenon of meaning itself. Pieces of experience are meaningful because they refer beyond themselves and, because they are meaningful, we can understand more than they immediately offer. These snatches of meaning give us a clue to the manner in which we may find a rational whole which will explain the part.

The second issue is really a more radical form of the first. Watson quotes James as conceding that he has had to throw logic overboard and take refuge in feeling. He finds James saying: "For my own part . . . I have finally found myself compelled to give up the logic (of identity) fairly, squarely and irrevocably. It has an imperishable use in human life, but that use is not to make us theoretically acquainted with the essential nature of reality."[57] Now part of this is Jamesian rhetoric. James does not mean that he has given up reasoning and he certainly does not mean that he has given up finding order in experience and determining ways in which one may seize upon the utilities of belief. But part of it is meant literally enough. It is hard to be sure what the "logic of identity" is—though Watson claims it is "the only logic that Mr. James recognizes"[58] but at least, no doubt, James means that he has given up propositions of the form "A is A" in the sense that he no longer thinks that entities in the world have unique and unequivocal characterizations. Giving up that form of the logic of identity is a necessary condition of being able to elide beliefs and utility.

Watson sees James, if he means to fall back on "relativism," as taking the "plunge into the abyss of phenomenalism, where we meet with nothing but the elusive fictions of an unintelligible universe."[59] If this is so, then: "The universe as known to us is, on his [James's] showing, utterly incomprehensible, and we must therefore abandon all the normal processes of reason and take refuge in a mystical faith."[60] Watson explores this notion as he thinks James wants to expound it in

57 Ibid., p. 117.
58 Ibid.
59 Ibid., p. 118.
60 Ibid.

terms of taking refuge in the "feeling"that we are all part of the "larger consciousness"[61] which is, ultimately, a finite God. But Watson finds this to conflict not with the truth of reason but with the "religious consciousness, which will accept nothing less than what the Shorter Catechism calls a 'spirit infinite, eternal and unchangeable in his being, wisdom, power, holiness, justice, goodness and truth.' "[62]

To get at the real issue which separates Watson and James on this point one must probe more deeply. To begin with, they have in common the rejection of certain views. Both really would reject the separation of reason and experience. It is just that the character of experience leads James to take one account of reason and Watson to take another. If James is rebelling against a kind of idealism like Watson's, it is not in the name of some common-sensical view that reality is simply given to us whole. Indeed, if anything, he thinks that our beliefs and our feelings are more deeply intertwined with reality than Watson does. What is at stake is the notion of a univocal reality. If Watson were prepared to say that he accepted the ultimate rational order of things as a *preferred* reality because of the experiences of value which he found in reason, James probably would have no objection. He would simply say there are other worlds, though they may not commend themselves equally to a rational man. Thus, if Watson were prepared to found his metaphysics on ethics and to call his metaphysics rational preference, he would be quite close to James. And, in a sense, Watson comes quite close to that very position. For he would admit that men habitually live out their lives in a world which is not, in his terms, the real world. These sub-worlds which frequently imprison men are not, for Watson, unreal, they are simply created by an unsatisfactory perspective. In the end it is the value he puts on reason which compels Watson to reject scepticism and compels him to reject every form of naïve realism. James was in no way insensitive to these values. The different emphasis which he gives to them reflects, in large part, a degree of certainty about them which is less than the one which Watson would ascribe to his own convictions.

What for James becomes a plurality of worlds is, for Watson, a plurality of perspectives all but one of which falls short of the ultimate reality. The reason in which Watson puts his faith is, however, the very reason which provokes James to ask the questions he does and must ask. It is partly a matter of the origin of thinking—in a variety of senses of the word "origin." We shall see some of these issues more clearly when we discuss Caldwell's attempt to make peace between the later pragmatists and the followers of various developed forms of essentially post-Bradleyan idealism.

61 Ibid.
62 Ibid., p. 119.

But the "logic of identity" is, in itself, still an important issue. Watson does believe that, at bottom, there is a univocal description of things and James does not. Watson is convinced that to adopt James's position is to lapse into a dangerous kind of relativism. James is convinced that to accept the logic of identity in this sense is to become committed to a view of reality which is altogether too narrow. Oddly enough, neither of them seemed very determined to explore the theoretical basis of this question about logic.

Watson was little attracted by the attempts of Bradley[63] and Bosanquet[64] to wrestle with the laws of identity, non-contradiction, and excluded middle. And he seems to have had no tendency to go back and reconstruct documents like Hegel's *Science of Logic*.[65] James provoked Royce[66] to numerous investigations about problems of formal logic but, for the most part, it was left to Dewey[67] to explore the pragmatist response to those problems.

Against this background, it will not surprise anyone to discover Watson in a hostile mood as he comes to review William Caldwell's book *Pragmatism and Idealism*. Caldwell was a fellow Scot and, at that time, was the Sir William Macdonald Professor of Moral Philosophy at McGill University. He was, thus, Watson's neighbour in space though they were quite unlike one another in cast of mind. Caldwell was impressed by pragmatism partly because it seemed to him to provide a new and interesting perspective from which philosophical problems could be freshly viewed and partly because he was interested in it, as he says, as an exhibition of the American mind at work. At the same time, he thought that many of the formulations originally given to it by James were vague, confusing, and, on their own ground, intellectually unsatisfying. He retained, what is more, a strong sympathy with the British form of post-Hegelian idealism. Consequently, he set out in his book to discover how one might reconcile the insights of these two views.

Watson was not impressed. He quotes with relish all of Caldwell's criticisms of the pragmatists and then expresses his "surprise" at finding that Caldwell says that what the pragmatists want to urge is "in the main"[68] true. He sniffs huffily at Caldwell's account of Bradley and

---

63 See footnote 55 above.

64 Bernard Bosanquet, *Logic, or the Morphology of Knowledge* (Oxford: Clarendon Press, 1888), and *The Essentials of Logic* (London: Macmillan, 1895).

65 G. W. F. Hegel, *The Science of Logic*, trans. W. H. Johnston and L. G. Struthers (London: George Allen & Unwin, 1929).

66 Josiah Royce, *Logical Essays*, ed. D. S. Robinson (Dubuque, Iowa: W. C. Brown, 1951).

67 John Dewey, *Logic, The Theory of Inquiry* (New York: H. Holt, 1938).

68 Watson, "Pragmatism and Idealism," p. 467.

Bosanquet—an account which he says is "little better than a travesty of their real opinions."[69] He can find praise only for the "singleness of heart" with which Caldwell has "proposed to himself an eirenicon."[70] Amidst all the hostility of tone, the less literate undergraduates confronting that issue of the *Queen's Quarterly* can be forgiven if they did not guess that an eirenicon is an attempt to make peace.

Indeed, Watson does not confine himself to assaulting Caldwell's conclusions. He rages on about the form of the book as well. The reader, he thinks, may well complain about the "somewhat inordinate length at which what are practically the same points are repeated in a different context without substantial change."[71] He even suggests that Caldwell is a little sneaky. "The manner in which he quotes sentences from these authors [Bradley and Bosanquet], without the qualifications that give to them their real meaning, is only calculated to produce exasperation and to defeat the object he has in view."[72]

One would have thought that there was room for significant debate between Watson and Caldwell and that debate might have led Caldwell on from his interesting beginning to a more satisfactory formulation of pragmatism, just as the debate might have led Watson to spell out, in a more adequate way, many of the details of his system. Watson, however, reacted much like an old wolf who has seen part of his pack under attack. Bradley and Bosanquet clearly belong to his pack. Caldwell was an upstart who wrote unattractive prose. What we have here is, at least, an exception to the general rule that Canadian philosophers do not read each other but not, alas, an exception to the rule that they seem to influence one another only indirectly.

Caldwell represented one of the very few major incursions of American pragmatism into Canadian thought. It might have proved significant and not merely a footnote to Watson but Caldwell seems to have been working largely alone and, whatever happened in the later development of his career, it seems clear that he was not significantly helped by reading Watson. In the difficult country which he chose for himself, one can forgive him his lapses into imprecision. It is difficult to forgive Watson for his lack of charity and helpfulness. At least, however, he saw the importance of nearly every question.

We must now turn to his philosophy of religion. Religion fascinated Watson all his life. His concern with it runs through all his philosophy like an ideological gulf stream. Like an ocean current, it is

69 Ibid., p. 466.
70 Ibid.
71 Ibid.
72 Ibid.

occasionally invisible and frequently beneath the surface. But the structure of his writings reveals, nonetheless, that it is there.

No part of his writing was more influential on the outside world. H. H. Walsh in *The Christian Church in Canada*[73] assigns him an important place in the creation of the climate of ideas which made possible the United Church of Canada. That most peculiarly Canadian institution no doubt had its origins in two situations. One of them, as Walsh points out, was the dispersion of the population with the coming of the railway. A population spread across western Canada in tiny tank towns at the railside could not afford the luxury of indefinitely many Protestant churches. But the other situation is equally important. It has to do with the changing climate of thought. Nineteenth-century science compelled the junking of much trivial mythology, at least in the popular mind. The throwing together of populations gathered from a wide variety of social and cultural backgrounds made irrelevant the particular history of denominations such as Methodism, Congregationalism, and, except in dominantly Scottish communities, Presbyterianism. The combination of these situations made whatever separated a Methodist from a Congregationalist seem unimportant. In a little prairie town, the difference between two such denominations was likely to be nothing more than the character of the minister. A good one would attract people from rival denominations. A bad one would reduce his congregation to virtual non-existence. To these was added a third factor: Canadians were coming to have an outlook of their own on the world. A Congregationalist might trace his origins to pre-revolutionary America, a Methodist might have been a Methodist because of a social or political situation in England or Northern Ireland. A Presbyterian was apt to remain one because he was a Scot. As these facts receded into the background, the new outlook, in the temper of the times, was bound to owe more to reason than to myth.

These facts—the cultural and ideological as opposed to the geographical facts—were reinforced by the character of the clergy at the end of the nineteenth century. They had been educated, over a span of time, by men like Paxton Young, John Clark Murray, George Blewett, and of course, in large numbers, by Watson himself. The fact that all these men were engaged in the deliberate creation of a rational religion gave a cast of mind to the young clergymen who moved west. They were, no doubt, most influential along the railway through the west, but they were not uninfluential in rural Ontario and even in the Maritimes. What they had learned made sense to their parishoners just because the cultural facts were what they were.

73 H. H. Walsh, *The Christian Church in Canada* (Toronto: Ryerson Press, 1956), pp. 212, 291.

That it was always Watson's intention, deliberately, to create a rational religion is beyond the possibility of doubt. He began his Gifford Lectures with an account of religion, claiming that religion and the nature of man as essentially spiritual were closely bound. He goes on to insist that religion, far from being the enemy of rationality, is the natural outcome of rationality. It is not that he is unaware that religion has functions which transcend those of the intellect. Indeed, he says, "So far as he is religious, man is raised above the divisions and distractions of his ordinary consciousness, and attains to peacefulness and serenity."[74] Religion has an obviously practical outcome. It was that peacefulness and serenity which men sought in carrying their religion with them to the prairie or into the mountains of British Columbia. But those feeling states, in Watson's view, were not to be distinguished from rationality.

In believing that, he had, however little it could be clearly articulated, the real support of Canadians engaged in settling a new land.

For the most part, they were or thought of themselves as tough-minded people. The man who sets up a hardware store or goes to run a bank in a town in Saskatchewan does not usually consider himself a sentimentalist. Nor, seeing that his business is the organization of technology, is he likely to regard himself as a traditionalist or as a man given over to superstitions. He wants his religion. But he wants it to make sense.

This demand made him impatient with denominational distinctions and receptive to the claims of reason. It did not reduce his demand for the solace of religion or his demand that it should, at least, once a week, take him out of himself. Watson's blend of hard-headed rationality and other-worldliness was exactly the commodity that the market demanded.

That is not to say that the founding of the United Church went smoothly. As one might have expected, the idea first originated on the prairies, indeed, in Winnipeg in 1902. By 1904, the committee on church union was at work. The actual union did not come about until 1925. Even then, a third of the Presbyterians refused to join and kept with them two colleges, neither of them Watson's Queen's. Half a decade later, they had nearly half of the original Presbyterians back in their fold. The Scots' culture, invariably, proved strong. But it is doubtful that the "continuing Presbyterians" turned out to have an ideology significantly different from those of the brethren who had joined the United Church.

74 Watson, *Religious Experience*, Part First, *Historical* [vol. 1], p. 1.

It is important, as part of the understanding of Canadian culture, to ask how successful Watson was in creating the synthesis that he wanted—the synthesis that would make religion rational but retain its solace. If the United Church had had patron saints, Watson might have been forgotten less quickly. But the importance of a task does not depend on its being recognized and Watson on religion is still a vital topic.

It will be helpful to begin our discussion by quoting at some length Watson's summary of the nature of religion and of its relations to other human activities.

> The possibility of religion is bound up with the essential nature of man as a rational and spiritual being, and rationality or spirituality presupposes as its primary condition the consciousness of a unity which embraces all distinctions, and more particularly the fundamental distinction of the world and the self. So far as he has merely immediate presentations or feelings, man is but potentially rational; it is only as these are lifted out of the flux of immediacy, and grasped in their relation to the world as a rational system, that he realizes his birthright as a self-conscious intelligence. It is in virtue of this inalienable capacity that he creates arts, sciences and political institutions, all of which imply the elevation of what immediately presents itself to the rank of an intelligible object. That object is possible at all only because of the self-activity which is implied in the power of turning immediate things into the means of expressing the will. Now, when man, as a rational subject, finds, or believes that he finds, the world to be a cosmos and human life intelligible, and refers both object and subject to a supreme principle, he adopts the attitude of religion. Thus religion is not one sphere along side of others, but the single all-embracing sphere in which all distinctions are but elements that have no reality or meaning when they are severed from the single principle upon which they depend. Religion cannot be subordinated to any higher form of consciousness; it is not a means to something else, but all else is a means to it. No doubt there are various forms of religion, but in all of them man has the consciousness of having grasped the inner truth of things and attained to the completion of his being. Whether the divine is believed to be immediately present or to be far off, there is never any doubt of its absolute reality.[75]

Religion, in this passage, sounds as though it is simply metaphysics. The familiar Watsonian theme occurs once again—rationality is part of the natural order of things, men realize it by grasping their true relation to the world, self-conscious intelligence is the result. The crucial factor is, as always, the process by which men rise beyond the "flux of immediacy." It is that which distinguishes men from other

75   Ibid., p. 2.

animals. But though, in this passage, the essence of religion is metaphysical, Watson goes on to distinguish two other elements in religion. The second he describes as worship and the third as a way of life. One must not only believe (and Watson thinks of belief as a kind of assent), one must also have a certain attitude to one's belief. More important than this is the way in which that attitude and the belief to which it is directed order one's life.

Watson will not have it that these elements are more than conceptually distinct. He admits that one might have a religion without a theology if, by a theology, one means a closely worked-out and detailed intellectual structure. But he says that this view must not be allowed to produce "the fallacy that religion does not in any way depend upon what a man believes, but is purely a matter of feeling or religious experience."[76] This proposition "is true only if by feeling or religious experience is meant the total concrete religious consciousness, including thought as well as emotion and will."[77] It is belief which makes worship and the shaping of one's life intelligible. They may disguise belief by embracing it in a single unity of consciousness. But that only helps make the fundamental point.

Because one might think of belief as expressed through the actions of ritual and through life as it is shaped by creed, one might also think of basic religious beliefs as capable of existing apart from their outcomes in action. But this is to deny a basic tenet of Watson's system. Watson holds consistently that the rational element in one's life *is* what shapes one's actions. There is not a dual reality of idea and act. It is those with fuzzy or irrational beliefs who are capable of bad action. Yet this almost hyper-rationality must be reconciled with the acceptance of religion as a crucial and intelligible element in our emotional life. Just how this reconciliation is developed is a crucial element in our inquiry.

Most of Watson's two-volume Gifford Lectures is devoted to an historical analysis of the development of philosophical ideas and their relation to religion. They cover the inevitable list from Plato and Aristotle, through Origen, Aquinas, Dante, Eckhart, Descartes, Spinoza, Leibniz, Locke, Berkeley, and Hume, to Kant and Hegel. Most of this long pilgrimage through the history of philosophical and theological disputes does not concern us here.

There is little doubt about the origins of Watson's own theory. Watson was a serious Kant scholar all his life.[78] He wrote about Kant,

76 Ibid., p. 6.
77 Ibid.
78 John Watson, *The Philosophy of Kant Explained* (Glasgow: J. Maclehose & Sons, 1908); *The Philosophy of Kant as Contained in Extracts from his Own Writings*, selected and translated by John Watson (Glasgow: J. Maclehose & Sons, 1888); and numerous

made extensive notes about Kant, lectured on Kant. Hume challenged the scope and use of reason more forcefully but did so, Watson seems to have believed, mainly on the ground of a too limited and even misguided account of experience. Kant, on the other hand, could hardly be faulted for a view of experience which closely coincided with Watson's own. Kant's efforts, therefore, to establish the limits of reason had to be taken with the utmost seriousness. In the chapters on Kant in his Gifford Lectures, Watson makes a determined effort to state Kant's position as strongly as possible.

Watson's summary of Kant's position on rational theology goes like this:

> Kant's objection to Rational Theology, then, is that, as we can have no knowledge of reality as a whole, we cannot establish the existence of a Being which contains all reality within itself. In the progress of our knowledge we never reach completeness. The reality that we know is "distributive," not "collective," being found dispersed among a number of individuals, not concentrated in one. Thus a Being within which all reality exists, and is known to exist, lies beyond the range of our knowledge. If such a Being exists, it must be as a perceptive intelligence, and a perceptive intelligence cannot be understood by beings like ourselves, whose perception and intelligence operate independently of each other. Though we are not entitled to deny the existence of such an Intelligence, it is for us merely a faultless ideal, that we can never verify by any extension of our knowledge of God, all so-called proofs of his existence must be sophistical, resting as they do (a) upon the confusion between the idea of completed knowledge and the actual completion of knowledge, (b) upon the identification of the idea of a Being which is the unity of all positive predicates with the knowledge of such a Being, and (c) upon the equalization of this totality of positive reality with an individual Being.[79]

Thus:

> At the close of the *Critique of Pure Reason* we seem to be left with an irreconcilable antagonism between the ideal of knowledge and the limited knowledge of which only we are capable. The Ideas of the Soul, the World and God no doubt reveal the limitations of our experience, but they do not enable us to go beyond it, valuable as they are in supplying us with ideals by reference to which experience is extended, specialized and systematized. But, while Kant has closed the entrance into the supersensible to knowledge, he has left the way open for a rational faith, as based upon the peculiar character of the practical reason or moral consciousness.[80]

other articles. For a bibliography of Watson's extensive publications, see *Douglas Library Notes*, vol. 16, no. 4, 1968, Douglas Library, Queen's University, Kingston.

79 Watson, *Religious Experience*, Part First, *Historical* [vol. 1], p. 270.
80 Ibid., pp. 270-71.

The essence of these Kantian objections, in Watson's eyes, is that reason is confined. Left to itself, it can produce ideals but, left to itself, it can also produce antinomies. It can show us that the world must have, and cannot have, a first cause; that the world must have, and cannot have, limits in space and time. When it perfects itself, it sees only its reflection. For its force comes only within the categories of the understanding which inform our sensible intuitions. The antinomies arise, most strikingly, because we cannot sum our experience in space and time. The phenomenal world is simply not that kind of thing. Now Kant's God resembles, most clearly, Anselm's God—that Being who,at least, is the sum of the largest set of compossible predicates. God cannot, therefore, appear as an object in the phenomenal world, in the world, that is, of sensible intuition as informed by the categories of the understanding. God is a unity unlike the fragmentary and fragmented experience which we encounter. Indeed, if there is such a being, he represents, for Kant, as Watson points out, a unity of perception and intelligence or perception and reason which is utterly unlike the disunity which, for us, holds in principle between these things. We must, Kant thinks, if we are to understand our phenomenal world, distinguish reason, the categories of the understanding which form structure and experience, and our sensory intuitions themselves. Hence God, if he exists, belongs to a domain in which the writ of reason, as we know it, simply does not run. Our reason, in that domain, erects only ideals which are reflections of reason itself or creates the contradictions of the antinomies.

In addition, Kant holds that we also know that the conditions which would be necessary for us to act as moral agents are actually met in the world. For it is Kant's view that "ought" implies "can"—that is, that no one has an obligation to do what he cannot, in fact do. Kant offers a variety of arguments in the *Critique of Practical Reason* and the *Critique of Judgment*. The most persuasive of them is the one which Watson summarizes this way: "The moral law prescribes as an ultimate end its own complete realization, and therefore we are entitled to assume that it is capable of being realized. Only on the ground of the moral consciousness can we maintain any ultimate end of creation."[81]

Watson realizes that Kant is here giving with one hand what he has taken away with the other and, in the discussion of Hegel's relation to Kant, Watson tries to seek out the ultimate basis of this seeming paradox. The explanation, in essence, is this: In the first *Critique*, Kant has painted reason as bound to our sensory intuitions. But in morality, reason, as pure practical reason, is entirely free. The moral law follows

81   Ibid., p. 278.

from the logic of the situation, from pure reason as applied to the practical situation. The moral law binds us, not as fat men or thin men, stupid men or intelligent men, emotional men or stoical men, but simply as moral agents. Since the essence of a moral agent is the same for us all—the potentiality of a good will—we act in and for all men, in acting in and for ourselves. Hence the problem is primarily a logical one, the problem of generalizing from the maxims of our acts to a universal law.

We can know this to be binding in and of itself and we can know, in this domain, that reason is efficacious. These rational commands, nonetheless, require a world in which they can be carried out. They demand an ideal and, if that ideal is impossible, they are a tissue of nonsense. Now we know that we cannot achieve this ideal state for ourselves as the argument above indicated and, thence, we know that something else must make it possible for us to do as we are commanded by pure practical reason. Only God would have power to arrange the situation. Hence, if we know both what our duty is and that what we know to be our duty could not be our duty unless God existed, we know, indeed, that God exists.

Watson, however, is persuaded that Kant does not mean to assert that God exists in this world—the phenomenal world in which we have our being. It is this phenomenal world in which pure reason can act only as it is informed by our sensory intuitions. In this, the phenomenal world, we know ourselves only as the empirical ego. That simply will not do as the explanation of morality. As the empirical ego, each of us is a different creature. What pure practical reason puts us in touch with is the noumenal self—the underlying of reality.

It is in that world that the moral agent, per se, has its being. But if that is where the noumenal self has its being, that is also where the God, demonstrated by the use of the postulation of pure practical reason, has His being. Hence, Watson says:

> Kant's opposition of nature and morality, instead of proving the existence of God, makes his existence incredible; for it is not possible to reason from a world that is essentially irrational and anti-moral to the existence of a rational and moral principle. To establish the existence of God, it must be shown that, properly understood, the world is rational through and through, and therefore that morality is the only principle which can possibly prevail.[82]

Watson finds, however, that as Kant goes along his view changes subtly. Because of this, the *Critique of Judgment* is "in some ways the most

82 Ibid., p. 326.

important of all Kant's works."[83] Watson interprets Kant's view this way:

> ... while understanding prescribes the laws of the sensible world, and reason as practical the laws of moral world, the two realms are separate and independent of each other. Nevertheless, these two realms must be conceived as not absolutely incompatible; for the moral law ought to be realized in the world of nature, and therefore nature must be conceived as admitting the possibility of such realization. The idea of the possible harmony of nature and freedom thus implies the idea of final cause or purpose, an idea which is the principle of reflective judgment, the faculty that mediates between understanding and reason, nature and freedom. The particular laws of nature must therefore be viewed as if they have been established by an intelligence other than ours with a view to their being comprehended by us. This idea of nature as in all its diversity purposive is, however, not to be regarded as objective, but only as a principle for the extension of our knowledge.[84]

Here Kant is approaching the unity of nature. Here, also, Kant is introducing yet another kind of fragmentation. It is now "reflective judgment"—a new device to mediate between the understanding, the set of categories which inform the phenomenal world, and reason as such. But this new reflective principle is essentially heuristic—designed, that is, as a desirable principle of inquiry in order to preserve the fundamental rationality of our claims to knowledge. Kant sees, in short, how his world must be made to fit together. But the continuous separation of reason and understanding forces him to hold it together with bits of intellectual sticking plaster.

Kant's later two *Critiques* must be answered, obviously, because they suggest what needs to be done in order to validate claims of reason. Reason must somehow be restored to nature—returned from its status as a kind of abstraction. Morality, too, needs to be brought down to cases and not left as a series of ideal rules for creatures who not only have one foot in each of the two worlds but, somehow or other, have their moral foot in another world. The flaw in Kant is in Kant's concept of reason. Watson reads Hegel as, at least, attempting to overcome this difficulty:

> The fundamental objection which he [Hegel] makes to it is that by its opposition of phenomena and noumena it creates a division that virtually splits up the universe into two discrepant halves. This division he regards as

83 Ibid.
84 Ibid., p. 327.

due primarily to the false conception of thought as in its own nature purely analytic, whereas he contends that thought always operates by way of a method which is at once analytic and synthetic or concrete. Thought is therefore, Hegel contends, adequate to the comprehension of reality, and in fact what Kant calls the categories of thought are the more or less adequate ways in which the human intelligence grasps the fundamental principles of a universe essentially rational.[85]

To say that reason is "analytic" is to say, in Kantian terms, that reason, as pure reason, deals always in formal structures which are tautologous. In Kant's terms, an analytic proposition is one, such as the proposition that all red balls are red, in which the assigned predicate already belongs to the subject. Watson would deny that this is the essense of reason and, rather, would regard reason as dealing with what Josiah Royce thought of as "types of order."[86] Reason is capable of discerning the order in what Kant would call an analytic proposition. But it is capable of discerning other kinds of order as well, and therefore of determining what successive positions in a given order must be like. Kant, in fact, frequently allows that this is so. In allowing for the postulates of pure, practical reason, Kant permits reason to determine morality because the issue about morality turns out to be purely formal. The issue is about universalization. It is the form of the rule as a rule binding on all moral agents which distinguishes it from other interesting phenomena such as pure prudential propositions. But what reason does here is not to grasp tautologies but to grasp what fits in a certain kind of order. Kant's claim that reason is simply empty as applied to nature when it is abstracted from the content of sensory intuition derives from his belief that it is only through the categories of the understanding that we are able to discern what types of order properly belong to nature and that this is simply a matter of fact.

However far Watson would or would not go with Hegel, he makes it clear that he will go far enough to admit Hegel's view of reason, for he thinks that Kant's restrictions turn out to be, to a large extent, arbitrary. Discerning the order of nature is, for him, as much an act of creative synthesis making use of reason as it is for Kant. He simply denies that it is arbitrary or that there is any reason to think that there is another world somehow quite distinct from the phenomenal world.

Another way of putting it is that Watson, throughout his writings, thinks that one may universalize from the data of nature much as one universalizes from the maxims of practical action. Just as a moral rule must be binding on all men as moral agents and therefore universaliza-

85 Ibid., p. 330.
86 Royce, *Logical Essays*, chapters 1, 9, and 16.

tion is a feature of it, so nature, to be nature, must exhibit certain standard features. Otherwise, we would regard it as chimera, illusion, or hallucination. Our belief that we have correctly described an individual element in nature is tied to our belief that we can universalize that nature so as to form a natural law. The process is much the same as the one by which Kant urges that, to be sure that we have a moral proposition, we must be able to universalize it. Nature exhibits, for Watson and Hegel, universals as much as morality does.

But, for both of them, it is not true in either case that the universal element is an abstraction. A truly moral act must fit into the pattern of all moral acts which would make up a moral universe and those acts must be acts of real flesh and blood persons, not the acts of hypothetically distant and abstract noumenal selves. For the moral question arises because there are choices to make in this world. Similarly, there are not, for Hegel or for Watson, abstract principles such as Kant's categories of the understanding or abstract laws of nature. There are merely ordered things and the things can no more be understood without the order than the order can be understood without the things.

This is the real point. The universal, for Hegel and for Watson, is only comprehensible as an ordered set of actual things. It is concrete in the sense that we must represent it to ourselves and our physical laws as an order of natural objects. We cannot understand that order apart from the objects or vice versa.

The incoherence in Kant, both of them think, is derived from separating these two elements. Reason, therefore, is sovereign only insofar as realities must always exhibit themselves as actual orders which can be discerned by reason and insofar as they are not real individual elements which could be described in some independent way. Kant seems to have a system which demands that the elements are conceivable without the order in which they appear but, at the same time, he is concerned to deny that we have any intelligible experiences without an order. The combination of these two propositions makes it seem as though we are trapped in the given phenomenal order of experience and that this order is, to an extent, conceivably not the order of reality. He thinks, in short, that the elements might have a different structure in a different world. But, in the end, he cannot make sense of this notion and is forced, with regard to nature, to postulate simply the possibility of an independent noumenal world. This breaks down when he turns to morality because he accepts a different view of the generality of moral rules. But Watson and Hegel would regard this choice as arbitrary and simply a sign of the incoherence in Kant's system.

It is quite vital to notice that Watson wants no part of Kant's other-worldly God any more than he wants any part of Kant's apparently other-worldly morality.

Thus, even if he rescues reason from Kant's assault, he is compelled to reconstruct it on its own in a way which will produce a rational theology. This is the point at which the discussion becomes most interesting both in Hegel and in Watson. Kant, essentially, in the second two *Critiques*, founds *his* rational religion on morality. It is because reason, viewed from the stance of morality, leads us to the noumenal world that we are able to reach such notions as God and so have a religion.

Hegel sought a quite different foundation for religion. He found it, in the end, in the nature of human consciousness as such. But it is not clear—and Watson sees this—that Hegel, himself, has escaped the further fragmentation of the world.

In general, Hegel's argument derives from the notion that we can see that human consciousness is, in a sense, unlimited and that to comprehend itself, it requires an infinite object of knowledge. Human consciousness is unlimited, in principle, because it always transcends the limits of any system within which it can be given a structure. Hegel's *Phenomenology*[87] paints the various modes of human awareness and understanding as various subject-object relations. The structure given to subject and object is determined, in each case, by the structure given to its counterpart in the dialectic. If the objects of knowledge are given the structures of ordinary material things, the subject comes to be conceived as a kind of ghostly mirror image of the thing—a pseudo-thing, a kind of Cartesian ghost. If the objects of knowledge are conceived as sensations, the subject will have to be conceived, as Hume suggested, as a bundle of sensations. But none of these pairs suffices. Consciousness is always capable of other modes, other structures. Our awareness is always coloured by this fact and, in Hegel's view, we search for a suitable infinite object which will match the real potentiality of the subject.

Historically, men have simply done whatever they could to satisfy this demand. The results, Hegel thought, generally have about them a revealing dialectical absurdity. The tendency is to associate infinite value with the most potent finite object that the existing structures of consciousness reveal. Hence, we have had a variety of religions which, when we look back on them, seem obviously to make the mistake of associating infinite values and finite objects. Hegel cites flower reli-

---

87   G. F. Hegel, *The Phenomenology of Mind* (London: George Allen & Unwin, 1966; first published in Great Britain in 1910).

gions, animal religions, religions based upon art, and, inevitably, the anthropomorphic superman religions which impinge on our own culture.

There is no avoiding these phenomena. One will accept some religion or make up one's own. It is a matter of the working of consciousness. Worst off of all, perhaps, are those who are not aware of the objects to which they attach infinite value and who may become the victims of greed, power, or some other pseudo-value designed, probably unconsciously, to encompass the infinite in some span of finite awareness.

Hegel thought that Christianity escaped this plague by a necessary ambiguity. On the one hand it understood that the infinite object of consciousness must appear in the world, and, on the other, that the infinite object of consciousness must transcend anything which is in the world.

Christianity therefore presents God as one who appears as the incarnation and who dies in an act of self-transcendence which reveals His ultimate nature.

Watson describes the Hegelian point this way:

> This essential unity of the divine with the human nature is possible only by God appearing as man and man as God. Thus the sorrow which arises from the division of the finite subject disappears when it is recognized that it is the essential nature of spirit to be conscious of the unity of the divine and the human nature.[88]

He adds that:

> The consciousness that it is the essential nature of God to be reconciled with the world only dawned upon the Church in its full significance after the death of Christ. For this reason the Church teaches that the death of Christ is the central point of the atonement, seeing in it the absolute love which even in finiteness overcomes finiteness, and negates that great negation, death.[89]

Watson depicts Hegel as going on to give a concrete meaning to all this.

> By the Kingdom of the Spirit Hegel means the realization in the spiritual community of the unity of the divine and the human nature. In order that this community may be realized in its definiteness and completeness, the utmost freedom must be allowed to all men, and no part of human nature may be regarded as common or unclean.[90]

88 Watson, *Religious Experience*, Part First, *Historical* [vol. 1], p. 351.
89 Ibid., p. 352.
90 Ibid.

In the second volume of his Gifford Lectures, Watson takes on the argument where Hegel leaves it. There is in the Hegelian view the possibility of a kind of mysticism which, in the guise of rendering an absolute unity, would succeed only in fragmenting the world in a new way. Watson insists, "Religion is . . . the supreme expression of man's rationality." He denies what the mystic maintains—that religion is "the form in which man completely transcends his individuality and is merged in God."[91] The Hegelian notion might, after all, tip the balance in this latter direction. For Hegel's doctrine seems to entail that the point at which subject and object finally merge is the point at which the individual consciousness finds the genuine infinite consciousness as its object of knowledge and so transforms experience. But, if this were so, our ordinary world of nature would be a set of mere appearances and, bound to them as we are, we would be, in principle, cut off from the final unity. Apart from the fact that this would impede Watson's constant attempt to demonstrate that reason arises in and through the particulars of experience, there would be, in his view, a moral objection to this position. If we are all simply finite appearances of the infinite spirit, our own affairs can be of no moment. Once the appearance has been overcome it is of no significance.

Hegel would have taken the same view about most of these issues. The dialectic of experience in the *Phenomenology* and the central dialectic of the *Science of Logic* both, however, seem to end with all their weight on one foot. The final transcendence is in the name of the subject rendered infinite through transformations of logic and experience.

Watson says, therefore:

> It is one thing to view his [man's] life from the point of view of the absolute spirit, and another thing to say that he is the absolute spirit. Hence the defect of mysticism, which abolishes the distinction of man from God, sublimating the consciousness of man until its distinction from the divine self-consciousness has disappeared. It is true that the highest life of man can only be realized through the consciousness that he has no true life which can be severed from life in God; but this consciousness is not the negation of his distinction from God; it is the consciousness that only in conscious identification with God can he realise his own deepest self.[92]

He goes on, more surprisingly, this way: "Religion, then, since it consists in identification with God, does not involve a process from lower to

91 Watson, *Religious Experience*, Part Second, *Constructive* [vol. 2], p. 125.
92 Ibid.

higher. God is not a Being who grows in experience, as some recent writers have suggested."[93]

Here, quite suddenly, in the middle of a chapter headed "The Religious Consciousness and Deism,"[94] we are introduced to a set of problems crowding in on Watson. If religion is not to involve "a process from lower to higher," what is the relation of God and man? If God is not "a Being who grows in experience," are we back with the God who is a mystical transcendent unity quite apart from nature which *is* a process?

The answer to these questions is to be found in Watson's own dialectic. A little later in the same chapter, he claims that religion exhibits three phases—a phase in which God is immediately experienced as present in nature, a phase in which God is exhibited in the moral order, and a phase in which we meet religion as "spirit in its concrete fulness."[95] It is this last phase which requires an explanation and analysis, but one may only get it by paying attention to the development of the earlier phases.

In the first phase God appears as a feature of experience—as that incomplete nature which appears in our experience, appears both rational and puzzling, both actually incomplete and potentially complete, both pedestrian and awe-inspiring. We seek to identify God with some feature of this nature, but we are always driven away from our positions as reason grows. But reason expands consciousness and gradually begins to reveal consciousness as, itself, at the basis of reality. Watson quotes Wordsworth:

> Something far more deeply interfused,
> Whose dwelling is the light of setting suns
> And the round ocean, and the living air,
> And in the mind of man.[96]

Wordsworth, here, can be read as expressing Watson's notion of the way in which nature gradually reveals itself as intelligible order. But, as in Hegel's dialectic of experience, the self always intrudes upon such schemes. When we turn inward, we meet God in the guise of morality.

Watson is, in this chapter, not very explicit about this process. He says,"... the subject becomes conscious of himself as that which is to overcome nature and subordinate it to moral ends. God is thus revealed, not as indifferent to the purposes of man, but as involved in

93 Ibid.
94 Ibid., pp. 129-42.
95 Ibid., p. 128.
96 Ibid., p. 127.

314

them."[97] This remark makes Watson sound like a typical turn-of-the-century believer in technological progress. But the next sentence appears to belie that: "Nature is not something which simply stands alongside of man, but its processes are in harmony with the ends of the self-conscious life."[98]

Probably we can make sense of these two sentences if we notice the thrust of the dialectic and its relation to the rest of Watson's philosophy. Nature is "overcome" only in the sense that, as our understanding of nature as rational order grows, we come to see that, as the next sentence says, nature is not something which "simply stands alongside of man," but rather something which proves to be continuous with the rational order in us. It poses a "moral" problem for us, precisely because it is not the case that it is something which we may do with as we please. The more we attempt to bend nature to some inner impulse, the more we distort nature and, ultimately, destroy ourselves. For once we are cut off from the ultimate rational order, we project ourselves into a self-made nothingness. Thus the contrast creates a responsibility in us. We use nature, but we must use nature only in the name of the rational order which we have in common with nature. In seeing this, we see that our moral commitments are not simply private but something which we share with all participants in the rational order. Thus we come to see God as within us. We can, if we wish, translate all our statements about nature into statements about our own discernment of the rational order but Watson, evidently, wants to make this a true dialectic. Properly grasped, an analysis of our inner states leads to nature and an analysis of nature leads back to us.

Thus, there is a third phase of religion. Watson says:

> In this stage nature is seen to have no independent being; it is in every part the manifestation of spirit. There is nothing common or unclean, because God is present in all things. The self does not stand opposed to nature, because nature is recognized to be a mode in which reason, as the essence of the self, is expressed.[99]

In short, the dialectic reveals to us our identity with nature. "Hence in his religious life man does not withdraw into himself, but 'lives in the world though not of it.'"[100]

Here we find "the religion of all men"; it is the religion of all men "because it is the religion of self-conscious spirit; and as the religion of

97   Ibid., p. 128.
98   Ibid.
99   Ibid.
100 Ibid.

free spirit, it is independent of all limits and restrictions, and therefore absolutely universal."[101]

But now, we can see that it is the character of God to be exhibited in nature and in our minds as well as to be in Himself. Without the variety of nature and without the variety of consciousness, God is simply a formal , empty unity of consciousness. We would not say, presumably, that God develops in time because the understanding of the rational order in nature and in ourselves transforms time. Once grasped, it is a timeless system. From the perspective of the psychologist, the system grows. From the perspective of the logician, it is a developing dialectic. From the perspective of the system itself, it is eternal.

Put another way, reason leads us to God but the understanding of the nature of God leads us back to ourselves. Nature reveals rational order. Morality reveals our commitment to nature. The two reveal themselves as an inextricable, ultimate unity, concrete spirit in its third phase.

Here we have, if anywhere, a religion of pure reason. Here the Kantian dichotomy of morality and science vanishes. Here, the hope of religion lies in the union of man and nature and in understanding the proposition that, since reality is a rational order, the irrationalities of limited experience can be overcome. But they can be overcome not by mysticism, not by a return to superstition, but only by the application of reason. It comforts us because we can understand that, from the perspective of God, irrationalities are already overcome. But the process of transforming our consciousness from its present irrational state to the ultimate rationality is identical with the process of overcoming the irrationalities as we face the natural world.

We can see then that Watson's view of Christianity is essentially that Christianity represents, sometimes in pictorial form, sometimes in mythical form, sometimes in rational form, elements which symbolize the ultimate rational religion. Jesus is the man who represents that God who is both in nature and transcends nature. The resurrection represents that transcendence in the ultimate eschatology of Christianity which, in turn, represents our ultimate hope that the irrationalities can be overcome in the immediate consciousness which we identify with ourselves.

Yet no consciousness will transform itself. The irrationality is of the apparent world and will not simply disappear. Nature will not yield to mere hope. Only the union of rational principle and rational practice will bring about the desired results.

101 Ibid.

We may still ask, however, whether or not this rational structure—however impressive one might find it—is genuinely the basis of a
religion or whether it is simply a pretty metaphysical device which
Watson has substituted for more primitive religious belief.

We must look more closely at the things Watson actually wants to
eliminate from religion as we have most commonly known it and then
consider the content of the residue. Watson tackles these questions in
the last chapter of the second volume of his Gifford Lectures.

He argues, in that chapter, for a number of propositions: There is
what he calls an "invisible church"[102] and this church represents the
spirit of goodness so far as it exists in all the forms of social organization. The visible church can at best be an approximation to this—the
invisible church may be concrete and manifest according to the abilities
of men to grasp its nature.

If God and man are not ultimately separate and the divine runs
through all those instances of rational order which exist in nature and
in man, then the divine appears wherever morality, the spirit of goodness, appears. But the invisible church can have no binding creed and
any visible church that seeks to have one must be resisted in its claims to
universality. For:

> The invisible church is not a community of slaves but of free men, and
> therefore men must be allowed freedom of action, even if it leads im-
> mediately to much evil. In no other way can a spiritual community be
> developed. The divine spirit cannot be externally imposed upon men. Com-
> pulsion and freedom are incompatible, and not less incompatible are com-
> pulsion and spirituality. For this reason the invisible church cannot be
> established once for all, and its lineaments fixed for all time.[103]

If freedom gives way to compulsion, the rational order cannot, ultimately, avail itself. For compulsion seeks to impose the understanding
of the moment and reason must always be its own guide. Thus organized religion, if not carefully monitored, is itself a peril.

Watson accepts the proposition that religion requires some ritual
but he insists, again, that the "invisible church" cannot "have a fixed
and unchanging ritual. As its fundamental principle is the essential
identity of the human and divine natures, any symbolical acts which are
fitted to body forth this truth may be employed as a means of educating
the young and reminding the mature of this central idea." But "We
must not overlook the danger that besets all forms of ceremonial—the
danger that, while in their first institution they are of service in sym-

102 Ibid., p. 298.
103 Ibid., p. 302.

bolizing the life of the spirit, they may degenerate into a dead and lifeless routine."[104] He thinks, however, that we may be protected from this danger partly "by contemplating the total sphere of art as the only perfectly adequate symbolism of the invisible church."[105]

Here he attacks the partisans of particular symbolisms—"those who would exclude all forms of symbolism but those employed by a particular ecclesiastical organization"—as driving religion back to the level of "mystical thaumaturgy."[106] He admits, too, that religion requires faith. But faith is not the belief in irrational propositions. That is mere superstition. Faith, for Watson, is rather what converts belief into action, and what "by its very nature must be expressed in action."[107] What he means is that since every action involved the bringing about of an unknown, every action involves the faith that the best rational proposition one has been able to assemble will, in fact, hold true after a given act of creation. Acting on the proposition that irrationality is itself the manifestation of unreality and must eventually perish is itself the supreme and primary act of faith.

Yet it is, of course, a faith in ourselves. It is the faith that we identify ourselves with God by becoming developed examples of our own fundamental rationality.

> Man is identical with God because he is a rational subject, not because the immanence of God in him abolishes his individuality. Under the imperfect conception of creation we think of man as projected out of God, or as formed out of a pre-existent material by the shaping activity of God, as the sculptor shapes a block of marble. But, when we discard this inadequate mode of conception, we find that for this external productive or formative activity must be substituted the idea of God as present spiritually in the soul of every man, and therefore as capable of being comprehended by every man. Thus, we must conceive of the relation of man to God as one which involves the independent individuality of each, but an individuality which implies the distinction and yet the unity of both. Man is most truly himself when he recognizes that in all things he is dependent upon God, and that he can only truly comprehend his own nature by conceiving it as in essence identical with that of God.[108]

He is thus able to find a place for ritual as art and for faith as action. But what of emotion? Surely, the reaching out of man beyond himself, the demand for religious objects, is associated with a feeling—a feeling

104 Ibid., p. 303.
105 Ibid.
106 Ibid.
107 Ibid., p. 307.
108 Ibid., pp. 291-92.

of limitation, a feeling of negation, a demand for comfort. Feeling, of course, in Watson's system is a mode of the presentation of experience. It is, indeed, the way in which experience is presented to us which gives rise in us to appropriate feelings. It is those feelings, in turn, which drive us onward.

Yet the solution, in Watson's view, obviously, is not to meet those feelings with other feelings—to create an emotional religion which fires us up like whiskey to enable us to overcome our confrontation with nothingness. Rather, Watson seeks to deal with the source of those feelings by extending reason. Reason, alone, is ultimately capable of giving us the sense of security and stability which religion demands. In part, therefore, religion proper *is* the process of the transformation of feeling into reason.

Watson, here, is evidently seeking to carry out the project which continuously occupied Canadian intellectuals from the first, tentative prospects of church union. He is imagining a religion for people who could take care of themselves—men who founded the little towns along the railroad across the prairie, families impatient with the trivial quarrels of competing sects, settlers conversant with nature, people unlikely to express a demand for thaumaturgy.

Ideas of this kind lay at the roots of the possibility of the church union in Canada and many varieties of them were to be developed. Watson and George Blewett, no doubt, were the most influential philosophical figures.

Those ideas survived World War I, despite the bitterness that was left in its wake, and survived even the frustrations of the Great Depression. In Canada, they continued to make sense. Church union came about, sectarian bitterness faded, but, until after World War II, organized religion continued to play a quite crucial part in the lives of most Canadians. Across the land, clergymen of the United Church provided a spectrum of belief and practice. Like Watson, they believed that faith was a matter of action and they provided a vast variety of public services at home and abroad. To intellectuals, they could serve Watson's rational religion undiluted. To the perceptive middle classes, they provided just enough colour and ritual to go with it. To an embittered Depression working class, they provided programmes for social change and much of the driving force behind the Co-operative Commonwealth Federation and even its successor, the New Democratic Party. As a rule, no one was excluded either because of his rationalist beliefs or because he wanted to maintain any part of the rich background which had belonged to the Methodist, Congregational, and Presbyterian churches.

The world outside, however, was less receptive, on the whole, to such notions. The new theological devotees of unreason—Karl Barth, for instance—proved more influential than Canadian philosophers, or indeed than those theologians abroad who, like Paul Tillich, were working in ways which, to an important extent, gave new underpinnings to those who wanted to expand Watson's rational religion.

A new and more "sophisticated" generation of young clergymen after the war, like many other Canadians, felt that the home-grown product was less desirable than exotic, irrationalist imports.

At the same time, the visible church was fading quite quickly into Watson's "invisible church." To an increasing proportion of young Canadians, organized religion seemed irrelevant. Its relevant features had, after all, merged into the social fabric. If one was to have this kind of religion, it was not obvious that it was necessary to gather on Sunday to hear it mixed with extracts from the Scripture.

It is not clear whether, if the United Church had remained more firmly committed to the philosophies of men like Watson, it would have increased rather than slackened its hold on the rising generation. In part, it could not do this because universities were no longer staffed by men like Watson. Increasingly, philosophy departments came to be staffed by young men, imported from the United States and England, who had no interest in such theories or in the kinds of problems with which Watson was concerned. There was no successor to the last "Watsonian" generation of the 1930s.

Whether, as Canadians increasingly look to their own traditions, all this will change and Watson's rational religion will, once again, become at least an object of interest is something which cannot be predicted. Would it be listened to, if our institutions gave it a hearing? Or is it merely a transition phase from primitive belief to no belief at all?

The answer depends, to some extent at least, on the assessment one makes of Watson's philosophy—a task which we can only, after all, begin in this book.

NINE

REASON, RELIGION, AND THE IDEA OF NATURE

George Blewett and James Ten Broeke

G EORGE BLEWETT WAS born in 1873—a year after Watson began to teach at Queen's. He died in 1912 in his thirty-ninth year. Though he was a quarter-century younger than Watson, he seems much more remote from us and his remoteness is accentuated by the elaborate Victorian prose of the essays in *The Study of Nature and the Vision of God*.[1] The simpler, somehow more modern, prose of his second book, *The Christian View of the World*,[2] brings him nearer to us, but even the titles of his books seem to isolate him from the contemporary philosopher and have left him too often buried in the musty shelves of second-hand apologetic theology.

All of this is a cruel trick of whatever fates govern popular and philosophic taste. For, in many ways, Blewett speaks more clearly and with more relevance to contemporary problems than any of the other participants in nineteenth- and twentieth-century idealist philosophy. In the current dilemma of our relations with nature—relations corrupted, on the one side, by those who believe in the myth of eternal technological progress and, on the other, by those who subscribe to the mythology of an eternally wise and beneficent nature which must be left untouched by man—he has much to say that is vitally important. Whether one accepts or rejects his theory, one must concede that one cannot review it with care without adding a significant measure of clarification to the problem. Again, whether one attributes the apparent decline of rational theology to a failure of nerve and imagination or to the development of an understanding of the world which makes all theology irrelevant or uninteresting, it remains true that Blewett's picture of the relation of nature, man, and God is refreshing and ought to open a host of issues which demand philosophical exploration.

1 George John Blewett, *The Study of Nature and the Vision of God* (Toronto: William Briggs, 1907). Hereafter referred to as *Nature and God*.
2 George John Blewett, *The Christian View of the World* (New York: Yale University Press, 1912). Hereafter referred to as *Christian View*.

Blewett's development of the idealist tradition stems from a position which he puts succinctly within a sentence in *The Christian View of the World*: "... it is plain that any Idealism which is to be of constructive value to the theologian, must have some deeper insight into nature than simply that it is a system of ideas in our minds."[3] The major themes in his philosophy revolve around three propositions: Nature is of value and importance in itself and not merely as something to be transcended in the development of experience. Nature and man alike constitute the necessary expression of God as the world: "... God fulfils Himself in nature."[4] The "primary reality" of the universe consists of "self-conscious and self-determining spirits" who form ideally "a certain state of character and society."[5] With these propositions goes the further proposition that reality is a developing process whose history and structure are, in themselves, of paramount importance.

Blewett was born near St. Thomas, Ontario, in the small village of Yarmouth. Like any farmer's son, his winters were busy with chores and his summers with haying and harvesting. Still, he found time to master much more than the official curriculum of the local collegiate institute, and he went on, in the fall of 1890, to University College at the University of Toronto.

He wanted to study politics and economics and then to go on to a career in law. But a shortage of money sent him to Alberta, first as a teacher of the children of missionaries, and then as a Methodist circuit preacher.

He continued to show his intellectual prowess. (In order to become a circuit preacher he had to write examinations set by the Superintendent of Missions at Calgary. He scored 100 percent in all subjects except Greek. His score in Greek was only 95 percent.) But he never did become a successful preacher. Each time he served a charge, the secretary of the local board wrote to the regional chairman asking for a change. Blewett himself reported that he had served three different charges in three months. (Years later, when he was appointed to the Chair of Philosophy at Victoria College in Toronto, he was invited to preach at a large and important church. He warned the minister that it was not a good idea, but the minister persisted. Blewett was not invited back.)

What kinds of problems confronted Blewett when he began his teaching career in Alberta? Certainly he was faced with a rugged frontier and a difficult contrast. The settlers understood the value of

3 Blewett, *Christian View*, p. 213.
4 Ibid., p. 192.
5 Ibid., p. 206.

learning. They wanted teachers and preachers who could match wits and ideas with any man. But the circumstances of their lives did not make for days spent curled up with a book and the learning they had been taught to value had no immediate practical outcome in their affairs.

It is little wonder that Blewett had them squirming in their seats when he came to preach, however diligently he tried to make himself clear. Many of them were lonely, some of them were fearful, some wished they were at home. On the whole, they wanted the old lessons, the old hymns, something for their emotions, something to make them feel better as they faced the next week.

Blewett's exposure to the Indian schools and missions in the west again revealed the sharp contrast seen in the confrontation of old and new cultural values in an uncompromising environment. Here were people engulfed by a new "civilization" whose scattered population had its hands full coping with its own problems. The French dream of another civilization, a "métis" civilization, which might grow out of the intermixture of European and Indian, taking on virtues of each and shedding the characteristics of each which made survival difficult in the new west, was already dead. One could neither make the Indian into a Scots Presbyterian or English Methodist, nor expect him to survive in the old way in a new situation.

Yet, so far, only a handful of men realized that that way of thinking would have to be reorganized. Blewett could talk to the Methodist superintendents, to a few clergymen, to some school teachers. But people busy surviving found him too "bookish," too absorbed in a kind of thought which, for them, was a luxury. Even more, Blewett knew that he had yet to think it all out for himself.

In 1895 both he and the church authorities decided that it would be best if he went back to Toronto to study. This time, he enrolled not in the secular University College but in the Methodist Victoria College in the third year of the honours philosophy programme.

He did join the college literary society, he did take part in all the discussions he could find. But mostly Victoria was attractive, as the university was attractive, because it had books. W. B. Lane, who was only slightly Blewett's senior, and who, oddly enough, was to succeed him in 1913 in the Ryerson Chair of Philosophy, was on the final examination board the year that Blewett graduated. He wrote, "His [papers] were easily detectable, for they were astonishing performances of accurate and brilliant thinking, linked to precise analysis and abundant quotation (both in English and Greek, as suited)."[6] He

6   William John Rose, "Brief Pilgrimage of George John Blewett, 1873-1912," bio-

graduated in 1897 with two gold medals, a silver medal, and an array of essay prizes.

He spent a year as a graduate student at Victoria. Then he needed to continue his studies or find another occupation. He still had no money and graduate fellowships and scholarships were a rarity. The obvious choice was to complete the necessary theology courses and become an officially ordained minister of the Methodist Church in 1898. No doubt, that made him respectable; but it still did not earn him anything to eat.

Eventually, he was rescued by a wealthy Toronto businessman who gave him money to go to Germany. He enrolled at the University of Wurzburg on May 24, 1899, and stayed there through that spring and summer. Meanwhile, his friends were at work in Toronto. He was awarded the George Paxton Young Memorial Fellowship in Philosophy and, in addition, a scholarship to Harvard, where he received his Ph.D. Blewett was awarded another scholarship—the Bowdoin prize for an essay on Spinoza. The Bowdoin prize, then worth about $300, must have seemed to him an incredible windfall. (His entire income for that year was $450.) The scholarship enabled him to travel to England and to spend a year at Oxford and Cambridge. At Oxford, he met Edward Caird who, by one of those quirks typical of the life of Canadian scholars, put him in touch with John Watson at Queen's.

In the spring of 1901, he was offered a post as lecturer in philosophy at Wesley College in Winnipeg—the predecessor of United College which, in its turn, was to become the University of Winnipeg.

Again, he found the west hard going. Students came from the farms with little clear expectation of university life. Whatever expectations they had did not often include philosophy. Blewett, furthermore, was not a popular lecturer. He spoke in a quiet voice, often hard to hear. His intellectual honesty precluded him from making things easy. (Later, he was to urge that Canadian universities should give serious thought to tightening their admission standards.) And once again he faced the violent contrast. All the records we have testify to the extent to which he found it difficult. He was a Canadian and at home in Canada, but in another sense, hardly at home in the only environment he could find for himself in Canada. He had to adjust. There is a good deal of evidence that he did. Gradually, he

graphical manuscript loaned to the authors by Constance Blewett, p. 4. Hereafter referred to as "George John Blewett." (Rose, a well-known Canadian Slavonic scholar, taught for many years at the University of London and later at the University of British Columbia. He was the author of works on Polish history.)

made friends and assembled an audience—never large, but frequently devoted. He seems to have been remembered in Winnipeg as a thoughtful, kindly, and patient man.

These two excursions to the west, first to Alberta and then to Winnipeg, no doubt had much to do with Blewett's continual fascination with nature and the struggle to survive.

Five years later, in 1906, the Ryerson Chair of Philosophy became vacant at Victoria College. He married, published his first book of essays, and settled down to a comfortable scholarly career.

The book of essays, *The Study of Nature and the Vision of God*, seems to have attracted some attention. At any rate, three years later, he was invited to give the Taylor Lectures at Yale. He gave them in the winter of 1910-1911 and they were published in Toronto the next year by William Briggs who had published the earlier essays. In those lectures, titled *The Christian View of the World*, Blewett seems to have found himself. The prose is clear, and generally relaxed. The themes of the earlier essays are brought together and made to form a coherent whole.

Canada's most distinguished native-born philosopher had come of age. But he was to write no more. In the summer of 1912, he drowned—leaving a pregnant wife and one child, and the hopes of his colleagues, but, as far as we can determine, no manuscripts. There is, however, a manuscript about Blewett, an unpublished biography, by W. J. Rose.

Rose talked to members of the family and to their friends who recalled the philosopher in his childhood. The result was predictable. An uncle said of him that "he had the least sense, for a smart man,"[7] that he had ever seen. Rose also uncovered the usual array of "crazy bookworm" stories. It was reported that Blewett rigged a frame over the front wheel of his bicycle so that he could read a book while he rode to and from school. Once, it was claimed, he rode straight into the farm gate before he noticed it was there. Nevertheless, the reports concurred that Blewett never evaded his share of the farm work and never lost his affection for it. Years later, when he was teaching, he would return home for the haying season. But as a teacher, his concerns with nature were rather more esoteric.

Rose's unpublished biography paints Blewett, in general, as a saint. The portrait may be exaggerated. Even Rose cannot help noticing the gap which always existed between Blewett and the men around him and there are strong hints that there was more than a little of the élitist in him. Yet that strand in his character, if it existed, seems not to have taken the form of looking down on people nor to have exhibited

7   Rose, "George John Blewett," p. 10.

itself in a failure to understand their concerns. Rather, there seems simply a strong sense of yearning—yearning for the company of men who shared his intellectual powers and concerns and also shared his background and outlook.

He could find philosophers to talk to. But they, generally, had not grown up in Canada, they did not share the intellectual difficulties which he had faced as a Canadian confronting nature. He found his share of promising and more than promising students but he found it distracting to confront them in the context of others who were more difficult to arouse.

Those who followed him were, indeed, apt to become his disciples. William Rose wrote his biography of Blewett forty-three years after his death. It shows his devotion on every page. In his search for recollections of Blewett, Rose had no difficulty in finding others who shared this devotion.

Blewett was a devoted Canadian patriot and made it clear a number of times that, at any cost, he would stay and teach in Canada. In the election of 1911, he said that he would vote, against his normal convictions, for the Conservative Party because the continentalist programme of the Liberal Party and its consequent stand on tariffs would imperil Canadian independence. But he took no active part in that raging public debate. More surprisingly, though Rose reports he was clearly on the side of liberty, he took no active part in the controversies surrounding George Workman and George Jackson. (He did sign the letter which defined the faculty position on the Jackson case.[8]) The Workman controversy erupted at Victoria College just before Blewett arrived to teach at Wesley College, Winnipeg. Workman had dared to say "that no scholar of repute today accepts the 'dictation' theory of inspiration."[9] That statement, though surely modest enough and implying only that God did not literally write the Bible, was enough to arouse the ire of the General Superintendent of the Methodist Church, Dr. Albert Carman. Students at Victoria were behind Workman and his entire attempt to get a more satisfactory and historical reading of the Bible. So was Dr. Nathaniel Burwash, the Chancellor of Victoria University. But Dr. Carman was determined to have Workman removed from office. So was John Carlisle who published, in Peterborough, a work with a splendid title: *An Exposé of and a Red Hot Protest Against a Damnable Heresy Smuggled Into Methodism and Taught by Profes-*

8   C. B. Sissons, *A History of Victoria University* (Toronto: University of Toronto Press, 1952), p. 236.
9   H. H. Walsh, *The Christian Church in Canada* (Toronto: Ryerson Press, 1968), p. 290.

sor Workman of Victoria University.[10] Workman was forced to retire from his chair in 1899 but he was then invited to become a member of the teaching staff at the Wesleyan College, Montreal. Naturally, this did not please Dr. Carman, who kept on with his activities and had Workman dismissed from that post in 1907.[11] Workman went on publishing and produced his last book, *Jesus the Man and Christ the Spirit*,[12] in 1928, eight years before his death.

Blewett was certainly in Toronto in 1907 when the final attack was made on Workman. Given Blewett's view, we must certainly believe Rose—Blewett always supported intellectual liberty. But he does not seem to have taken a part in the affair or in the overlapping "Jackson Affair." George Jackson was brought from England to the Sherbourne Street Methodist Church in Toronto. In public lectures Jackson announced that the early narratives of Genesis could no longer be regarded as "literal history." They were well received by the audience and it was thought that Jackson would persuade the Methodist contingent in the new joint committee on church union to take a very liberal stand on doctrine. Yet, once again, Carman was able to rally strong support for his stand when the Methodists met in their general conference in 1910. Rose reports that Blewett was certainly on Jackson's side but took no active part.

In retrospect, it is astounding that Blewett should have survived in a situation in which a man like Workman, who would seem today so much more orthodox, was in constant trouble. Rose recounts an evening discussion, in Toronto, during which Blewett was asked to define "God." He replied, "God is the Home of all relations."[13] Surely that is much more astounding than the mere suggestion that God did not literally write the Bible.

The explanation, no doubt, is quite simple: Workman was saying things which everyone understood clearly and was saying things about which everyone felt clearly entitled to an opinion. Whether or not

10 John Carlisle, *An Exposé of and a Red Hot Protest Against a Damnable Heresy Smuggled into Methodism and Taught by Professor Workman of Victoria University* (Peterborough: Examiner Print, 1891). In 1884 Victoria College was designated Victoria University by charter. The two terms, however, continue to be used interchangeably.

11 Dr. Albert Carman was a long-time head of the United Methodist Church and also had been the last bishop of the Methodist Episcopal Church. When the Workman controversy erupted he was the general superintendent of the Methodist Church. He represented "an older generation of circuit riders who had little patience with modern Biblical scholarship which seemed to them to be undermining the very foundations of belief" (Walsh, *The Christian Church in Canada*, p. 290).

12 George Workman, *Jesus the Man and Christ the Spirit* (New York: Macmillan, 1928).

13 Rose, "George John Blewett," p. 41.

Jonah was swallowed by a whale or heaven might be reached with a suitable ladder are questions to which one may turn for answers in the Scripture. If someone denies the immediate truth and validity of the Scripture, one knows, at least, what one is saying. Furthermore, the question of the "dictation" of Scripture is not a simple matter of "scientific" fact. It is a matter of how one takes the text, of what one's attitude is.

When Blewett said, "God is the Home of all relations," it is very doubtful that many people, if any, understood what he meant.

It is an odd fact that the most bitter and heated turn-of-the-century religious controversies, in both Protestant and Catholic denominations, seem to have taken place over historical scholarship and over attempts to reinterpret the Bible. Philosophical interpretations of more basic concepts seem, then at least, to have aroused far less concern.

But there is little point in speculating about whether or not Blewett would have been able to defend himself. The fact is he did not have to. He simply did not try to reach the audience represented by Carman and his friends. Rose reports that, indeed, some people thought Blewett was "too little of a fighter"[14] in these circumstances. But it would be foolish, as well, to castigate Blewett for lack of courage.

These events can scarcely have encouraged Blewett. That radical intolerance should turn up even within Victoria College, that the distrust of reason and scholarship should seem so deeply engrained in a religious denomination within which he was an ordained minister, that men as forceful (and indeed powerful) as Burwash and Massey should seem incapable of dealing with the situation, would be depressing.

All these forces and contrasts are behind Blewett's crucial break with a kind of idealism common at the time. They are part of the source of his remark which we quoted earlier: ". . . it is plain that any Idealism which is to be of constructive value to the theologian, must have some deeper insight into nature than simply that it is a system of ideas in our minds."[15]

It is important to see that this issue, so basic to Blewett's philosophy, lies at the root of an important aspect of the Canadian experience. Nature had to be conceived not simply or primarily as a neutral background against which engineering technology might have its way, and not, on the other hand, as a charming though primitive delight, perfect in its own right until despoiled by the hand of man.

14 Ibid., p. 60.
15 Blewett, *Christian View*, p. 213.

Not only did nature shape the life which man must lead in Canada; it also shaped the nature of man himself. At its crudest, loneliness breeds a demand for certainty and, if that certainty is challenged, it will lead to ugly intolerance. Men too busy fighting nature to have much time to think, and men fearful that their small certainties will be successfully challenged, may easily find an Albert Carman more persuasive than a George Workman or a George Jackson. But if they are to be persuaded to a more rational stance, it will have to be by someone who understands what they have faced and are facing. One who thinks that nature is an idea in our minds will not find a large audience amongst men whose crops have just been wiped out by hail or amongst men who must count their meagre supplies in September and wonder whether they will last through until May. Nature had to be accounted for in its own right both to make a case to which men on the frontier might listen and to explain many of the most obvious features of everyday life in Canada at the turn of the century.

Man's relation to nature—"nature in all her processes, all her strange blending of apparent indifference and cruelty with unspeakable tenderness and grace"—was, for Blewett, "a relation to God and to the purpose and the ways of God."[16] The kind of idealism which he wants to avoid he calls "an immature Idealism which falls helpless at just this point"[17]—the point at which a real understanding of nature is essential. To some extent, it is John Stuart Mill and his "permanent possibilities of sensation"[18] who seems to be the target of Blewett's attack here, but he also means, to some extent, to set himself apart from the British Idealists who were commonly called "Hegelians"—Green, Bosanquet, Bradley, McTaggart, and, perhaps, even the Cairds and Watson himself. He respected Green, the founder of the British Idealist movement. Yet, after comparing Hegel to Aristotle and Thomas Aquinas, he says:

> The late Professor Green had not the special gifts of the men to whom reference has just been made: not the remarkable blending of profundity and subtle keenness which characterises one of them; not that union of philosophic insight with the whole breadth of humane learning which gives charm to all the work of another; not the vast and systematic range of thought which makes a third the representative of philosophy in its true greatness as a rationally articulated view of the world and of life.[19]

16　Ibid., p. 208.
17　Ibid., p. 210.
18　John Stuart Mill, *Philosophy of Scientific Method* (selections reprinted from Mill's *An Examination of Sir William Hamilton's Philosophy*, 3rd ed.), ed. and with an Introduction by Ernest Nagel (New York: Hafner Publishing, 1950), p. 369.
19　Blewett, *Nature and God*, p. 63.

He excuses Green on the ground that "his life was weighted with labour and his day was short."[20] But he says that Green wrote no completed system of philosophy and he remarks that the "technical apparatus" of Hegel is "peculiarly distasteful" to the " 'Anglo-Saxon'—or at any rate to the specifically English—intellect."[21] Thus he says of the English Idealists:

> ... they have gone forward with the sober caution of their race, and have steadily avoided any such immense technical apparatus as that of Hegel. This has involved, it is true, the loss of much that was possible to him; the great sweep of his system, his vast and orderly outlook upon history, upon nature, upon all the departments of man's life and society.[22]

Though Blewett is prepared to admit that the British Idealists had been wise to adopt a simplicity of thought which put the crucial ideas within reach of many, he remains unsatisfied. His dissatisfaction with some of Hegel's German successors, notably Lotze and Paulsen, has some relation to this unease. Both of them recoiled against Hegel's technical apparatus. Blewett says:

> In them philosophy was unnecessarily crippled: not altogether, but to some extent, philosophy in them defeats itself; in the name of the ordinary consciousness and of everyday interests, of the "solid ground" and of "plain facts," they recoil from precisely those scientific insights which show us what those everyday interests and ordinary facts really are—the body, namely, of an eternal reason, the media through which and in which an eternal purpose is being realised.[23]

Thus, in two ways, the idealists and other post-Hegelians Blewett was confronting seem to fail. On the one side, by presenting reality as a simple rational system, they failed to deal with the extent to which nature is other than us. On the other, by "recoiling" from Hegel's technicalities, they avoided stretching the human understanding so as to uncover the basic difficulties.

But, here again, we have the seeming conflict in Blewett's philosophy. He wants both to hold that nature is not simply a set of ideas in our minds, *and* that the primary reality is a set of spiritual substances. He wants both to hold that one must take account of our immediate confrontations with nature, and that if need be through the adoption of elaborate technical apparatus, one must somehow tran-

20 Ibid.
21 Ibid., p. 61.
22 Ibid., pp. 62-63.
23 Ibid., footnote p. 61.

scend the limits of the so-called "plain facts" which represent the ordinary uneducated human consciousness.

Is he both announcing and denying a duality of nature and mind? Is he both calling upon us to take account of the kinds of experience that men really have when they are face to face with nature and demanding that we escape from the parochial bounds of the human intellect?

Obviously, these questions are related. The solution to them has to do with one's understanding of a kind of Hegelian dialectic. It is this dialectic which Blewett demands. He does not demand that one adopt Hegelian language. Indeed, he remarked once that Hegel "appears to be mounted upon a very high horse indeed"[24] and he proposed that it would be as well to bring him down from it. But he is not to be brought down by simple-minded homilies, he is not to be brought down by using reason as a device to paper over the cracks in human experience, and he is not to be brought down by avoiding the hard questions.

We shall have to look at Blewett's metaphysical system in some detail. Our best guide is the text of *The Christian View of the World*. Blewett's account of God and his subsequent discussion of the nature of religion itself will form a separate topic. The metaphysical theory involved in his Taylor Lectures at Yale divides into four parts: the theory of nature, the theory of human nature, the theory of the Absolute, and the problem of freedom. We shall discuss each of these.

In order to understand Blewett's view of nature, it is necessary, first, to sketch important alternative views, particularly those which Blewett himself frequently mentions. Without some such background, we cannot tell what Blewett's arguments are directed toward or against.

There seem to be four of these and each of them, in Blewett's view, represents simply an over-estimation or over-extension of a grain of truth. For convenience, we can label these theories, without straying too far from Blewett's actual language, the machine theory, the divine machine theory, the sensible frame theory, and the pantheist or Nature-God theory.

The machine theory, of course, was widely championed by the practitioners of nineteenth-century science, though Blewett notes that it was not as widely believed amongst practising scientists as the general public might have thought.[25] It is still with us, usually in the form of reductive materialism which seeks to reduce psychology to physiology and physiology to physics and then to interpret physics as an essentially determinist and mechanical system. Most contemporary defenders of

24 Ibid., p. 61.
25 The most famous example, of course, is Laplace.

such a programme would concede that there are elements of randomness or indeterminateness at the lowest level of such systems but they
would urge that, when the most basic particles are arranged in systems
of a certain amount and kind of structure, they form systems within
which accurate predictions can be made. On this view, human beings
are part and parcel of the system. Nature simply *is*. It has no purpose,
no meaning, no hint of values of its own. Apart from our preferences,
one arrangement of it is as good as another. Our preferences, themselves, would be held to be determined by other features of the system.
Contemporary champions of our technology usually hold this position
or a somewhat inconsistent variant of it which is seldom worked out.
The variant would hold that, somehow or other, we are ourselves
"free" in the sense that we can conceive the kinds of alternatives to
nature which constitute the basis of our engineering projects. We are
not to be praised or blamed for what we do to nature because nature
itself is entirely indifferent to our preferences. We may suffer from or
enjoy the consequences of our acts, but that is as far as it goes. This
variant takes account of the fact that we seem to be able to conceive of
alternatives to "nature" in the form in which we find it but the variant
becomes inconsistent in our attempts to explore the basis of this "freedom."

It is this fact which leads Blewett to complain that theories of this
kind turn out to be abstractions. He says: "On the one hand, there is
'nature.' Nature, under the aspect of necessity, surrounds us; not only
surrounds us but is so in us, that its breath of life is in some sense our
breath of life, and the revelation of its being given by the special
sciences a revelation to us of our own being."[26]

The view starts out by holding that we *are* simply what the descriptions of us given by the special sciences say we are. But Blewett notes:
"On the other hand, there is our assertion of ourselves, not merely in
the presence of those necessities of nature, but also upon the basis of
them.[27] *We* announce those necessities and then we announce our
proposed course of action in terms of them. That we are free to do this
is *not*, however, based on a "merely abstract and indifferent power of
volition."[28] (Ultimately Blewett is concerned with explanation.)

The original "machine" theory thus constitutes an abstraction
because we fail to take account of its basis. We could put this in our own
terms by noticing simply that what physics does not explain is the
occurrence of physics itself. It is as if one had a map of the world and

26 Blewett, *Christian View*, p. 59.
27 Ibid.
28 Ibid.

then attempted to show, on that map of the world, the map itself. There are two things wrong with such a proposal. One is that the map within the map would have to have another map within it and so on to infinity. The other, much more important, and noticed by Blewett, is that if the theory explained itself, it, itself, would be predetermined, and so, untrustworthy. We put ourselves thus into our science and find ourselves in the outcome. But we cannot look at it apart from ourselves as if it were capable of taking on this intelligibility without any human activity. Theories must be accounted for, too. The act of freedom which makes the theory possible must be something more than a free and abstract volition. It must be, in Blewett's words, the coming-to-be of reason in concrete form.

Religious men, Blewett says, are prone to get out of this difficulty by making of nature "a divine machine"; they simply want to hold that it is all the things which the first theory maintains except it is a machine created by and, perhaps, maintained by God. The first theory emphasizes the truth that nature does have a structure of its own, but misconceives that structure. The second theory seeks to explain the intelligibility of nature by supposing an intelligent creator who occupies it. It is this view which Blewett sums up as "Nature may indeed be a machine, but then it is God's machine."[29] He says that this thesis "has secured an enormous, I am tempted to say a monstrous, expression of itself in the literature of that cross-grained department of theology, Apologetics."[30]

It is "monstrous," apparently, for two reasons: One is that it implies that God simply created nature as a background for whatever activities He had in mind. But if so, He did it by Himself, without the need for us, and whatever He is doing with us is some kind of game. The world, perhaps, is a sort of training course and we who are its pupils are also its victims. The other more profound difficulty is that it makes of nature a kind of contrivance which God made rather arbitrarily. So long as we fulfill our religious obligations, we can, apparently, do with it what we please. In particular, we can do with it what we please if it seems to advance our own interests. Blewett finds this view all too frequently held even by men with a serious concern with religious matters.

In a passage that seems, perhaps, more telling now than it did in 1912, Blewett says:

> One of the unconscious vices that do us wrong to-day, is our impiety toward the earth. I mean not now the impiety of hasty and preoccupied minds, to

29 Ibid., p. 171.
30 Ibid.

which the perpetual forms about us can never utter their voice of memory, of consolation, of rebuke. I mean the more terrible impiety practised toward the earth by a race that, after age-long struggle with hunger and with cold, has entered at last upon a day of natural opulence, and in that day has built up a civilisation wherein one knows not at which to be the more amazed; the wonder of the achievements; or the incredible profligacies of waste, and the social injustice, the oppression of class by class, which is the inevitable outcome of the spirit of unashamed and wasteful expense. In such a time, no one who wishes to see our practical life and its arts put upon just foundations can feel any vocation to encourage by so much as a syllable the laying aside of what fragment still remains to us of the bygone reverence of men toward their ancient mother, the dust of the ground. To-day, after having been to man his foster-mother, genial or cruel, his sublime and dread teacher, sometimes his kindly companion, sometimes his terrific enemy, she has become to him something like his slave, the object of his cleverness, the object of his prodigality. To-morrow, for our salvation, our devices outworn by the march of her ages, it may be that she will hold once more, terribly in her inexorable arms, her proud and frail child.[31]

Nature does not seem, to Blewett at any rate, to be either a machine or a divine machine. One of these views is, as he says, simply an abstraction. The other, apart from its dire consequences, fails, because it does not explain anything. To say that God simply created nature does not add anything to our understanding of nature or to our understanding of God. It is merely an attempt to take account of freedom but to degrade it to the level of empty "volition"—though, this time, the volition may seem more acceptable because it is ascribed to God.

If we are to progress, we must have a better understanding than these theories produce of the demands which a successful theory must make. First of all, Blewett writes of truth, in this context, in these terms:

> . . . reality as the object of intelligence, the concrete facts of the world in their concrete relations—nature, for instance, not as a set of hypothetical constructions, but as an actual world of experience, a world of sound and colour, taste and odour and visible form, with all its sensible frame organised and governed by an inner constitution of intelligible principles.[32]

If we seek this, we will come back, at least, to nature in its concrete form. Nature includes physical particles, but it also includes shores and mountains, small animals scurrying across the prairie, the wheat ripening in the August sun, and the hail which smashes it to the ground. If

31 Ibid., pp. 197-98.
32 Ibid., pp. 132-33.

we proceed on this level, we might come to think of nature somewhat in the way that the British philosophers who attempted a return to "common sense" later in the twentieth century did. Nature is a collection of objects, each of which has its own description, each of which is a thing in its own right, each of which requires its own understanding. To find some set of common properties from which we can make predictions about its future is not, particularly, to understand nature though it may well be to increase our control over it. If we took this view, which we might call the "sensible frame" theory, we might eventually come to the view that there is not a single understanding of nature; there are simply, after all, many things to be understood and the criteria for understanding them vary from case to case.

Blewett thinks that this is an important ingredient in correcting the various machine theories. But it, in itself, also represents a misunderstanding. So we would find that each and every one of these things is comprehensible only in terms of some system. To think of the rabbit as a rabbit, then consider it in its own right and against its own background, is an improvement, in some respects, over thinking of it as a collection of atomic particles or a system of electrical charges. But so long as we merely think about rabbits, we will, probably, ultimately fail in our duty to understand the significance of the situation, to have that respect which Blewett calls the respect for the "dust of the ground." We have learned painfully that rabbits cannot be understood apart from their environment. And that is true of everything that we face. Even our attempts to stamp out the lowly mosquito resulted in changes in the environment which affected creatures we gave no thought to. The hummingbird which eats the mosquitoes may be the first victim, but other life-forms may be wiped out by the growing accumulation of insecticides too. The rabbit may perish from disease and overpopulation if we wipe out its natural enemies. Somehow the whole system works together. Blewett was fortunate in living before many of our schemes to alter the environment had come home to roost but he grasped that we must, if we are to understand nature, come to regard it as a significant system. Return to the "sensible frame" will at least get us to confront the facts. Yet the facts cannot be confronted one by one.

Moved by our failures, we may revert to the Nature-God theory—to the point of view which regards nature as a self-contained system, never to be tampered with, always capable of solving its own problems, perfect apart from our intrusions in it. Yet we find that the meaning of nature is not plain on its own terms. This assemblage of facts fails to bring out its significance. Elaborate ecological theories fail to give us much guidance as to what attitude we ought to take to nature. Whatever values we find in nature, we find, also, that nature is capable of producing counter values. It produces the rabbit. It also destroys it. The joint efforts of animal and man are capable of being wiped out by an ice age and may be capable of being even more decisively wiped out by disasters on a cosmic scale—a super-nova, a voracious black hole, a sudden increase in cosmic radiation. To equate nature with God would give us no understanding of these conflicts. Furthermore, such a view makes us mere spectators in the process and yet, obviously, we are part of the system itself. We contribute to it, suffer from it, we have a stake in its own outcome, and we can play a part in that outcome. The Nature-God theory is much like the divine machine theory except that the Nature-God theory seems incredibly inconsistent, confused, and incapable of holding our allegiance.

What Blewett wants to do is clear enough: He wants to maintain the unity of man and nature, he wants to maintain the notion of nature as something important in itself, he wants to restore our failing respect for nature, and he wants to develop a position within which it can be seen that nature is meaningful. What he does not want to do is also clear enough: He does not want to give in to the temptation to achieve the unity of man and nature through a simple reductive materialism, he does not want to give nature a spurious meaning by making it a plaything of God, he does not want to ignore the fact that our ideas and attitudes are, themselves, a part of nature or the fact that nature and our theories about nature are only separable by a kind of abstraction. He does not want to ignore any of our involvements in nature and he does not want to make of nature something fixed.

The theories which he has been concerned to deny seem to exhaust traditional pairs of attitudes. He has rejected the theory which comes naturally to one who thinks that nature ought to be left alone along with the theory which comes naturally to one who sees nature as something to be subdued. He has rejected the traditional position of the believer in Divine Providence along with the traditional position of the non-believer. By insisting on the unity of man and nature but denying the possibility of reductionist positions, he has rejected the position of both the naturalist and the super-naturalist. By denying that nature is a plaything of God, he has denied the most common device by which men have sought to find a "meaning" in nature. But by insisting that nature is "meaningful," he has rejected, as well, the position of those who think that finding meaning in nature is simply an anthropomorphic projection.

What possibility, then, remains? The possibility which Blewett insists upon is, essentially, this: Each of the theories he has rejected stems from some of our transactions with nature. In one sense, nature *is* the structure of these transactions. In another sense, we are the outcome of nature. For we are, ourselves, intelligible only in and through these transactions. The reason which animates us is, in another guise, the structure of nature itself. We add consciousness to that structure but we do not make it. He quotes with approval Hegel's remark that we are nature made conscious of itself, but he does so with a caveat. "But in Hegel the logical method is a tyrant, and at the end the emphasis falls wrongly"[33]—a caveat which has something to do with Blewett's theory of religion which we shall discuss later, and something to do with his view about the primacy of experience. More clearly, he gives weight to an insight which he ascribes, in a sense, to Kant:

> To put it more fully and more fairly, things are elements in a spiritual process which is at once cognitive, moral, religious; a process in which the experiencing subject comes gradually to know a world and to apprehend the principles of its natural and social order; and by ideals and impulses which constitute his very nature, is called to a unity of thought and affection and character with that order and with its creative source.[34]

He explains: "Things are thoughts—they have an ideal or spiritual nature as elements in experience; but thoughts are objective."[35]

If this seems a tangled web, it can be disentangled with relative ease. Blewett is simply saying that ideas, including our theories of nature, our concepts of nature, and the values we find in nature or rightly ascribe to it, *are* objective entities in nature. We bring them together in consciousness but the order which we represent in consciousness has its own structure. Our ideas and theories represent one set of relations; without us there is another set of relations. But what is real is the rational order itself. When we are wrong about nature, we are wrong because we abstract parts of that order or because we organize subsets of it in a misleading way.

Thus we always face a number of options. We could regard nature as the eternal set of ideas in the mind of God and, if we mean by this the most pervasive and rational order which we can ascribe to the universe, this is not literally wrong. For such an order will contain everything which there is and nothing in our experience suggests the impossibility of constructing such an ideal order. Yet we would still be wrong if we believed that that was *all* there was to nature. Again, we can regard nature as the sum of all our possible transactions with it—we can look at

33 Ibid., p. 188.
34 Ibid., p. 87.
35 Ibid.

nature as the sum of our idealized knowledge combined with the state of affairs which would result from our performing the best possible acts. We would not be wrong, for we cannot meaningfully assert anything to be real without asserting that it is a possible object of knowledge. Nor could we imagine ourselves to know the real potential of nature unless we acted in an optimal way so as to bring out the optimal potentialities of nature. Still this is an abstraction. For that same order can be grasped from the perspective of a wolf or a jackrabbit or a mosquito and part of the potential of nature *is* to be grasped in these ways. Without those potentialities being actualized *in themselves*, nature is distorted. For every natural order which we can grasp there is the possibility of that order from its own perspective. Even God is *not* in a position simply to create his own universe. He can actualize the potential of God, but only the jackrabbit can actualize the potential of the jackrabbit. Hence Blewett says:

> Nature, then, has its being in a process in which God fulfils Himself in the gradual creation of a spiritual society. But, as we have had at every point to notice, we ourselves are active in that process. To have knowledge of nature the human soul must exert energies of its own; although those energies of its own could neither exist, nor have any effect in the way of knowledge, unless similar energies were working on a greater scale through the whole of nature. And if this is true of the knowledge of nature, still more is it true of that practical intercourse with nature—the labour and wrestle, the steadily growing mastery crossed by occasional and terrible defeat—which has an even greater place than knowledge in the total process in which we at once receive and achieve our spiritual being.[36]

Nature must be a developing process. For some of the perspectives which are crucial to its essence can only be brought to light in the course of a long and elaborate development. God cannot create the wolf without trees to hide in, ground to dig holes in, and prey to chase. And each of these things is possible because it has a place in the order of things. Furthermore, each such development adds something to reality.

All this, of course, assumes that there is a total, ultimate, and unified view of nature which has as its meaning the development of all the values in the system. But who is to say there is such a total perspective?

Hegel would have argued that that perspective is, itself, guaranteed by the logic of the situation and Blewett would not deny this but he is afraid to make that logic "a tyrant" and to make *it* the end of the

36   Ibid., pp. 188-89.

process. Logic for logic's sake is not, to him, an appealing notion. Rather, the guarantee is in our experience and in what happens to our ideas.

Blewett believes that the fundamental dialectic is in our experience itself. The crucial part of that experience is our experience of personality. He says:

> By personality one properly means that which is suggested, but not fulfilled, in our developing human experience upon the earth; a principle which, in possessing itself and possessing a world, is self-distinguishing, self-objectifying, self-determining; a principle wherein many distinguishable elements of experience, many different facts and actions and kinds of facts and actions, are present in a unity not merely of consciousness but of self-consciousness.[37]

Put another way, Blewett is saying that we discover our personality in the process of "possessing a world," the process of self-objectification, and the process of distinguishing events and actions. We find ourselves in and through the world. We find the world in and through ourselves. The process is a dialectical one. To reduce either side of the dialectic to the other is to destroy the point. If we regard the world simply as "a set of our ideas" then we are left with no notion of objectification and identification. If we regard the world simply as a set of elements of nature, then we are unable to explain how we come to know the set of those elements. On the face of it, it is paradoxical that one finds out about oneself by doing things in the world—that one finds out about oneself not by immediate introspection but by noticing what goes on in nature. And it is equally paradoxical that one finds out about nature by discovering how one's own thought processes, one's own investigative techniques and procedures, actually work. But if reality always involves the interplay of such subject and object, this dialectical shift is not surprising. It is because we find ourselves through nature and in the world that the temptation arises to reduce the subject to the object, the self to the world. This temptation results from a very obvious experience and its misunderstanding leads to various pieces of the "machine" theory of nature. Yet when we try to substantiate our knowledge of nature we find that knowledge is the result of the transaction between us and nature and that all the facts we can discover can always be regarded as parts of our own experience. This discovery, in practice, can lead to what Blewett thinks is the kind of idealism which is simply the characteristic mistake of one who accepts the machine theory. It, too, is just the result of misunderstanding the

37 Ibid., footnote p. 12.

dialectic. Both these experiences are combined with the experience which Blewett thinks is fundamental to all investigations—the experience of finding that there is a rational self revealed equally in nature and in human life. We do not find literally inexplicable phenomena, we do not find that our various theories will not fit together. We find, on the contrary, that between any two pieces of knowledge there is always a path of rational inference. As such, this is simply an experience that we have and we might agree with Hume that, as experience, we are entitled to say no more about that than that it happens. It may not happen with the next two pieces of knowledge which we attempt to join. Yet, when we can join that experience with the experience we have of finding ourselves in nature and nature in ourselves, we begin to understand that the situation is not merely fortuitous. The rational order which we find in our own lives cannot be something other than the rational order which one finds in nature. The two are unintelligible if they are taken apart from one another. Thus, if all the experiences are taken together, Blewett thinks, we *are* entitled to believe that there is a final rational order.

We might be tempted to the false conclusion that the final rational order is something ready-made, stored up in heaven, created originally by God. The combination of these experiences could easily mislead one into accepting the divine "plaything" theory of nature once again.

But this notion will not withstand very much careful analysis. For it implies that there is a ready-made rational order which we use as a path between event and event.

This, however, is incompatible with a proposition which Blewett holds very firmly—the proposition that freedom is indispensable to knowledge. If knowledge were merely "a series of feelings and sensations, determined in their succession and combinations by some alien or impersonal necessity," then knowledge in the sense of science would not be possible. It must be "an active process, animated from within by implicit but effectively operative ideals, in whose operation we apprehend an objective world and have continual commerce with it,"[38] if we are to have knowledge in any serious sense. The element of what Blewett calls our "self-communication"[39] is not fortuitous to the possibility of genuine knowledge. The alternative is knowledge as a pre-determined entity and investigation as a series of trials before bought juries. Thus one may well argue that we transform nature in the course of knowing it. Though such assertions are true in isolation, they represent a perverse misunderstanding of the situation. For to say that, since there is

38 Ibid., p. 256.
39 Ibid.

an active element in all knowing, we must transform nature in the course of knowing it, is to urge that nature has, from the beginning, a wholly independent existence. This is to deny the dialectical reading of the situation. If that dialectical reading is correct, nature in the sense of something to be transformed is only the objective side of a subjective principle. True, we are not and cannot be the only instantiations of the subjective principle. The belief that we are would seem to be one of the mistakes of the kind of idealism which Blewett wants to oppose.

Some understanding of this situation should develop in our discussion of Blewett's theory of the Absolute and of his natural theology. *The Christian View of the World* develops only a portion of a philosophy of nature. Though nearly a hundred of its three hundred and forty-two pages are devoted overtly to the topic of nature and the topic is alluded to frequently in the other portions of the book, the work was, after all, intended to justify its title. As a consequence, one must speculate a little as to some of its implications if one is to guess what Blewett is really driving at. The nature of our knowledge requires that nature itself is an ongoing and creative process. Essentially, our knowledge is the objectification of the subjective principle as it is manifested in us. But, from Blewett's frequent statements about the independence of nature, one must assume that he means to assert that the subjective principle has many other manifestations as well. The most dramatic is the manifestation of the principle in the Absolute itself but that discussion will have to wait its proper place. More germane here is the likelihood that Blewett means to assert that all aspects of nature represent instantiations of the subjective principle in their own right. We could easily understand that the rabbit and the wolf instantiate the subjective principle in their own way. In their case, its objectification will take the form of the unity of feeling and experience which gives them their individuality. But Blewett insists that even the earth is to be regarded as something individual and important in its own right and that our failure to grasp this lies behind much of the evil which industrial society has brought upon us. Our knowledge of the earth is as a collection of fragments—incomplete, imperfectly assembled, poorly grasped. But the earth itself is a unity, a functioning system, an objectification of rational principles. The same rational principles are capable of being objectified as another planet somewhere else in the universe and no doubt there are many such planets. But they will not be literally identical. They will not, for one thing, occupy exactly the same place in the system. They will not be the same concrete individual. We cannot simply, without loss, blow our planet up and replace it with another. It has its elements of uniqueness, its parts function together in a certain

341

way, it is an identifiable individual. As such, the earth instantiates the germ, even if only in the most rudimentary way, of the subjective principle. If our world plays its part in the system, the system would be different without it and, if that is true, it is literally irreplaceable. Hence, our knowledge, if it is genuine knowledge, must reckon with the creative process by which the general principles of physics come to manifest themselves in a unique state of affairs. Before it existed, one might have known all of its elements and all of the principles. One would not have known exactly what it was as a concrete actuality.

Against this background, we can begin to look at the two further facets of Blewett's system—his theory of the Absolute and his theory of human nature.

If he is right in believing that experience invariably forces us to the notion of a complete system of things, if nothing is intelligible except by relation to its place in the system, if every individual thing instantiates, in some way, the subjective principle as well as the objective principle, then there must be a perspective which is a perspective of that total system. For there is a basic duality in all such explanations. One may say that each thing is simply what it is. And that is true not merely in the trivial sense but in the sense that each thing is a manifestation of a subjective principle which is its own. Yet, to see that it is that, one must exhibit it as occupying a place in a system of things. I acquire my identity in the social intercourse within which I distinguish myself from you. The earth acquires its identity by instantiating some of the properties made possible by the rest of the solar system. It cannot be what it is without that system nor can that system be what it is without the galaxy which surrounds it and so on. The system of which they are all parts needs to have some characterization if the parts are to be intelligible at all. It is that characterization, as best we can make it, which is the characterization of the Absolute.

Blewett tackles this difficult task in his own way. He points out, first of all, that the problem arises in our own knowledge. It arises in the course of our attempts to objectify our own instantiation of the subjective principle. It arises, therefore, in the domain of what he calls "spirit." Sometimes he equates "spirit" simply with "concrete consciousness"[40] but he means, more generally, the combination of consciousness and value—consciousness directed in a certain way at a certain end. As creatures whose objectification becomes knowledge, we search for the characterization of the system in which that objectification, along with all other objectifications, is possible. Hence we need to

40 Ibid., p. 82.

locate a principle which accounts for the system and is capable of accounting for the fact that it is conscious.

Blewett puts it this way:

> Since what is developed is concrete consciousness or spirit—consciousness which has an intellectual, a moral, a social, history—the *prius* for which we are asking must be adequate to the gradual production of such consciousness, either as being itself conscious, or as having a nature which is still higher than the nature of spirit. It cannot be a principle lower than spirit; and the man who holds that it is higher must be invited to explain, as exactly as he can, what he means; in which case one of two things is likely to result. Either he will be found to hold that the source (or, as he may put it, the genuine reality) of ourselves is something intrinsically above spirit, so that only by rising out of our spiritual individuality can we enter into true communion with it. That is, he will come to Mysticism; and then the problems of theology will be problems for him no more; in him, so far as he can attain his goal, the unquiet spirit of man will have entered upon the rest which lies the other side of reason and all its searchings. Or else his meaning will be found to be simply this: that the principle in question is self-conscious, is spiritual; but, as the *prius* of the whole movement of spiritual development in individuals and in all their history, is free from the limitations under which spirit moves in its gradual development in man. But that position we are concerned, not to deny, but to affirm.[41]

We must keep reminding ourselves, of course, that Blewett does not mean to assert that reality is carved out of something like *our* consciousness or that it is in some sense the product of another consciousness which functions magically like the genie in Aladdin's lamp. He has, after all, denied both subjective idealism and the "divine machine" theory of nature. The difficulty with the paragraph we just quoted lies mainly in one sentence: "It cannot be a principle lower than spirit. . . ." Indeed, within that sentence, the problem centres on the word "lower." Blewett never explains precisely what this word means but he seems to have packed within it several crucial notions. The simplest of them is just the notion that spirit is inherently richer than anything else of which we are aware. It is richer because, within it, the subjective and objective principles can both be discerned. Now any universe which is explicable in his terms will have to include both these principles and anything lacking some of the properties of spirit will fail. It is within spirit, as he understands it, that the distinction between the subjective and the objective can be grasped because it is within spirit that the possibility of perspective arises. The principles may well

41 Ibid., pp. 82-83.

adhere jointly in what we think of as simple material objects but they are not jointly discernible except in spirit and, if spirit did not exist, it would make no sense to talk of the possibility of alternative perspectives. But he means more than this, evidently, by "lower." The notion of value plays a clear part in his use of it. The notion of value he is implying, however, is not the notion of a scale of values on which spirit ranks higher than material object. It is rather that the possibility of value involves the possibility of intention and it is only in spirit that intention can manifest itself. Blewett would no doubt agree that we may easily dispute about values. We may lack certainty as to how any given claim to value is to be substantiated and, given the substantiation of any claim, we may lack certainty as to where the value referred to ranks in a scale of values. But it is not the case that we are in doubt about the objective existence of values as such.

The situation is one which reveals a constant dialectic. Were there no objects to be confronted in nature there would be no way in which spirit could reveal itself except through the process of thought turned inward on itself. Thought would, then, become the prisoner of its reflection. Actual reflection, however, reveals the structure of objects against the possibility of other structures. We look outward on our world and seek to find its intelligibility in our reflections on it.

In creating the context for reflection we can, of course, "explain" events by reference to each other. When we do this, we make it seem as though thought itself is one of the events in the sequence. Thought appears in the history of the world as one stage in a natural evolution. The aim of the process is the revelation of all knowledge as part of a single, unified, self-contained, rational system. Whenever we encounter gaps in such a system, our explanations break down. We explain A in terms of B, B in terms of C, and so on until, at length, we come to what cannot, as yet, be explained. If we accept that lack of explanation, the whole chain of explanation breaks down.

If one ingredient in the system just "is" and has no explanation then, perhaps, we are deceiving ourselves about the things which seem to have explanations. Perhaps they are really irrational as well. The ultimate test of the system we impose is its ability to complete itself.

Yet, if spirit itself is to be explained by other things and if thought is the manifestation of spirit, then, if thought is explained by something else, thought cannot explain that something else. Intelligibility is the breaking into the open of values which either are within nature all along or else are simply *ad hoc* superimpositions upon it.

Blewett's contention seems to be that we cannot accept the latter hypothesis for, to sustain it, we would have to show that thought did arise (along with the "spirit" of which it is a form) from something else. And that amounts to a self-contradiction. For our theory about the origin of spirit and thought is, itself, a reflection of thought and spirit.

Since, however, his object is to show the nonreducibility of thought and spirit—to show that they are not manifestations of something else—it would be open to him to argue that there are two alternative hypotheses and that either of them will make his point. It is either true that thought and spirit must be constantly in the structure of things in the order that we find in nature, *or* it is true that thought and spirit are independent of nature.

What *cannot* be true is that thought and spirit develop out of something else. For they embody the objective values which lead us to prefer one explanation over another. They set the conditions for what counts as an explanation and they, consequently, contain a crucial element which cannot be in the object to be explained if that object is conceived as wholly alien to thought and spirit.

Blewett dislikes the dualist side—evidently because he is convinced that that would leave the objects of nature as an irrational surd which simply *is*. That possibility is severely undermined by virtually all of the evidence that we have been able to accumulate about nature.

The argument, as he states it, is much involved with notions of time. Blewett does not argue that time itself is revealed by the way in which spirit organizes the world into explanatory sequences. Rather, he appears to argue that the coming to be of consciousness in the world is simply the transference of the rational structure from things into thought through the natural process of reflection. In that process, spirit gains its freedom in time. Reflection frees the rational, intelligible structure and makes possibility real and effective. For reflection on rational structure makes us aware of the possible as well as the actual.

Hence he argues that nature, man, and God are all bound up with one another in a process which is necessary to each. Nature becomes rational order and not mere happening as reflection comes into play. Rational reflection is possible because there is an order in nature. God can play a different role in the world as its possibilities open. Value, which is merely latent when nature is considered in and of itself, becomes actual in experience.

The Absolute is complex. Considered as nature, it is simply the rational order in things—the final system of the world. In reflection, a duality between thought and thing becomes a possibility. As nature is transformed into knowledge through reflection, the Absolute begins to reveal itself as intelligibility. In its final form, it is seen as a self-explanatory unity in which the subjective principle in things is revealed and they are seen to be jointly necessary in the creation of an ultimate system.

In one sense we can regard the Absolute as represented by an original "nature" which is not relative to anything. It is simply a system which has its own being and its own integral structure. In another sense, the Absolute is revealed to *us* as the demand that the fragmentary systems which we have been able to grasp be completed so that they can be rendered self-explanatory. It opens to us choices and values in the demand that the subjective element in us and in other things have expression in a way which will make for a complete and intelligible system. As we see that we can express ourselves through acting in the world we see, as well, that that objective background has its own values—that the other components of nature must be given expression if nature is finally to make sense. If we simply transform nature in the quest for our own ends, we merely internalize ourselves and face the emptiness of reflection turned back on itself.

In a different sense, the Absolute is to be found in the revelation that the entire system has a unity of its own—not a unity which obliterates all the particularities of subjective existence but a unity which reveals the significance of each of its components. It is this third sense of the Absolute which Blewett apparently associates with God. The unity of perspectives is the natural history of God. Human beings stand at an intersection of these perspectives. One perspective presents reality as an ordered set of objects within which rationality may be discerned; the other presents reality as a rational order in thought which manifests itself to us as a set of objects. There is not an ultimate duality in our nature, but there are two perspectives on that nature as on anything else. Without creatures who can sense, feel, and think, the values latent in nature would simply remain latent. Without nature to reflect on, we would remain merely empty.

Blewett argues that human beings are neither an inessential nor a merely transient part of the system. True, since we must reflect that system from a point of view, there is always a facet of incompleteness in our affairs. That incompleteness is potentially overcome because we are not alone. There are all the human and other sentient beings in the universe and we can share one another's perspectives in the creation of what he calls "the concrete and many-sided communion of a spiritual society."[42] The system cannot have only one reflective self, even if that one reflecting self is God, for any one perspective is ultimately a distortion.

Nor is it true that we are simply a brief phase in the development of the ultimate reality. When we conceive ourselves in time as part of objective nature, we see that the part of that system which defines our

42   Ibid., p. 207.

immediate perspective is transitory. We shall all die. But that is not the whole of the story. ". . . the soul of man . . . is not merely a part of an eternal system, a mode in a system of modes; it has within itself, under whatever present limitations the principle of that eternal system."[43] The "principle of that eternal system" is, of course, reason and reflection. In a sense, each of us is a microcosm of the whole reality and each of us is capable of regenerating that whole system in knowledge. Hence we transcend the immediacy of our perspective. It only appears that we are transitorily confined to the immediacy of space and time because our position in that system generates a perspective from which we locate ourselves.

Only God—who sees the system from another level, from a level of reflection on reflection—can know just what the form of our future experience is to be. Blewett's God stands in a complex and, one must suppose, not very orthodox relation to the world. Blewett speaks of God this way: ". . . what this means is that God, under forms of externality and necessity, continually is manifesting Himself to us and in us, and by that manifestation is continually developing in us our own capacities."[44]

God, in short, is not another thing added to the universe beyond the domain of rational order and reflective spirit. But He is also not simply the structural properties of that system. Blewett repeatedly denies that his philosophical arguments should be understood as tending toward pantheism.

Rather God manifests Himself through the system of reality. God is the explanation for the fact that reality is an actual unity and that the development of the world appears to us to have a direction—roughly a direction from the discrete and fragmentary, through higher forms of unity which characterize the organic world, and finally, to the kinds of unity which is nature reflected in systematic knowledge. But that history of the world is only its structure as it is seen when the pattern of its development is given a temporal axis.

Blewett is concerned, ultimately, to insist that God must exist in a mode beyond time, as eternal and complete. The problem is to make this consistent with his view of the world as a process whose components are necessary to its development and an activity within which human beings play a role which is as vital to God as God is to them.

He is clearly aware of the problem and devotes considerable space to it in *The Christian View of the World*. He speaks of God as the Absolute Spirit (in the third of the senses which we noted above) and says:

43 Ibid.
44 Ibid., p. 214.

It is often said that the reference to an Absolute Spirit, in our attempt to understand how our experience is possible, involves denying the reality of change; involves taking the world to be a static universe, . . . But the reference to an Absolute Spirit really involves the opposite of this; it means that change is intelligible at all, is possible at all, only in and as and through the activity of a spiritual being who has all the changes present to him eternally or *totum simul*. We begin with change as a fact; and Absolute Idealism might be summarily described as the most reasonable hypothesis that men have so far been able to make as to the possibility not merely of change in the abstract, but of the actual changes which are the history of the world.[45]

He remarks that the alleged problem "is really not a difficulty at all."[46] He explains:

The actual temporal movement of the world, as a single history and not a succession of absolutely discontinuous universes, each arising unintelligibly from the void only to return at once to it, is possible only because a single supreme subject of the world constitutes and holds together as one all that movement. That, indeed, is a truth so elementary that it has its witness in our most ordinary consciousness. A man can apprehend events in temporal succession only because he has time in him (as a form of the synthetic unity of his consciousness) as well as being himself in time; he could not so apprehend events if time were an independent existence and he were situated at some point in it.[47]

Blewett seems to have been telling us that human acts make a difference to the universe and that the universe is to be regarded as seeking a goal which is furthered by God and man in co-operation. We are working toward a reality which is a "society of spiritual beings";[48] we are not there yet. The universe for Blewett has a direction and not merely man but nature as well plays a part.

It seems evident that we could not know this if we were trapped in a world of Kantian phenomena which we could not transcend. It seems also that, for Blewett, time is real and God is in time. It does not help us very much at this point in the argument, to learn that time is in God and God is perfectly all right on His own and really quite distinct from the little times which are internal to us.

Blewett never quite comes out to meet this challenge head-on. Rather, the discussion sounds as if he is standing in his corner and telling his trainer that he will, indeed, pound the daylights out of the

45 Ibid., pp. 120-21.
46 Ibid., p. 120.
47 Ibid., p. 121.
48 Ibid., p. 184.

enemy when he meets him. Actually, it seems that Blewett does have the necessary apparatus to do it and since the resolution of the problem is so evidently important for Blewett, it may be fair for us to speculate here about how that apparatus might be put to use.

One of Blewett's most important concerns might be put this way: Nature has its own properties and its own perspectives. In consciousness, however, nature is restructured reflectively as systematic knowledge. When one knows something, that thing, considered as the object of knowledge, is abstracted from time. It becomes available not just at the moment of its happening but, as an element in reflective consciousness, as a feature of what Blewett calls spirit, it becomes available at any time. Human knowledge is, to be sure, imperfect; and the object of knowledge never reflects the whole of the reality known. It is one thing in and of itself and another as an element in knowledge.

Yet we must be able, in principle, to represent it as a unity. The fact, as he says, that we regard the whole of time as a unity and not merely as a set of disjunctive happenings entails that that unity, itself, has a place as one of the perspectives in and on reality. The point about the unity of time may be difficult to grasp. It seems so obvious that successive events belong to the same time—are elements of the same system—that we do not normally give it any thought. But Blewett is right to call this thoughtless acceptance into question and to demand that we face up to its implications.

If events were simply discrete, we could not say that they belonged to the same time. They would simply be discrete occurrences which might come in *any* order. Now the unity which is in question is not, literally, the unity of consciousness or Kant's transcendental unity of apperception. Those unities may or may not represent the unity and order in nature. In practice they do not. One's position relative to distant objects determines the order in which one perceives them and one must make adjustments in constructed knowledge to get anything like a "real" order. That "real" order, anyhow, will be relative to the frame of reference one adopts. We normally assume that the "real order" of things is the order which would be given by our best explanatory system. (Traditionally, it is assumed that the "real order" is the "causal order" but causal explanation represents, itself, one option out of many even if we can arrive at a settled meaning of "cause.")

The notion that there is a preferred order is the notion that there is a coherent story to be told about nature. But coherence is a coherence of intelligibility. The order of intelligibility is the order of effective knowledge—and knowledge, as we said, seems to transform or transmute time so as to make the objects of knowledge timelessly available.

The function performed in Blewett's metaphysical system by his concept of God is, precisely, the function of providing intelligibility—the function of providing the notion of a preferred order for the understanding of nature and man. The best argument that Blewett could provide, consequently, would be the argument that, finally, the unity of time is a unity of knowledge.

Though events do "unfold" in time, they are, he might argue, transformed by God in his knowledge into a system which, seen from the point of its completion, is eternal. Once it *is* complete it will seem as if it always *was* complete. For it will be exhibited as an order which is timeless (in the sense of not undergoing change) and as eternal in the sense of being what Blewett, borrowing from the obvious tradition, calls a *totum simul*—a situation in which everything is given at once.

He is evidently torn between wanting to take time seriously, wanting to take man seriously as a contributor to a cosmic intelligibility, and, from the other side, wanting to retain more than a little of the traditional and orthodox notion of God. The suggestion we have made here as a way around the paradox would, certainly, make Blewett sound more like Whitehead than like Bradley or McTaggart.[49] But it should be admitted that his various convictions about nature, process, and the relation between man and God do make him sound more like Whitehead than one would expect.

This brings us to Blewett's views on religion. The remark attributed to him by Rose—the remark that God is the "Home of all relations"—makes a kind of sense in the light of the things we have him saying about God. For it is the kind of unity which God gives to the world which, in its turn, makes nature and our own condition intelligible. This unity is, no doubt, a set of relations—it provides the framework within which the light dawns. Without it, our claims to knowledge dissolve into claims to have grasped fragments unrelated to one another. Furthermore, it seems very clear that Blewett's God is not, as we have said, another object to be added to the list of things in the world. Nor is He a mere idea or a psychological projection of ourselves. But that leaves us with, so far as one can see, only the option of taking God to *be* that complex of relations which provides intelligibility.

Blewett, nonetheless, claims to be a Christian. It would be pointless to deny, despite that, that many Christians then and now would have found his views about God and the world somewhat puzzling. The traditional Christian God is both transcendent and immanent—both to

49 Compare the last chapters to Whitehead's *Process and Reality* (London: Macmillan, 1929) and McTaggart's *The Nature of Existence* (Cambridge: University Press, 1921, 1927).

be found in the world and to be rightly described as transcending the world, as its creator, its judge, and its motivating force.

Blewett's God, strictly speaking, is neither immanent nor transcendent. He is not an additional object standing outside the world, but He is not revealed solely in the development of the world either. He is the "creator" of the world only in the sense that His nature is the best example of that "spirit" which is *ground* of the world. He is its judge, one would guess, only in the sense that the standards of divine reason must be the standards which set the rule—since the divine consciousness is the best and fullest example of spirit.

Yet He has, according to Blewett, co-creators—us. For what we do, Blewett insists, is vital to God just as God is vital to us. The test of a right act is reason. God is simply the best exemplar of that reason. It does not seem likely, in Blewett's world, that God will descend upon us in a thunder-clap or that He literally casts us into hell or elevates us to membership in the community of the saints. If anything, we do those things for ourselves. The nearest thing to hell which Blewett's world can accommodate, seemingly, is irrational and disorganized perception. Heaven is a community of spirits but it comes about through our acts and through our ultimate ability to grasp ourselves as we really are and not merely as phenomenal reflections in a transitory experience.

The core of Christian belief, presumably, has to do with the persons of the Trinity. In particular, it has to do with the proposition that God became man while remaining God; that there is an identity of some kind between God the Father and God the Son. As a result of this event, Christians hold, salvation is possible and the reunion of God and man is feasible.

All this is perfectly *possible* given Blewett's view of the world. Since God does manifest Himself through consciousness, He might manifest Himself through a human consciousness. It might well be that a rather superior human consciousness would provide a feasible path to salvation because salvation, for Blewett, is to be achieved through the actual instantiation of a "community of spirits."

The natural path, however, is through reason and a reasoned morality. Moral practices, for Blewett, are, presumably, just those practices which do develop the appropriate self-realization—those practices which being inherently reasonable bring about the actual "community of spirits." But they mostly have to do with acting reasonably, attempting to bring about the development of oneself along with the development of others, and developing a suitably expanding experience.

This all sounds rather unlike the collection of parables, oracular utterances, and occasional moral commands which constitute the relevant portions of the New Testament.

If Blewett's philosophy is correct and God exists, then God, presumably, subscribes to the philosophy of Blewett. How is it then that if, in addition, God manifested Himself on earth in the Incarnation, He did not talk more like Blewett? Why is there not in the New Testament more of an account of the role of reason, the historical development of consciousness, the phases of the Absolute? We seem not, there, to be told to reason our way to salvation. The praise of intellect is, as Russell remarked, curiously absent from the New Testament.

Blewett speaks about the Incarnation in twelve different passages scattered through *The Christian View of the World*. His principal argument is that the significance of the Incarnation is that, through it, we are able to understand our own consciousness as something through which God "seeks a realisation of Himself."[50] The Incarnation, then, is a kind of model. Since the principle of spirit and consciousness is always and everywhere the same, we can see how it is that there is one God but that that God can be exemplified wherever spirit is exemplified. The principle remains unfragmented even though its expression is imperfect.

Blewett also insists that it is through the Incarnation that we acquire our own "sense of sin."[51] There are many long discussions of sin in *The Christian View of the World*, but the upshot of it is that sin is the result of a kind of imperfection which comes from our incompleteness. That incompleteness is determined by the fact that we appear to ourselves as finite creatures caught in a finite world. What the Incarnation provides us with is a sense of that principle of consciousness and spirit which really animates the world.

Moreover, Blewett thinks that, if we can see the world as ultimately "spiritual," we can see that "the broad antecedent probabilities would . . . seem in favour of the great body of the New Testament miracles."[52] What he seems to be arguing is that, if the ultimate reality is not material, then our normal presumptions against those miracles will dissolve. This must be the most curious section of *The Christian View of the World*—a work in which, otherwise, reality is described as a close-knit, rational, and coherent order. It might be that those very miracles would represent the most orderly course of events conceivable *if* we knew the facts. But this view of the relation of "appearance" to "reality"

50 Blewett, *Christian View*, p. 164.
51 Ibid., p. 302.
52 Ibid., p. 234.

seems to go against the whole grain of Blewett's thought. If we are to regard the surface appearances of things as mere coverings for a "spiritual" reality, then what becomes of the importance of "nature"— the very importance which Blewett emphasizes so strongly elsewhere in the book? There is, to be sure, another possibility: As a good Christian Blewett may simply regard the "givens" of the New Testament as a basic part of the data one must work with. If it is a general revelation, then its claims will have *some* meaning. He does not tell us, for instance, whether the "miracles" are to be taken literally or symbolically. But he does not suggest that they are to be taken other than literally.

What he says is that the probability that God would act in this way "appears in its full strength only when considered in the light of the grave and deep need of humanity through sin."[53] The argument is that, given that men are so bad, God will most likely be inclined to intervene. But isn't this a *different* God—not at all the God who animates Blewett's metaphysics? This is now God conceived as a wholly separate entity and given to wilful (arbitrary if you like) interventions in the natural world. Is this the God who can "realise Himself—can give to His own nature its appropriate expression and activity—only in and through the life of a society of freely creative spiritual beings; whether that society have its being eternally, as in the Trinity; or under a form of development, as in the world"?[54] One must admit that there is, at least, some difficulty in reconciling the two.

His most "fundamentalist"[55] mood is the one in which he undertakes to subscribe to the New Testament miracles—but, even then, he talks only about the "antecedent probabilities."[56] He appears to be doing what Bishop Berkeley once did in one of his sermons—giving betting odds on the truth of the Scripture. Perhaps Albert Carman would have liked it better if he had repudiated them altogether.

Blewett's account of religion, then, is at least persistently oriented to and by reason. It would seem, also, that his is a rather open religion, one which is, probably, subject to amendment as we learn more about the antecedent probabilities and about other things. Blewett is caught here between two competing demands in his mind. He did not succeed, quite, in reconciling them nor in making a coherent adjustment to them. But one must concede that he is, at any rate, reasonable in the face of them.

53 Ibid., p. 235.
54 Ibid., p. 241.
55 We must remember that, given the controversies of the time, Blewett is never far from questions about the truth of the Scriptures.
56 Blewett, *Christian View*, p. 234.

This chapter cannot be closed without reference to James Ten Broeke, who was nearly Blewett's contemporary and who carried on the idealist tradition in Canada into the 1930s. Ten Broeke, like Blewett, saw his main task as bringing about the reunion of the fragmented forms of human knowledge. He was inclined, however, to place even more weight on the problem of religion for, as the twentieth century went on, he increasingly felt that it was religion which was in danger of losing its place in the affections of intelligent men and that the greatest challenge was to show that religious claims still figure amongst *bona fide* claims to knowledge.

Born in Vermont, Ten Broeke studied at Yale, Berlin, and Oxford. He took the Chair of Philosophy at McMaster in 1898, seven years after completing his Ph.D. at Yale. It was a radical departure from the Scottish connection that dominated the Baptist university, to have this European name added to the faculty. A retirement tribute in the *McMaster News* notes that "the name 'Ten Broeke' left the genealogical experts speechless. . . . Indeed it was somewhat of a relief to some to be assured that he was of New England stock."[57]

McMaster seemed not yet as philosophically emancipated from theology as Toronto and McGill and much of what Ten Broeke wrote is riddled with the religious clichés and phrases of the preacher. Ironically, this same tendency made him more than acceptable to the surrounding community. His classes were full and his students attentive. Yet if one ignores his style in his books, *A Constructive Basis for Theology*[58] and *The Moral Life and Religion*,[59] one finds a serious scholar of philosophy.

He was an idealist and well schooled in the thoughts of his predecessors. His *Constructive Basis for Theology* is an attempt to show that modern thought afforded a superior constructive base for Christian faith. Hegel and Lotze, he thought, provided a better metaphysical foundation for legitimizing theology than did Plato and Aristotle.

In addition to his interest in idealism, Ten Broeke had a strong interest in the new advances being made in psychology. His involvement was more extensive than John Watson's and we find General Psychology and Advanced Psychology among the courses he taught. Many of the universities in the early 1920s and 1930s combined philosophy and psychology in one department and McMaster was no exception. His concern with principles of psychology is evident in both books. His conception of God, as we shall see, is a very personal one and

57 "Dr. Ten Broeke Retires," *McMaster News*, vol. 3, no. 3 (July 1932).
58 James Ten Broeke, *A Constructive Basis for Theology* (London: Macmillan, 1914).
59 James Ten Broeke, *The Moral Life and Religion* (New York: Macmillan, 1922).

his theories about epistemology and reality are heavily influenced by a strong awareness of individual differences.

The major portion of the *Constructive Basis for Theology* illustrates the rise of Christian theology under the influence of the philosophy of the Greeks and Romans. Their philosophy championed the universal as the true reality and the highest universal as the most real Being. Individualism was a feature of later revolutions. Early theology formed under Greek and Roman philosophy emphasized the absolute sovereignty of God. Ten Broeke's purpose was to set out the foundations of modern philosophy which make possible a Christian theology more suited to the needs of the individual.

Ten Broeke was intensely interested in making religious consciousness both natural and individual. He discussed at length heredity and developmental influences which would contribute to this conceptual growth as children mature. It is a simplistic psychology that he lays out and at times rather far-fetched. But it is a real attempt to theorize scientifically about theology. Perhaps his most distinguishing feature as a philosopher is his view that the individual's perception of reality is what is real. Nonetheless, because Ten Broeke sees the individual as primarily a social being, he avoids the "many worlds" problem.

A basic unity of consciousness provides the background to all experience. Hence subject and object (which require each other) are but different aspects of experience. (For example, the body is an objective aspect of conscious experience, whereas the mind, so far as we know, is the unity of thoughts, feelings, and volitions directed towards objects and inseparable from objective experience.) The psychological difference between the body and other objects is that body-percepts are a little more constant and interesting than other percepts. Whatever dualism there is between subject and object occurs within experience of which self and world are aspects. Each world, mathematical, chemical, or supernatural is clearly "as much a mental construction"[60] as any other. Yet each mind can experience and/or construct only a partial aspect of the whole. What enables us to share reality if we are confined to our individual percepts, or to know that we experience only a part of the whole? That we are social beings is his answer. There is no individual apart from social relations. What we do and think is a product of the relations we stand in to the community of which we are a part.

As members of a community, personal growth becomes a dialectical process. Language is a co-operative social product and public opinion expresses the common social consciousness which forms and is formed by the individual. It is the uniqueness of one's manner of

60 Ten Broeke, *A Constructive Basis for Theology*, p. 260.

responding to one's social environment that distinguishes one and determines reality as it is for the individual. Reality, then, for Ten Broeke is the community awareness of shared experiences. Its unity is a conscious one. Its differences are in the individual's responses to and comprehension of that unity.

Ten Broeke does not ignore the responsive side of experience. Often belief depends upon the degree of our emotional arousal to the experience. "The more intense the emotional element becomes, the more the self is laid hold of and called into action, the more reality the objects of experience acquire."[61] To ask whether our thoughts apprehend reality is, for Ten Broeke, a question which grows out of a misconception of the relation of thought to being. The world about us is a world of meanings and ends so intimately connected with belief and reality that the question never arises. The physical world is none other than a scene of moral struggles. It is the world to which I must relate and account for my actions and the actions of others. It is a world of meaningful moral relations, not simply abstracted tables and chairs. Tables and chairs have no meaning independent of the experiencing agents, hence no reality as such in Ten Broeke's terms. For him the meanings of the world are inexhaustible. Interests and purposes determine these meanings, hence the value we place on things. Emotional involvement affects how strongly we defend those values and communicate them to others.

Three important features are involved then in Ten Broeke's view of reality: individual differences, emotional factors, and shared thoughts—the basis for morality as well. Products of thought cannot be separated or abstracted from the primary unity of experience. Platonism, in Ten Broeke's view, neglects the emotional and volitional factors in its conception of the true reality. They are, he insists, equally essential factors of experience.

Ten Broeke's theory of the self falls easily into this analysis. Our awareness of self is organized around our goals and ends. To remember or know who one is, is to remember the set of goals one has attempted to realize. If these purposes are indefinite and unorganized, we "fall back into the ceaseless flow of mental states and have no proper individuality."[62] Ten Broeke concludes, "Thus the permanency of the end becomes the permanency, indeed the substantiality, of the self."[63] And we must try and allow each person or personality to live out the meaning in which his reality subsists.

61   Ibid., p. 266.
62   Ibid., p. 270.
63   Ibid., p. 271.

Ten Broeke's theory of the self is fundamental to his moral theory, which he develops in a book written subsequent to *The Constructive Basis for Theology* called *The Moral Life and Religion*. If to be a self is to be a being whose reality is grounded on goals and values (and that reality is such in terms of our emotional commitment to it), and if as social beings our being is bound up in the maintenance and promotion of the being of others, then the only possible relation which can hold between persons is a moral one. Furthermore, other persons necessarily have a value which requires that one thinks of their reality in a way that cannot be applied to objects of the real world. (For Ten Broeke, to value one's car more than one's family would indicate a serious misunderstanding of what one's own self was.)

When it comes to moral laws, Ten Broeke is understandably cautious. Because we will all respond differently to our situations, we must talk in terms of moral laws or universal moral rules only tentatively. Laws, he suggests, "are not existing things but formulations of experienced processes."[64] Thus moral laws are only rules of action which undertake to formulate the relation of certain acts to their motives and effects upon the welfare of the agent and of those with whom he has to do. In each case the experienced facts are primary, the rules or laws secondary. It is not surprising to find Ten Broeke questioning the notion of the Kantian Moral Law, or the universal dictate on which all men can rely. Law requires some kind of repetition and there seem to be no repetitions in the moral sphere. Each person feels that no one could have had just the crisis to face that he has had to meet.

> Still more precisely, how can the same individual have a rule of action, for is not each modified by his own responses to the environment which constantly changes and is affected by the agent's own action?—but change involves time while a rule or law of action implies sameness at different times apparently making real change impossible.[65]

Ten Broeke recognizes the age-old problem of trying to provide for objectivity and universality required by moral theory. One is either left with a universal principle, abstract and rational but devoid of normative content (as with Kant), or a set of particular occasions so distinguishable that no bond between them can be found. How then is morality possible in his view?

It is a refreshingly simple answer that he gives. The ground for the universality of ethical ideas is in their "sensuous and social origin."[66]

64   Ten Broeke, *The Moral Life and Religion*, p. 59.
65   Ibid., pp. 60-61.
66   Ibid., p. 62.

This origin presupposes fundamental capacities and needs and these needs and what satisfies them afford a basis for the construction of a universal. It is evident, he observes, that men have original and acquired needs much alike and capable of being satisfied in similar ways. Our choices and interests will be more or less similar to and representative of the needs and choices of everyone. Hence the community consciousness and social mind will reflect rules of behaviour required of all for each individual to act out his own role. The maxims of our actions are only tentative working hypotheses whose consequences must be assessed (and re-thought) in terms of community well-being. There will always be a certain amount of guesswork in moral behaviour (a fact few theorists are prepared to acknowledge) and each individual's uniqueness will produce a variety of moral responses. Ten Broeke himself raises the obvious when he asks, ". . . how can a rule of action be universally valid, since circumstances are never twice identical?"[67]

With so little to go on one can understand why our self-concepts, as social beings, are so crucial to Ten Broeke's position. Only in terms of the opinions of others do we judge our own worth. When we see ourselves as beings with purposes and recognize others to be the same, then the identical nature of our good and theirs will result in a moral consciousness in the community.

Ten Broeke relates his moral theory to God, but does not rely on God as a crutch for good behaviour. Action takes place according to what is believed (and what is believed is what makes the strongest claims of realness). We find Ten Broeke suggesting that moral actions will accord with the reality of the objects of religious beliefs.

Reality is but a category of response of a subject to certain experience. "Whatever is real is . . . a subordinate form of self-conscious experience and properly has no existence elsewhere."[68] "Hence the real, the true and the valuable or good are unified in the same object through the subject's attitude and action, and the object has its determinate place for the subject in a unity of reality."[69] The force with which religious objects strike us as aspects of our experience will determine their reality. Action in accordance with a belief in religious objects will be of the highest moral standard. Although he suggests that a man who has no supernatural world in his experience, whose moral beliefs are not religious ones, is deficient in the scope of his thought, his position is sufficiently grounded in his theory of the self to explain moral behaviour without resort to a belief in God.

67 Ibid., p. 65.
68 Ibid., p. 211.
69 Ibid., p. 212.

Ten Broeke's emphasis on the self as worthy and social extends to his analysis of God as well. As an idealist he is committed to the unity of rational thought. But he would have more than the rational Absolute as his God. An inexhaustible Reason in which our rationality participates and an infinite self of which we are the expression are part of the explanation of God for Ten Broeke, but such idealism seems to lack the teleological nature of experience—the purposes which give value to our activities and bring forth their reality. When we see ourselves as valuable, we have the clearest self-concept. And it is through participating in a society with moral goals and ends that we truly express the existence of universal value and worth—namely God.

Ten Broeke's arguments with the absolute idealists focus mainly on the difficulty of making God other than self—(or other than our experience of what *is*) and yet related to all selves. To suggest the Absolute as some transcendent being that is in and yet is other than the whole of reality lands one in conceptual difficulties. Even to rely on the concept of creation as a foothold for God is to tread on shaky ground, for there is nothing in our experience of the physical world to suggest this. The finite world cannot just be posited as depending on the infinite God, or the Absolute, willy-nilly.

It is primarily the force of our feelings of worth and value in experience that produces religious feelings—indeed, that is what constitutes religious experience. An identity between reality and value seems necessary to Ten Broeke (as it did to Bosanquet and Lotze). Such a position born out of modern speculative thought, in Ten Broeke's eyes, legitimizes the theological concept of a self-conscious personality as God. His point is that it is not unreasonable to entertain such a religious idea.

Ten Broeke has gone to great lengths tracing through the history of thought to make theology more intellectually respectable. In spite of McMaster's Baptist biases he was not, in spirit, the evangelical preacher that some of his writing would at first glance suggest. His position, were it fully understood, might have raised the eyebrows of many of his colleagues, for he wrote: "In the first place, the term God is the expression of the immeasurable need of life in its fulness, the persistence of the belief in God is due to the strength of the conviction that there is such life for us, and the difficulty of explaining the nature of God is commensurate with the difficulty of telling what this need of eternal life is."[70]

He was not a dogmatist. And he was far too interested in the human side of being to let God become just an abstract symbol. Ten

70 Ten Broeke, *A Constructive Basis for Theology*, p. 282.

Broeke had no Bible up his sleeve. His belief in individuals, their differences, and their own realities makes him a most appealing theoretician of theology. ". . . no one can be a self-conscious personality without striving to unify his religious ideas in some sense with his entire complex and diverse experience, but this does not mean that he reproduces the idealist's 'absolute' theology, if such there be."[71] Every theology must have some relation to personal experience, not symbols. And for each theological utterance: "Let it be welcomed as the utterance of some mind that has had precisely that experience of reality."[72] That should be the fate of any theological system constructed by a given individual or generation in Ten Broeke's view. It was a liberal and tolerant thinker who gave McMaster thirty-seven years of his life.

Ten Broeke died still wondering about the reality of God, morality, and goodness. There is an unfinished manuscript of his, far too illegible to decipher, in the McMaster archives. Although it is titled the "Finality of Faith" one can speculate that it offers no firmer ontological commitment than before. Near his death he continued to ask: "How can we know God? And what do we mean by God? I can only ask the questions."[73]

The chapters of his unfinished book have titles about teleology, the self, the world as a system of ends, the self as an end—all of which suggest that the work continues his earlier commitment to individuals and their value in terms of the community, a belief in the strength of differences and the common good. Ten Broeke would have agreed with St. Augustine—that any statement about existence or what is, requires a commitment or act of faith.

> It is always possible that the fulness of God should be revealed in some individual so uniquely that the intellectual formulation may rightly differ from that of other minds. But, when severed from the living experience in which they were born, theological doctrines are like branches cut off from the vine. There is no life-current running through them.[74]

His belief in the reasonableness of mankind precipitated his efforts to justify that faith in a universal order.

71 Ibid., p. 374.
72 Ibid., p. 375.
73 F. W. Waters, "A Former Student's Tribute," *The Canadian Baptist*, November 11, 1937, p. 6.
74 Ten Broeke, *A Constructive Basis for Theology*, p. 375.

TEN

THE SELF-TRANSCENDENCE OF REASON, AND EVOLUTIONARY MYSTICISM

Richard M. Bucke and William D. Lighthall

BUCKE AND LIGHTHALL hold a curious but important place in this story: Bucke's *Cosmic Consciousness*[1] has had a continuous and large audience in Canada, the United States, and England since its publication in 1901, shortly before his death. The first edition of 500 copies sold out slowly, but word of it spread and, through a variety of publishers, it has remained in print ever since. Lighthall, as poet, anthologist, and literary organizer exercised a lasting influence on Canadian literature.

Yet Carl Klinck's *Literary History of Canada* contains only one mention of Bucke—a casual remark in an essay by Northrop Frye.[2] In the chapters which form the telephone book of Canadian philosophy, he is altogether omitted. Lighthall's name is scattered through several essays in that massive volume, but he, too, is missing from the list of philosophers—though philosophers as different as John Laird and F. C. Schiller seem to have found something of interest in his work.

There are evident reasons for this. Neither Bucke nor Lighthall was a professional philosopher, though Lighthall frequented philosophy conferences and is reputed to have corresponded with a good many "professionals." Bucke was a physician and the director of a large mental hospital. His contributions to the treatment of mental illness continue to be remembered. Lighthall was a lawyer, a patron of the arts, a friend of learning, and, beyond doubt, a learned man.

1 Richard Maurice Bucke, *Cosmic Consciousness* (Philadelphia: Innes & Sons, 1901; reprint paperback ed., New York: E. P. Dutton, 1969).

2 Carl F. Klinck, general editor, and Alfred G. Bailey, Claude Bissell, Roy Daniels, Northrop Frye, and Desmond Pacey, eds., *The Literary History of Canada: Canadian Literature in English*, 1st ed. (Toronto: University of Toronto Press, 1965), p. 832. (Second edition published by University of Toronto Press in 3 vols., 1976.)

Both of them were influenced by the current of ideas in the later nineteenth century and Lighthall followed the development of science through the first third of this century. Both of them were attempting to paint a world picture which would be acceptable to a generation for whom traditional religious beliefs had often become meaningless[3] but for whom it still seemed important to form a general estimate of the significance of the universe—to locate, if you will, a meaning for human life against a very large background. They accepted biological evolution as a key to reality and they inferred from some of its features that the mechanistic materialism of an earlier science was not merely repugnant to human sentiment but intellectually unviable as well.[4] They both rejected the notion that men could make up their values for themselves on what to them seemed an evident and obvious ground— each of us, evidently, is a feature of a larger process and our own lives are unintelligible without reference to the process. Lighthall (waxing uncharacteristically poetical in a generally dry philosophical work) likens us to leaves on a tree.

Both of them came to the view that there is an evolutionary process which will lead to a higher order of consciousness. The interest in their work lies largely in the special twists which they give to this notion and in the way in which they bring to bear universal knowledge and experience on philosophical problems. They have in common that they use reason to show its own limitations, its place in a larger scheme, and that they suggest a kind of rational mysticism which has been a part of the history of Western thought since Plotinus.

In other respects, they differ. Lighthall was an outspoken Canadian nationalist, though he continued to see Canada in an essentially British tradition. Bucke, so far as we know, had little or no interest in such questions—though, after a period of adventure in the American west, and study in England, he settled in London, Ontario, and stayed there. Despite his close friendship with Walt Whitman and his connections with a variety of American literary figures, nothing enticed him to leave his work in western Ontario. Once again, we find two Canadian philosophers of much the same period (Lighthall was twenty years younger than Bucke) who appear to have known nothing of each other. In the long list of "sources" published as an appendix to Lighthall's *The Person of Evolution*,[5] there is no mention of Bucke. Indeed, though the book is dedicated to John Clark Murray (along with Sir

3   Neither, however, seems to have had a scholarly interest in theology as such.
4   But though both were interested in ethics, neither seems to have had an interest in Social Darwinism.
5   W. Douw Lighthall, *The Person of Evolution*, Definitive Edition (Toronto: Macmillan, 1933).

William Osler), there is little mention, there, of any Canadian philosopher.

Bucke, born in 1837, was just a year old when his family moved from England to "Creek Farm," a spot which then seemed remote but long since has been absorbed in the suburbs of London, Ontario. They did not come empty-handed. His father brought a library of several thousand volumes—not, perhaps, the best equipment for a pioneer farmer, but reasonable for a graduate of Trinity College, Cambridge. His mother, the grand-daughter of Sir Robert Walpole and the sister of an eminent Q.C., also seemed an unlikely candidate for her new role. We know nothing of their motives, but they did succeed as farmers. Maurice was taught Latin by his father but otherwise left to educate himself in the library between the more pressing chores.

At seventeen, he decided to see the world. Whatever the family had, cash seems not to have been readily available. The young Bucke worked as a gardener in Columbus, Ohio, a railroad worker in Cincinnati, and a deck hand on a Mississippi river boat. But he wanted to see the real west. He offered his services as a wagon driver for a journey from the central plains to the far edge of the Mormon Territory—now western Nevada. He did get to the Carson River, but at great risk. Indian attacks exhausted both ammunition and supplies and, at one point, he travelled 150 miles on nothing but flour mixed with hot water.

There he settled down to mine gold and silver. He was with the Grosh brothers when they discovered the Comstock Lode, but disaster overtook them. In an effort to replenish their supplies, they decided to cross the mountains to the coast during a severe winter. One of the Grosh brothers and their partner, a man called Brown, died on the trip. Bucke arrived with severe frost-bite, so severe that one foot and part of the other had to be amputated.

By then he was twenty-one and it turned out that there was some money in his mother's estate, enough to put him through McGill medical school. He graduated with an essay prize and honours and went on to England for two years of postgraduate study. Nevada had cured him of the taste for physical adventure and he came home, married, and started a practice in Sarnia, Ontario. A few years later, he became Superintendent of the new Asylum for the Insane in Hamilton and after a year there, he became, in 1877, Superintendent of its twin in London.

Even now, the yellow brick buildings of the London Hospital are not a very prepossessing sight. When Bucke took it over, it was primitive in many senses. Inmates were—if we may judge from its supply records—frequently kept sedated with alcohol. The hospital's function was custodial—to use a euphemism still current in the trade (though not at that hospital now).

Bucke set about a programme of reform which won him a permanent place in the history of public psychiatry. He believed that mental illness had a cause, that it could, in many cases, be cured. His general beliefs inclined him to the view that the problems were to be found in the physiology of the nervous system.

The notion that madmen are wicked dies hard. They are sometimes violent and therefore dangerous, often unpredictable and therefore difficult to handle, quite commonly unable to face reality and therefore impervious to rational persuasion. Behaviourally, in short, they are frequently indistinguishable from those on whom we commonly pass adverse moral judgment. It was obvious to Bucke that this fact in itself tended to make the care of the mad—or of those whom society thought mad—extremely difficult. The mentally ill, however much persuasion is exercised on their behalf, do not attract the natural sympathy which is extended to the physically ill. Much of the staff which is engaged to treat them consists of people of limited education who must be hired to perform essentially menial chores. It is no easy task to arouse in them the necessary sympathy. The general public, even now, is frequently glad enough to be spared contact with the inmates of mental institutions.

It is against this background that we must view Bucke's first major work, *Man's Moral Nature*,[6] published in 1879, two years after he took over the London Hospital and three years after he first became engaged in the treatment of insanity.

One event in Bucke's life is also essential to an understanding of the book. In 1867, he had been introduced to the works of Walt Whitman and had come to associate with a group of admirers of the poet and to ponder carefully the received view of the nature of human experience. Five years later, after an evening of poetry reading with some friends in England—an evening which included a good deal of Whitman as well as some Wordsworth, Shelley, Keats, and Browning—he had a curious experience. It was described later to the Royal Society of Canada in these terms: "All at once, without warning of any kind, he found himself wrapped around, as it were, by a flame-colored cloud. For an instant he thought of fire—some sudden conflagration in the great city. The next (instant) he knew that the light was within himself."[7] This mystical experience, one of the few ever de-

6   Richard Maurice Bucke, *Man's Moral Nature* (New York: G. P. Putnam & Sons, 1879).

7   Richard Maurice Bucke, *Cosmic Consciousness*, New Introduction by George Moreby

scribed to a body so stuffy as the Royal Society, effected an important transformation in him.

It did not set him on a religious career. No doubt men who have strange experiences tend to assimilate them as best they can to the age in which they live. A mediaeval man would have thought himself chosen for some special religious revelation. A contemporary man might set in train an analysis of his blood chemistry. For Bucke, this seemed a sign of evolutionary progress: He began to inquire as to whether or not such experiences were common, whether they were becoming more or less common, and what happened, in general, to those who had them. It seemed to him that he was likely facing a change in the structure of the organism and not simply a change in the relations between the organism and its environment. It should be admitted, however, that, though we might now look for an explanation in neuro-pharmacology or, at any rate, in some aspect of body chemistry, there is no evidence in Bucke's case or in the many cases he was later to cite in *Cosmic Consciousness*, of drug taking, of disease which might produce an important change in the body chemistry, or of any of the usual kinds of mental illness.

Bucke therefore set out to write *Man's Moral Nature* with two problems in mind: How do we explain the proclivity to behave well or badly? If we can explain that, is it likely that this proclivity has remained constant in the past and will remain constant in the future or is there in prospect a pattern of human evolution? We must remember that, in his growing psychiatric practice in the later 1870s, Bucke was hoping to bring about a change in public attitudes toward those who in certain respects fell short of public expectations for normal men. If immorality was *itself* a physical dysfunction, then behaviour which, to one degree or another, merely *resembled* immorality, could more readily be understood as something which entitled those who exhibited it to humane and responsible treatment.

It is impossible not to ask whether Bucke read Samuel Butler's *Erewhon*,[8] published seven years before *Man's Moral Nature*. Butler's tongue-in-cheek account of a society in which wickedness is treated and illness punished is, of course, only a half-spoof. Butler seriously believed in the dangers of the machines which he satirizes in the book and more than half-seriously believed that wickedness should be treated. It is only when we find that the Erewhonians punish illness that we find

Acklom (New York: E. P. Dutton, 1946). The quotation is taken from the new Introduction "The Man and the Book," the pages of which are not numbered.

8   Samuel Butler, *Erewhon, and Erewhon Revisited* (London: Paul Trubner, 1872; Dent, Everyman's Library, 1932). This book has been edited, revised, and published many times.

them silly—but silly as a mirror image of ourselves. Butler, too, believed in the evolution of consciousness. He does not figure, however, amongst those to whom the new illumination has been granted and his are not amongst the works cited in *Cosmic Consciousness*.

With this much background, we can turn to an examination of the argument in *Man's Moral Nature*—perhaps the only treatise on moral theory to be equipped with detailed diagrams of the sympathetic nervous system. Bucke begins his inquiry with some rather general assertions and disclaimers. A human being is a unity and, itself, a phase of a larger unity. Though we represent aspects of this unity to ourselves as "matter" and other aspects of it in quite different ways, we have no sanction for this. Matter is not the essential feature of reality; the distinction, rather, is between our inner awareness and the background against which that awareness takes place.

> Man himself . . . is divided, first, into structure and function—in other words, he is a static being and a dynamic being. Of this static being, however, we really have no knowledge, and its existence is open to the gravest doubt. . . . Did it exist it would correspond with what is called matter in the external world. . . . The first line of cleavage, then, in man, is that which may be drawn between his receptive and his reactive functions.[9]

It is not entirely clear how Bucke wants to conceptualize the "one great whole"[10] of which man is a part; but it is clear that he wants to insist that divisions within it are provisional and may be misleading and, later in his writings, he makes it clear that the unity which is reality has a significance which provides grounds for the grave doubt about the independent existence of matter.

Nonetheless, he wants to make distinctions which will open his immediate problems to potential solution. And he insists that there is a distinction between our intellectual and moral natures. Drawing on the logic of Mill, he urges that the reason for this is simply that one of them is capable of development without the other. The best intellects do not always go with the best moral natures. On the contrary, he says, women generally have better moral natures and worse intellectual natures than men. (Apparently, however, the understanding of the moral nature is a work of the intellectual nature. He does not urge that we should leave moral theory to women!)

More importantly, he claims that our moral natures are compounded out of certain basic emotions: love, hate, fear, and faith. They are capable of numerous combinations and they are also capable, at the

9   Bucke, *Man's Moral Nature*, p. 4.
10   Ibid., p. 3.

level of ideas, of forming still more complex compounds of varying degrees of stability. Though he admits to some doubt that his four "elements"[11] (which, in turn, form two natural pairs) constitute the whole of the table of moral elements, he does not think this doubt needs to be taken seriously. The independence of our moral natures is, therefore, given in another way: None of the elements, he says, are elements of our intellectual life and our intellectual life influences them only in the sense that compound ideas can be formed out of moral and intellectual elements. A man is properly said to have a good moral nature in so far as love and faith predominate over hate and fear. At any rate, Bucke habitually uses the expression "high moral nature" in a sense which implies this conclusion. He insists that "to have a high moral nature and to be a good man are not synonymous terms"[12] but he apparently means by this only that the common usage of the expression "good man" is confined to occasions when conduct is being approved.

> It will be remembered by all that many men with the highest moral natures have been put to death as bad men, the reason being that the adhesions and want of adhesions in their minds between moral states and concepts were such as current opinion could not tolerate. . . . Given two men with equally high moral natures, and it is plain he will be called the better man of the two in whom the intellectual and moral associations are most similar to those of his contemporaries.[13]

Statements about moral natures, then, whether "high" or "low" are to be understood as statements about the actual predominance of certain emotional states. Statements about "good" and "bad" *men*, however, are to be taken as statements about the conformity of conduct to standards generally held in a given community.

Good and bad *acts* and good and bad *consequences* are to be identified only after an analysis in which the components of the moral nature, the components of the intellectual nature, and the probable references to community standards of acceptance have been identified.

What we might hope for, Bucke thinks, is a world in which we might arrange for love and faith to predominate over hate and fear *and* a world in which our opinion that love and faith *ought* to predominate has a justification. The question really is: "Does the central fact of the universe, as it stands related to us, justify on our part fear and hate, or love and faith, or does it justify neither? I believe, and I believe I shall show before I finish this book, that it justifies love and faith."[14] This col-

11 Ibid., p. 20.
12 Ibid., p. 34.
13 Ibid., pp. 34-35.
14 Ibid., p. 40.

lection of doctrines is, of course, so complex and gives rise to so many difficult questions that it is tempting for the contemporary philosopher to write it off as a hopeless confusion. Bucke does, however, have something to say.

The only question which we can ask, according to Bucke, has to do with the relations between the moral nature and its natural objects. Love and faith are justified if what Bucke calls the central fact of the universe justifies them—if there is a suitable object for them. It is not that hate would be preferable to love if such a situation did not obtain. It is rather that the human condition would, in that case, be incomparably tragic. Our moral natures appear to us in the guise of a struggle between opposing elements because the opposites of love and faith have been necessary conditions, at times, for our survival and not because there is any doubt as to which we should prefer or which we should regard as "higher." That is an insight which is either justified or a source of human tragedy.

The problem is not, he constantly asserts, an intellectual one at all. The intellect is powerless against the moral nature whether higher or lower. Reason, here, reaches its own limit in seeing that the moral nature is something in itself and not a fiefdom of the intellect. Hence we are not to be given *reasons* for the preference.

It is here that Bucke presents to the moral philosopher his biggest surprise: He insists that there is a *physiological* difference between the intellect and the moral nature. The source of the materials upon which the intellect works is in the sensory apparatus and the cerebro-spinal system to which it is linked. The intellect generates concepts out of sensations and it makes use of a nervous system which has many close connections not just with the central nervous system which processes incoming data but with the motor system which dominates action. One of Bucke's arguments, indeed, against the practice of judging actions is that action is dominated by the intellect because of the connections between the motor system and the data processing function.

Much of what Bucke has to say about the sympathetic nervous system has survived as general doctrine in neurophysiology. (The interested reader may want to compare the appropriate sections of *Man's Moral Nature* with a standard work such as Brain's *Diseases of the Nervous System.*[15]) In general, the sympathetic system has no inputs from the outside. Its links are nearly all with our internal organs. It controls, substantially, the working of various glandular systems and monitors the production and distribution of the associated hormones.

15 Sir Walter Russell Brain, *Diseases of the Nervous System*, 7th ed., revised by the author and John N. Walton (London: Oxford University Press, 1969).

It is connected to a part of the brain, the hypothalmus which can be altered surgically so as to render monkeys and men tame and quiet. It *is*, therefore, connected with feelings of various kinds and with sexual functions and organs. Bucke wrote before many discoveries about the glandular system and long before the relevant discoveries about brains. But what has been discovered seems to bear him out,—most importantly, in the sense in which he is talking about our "moral nature"— that nature can be altered by making physical changes in us associated with the sympathetic nervous system.

It is harder to guess what uses he would or would not make of this information were he with us now. Would he be one of those who welcomed pre-frontal lobotomies—operations which have so often, it seems, dampened feelings of fear and hate and rendered difficult human beings tractable if somewhat damaged in character? Would he have welcomed all our findings in neuro-pharmacology and sought to improve our moral natures with drugs? Would he, indeed, like Butler's Erewhonians, actually *treat* immorality and, if so, how?

It is easy to get from the starting point—that the moral nature is distinct from the intellect—to the further point that, if that is so, we ought to expect that we could find a physiological path through which this distinction becomes manifest. It is much harder to decide what the moral implications of all this really are.

Is Bucke, then, the prototype of the psychiatrist of *A Clockwork Orange*?[16] Yes and no. Yes, if one means by that the proposition that our moral natures may well be distorted by our physiologies and that we would be better off doing something about what we can actually change than muttering dark imprecations at those whose moral natures seem to us unsatisfactory. No, if one means that all we need do is to discover what behaviour *society* approves and then proceed to reconstruct human beings to fit that description. Evidently, a great upsurge of love and faith *might* lead to much conduct of which society would clearly disapprove. One who achieves a high moral nature may, as Bucke points out, be crucified and is very likely, as a matter of fact, to run into substantial opposition. But there is no *necessary* connection between one's moral nature and one's behaviour. For action, on his theory, is conditioned by the intellect as well as by our moral natures.

Bucke does not put it so bluntly, but the text shows him clearly aware of what we might call the paradox of the insane: A person insane must first be taught to behave rationally but then, if he *is* rational, he will have great trouble with a world which is irrational. The

16 Anthony Burgess [John Anthony Burgess Wilson], *A Clockwork Orange* (London: Heinemann, 1962).

therapist faces the conundrum which stems from the need to make his patients more rational but not so rational that they cannot get along in the world as it is. There is, if Bucke is right, an even worse dilemma about the moral nature. One who is dominated by fear and hate (whose "adhesions," to use one of Bucke's favourite words, are to low moral states) will eventually require help. The help must take the form of generating, by physiological or psychological means, greater awareness of love and a more substantial capacity for faith. But if one becomes too clearly aware of love and too much given to faith, one may be in peril in the real world. One may be judged mad by one's fellows if one rises too far above or falls too far below the normal standard for a moral nature.

If Bucke were a consequentialist, if he calculated utilities as a feature of his moral system, he would have to hold that *both* extremes by way of a moral nature ought to be shunned. He is not a utilitarian and at least part of the reason is that he cannot bring himself to believe that a high moral nature ought to be shunned.

He claims that whether or not we should seek a "high" moral nature depends very much upon the facts of the case. While one cannot bring oneself—or Bucke cannot bring himself—to believe that an excess of love or fear should be regarded as worse than any other conceivable state, there arises the *intellectual* problem as to whether, rationally, we ought to pay any attention to the moral nature. This is a very evident human problem in most well-developed societies. For most such societies are characterized, in fact, by a conflict between moral expectations and rational prudence.

Bucke could see, indeed, that he would have to face the very question which, nearly a century later, Anthony Burgess was to confront us with in *A Clockwork Orange*—shall we remake men according to our own principles? One can only answer this question if one knows something about the state of the world. If the world is organized so that it is, ultimately, a suitable object of love and faith and not a suitable object of heat and fear then we are justified in freeing men from the burden of hate and fear by whatever means are consistent with our views of the surrounding moral questions. If we must conclude either that we have no means of knowing or that the world is not a suitable object for love and faith, then we shall have no such justification.

The patients Bucke was given in Hamilton and in London were, so far as we can tell, in pitiful condition. The society which locked them up and filled them with booze was largely concerned only that they should stay alive and out of sight. It is not surprising that Bucke had very little concern for the possibility that one might deprive human beings of something important by improving, as he thought, their "moral natures." But there is no suggestion that he proposed to undertake a wholesale reconstruction of human beings as he knew them.

He merely sought evidence for one proposition or another which would give some guidance as to how one might proceed. It was this hunt for evidence which led to the later chapters in *Man's Moral Nature* and led directly to the still popular *Cosmic Consciousness*.

The evolutionary model dominates Bucke's later work in *Cosmic Consciousness*; it also forms the central focus of the last third of *Man's Moral Nature*. We have already seen one of its functions: Bucke needs to explain why the moral nature of most men is what it is. So long as the world is fraught with peril, the ability to fear and hate is of great value. That being so, those whose moral natures are of a certain sort will have advantages. They will live longer, be more likely to attract those of the opposite sex and so have more children, and they will rise to dominant positions in society. The world in which we live, Bucke thought, tends to favour a moral nature which is between the possible extremes.

A very popular intellectual pastime, in Bucke's time, was the search for some clue as to the direction of human evolution. Bucke took up this activity not out of curiosity (his curiosity was most strongly aroused by problems in physiology and by the mystical experiences which he himself had) but because he urgently needed an answer to the questions which his moral theory posed. The most pressing issue was this: If the universe has an intelligible core, a "central fact" which would make love and faith genuinely acceptable, natural forces might, nonetheless, conceal that "central fact" from us because evolution, as we have seen, might tend to favour one moral nature over another. But, as civilization progressed and the premium on fear and hate was lowered, our moral natures ought to change. In a civilized society, fear and hate are less and less useful. Indeed, they may lead to the insane asylum. In those conditions. evolution would more likely favour a change in our moral natures—we ought to be seeing the development of a higher moral nature. Better information should come through to us about the real nature of the universe.

Bucke had a shrewd idea of the time span involved. He did not think that such evolutionary changes would appear in a single generation. Since human beings are fairly long-lived and must develop for fifteen to twenty years before it is likely that they will reproduce, a long time will be required for any change to show itself. Men are poor candidates, as well, for biological experimentation. It is because they do not relish the thought of themselves as subjects for experimentation. One man cannot usually perform a genetic experiment on another and live to see its ultimate outcome. Bucke therefore turned to history and began to search the records for any significant changes, especially in man's moral nature. He found, easily enough, what he was prepared to accept as the necessary evidence and much of the rest of his life was devoted to attempts to locate its significance.

He puts it this way:

> ... speaking generally, all the religions which have originated subsequently to Buddhism, and which have been held by the foremost races of men, such as the various forms of Christianity and Mahometanism, all differ from Buddhism and Zoroastrianism in these two essential particulars—first, that they declare the good power or principle in the government of the universe to be stronger than the evil power; and, secondly, that they represent the state beyond the grave to be, for the good man, more to be desired than feared. The meaning of this, of course, is that with advanced nations ... in the last two thousand years, the scale has turned, and faith is now in the human mind in excess of fear and consequently the ideas projected into the unknown world by man's moral nature, are, on the whole, a plus quantity instead of being, as with the lower races, a minus quantity or simply equal to zero.[17]

It is all very well to quote those long sentences, odd syntax and all. For they both present a case and expose a problem. The case is that in certain places (principally western Europe and the near eastern regions which are dominantly Moslem) men have changed in the last three thousand years. Their moral natures are different. The problem is that Bucke is compelled to speak of "advanced races"[18] and to make a wholly different kind of value judgment. Earlier, he had warned about a mistake which seems to have close affinities to the doctrine he now announces:

> It seems to me that the question: "Is the moral nature a fixed quantity?" has not been answered because it has not been properly asked. The usual form of the question is: "Is mankind becoming better?" or "Are men more or less moral now than they were formerly?"[19]

He complains that these questions usually lead to a search for *acts* and that the search is, in his terms, irrelevant. The question is not whether men have come to behave better but whether they have changed their moral natures. But when he speaks, in the passage we cited from a later part of the chapter, of "advanced races," what is he speaking of? What

17 Bucke, *Man's Moral Nature*, pp. 139-40.
18 Ibid., p. 140.
19 Ibid., p. 131.

372

are they "advanced" in? Perhaps their moral natures have shown improvement, but one could hardly know that in a general way without reference to the doings of the people concerned. Mostly, the "advanced races" turn out to be those associated with technological improvements or intellectual advances—British steam engines and Arab arithmetic.

In *Cosmic Consciousness*, the time scale has been extended a little so as to include Moses; Gautama the Buddha has been generally rehabilitated and allowed to be a recipient of the new consciousness. The horizon, in some respects, is broader. But African "bushmen" are likened to "idiots" and said to lack even the old "self-consciousness."[20] The classification, to say the least, is difficult. But that is a story which we shall develop later.

It is not absolutely clear just how Bucke views the evolutionary process. He seems to be a Darwinian and not a Lamarckian. Assuming he is a Darwinian, he has to hold that it simply happened that men were born whose genetic heritage strengthened some features of their moral natures or some features of their consciousness in general. These were better adapted in the long run to survival—i.e., on the whole, they prospered more, had more offspring like themselves, and generally became increasingly dominant. It turns out in his later writings that the improved, rather general, moral nature of the "advanced races" of *Man's Moral Nature* is not to be equated with the "cosmic consciousness" of men like Moses, Jesus, Paul, and Francis Bacon, who were special cases of a wholly new consciousness. The general advance alluded to in *Man's Moral Nature*, we must suppose, was largely an advance in the structure of the sympathetic nervous system combined with a general improvement in consciousness. It need not have been that complicated: Our moral nature might have remained the same while our general awareness improved so as to make more use of the moral nature's offering of faith and love and less use of its offering of hate and fear. But since he insists on a change in our moral natures, Bucke most probably intended the more complicated claim. (Without some change in consciousness, one must suppose, the general tendency to ignore much of the moral nature's "faith and love" output would likely have persisted.)

We have, therefore, a rather widespread genetic change and a resultant change in human attitudes. What is important according to the last chapter of *Man's Moral Nature* is the fact that this change in attitudes is justified because the universe turns out not to be a place so appropriate to fear and hate as we had thought. Had it been, those who

20 Bucke, *Cosmic Consciousness*. See pp. 46-47, including the footnote on p. 47, for a discussion of African bushmen.

underwent the new change would have been mutants destined for oblivion. Those who clung to their fear and hate would have prospered far better.

What Bucke wants to claim as the "central fact" of the universe should by now be quite obvious—vast logical leap though it may be: He wants to claim that the universe as a whole is a fitting object for love and faith.

He is not alone in this, of course. Augustine would have agreed. But Augustine's reason[21] for thinking that his case was sound depended upon his belief that he could give reasons which would satisfy the sceptic about the existence of God, our ultimate possible re-union with God, and about the fact that the causal connections in reality depend upon love rather than upon any other mechanism. McTaggart also thought that love was a suitable attitude to take in the present universe, but that is because he thought he could demonstrate by formal reasoning that reality consisted of timeless loving spirits.[22]

There is nothing unusual about Bucke's conclusion. What is unusual about his position is that the reason he thinks adequate is, apparently, that those who adopt a certain position about love and faith are likely to give rise to a society which can take its place amongst the "advanced races." Crudely, love and faith work.

Cosmic Consciousness is a very different kind of book. There are no diagrams of the sympathetic nervous system, no complicated discussions of physiology. The issue is plain and simple: What are we to make of the mystical experiences which had transformed his life as far back as 1867? We must infer that Bucke was to some degree suspicious of each experience—in just the way that anyone who had devoted his life to the practice of science might well be expected to be. It was only when he had satisfied himself that he could find a context for it that he was prepared to give it a major part in his theories about men and morals. The transformation from the subjective to the objective is, after all, one of the characteristics of science in general. It is the transformation which Russell called the replacement of names by descriptions.[23]

On this issue Bucke faced his most intractable problem. He did not doubt the significance of his own experience. If he doubted anything, it

---

21 See, e.g., *De Civitate Dei* 11, chapter 26, *Corpus Christianorum, Series Latina*, vol. 48 (Turnholti: Brepols, 1955), pp. 345-46.

22 John McTaggart Ellis McTaggart, *The Nature of Existence*, 2 vols., ed. C. D. Broad (Cambridge: University Press, 1921, 1927).

23 Russell's argument can be found in chapter 5, "Knowledge by Acquaintance and Knowledge by Description," in his book *The Problems of Philosophy* (London: Oxford University Press, 1970), specifically pp. 28-29.

was the place which such an experience ought to occupy in the *theory* of mind and nature.

But the replacement of "names" by "descriptions" is exactly that problem and the difficulty with mystical experiences is that they defy description. The Royal Society note spoke of being "wrapped around, as it were, by a flame-colored cloud," but that is not very helpful. Nor are phrases like "one momentary lightning-flash of the Brahmic Splendor."[24]

Bucke decided that a first step in scientific practice would be a search for like cases. His long list was eventually to include not only, as we have seen, Gautama the Buddha, Jesus, Paul, Plotinus, Mohammed, and St. John of the Cross, but perhaps less likely figures such as Francis Bacon, Dante, and Balzac. Moses is admitted as a more doubtful case, as are Socrates, Pascal, Pushkin, and Spinoza. Swedenborg might seem a more natural candidate for the list of clear cases than for the "lesser, imperfect and doubtful instances"[25] amongst which we find him. But Thoreau, Emerson, Roger Bacon, and Wordsworth, though they are men who had unusual experiences, may seem a little surprising even in the list of candidates of the second class.

Bucke gives us a reasonable list of the criteria which the candidates ought to meet. The "awakening" should be sudden, others should notice the "transfiguration," and there should be a strong, noticeable added "charm" to the personality. The "awakened" should claim a subjective "light," exhibit moral elevation, intellectual illumination, a sense of immortality, and a loss of the fear of death, and should, previously, have exhibited appropriate moral, intellectual, and physical characteristics. More surprisingly, they should exhibit a *loss* of the "sense of sin."[26]

The difficulty with this list is that, though reasonable, it is vague. Plotinus and Spinoza no doubt had in common a claim to the title "rational mystic"—they both thought that after a long period of vigorous and sustained intellectual activity one would reach a stage of more direct (or absolutely direct) knowledge. But Pascal and Francis Bacon seem scarcely to have much in common with each other, much less anything in common with Plotinus or Spinoza. Are any two men in history less alike than Spinoza and Jesus in their intellectual attitude, their sense of the order in the universe, their approach to the problem of conveying their enlightment to others? It is all well and good to say that they were both unusually good men who endeavoured, according

24 Bucke, *Cosmic Consciousness*. See New Introduction by George Moreby Acklom.
25 Ibid., p. 255.
26 Ibid., p. 74. See pp. 72-76.

to their different lights, to see the world and see it whole. If Jesus is on
the list of candidates certain to pass, Spinoza seems unlikely to meet
even the doubtful list.

Francis Bacon, admittedly, is there because Bucke thought he was
the author of Shakespeare's plays and sonnets. But the playwright
seems hardly to have been a saintly man or a man who would have had
much if anything in common with Moses on the one hand or Plotinus
on the other.

The lists are comprised of the names of men who claimed to have
insights into the nature of reality or, if they made no such claim, acted
or wrote as if they had such insights. Beyond this, they are all men
whose claims deserve to be taken seriously. But the reason for our
belief that we should take account of these men does not seem to have
anything to do with the content of their doctrines or the content of the
background belief which animated their actions. Spinoza may have
been a man whose life was more edifying than that of Leibniz (who does
not figure in Bucke's lists), but we would not, I think, appraise his
insight into reality differently had he lived Leibniz's life. Indeed, Leibniz surely has a claim to our attention which is every bit as strong as
Spinoza's. If the interesting issue was strength of claim on our attention, philosophers such as Thomas Aquinas, John the Scot, John Duns
Scotus, George Berkeley, and René Descartes would have to have a
place. And surely Plato belongs as much as, if not more than, Socrates.

We ought to remember that some people on the list—Francis
Bacon on the first and Spinoza on the second, for instance—made no
claim to anything much like a mystical experience. Bucke notes that
Bacon took up a secluded life of meditation for a time in 1590 and 1591
and that, perhaps, something dramatic had happened to him to make
him imitate in a modest way the flight of Jesus into the wilderness. But
that does not seem to be enough to convince us. Nor is there much solid
foundation in Shakespeare's life if we should prudently amend Bucke's
list by replacing Bacon with Shakespeare.

The detailed pursuit of all the cases would make an interesting
study in itself, but it is hardly germane to our purposes here. What *is*
germane, perhaps, is that those philosophers, writers, and miscellaneous thinkers who have set out to take a systematic view of the
universe have frequently, in the end, come to a certain sort of experience which might be described as something like Plotinus' rational
mysticism or Spinoza's third kind of knowledge. On the other hand,
those philosophers, writers, and miscellaneous thinkers who have persistently pursued an analytical tack and insisted that the world was not
to be seen "whole" in that sense have, frequently enough, found that
their experience remains in a mode which offers no suspicion of the

376

possibility of the kind of knowledge at issue. Bucke might, therefore, have claimed that a certain kind of validating experience is often available to those who search for it in certain ways.

Such a claim would have something to be said for it: We might seek a detailed account of the specific inquiries which led to the result and try to see whether those thinkers who have rejected the kind of knowledge claimed by Plotinus or Spinoza failed to carry out the necessary regimen. If they did, we might be able to take the inquiry further. If the thinking and other activities of philosophers like Hume turned out, on the other hand, too much like those undertaken by philosophers like Spinoza, we might want to abandon the quest.

Even this, however, would not get over the fact that we cannot move from subjectivity to objectivity very effectively because we cannot offer a sufficiently detailed description of the experiences in question. We can only *name* them as the transforming experience Bucke had in 1872 or whatever. It does not seem to do much good to list the characteristics—loss of fear of death, general sense of uplift and illumination, transformed moral character—because it is quite possible to meet all the conditions without ever having had the necessary experience and, so far as the historical data go, we cannot demonstrate that anything like all the men on the list had experiences in common.

In any case, Bucke specifically does *not* want to associate his case with the claims of men like Plotinus and Spinoza who seem to have regarded their insight as the outcome of a set of activities which were dominantly intellectual. Both speak of stages and steps and both find serious mysticism to be an outcome of the stages and steps.

Bucke wants to claim a sudden transforming experience which is the outcome of an evolutionary process in consciousness—technically, a mutation which has genetic consequences. (Though the word "genetic" was not invented at the time he was writing, the sense of a leap which has consequences for subsequent organisms of one's kind is clearly there.)

He is impressed by the fact that the characters in his cast have in common that they mostly attained to their insights sometime after the age of thirty and well before late middle age, a fact which suggests to him a biological development. He is also impressed by the fact that he can find more names for the list at later times than at earlier times. His result is thus compatible with some mode of genetic transmission. He admits that we may only think this is so because we have more information about later times than about earlier ones, but he thinks that will not wholly account for the proliferation of instances.

Oddly, however, he makes no attempt to link any successive names in a genealogical tree though, if he is right, there ought to be more likelihood of two men who were directly descended from one another exhibiting the same mode of consciousness than of two wholly un-related men sharing the same consciousness. We must remember that he was not aware—so far as we can tell— of Mendel's findings and therefore would not have known about dominant and recessive charac-teristics or of the probability tables of modern genetics. In any case, if modes of consciousness are inherited at all, the mechanism of in-heritance is probably multi-genetic and very complicated.

Bluntly, Bucke simply thought that the experience which he had in 1872 represented a biological development and sought to find others who had had similar experiences. Since the experience was not easily describable—even by a trained psychiatrist—he allowed himself rather a lot of latitude in his identifications though he honestly and scrupu-lously admitted his doubts about many cases.

We should admit that many people have held that evolution is "progressive," that the next stage in human development is probably the development of a new consciousness, and that mystical experiences are self-evidently important. Few people have held this belief about evolution together with this belief about mystical experiences, but putting the two together patches a bad tear in many people's lives. The tear is caused by the fact that they have a general faith in "science" and a general belief in the importance of essentially religious experiences. Bucke's patch makes it possible to hold these beliefs in common without embarrassment. The reasons for the continuing popularity of *Cosmic Consciousness* are, therefore, not far to seek.

The problem, however, is that both beliefs are rather vague. Bucke does very little, in the end, to make precise his belief in evolution. He would surely have welcomed the work of Bergson and Teilhard de Chardin had he lived into our century. But he would have taken seriously their critics (including Sir Peter Medawar) who have doubted that much sense can be made of these attempts to build a metaphysics out of the theory of evolution, modern genetic theory, and the details of developmental biology. But Bucke did not live to see the general understanding of Mendel's work, much less the more startling work of Crick and Watson, and he was really in no position to be much more precise about his biology. Who knows what speculations all these dis-coveries would have set in train in Bucke's mind? Faced with all these technicalities, he would certainly have coped, though he probably would have lost much of the general audience he still retains.

The position about mystical experiences remains much the same as it was in Bucke's time. If there *is* a major change in human con-sciousness afoot, Nature is taking her time about it.

Bucke's death in February 1902, as a result of a fall on the ice outside his house, deprived us of much which might have rendered his theory interesting. At the beginning of *Cosmic Consciousness*, he predicted two other major changes in human affairs. "They are: (1) The material, economic and social revolution which will depend upon and result from the establishment of aerial navigation. (2) The economic and social revolution which will abolish individual ownership and rid the earth at once of two immense evils—riches and poverty."[27] Of the first there is nothing to say except that it happened. Of the second, we would surely have liked to hear his social and political theories. For the rest, we can only say that he staked his moral theory on his metaphysics and his metaphysics on his account of the evolution of consciousness. The point of it all was to reconcile faith in science with the acceptance of religious experience of the sort which suggests that faith is justified and love is at the centre of reality.

William Lighthall illustrates, more clearly than any other Canadian philosopher, Northrop Frye's remark that: "The sense of probing into the distance, of fixing the eyes on the skyline, is something that Canadian sensibility has inherited from the *voyageurs*."[28] Most likely, Lighthall would have rejected the claim to mysticism which is implied by the title of this chapter, but there is little reason to deny it unless one supposes that the very word is derogatory. Others—from Lyall to Watson— attempted to frame metaphysical pictures which would include the whole of reality. But their portraits are cosy and woven from threads of human reason. Rupert Lodge, whose work extended two decades after Lighthall, also sought a schema which would be all-encompassing, but it turns our attention to the mundane. Lighthall wants a single vision in which reason leads to the importance of feeling and feeling reveals our kinship to the universe as a whole and to what he calls the Superperson. (The word, no doubt, sounded less bizarre to those who lived before Superman.)

As Frye implies, the sensibility of the voyageurs may seem natural enough in Canada and Lighthall can hardly be accused of doing much more than applying a way of organizing experience which ought to come naturally to those who wander over vast spaces and have a genuine need to speculate about the horizon: A sharp eye for detail, a knowledge of the way things fit together, and a capacity to extrapolate forward from what one sees in the foreground need to be supplemented by a strong feeling for what seems right and makes sense.

27 Ibid., p. 4.
28 Northrop Frye, *The Bush Garden: Essays on the Canadian Imagination* (Toronto: House of Anansi Press, 1971), p. 222.

Lighthall uses reason to open the possibilities of philosophical synthesis; but it is his feeling for what is right and makes sense which dictates the final form of his world picture.

From the beginning of his philosophical writings, Lighthall seems animated by a conviction that things are not what they seem to be. His early moral essays—beginning with "The Altruistic Act" in 1884[29]—exhibit a strong sense that the casual observer of human nature is apt to get things wrong and the philosopher is apt to erect clever theories around casual observations which merely serve to conceal the truth from us. Mill is right, he thinks, in observing that men do seek pleasure and that it is good to do so; but this conceals from us the fact that they do not necessarily seek their own pleasures or even a well distributed set of pleasures like their own. Rather, their attention frequently moves from the field of self to what he calls the "world-field," and "when a man recalls . . . the happiness of all society . . . he experiences a feeling of vastly finer quality and greater satisfaction than when he turns his thoughts upon himself."[30] A year later in an expanded essay now entitled "An Analysis of the Altruistic Act in Illustration of a General Outline of Ethics,"[31] he speculated that there may be a "deeper self" which connects us all and which can perhaps explain why the contemplation of our own pleasures is different in kind from the contemplation of the larger good. Similarly, Kant is right, he thinks, in connecting reason, generality, and duty, but this obvious truth, buttressed by a theory, also tends to obscure what is really at issue. Kant's theory, Lighthall complains, is lacking in a sufficient "analysis of the motive."[32] Reason, he complains, is "always a Hypothetical, never a Categorical, Imperative."[33] We must know what is the case in order to have a motive adequate for action. Moral action must take us out of ourselves and Kant's theory does *that*, but in reality, "reason in 'giving a maxim,' is simply placing before us an *object—a thing*."[34] Thus both Mill and Kant make us think that we need simply generalize from our surface consciousness, and both theories are false.

29 W. Douw Lighthall, "The Altruistic Act" (Montreal: "Witness" Printing House, 1884). The title page of this essay reads: "The Altruistic Act" by Alchemist, Montreal. The pamphlet was identified as Lighthall's and loaned to us by his daughter, Alice M. Schuyler-Lighthall.
30 Ibid., p. 9.
31 W. Douw Lighthall, "An Analysis of the Altruistic Act in Illustration of a General Outline of Ethics" (Montreal: "Witness" Printing House, 1885), p. 16.
32 Ibid.
33 Ibid.
34 Ibid.

In these earliest essays and the slightly later "New Utilitarianism,"[35] Lighthall is feeling his way. In the end, his complaints about Mill and Kant amount to this: They see the human person as the self which figures as an individual in the world and the self of immediate experience. But this does not explain why it is that something urges men to martyrdom.[36] Or, more simply, why it is that even for Mill we need to be concerned with the happiness of "the greatest number," or why we should follow the dicta of the Kantian reason and seek to universalize our maxims.

Lighthall does not always make his moral point perfectly clear, but it seems quite certain that what bothers him is not that we should have reasons for being altruistic or for universalizing our moral claims, but that we should at once grasp that it is right to accept those reasons. The altruistic claim, he says, and repeats in all his writings down to the final version of *The Person of Evolution*,[37] is always based on a kind of intuition. But he will not accept Moore's claim that all we have to go on is moral intuition. He does not directly deal with Moore's doctrine that the reason we are left with intuition is, at bottom a logical one—that any attempt to provide a foundation for it in terms of something else would commit the "naturalistic fallacy" and result in goodness being defined in terms of something else. He does, however, accuse Moore of confessing an "inability to analyze the basis of value-judgments."[38]

The repeated emphasis on altruism as the crucial problem in ethics suggests Lighthall's position on morality. Morality consists in the transcendence of the individual viewpoint and in the acceptance of the proposition that the only acceptable motive for such a transcendence would be provided by knowledge of the fact that our surface individuality is only a feature of a larger personality. Thus he claims that Moore would not have been troubled by the problems which animate *Principia Ethica* but for the fact that he was "skimming about on the surface of an individual consciousness . . . for solutions of a matter the roots of which lie beyond the surface."[39]

While this does explain the motive which lies behind Lighthall's move from ethics to metaphysics, it does not seem to offer an answer to Moore's complaint about the naturalistic fallacy. Plainly, Moore would

35 W. Douw Lighthall, "Sketch of a New Utilitarianism" (Montreal: "Witness" Printing House, 1887).
36 Ibid. Reference to "martyrdom" on p. 37.
37 See footnote 5. The book from which the authors have quoted is one of ten copies issued privately in Montreal, 1930, printed in Toronto (Warwick Bros. & Rutter) and loaned to the authors by Lighthall's daughter, Alice M. Schuyler-Lighthall.
38 Ibid., p. 108.
39 Ibid.

have said that it does not matter what consciousness one is skimming about on, the question is about the definition of goodness. However interesting and extensive a given consciousness might be, Moore would say, we can still ask "Is it good?"

Whether or not Lighthall has available any response to this depends upon whether or not he can develop, within his metaphysical system, a context within which questions about value can be asked. Moore usually supposes that at least some value statements—those which seem to him interesting—are intelligible on their face and suppose no particular context for their understanding. For Moore, the question: In what kinds of world can one raise questions about value? seems only marginally interesting. One must suppose that, for Lighthall, it is of crucial importance. For what Lighthall does is to embed his moral theory in a metaphysical theory and then claim that this theory renders it intelligible and provides evidence for its soundness. It seems unfortunate that Lighthall should have chosen to discuss Moore and yet omit serious discussion of the doctrines for which Moore was best known. It seems barely possible that Lighthall was not familiar with *Principia Ethica* or that he simply did not understand Moore's point, but more likely, he supposed that the reader would discern an answer to Moore in the structure of *The Person of Evolution*. It is, in any event, to that book that we must turn.

The Person of Evolution is evidently the culmination of Lighthall's philosophical work, published first privately in 1930 and then by Macmillan three years later. Parts of the work had been published in 1926 as "The Outer Consciousness,"[40] while some other portions had appeared over the previous thirty years as papers in *The Philosophical Review*. Essentially, it sets out to give additional reasons for thinking that all of us are features (in a sense) of a large person or "Superpersonality"[41] who is responsible for the development of a whole and in whose affairs the meaning is to be found. It purports to render comprehensible some real or alleged problems about the biological theory of evolution as well as to make sense of a range of claims about human beings which arise from our moral, social, and religious life.

It is best, since we have already dealt at length with the theories of Schurman and Bucke, to begin with an account of the ways in which Lighthall differs from both of them. Schurman's procedure was to try to understand biological evolution within the context of a metaphysical system, essentially idealist in kind, which would give us reason to think

40 W. Douw Lighthall, "The Outer Consciousness," published privately in Montreal, 1926. See Preface to *The Person of Evolution*, p. 13.
41 Lighthall, *The Person of Evolution*, p. 15.

that, whatever reality is like, it *must* take a form which exhibits itself in time even though, in some sense, it transcends time. The theory of evolution, then, does not necessarily interfere with the logical priority of mind or the moral stature of man. Rather, it explains the order in which development makes possible knowledge of reality. The world described by the biologist, on this view, like the world described by the physicist, is simply an aspect of reality and one which is rather misleading if taken in isolation.

Bucke sought to find out where evolution was leading us and seemed prepared to accept the biological picture of the world as primary for our present consciousness. Even moral values turned out to have, if not a biological basis, at least strong connections to our physiological structures. He did not see how we could reason ourselves into a new understanding. Reason reveals its own limitations and turns out, as we can use it, to be closely tied to our physiological structures. It can inform consciousness, but it cannot, in Bucke's view, transcend it.

Lighthall's approach to the problem—at least in the development of his thought—begins by seeming to have affinities to Schurman. Like Schurman, his first point of attack is in moral theory and, like Schurman, he thinks our picture of the world has to be tailored to fit our moral knowledge. But where Schurman's critique of values as of metaphysics is, in important ways, rationalist, Lighthall bases his claims upon experience. We know that men are impelled toward altruistic acts—even philosophical theories like those of Mill and Kant have to be formulated in such a way as to make sense of the fact that, however we may behave, we generally disapprove of selfishness, and simple psychological hedonism is repugnant to mature reflection. Lighthall is, therefore, close to Bucke in his insistence on the primacy of experience.

Unlike Bucke, he does not seek special experiences or claim that a new consciousness is gradually appearing. His claim more nearly is that we all have, below the immediate surface of consciousness, a strong sense of our unity with other persons and of our ultimate unity with reality.

He thinks this can be explained if it is assumed that evolution is working in a certain direction. If we take it that evolution proceeds to develop the possibilities in the underlying reality by a process of differentiation, we can understand how it is that we are at once keenly aware of our individuality and of our unity with reality. If we accept the proposition that this differentiation makes possible a new and more satisfactory unity, we can then see the meaning of the direction.

He likens us to the leaves of a tree. It is true that a tree is a fragmented entity in a way that a unicellular creature is not. But it is

also true that a tree forms a kind of unity which the unicellular creatures lacks. The tree, as a unity, can modify significant parts of the
environment, can hold together many disparate kinds of activity, and
can aim at complex goals.

Similarly, we seem to be differentiated from each other. Yet this
differentiation itself makes possible a range of activities which no
individual could finally perform. ". . . as we are an unfolding of the
Tree, so all that is in us helps to explain the Tree and is all packed into
the earliest seed of terrestrial life. Our Tree of origin is the life of the
outer universe."[42]

It is no doubt true that evolution does develop through a process
which leads to differentiation and that the path is one of increasing
complexity and individuality. It is also true that there is a certain unity
to this process—at least whatever unity it is that makes it possible to say
that evolutionary theory links all life forms to a single process. Lighthall
is generalizing from these facts, however, in a way which is slippery,
and he is at least partially aware of the difficulties he faces.

One chapter of *The Person of Evolution* is devoted to a critical
analysis of L. T. Hobhouse—the widely influential author of a theory
which is overall much more cautious and modest than Lighthall's,
though the two are certainly relatives of one another. Hobhouse had
rejected the more dramatic attempts to make metaphysics out of
evolutionary theories on the ground that the evolutionary process has
too much randomness, too many twists and turns, and conforms most
readily over much of its course to the notion of random change of
genetic material combined with natural selection by the environment.[43]
He thought, however, that there were special and interesting problems
connected with the evolution of mind. The development of mind tends
to give the process a firmer direction. As conscious mind begins to take
over from instinct, the range of forms which can be adapted to a given
environment tends to expand. Furthermore, as he conducted his researches, Hobhouse began to think that mind goes very far into the
development of life—back to its original "germ."[44] By the time Lighthall wrote the 1915 edition of *Mind in Evolution*, Hobhouse had read
the work of H. S. Jennings[45] and remarked:

42   Ibid., p. 146.
43   Leonard Trelawney Hobhouse, *Mind in Evolution*, two editions (London: Macmil-
     lan, 1901, 1915).
44   Lighthall, *The Person of Evolution*, p. 175.
45   H. S. Jennings, 1868-1947, was a major American zoologist and one of the first
     scientists to be subsidized by the Carnegie Institution of Washington. His major
     books were on the behaviour of lower organisms, and genetics and evolutionary
     theory. Most widely read was *The Biological Basis of Human Nature* (New York: W. W.

His results, together with other work in general psychology, have led me however to extend rather than to narrow the view taken in the first edition, and even to raise the question whether Mind, in the infinitely varied forms of its activity, from the groping of unconscious effort, to the full clearness of conscious purpose) [sic] *may not be the essential driving force in all evolutionary change.* [46]

Even in this expansive mood, however, Hobhouse was fairly cautious. He did not think that the analysis of sociological laws revealed any *"superhuman monster,* but only human beings,"[47] even though it is true that the fact that consciousness leads to the possibility of genuine co-operation makes for a kind of unity not possible on the lower rungs of the evolutionary ladder. This new unity does not, so far as Hobhouse could see, transcend the individuals concerned, though it may surely change them by changing their relations to one another.

Lighthall finds Hobhouse much too mundane. The cautious Hobhouse, he says, propounds a theory which "hangs in the air."[48] He means by this that Hobhouse does not explain how it is that minds come to be purposive and how it is that the universe gets to be in that state which produces minds at all. Hobhouse thinks that mind may always have been latent in the possibilities of the world (hence his remark that mind may be the "essential driving force") and, if that is a possible position, it is one which, despite Lighthall, does not need explanation. Things in the ordinary sense cannot come to be possible or impossible.

Furthermore, Hobhouse's "monster" is a close relative of Lighthall's "Superperson" and the choice of language simply indicates a difference in appraisal. It is probably pointless to follow this debate through all its possible details. Indeed, Lighthall's account of the matter is singularly lacking in detail itself and the reader is left with the impression that, for him, the real issue is still the explanation of certain kinds of moral experience. If the debate over how one should "read" evolutionary theory were to be given form, sense would have to be made of the notion of direction in biological development. We would also have to decide whether or not the apparent unity of the evolutionary process is simply an heuristic principle—we get the tidiest theory and the best frame for *comparing* data by assuming that there is one process and one set of principles rather than many—or whether we

Norton, 1930). An experimentalist, his work was systematic and descriptive, and he made contributions to problems of physiology and adaptation, variation and reproduction, and genetics.

46 Quoted in Lighthall, *The Person of Evolution*, p. 179.
47 Ibid., p. 181.
48 Ibid., p. 184.

have enough information to be sure that there is a single process. But there is no sign that Lighthall really wanted to tackle these questions.

We are forced back, therefore, to the moral argument. This argument is begun by the second chapter of the book and developed (somewhat sporadically) up to the seventh chapter. It is repeatedly urged that however much we may wriggle on the hook, we all know that altruism is good. "Altruism, even in its most clearly reasoned forms, always retains at least a part of its instinctive basis: for it is always Outer Conscious in its *point of view*."[49] Lighthall thinks this to be an advantage, for we have no control over instinct. We could not have invented altruism, it must be built into us. If it is built into us, it has a factual basis. And what could that factual basis be but the fact that we are all parts of a larger and more real entity?

It is difficult to be sure what Lighthall wants to say or what he would say if he were challenged directly by someone like G. E. Moore. The difficulty is created by the fact that he relies heavily on what makes sense to him—on the voyageur's eye on the horizon—and he appeals to the reader to take a long and appraising look at his own experience. Lighthall's general conviction is that, once we have seen his schema for ordering reality, we shall be able to use it on our own experience and we shall find that it makes sense.

Fairness demands that we make some attempt to estimate his likely responses to criticisms of which we suppose he was aware. To Moore he might very well have said something like this: The prior question is, after all, why do we take moral discourse seriously? In what circumstances could it be the case that moral questions are pressing? They could not be pressing in a world in which we had no choices to make nor in a world in which the conflict between altruism and naked self-interest could not arise. (Other value questions might be pressing in such circumstances but not, if what Lighthall insists upon is right, moral questions.) We would not have failed in our duty to anyone in such a world. Now one might make a case for the proposition that a world which contained either one and only one conscious and free being or several such beings who stood in no inter-personal relations with one another could not give rise to moral questions. (Altruism and self-interest are the same in the first world, and in the second—suppose it to be a world in which each person inhabited a planet of his own and could not communicate in any way with any of the others—it is difficult to conceive of a genuinely altruistic act.) The problem, therefore, arises only in worlds like ours where there are inter-related beings whose relations are of a certain special sort. If we are quite independent of one

49   Ibid., p. 111.

another, there may be genuine clashes between self-interest and altruism, for the notion of independence implies at least the possibility of
competing interests each of which is independently valid. If we are not
independent of one another then, depending upon the degree of
interdependence, there will be more or less of a case for supposing the
superiority of altruism.

Lighthall's intuitions supply him with the belief that altruism is
generally preferable, indeed with the notion that morality derives from
the transcendence of self-interest. This implies that our intuitions
suggest strongly a high degree of interdependence.

The interdependence, he argues explicitly, cannot be explained by
such notions as the general equality of human beings—for human
beings are not all equal "in this life."[50] Nor, in general, will any of the
facts about individual human beings and their social relations suffice.
The only explanation that there can be is that we are all facets, in some
sense, of *one* person.

The function of the biological arguments is this: They rebut objections to the moral arguments. Objections to them must take the form
of claims that our intuitions (or Lighthall's) are wrong or misleading.
To accept them, we would need a reason to think we could conceive of
ourselves clearly as distinct individuals with distinct interests. But
evolution shows generally—in Lighthall's view—both the unity of life
and the unity of its purpose. We do not, at any rate, find any strong
counter-evidence in our study of the natural world for, if evolution is a
unity, it must form another kind of unity with the physical universe
which makes it possible. All our studies of bio-chemistry show that this
is so.

We cannot, therefore, find reasons to doubt the intuition about
altruism and we are compelled to accept it or, if not, to condemn
ourselves to a life in which what we do constantly feels wrong to us.
Suppose a follower of Moore asks: Is acting so as to create a unified
view of the world in which the Superperson stands out clearly "really
good"? Lighthall has an answer: If it isn't really good it is because there
are real interests which attach to genuinely independent individuals.
Altruism is as certainly good in his world as self-interest is good in a
world in which there is only one individual. Moore's problems have
force, perhaps, only in worlds which are more complex than those with
a single agent or those with an over-arching Superperson.

Like Moore, we may not think we live in Lighthall's world but that
world is not without its instructive features.

50 Ibid., p. 112.

ELEVEN

REASON, REGIONALISM, AND SOCIAL POLICY

Wilfred Currier Keirstead, John Macdonald, and Herbert Leslie Stewart

IDEALISM IN CENTRAL Canada remained, in its academic dress, very much the idealism of Watson and Blewett. Its central problem, even when the authors were writing directly about politics and morals, remained the problem of informing religion with reason. From the relative prosperity and security of central Canada, a thoughtful man might still make salvation his central concern.

But as the doctrine took root in the Maritimes and in the prairie west, the emphasis tended, as one might suspect, to shift. Indeed, where Watson's federation of the world is a kind of heaven on earth as it might have been envisaged by a United Church theologian, Keirstead's criticisms of the social order are pointed, directed at particular and limited issues, and conveyed in something less than Watson's magisterial tones of certainty. Where Blewett worries about the perfection of the human soul, Macdonald, evidently, is more concerned with establishing a democratic social order out of the ranks of frequently embittered farmers and businessmen, and with establishing a practical school system capable of sustaining the openness demanded of a democratic society and, at the same time, inculcating the values necessary to maintain a working social order.

The Maritimes have had periods of great prosperity but they have suffered since their settlement from political manipulation by outsiders, from the economic uncertainties which beset producers of raw materials who must compete in world markets, and from a climate and a geological heritage which places severe limits on agriculture. In the end, one could say much the same of the prairie west. The promise of endless prosperity in the wheatlands ended in the dust-bowl of the thirties. The oil of Alberta and the potash of Saskatchewan did not become significant counter-balances until after World War II. Even when crops were good, prairie farmers were tied to a world price which fell just *because* crops were good. Yet the price of farm machinery made in Ontario rose if the crop was good and farmers needed more machines to harvest it.

Whether one lived at one end of the country by catching codfish and growing apples or at the other by raising wheat and cattle, the economic order did not seem to exhibit great rationality and the political order was not much better. Alberta was a favourite stamping ground for political magicians with new rabbits in old hats. The Maritimes, tied much more closely to a very old social order, were, for the most part, merely treated to the most traditional kinds of political incompetence and petty corruption.

A philosopher in this century was not likely to react to such situations as William Lyall had. For Lyall, Halifax was something of a refuge to which a man might withdraw without too much concern about the immediate and pressing. There were real enough problems but, given the time, Lyall was a long way from most of them: The bitter adventures of the Acadians must have been remote from him in space and time. A very small population hardly overtaxed what good farmland there was. The hardships of fishermen were in no sense unusual. Halifax itself was a prosperous port and a garrison town supported in large measure from outside for purposes associated with political ambitions. (Relations between the populations of Maritime Canada and the northern New England region of the United States had always been and continue to be close and the settlement of United Empire Loyalists in Maritime Canada only strengthened that tie.)

Eventually, however, outside powers lost some of their interest and the region was left increasingly to its own devices. From time to time the larger political machines which developed in central Canada had to depend on the Maritime vote to provide a working majority in the House of Commons. But mostly the Maritimes were increasingly regarded as picturesque places in which interesting specimens of Celtic culture were preserved for the benefit of tourists. Halifax remained a port and naval centre, valued along with St. John for its harbour, cursed for its climate, hated by sailors for its tight-fisted ways. But that changed as the role of the Canadian navy came to be viewed more and more narrowly and the opening of the St. Lawrence as an all-year waterway diminished interest in the Maritime harbours.

It is not easy to compose a simple picture of life and society in New Brunswick as Wilfred Keirstead must have experienced them. He was born in a period of relative prosperity, four years after Confederation, attended rural schools, and finally made his way to a provincial normal school. From there, he worked his way through the University of New Brunswick by preaching in Baptist churches and finally received his bachelor's degree at the age of twenty-seven. Those facts speak of a kind of hardship which has been common in the lives of scholars—

particularly in the lives of those scholars who choose fields like philosophy and classics. The fact that the University of New Brunswick, though long established, had only about 150 students is also evidence that education must have been beyond the reach of most young men. It was not only money which kept them from the university. The poor quality of rural education guaranteed that only those who were willing to undergo the arduous process of filling in the gaps in their schooling or could afford private schools were likely to prosper at any institution of higher education. Fundamentally, the social process did not exhibit the kind of rationality which a young man moved by Hegel might hope to introduce. The differences in prosperity and outlook which later would distinguish most of Maritime Canada from central Canada and from the more prosperous Great Lakes region of the United States were not, in Keirstead's youth, marked as they would be later, but there were enough problems to raise serious questions in his mind.

To begin with, we find Keirstead devoting his master's thesis at the University of New Brunswick to problems of the inner life—specifically to "The Light which Self Consciousness sheds upon the Existence of God."[1] If the social order does not reveal that rationality is consistent with divinity, if nature is hard and usually unsympathetic, one must look to another address for one's answer. But the only other address seems to be the inner life.

Later Keirstead was to devote his mind mainly to social problems—the nature of democracy, the bases of social theory, the fundamental terms of human relations—but his first sustained work had to do with evidences for the existence of God and their relation to human consciousness. One must bear in mind that he was twenty-eight years old when he submitted his thesis on this topic—in no sense a callow youth.

The message is conveyed, not so much through the specific arguments with which the paper is filled, but through the shape which Keirstead gave to his topic. Clearly no friend of Tertullian or Kierkegaard, Keirstead firmly believed that, wherever real evidence of the existence of God might be found, that evidence would have to be accompanied by a perfection which included, even if it transcended, rational order. Were it otherwise, we should not be able to claim "evidence" but only conviction. We have to cope with the fact that all knowledge is knowledge which someone has—and therefore condi-

---

1 Wilfred C. Keirstead, "The Light which Self Consciousness Sheds upon the Existence of God," Master's thesis, University of New Brunswick, Fredericton, Harriet Irving Library, Acc. No. 7016, 1899.

tioned by the individuality of its possessor—as well as with the fact that coming to know is a process. It therefore changes inevitably and is relative to some time span or, as Keirstead puts it, subject to evolution.

The states of affairs which we call knowledge are subject to reservations which may make for scepticism. Knowledge itself, along with the rest of the world, Keirstead thinks, is involved in a process of evolution. One of the lessons which he seems to have derived from his traffic with evolutionary theory is that the objects of knowledge can only be understood over a span of time which reveals the nature and direction of the process they are involved in. But this means that ordinary objects of ostensible knowledge—things and states of affairs in the material world, for instance—are flawed. We do not know them except in terms of their present and in terms of their inferred past. (A being who lived before there were mammals could not have foretold the possibility that the earliest protoplasms would develop into tigers.) The possible objects of knowledge include not only the material and the biological orders but the social order as well and, at the end of his thesis, Keirstead introduces, briefly, a discussion of the development of "civilized"[2] man. Even then the fact of evolutionary development serves to limit our claims to knowledge.

The standard for knowledge, therefore, is one of intelligibility: What is at issue is whether given the experience we have, we can, in the end, make sense of it. He concludes that it is the intelligible which must be claimed as real. To deny this claim is to insist that what is real may not be susceptible to the kind of description which can be formulated in intelligible discourse. Logically, the difficulty with such an insistence is that it conflicts, in the nature of the case, with the very thing it is trying to insist upon.

Much of the thesis is devoted to claims about the consequences of theories which are, in Keirstead's words, "suicidal." Materialism, for instance, seems to him self-destructive because its assertion involves the denial of the possibility that intelligible theories can be formulated. If materialism were true the expression of the theories must be no more than matter in motion. Even if rational intelligibility were to entail the occurrence of matter in motion, it could not be reduced to such motion. If materialism were true, no theory could be known to be true—at any rate within the scope of what Keirstead is prepared to concede as knowledge.

Keirstead, however, wants to take the argument one step further: to argue that in the rational order which consciousness is able to supply there lies, in fact, the ultimate reality. Basically, the argument becomes

2   Ibid., p. 62.

more Platonic than Hegelian. The real turns out to be whatever it is which *could* be an adequate object of knowledge. Such an object will have to have in it an element of objectified reason and will have to have, as well, a decision maker—someone for whom intelligibility exists. So long as there is a gap between knower and known, he argues, the necessary unity required to support a significant claim to knowledge will be lacking. In so far as the object is indifferent to or alien to the knower, there is a feature of it which cannot be known and so there is a feature of what can be known—the relation of what is known to what is unknown—which remains dubious. If there were real objects which exhibited the property of unknowability, then reality itself would have the property of being closed to systematic reason. But that could only be true in so far as it, itself, lacked the properties necessary for a logically coherent description. Such a supposed reality would meet the ordinary conditions for impossibility.

The world, therefore, is to be divided. There is a reality which consists of the idealized forms of human consciousness or the divine forms of ideality. (They seem to come to the same thing in Keirstead's mind, for on the cover of his thesis he quoted Genesis 1:27: "So God created man in his own image. In the image of God created he him."[3]) There are then approximations to that order—immediate human consciousness, the social order, the biological order, the material order. The finally real is very close to a Platonic form and the distinction between the real and the apparent is more the Platonic one of order and chaos than the dialectical one of complementary form and content. (It is at least interesting to notice that this pattern was probably not rare. A generation after Keirstead, a Platonized Hegelianism is to be found in the writings of George Grant.)

When Keirstead turns to morality and the social order at the end of his thesis there is little doubt about what really interests him most. What he is seeking to do is to reconcile, as Kant had tried to do before him, the goodness of divine providence with the badness of a social order which he found all around him.

What he wanted was to understand the social order in a way which would enable him to accept it and, at the same time, to have at hand a strategy for social reform. Virtually the whole of his later philosophizing has to do with that strategy. If reality is accessible to human beings but has not been reached effectively, one must expect that, even if men are doing the best they know, they will achieve a social order which is less than optimal. In that case, one need not despise them. One may approach them with compassion and also with hope. Education and the

3   Ibid., p. 1.

development of moral understanding will be the best and clearest hope.

Most likely these considerations led Keirstead from New Brunswick to Chicago. John Dewey had gone to Chicago in 1894 and, by 1899 when Keirstead finished his work for the master's degree, was already making his name. Dewey and Keirstead had rather a lot in common and, though Keirstead would not have called himself a devotee of Dewey's instrumentalism, the years of study under Dewey had an impact which proved permanent. Both of them had been devoted to a form of Hegelianism; both came from rural backgrounds in what, to an important extent, is the same region. For the most part, the differences between American and Canadian culture are strongest in the region in which central Canada meets the American mid-west and weakest along the Pacific Coast. The extent to which Maritime Canada is like the New England region of the United States is great enough so that it is fair to say the two regions, though culturally different in important respects, have more in common with each other than either has with its own nationally affiliated regions on the Pacific Coast. More importantly, both Dewey and Keirstead had been raised in a philosophical tradition in which the connections between philosophy and religion were very strong, and each of them was trying to make philosophy more immediately responsive to social problems whose basis was secular. Finally, each of them had already set out in search of a way of formulating the problems of truth and knowledge which would relate both truth and knowledge to the inner states of the individual.

Dewey, therefore, was one of the sources of the pattern which Keirstead's thought was to take. Far more than Dewey, however, he retained the conviction that the basic insights of Protestant Christianity were sound and far more than Dewey he retained his original conviction that our inner life could be a source of standards which, if they were not absolute, were at least very unlikely to be modified by any earthly experiences which might come our way. Clifford Williams,[4] whose master's thesis is the only extended study of any of Keirstead's work, found that, in an examination which centred on political and social topics, it was unreasonable to say that Keirstead remained finally committed to any metaphysical position. An examination of Keirstead's published writings does not show any sign that he deviated to any important extent from the position of his own master's thesis and does seem to indicate that he believed that he could produce an ulti-

---

4 We are deeply indebted to Clifford Williams whose thorough research into early Canadian philosophers made our task much easier. He kindly provided us with his notes and theses of graduate work done at the University of Toronto.

mate justification for ethical and political positions which are frequently stated without much backing.

Keirstead was interested in metaphysical theories even though he himself shied away from them. His Doctor of Divinity, earned at Chicago, was awarded after he wrote a thesis called "The Metaphysical Presuppositions of Ritschl." He left those concerns behind when he returned promptly to the University of New Brunswick, although he reportedly turned down an academic post in Chicago. At home the conditions of his life were to dictate a certain pattern to his thought. There he had to teach all the major branches of philosophy and to tackle economics, psychology, and sociology as well. Accordingly, he sought to find links between them and he became known to the general public of the province as a social scientist more than as a philosopher.

During World War I he served as provincial administrator of the Federal Food Board and later chaired a commission on mothers' allowances and also a commission on minimum wages. His writings included papers on the theory of taxation, on succession duties in Canada, on rural taxation in New Brunswick, on education, and on the justification of provincial subsidies. These writings in applied economic theory or descriptive political science frequently draw upon his growing fund of political principles and relate to his overall political philosophy. It is from them and from a brief essay or two on the nature of democratic theory that his political thought must be reconstructed.

Most immediately, the whole bent of his own thought and the whole bent of the lessons he learned from Dewey set him against the kind of philosophical economics which he thought he found in the writings of Adam Smith. It seemed to him unlikely that there were any inexorable or even invariant laws of economics. As the social order changed, he supposed, so would the laws which applied to it. Secondly, he was unable to see that there was any intrinsic merit in competition. Competition rather than co-operation would surely be felt, and lead to the warping of human beings. For him, men are not, in any final sense, competitors at all. Each of us, after all, is created in the image of God and may be thought of as having an ideal and ultimately real nature in which that image becomes our dominant reality. If that is so none of us finally can attain more than any other and all of us together represent the divine reality.

Keirstead took seriously the possibility that taxation might be used as a device for bringing about something more closely approximating genuine economic reality than anything hitherto achieved. He did not think that our central concerns ought to be with providing incentives. Indeed, he thought that existing riches frequently far outweighed anything which sound social possibility could possibly endorse. Those who believe that economic incentives help to ensure a more abundant production from which all might prosper frequently fail, he thought, to notice the bad social and psychological effects of competition on those who take part in such authorized struggles.

Similarly, his emphasis on the relation of truth and knowledge to our idealized inner states undoubtedly influenced the account he was inclined to give of democratic political theory. Commonly, democratic theory—at least in its eighteenth- and nineteenth-century forms—has concentrated on the formal mechanics of political relationships. It has directed itself to questions about who may vote, how votes may be freed from organized pressure, how elected officials should be made continuously responsive to the popular will, and so on. Keirstead sees the essence of democracy in something quite different—essentially in the process of discussion. A real democracy, he thought, would be one in which decisions had to be discussed in a way which involved all its participants. The best approximation to such an ideal is probably, in ordinary and realistic terms, a society in which freedom of discussion is ensured, in which the participants are sufficiently well educated to understand the ideas crucial to the necessary decisions, and in which facilities exist which will foster such decisions.

But Keirstead found that modern devices of mass communication were used, not to promote discussion (much less to provide effective forums for discussion), but for whatever ends their owners or controllers happened to have. Writing in *Canadian Forum* in 1939, he apparently sided with a "recent writer" (whom he did not name but who was probably Harold Innis) who had "pointed out" that "the press, the radio and the cinema have been appropriated so largely for propaganda purposes by great pecuniary interests."[5] The then infant broadcast industry was in Canada destined to fall, in part, into the hands of a public trust which could hardly be accused of being a "pecuniary interest," but it is probably fair to say that the CBC has not been governed by anything like Keirstead's participatory democracy. The public has been given what the public trustees have thought was good for them—and, in their millions, they have turned their dials to stations tolerated by "pecuniary interests."

For the most part Keirstead's point has stood the test of time. Our democracy has been rather formal; our choices in politics have been between pre-packaged proposals made by political vested interest; our choices in the arts and in entertainment have been between what the

5 Wilfred C. Keirstead, "Discussion in Democracy," *Canadian Forum*, vol. 18 (March 1939), p. 377.

public trustees have thought good for us and what pecuniary interests (advertisers) have thought good for themselves. He would claim that this is in no way surprising: We think of democracy as a system of rules which govern a world essentially external to us and not as an account of a state and condition of the human mind. In Keirstead's view of the ideal state, democracy is not so much a system as a way of being. There are not democractic systems but democratic men. He wrote in the *Educational Review* on the eve of World War II: "The democratic state places supreme value upon personality. Its goal is the development and happiness, according to potentiality or capacity, of each individual. The person is the end, and the state is the means."[6]

This emphasis is by no means unimportant or without consequences of its own: It implies that it is perfectly possible to have the outward trappings of democracy without having any real democracy at all. If all our public demands and public yearnings can be met with systems which turn out to be empty in the end, it is difficult to know how such a result is to be avoided.

It is worth noticing that this stance tends to de-emphasize large-scale theoretical issues and to re-emphasize small- and medium-scale practical issues: For it is not the large systems, the foundations of the social structure, which are ultimately important but, rather, the states of mind of individual men. Theoretically, the difficulty with such notions is that they lead both to a commitment to individualism and to a commitment to a kind of communitarianism. Individuals are, ultimately, what counts—as Keirstead repeatedly says. But the implied notions of egalitarianism, mutual responsibility, and social welfare are surely going to tell against applied individualism. Keirstead decries repeatedly the evils of competition, the unfairness of various forms of wealth, the irresponsibility of capitalist institutions.

Keirstead's ideas are instructive more for the way in which they illustrate the development of certain forms of thought under evident kinds of social pressure than as original philosophy. The parallels between Keirstead and John Macdonald are both remarkable and puzzling. They are remarkable because both men undertook to apply their philosophical positions to immediate and practical problems connected with education and with the development of an effective "grass roots" democracy and both came to emphasize strongly the place of discussion, of personal interchange, and of effective individuality in the development of a democractic theory. They both wanted a theory

6   Wilfred C. Keirstead, "Ideals in Dictatorships and Democracies," *Dalhousie Review*, vol. 19 (April 1939), and *The Educational Review*, Fredericton, N.B. (May-June 1939), p. 6.

which would be proof against the manipulations of political and social institutions. The parallels are puzzling because, while Keirstead has sometimes been associated with Dewey (see, for instance, the obituary in the *Canadian Journal of Economics and Political Science*[7]), Macdonald's *Mind, School and Civilization*[8] has generally been taken as an attack on Deweyite educational practices and principles.

We need to recognize that Keirstead was not, in any obvious way, a follower of Dewey. He shared many of Dewey's immediate concerns and, like Dewey, he spent much of his life puzzling over the confrontation between individualism and communitarianism. But Keirstead is much closer to the kind of Platonized Hegelianism with which he started his philosophical career than Dewey would admit to being. The issue is further confounded by the fact that many scholars would now be inclined to see in Dewey's thought strands which remained fairly close to his original Hegelian convictions. Macdonald, on the other hand, is not rebelling against the values to which Dewey subscribes but rather against Dewey's account of the nature and origin of value. It is to this which we must turn for an understanding of Macdonald's concerns.

Something of Macdonald's background and of the general situation in Alberta may help to make all this comprehensible. Macdonald was more than ten years younger than Keirstead and graduated from the University of Edinburgh in 1911. He taught for a time at Bristol and came to Edmonton (then the only university centre in Alberta) in 1921. There he met J. M. MacEachran, who will figure later in this chapter. MacEachran had studied at Queen's under John Watson and they were, for many years, a mutual influence on one another.

The first flush of enthusiasm for theories such as Dewey's had already passed when Macdonald turned his mind toward problems of education. But there seems to have been a larger issue—one which appears sometimes overtly in his writings and sometimes between the lines. Alberta presented a special challenge. It had a far smaller core of population from the various "British" cultures to which Canadians tended to look for their identification. The waves of immigration from eastern Europe left their mark firmly on the Alberta society and figure largely in the struggles of its peoples. Many of them came from peasant and working-class stock and lacked extensive educations. Their children depended very heavily on the public school system as a device for

7   "Obituary," W. C. Keirstead, 1871-1944, *Canadian Journal of Economics and Political Science*, vol. 11 (1945), pp. 111-14.

8   John Macdonald, *Mind, School and Civilization* (Chicago: University of Chicago Press, 1952).

transmitting the culture they would need to survive in the new country. Inevitably, that was an uphill struggle—carried on by poorly paid teachers, many of whom had only rudimentary education themselves. The creation of a university which would effectively serve these people—a university which would make real the rhetorical promises of equality which politicians in election years and immigration officers on recruiting drives spoke so freely of—was, indeed, an heroic task. The infant University of Alberta was, itself, still struggling when Macdonald came to it.

All of this focussed his attention on two questions—the idea of a "western civilization" which had values worth learning and capable of being taught, and the idea of a genuinely free man who might live, work with, modify, and sustain those values.

Dewey's programme seemed to Macdonald a mistake. Dewey's claim, at least as Macdonald expressed it in works like *Mind, School and Civilization* and in his extended lecture to the University of London Institute of Education,[9] was that one should attend to the natural needs of the child. But Macdonald urged that there are, in the crucial sense, no such things if, by that, one means that there is a unique set of needs which are those of a human being. If you ask what are the needs of a civilized man, that is different, but one must not be misled into thinking that they are unique and necessary. Valuable, yes; necessary, obviously not. Dewey had thought, according to Macdonald, that one developed the interest of the child by focussing on his real needs and by duplicating, in the school, the child's natural environment.

To Macdonald, however, that seemed highly questionable. What environment? The fairly sophisticated middle-class environment of Dewey's Vermont boyhood? The ultra-modern environment of the urban Chicago in which Dewey first ran his laboratory school?

Dewey saw values as created out of the development and interplay of human experience. But suppose one chose to duplicate, in the school, the harsh environment of the immigrant Alberta dirt farmer. Would that really have the liberating effect the school was supposed to have? Would the values in question be *created*? Was it not true that one had to confront the important values before one could decide whether or not one wanted to adopt them?

At this point, the line of thought in Macdonald's educational writings becomes somewhat difficult to disentangle with any certainty. His position does not seem to be—despite references to Plato—the

9   John Macdonald, "Some Suggestions Towards a Revised Philosophy of Education," a lecture given at the University of London, Institute of Education (Oxford University Press, 1938).

literal Platonic one that values are not created at all but are permanent denizens of a realm which is special to them. It seems more nearly to be the quasi-Hegelian one that values develop over an historical period as a result of a community activity: They are not expressions of the individual but of the community. For it is in the options which a community makes possible that values can take root and grow. The individual has desires and performs actions; he adopts values as a means of reconciling his own behaviour or conduct with that of others. In a sense, the values are endemic to the idea of a community, but they emerge historically. In his brief political writings, especially in *The Expanding Community*,[10] a little book intended to introduce students to philosophy, even before they reached university, Macdonald emphasizes the inter-relations of individual and community and suggests, without any technical apparatus, the kind of political philosophy which had been urged by Watson.

If anything, however, Macdonald is more radical than Dewey and the fact that he championed a rejection of what had come to be called "progressive" education should not disguise that fact. Excessive individualism, obviously, would simply entrench the advantage of those who dominated society already. Excessive reliance on the "creation" as opposed to the inculcation of values can only emphasize the advantage of those who find the requisite values already present in their daily lives over those whose basis for invention is already impoverished.

In his lecture to the London Institute of Education, Macdonald remarks that when he first came to North America he tended to despise organized group action and to regard significant action as inevitably individual. His experience in Alberta changed his mind. He recalls that the event which brought the change home to him most strongly was an organized movement amongst Alberta women which demanded adequate birth control information.

In *Mind, School and Civilization*—published when Macdonald was in his sixties and evidently intended to be the culmination of a lifetime of thought—he tries to put together an all-embracing theoretical structure which will link value, knowledge, and the human condition. He distinguishes primarily material values; the knowledge of value which emerges as science and art; and philosophy, which essentially investigates, on the one side, social and political values and, on the other, metaphysical values. Much of the underpinning of this structure remains, like the iceberg, under water, because the alleged concern of the book is, after all, with education. Macdonald's attempt, however, is to attack the separation of fact and value by maintaining that value judg-

10   John Macdonald, *The Expanding Community* (Toronto: J. M. Dent, 1944).

ments enter into all propositions. Like many others before and since, he gets rather tangled in the different senses of value and in the ambiguities which arise when one insists that science has a value structure because it values certain perspectives on the world which it then takes as reality. The preference for objectivity, which concerns Macdonald, is contrasted with the preference for the morally and the aesthetically satisfying. All three are then linked to the notion of system and to the proposition that science is not concerned with individual propositions. Science he paints as, in part, the refusal to take custom and authority as definitive. This is followed by the logical extension of that principle in the refusal, equally, to take one's own perspective as definitive. Thus we may see science as a stance which has a valuation within it. But the scientist may reply that all has to do with the manner in which we value scientific propositions and not with the different question of whether or not there are values embedded in scientific propositions.

If Macdonald could sustain his position, he could link the objectivity of science, the altruism necessary for an acceptable political theory, and the objective extending of one's experience beyond oneself in art and philosophy into a coherent structure. He is evidently aware of the most likely difficulties and objections and he devotes considerable space to the analysis of language as uniquely, in its ultimate written form, the condition of civilized reflection.

Stability (the power to control time), coherence (the power to hold together the thoughts of many occasions), and effective reflection all come with language and build into all our propositions the unique virtues of civilized man. Thus, in fact, values are built into language and are built, therefore, into scientific propositions as well. Though the sciences may seek to have a logic and a form of their own, they do so only by building these values even more firmly into their specially contrived languages. Unhappily, all this is more suggested than worked out in what, to repeat, was necessarily a book with a limited intention.

It would have been fascinating to see Macdonald in active debate with Marshall McLuhan over the virtues of the written word or with the more modern linguistic theories over the question of the relation between written and oral languages. Alas, the public which danced to McLuhan's strange pipe had forgotten Macdonald.

No doubt it had also forgotten James MacEachran who had preceded Macdonald and had brought the Watsonian doctrine west. MacEachran will be remembered most, however, for his work in founding philosophy's sister department, psychology, at Alberta. He had studied in Europe with Wundt and Stumpf at Leipzig, Durkheim and Bergson at Paris, and felt that there remained a natural connection between philosophy and the social sciences. Though devoted to practical questions, including the reform of prisons and the criminal law (one an Albertan and one a federal concern), he continued to have general interests in philosophy, and wrote a long essay in a volume presented to Watson.[11]

The old questions and old conflicts continued very much to agitate him and, in the essay in the Watson volume, he returns to the question of religion, philosophy, and science. He no longer thought that traditional metaphysics could restore the damage done to much religious belief by science but he also did not think that religion was to be abandoned. Rather, he saw a coming together of science and religion. Philosophical principle would become more precise and scientific principle would be rendered more general as knowledge advanced. Hence there might be a *new* metaphysics—much, one gathers, like Whitehead's—though, in fact, the base on which he would continue to build was that of Bradley.

Pressure of other concerns prevented him from developing the philosophy hinted at in that essay. But the base for philosophy had been built in Alberta. Later, others, from outside, chose to sweep it away rather than build on it. But that is another story. In retrospect, some of MacEachran's enthusiasms seem curious. In an address to the United Farm Women's Association of Alberta, published in *The Press Bulletin* (a journal run by the university extension department) in May, 1932,[12] he advocated the sterilization of criminals as a device to ensure that, one day, prisons would be unnecessary. The essay, with its strong humanitarian concern for men and women in prison—in Alberta in 1932 they would have been almost entirely the feeble-minded, the mentally unstable, the poor driven by circumstances to petty crime and hardly at all "gangsters" or even professional criminals—provides a sharp contrast between its feelings for the oppressed and its willingness to trust some surely pseudo-scientific mixture of sociology and genetics. (Alberta did adopt sterilization laws and the arbitrary application of the Alberta Sterilization Act has been a subject of controversy from that time since. MacEachran was writing when the act was already passed and the authors have not been able to determine whether or not he had any influence on its passage.) The written record we have been able to

11 J. M. MacEachran, "Some Present-day Tendencies in Philosophy," in *Philosophical Essays Presented to John Watson* (Kingston: Queen's University, 1922) pp. 275-97.
12 J. M. MacEachran, "Crime and Punishment," *The Press Bulletin*, vol. 17, no. 6 (Alberta: Department of Extension, University of Alberta, May 1932), pp. 1-4.

locate also does not tell us whether or not he later changed his mind. It is hard to imagine that he would have applauded many of the applications of the Act.

In the work of Macdonald and MacEachran idealism was established near the extremities of Canadian settlement and it mainly took the form, as we suggested, of the application of general principles to more particular issues and occasions. The needs of the frontier were "down-to-earth" and reason took on, inevitably, a more practical guise.

As good an example as any of that tendency is to be found in the career of Herbert Leslie Stewart at Dalhousie. Stewart had come to Halifax from Ireland via Oxford, a convinced realist of the turn-of-the-century sort—one of those who reacted against the central idealist claim that there is a unity of man and the world, of consciousness and object, of reason and its subject matter.

He had expressed these views in a book called *Questions of the Day in Philosophy and Psychology*,[13] published in London in 1912, the year before he came to Halifax. The coming of World War I changed the immediate direction of his philosophical concerns in a way which was perhaps understandable enough at the time. He began to search for the causes of the war and, though he was by philosophy then a "realist," he sought them out in the ideas which animate men's minds.

Like others, he found this set of ideas in the writings of Nietzsche—the romantic nihilist of mid-century. Stewart's book *Nietzsche and the Ideals of Modern Germany*,[14] clearly has a cause in mind: Stewart is concerned about the fragmentation of modern thought and he thinks that Nietzsche is a good example. While he is careful to note that Nietzsche attacks militarism, sneers at Bismarck, and disowns the name of patriot, he finds so many contradictions in his thought that he believes one can justify most anything by quoting from its expressions. By undermining the power of reason, Nietzsche tended to justify war.

At any rate, Nietzsche does not emerge a hero. And, while one must distinguish Stewart from those who simply found in Nietzsche a militarist monster and the cause of World War I, it is fair to say that Nietzsche's writing turns out to be, in Stewart's view, the result of a way of thinking which Stewart believes must be combatted. The book is therefore not so much reflective or contemplative as an honest attempt to rally the troops for a battle, not against a dead German philosopher, but against a live calamity in the history of ideas.

13 Herbert Leslie Stewart, *Questions of the Day in Philosophy and Psychology* (London: Edward Arnold, 1912).
14 Herbert Leslie Stewart, *Nietzsche and the Ideals of Modern Germany* (London: Edward Arnold, 1915).

The book, however, probably brought about the beginnings of a change in Stewart's larger philosophical outlook if only because in that writing it forced him to re-assess the power of ideas and the nature of competing claims about the nature of reality. There seems little doubt (from the word of his students) that, by the twenties, Stewart was a devotee of the sort of idealism practised in England by the followers of T. H. Green. In him, however, the effect of it was quite different from the one it had generally seemed to have on philosophers in Canada, for in many ways Stewart was to become an arch-conservative. Toward the end of his life, he devoted himself to warning the public in his radio broadcasts of the dangers of communism, to championing all the forms of military preparedness, and even to the support of capital punishment.

The transition is an interesting one but one which it is difficult for anyone, now, to document effectively. There is a clue in his growing interest in religion[15] and in his growing interest in Nova Scotia history and the ways in which the communities and cultures which had been transplanted to that soil had managed to survive.

Both concerns indicate a strong interest in tradition, in the continuity of culture, and in the threats to cultural continuity and the development of bulwarks against them. All this is a possible reaction to the "new world" which, up to now, we have not found in philosophers in Canada. But none of it comes out directly because Stewart's published and specifically philosophical writing was, after this period, fragmentary, occasional, and rarely devoted to the most basic and central issues.

Such concerns can be set in train by an extremely conservative turn of mind and they are by no means unusual in immigrant populations, amongst which traditional values and virtues are apt to seem constantly in danger. It seems, however, somewhat odd to impute such a state of mind to Stewart who, after all, was well established in a community strongly British in origin and orientation, and which seemed to have preserved (some would say all too well) the values of its original culture.

Stewart did write an essay as World War II neared in which he explained the curious conversion to "imperialism" of an Irishman who had started out without much love for the British Empire.[16] The Irishman, of course, was himself. The explanation was essentially this: It had become increasingly clear that the world could not survive

15 Herbert Leslie Stewart, *Modernism, Past and Present* (London: John Murray, 1932); *A Century of Anglo-Catholicism* (London and Toronto: J. M. Dent & Sons, 1929).

16 Herbert Leslie Stewart, "The Imperialist Faith as Seen in Canada," in *From a Library Window* (Toronto: Macmillan, 1940).

without effective international organizations. Experience had shown that the application of contractarian theories of public order to that problem produced ineffective structures such as that of the League of Nations. Such structures might grow and take root in human tradition, but they were unlikely to be given the chance.

The alternative was to adopt (and adapt) existing orders, of which the British Empire (by then close to our Commonwealth in outlook) was by far the most effective. (In other casual writings of the time, Stewart wrote off the French Empire as a model.)

The significance of the British Empire was its ability to give official status to the opposition—indeed to reconcile irreconcilables in a form of government in which the losers always keep some power. (He speaks of English and French Canada as standing, as seen by the French habitant and the Ontario farmer, "on a firm foundation of mutual contempt."[17])

What is clear is that Stewart felt his philosophical energies should be channelled largely toward immediate or middle-range concerns and that the need to do this took precedence over the development of a formal philosophical system. There is little doubt that World War I came to him, as to many thoughtful men, as a profound shock and that much of his later life was reasonably spent in trying to salvage something from the wreckage of human hopes. The events of the 1930s seemed to make a mockery of the Soviet experiment and World War II threatened, quite literally, to extinguish human civilization.

The fact that his philosophy was essentially idealist probably had little to do with it. The sense of a strong community can either take a progressivist form as it did in most of the Canadian philosophers to whom it appealed or, since the community is a given—something inherited, and something to be preserved—it can take a conservative form. The difference seems less to be involved with idealist meta-physics—though some thinkers have thought otherwise—than with questions about the manner in which communities are expressed through historical and temporal processes. The nearer one moves toward an original Platonic idea of a perfected community, the more conservative one's outlook is likely to be. The nearer one moves to a notion of the community as something constantly changing and having a direction of development, the more progressivist, perhaps, one is likely to be.

17 Herbert Leslie Stewart, "Philosophy in a World Crisis," in *From a Library Window* (Toronto: Macmillan, 1940), p. 223.

TWELVE

THE FRAGMENTATION OF REASON

Rupert Lodge and Henry Wright

L ODGE AND WRIGHT came to Canada within a year of one another, arrived at the University of Manitoba in the same year, 1920, and served as joint "heads" of the Manitoba philosophy department for fourteen years. Both spent their whole careers there, though after 1934 Lodge became sole head of the philosophy department while Wright went to the psychology department.

Lodge had come to Manitoba from England, by way of Germany, Minnesota, and Alberta. He had already distinguished himself as the author of a work on modern logic,[1] an expert on Locke, and the translator of the now largely forgotten Italian philosopher Bernardino Varisco.[2] Despite this array of interests, he continued to be a proponent of the Oxford idealism.

Wright had been educated at Cornell, taught there briefly, and then became professor of philosophy at Lake Forest College in Illinois where he had written books on ethics and religion and distinguished himself as an expert on self-realization theories. He, too, had been reared on the moderate kind of idealism, sustained at Cornell by Jacob Gould Schurman. In a way, Schurman's idealism had come home, but Wright had become interested in Dewey (himself a breakaway from the then fashionable idealism) and pragmatic thought played, by 1920, a significant though not dominant role in his philosophical criticism.

Both wrote continuously and extensively and remained amongst the most productive philosophers in Canada for nearly thirty years.

Lodge and Wright, apparently, were men of different temperaments and, to some extent, of different outlooks. Those who remember them recall that there was some tension between them, though, given the peculiarities of two-headed institutions and the

1 Rupert Clendon Lodge, *An Introduction to Modern Logic* (Minneapolis: Perine Book Co., 1920).
2 Bernardino Varisco, *The Great Problems*, trans. Rupert Lodge (London: G. Allen, 1914).

normal difficulties of academic administration, it is perhaps more to be wondered at that they survived as joint heads for fourteen years.

Both developed in various ways during the decades in Winnipeg. Lodge's philosophy underwent a dramatic change, while Wright's developed in scope largely through his growing interest in psychology, an interest which was very much a feature of his philosophy.

Lodge became a central and controversial figure in Canadian philosophy, while Wright faded slightly from view as a philosopher. His central concerns, the detailed critique of a psychology of knowledge, a certain kind of ethical theory, and a certain facet of the philosophy of religion, were not dramatic and became rather unfashionable amongst professional philosophers.

Whatever their personal relations, they were both involved in the philosophical and cultural crisis of the post-war world and they both figure in the movement away from the pre-war versions of idealism. Both reacted to the social crisis in a way which seems to have been characteristic of philosophers of most schools in Europe and in North America: They began to examine the scope and function of reason and saw rational analysis as limited to a set of rather specific functions. More than any other philosophers in Canada, they typify the fragmentation of reason. There is a continuity to Wright's work which diminishes the extent to which one can ascribe his development to the characteristic difference between pre-war and post-war philosophical outlooks and makes it less likely that the influence of Lodge on him was dominant. But it is almost impossible to escape the view that Wright's influence on Lodge was considerable and that Lodge's influence on Wright was discernible.

The differences of response can be explained by a complex of factors: Wright had begun to make philosophical adjustments before World War I and was in a good position to pursue the line he had already taken. He was much closer to his native culture than Lodge. (Manitoba was significantly influenced by the populist movements from adjacent Minnesota and nearby Wisconsin and had a large immigrant population fairly newly arrived from Central Europe which had much in common with similar American immigrant groups. Traditional Canadian influences reached west with at least as much difficulty as American influences reached north.) Furthermore, Wright could easily maintain contact with his former colleagues, teachers, and graduate student classmates from Cornell.

Lodge had graduated from Oxford, taught in Manchester, and studied in Germany. The discontinuity in his life was necessarily great. Winnipeg was surely like none of them: The accents, the faces in his classes, the cultural traditions of a polyglot community then beginning to make itself felt in the university must have been wholly strange to him. Only a little earlier, a native Canadian, Blewett, had found Winnipeg hard going, and at that, he was attached to a religious college of his own denomination while Lodge faced classes in the much more heterogeneous University of Manitoba.

Lodge faced a new world. It is difficult now to put ourselves in the place of a philosopher who had to confront the world after the war. World War II, coming when many thinkers had already grown cynical about the human situation, had no comparable effect.

The last decades of the nineteenth century and the beginning of the twentieth century had seemed, most of all in the English-speaking world, to usher in an era of consistent, persistent, and irreversible progress. Hegelian idealism, read as a story about the gradual unfolding of the Absolute Idea in the formation of the world, seemed to lend substance to this idea. So did popular readings of the theory of evolution.

It is true that the more cautious readings of Hegel (who said the history of the world concerned only what is present, and reminded his readers that "The owl of Minerva spreads its wings only with the falling of the dusk"[3]) supported no such simple vision. It is also true that some of the post-Hegelian idealists—Bradley in his more cynical moods, McTaggart, if read with care—cast considerable doubt on the notion of linear progress. Even Bernard Bosanquet does not produce a very comfortable certainty if one prods beneath the surface of his confident Victorian prose. The picture which Bradley and McTaggart paint is, in fact, metaphysically and practically different.[4] They argued that we need not worry about *reality*. It has its own perfection. What we need to worry about is our own illusions from which escape is difficult and perhaps, for now, impossible. But they did, at least some of the time, create the impression that there was some reason to think that increasing human rationality would make that escape easier as time went on.

We need not, however, go far afield to get a sense of what the pre-war philosophical consciousness was like. The zest with which John Clark Murray plunged himself into essentially educational causes indicates that he believed firmly in the perfectibility of man through enlightened reason. John Watson remained serene even in the face of

---

3   George Wilhelm Friedrich Hegel, *The Philosophy of Right*, translated with notes by T. M. Knox (London: Oxford University Press, 1962), p. 13. First published in 1821; first published in Great Britain, 1942.

4   See F. H. Bradley, *Appearance and Reality* (Oxford: Clarendon Press, 1897), especially the preface; J. M. E. McTaggart, *Some Dogmas of Religion* (New York: Greenwood Press, 1968) and Bernard Bosanquet, *The Philosophical Theory of the State* (London: Macmillan, 1923).

the war: The growing rationality of man might face difficulties, but it would surely triumph. George Blewett seems to have had few doubts, either, about the eventual direction of events.

They all saw progress as a natural concomitant of the development of reason and the spread of rationality through educational, political, and religious processes already under way. The spread of education must make men better; politics suffered mainly from a failure to apply reason in its proper context. Even religion was to be made effectively rational.

All of them lived through a time when, indeed, these things seemed to be happening. Education did grow, governments were becoming more responsible, scholars travelled freely about the world. Even at Victoria College, the fundamentalists did not finally triumph.

For many if not most people, the world war shattered that whole dream. Better educated than ever, men turned out to be more given to insane brutality. Richer than ever, whole countries channelled their riches into guns and tanks and aeroplanes. Faced with a stand-off war in the trenches, governments sent growing thousands of men to their deaths and proved, perhaps, less willing and able to negotiate a solution than any group of leaders in modern history.

The post-war period brought with it not a return to the normal pattern of "progress" but a period of economic uncertainty, growing disorder in the conquered countries, and in England, Canada, and the United States a period of sterility in politics and uncertainty in the whole realm of human values.

A period which now seems to us perfectly normal seemed to those who sought to make sense of it a radical departure from what they had imagined to be a pattern fixed for a long if not eternal future. The failures of the League of Nations, the uncertainties of the Weimar Republic, the politics of Warren Harding, the misuse of land which led to eventual disaster on the Canadian prairies all seem to us ordinary events in a normal human life. The momentary courage which led men to talk of World War I as "the war to end all wars" now seems to us touchingly naïve. For anyone who made his living by thinking in the 1920s, however, those events provided a severe challenge.

The challenge as it was seen, generally, by philosophers can be summed up quickly:

The Hegelian equation of the rational with the real became deeply suspect. Human nature must be a part of reality. It seemed that human nature was not rational and could not, likely, be made rational by any available process. If there were not areas which were immune to rationality, how could it be the case that intelligent and educated men could conduct themselves in the way that the war had revealed?

The failure of rationality to maintain itself in a crucial human situation at least called for an explanation. There was no shortage of explanations ready at hand. Though various kinds of idealism had tended to dominate philosophical thought in the pre-war period and though all of them owed much to Hegel, they did not exist to the exclusion of other ideas. Marx and his followers had argued that the capitalist system, its attendant class structure, and the tendency to dress social and religious institutions in the clothes of a pseudo-rationality all prevented reason from manifesting itself in human affairs. They also argued that one could not correct the situation by rational persuasion but only by action which altered the physical basis of human existence. Nietzsche (who was blamed by philosophers, of whom Herbert Stewart is typical, for the state of mind which helped make possible the war itself) had urged the transcendence of rational morality itself and recourse to basic human intuitions.

Kierkegaard had claimed that the Hegelian rational synthesis provided a convenient cover for the basic irrationality which defined the human condition. Philosopher psychologists like Brentano and Meinong had pointed to the importance of intentionality in structuring the world of objects which human beings faced.

Many of these currents of thought had their origins in the writings of Hegel, who continuously emphasized the elements of logical tension in both reality and thought and claimed that they could be rendered intelligible only as a dynamic system which underwent constant change to keep them in balance. His message was that only by continuous and creative rethinking of our situation could we keep a grasp on the ultimate developing rationality of the universe. But each of the conflicts he discovered in human thought and affairs could also be used against him, as evidence against the claim that everything was to be reconciled in a transcendent rationality.

The effect of the war, in part, was to give each of these currents of thought a new importance—not always for philosophical reasons. Marxists were politically triumphant in Russia, and Marxism ceased to be another curiosity on the philosopher's shelf and became a political force. Combined economic and political force rendered German institutional life a shambles and made the claims of opponents of reason immediately important. The accelerated technological development of the war years increased the prestige and practical power of scientists and engineers and, in contrast to the failure of other attempts at reason, science seemed overwhelmingly successful. The sense of success in science was buttressed by the fact that, technology apart, very real and basic scientific advances characterized the pre-war and post-war years. Those who felt a need to defend religion, consequently, were inclined to leave reason to the physicists and to seek refuge in new kinds of subjectivism.

Furthermore, philosophical notions like those of Russell and Moore, which before the war were, for the most part, curiosities studied by professional philosophers, were available for consumption and took on a new importance. Moore, in the years just before the war, had argued for a kind of moral intuitionism and substantially against the prevalent forms of philosophical rationalism. *Principia Ethica*, with its insistence that "good" was indefinable, its return to a practical utilitarianism, and its insistence on immediate experience seemed by 1920 less a brilliant but eccentric piece of philosophical reasoning and more a revelation of the actual human condition. Russell's gradual (if partly temporary) retreat from Platonism, insistence on logical atomism and radical empiricism, and tendency toward moral emotivism seemed to parallel the needs of the time.

Russell and Whitehead, in *Principia Mathematica*, had sought, formally, only to lay bare the logical underpinnings of ordinary arithmetic, but the "new" logic appeared to confine formal reason to a special and restricted sphere and so, in a curious way, to explain why reason did not run effectively through human affairs. It presented a universe of discourse fragmented into logical atoms and a restricted set of logical moves which handle only a special, perfected, and necessarily limited set of concepts.

In the United States, James and the now de-Hegelianized and not yet metaphysical Dewey emphasized the practical in thought, the limits of speculation, and the tie between theory and human satisfaction. (The fact that both had in them a deep itch for speculation and a profound concern with theoretical issues which showed itself in metaphysical and even theological writings attracted less attention than the attempts to recall attention to concrete experience, short-range goals, and practical results. In the immediate post-war world James seemed to have been disreputably inclined toward rash speculation and the sober if convoluted prose of Dewey attracted more attention. Dewey's major efforts in large-scale speculation were still to come.)

In Europe, the ideas of Brentano and Meinong had developed into the intricate and formal phenomenology of Edmund Husserl, and efforts to establish the limits of reason led gradually to the preeminence of philosophers like Heidegger and Sartre. Despite a small movement of students and scholars to and from continental Europe (one of Husserl's pupils, Winthrop Bell, returned to Canada after the war, but he did not practice as a philosopher), these ideas had a very

410

limited impact on thought in the United States and Canada until the end of the inter-war period.

In the English-speaking world, moderate shifts toward subjectivity and serious attempts to chart some of the limits of reason were the most obvious outcomes of the shock brought by the war. In England, the death of the great idealist philosophers, McTaggart, Bradley, and Bosanquet, marked the end of the idealist ascendency—though not the end of idealist philosophizing. Their greatest successor, R. G. Colling-wood, turned to history, worked largely alone, and developed a system whose importance was not widely recognized until well after World War II. In the United States, idealism continued to have an effect, and important figures like Brand Blanshard developed in the late nine-teen-thirties while others, like Alfred Hoernle, came from abroad to join them. But instrumentalists, pragmatists, logical pragmatists (like C. I. Lewis and Willard Quine), and assorted species of realists rapidly became dominant.

In Canada, Watson worked on though he published less, Herbert Stewart influenced philosophy in the Maritimes, and John Macdonald had a regional influence in the western prairies. (More, perhaps, than anywhere else, idealism flourished with reasonable continuity in Canada.)

For Rupert Lodge, however, discontinuity must have been acute. He was largely on his own. He was in a small department, hardly more easily in touch with the nearest large concentration of philosophers in Canada (in Toronto) than with his colleagues in Oxford. He could read the journals, talk to his immediate colleagues, and meet with his students.

Everywhere he looked were signs of plurality of belief, of un-certainty, and of change. Lodge adopted two strategies, both of which produced substantial amounts of philosophical literature and one of which finally produced an explanation for the chaos—an explanation strong enough to satisfy him most of the time, though there are signs that he had doubts about it.

The first of them was one which usually seems natural to philosophers in a time of intellectual crisis: He turned to the history of philosophy. Out of that came books which continue to be republished and read—*The Philosophy of Plato*,[5] *Plato's Theory of Education*,[6] *Plato's Theory of Art*,[7] and a brief history of philosophy published as *The Great*

---

5   Rupert Lodge, *The Philosophy of Plato* (London: Routledge & Kegan Paul, 1956).
6   Rupert Lodge, *Plato's Theory of Education* (London: Kegan Paul, Trench, Trubner, 1947).
7   Rupert Lodge, *Plato's Theory of Art* (London: Routledge & Kegan Paul, 1953).

Thinkers.[8] These were evidently satisfying works to author and readers alike. Lodge wrote easily, read widely, and could find his way about in the thickets of ideas in a way which was helpful to students and, in the case of the Plato books, to scholars as well. But these books did not solve the larger problem of the meaning in the chaos, the reason for the plurality of ideas, the explanation of the uncertainties to which his generation was prone.

The Great Thinkers is a straightforward run-through of the classical canon, excluding only the mediaevals. The classical age ends with Plotinus and the modern begins with Descartes. The thirteen hundred years between are left blank.

Plato, Aristotle, Plotinus, Descartes, Spinoza, Leibniz, Locke, Berkeley, Hume, and Kant each receive a chapter. In the last chapter entitled "Post-Kantian Movements," Fichte, Schelling, Hegel, Schopenhauer, Comte, and Spencer rate a few pages each and some of the post-Hegelian idealists are given a brief mention. Then Lodge comments on the fragmentation of philosophical thought into its idealist, realist, and pragmatist strands. He confesses that "transcendental idealism" is his "natural bias" but he adds that he cannot believe that "any one-ism is 'absolutely right.' "[9] The reader is given only a hint of the theory which dominates *The Questioning Mind*[10] and Lodge's "practical philosophy books," *Applying Philosophy,*[11] *The Philosophy of Business,*[12] and *The Philosophy of Education.*[13]

Lodge says that the history of philosophy is to be read for its continuing insights, its suggestive ideas, its constant reminders of ideas which refuse to die. The book is rather full of metaphors which suggest that ideas have a life of their own.

> Realism, one would think, had been done to death for ever and for ever, by Kant and his successors. But in the middle of the burial service, to the great scandal of the congregation, the alleged corpse sat up and gave notice that the reports of its timely decease had been much exaggerated.[14]

He calls pragmatism "an unwanted child which has come of age and repudiated its parents with a vengeance."[15] (Its parents are described as

8   Rupert Lodge, *The Great Thinkers* (New York: Frederick Ungar, 1964). First published in 1949 and republished by arrangement with Routledge & Kegan Paul.
9   Ibid., p. 300.
10 Rupert Lodge, *The Questioning Mind* (New York: E. P. Dutton, 1937).
11 Rupert Lodge, *Applying Philosophy* (Boston: Beacon Press, 1951).
12 Rupert Lodge, *The Philosophy of Business* (Chicago: University of Chicago Press, 1945).
13 Rupert Lodge, *The Philosophy of Education* (New York: Harper & Bros., 1937).
14 Lodge, *The Great Thinkers*, p. 284.
15 Ibid., p. 292.

rather numerous: Protagoras, the Greek Sophists, the German philosopher Vaihinger, the Americans—Peirce, James, and Dewey. Fortunately, he does not pursue the metaphor into the details of schemes of reproduction.) These metaphors, however, seem to dot the text for comic relief.

What *The Great Thinkers* illustrates is that his historical work solved no problems for Lodge. For him, one will not find in the history of philosophy the necessary explanations unless one is content with negatives. Admittedly, one theme of *The Great Thinkers* is that one who reads the history of philosophy will find a substantial plurality of well-designed rational schemes each of which has very considerable power to hold the imagination, to confront basic human problems, and to provide a framework for a civilized life. One *could* take this as evidence for two propositions: Since we cannot easily demolish such schemes by critical analysis, we ought not to be surprised by the plurality of systems of ideas which we find in circulation, and since human reason is so obviously capable of designing many intrinsically plausible schemes, we must accept that it cannot finally solve our problems. It can only give us new choices. Lodge toys with both propositions in *The Great Thinkers* but he does not hunt for their theoretical underpinnings.

The history of philosophy is simply given. Lodge feels no need to explain his choice of figures and no embarrassment at the notion he generally conveys. Philosophy does, perhaps, just leap from great man to great man. Lodge had certainly become learned and he could put his learning to a publicly useful task. *The Great Thinkers* can still be found with ease in American (though not Canadian) bookstores and it continues to do its work.

The theory which held the centre of his attention was developed through a number of papers and minor publications but stated most extensively in *The Questioning Mind* and most clearly, perhaps, in *The Philosophy of Education*.

Both books set out to discover why people are interested in philosophy, what the limits of philosophical speculation are, and, most of all, to determine why there is chaos and uncertainty in philosophical certainty and what bearing that has on the practical conduct of life. The related books—*Applying Philosophy, Philosophy of Business,* and *Philosophy of Education*—pursue these themes and provide a more detailed analysis of some of the material.

Lodge develops his solution from a notion of Fichte's, the notion that one must choose between idealism and dogmatism. Fichte did not mean "dogmatism" in its current pejorative sense. A dogma is simply a received teaching and the "dogmatism" he speaks of is the acceptance of a philosophical system as something given, i.e., as something which cannot ultimately be explained. The "idealism" which Fichte painted as the other choice is a rather special sort of "idealism," the view that the world can be understood as the unfolding of the self or the pure ego, though that doctrine is to be understood with many qualifications. In contrast to "dogmatism," "idealism" is capable of offering an explanation. Since it relates both world and theory to the inner structure of our own affairs, we are capable of understanding it in the sense of embracing it as a system no part of which is inherently alien to us.

Fichte saw all philosophical theories as being of one sort or the other: Either they descend from original first premises which are just "given" or they seek to generate their premises by some intelligible process of development which has its origins in the philosopher. In the first case, the philosopher is part treasure seeker and part logician. He hunts about for first premises of great clarity and great scope. Then he attempts to develop their most salient implications. But, challenged by the first premises of a rival, he can only respond by appealing to the structure and powers of his own. In the second case, the philosopher is seeking one form of the Socratic wisdom and in so doing, hopes to illumine the world by reference to himself.[16]

Lodge appeals to Fichte's dichotomy as a basic insight. He proposes, simply, to make it into a trichotomy and so tidy up its terms of reference. The third term which he adds is a kind of pragmatism (indeed it is pragmatism as Lodge understands that expression). The tidying is mainly the result of his identification of Fichte's "dogmatism" with philosophical realism of a certain sort (again, Lodge just calls it "realism" without much reference to the various species of that doctrine) and his identification of Fichte's "idealism" with some features of a rather standard post-Hegelian idealism together with some features which are evidently his own.

He then argues for two propositions which, if true, will solve his explanatory problems: First, he claims that all philosophers, ultimately, are realists, idealists, or pragmatists. Then he argues that there is no ultimate way of determining which of these positions is adequate, essentially because they represent rather basic conditions of human

16 See J. G. Fichte, *New Exposition of The Science of Knowledge*, trans. A. E. Kroeger (London: Trubner, 1869). The Fichtean analysis is surely crucial as the source *both* of Lodge's bent toward idealism and his belief that, in a certain sense, realism and pragmatism are not to be disposed of. Fichte, too, finds that idealism explains but does not dispose of a kind of realism which takes on a life of its own since it arises from the self positing its own object. There is, in Fichte, as well, the seeds of a kind of pragmatism since the test of the postulated object world is, in part at least, its outcome for experience.

414

life. He sticks with this position almost all the way through *The Questioning Mind* and the three related books. Toward the end of the former, he almost suggests that there may be a synthesis, though he does not develop it.

As usual, Lodge writes easily and without recourse to jargon or technical detail, but it is not a simple matter to be sure what his original terms mean.

Generally, "realism" is primarily the doctrine that there are objects which are independent of us—or at least independent of our minds and not related by their nature to our knowledge of them. Pragmatism, for the most part, is the doctrine that truth and falsity are not independent of us in the sense that the truth of propositions (or their fitness as objects of belief) depends upon the work which they do for us and the satisfaction which they bring. Idealism, in its turn, is most clearly the notion that reality is mind-dependent, though that sometimes is taken to be equivalent to a perfectly rational system or whatever is a fitting object for the human spirit. The reader is never completely sure whether Lodge means to lump together disparate doctrines or means, rather, to show that seemingly disparate doctrines have family resemblances of one sort or another.

As the book and its shelf-mates develop, there seem to be other senses given to the terms. "Realists" are painted as hard-headed, anti-dreamers, tamers of speculation, champions of public order, and so on. "Idealists" are painted as rather high-minded, given to human sympathy, champions of assorted kinds of free thought, a trifle disorderly (perhaps), and given to large and distant goals, while "pragmatists" turn out to be oriented toward more immediate goals, more concerned with personal satisfaction, people who can make things go.

In other words, there is a steady shift from readings of philosophical theories which are technical, formal, and define well-known epistemological and metaphysical positions to popular notions of what it is to be a "realist," an "idealist," or a "pragmatist." The shift aroused some bewilderment (and mirth) in an anonymous reviewer in the *Times Literary Supplement* who said he was not sure that he should (or could) take *The Questioning Mind* seriously. But Lodge certainly meant what he said seriously and took very seriously the proposition that between technical philosophical theories and popular "casts of mind" which we can all recognize, there is a connection. Sometimes it is thought to be an explanatory connection. When he says at the end of *The Great Thinkers* that he has natural bias for transcendental idealism, he means to link his theory to the view that there are natural casts of mind.

It is not, therefore, always easy to discern the path of the argument which he wants to follow. Nor is it the case—if one takes together all the books in question—that one can frame very precise accounts of the basic human experiences from which he thinks the fundamental philosophical theories stem. Fichte was evidently impressed by the subject/object and knower/known dichotomies which characterize common accounts of awareness and knowledge. Hegel tried to transcend these dichotomies by insisting that subject and object, knower and known are co-determinants of one another. It is from the form or structure of the object as known that we come to grasp ourselves as knowers, but it is from the grasp we have of ourselves that we come to grasp the meaning or significance of the object. Hegel, like Fichte, thought that the dispute between "subjectivists" and "objectivists" stemmed simply from the fact that one and the same situation always has two basic characterizations. In one it figures as an object or set of objects; in the other it figures as the outcome of a knowing process. Fichte thought that over-emphasis on the object would lead to a "dogmatism" while a grasp of the knowing process itself would lead to a form of idealism which could "explain" the objects of knowledge. Hegel insisted that only if one could find a mode of knowing in which the subject and object coincided—only if one could somehow reach the Absolute, the unconditioned—could one overcome the relativity of subject and object.

When Lodge takes his starting point in Fichte and not in Hegel, we must suppose that he does so deliberately, for he knew Hegel's writings well. He does not in *The Questioning Mind* argue against Hegel, most likely for the reason that he wants to resist as much technicality as possible, but we can take it that he does not think the Hegelian synthesis will ultimately succeed. Furthermore, in describing himself as a "*transcendental* idealist," the adjective suggests either Kant or Fichte and not Hegel who, insofar as he was an idealist at all, would not have approved that term. Hegelian "idealism" locates reason in objective reality. The Hegelian Absolute appears through the order of a natural world which is not to be found in the analysis of subjectivity. Transcendental idealism is essentially the doctrine that reason is to be found in the structure of subjectivity, in the mode of knowing rather than of the known. Hence Kant argues that objective reality is beyond the grasp of pure reason and knowledge is confined to the phenomenal world. Fichte goes beyond this to hold that the structure of knowing yields the form of the objects of knowledge and Fichte is a fore-runner of the philosophers who were to make so much of intentionality as a characteristic of objects of knowledge—Brentano, Meinong, and Husserl.

Lodge wants to decline the invitation to Hegelian synthesis but also, while admitting the attractiveness of a Fichtean scheme, to insist

416

that Fichte should neither offer a simple dichotomy between idealism and dogmatism nor finally substantiate the claim that he can refute one of them.

Part of Lodge's argument is evidently the claim that philosophers simply have not been persuaded either by Hegel's synthesis or by what might best be called Fichtean reductionism, the elision of the objective world into the knowing process. Thus a plurality of world views has persisted. At least as historical fact, what Lodge urges is true though one may well suspect, as did George Brett, who figures in the next chapter, that the story is more complicated than Lodge will allow. While contemporary "phenomenologists" continue to be interested in Hegel, at least some of them are inclined to find a major source of Husserl's programme in Fichte and, if, as is sometimes argued, Husserl was an idealist, he was an idealist more nearly in the sense that Fichte was. But a sharp edge of realism crops up in Meinong and in Husserl, if by "realism" one now means a sense of the human experience of irreducible confrontation. Thus, even those philosophers most sympathetic to Fichte would not be strongly inclined to accept the whole of his position and would, in modifying it, be inclined to move in a direction which is not Hegel's.

In a much less arguable way, Russell and Moore can be characterized as flatly opposed to idealist doctrines, though Russell has moods in which he comes close to being, by turns, subjective idealist and Platonist. If one had to characterize their refusal to accept those doctrines as stemming from some ground other than their criticisms of idealist attempts to *prove* their case, it would be fair to claim that both were impressed by an experience of confrontation. Moore, indeed, was particularly concerned to press very hard the case that the knowing process is not to be confused with the object of knowledge. At the level of immediate perception, he argued that the perceiving process is not what is perceived. Russell inclined to the view that some objects of knowledge are just given.

Lodge seems to rest much of his case on features of the human situation which are reasonably characterized as the experience of confrontation and the sense of self-awareness and of involvement in the whole of the perceptual world. But these experiences lead inevitably to a third: Because we are both aware and aware of a world which we evidently do not "make" by any readily discernible internal process, we are inclined to act *in* the world and to set goals for ourselves there. The knowledge which is the basis of this action is tested by the satisfaction which it brings. Hence, if the original dichotomy is irreducible, a third position, that of the pragmatist, arises naturally.

417

Thus one would think it is a set of features which are basic and natural to human affairs which leads to the three-cornered dispute between realists, idealists, and pragmatists. The next move in Lodge's investigation has to be to decide between two possibilities: Either these positions are accounts which are true of parts of human knowledge but must be combined to get a complete picture, or else the basic human experiences which we all share give rise to different and incompatible total world views.

This step in the inquiry occupies rather large tracts of the works in question. Lodge does not argue in detail that no simple "eclectic" position will hold. Rather, he seeks to show how idealist, realist, and pragmatist stances structure the whole of our outlooks—moral, social, psychological, and so on. Even the preference for various disciplines comes to be influenced by these stands. A realist is more likely to be a chemist than a practitioner of the humanities. A pragmatist will have little sympathy for those disciplines which entail major amounts of detailed description.

It is because of this phase of the inquiry that the slide from the technical philosophical meanings of realism, idealism, and pragmatism to the "common sense" meaning of those expressions takes place. Lodge does not argue *for* this shift. (He seems to suppose that, on the evidence presented, the reader will find it a natural one. Lay readers often do; professional philosophers are more resistant.)

The assessment of the philosophical situation Lodge has created is not easy—at least not for those who resist the temptation to conclude that Lodge is being merely silly or downright careless.

He claims that the realist thesis can only be understood in terms of a set of structures which determine not just a technical position but a whole set of responses to life. The "realist" sees values as objectively imposing themselves—as objects to be confronted—and knowledge as something "there" to be learned. In education he favours structured curricula, carefully ordered systems of learning, and "objective" tests. In business, he is apt to see the whole enterprise as an objective entity, to be considered independently as something important in itself and not merely as a source of satisfaction to its employees and customers. The idealist, by contrast, sees values as something we impose on ourselves, favours independent development in education, and sees business in relation to the people involved in it. But he differs from the pragmatist, in turn, by reason of his insistence on seeing all these activities as parts of an interlocking whole and by his general refusal to be content with a fragmented set of ad hoc solutions to the problems he confronts.

Lodge's point is that the realist is not just one who sees objects and perhaps values as technically independent entities. Rather, he sees them that way because he centres his philosophy around a crucial kind of experience. The idealist, similarly, is not one who has a certain set of technical solutions to particular problems. He develops those, rather, in order to make general sense of his outlook on life. The pragmatist adopts his position not because he cannot develop technical solutions which would satisfy a realist or an idealist, but because, essentially, he cannot abide such solutions.

The systems collide because they take different experiences as crucial, basic, and not to be explained away. The idealist is impressed by the fact that the act, the art, and the process of knowing enters into every attempt to describe the objects of knowledge. The realist refuses to accept that anything is more basic than immediate confrontation. The pragmatist sees every problem and every description and pre-scription as aimed at some definable and particular issue which gives it meaning.

Hence the philosophical theories never finally diverge from the popular senses of the expressions which are used to define them. They resist dissolution because nothing ever counts as a sufficient reason for not taking one of the primary facets of experience as crucial and basic and because it is always possible to develop a coherent realist, idealist, or pragmatist solution to any problem.

There are not more basic theories than these because there are not more aspects of the human situation which can be taken as basic and crucial in the relevant way. There are not less because none can be explained away.

Lodge seeks to demonstrate this by developing appropriate triads of theories for each of the major areas of philosophical inquiry. But he insists on more than this.

He claims that philosophy, ultimately, is a practical *activity*. It seeks to produce coherent ways of confronting the tasks of life and its motivations are, in any case, basically practical.[17]

In the end, it does not so much solve problems as inform life. It enables the man who insists upon reflecting to develop a policy. But it cannot finally decide that policy.

Reason is finally fragmented and confined. It can shape experi-ence; it cannot provide final solutions. It imposes different demands on the realist, the idealist, and the pragmatist in the light of the choices they have made or in the light of the different species of "natural bias" which they inherit.

17 Lodge, *Applying Philosophy*, p. 1.

A plurality of competing schemes will, in all likelihood, continue and reason cannot be the final arbiter. It does not penetrate the depth of human nature but rather structures the surface of that nature. Below it is something more direct and, conceivably, more powerful.

Lodge nevertheless remains both optimistic and a little wistful. He is optimistic because he appears to think that once we understand the situation, we can better understand one another and communicate to one another our various understandings. The four "practical philosophy" books seem, more than anything else, to stress this outlook and the possibility that in it lies the solution.

The realist may understand why the idealist is what he is, may come to appreciate the values which are paramount to him. The idealist may similarly understand the realist; both may understand the pragmatist and he may, in his turn, gain a sympathetic understanding of the positions of his rivals. Furthermore, the more completely each basic outlook is developed, the more clearly, Lodge hopes, its limitations will be understood and the more we come to see that the world will run better if it has representatives of all three sorts of mind in it.

Lodge may envisage a solution which would go beyond "comparative philosophy." There is never much doubt that *he* is an idealist and the solution seems evident: All the schemes as he described them seem to be merely different ways of putting coherent order on our experiences. They offer different perspectives but he always treats them as things that we do. Even the dialectic immanent to idealism is "life becoming conscious of itself, life expressing itself through the medium of language."[18] But it is never clear whether or not he wants to press this enthusiasm and to say that idealism is true. If it is true, that does not make it impossible to say that, nonetheless, the *idea* of objectivity in its "realist" form has precedence over the *idea* of subjectivity, or the *idea* of satisfaction in its "pragmatist" elucidation has precedence over the *idea* of coherence in its "idealist" delineation. The realist wants to argue about the ultimate referent of the idea of objectivity while Lodge only wants to argue over its relative pervasiveness in any scheme which seeks to order human experience.

It is this problem which finally leads to suspicion about Lodge's basic scheme. It is not clear that anyone is "really" a "realist" on Lodge's reading. A "realist" is just a man with a taste for certain ideational structures. But if no one is "really" a realist, then a "real" idealist is one who grasps just why this is so and what Lodge calls an "idealist" is someone who is trapped in a special illusion—one who would not hold

18 Lodge, *The Questioning Mind* (New York: E. P. Dutton, 1937), p. 117.

his position in the way he does could he but understand Lodge's position.

There is a genuine danger that all this will collapse into nonsense. Furthermore, it does not seem to help in deciding where the philosophers "really" go in this classification. Is Spinoza an "idealist" because his system champions ultimate coherence as a kind of final test, or is he a "realist" because he sees everything as "objectively" there in its place? Is Hegel a pseudo-idealist who is "really" a "realist" or is he a real idealist because he grasps that the distinctions are shams?

And are there not many more possible positions if we allow ourselves finer distinctions and struggle successfully to escape the associations with popular terminology which enmesh Lodge?

When Bradley wrote, "Metaphysics is the finding of bad reasons for what we believe upon instinct,"[19] he was being cynical but also enjoying the tongue in his cheek. Lodge seems often to take this as gospel. Lodge's philosophers (in the "practical" books much more than in *The Great Thinkers* and the Plato books) seem to be people who set about spinning great philosophical webs in order to catch the small flies of their original beliefs, and, on close inspection, Lodge's surface optimism may turn into a rather bitter cynicism.

His theories are, at any rate, rather more complicated when one comes to analyze them than they seem to be as the charmingly simple prose flows through one's mind. Lodge himself was a complex man— easy-going and friendly but inclined, when pressed, to retreat behind a formal façade. He liked to invite students to his house, but things were organized there with formal tea parties, piano recitals, and a traditional academic dignity which did not invite much probing of his intimate thoughts.[20]

He came to terms with a pluralistic society by producing a pluralistic philosophy. He came to terms with his colleagues by finding a place for their philosophy in *his* philosophy. He democratized reason by allowing that it might serve any of the basic causes. But one gets the feeling that Lodge thought he could see through the pluralism to another meaning, that other people's philosophies might have a place in his philosophy but that did not make them satisfactory. And reason, having been democratized, was also fragmented and deprived of the powers of settlement.

19 F. H. Bradley, *Appearance and Reality* (London: Oxford University Press, 1969), p. xiv.
20 Lodge was very interested in music and was instrumental in establishing orchestral groups amongst the students. Often his office was used as a rehearsal room for aspiring quartets during his stay at the University of Manitoba. (We are indebted to W. Briggs, a colleague and personal friend of Lodge's, for information about the man and insights into his mind.)

There is a serious point to Lodge's undertakings. It represents an attempt at a kind of philosophical federalism as that which might be opposed to philosophical dogmatism on the one side and old-fashioned eclecticism on the other. It might have been developed to show how many theories can be created in a way which enables them to cast light on one another, regulated only by a common theory which limits the claim that they destroy each other. He does not really achieve this because there is too much puzzling philosophical sleight of hand at work and the basic problems are sometimes not confronted.

Whatever we now think about it, Lodge's thesis was a bold and intriguing assault on the philosophical situation of his time, one without exact parallel elsewhere, and it did have a practical result: Lodge reached a wide audience through the many editions of his numerous books and evidently succeeded in interesting in philosophy a public otherwise puzzled or bored by the whole thing.

Henry Wright, by contrast, is characterized by caution, attention to detail, persistence, and growing involvement in smaller scale philosophical activities which impinged strongly on psychology.

Up to the time of his arrival in Winnipeg, Wright's central interest had been in ethics and in the philosophy of religion. He had written books with a broad swing and scale: *Self-Realization, An Outline of Ethics*[21] and *Faith Justified by Progress*.[22] The first, as its name implies, seeks to relate the problems of ethical theory to self-realization theories (partly in the literal sense of examining the kinds of theories which go by that name and partly in the extended sense of regarding the study of ethics itself as a process which leads to self-realization). The second tries to show how faith—essentially religious, Christian faith—may be justified by a study of human developments and prospects. The first book just pre-dates World War I and the second emerged in the middle of that war.

They were followed by two general "survey" books, *The Moral Standards of Democracy*[23] and *The Religious Reponse*,[24] both published in the years after Wright's arrival in Winnipeg. But there is a marked difference in tone between the two pairs of books.

21 Henry Wilkes Wright, *Self-Realization: An Outline of Ethics* (New York: Henry Holt, 1913).
22 Henry Wilkes Wright, *Faith Justified by Progress*, The Bross Lectures, 1916 (New York: Charles Scribner's Sons, 1916).
23 Henry Wilkes Wright, *The Moral Standards of Democracy* (New York and London: D. Appleton, 1925).
24 Henry Wilkes Wright, *The Religious Response, An Introduction to the Philosophy of Religion* (New York and London: Harper & Brothers, 1929).

The difference Wright explained in an essay which he wrote for Edward Leroy Schaub's *Philosophy Today*,[25] a volume subtitled *Essays on Recent Developments in the Field of Philosophy*. There Wright, though he claims to be characterizing others, clearly enough characterizes himself:

> Ethical thought in English-speaking countries has been strongly affected for the past few years by two influences. One is the general concern over the application of ethical principles to problems of social and political organization which was a natural consequence of the war. The other is the recent dramatic swing of psychology away from the analysis and description of mental processes to an experimental study of behavior, in whose motivation and control ethics is profoundly interested.[26]

He adds:

> The war has not simply directed attention to pressing problems of political and economic organization; it has led, at least in the countries now under consideration, to a wide-spread movement away from idealism in ethics and in political and social theory.[27]

The first ethics book, *Self-Realization*, treats moral problems as though, at least, the idealists had defined them correctly. Self-realization *is* the problem. And in other writings of the same period Wright subjects such theories to an analysis which questions such theories in a technical way, but suggests that the idealist account is a natural and attractive one. He is concerned whether the self to be "realized" is the self which confronts the problem of something essentially different, about the way in which the ground shifts from an individual self to an Absolute self in T. H. Green's theory, and about the precise ways in which reasoning bears upon decisions about particular goals.

But, in 1913, his concern was mainly to show how all these issues can be made to fall into an ordering which, nonetheless, leaves self-realization as an intelligible goal. He canvasses the self on many levels and attempts to trace it from perceptual immediacy, through a social structure, to a religious notion in which self-realization involves—if a

25 Edward Leroy Schaub, *Philosophy Today: Essays on Recent Developments in the Field of Philosophy*, collected and edited by Edward Leroy Schaub (Freeport, N. Y.: Books for Libraries Press, 1968). It was also published in *The Monist* (October 1926).

26 Henry Wilkes Wright, "Ethics and Social Philosophy" *The Monist* (October 1926), p. 627. Also referred to in Schaub's *Philosophy Today*, p. 87.

27 Ibid.

real self is to emerge in the literal sense—a natural relation to a transcendent unity.

Though there are references to Dewey and Tufts,[28] the main line of the idealist case largely emerges intact: Morality is concerned with the rules for determining right human conduct and so involves the development of a self which is capable of being regarded as a centre of value. Egoistic self-interest will not suffice in such a development because there is no guarantee that any self in such a system or all of them together will form a structure which is rightly valued. Mutual self-interest and prudence might develop a structure which we would all accept; but it would not, even then, guarantee that we ought to accept the system produced.

Merely adding altruism to the list of desirable motives will not suffice. Concern for others is a virtue but it does not tell us whether that concern should be for others as they are or for their reform in some way. It is only if they are developed in such a way as to merit our support that the question can be settled; but that is what is at issue. The implication is that self-realization is more basic than altruism and the concern for self-realization must be mutual since it requires the development of others if one is to know how one ought to treat them.

What emerges gradually is the notion of a community of selves which develop together and the members of which depend upon one another for their mutual self-realization and for the development of the appropriate notions of self-interest and altruism, of individual and community. The ideal of such a community is fully actualized selves, an ideal which Wright saw, at least in 1913, as basically religious.

Insofar as the book differs from rather typical accounts of idealist ethics of the time, it does so mainly by putting more emphasis on levels of self-development and awareness, on the psychology of motives, and on showing how various ethical theories fit as aspects of the central theory. The self, as Wright describes it, is more complex, more like the self of ordinary reflection, less a rational construct than the self as it is dealt with, say, in Green's *Prolegomena to Ethics*. Wright's interest in psychology had already begun to show itself and so had his tendency to carve away at the details.

The theme of the 1916 book, *Faith Justified by Progress*, is more interesting as an item in the history of thought. In many ways, it anticipates—but does not go so far as—Dewey's much later *A Common Faith*.[29] But, in other ways, it is, though it must have been finished after

28 John Dewey and James Tufts, *Ethics* (New York: Henry Holt, 1929; first published in 1908).
29 John Dewey, *A Common Faith* (New Haven: Yale University Press, 1934).

424

World War I was well under way, a testament to what we have come to think of as the central late-Victorian notion of progress.

The doctrine which it advances is that human history sustains at least some of the crucial notions of the Christian religion if that religion is seen as ethical and social and not as a super-natural system. Like Dewey's much later work, it takes as central the notion that the objects of religious faith are not actual but ideal. Human immortality is to be found in the effects of great men on the structure of society. The perfected good is not a super-person but an ideal whose existence is or can be in the future. Ideals *do* influence actuality but that is not because they are actualities of another sort but because they are organizing and directing features of the structure of our experience.

Wright generates the whole notion of a spiritual world from the concept of a universal. He holds that, from seeing many houses, we generate the general notion of house. That notion helps to organize our experience and, as we add to it, it may become not merely a universal in the sense of what is actualized in many instances but also an ideal—the notion of that which *should* organize our experience. The Platonic universal, he thinks, was both a universal in the first sense and a standard in the second sense and the transition is inevitable because our experience is always changing and demands a direction.

In human affairs, the gradually developing ideal is that of a democratic society—a community of equals, of moral concern, of a common experience commonly felt as actualizing the ideal which is potential in each human being. But there is a temptation to regard this as actual rather than as something ideal and which is to be. If it is to be real, it is to be through *us* and the confusion between the two, Wright says, is a great danger. (Here there is at least a difference of emphasis between *Faith Justified by Progress* and *Self-Realization*. In both books, it is the socialized man who is to be preferred and the social ideal of God is to be fostered. The connection between the divine nature and the ideal community had, of course, been made by Royce and we have seen it in the Canadian idealists as well. But in *Self-Realization*, we seem to be given a choice between naturalism and supernaturalism.)

The existence of a Universal Purpose which is striving to adapt the natural world to the needs of a society of free, self-developing persons has, to be sure, not been demonstrated. Complete proof of the working of such a Universal Purpose whose aim is the welfare of all intelligent beings, will be given only when this purpose is itself realized. The realization of the purpose awaits the fulfilment of the process of Self-realization which is being accomplished in the moral development of man. But faith in the existence of a universal principle which makes for righteousness is being justified, belief in a God of universal benevolence is receiving verification.[30]

Whether the message is rather strongly naturalist as in *Faith Justified by Progress* or potentially (if a little ambiguously) supernatural as in *Self-Realization*, it is clear that both books announce with vigour the doctrine of progress. Indeed, it is the fact of progress which Wright thinks justifies the belief in the ideals which he takes to be Christian. Though he is a little puzzled by the natural and the supernatural, he does not pursue the notion of the reality of the ideal as far as Dewey was to do in *A Common Faith*.[31] He does think it is the fact that human experience has a direction which enables us to take the ideal seriously as an influential force in human affairs. (Dewey gave himself more manoeuvering room on questions of this kind.)

Both these books then set the stage for a shock which Wright felt deeply and expressed with some eloquence when the war was over and the extent of the damage to human self-satisfaction could be estimated. Both, too, show him moving in a direction influenced a little by pragmatists and more, no doubt, by the development of psychology as an extensively pursued intellectual activity.

The effect of the war shock, however, was not like the effect on Lodge, who set out to explain the limits of human reason and to come to terms with a world in which general agreement seemed more and more a pipe dream. Rather, Wright dug more deeply into the details of his own positions and came up with imaginative and fairly detailed solutions.

The Moral Standards of Democracy, published in 1925, differs from *Self-Realization* mainly in details and emphasis. The democratic community is still the ideal through which self-realization is to be reached. There is, however, more emphasis on psychological detail. Wright here asks why men fail to co-operate, what might motivate them. He looks (sometimes a little nostalgically) back on simpler agrarian societies in which men worked together at common tasks, knew one another well, and had more concern for each other than for their machines. He notices the conflict between the human talent for imposing human wishes on nature—and so building the potential for effective individuation—and the failure of humans to react effectively when they are insulated from each other by technology. Reason, now, is not to triumph in one move through the creation of philosophical under-

---

30 Wright, *Self-Realization: An Outline of Ethics*, p. 420.

31 Dewey (see footnote 29 above) argues that religious realities have the status of ideals though their place in his ontology is unclear.

standing of morality and the nature of ideal objects. Reason, rather, is to work piecemeal on the findings of empirical psychology, taking account of the actual limits of human beings as we find them. There is more serious talk of concrete problems and short-range goals and less general talk about moral theory.

Wright is simply a little more cautious. It is in *The Religious Response* three years later and in papers such as "The Metaphysical Implications of Human Association"[32] and "Dualism in Psychology"[33] that he extends and reconstructs his position in a new way.

He argues that "dualism" is to be revived. But it is not the Cartesian dualism of mind and body—or at least not literally—that he proposes to defend. That theory, he claims, belongs to a stage in human development—the stage at which we construct our picture of the inner on the model of the outer world. The mind as ghost strikes him, as it had Hegel (and as it later would strike Gilbert Ryle), as a conceptual mistake which results from turning consciousness into a thing.

On the other hand, the psycho-physical reductionism which seemed to attract so many of the behaviourist psychologists whose work he read avidly (and with whom he mingled) struck him as merely silly. The view that men were merely material objects, he thought, was one which would not last or even make much of a mark on the history of thought. It collided with too many facts.

What, then, was left? The idealist claim that both mind and matter are simply fragments of a larger rational order which *seems* divided into two orders he rejected on the ground that it was growing difficult to sustain belief in the underlying rational order. That order could be known only if human reason, as a manifestation of it, could be turned on itself in a way which would reveal the ultimate structure. But human reason now seemed to him too limited for the task or, at least, in present circumstances, too weak to do the job.

With a few deft arguments, he had rejected traditional dualism, classical materialism, and the idealism which if not dominant had at least been a significant force in his way of seeing problems. In his own work, the problem presented itself, still, as the rather ambiguous line between the natural and the supernatural which is sometimes crossed in *Self-Realization* and fenced with in *Faith Justified by Progress*. The solution which seemed to be implied by that ambiguity was the one he adopted: The distinction between the two realms wrongly marked out by Descartes depends on the nature of value.

32 Henry Wilkes Wright, "The Metaphysical Implications of Human Association," *Philosophical Review*, vol. 38, no. 1 (1929).

33 Henry Wilkes Wright, "Dualism in Psychology," *American Journal of Psychology*, vol. 53, no. 1 (January 1940), pp. 121-28.

Consciousness reveals a link, he says, with a "cosmic reality . . .[a] Universal System"[34] which is not the one of physical science and not the one implied by the old notion of the supernatural. "We have no acquaintance with this objective value-system apart from the activity of conscious intelligence."[35] Values form a realm of their own as a link between things, which renders directional and directed change possible.

In consciousness we are confronted by values: In being aware, we direct ourselves, become open to possibilities, meet the line where ideal and actual intersect.

We are ignorant neither about values—we confront them all the time—nor about the moral question: How shall we order them? For to order them is to order ourselves and to order ourselves is to seek to realize ourselves in the actual world. We can only confront these problems as a community. The consciousness in question is ultimately, he says, a social intelligence and not an individual one, for it is in the social situation that the ordering of values is confronted. The problem, in part, is empirical. Just as, in *Faith Justified by Progress*, he argued that universals are first assembled from experience and then come to structure it and be its standards, so values as public objects are like those universals. We find, by experience, that to actualize ourselves we must work with others and the awareness of that situation is the basis of the social intelligence.

Metaphysics and ethics come together and both become open to evidence from empirical psychology. We understand the nature of the process of valuation and evaluation by confronting those facts. By seeing the limits of purely physical explanations, we come to formulate hypotheses about the realm of values. By acting on those we bring about an actuality which sets the process in train once more.

This sounds like a convenient route from an Hegelian theory to a Deweyite theory. But Wright differs from Dewey in what seems to be his insistence on the metaphysical reality of the realm of values. It is not just that we react against the world and test the result by our own response to the subsequent states of consciousness. We actually encounter values which become actualized in real social situations. Consciousness really *is* enmeshed in values and the expression does not seem to be metaphorical.

Reason once again is fragmented. There is no single system. There is no characteristic of reason as such—only the shapes which reason takes as the twin orders of the cosmos intersect and interact. But the

34 Wright, *The Religious Response*, p. 157.
35 Ibid., p. 158.

hope of rational solutions remains and so does Wright's belief in the possibilities of human progress.[36]

Wright's enterprises, unhappily, tended to fade somewhat from the centre stage of philosophical interest. Theories about the place of religion in human life and philosophical attempts to make it respectable again became, on the whole, between the publication of *The Religious Response* and Wright's death, something of a minority taste. Questions about human motivation and its relation to value theory were largely lost sight of in a period characterized by philosophical doubts about the possibility of moral knowledge in any form and growing acceptance (only recently undermined) of something like G. E. Moore's dichotomy between facts and values. In the 1920s many psychologists had a real interest in the philosophical basis of their subject matter and in the possibility that it might involve a realm not reducible to physiology and then to physics. The popularity of behaviourist psychology, however, stemmed as much from the desire by psychologists to be acceptable as "scientists" as from the success of their endeavours, and such interests become distinctly unfashionable.

Wright had something in common not only with Dewey and the pragmatists but also with the Husserlian phenomenologists who, as successors to Brentano and Meinong, continued to have an interest in the metaphysical dimensions of value. Their language and their practice made contact difficult and there is no evidence that Wright drew much sustenance from their work.

He himself became more interested in psychological practice and the development of his theories remains in important respects incomplete. The problems will suggest themselves readily to the reader.

There are still difficulties with his theory of universals. Was he finally a realist about universals despite his earlier disclaimers? There are difficulties in connecting the concrete content of consciousness with the realm of values. The theory of society and of individuation remains incomplete and, in particular, though he wrote about democracy, he was inclined to leave the connection between economics and politics a blank. (In that he follows the common American practice, until recently incomprehensible in Canada, of thinking that economics and political science are completely separable disciplines.)

The difficulties are finally too numerous for us even to suggest how he might have responded. But, at least, some of his concerns are returning to fashion and we may yet find him widely read.

36　Wright's discussion of value is found primarily in chapter 9 of *The Religious Response*.

THIRTEEN

REASON, HISTORY, AND THE SOCIAL SCIENCES

George Brett, John Irving, and Harold Innis

B RETT AND IRVING had much in common as philosophers, little in common as men. Innis, who would not have called himself a philosopher at all, had little in common with either of them.

But it is not mere whimsy or convenience which puts them together in a single chapter. Together they represent the absorption of philosophical reason into other subject matters—attempts, conscious on the part of Brett and Irving though less so, perhaps, on the part of Innis, to regenerate philosophy by using it as a device for reflecting on something else.

Brett sought to anchor philosophy in the history of ideas, to expose its meaning by showing the historical development of significant strands of it. Irving sought to confront philosophy with the practice of the social sciences. Innis developed a philosophy out of the practice of the social sciences and, more than that, out of the problem of the nature and validity of the social sciences.

Brett and Irving praised philosophy but seemingly practised something else—the former wrote the history of psychology[1] and the latter investigated the development of the Social Credit movement in Alberta.[2] Innis damned philosophy—said it was "stuffed"[3]—but reinvented it in his own way.

All of this is surely puzzling though it becomes comprehensible when one sees it as one of the adventures of reason in our place and time. Perhaps it could never have been predicted, but it may now be possible to understand it.

1   George Sidney Brett, *A History of Psychology*, 3 vols. (London: G. Allen, 1912, 1921). Hereafter referred to as *History of Psychology* or *Psychology*.
2   John A. Irving, *The Social Credit Movement in Alberta* (Toronto and Buffalo: University of Toronto Press, 1959).
3   Robin Neill, *A New Theory of Value: The Canadian Economics of H. A. Innis* (Toronto: University of Toronto Press, 1972), p. 78. Hereafter referred to as *A New Theory of Value*.

In the last chapter we discussed the intellectual upheaval which eventually was ushered in by World War I and the decline of the idea of progress. But there was something else at work which must be brought to light if we are to understand the philosophers who figure in this chapter.

One of its manifestations was the development of psychology and of the other social sciences as enterprises quite separate from philosophy. Another was the development of purely formal logic in ways which probably represented the greatest single advance of that subject since Aristotle. A third was the development of the mass culture represented by the movies, the greatest return to mass spectator sports since the Roman Arena, new mass circulation magazines, and new mass political movements which were to make this the century of communists, Nazis, fascists, and the political image makers of the United States.

All three of these manifestations seem to be features of a new, fairly pervasive, relation between man and his universe. Men seemed to themselves to be small, insignificant features of a vast universe. That image was created through the gradual movement of the sciences of physics and astronomy toward the centre of western culture. The same cultural paradigms created the notion of man as an object like other objects, to be studied in the laboratory. That was the demand for the creation of sciences of society and for human nature to be forged in the image of physics and astronomy. The mass culture exploited the notion that men, as objects, might be thought of as resembling one another nearly as exactly as one hydrogen atom resembles another—a notion which finally emerged as the public opinion poll in which the beliefs of millions are inferred from the known beliefs of hundreds.

What was philosophy to do in the face of these demands? It could adopt the "realist" stance and support the new social sciences. It could retire into formal logic and become a branch of mathematics. It could lead the pack in extolling the virtues of the useful. Thus one might become a Moore, a Frege, a Dewey, or (like Russell) a little of all three. Such men were hailed as the new breed of great minds—an adulation which the mob generally reserves for its own reflection in the mirror. There were a few other options. One might seek new reason-transcending intuitions. France expected its thinkers to be unlike the others and revelled, for a while, in its Henri Bergson,[4] though it finally found

4 Henri Bergson, *Creative Evolution*, Authorized Translation by Arthur Mitchell of Harvard University, Foreword by Irwin Edman of Columbia University (New York: Random House, The Modern Library, 1944). Copyright 1911 by Henry Holt.

431

him too tough to understand and, when it was presented with a truly great and original thinker in Louis Lavelle,[5] almost failed to recognize him.

In Canada, however, none of these movements caught on. Older views of the function of reason, more traditional accounts of human dignity, a culture which had never been exposed to revolution and valued continuity still managed to assert itself. Watson flourished still. Blewett was still fresh in mind. Rupert Lodge was yet to come.

In the centre of the movement of ideas and population, however, some response seemed inevitable. In Winnipeg or Kingston, Halifax or Edmonton one might, from the superiority of distance, call fads fads. In Toronto one was expected to have a sense of the movements of thought in the world.

Brett's response was to moderate the new upstart claims; Irving's was to carve out for philosophy a small place in the social sciences. Innis, unrepentant in his suspicion that there was a grain of truth in his Baptist upbringing, that his old teacher James Ten Broeke had caught a glimpse of a larger reality, that human dignity could only be protected by a deep inquiry into the nature of values, cheerfully set off to capture the social sciences and re-invent philosophy.

All three present problems for us in this book. The real subtleties of Brett's *History of Psychology* are beyond the scope of anything but a detailed chapter-by-chapter commentary on its three volumes—a task which cannot be accommodated here. Irving's own attempts at social history invite a kind of response and debate which is inappropriate to a history of philosophy. Innis' work spans a compass which, similarly, will not fit here. At the same time, all three had philosophical views and raised problems which belong here. We can try to do justice to an aspect of the work of each if not, in any of the cases, to the man involved.

Brett came to Toronto from Oxford via India—originally as a librarian and lecturer in Classics at Trinity College. He was soon to move to Philosophy as Professor of Ethics and Ancient Philosophy. He began to lecture in the University College as well. By 1921 he had severed his connection with Trinity and five years later he was appointed Head of the Department of Philosophy, University College.

Slowly and quietly he became the dominant force in philosophy at Toronto, leaving his mark on the curriculum, influencing the choice of staff, and shaping the outlooks of students and junior philosophers alike.

5   Louis Lavelle, *La Présence Totale* (Paris: Editions Montaigne, 1934; 3rd ed., Paris: Aubier, 1962).

He was a quiet, almost secretive man—his friend and chronicler John Irving described him as "one of the most impersonal of men"[6]— whose opinions emerged only obliquely even in his writings. Another friend remarked that "though he lived in Toronto for nearly forty years, had his cottage on the lakes where he spent his summers like everybody else, he was always an Englishman."[7]

His effect, however, became obvious and made philosophy at Toronto something which, if not unique, at least had a special cast of its own. Philosophy became dominantly the history of philosophy. Brett's own work was almost wholly historical and, after George Blewett (who died in 1912), there were to be, at least for the rest of Brett's lifetime, no major speculative philosophers there. The curriculum stressed the detailed study of the history of thought, problems generally tended to be placed in an historical context, and students were encouraged to think of philosophy as a main rubric of the evolution of thought.

By comparison to other universities in Canada, Toronto was large and rich. Only McGill vied with it for prestige at a national level. Philosophy prospered as much as, if not more than, any other discipline. There were seven philosophers when Brett arrived in 1908 and the department was to grow to be one of the largest in the world. But, though it produced much scholarship and was in the literal sense a great centre of learning, its staff produced relatively little original philosophy. It had no Watson, not even a Lodge or a Wright.

During Brett's lifetime, the Institute for Mediaeval Studies brought philosophers like Gilson and Maritain to its campus, but the Institute and its spiritual affiliate, St. Michael's College, were outside Brett's grasp.

It is not fair, as we shall try to show, to paint Brett *only* as a dour, introspective man whose interests were in a selective vision of the past, immersed always in an alien culture which he brought to Canada. He was immersed in a very special view of the past. His influence on the Canadian scene owes much more to the fact that some facets of the culture in which he grew up meshed perfectly with some facets of the culture of Toronto as he found it, than it does to any changes or adjustments which he made during his thirty-eight years amongst Canadians. He was not, like Blewett, a source of the Canadian vision, nor, like Watson or Murray, a man who broadened greatly out of interaction with the Canadian environment, nor, like Lodge, a man

6   John A. Irving, "The Achievement of George Sidney Brett," reprint from *University of Toronto Quarterly*, vol. 14, no. 4 (July 1945), p. 329.
7   A remark made during an interview by one of the authors with a personal friend of Brett's.

whose views underwent dramatic change as a result of the cultural crises of the time.

His upbringing continued to influence his work until the end and it is important to understand his background.

Brett was born in South Wales at Briton Ferry in 1879. His father was a Methodist minister who sent him to Kingswood where he received a stern Methodist education. Though science was creeping into the curriculum and Brett was exposed to some of it, his first and abiding love turned out to be the classics.

From Kingswood, he went to Oxford on a scholarship and received that curiously narrow official education which Oxford tends still to impose on young philosophers—a massive dose of the ancients under the guise of Classical Moderations and Literae Humaniores. Less officially, he began to develop his interests in the history of science, especially medicine, and to acquire a taste for history in the larger sense.

The Oxford of the turn of the century was still under the spell of Bosanquet, Bradley, and Green, though occasional glimpses of philosophical realism must have emerged. Brett was later to be described as a "realist" though, insofar as he was, his "realism" had little to do with the Oxford programmes developed by Cook Wilson and others and he remained fascinated with, but uncommitted to, the idealism of the great Oxford figures.

He seems to have emerged, indeed, with many interests and a great fund of historical education, but few convictions of the sort which would count as a commitment to a philosophical position. Irving remarks that Brett overcame the characteristic weaknesses of his Oxford education partly through the influence which W. P. Workman, his headmaster at Kingswood, exerted over him (Workman had interested Brett in science) and partly through his wide reading. There is no reason to quarrel with that verdict from a scholarly point of view.

He was exposed to tutors whose view of the philosophical education reflected much more nearly than most the stance of the official curriculum. John Alexander Stewart was the author of books on Plato and Aristotle, and Herbert W. Blunt, who officially supervised the philosophical part of Brett's education, wrote mainly articles on German philosophers and is said to have warned him against hasty system building.

After a brief experience as a schoolmaster, Brett, when he was twenty-five years of age, joined the Indian Educational Service as Professor of Philosophy at the Government College at Lahore, the Punjab. The "government colleges" were devices by which the British proposed to export higher education—mainly in the red brick style of the English provincial universities—to the inhabitants of India. During his four years in India he learned to speak Hindustani and applied himself to learning Sanskrit and Arabic.

Brett delved fairly deeply into Indian thought and developed an interest in Indian politics which was to last the rest of his life. Though he frequently defended Indian ability and talent, he also frequently deplored the activities of Indian "agitators" against the British and felt that India's best interest lay in a continuing relation of some kind with the British. His sensitivity to ideas of all kinds made him see that India was hardly a country full of backward savages who needed the British to civilize them, but his own reticence and his general and life-long respect for authority made him suspicious of the kinds of political activism which people in India found increasingly necessary. Out of the conflict, he became a "moderate" on the Indian question, a source of general enlightenment, but not exactly a friend of Indian liberation.

When he came to Canada, Trinity at first put him to work teaching classics and playing a role in its library—tasks for which he was equipped both by his general knowledge and by his interests. His gradual shift to philosophy, first at Trinity, and then at University College, represented a general recognition both of his knowledge and of his scholarly capacities.

In Canada, he gave up Methodism and became an Anglican. There is little doubt that in 1908 the Anglican Church provided a stronger sense of being at home, of being in the British Empire, and of being a force for tradition and order than its methodist counterpart. Brett thus fitted into a comfortable anglophile niche in the Canadian culture.

By then Canadian culture had deep roots of its own, and a rather traditionalist outlook came naturally enough to a people who tended to see themselves, in fact, as the defenders of tradition by contrast to the American preoccupation with the future and with the prospects for rapid social change.

Furthermore, history seemed unusually important to those who thought of themselves as maintaining standards in a lonely part of the world which had a brief history of its own. Maintaining tradition in such an environment is apt to be seen as a task to be undertaken deliberately and buttressed with a substantial formal structure.

The curriculum at Toronto became highly structured principally around an historical ordering of courses, and faculty were recruited to teach the curriculum as it stood. Irving remarks that during Brett's administration "new appointments were discussed with members of the permanent staff."[8] But he also says Brett, "having chosen a man for the department . . . assisted him. . . ."[9] There is little doubt that Brett chose. Discussing is not deciding and Brett hovered over his new appointments with gentlemanly courtesy which seldom left much doubt as to what was expected of them.

There is no feeling that Brett ever struggled to obtain power or to keep it. He simply seemed a natural choice for the time and place, devoted himself to scholarship with such assiduity that his learning commanded constant respect, and created a climate of opinion in which what he expected happened.

The record shows that he was, almost always, magnanimous and charming. Though he had grave doubts about the worthwhileness of enterprises in philosophy like those of Rupert Lodge, his review of *The Questioning Mind* and *The Philosophy of Education* in the *University of Toronto Quarterly*[10] was kind and thoughtful and showed that he grasped clearly what Lodge was about. He could be acid—as he was in "Aquinas, Hollywood and Freud,"[11] a review of two books by Mortimer Adler. But Adler was outside the scope of Brett's immediate sense of obligation while Lodge, writing in Manitoba, was a brother department head in the same country. Furthermore, Brett saw Adler as a doctrinaire Thomist and he had little use for anyone who was a doctrinaire anything and little affection for Thomism itself.

Brett simply did not have to fight and did not fight. When he became Dean of Graduate Studies at Toronto, the appointment again seemed natural. He was, perhaps, the most learned man in the university; his interests in the history of science and medicine, in literature and in languages made him, very likely, the man most likely of all those in the university to understand the range of disciplines which a graduate dean must confront. What is more, the business of a graduate dean is to maintain standards where they matter most.

His assorted administrative duties did, evidently, take their toll. When one adds to his formal duties as a university administrator the duties which went with his work as a founder of the *Canadian Journal of Religious Thought* and as a member of the board of editors of the *Journal of General Psychology* and the *International Journal of Ethics*, as well as the tasks associated with being the first editor of the *University of Toronto*

8   Irving, "The Achievement of George Sidney Brett," p. 341.
9   Ibid.
10   George Sidney Brett, "The Classifying Mind," *University of Toronto Quarterly*, vol. 7 (October 1937).
11   George Sidney Brett, "Aquinas, Hollywood and Freud," *Ethics*, vol. 49 (January 1939).

Quarterly, one can hardly help wondering how he could have had any time for scholarly writing.

He talked much about setting down his own views on epistemology and metaphysics, but nothing came of it. He went on writing but his writings were mostly book reviews, short, incisive articles, and by-products of his concern with the *University of Toronto Quarterly* and the literary and cultural concerns which that journal provoked.

His major works—*The Government of Man*[12] and the massive three-volume *History of Psychology*—were written before he assumed any of these duties. The first volume of the *History of Psychology* was complete when he came to Toronto in 1908 and the last volume appeared in 1921. *The Government of Man* was published in 1913. The *History of Psychology* was designed as a parallel work to the three-volume *History of Philosophy* by Eduard Erdmann whose English translation had already appeared in the "Library of Philosophy," edited by J. H. Muirhead for George Allen in London. It is important, probably, to see it in its original context, for it seems likely that that arrangement with the publishers had an influence on its design and intent.

It is not now easy to imagine just what "psychology" would have meant to philosophers at large, to publishers, or to the general educated public in 1908. Psychology had been taught in one way or another in universities for fifty years and more but it was generally regarded as a branch of philosophy, essentially the philosophy of mind, and a branch of the philosophy of conduct which dealt with motivation, habit, and modes of regulated behaviour. A history of psychology might have been many things. It might have been an attempt to chart the course of the growing—though not powerful as yet—movement to conduct organized observation of human behaviour. It might have been a study of the relation between certain kinds of philosophical theories about minds, and incidents and theories in medical practice. It might have been simply a history of the philosophy of mind.

Brett, in short, had decisions to make. As one finds that his history contains what is, in large measure, a review of philosophical theories beginning with a brief account of "primitive thought"[13] but moving quickly to the pre-Socratics and on to discussions of Mill, Bain, and Spencer, one is inclined to suppose that it must, really, be a history of philosophy with emphasis on the philosophy of mind.

And, indeed, Volume 1 is enough like that to justify such a description. It soon becomes obvious, however, that Brett is up to something else. Though he himself said that history ought, essentially, to be

12 George Sidney Brett, *The Government of Man* (London: G. Bell and Sons, 1913).
13 Brett, *A History of Psychology*, vol. 1, p. 3.

descriptive and that the historian ought never to anticipate but always exhibit his subject matter in an evolutionary guise, he does, in fact, gradually unfold a theory and even a purpose. By the end of Volume 3, one knows what it is.

To announce it baldly is to risk a misleading impression—especially because the theory both emerges from the data and then is used to order further data, and Brett was much too cautious a man to let it stand naked on the page. Our task, however, allows for no such caution.

In the end, Brett wants to say this: There *is* a subject matter which, properly speaking, is the subject matter of psychology. It is the immediate data of the inner life. But it is not a subject matter like the others if, by the others, one means such subject matters as astronomy, geology, or the physics of solid states. Astronomers gather data about stars and planets, geologists about rocks, soils, and interacting structures of the earth. The physics of solid states is about a determinate set of objects which, at any moment of time, form a discrete set of the portions of the universe.

Subject matters in that sense are to be distinguished from subject matters like physics in general or chemistry in general which, in a sense, embrace all the objects in a natural universe but do so from a special perspective. Two such subject matters may, thus, embrace the same objects but organize them in different ways.

There is a sense in which the subject matter of psychology is like the latter in that it embraces sets of objects as they turn up from the perspective of human beings or animals who know them and thus there is a sense in which psychology forms a perspective on epistemology. But, though Brett concedes that, to the psychologist, everything may be relevant, he thinks that is not a correct or reasonable characterization of psychology either. For the focus of psychology is on the knower and on the inner life and phenomena which make that life intelligible.

This might make it seem as if psychology were essentially a matter of immediate introspection and as if Brett were embarked upon a project which was, indeed, characteristic of nineteenth-century psychologists. But this would not explain why much space is devoted to Plato, why Plotinus plays an important part in the story, or why we should trouble with an introduction about primitive thought.

No doubt Plato and Plotinus, for instance, did introspect and they sometimes reported what seem to be introspections, but their claim to fame is not that they were particularly skilled introspectionists. Furthermore, the making of lists of introspections does not seem to be—as most contemporary psychologists would testify—a really fruitful activity.

Brett wants to make a point about the significance of the history of psychology. For there is something crucial to be said about psychology without which the kinds of things we have been saying about its subject matter are apt to degenerate into mere silliness.

The missing piece of the account is this: In the history of human thought, there is a development in our ways of conceptualizing our own inner life. That, in its turn, has an important effect on the ways in which the immediate data of introspection appear to us. Without the context, introspection yields little or nothing by way of information about the significance of the data it produces. With the context we can see the pattern of development and, gradually come to see the possibilities which are open to human beings.

There is little in Brett's three volumes which, finally, sustains the view that this process is progressive. Since he has the philosopher's habit, very often, of presenting one thinker as responding to or providing solutions to the problems posed by or left by his predecessors, the impression is sometimes created that the chain of developments is progressive. Since, as we have said, he had his own biases, one can easily form the view that he means to say, for instance, that thought in the Middle Ages was back-sliding. But while he may paint us as freed from presuppositions which, perhaps, Plato was not clearly aware that he suffered from, he also frequently tells us that what may be a problem for us is not necessarily a problem for Plato.

It would be difficult, in fact, to paint Brett as a subscriber to the most popular nineteenth-century notions of progress or to fit him into the pattern of those who, like Lodge and Wright, were shaken by World War I into a new philosophical stance. There is little evidence that the events of the twentieth century influenced him in any deep way.

This is important to an understanding of Brett's theoretical account of psychology. If the phases were necessarily progressive, we might content ourselves with the latest ones leaving the past to itself and to the curious. But the significance of the present, he thinks, is partly in its relation to the past since the data of introspection represent one set of possibilities out of many and they are meaningful only if we have understood what we have done.

Brett, for all his reluctance to unfurl his colours and sound the trumpets, was engaged in an intellectual battle. The enemy was one branch of the new science of psychology. Irving notes that Brett was firmly opposed to the "'brass instrument' psychology"[14] of the laboratory—an expression which oddly connotes both luxury and dig-

---

14 Irving, "The Achievement of George Sidney Brett," p. 351.

nity in these days of cheap plastic and rat laboratories full of galvanized wire cages.

His objection was not to the study or even the measurement of human behaviour, but rather to the abstraction of such studies from their intelligible context. If one simply measures and correlates the movements of bodies—if one does essentially physiological psychology—the peculiar nature of the subject matter of psychology is lost. One may do something which ultimately could turn out to be a branch of physics, but that is to stand on two sides of the issue at the same time. If one really wanted to do physics, one would deal with human behaviour in terms of the distribution of fundamental particles. (Equally, one might do organic chemistry and treat the phenomena at a molecular level.) But the psychologist who thinks that he has a separate discipline *and* that that discipline is adequately dealt with by attending to measurable external behaviour, would be contradicting himself. One or the other might be true, not both.

What has to be added to the "brass instrument" approach is an understanding of the conceptualizations, their history, and, most crucially, the immediate data of introspection—as far as possible, present and past. Brett treats the whole history of thought (especially western thought) as evidence for his propositions. We can see real men coming to grips with real problems. We can understand that their immediate introspections did not necessarily produce what ours do and we can come to understand something at least of what their data were like by patiently unravelling their conceptualizations. The history of psychology is evidently, for Brett, *part* of psychology in the way that the history of philosophy is part of philosophy and in just the way that the history of physics is *not* part of physics.

In many ways, Brett was an unworldly man if, by that, we mean that he lived importantly in a world of his own, dominated by ideas, literally absorbed in history and rather detached from many things going on in the culture around him. But it is important to notice, as he himself did, that his theory about psychology had very practical and even immediate implications.

The clue is in a paper he wrote for the *Canadian Journal of Religious Thought* in 1924. The paper, entitled, somewhat blandly, "Some Beliefs About Psychology,"[15] is a frank reply to an assault on recent psychology. Brett concedes that psychologists deserve a large part of the criticism they get, but he insists that it is of the utmost importance not to go on from this to the denigration of psychology as such. For, he says, political democracy depends upon psychology.

15 George Sidney Brett, "Some Beliefs About Psychology," *Canadian Journal of Religious Thought*, vol. 1, no. 6 (1924).

Roughly, he claims, the extent to which men seek to rule each other by persuasion rather than by force is a function of their interest in and knowledge of psychology. If we want a democratic society, we must know enough about men to have a society in which they can persuade one another well enough to create an order without rule by force.

On some accounts of the nature of psychology, a statement of this sort is evidently a prelude to *Brave New World*, *1984*, and *The Clockwork Orange*. If psychology is a set of devices for ordering and controlling human behaviour then applying psychology is a way to obtain a society which looks democratic and is actually wholly authoritarian.

But what Brett is talking about is the possibility that psychology will provide us with the means for developing the social context for a genuine democracy. Though he there defends the physiological psychologist (provided the psychologist realizes the connection between, for instance, sensory physiology and the inner experiences of his subjects), he reminds us again that the past is related to the present. The psychologist examining religious phenomena, he says, cannot ignore the experience of St. Paul or St. Augustine. If we do not now have their experiences, psychology may at least enable us to understand those experiences and "elevate the idea of human activities."[16]

The same general attitude dominates *The Government of Man*. The book is dedicated to the proposition that human societies are not made, they grow and that, therefore, their present is to be understood only in terms of the past.

The Government of Man follows, though with less detail and significantly less scholarly craftsmanship in the construction of its development, the same general plan as the *History of Psychology*. It, too, begins with a notion of "primitive"[17] thought but passes quickly (after twenty-seven pages) to the Greeks and a more technical notion of philosophical ideas.

It also follows the development of thought through the Middle Ages, the early modern period, and the nineteenth century. Rather more space is given to Roman ideas, the structure of life in the Middle Ages, and the currents of thought which surrounded technical philosophy in the early modern period. Its basic notion is that societies change in a way which creates an interaction between conceptual structure and the inner life as well as through an interaction between conceptual structures and the objective social order.

The message, significantly, is that, as with psychology, we gain a measure of freedom—freedom in a sense closely associated with

16   Ibid., p. 480.
17   Brett, *The Government of Man*, p. 7.

441

understanding—through a process of development which is fundamentally rather than accidentally historical.

Both these notions, freedom as a species of understanding, and the distinction between the intrinsically (or fundamentally)and the accidentally historical, play a role of great importance in both works. The difficulty for an interpreter is that, like almost everything else, Brett approaches them obliquely and develops them in a context which is, especially in the *Psychology*, rich in detail.

It seems clear that, insofar as there is a direction in the *Psychology*—a direction not, as we have suggested, to be facilely associated with common notions of progress—that direction is from the less to the more free. Thus, when Plato has conceptualized the soul as a metaphysically distinct entity, it is possible for Aristotle to take the counter position that the soul is the form of the body. It was not until the notion of soul as special bodily function had been contrasted with the Platonic notion that Aristotle's thesis could have been formulated in a way which would have distinguished it from the bodily function theory. Aristotle would have sounded like someone advancing a vague form of the theory that the soul is breath but for the distinctions provided by the Platonic notions of form and of soul. When Plotinus had developed a more mystical view of the soul, the Platonic notion of its associations with a rational order reached by using the incomplete order of the sensory world as stepping stones could become, in its turn, clearer.

The thesis is not that Aristotle improved upon Plato or that Plotinus improved upon Aristotle. On the contrary, one gets the feeling that, as it becomes clearer, Brett would have concluded that there is more to be said for the Platonic theory. (Certainly his return in each case to new facets of the Platonic case would leave that impression.) The thesis, rather, is that we become increasingly free. We can now understand Plato a little better. After more contrasts have been introduced we shall grasp Plotinus better.

This understanding is liberating not in the sense that it enables us to assemble a greater array of ideas for contemplation but in the sense that it creates in us a greater capacity for experience, literally a richer inner life within which we can move more freely. For all his introspective focus on learning as such, Brett is not, in reality, much attached to the notion that the passive contemplation of ideas is to be recommended. It is not, if we understand his psychological theory (or psychological meta-theory as it turns out to be), even possible, on his view, to engage in the purely passive contemplation of the conceptual forms which generally, now, seem to be what is meant by "ideas." These

442

structures shape and govern the immediate experiences which are our inner lives and, as our understanding of them changes, so do our inner lives.

This notion of freedom is a feature of the meta-theory which turns out to dominate the three volumes. The meta-theory is, after all, that the arena in which the psychologist works is one which is governed by these developing conceptual frames. At any moment, what psychology investigates—the first-order subject matter of psychology—*is* the immediate experience. But what makes this experience possible is the developing conceptual frame.

We must, Brett seems to imply in his minor writings on psychology, be rather careful about this. Were we to ask whether or not the psychologist can establish the fact of human freedom, the question would be ambiguous to the point of being inappropriate. The psychologist will investigate, first of all, a certain class of immediate first-order experiences, secondly, a set of relations between these and other events in the world and human life, and thirdly the relation between these and past experiences which men are to have had. Freedom might or might not be a sensible characterization of certain features of first-order experience, but that is independent of freedom as a characterization of our ability to understand a range of conceptual frames. As our understanding of those conceptual frames grows, we shall become more or less able to control the shape in which some of our experience strikes us and more or less able to imagine other modes of experiencing. One sense of freedom is the state of not being bound by a single understanding.

Similar conditions apply to political arrangements. Being able to choose implies having a choice. Having a choice implies both a variety of possible understandings of a given situation *and* being able to generate the requisite first-order experiences so as to have something on which that understanding might be able to operate. We can be free or not free in any of these senses but as history develops—and as our understanding develops—we at least multiply the possibilities. Hence Brett's belief that a democratic society depends, in all likelihood, on the development of an effective psychology and on the development within a tradition of ideas of an understanding which has an historical frame.

The notion of what is intrinsically or fundamentally historical is also, one would think, of the utmost importance. As we study the history of ideas we can see that they come *only* in a sequence. They cannot suddenly be brought into existence nor can they, since their successors depend for their intelligibility upon them, be suddenly withdrawn from existence. Psychology, politics, and philosophy are, therefore, intrinsically historical if they are understood as a network of interlocking ideas.

Brett is not only laying the foundations for his meta-psychology; he is, in tracing these ideas, trying to show *how* philosophy itself is intrinsically historical. To try to understand present ideas without their historical context is, he invariably thought, a forlorn enterprise.

A final twist to the theory needs to be unravelled, however, before one can grasp Brett's relative lack of interest in contemporary speculation: He was gradually developing a philosophy out of his meta-psychology and its implied meta-philosophy. When we are faced, after a long history of thought, with a very complex and inter-related set of ideas, the task becomes one strongly related to the history of ideas. In a minor way, we can see that after Plotinus, one could understand Plato better. Looking back, now, we can see still more in the possibilities. We could choose simply to forge on into an unknown future, but since the developing inter-relations of ideas constrain the path into the future we also want to win our scholarly independence from that path. Only by deepening our sense of the past can we become its rightful heirs and not simply its victims. The wise philosopher, therefore, will build onto the meta-theory as well as onto the original historical dimensions of the ideas.

Evidently, this sets a new task for philosophers—new in kind as well as in detail. Once we have grasped the additional dimension we can see why it would be foolish to imagine that philosophy has as its task the refutation of old theories and the building of new ones. Each new theory deepens the possibility for understanding old ones and, if properly understood, gives them new life which must itself be assessed.

In Brett's view that philosopher who thinks that he can sit down at his desk and refute all the theories, sweeping them away in favour of the new dispensation, is a fool. Before he even entertains a new theory he must see how the old ones appear in its light. His contribution really *is*, however little he knows it, the creation of a new historical perspective. His ideas, after all, did not arrive *ex nihilo*. A theory which seemed to render nearly all the old ones meaningless would be one which represented a profound misunderstanding. For the old theories in their development represent the very conditions of understanding, whether that notion is taken philosophically or psychologically. There is a place for wrong turnings in such a theory and Brett, for the most part, remained tolerantly amused rather than outraged by the positivist attempts of the late twenties and thirties to demolish philosophy.

It is a great tragedy that we lack Brett's promised developments of his own philosophy. One suspects that it would have been, in the end, a commentary on his own *History of Psychology*, extracting the meanings and lessons from it, or, just as likely, a commentary on the history of philosophy. The fact that such a commentary does not occur within the *Psychology* is partly due to the fact that the ideas are developing within the book, partly the result of its place within Muirhead's "Library" which did not allow him to trespass too much on Erdmann's *History*, and partly, one suspects, the outcome of his own rather strong feeling that the message should carry itself to the alert reader. But, since one can hardly imagine that he would have accepted our rendering of his enterprise without at least important qualifications, riders, new insights, and his own ordering, the tragedy remains.

Part of the puzzle concerns the extent to which we can, in Brett's view, attain anything like a systematic understanding of the situation either in philosophy or in psychology. In some respects, Brett clearly adheres to doctrines which one might associate with Hegel: The reliance on history and the development of an historical method, the notion that ideas are mutually illuminating, the desire to see how one position, on close analysis, reveals the possibility of others are all Hegelian. The insistence on the particularity of ideas, the apparent insistence that historical development is not a surrogate for logical development, the general lack of interest in formal systems are all anti-Hegelian.

Volume 3 of the *History of Psychology* contains at least three widely separated sets of derogatory remarks about Hegel. The anti-Hegelian stance is here, admittedly, brought out rather starkly because of the nature of the subject matter. However philosophical he may at times wax, Brett does not forget that the subject is psychology and that psychology is about the immediate data of the inner life even if "about" should be interpreted with as much latitude as possible. Hegel's *Phenomenology* exhibits or seeks to exhibit those data under the shaping guise of general categories which emerge in the development of human thought. If one destroys them in their particularity, one destroys their value as objects for psychologists even if not as objects for philosophers. Brett is inclined to be much kinder to materialist reductionists, associationists, and even the "brass instrument" workers, if only because to look for the psychological data in a body, as an association of sensations, or with the tools of laboratory measurement is, at least, to maintain crucial aspects of their links to a here and now and so, in principle, to their particularity. The Hegelian synthesis simply would not, in Brett's view, sustain what seems to develop as the all-important distinction between first-order psychology and meta-psychology.

But does this carry over into a critique of systematic philosophy? Brett is never very clear. The fact is that he does not produce a systematic philosophy. (Nor does he always carry out his own small-scale enterprises in a way which would settle the question for us. In his essay on Berkeley, a Presidential Address given before the Royal Society of Canada in 1933, in which he promises to "give some account of . . . the present value of his [Berkeley's] philosophical works,"[18] Brett concentrates on biographical matters.)

He did insist that system had its place. He remarks at the beginning of *The Government of Man* that "the life of the individual is a series of events more or less capable of becoming a system"[19] and he implies that the meaning of such a life depends upon the extent and mode of that system. Irving argues that Brett maintained that "two great ideas of Hegel's philosophy of history, the idea of continuity and the idea of the organic totality of life, are essential to the historical approach not only in science but in all other fields of inquiry as well."[20]

But in order to make those notions work we have to know where the cutting of history is and we have to seek an organizing principle for it.

Brett is thus torn between the view that the study of history, especially the history of ideas, will impose its own system on us if we grasp the way in which the ideas come together and the view that there is an ordering principle. There are passages which, by implication, sustain Irving's reading and may suggest that it is not just freedom in a special sense which may emerge from history, but that the direction toward freedom is the guiding and directing force behind history. But there is no more to this reading than implication.

If it is the right reading, then the freedom is not that of Hegel's Absolute Idea coming to be in the world and coming to be aware of itself as we become aware of ourselves, but something more concrete— the coming into actuality of a nexus of possibilities which lead into one another and produce the possibility of an order which transcends the old bonds.

It would be tempting to read Brett as close to Collingwood, except that there is nothing in Brett's historical analysis which makes him sceptical of objective truth or bound by anything like Collingwood's

---

18 George Sidney Brett, "Bishop Berkeley," A Presidential Address, *Transactions of the Royal Society of Canada*, vol. 27, section II (1933), p. 109.
19 Brett, *The Government of Man*, p. 1.
20 Irving, "The Achievement of George Sidney Brett," p. 356.

absolute presuppositions. Indeed the ideas of objectivity and truth for Brett seem to be amongst the ideas which develop in history. One is objective insofar as one instantiates an acceptable idea of objectivity. Truth is an idea associated with the experiences of inquiring and finding and has its meaning in the historical context. But the historical context does not for Brett, as it did for Dilthey and in a different way for Collingwood, destroy some of the validity of the ideas. Rather it opens possibilities for their further understanding and those ideas, too, we may expect to go on growing. Nor, a fortiori, is history, as Croce might have had it, a connected story which we tell to ourselves. Rather, since our self-concepts are part of the development, we are a story which history tells to itself. Surely, Brett would not have put it quite that way; but an implication of his theory is that we must remember that *we* shall be intelligible as part of the unity of history. We are made by it every bit as much as we make it.

The sense in which Brett thought of himself as "realist" emerges rather strongly from such an interpretation. We confront history; it enables us to make ourselves intelligible to ourselves and that understanding, itself, makes us anew. It is not what we impose on history that necessarily matters—that *may* pass into unintelligibility—but what history imposes on us. It may be that out of our freedom we shall make history different but, if so, that will be because of the historical process itself.

Furthermore, though history is the dimension of ultimate intelligibility whether in philosophy, psychology, or science, there is the immediacy of experience which *can* be rendered intelligible by a systematic psychology. That is another—and less crucial—dimension of reality. Reality in Brett's theories evidently has more than one dimension and the sin of the systematic philosophers has often been to reduce one dimension to another, a process which he sometimes illustrates along the way in the *History of Psychology* as in his discussion of the sins of Hegel.

One could, however, call him not a realist but an objective idealist. For the moving forces in the world are, for him, the interconnections of ideas, ideas as objective and not merely as subjective components in immediate experience. His reality, after all, seems to be composed of that objectivity together with immediate experience. He cannot be a Berkeleyan (despite his long interest in Berkeley) because reality for him does, obviously, transcend immediate experience. He cannot be a follower of Bradley, Green, or Bosanquet because system cannot swallow the immediacy and particularity of the givens of experience. But he is no materialist and no realist in the "critical realist" sense either. Even science is to be understood within and not as transcending the historical scheme. In 1925 he told the Royal Society of Canada that science was cumulative, had a principle of growth, and was therefore "historically determined."[21]

In all likelihood, even such an expression as "historical objectivist" would not please him much more than "objective idealist," for those terms, too, would imply that his theory had descended from the meta-level to the first-order level of philosophical debates where the theories are simply part and parcel of the organic historical development. Marxists would have no trouble in identifying him as the very epitome of the bourgeois idealist philosopher, for he did think that the moving and shaking was done by ideas, that revolutions in ideas are hardly feasible and therefore revolutions amongst humans are probably productive of illusions. There is certainly no call to revolution to be discerned in *The Government of Man*.

Brett would only have been amused at such a characterization. One can only wish that he had produced, stimulated, or set in train a substantial work of philosophical synthesis which would have made clear the details.[22] But one *can* grasp what he was up to and, if we can find a philosopher with enough learning, the work may yet be done.

John Irving fits naturally into this chapter not merely because he was Brett's biographer and annotator but also because, more than any other philosopher, he was markedly influenced by Brett. The two men, however, were remarkably unlike in everything but philosophical outlook.

Irving enjoyed—and played to the full—the part of the public philosopher. He mastered the technique of broadcasting soon after the widespread introduction of radio, switched to television when the Canadian Broadcasting Corporation introduced talk shows, and served for nearly a decade on the editorial board of the (then) weekly magazine *Saturday Night*.

Born at Drumbo, in Oxford County, Ontario, in 1903, he went to school in Galt and then went on to Victoria College. In 1927 he left Toronto with a Master's degree and was accepted at Princeton as Proctor Fellow. From there he went to Cambridge where he completed a second bachelor's degree, and in 1930 returned to Princeton as an instructor in philosophy. After eight years at Princeton he moved to the University of British Columbia as Professor and Head of the (com-

21 George Sidney Brett, "The History of Science as a Factor in Modern Education," *Transactions of the Royal Society of Canada*, vol. 19, section II (1925), p. 42.
22 But this is not to ignore his careful scholarly work as evidenced in his book on Gassendi. George Sidney Brett, *The Philosophy of Gassendi* (London: Macmillan, 1908).

bined) Departments of Psychology and Philosophy. He spent the war years on the west coast and then accepted an offer to return to Victoria College as Head of the Department of Philosophy. There he continued to teach until his death in 1965.

Throughout his thirty-five-year teaching career, he was active not only in public debates but in every available professional association. He served as an officer of both the Pacific and the Eastern Divisions of the American Philosophical Association, as President of the Pacific Congress on the teaching of philosophy, and as a founder of the Canadian Philosophical Association.

Brett's influence on him seems to consist mainly in this: Irving became substantially convinced of two propositions: Few if any human phenomena can be grasped outside their historical context, and philosophy invariably requires another subject matter in which to work.

The first of these is responsible for Irving's long concern with the history of philosophy in English Canada. It is, indeed, to him that we owe the fact that it is possible at all to piece together that history. He seems to have been the organizer and moving spirit behind the project which resulted in the development of the publication of *Philosophy in Canada: A Symposium*. That work appeared in 1952 as a pamphlet in a series published by the University of Toronto.[23] Though its contributors included Charles Hendel, Allison Johnson, Rupert Lodge, and (as author of an Introduction) Fulton Anderson, the basic work in putting the picture together is clearly Irving's. The same material figures again in his essay on "Philosophical Trends in Canada" in *Science and Values*[24] and in the appropriate chapters in Carl Klinck's *Literary History of Canada*.[25]

Admittedly, in his attempt to get much material into focus in a small space, Irving too easily lumps philosophers together into schools, and leaves the impression that the Canadian idealists owe more to their British counterparts than is the case. But without his work, the rest of us might well have been unable to find our way.

He saw philosophizing as a particular response to a particular situation, as something which needed to be explained and understood in its place and in its context. Thus early Canadian philosophy, at least in English Canada, revealed the way in which various British

23 John A. Irving, *Philosophy in Canada: A Symposium* (Toronto: University of Toronto Press, 1952). See also "The Development of Philosophy in Central Canada from 1850 to 1900," *Canadian Historical Review*, vol. 31, no. 3 (September 1950).

24 John A. Irving, *Science and Values* (Toronto: The Ryerson Press, 1952).

25 Carl Klinck, *A Literary History of Canada*, 1st ed. (Toronto: University of Toronto Press, 1965).

cultures—especially Scottish culture—had come to Canada and the adjustments they were compelled to make here. His essay on Brett, however, seems to view Brett as something different: Here was a man clearly aware of the effects of history and culture and therefore, one infers (though Irving does not say it outright) no longer the creature of his culture.

Interestingly, it is not in such freedom that Irving himself seemed to see the future of philosophy. In 1952, he wrote:

> There are certain indications that philosophy will play a much more dynamic role in Canadian civilization in future than it has played during the past hundred years. Its emphasis on intellectual history will continue to bring it into more vital relationships with scientific and humanistic interests; an emphasis on social philosophy will build up more intimate connections with the educational, social, economic, and political problems of the wider community. There are also indications that in future Canadian philosophy will be brought into closer relationships with American philosophy. . . . There is also an increasing awareness that Canada is a North American nation.[26]

It may not be clear to one not familiar with Irving's career just what this means, but to Irving, it had a vivid and direct meaning. In pursuit of "intellectual history" and "social philosophy," he set out on a long detailed study of a brief period in the history of the province of Alberta.[27] He produced, in 1959, his book on the Social Credit movement there—the only book he produced other than the volume of essays entitled *Science and Values* and the volume of essays (mainly by others) which he edited.

The Social Credit project is a difficult one for a philosopher to evaluate. It seems, almost entirely, to be just what it purports to be—a history of the brief period in which William Aberhart, an obscure Ontario school teacher who had moved to Alberta and became a school principal and fundamentalist radio evangelist, rose to political dominance in the province.

The period is, indeed, a fascinating one. Though debates about monetary and fiscal policy must be as old as the invention of money

---

26 Irving, *Science and Values*, pp. 81-82.

27 John A. Irving, *The Social Credit Movement in Alberta* (Toronto and Buffalo: University of Toronto Press, 1959). Hereafter referred to as *Social Credit*. The Social Credit movement flourished in Alberta from its inception in the autumn of 1932 to its achievement of political power in the summer of 1935. The movement "owes its origin to a Scottish engineer, Major Clifford Hugh Douglas (1878-1952), who was impressed by the fact that many developments *physically* possible from the engineer's point of view are *financially* impossible" (*Social Credit*, p. 5). William Aberhart led the Social Crediters to victory and became premier of Alberta on September 3, 1935. (See *Social Credit*, pp. 3-5.)

and, at least since Adam Smith and the development of modern economics, there have been frequent political resorts to monetary solutions to social problems, the Social Credit success is one of the very few which accrued to political parties which have claimed that virtually all social problems could be solved by changing the nature of the money supply.

Irving does discuss, briefly, the monetary theories of Major Clifford Hugh Douglas, the real or apparent changes made in them by Aberhart, and (much more briefly) the objections to them made by orthodox economists.[28] But he makes no attempt to assess the real relation between money and social form.

The period is also fascinating because it represents a clear example of widespread popular belief in a theory which (one would guess) few people actually understood, an example of the way in which one Canadian province can be set on a course dramatically unlike those of its neighbours which seem to have much the same demography and history, and because of the lessons it teaches about the art of political organization.

The surprise in store for the reader is that it is mainly the last of these that concerns Irving. A philosopher, one might think, would be interested in problems about belief or in problems about the central notions of historical explanation. But political organization?

Yet the bulk of the book simply recounts the way in which Aberhart first built a following for his radio talks on the Bible, how he gained control of the Bible School which grew out of these activities, and how, as he began to read Major Douglas and to muse on the growing disaster of the Depression, he came to use the framework he had built as a device on which to predicate a political movement.

Is Irving, then, writing a treatise on human motivation, on the now fashionable distinction between behaviour and action, or on the doctrine that historical events are essentially unique?

It is not obvious that any of these things is really going on. Aberhart is painted as a man who only gradually came to understand his own capacities and the power which they might bring him, who genuinely set out to instruct others about the Bible and only under severe pressure came to accept the proposition that he might use the hold he had on his audiences for political ends, and who, for the most part, lacked both the imagination and the reflective powers which would justify us in claiming that he was a deliberate manipulator of other human beings.

28 Ibid., pp. 6, 54-57, and appendix IV.

451

More puzzling, still, is Irving's apparent assumption throughout the book that we (the readers) share with him the superior knowledge and wisdom which enable us to understand that Social Credit theory really doesn't merit a thorough analysis—that it is silly rather than wrong.

Thus the "explanation" for the Alberta phenomenon seems to be the usual mixture: Albertans, oppressed by Depression, drought, and lack of education, were mesmerized by a rather ordinary school teacher who mixed the Bible with the crank theories of a rather absurd Scot. Irving noticed that there was something rather odd about this. He devotes considerable space to the development of the co-operative movement, the social and economic theories of Henry Wise Wood[29] (an American immigrant), and the political downfall of the United Farmers of Alberta.

How did it come about that a people capable of the great sophistication needed to create a flourishing economic institution like the agrarian co-operative, to sustain a substantial reformist political movement and an impressive array of public services, suddenly became prey to what Irving leads us to believe was a simple-minded purveyor of pseudo-panaceas? It is possible that, in that question, there lies buried a philosophical issue or series of philosophical issues which must be confronted before one can do very much by way of orderly social science. For the question seems to suppose a distinction between people as a mass political public (a statistically defined entity of rather large dimensions), people organized efficiently into responsive institutions, and people as individuals. One might have argued in the Alberta situation that the institutions which should have prevented the lapse or collapse of the people into a mass or politicized public simply failed and that, therefore, the range of individual intelligence was not brought into play. But, though Irving does imply something of the kind in his preface and in the long descriptions which he offers of the failure of various groups and institutions to solve the pressing problems, he does not raise these large issues in a specific way.

More particularly, he does not raise the issues in a philosophical way. The philosophical issues have to do with the methodology by which one would inquire into such matters, the problem of individuality, the nature of causes, and the nature of human action. But Irving adopts a kind of historical methodology without seeking to defend

29 Henry Wise Wood (1860-1941) was the dominant agrarian leader of the province from 1916 to 1937. Statements of his social and political philosophy can be found in his presidential addresses to the U.F.A., 1917-1931, on file at the Head Office of the United Farmers of Alberta Co-operative in Calgary. For further information on Wood see Irving, *Social Credit*, pp. 230-32.

it—at least if one thinks of a defence as something explicit. He simply tells the story, mostly in chronological order, and seeks to provide us with explanations only in the way that a novelist might be said to provide us with explanations for the behaviour of his characters if and only if he leaves us with no loose ends.

But he insists that there is a philosophical point to what he does and we can do no better than to quote him:

> The importance of the study of collective behaviour is immediately apparent to most psychologists, psychiatrists, and social scientists. It should be equally apparent to moral and political philosophers. The rise of the Social Credit movement in Alberta illustrates, in eminent degree, the social context in which democracy functions under stress. The functioning of the democratic process in Alberta during the rise of the Social Credit movement provides a much needed corrective to the abstract concepts of the classical philosophers of democracy from John Locke to John Dewey. No interpretation of democracy which ignores the phenomena of collective behaviour can hope to stand. In its wider implications this book may therefore be envisaged as a contribution to the democratic philosophy of society and the state.
>
> In the twentieth century several large-scale movements based on philosophies such as socialism, communism, fascism, or Naziism have sought to transform society through the attainment of political power. Owing to its more limited objectives, the Social Credit movement provides an unusual opportunity for a study of the formative role of ideas in the process of social development.[30]

Much seems to depend on the proposition that the story from the time of Aberhart's arrival in Alberta to the night of his victory in the Alberta election in 1935 is a story of general deterioration in the quality of institutional response. Irving's expression—"under stress"—in the Preface bears this out and the whole tone of the text is one of general praise for the words and works of Henry Wise Wood and general condemnation of "Bible Bill" Aberhart and his friends. The fact that Irving's language is invariably temperate and that he plays down Aberhart's character flaws does little to disguise this conviction. If the story was one of a general fall from rationality to emotionalism, from reasoned solutions to pseudo-panaceas, from demands for orderly change to demands for instant utopias, then the proposition that collective behaviour is not always or merely the sum of individual behaviour would be sustained. The difficulty is about Social Credit ideas as "ideas."

We need to know how to take "ideas." Are they Platonic ideas, Cartesian ideas, Lockean ideas, or what? (Are they, that is, archetypes

30 Irving, *Social Credit*, Preface, pp. ix-x.

which are basic features of reality, mental entities which are direct objects of cognition, or associative assemblies of sensory impressions?) The Preface cannot help but tantalize the philosopher who may expect that something exciting should follow. Is it not true that the concept of money seems to provide an extraordinary opportunity to investigate the sense in which ideas—as opposed to something other than ideas—might influence the course of human events? For is not money a "pure" idea? Everything which is money is also something else which has physical properties, interesting or otherwise. But these physical properties seem to have little to do with the behaviour of the "monetary" properties. Could we not now see how a non-standard idea of money functioned in the political arena and what the implications of that functioning are? Furthermore, the orthodox economists have frequently written as though "real" money was a kind of Platonic idea which obeys its own laws and has its own way in the world independently of us.

Major Douglas, William Aberhart, and their friends may have been woolly-headed, but one of the things they seemed to be trying to say was that the orthodox economists were under the spell of a Platonic superstition. They took, instead, an empiricist view of the idea of money. They thought we made and could change it at will and that, if it caused social problems, then social problems could be solved by changing it.

Here, in short, we find a classical philosophical dispute being thrashed out in public by men and women who, for the most part, would not recognize the technical vocabulary of the philosopher nor care a whit if they did. But the circumstances of their lives formed, unwittingly, an arena for the investigation of that issue.

Irving, however, tackled the issue indirectly. His account is something like this: The dispute is not really about the idea of money but about the distribution of goods and services. The economy in Alberta in the early nineteen-thirties reached a point at which it was difficult to acquire or maintain operating capital, unlikely that, if one did, one would produce efficiently either in agriculture or in most available kinds of industry, and less likely still that one would find an acceptable market for what one did produce. All these ills might—irrationally—be lumped together as the "lack of money" and the Social Credit proposal might be understood as an undertaking to provide money. Earlier, when men and women were less desperate, they indulged in better analyses of the economic problems they faced and produced more sophisticated conclusions, though the conceptual mistake of regarding all economic difficulties as "lack of money" was always possible and had, in fact, a long and quite depressing history.

Ultimately, Irving claims that his study can produce "a much needed corrective to the abstract concepts of the classical philosophers of democracy from John Locke to John Dewey." He does not overtly draw any morals from his story about what this "much needed corrective" might be, but we can, perhaps, infer what was on his mind.

Locke regarded democracy as the outgrowth of a set of claims to the ownership of property. Everyone who laboured to transform raw materials into finished and marketable products had, on Locke's view, a claim to the ownership of his production and to whatever he might obtain by fair trade for it. At the same time, there remained a community claim to the property because all men had a common right to what God had granted equally to all. Thus men were involved with individually defensible claims to property and with a community which must arbitrate those claims and which retained—on behalf of all—a residual right of its own. Democracy seems a fair and reasonable response to this situation though it may not, perhaps, be the case that one who accepts the Lockean view of it can produce a logically unexceptionable case. Dewey, by contrast, views democracy as the reasonable outcome of the fact that truth, including political truth, is relative to the ability of propositions to produce appropriate results for their users. Propositions, he most often thinks, are used much as tools are used and the question is about whether or not they perform in the way that we expect of them. In these circumstances the arbiter of the truth becomes the individual and democracy is the only evident way in which individuals, so constituted, can ultimately reconcile their conflicting claims. Dewey certainly would admit that there is a community within which the individual finds himself and that the community represents the acceptable trade-offs between individuals in terms of interest and intelligibility.

These, then, are examples, perhaps, of "abstract" democratic theories held by philosophers actually named by Irving. In what sense are they abstract and in what sense does Irving's study of the Social Credit movement really provide "a much needed corrective" to them? Neither shows, as a theory, just how it is that individual interests are actually reconciled and neither, considered simply as a theory, gives a detailed explication of the way in which the concept of community is related to the concept of individual. Each, however, offers a way of construing individual interests; each tells one how meaning is to be given to the notion of community, and each has provided fairly effective inspiration if not actual guidance for individuals who have sought to democratize various kinds of institutions.

The suggestion of Irving's study is that democracy sometimes (or at least on one occasion) works by reducing interests which are individual and rational to interests which are collective and irrational. There is a strong sense in Irving's account of the matter that the Social Credit movement was successful very largely because it dealt with ideas which no one understood very well. Where no one understands very well, each may understand in his own sense without seeming to clash with the understandings of others. But there is also a sense from his narrative of the likelihood that most people in Alberta found the condition of the economy in those years utterly unintelligible. Some of them were, one must suppose, inclined to the belief that there must be something which they did not understand well and which, if exposed, would explain what seemed unintelligible. What could be a better candidate for this dubious office than the concept of money?

Is it, then, Irving's claim that classical philosophers placed too much emphasis on the rational and the intelligible and not enough on the irrational elements? It is tempting to think so, but Irving does not say that. He leaves the reader to draw his own inferences and the reader may well suspect that the failure on Irving's part to tackle the theory of money head-on gives a spurious look of irrationality to the whole situation.

Talking about money had become in those years in Alberta a familiar enough activity. If you knew nothing about Canadian football and dropped into a little Alberta town during Grey Cup week, you would also be baffled by the strange terms, the statistics, the predictions, the whole way of looking at a department of human behaviour. Street talk during Grey Cup week may, of course, *be* irrational but the fact that we fail to grasp the jargon does not make it so. Similarly, we may now infer from Social Credit literature, private letters, newspaper editorials, and so forth that the Albertans did not know what they were talking about and (though he is careful to suggest rather than say) Irving seems to have come to believe that. He may well have been right. But it is hard to be sure.

Furthermore, we are not given any theoretical structures which we can use to supplement Locke or Dewey, to decide on the place of economics in social theory, to develop norms for rational group behaviour, or, for that matter, to distinguish clearly between collective behaviour and aggregates of individual behaviour.

John Irving was not deeply committed to the most popular kinds of current philosophy outside Canada. Despite at least two mentions of Wittgenstein,[31] Irving mostly ignored logical positivism—whether or not some versions of it had irrationalist tendencies—and his essay on existentialism makes it clear that he thinks its future in Canada is

---

31 Irving, *Science and Values*, pp. viii, 90. Professor Martyn Estall recalls, however, that Irving returned from Cambridge in 1930 "much taken with Wittgenstein."

confined to certain kinds of theology and that it has in any case a "serious weakness,"[32] that it cannot pass the test of the views of human affairs supported by the social or the natural sciences.

We think one can only understand Irving's theory in terms of an extension of what seemed to be Brett's hypothesis—that philosophy itself can only be understood as an historical process. Irving claimed that Brett should be acclaimed the "founder and chief inspiration of the first indigenous philosophical movement to develop in Canada, the Toronto school of intellectual history."[33] He included Fulton Anderson, Thomas Goudge, George Edison, D. R. G. Owen, Allison Johnson, R. F. McRae, and Emil Fackenheim in that "school." Irving did not mention himself in the list, though his own work comes closest to what one would expect to find canonical in such a school. There is little of Irving's writings (unless one puts weight on some essays which are, in fact, book reviews) which does not have an historical slant.

But what does "intellectual history" in this sense do? Brett, as we saw, can be read in several different ways but at least it would seem to be the case that (part of) his method in the history of philosophy was to insist that one philosophical proposition should be contrasted with another of the same logical type or kind. Thus his *History of Psychology* does not so much confront theories of mind with critical statements which are about them as confront theories of mind with other theories of mind, with ideas which form the context for them, and with a succession of such theories spread over a span of time. (Even if one objects, as one may, to the reading which we gave to Brett's theory, it seems reasonable to admit that, descriptively, this is part of what Brett *does*.) But this means that, to an important extent, the philosophizing is oblique. It comes out in the ways in which one juxtaposes ideas, in the way in which one orders concepts, in the historical path one chooses to cut through the history of ideas.

Irving evidently wanted to confront a more difficult problem: How does it come about that we have philosophical ideas or concepts and what constitutes their legitimacy? In that light, the work on Social Credit in Alberta can be read as a first-order enterprise out of which one might eventually engender a second-order enterprise like Brett's. In the first-order enterprise, however, the philosophical ideas are engendered not directly but indirectly in the way in which one orders the facts and the issues.

Thus, no doubt, what the Preface says is correct: The facts about the rise of the Social Credit movement are ordered so as to force the

32 Irving, *Science and Values*, p. 44.
33 Ibid., p. 78.

457

questions about collective behaviour, democratic practice, and the place of rationality in the determination of social values.

It was, to an important extent, against philosophy as Brett, Irving, and others like them had reconstructed it, that Harold Innis reacted. Innis will be claimed as an economist, historian, theorist about the social sciences—almost anything but a philosopher. And it is true that much of his writing lies outside the scope of the technical philosopher.

Whatever Innis might have called himself, the fact of the matter is that his own career was given its direction essentially by the fact that philosophy had abandoned the task which he wanted it to perform and, therefore, by the fact that he was compelled to invent a discipline of his own in which to perform that task. The choices which he made did open important vistas which, if philosophers would only look, might very well give the discipline a new shape and make possible the achievement of some of the tasks which Innis did not live to complete.

Innis, like Irving and Blewett, was an Ontario farm boy. Born in 1894 (and thus fifteen years younger than George Brett and nine years older than John Irving), he grew up before the Ontario school system had extended its collegiate institutes effectively into the countryside. Commuting twenty miles each way every day by train to high school at least gave him time away from farm chores and an opportunity to think. When he went from Woodstock to Toronto to study at McMaster University (an institution defying the increasingly godless University of Toronto), the journey and experience were wholly new to him. Innis was attracted there (as were so many of its best students) to James Ten Broeke and the philosophical questioning of the simple and common-sense view of the world. Ten Broeke, as we have seen, was strongly given to what seem, to the contemporary ear, orthodox pieties and it is a measure of McMaster at the time that Innis described him as "by far the most heretical thinker in the university."[34] In his unpublished autobiography Innis remarked that Ten Broeke "opened the subject of philosophy in such a way as to free those who sought to be free from the conventions of philosophical thought."[35]

Evidently, however, he acquired from Ten Broeke the philosophical conviction that there is an ultimate importance to system and that very few facts can be understood except in terms of a system which unites them to all other facts. Thus, much of Innis' life as a social scientist was to be devoted to an attempt to discover why there are several social sciences and not one, to a search for an answer to questions about the relation of fact and value, and to an understanding of

34 Robin Neill, *A New Theory of Value*, p. 10.
35 Ibid.

the relation between the physical and the social sciences and between both of those and the humanistic activities which more naturally go under the name of "culture." All of these themes lie very close to the surface of every one of Innis' major writings and all of them are, traditionally, philosophical. If we are prepared to accept Irving's claim that his work on the Social Credit movement in Alberta has something to do with philosophy we can hardly reject Innis' work as a prospective source of philosophical ideas.

Innis' studies were interrupted by World War I and he returned to civilian life, limping from a wound inflicted in the bloody assault on Vimy Ridge, determined to find a way to investigate the questions which his work at McMaster had suggested to him. In the end, he chose the University of Chicago, partly because it was not far from home, partly because it gave him a chance to work his way through graduate school as a teaching assistant, and partly because it had a reputation of openness, innovation, and a willingness to let students follow their own bent.

Nominally he studied economics, wrote a thesis on the development of the Canadian Pacific Railway, and acquired the tools of the trade then expected of a young man setting out to practise the most formally ordered of the social sciences.

In fact, this conventional façade conceals the development of a set of ideas which dominated his thought and work for the rest of his life. For one thing, he was influenced by Robert E. Park,[36] a reformed philosopher and the leader of a school of sociologists who were coming to see human and social problems as issues in communication. For another, the thesis on the CPR had its origin in his belief that classical economics—with its foundation in price theory—failed to mesh with reality because the evolution of institutional change constantly upset its hypothetical or prophetic equilibrium, and in his belief that there is a basic connection between communication systems and economic development. Finally, the building of the CPR is a classical case of the problems involved in choosing social values: Promised as a device to make possible Confederation, built at considerable public expense and with land grants and other favours as a device for private profit, completed on a route which brought a population guaranteed to produce the dust bowls of the 1930s, what could offer a better purview of every sort of value conflict? Innis, of course, did not raise all these questions in his thesis, but they all emerged in his later writing

36   Robert E. Park was a philosopher who became a sociologist and is widely regarded as a founder of what is now thought of as the science of communication. See his *The Crowd and the Public*, ed. H. Elsner, (Chicago: University of Chicago Press, 1972).

and that first study of the CPR was an experiment at finding the forms which would later go into his studies of the fur trade, the cod-fisheries, the lumber and pulp and paper industries. And even though the prairie dust bowls were yet to come, the problem of the railway and its creation of a force which stripped a narrowly focussed region of its immediately pluckable resources could not have escaped a man who was to make conservation one of the chief issues which would force a revision of classical economics.

Luckily, he was able, when he had finished his studies at Chicago, to find a post in the University of Toronto's department of political economy—a place in which, at least, the separation of the social sciences into competing abstractions had not severed the traditional connection between political science and economics.

He was eventually to become head of that department and Dean of Graduate Studies, but years of serving under successive imported "heads" who generally knew little and cared less about Canadian problems left him with a bitterness which never quite wore off. Indeed, toward the end of his life in an essay included in the posthumous *Essays in Canadian Economic History*, he wrote, "I am unhappily aware too of the fact that I am the first Canadian to be appointed to the position which I have the honour to hold...."[37] Significantly, he blamed this, however, not on the Englishmen and Americans who came to dominate Canadian universities but on Canadians themselves. He thought that those in a position to influence crucial appointments in the social sciences feared that Canadians in such posts would become forces for social change. Foreigners, most often, knew little about the Canadian scene and were reluctant to make public pronouncements about it.

This experience seems to have been decisive in the forging of the remaining crucial idea which continued to influence his work: the idea that, as Canadians, we must understand the world for ourselves—that no one else, however clever, can do it for us because our understanding is uniquely related to concepts which do not have exact counterparts in any other culture.

Two issues concern us here as representative of the philosophical outcome of his work: his theory of the historical development of the social sciences and his theory of the inter-relation between those sciences themselves and between them and other kinds of knowledge.

The difficulty involved in getting an accurate account of these themes should not be underestimated. All his works have scattered through them philosophical references, quotations, and asides, and

37 Harold A. Innis, "The Church in Canada," *Essays in Canadian Economic History*, ed. Mary Q. Innis (Toronto: University of Toronto Press, 1956), p. 387.

there is plenty of evidence that he went on reading philosophy until the time of his death. But not only is there no single work devoted to specifically philosophical issues; there is also no single work in which he sets out his philosophy of history or his philosophy of the social sciences.

The nearest thing to the former is *Empire and Communications*,[38] originally a set of lectures given at Oxford and published there but revised after his death by his wife and re-published by the University of Toronto. Like any book given to the exploration of a single theme, it accords an exaggerated importance to its theme—in this case the ways in which changing modes of communication have brought about socio-political structures. From it alone, one would get a distorted picture of the shape of Innis' thought. Such a shape brings out clearly the relation between Innis, his predecessor Robert E. Park, and their successor, Marshall McLuhan, but McLuhan and his followers have, after all, exploited only a rather special part of the Innis legacy. The complex inter-relations between the forms of the social sciences and the structures of space and time are better emphasized in many of the essays of the same period (including the difficult and obscure Royal Society presidential address called "Minerva's Owl" which is unashamedly philosophical).[39]

The most valuable assistance we have found in understanding these issues is in Robin Neill's *A New Theory of Value: The Canadian Economics of H. A. Innis*. Much that follows derives from his serious attempt to put things together.

In the most general way, Innis' thesis about historical change is that it comes about as a result of changing capacities for the control of space and time. Time is not, for Innis, the metrical linear order of the physicist but, essentially, the psychological time of immediate experience. We are able to give meaning to events or to components of immediate experience insofar as we can control time—insofar, that is, as we can create occasions of intelligible repetition or recurrence. In terms of these we agree on one or more structures which might be thought of as objective time.

It is here that the value question at once presents itself: As soon as we adopt a way of controlling time and mastering space, we change the likelihood of events—we create opportunities where none were before and, on a statistical basis, we can bet that some of those opportunities will be acted upon.

38 Harold A. Innis, *Empire and Communications*, revised by Mary Q. Innis with a Foreword by Marshall McLuhan (Toronto: University of Toronto Press, 1972).
39 Harold A. Innis, "Minerva's Owl," *Proceedings of the Royal Society of Canada*, vol. 41, series III (May 1947).

If, therefore, we build a railroad across Canada, or create in Egypt an abundant supply of papyrus, or confront Europe with the printing press, we open the way for a dramatic change in the pattern of behaviour. These events are crucial, more crucial than any others because the opportunities to act are, after all, definable in terms of the available regions of space-time within which actions can take place. (Innis, so far as we know, never confronts the issue directly but he seems to see human behaviour statistically—i.e., as a set of opportunities some subset of which will be instantiated—and never in the context of a strictly determined pattern of causes and effects.)

In *Empire and Communications* he repeatedly probes historical occasions on which communications opportunities changed and resulted in important changes in the social structure. The more common view had been, of course, that pre-existing social forces created a demand for more or better communications and thus brought about the necessary changes and inventions. Factually, this is not in Innis' view what generally happens, for a new social force seems to imply a new pattern of human action. But how can that be without the opening of a new way of structuring space or the extension of an existing space? It seems, in this case, that Innis' concern with Canadian problems put him on the track of this notion. Consider: With the coming of the transcontinental railway, the route from Halifax to Vancouver ceased to be by way of Cape Horn and came to be by way of Winnipeg. In human experience, the space between Halifax and Vancouver was changed dramatically and so was the structure of important features of experienced time. It was within this humanly created space and time that a whole country was born. Winnipeg as a place impossibly far from any other human settlement was not the same place as the Winnipeg whose distance from a point from which to ship wheat could be measured in hours on a train.

Space and time are not only influenced by communications systems or devices, and if *Empire and Communications* suffers from some overemphasis, Innis' writings, taken as a whole, do not. There are also social systems which determine the dominant positions within such communications systems. One of the peculiarities about Canada, Innis thought, was that our social space and time do not have their roots in a revolutionary tradition. The French Revolution passed by the French Canadians who were isolated by an ocean. The American Revolution was deliberately rejected by Canadians. Even the English Revolution of 1640 had little influence on the peoples (heavily Scots and Irish) who settled in Canada. Subsequently, almost everyone else in the world (outside the older units of the British Commonwealth) has had a revolution. But Canada remains immune. This means, of course, that for Canadians it usually does not seem true that the dominant regions of space-time are those commanded by instruments of force and, in general, one region of that social space-time seems connected to another by an orderly route of decision making. (Though Innis worried rather extensively about the lack of effective action taken by Canadians and their governments against the ravages of the Depression of the nineteen-thirties, it does not seem to have occurred to him that the absence of a revolutionary tradition may have made Canadians less likely than, say, Americans to believe that their fate was in their own hands, and more prone to inaction.)

What all this means is that knowledge about society has a temporal orientation and it is not irrelevant that societies have histories and are composed of human beings. The mechanisms of social change cannot be understood *sub specie aeternitatis* or in mathematical formulae which are abstract and link any pair of events to any other pair within the same region (as, in principle, a law of physics might). Since human actions are involved, the shaping of events is unique and, at most, intelligible through the systems of common meanings which define cultures. There may be very general rules (such as Innis' own rule about space, time, and social change) but those only give the most general shape to human history. The detailed accounts of them have to be as voluminous, patient, and full of particulars as, say, Innis' own account of the history of the cod fisheries.

Furthermore, the understanding of the situation is no more value-neutral than the situation itself—and the understanding of the situation may bring about a significant social change. To choose to understand, say, the uniqueness of Canadian society and its culture is to open the way to its recognition and the way to actions which may help to sustain it. To treat it, instead (as in Innis' view often happens), merely as an extension of British or American society and culture is to bring about a situation in which Canadian individuality may really be obliterated. For to ignore its nature is to create a space-time in which the necessary acts have no place and no meaning. Hence one of the problems of any social science is that to describe a situation is (at least potentially) to change it, for, to revert to what seems to be Innis' basic thesis, descriptions are meaning structures which *themselves* add to or at least complicate an existing space and time.

It should be evident that if this is a fair account of Innis' later writings and their emphasis on time, space, culture, nationalism, and communications, there is a basic ambivalence about the situation as he describes it.

On the one hand, it would seem that a social science of some kind is possible because there are general principles of social change, crucial

463

features of causal relations (even if they are statistical in kind), and objective features of the growth of value systems. On the other, we must fear that such a social science will necessarily founder on the rocks of uniqueness and be swamped by the waves of arbitrary value systems. If events are really unique how is it that they can be linked by law-like formulae? If we change situations—at least potentially—by our descriptions of them, how is it that we can claim to have knowledge at all?

These, to be sure, are simply two of the questions which had philosophers in the same period doubting whether or not it would ever be possible to create a social science. Innis found their despair, their retreat into the history of ideas, their creation of ever more exotic and eccentric symbolic devices for linking tautologies, sometimes amusing and sometimes infuriating. He believed that philosophy ought to have been the device for linking the social sciences—or ought to have been that social science which established the place of all the others. Yet Neill quotes him as saying that philosophy was "killed, stuffed and properly labeled"[40] and that:"Exponents of the individual disciplines of social science, including philosophy, one by one, wash their hands of the problems of philosophy or offer spurious remedies and alternatives."[41]

We must, therefore, look at Innis' own "remedy and alternative." The best route to that alternative is through his account of the relations between the social sciences. It is worth quoting Neill's summary of this:

> At one extreme geography, demography and the history of technology deal with the physical limitations within which human behaviour takes place. Geography is the purest type at this extreme, since it is concerned almost exclusively with physical quantities and is largely descriptive in its mode of procedure. It comes closest to being a natural rather than a social science. At the other extreme, philosophy and cultural history deal with human activity from the point of view of values. Philosophy, the purest type in this case, proceeds by insight and deduction. Between the extremes of geography and philosophy, social science has two other focal points of interest, each being an extreme in another logical dimension. These are two principles of social organization: coercion, which is the principle of politics; and exchange, which is the principle of economics. Politics, dealing with institutions, proceeds largely by the historical method. Economics, dealing with society from the point of view of price, proceeds largely by way of logical elaboration or mathematics.[42]

For the most part, this summary of Neill's is made up from actual passages of Innis', though the "insight and deduction" account of

40 Neill, *A New Theory of Value*, p. 78.
41 Ibid.
42 Ibid., pp. 83-84.

philosophy admittedly has no foundation in any specific text. Neill describes the result as a "six-dimensional concept of social action"[43] and it is fair to emphasize the dimensional aspect of it. More importantly, it is a scheme for coping with the problems posed by uniqueness and by the openness of the value structures which are inevitably involved.

The point of the scheme, roughly, is this: We have to admit the uniqueness of human actions and meanings but both actions and the assignment of meanings take place within an arena which is circumscribed in a way which can be expressed within law-like formulations. First of all, there are physical parameters to behaviour. True, they do not determine acts but they do determine the likelihood of acts. Communication may take place between two peoples separated by an ocean or a mountain range without easy passes. It seems more likely to take place between two groups who inhabit the same plain—especially if they are brought together by a single source of water or food. These examples are simple instances of the relation which is generated by putting together demographic and geographic facts and, indeed, much history and much social science seems to proceed in just that way. We might notice, though, that it deals with the obvious and does so in a way which is very misleading. The practitioners of this kind of social history (or whatever it might be called) have formed the most obvious opposition party to such theses as that the Egyptians had a culture related to that of the Aztecs and that the structures at Stonehenge were an instance of a computing device for astronomical forecasts. The Egyptians *might* have made their way to Central America, but the partisans of demography and geography see that as a rather strange way for them to spend their time. The ancient inhabitants of Salisbury Plain may have designed sophisticated devices for the making of astronomical predictions but isn't it easier to think of them as doing something of which *all* men are capable (making religious sacrifices?) than to think of them as doing something which only rather advanced cultures usually manage? It is here that an understanding of the value situation is crucial, and here that knowledge of the way in which spatio-temporal understandings change becomes crucial.

The social science of the obvious perishes as soon as one adds the value dimension to the scheme. We would have to know—surely—what the Egyptians valued before we could know whether it is probable or not that they were likely to cross the Atlantic. We would have to know what the peoples of Salisbury Plain valued before we could judge the likelihood of their interest in astronomy. But this is just the question which we seemingly can't answer. How could we know what anyone did

43   Ibid., p. 84.

or was likely to value if values are wholly arbitrary and indeterminate? And what kind of question are we confronting? There seem to be at least two questions. In each question, the problem of value arises differently. One of them has to do with the kind of knowledge at issue when we ask, What was it that the Egyptians valued? The other has to do with the kind of knowledge involved when we ask, What ought *we* to value as a kind of knowledge when we seek to "know" the behaviour of others? Both questions have to be answered before Innis can begin to escape from the social science of the obvious on the one side and the trap of speculative fantasy on the other.

It is here, one must suppose, that the issues about space and time become more pressing. Innis—so far as the present authors can discover—never finally says so but his later writings seem full of hints to the effect that, ultimately, the mastery of space and time is the condition of human freedom and the basic direction of human value structures. Such a proposition would not, any any rate, be frivolous: Innis likes to remind us that writing is a device for mastering time. But so, one might add, are the arts in general. Music is a way of binding together a fragmented time and of transcending its arbitrary order. Literature creates its own space and time. Poetry rivets together widely disseminated experiences and so creates a unity in space and time. Politics and economics bind men together so as to give meaning and to transform regions of space and time.

On that basis, we might, after all, expect that where it is possible to do so at least some human beings in any large group will always act so as to increase their mastery over space and time. Given an ocean, men will build boats. And given a wind or a current, someone will follow them to whatever destination they lead. *If*, then, as Thor Heyerdahl set out to show, the Egyptians could have reached Central America, we can be sure they did so. Given that one can master time by marking out the patterns in celestial motions, someone will do so. We are, after all, extremely clever at what really matters to us. Surely, at least, these speculations are more plausible than the thesis that two very distant groups of people just happened to contrive elaborate artifacts with great similarities to one another and the hypothesis that Stonehenge was intended for some dark religious observance. (We seem to like the thesis that people more "primitive" than ourselves are most likely to have strange vices, but, while it would be hard to find human beings anywhere with no interest in astronomy, it is easy to find groups of people, primitive or not, who do not indulge in religious sacrifice.)

We would want, no doubt, to press further the connection between values and spatio-temporal systems, and though, again, Innis attacks these questions obliquely, it is certainly fair to point out that his many discussions of communication are full of accounts of the associations which exist between our efforts to create meanings and our efforts to master space and time. Writing, trades, games of all sorts circumscribe regions of space, order temporal sequences into bound repetitions, and so on. Might one not speculate that the giving of meanings is what is characteristically human?

Meaning, intention, value, and the escape from imposed spaces and times are, clearly, associated. And what this means is that, in answer to the first question, there are certain events which, if they are possible, are likely to happen even though they fall within the domain of free human acts. There are others which are less likely to happen. Some values, furthermore, are surely more fundamental than others. Hence we are not completely in the dark in our attempts to escape the social science of the obvious.

The second question, however, is more difficult. What should we value as knowledge in order to create the necessary understanding? One result of the escape from the social science of the obvious seems to be that we will need to develop insight, taste, sensitivity, and the ability to manipulate large systems of concepts if we are to succeed at all. It will not be enough to measure and count—for measuring and counting will never tell us why it is that two peoples inhabiting the same basin or plain in Hungary or in the Punjab should have cultures with little in common, while two peoples separated by an ocean should turn out to have cultures with marked overlaps.

But the insights, sensitivities, and abilities to handle concepts must be applied to something. Again, Innis thinks this is not a hopeless problem. It is not that classical economics, with its price mechanisms and its quaint beliefs that demand would be met with supply at a point which tended to fix a price, was utterly wrong. Given that we know that we have a culture in which people regard ducks' eggs as a delicacy and that the art of raising ducks is well known in that culture, it *seems* reasonable to predict that one will find duck farmers there and that their numbers will increase until the price of ducks' eggs begins to fall toward the limit of profitability. Here, again, we have the social science of the obvious in another dimension—the dimension which, in Neill's summary of Innis' theory, is called exchange. The remaining dimension—the dimension of coercion—will produce yet another social science of the obvious.

If, as Hobbes thought, men are roughly equal in strength and cunning, then one man can always hide behind a bush and successfully assault another. And any two men can probably subdue a third man. If the world is so organized that some states of human experience are preferable to others and if the preferable ones are in short supply, it is reasonable to suppose that some two men will, indeed, coerce the third.

In both these cases, measuring and counting will provide alleged parameters of likelihood. They will usually be wrong, as was the social science of the obvious which arose out of demography and geography. But it would seem to be Innis' view that we need not despair about that. What we need is a clue to the way in which the bias will fall so that we can tell, for a given occasion, how the social science of the obvious will fail. (Presumably, that is why he entitled one of his more important collections of essays, *The Bias of Communication*.[44])

We can guess, of course, that in the duck egg case something will go wrong: Too many people will find the duck business boring, speculators will get into duck egg futures, people who publicly claim an interest in ducks' eggs will privately spend their money on race horses and wine. Something will happen. The economists of a classical bent will urge that, in the long run, the oddities of the egg market will even out and an order will come forth with a projectable equilibrium price. Similarly, we shall not really get, in our political situation, Hobbes's war of all against all. There will be conflict, but it will always take some rather specialized form—class war, race war, religious schisms. And the political structure will not be Hobbes's *Leviathan* with its absolute monarch and its citizens who have contracted away their freedoms, but some temporary, jury-rigged, jerry-built political mess which is called a corporate state, a people's republic, a liberal democracy, or whatever. Again, the classical political theorist might say that the Brownian movement of human atoms will tend over the very long run to reach the equilibrium described by Hobbes.

Though he never quite stops long enough in one place to do a thorough analysis, Innis seems to notice, indeed, that all these classical theories leave themselves an unconditioned time (is it William James's splendid "long run"?) for their statistical manipulations to work out. One might guess that where they are wrong, therefore, is in supposing that we live in a time-frame in which that historically unconditioned time has a place. The more one stands back and takes a hard look at the whole canvass Innis is painting in his later writings, the more comprehensible one must find his continuous insistence on the problem of time.

Classical political and economic theorists suppose that we live in a world with a bias toward the long run. Innis would argue that we live in

44 Harold A. Innis, *The Bias of Communication*, with an Introduction by Marshall McLuhan (Toronto: University of Toronto Press, 1951).

a world with a bias against the long run. We live, that is, in highly structured, stylized, and restricted regions of cultural time and it is these biases which determine to a large extent the pattern of social change.

Now, it turns out, we *do* know where to look: We need to look at ways in which our societies structure their time-frames. But this is very difficult.

It is (as usual) difficult to pick out from the welter of Innis' discussions examples which are simple enough to make the point quickly and easily. In a textbook for engineers, however, Innis discussed the patterns and difficulties of canal and railroad building in North America.[45] The canal and some early railroads were built either by governments or by private enterprise underwritten by governments. The future to which a government may look for a return on its investments is very long—governments are never supposed to imagine their own demise. (Indeed, such discussions are strictly taboo: During the Canadian centennial or the American bicentennial it would have been thought boorish in the extreme to devote serious attention to the question of what might reasonably replace the existing political structures.) As a consequence, these enterprises tended to be very solidly built, very expensive, and very slow to generate any reasonable return on capital. Private entrepreneurs, however, took a very different attitude as the railroad boom grew. They realized that they could build cheaply, stimulate business in the areas they reached, and rebuild again out of the profits. The future which they were willing to contemplate was only that future which their shareholders proved willing to accept. Such futures, of course, rebound on themselves: The greater the demand for capital—and capital demand will generally be strengthened by the improvement of communications systems—the more those who want some must compete not only in large returns but in quick returns.

In the text, Innis' message seemed to be the happy one that private enterprise generates capital as it foreshortens the future, while monumental governmental building projects tend to absorb it. It does not disturb him too much that, in fact, the railroads in Canada which set out to compete with the original CPR ultimately ran out of futures and had to be absorbed by the government and seen again in the original open-ended time-frame. Nor does he there draw the message that all this may lead, over a whole economy, to a shoddy, quick-return,

---

45 Clarence Richard Young, *Engineering & Society, with special reference to Canada*, Part I by C. R. Young: Part II by H. A. Innis and J. H. Dales (Toronto: University of Toronto Press, 1946).

obsolescence-bound society in which tomorrow is the last imaginable day—and ultimately, perhaps, the last possible day. Elsewhere, though, conservation is one of his evident concerns and it forms, for him, a crucial determining value. If one ignores it as a problem, the future goes on foreshortening. If one makes it an absolute value (as Innis suspected some Canadians of doing during the Depression), one's world stagnates. The problem is to create a time-frame in which use may match regeneration.

The complexities of all this explain the puzzlement which some of his readers felt at his increasing preoccupation with the notion of time. In fact all the examples seem to suggest that from his first work on the CPR to his last essays on the nature of the social sciences, his interests changed very little. At first glance, it is not easy to see how his worries about railroads, cod fish, and pulp mills tie together with his essays, say, on the impact of American publishing on Canadian literature.

The reader who soaks himself in the later essays, however, gradually comes to grasp the connections. What stands between us and a truly disastrous foreshortening of the temporal horizon brought about by economic forces which tend to compel quick returns on capital, is what, vaguely, we call culture. The essence of that culture is also found in the social space and time in which it operates—a structure which comes out in literature and poetry even if it is suppressed in the "long run" mathematical time of the classical social theorist. But the technology of communication, according to Innis, has threatened that culture, in Canada, with extinction and, where it has not obliterated that culture, it has reduced it to mediocrity. A book is only feasible as a commercial publishing venture if it can be densely dispersed in the space within which the nearby relevant economic system prevails or if it can be very widely distributed in a very large space. Furthermore, the distribution must take place quickly so as to keep the necessary capital circulating at an acceptable rate.

The characteristics of social space in Canada usually do not meet these conditions and so we are prey to publishing ventures (and other media interventions) from the United States. Insofar as Canada can be made into an effective receptable for such ventures at all, it can only be by selling books or whatever to a relatively high proportion of the population in a very short span of time. Successful Canadian books, in other words, have to be fads. Oddly, Innis does not usually discuss the possibility that technology might respond to this situation by producing cheap printing, paper, efficient systems of distribution, or whatever, which would allow small ventures to survive more readily. In fact, in recent years, fairly small publishing ventures have had at least some modest success in Canada. The two reasons Innis ignored this possibility are, presumably, that technological victories usually go to those able to make the largest investments in development and therefore favour large producers over small ones, and the fact that sporadic small-scale revolts in the name of a local culture are unlikely to survive determined large-scale assaults against them. (In any case, they have difficulty in generating the perspective from which to distinguish the really worthy and significant.) Most of Innis' writings pour scorn on these little displays of Canadian defiance and, for the most part, he expresses a deep pessimism.

The explanation for this is partly that in Canada it seemed unlikely that the cultural strength to ward off economic disaster was to be forthcoming and the undermining of public values seemed, therefore, to be a continuous process. Partly, however, Innis was beginning to struggle against the technical problems which stem from applying his theories reflexively to themselves. Surely, Innis and *his* theories have a history just as the others do and surely, too, Innis and his theories are the outcome of the ways in which experienced time and space get structured. To look at this, one would expect to turn to the literature, poetry, and philosophy which belong to one's culture—to look at what is beyond theory or to look at theories about theories. For a Canadian this seemed a difficult task, especially in the years just after World War II. Was not our literature imitative of its American, British, and French counterparts and were we not importing our philosophers from the same regions which produced the social forces which threatened to obliterate us?

Throughout this period, Innis did scatter his writings with accounts of phases of the history of the social sciences. He noted that economics arose at the time of Adam Smith in response to the fact that there was a growing and effective commercial interest which ran counter to the interests of the state and its traditional mercantilist policies. If political science has its roots in the works of thinkers like Hobbes, it must also be conceded that it arose as a way of specifying (and trying to legitimize) the role of the nation state in the confusion of post-mediaeval Europe. There is a strong suggestion then that the social sciences at least start not as inquiries into subject matter but as defences of an interest. No doubt, as rival practitioners attempt to reconcile their differences, one of their strategies will be a search for objectivity, but the victory may well go to the party which has most success at academic politics. Innis was clearly aware that the refuge of the academy does not guarantee objectivity.

How then, should we see Innis' own effort? Is it the product of an interest not yet clearly identified? Is it biased by a value structure which arises out of the curious plurality of time-frames and social spaces which must form the background of a Canadian scholar whose culture is under continuous assault?

Is not his pretty six-dimensional scheme for the assimilation of the social sciences itself a reflection of the urge to pretend to objectivity by covering up the historical origins of the social sciences?

The answer must be that one ought to try as hard as one can to subject one's findings to all the implied tests, but the truth lies in the systematic nature of the conceptual structure one generates. Innis was looking for coherence and for a conceptual structure which would free human experience and generate a culture actually capable of dealing with the mindless social forces which classical theorists have discovered. When men are really free, they move through time-frames of their own making and time as master has an end. In a London lecture in 1949 he recalls his thesis that "civilization has been dominated at different stages by various media of communication such as clay, papyrus, parchment, and paper...[each making a] monopoly of knowledge." He ended his lecture by quoting the title of a novel by Aldous Huxley, "*Time must have a Stop.*"[46]

Behind this, no doubt, is the residue of his boyhood Baptist belief in the millenium and the transformation of time at the end of the world, made sophisticated by the Hegelianism of Ten Broeke. Both these forces he subjected all his life to a continuous sceptical analysis. Though Vincent Bladen[47] seems to have remained convinced that Innis, inwardly, was still a Baptist, his biographer, Donald Creighton,[48] came to believe that Innis had become a religious agnostic. And, though experiences from Hegel are scattered through his works, it would be strange to call him an Hegelian.

Like Brett and Irving, Innis sought the re-integration of reason and the object reasoned about. But where Brett and Irving seem, finally, to conclude that the powers of reason are restricted to the determination of right (essentially historical) order of experiences, events, and concepts, Innis saw the emergence of reason again as a source of values. He evidently believed not only that he had at least an important clue to the nature of value, but also that he could explain, at

---

46 Harold A. Innis, "The Press, A Neglected Factor in the Economic History of the Twentieth Century," *Changing Concepts of Time* (Toronto: University of Toronto Press, 1952), pp. 78 and 108. (Originally The University of London Memorial Lecture, 1949.)

47 Neill is referring to a remark made by Vincent Bladen about the attitude of Harold Innis. See *A New Theory of Value*, p. 10, footnote 3.

48 Donald G. Creighton, *Harold Adams Innis: Portrait of a Scholar* (Toronto: University of Toronto Press, 1957).

least in part, the curious ambivalence of values between the subjective and objective. Out of that came the possibility of reasoning about values and so the possibility of reason as a positive and constructive force.

That force, however, continued to have limitations: It must start from (and could never wholly escape from) the limitations of one's own culture. It must always precede a situation in which freedom played a part—one may reason about social processes and forces but only from a conceptual position which makes one aware of alternatives between which one may choose. The possibility of choosing retains what Neill quotes Innis as calling the "indeterminateness"[49] of values. That means that all propositions about values can be questioned. It does not mean, for Innis, that all propositions about values are equally sound or unsound. (To the social scientist accustomed to regarding the most important of his propositions as having a statistical degree of reliability, the temptation of some philosophers to hold that what cannot be completely determined is completely indeterminate usually seems incomprehensible.) But, in this case, what is involved is not merely a logical misunderstanding. The philosopher who is sceptical about the knowledge of values will, of course, point out that, if we knew what certainty about such matters would be, we could not claim a statistical approximation of it. But we could only know what the standard of certainty was if we actually had some piece of the required knowledge—i.e., if we were certain about at least one value proposition. Hence to hold that all value propositions were in some measure indeterminate with respect to truth and falsity would seem to be to claim that they were completely indeterminate. Very likely Innis usually had in mind something very different: He meant that value characteristics had more than one dimension and, with respect to one of these dimensions, values themselves remained indeterminate.

This issue is important in itself and deserves, before we leave Innis, some independent consideration. For, if the reading we are inclined to give Innis is correct and if the propositions which feature in its formulation are true, the implications both for the understanding of Innis and for the development of the social sciences are considerable.

Most philosophers would agree that values have to do with the ordering and grading of things, events, courses of action, or whatever. They would also agree that in general, therefore, nothing has *only* value properties. Nothing is just good or bad. It is, say, both good and a humane desire, or bad and a cruel intention. (Whether it is generally characteristic of the situation that there are two sorts of apparent value properties—"good" along with "humane" and "bad" along with

49 Neill, *A New Theory of Value*, p. 84.

"cruel"—and whether or not entities might be said to have one of these properties in virtue of having the other are, to be sure, matters of dispute.) To say, therefore, that whatever has value properties has more than one dimension (here "dimension" as used by Neill in his account of Innis apparently means "independently measurable variable") is not, in itself, to say anything very surprising. Nor would it be very surprising to add to this the proposition that, with respect to value-possessing entities, there is generally an objective dimension and a subjective dimension. The kinds of contentions which *would* be important would either involve the notion that the value dimensions of a value-having entity are in some way determined by objective and non-value dimensions, or the contention that the value properties of a value-having entity themselves have more than one dimension and that one of these dimensions is, in fact, objective.

Innis' position seems to be this: Values are exhibited in our ways of organizing experience through the development or imposition of space-time frames. Objective factors such as the available technology, the topography, and the range of biological responses severely limit the alternatives. The content and strength of our inherited culture determine the options we have for assigning meanings to these alternatives. Given this we can reason about the alternatives by considering, for instance, how they are related to one another as option sets (does choosing one leave us free to choose another or does it give us a closed future?), how they will reinforce or weaken our cultural potential, and so on. These are all "objective" questions, though no one would say they are irrelevant to the appropriateness of values. The question really becomes one about what it is that one might want to say about values and how it is that a given claim might be justified. One may well say that to claim a value is inappropriate to one's culture and potential future (i.e., that acting on it may leave one's life meaningless and one's future without options) is not to make an "evaluation" but to offer description and prediction. The rejoinder might be that to evaluate values is to do something very queer and perhaps logically absurd. As a matter of fact, descriptions and predictions are usually, for sensible people, what determine which values they will choose. To leave the question like this is, certainly, to irritate nearly all philosophers but we ought to give some weight to the fact that Innis showed no desire whatever to debate with philosophers on the question. There is plenty of evidence that his unconcern was not predicated on ignorance of philosophical habits. Nor is it reasonable to think that it was based wholly on arrogance—though Innis seldom showed much patience with what he took to be nonsense.

The situation may become clearer if we look at one of the characteristic ways in which value problems arise in classical economic discussions. One of the questions asked by classical economists seems to have been What is it that confers value on commodities which enter into exchange? and one of the answers—given with various sorts of emphasis by Adam Smith and John Locke and historically favoured by Thomas Aquinas—was "labour." Now it is true that one way in which one may command a price for one's effort is to put it into turning some raw materials into a desirable or useful object—writing a novel, or singing a song, raising a crop, or designing a widget. These are all examples of ways in which, very often at least, something worthless can be made to fetch a price or something which already fetched a price can be made to fetch a higher one. It is not foolproof, of course. One's crop may bring nothing, the market for widgets may have declined to nothing, one's novel may be terrible, one's song hideous to the ear. The "labour theory of value" is, therefore, ambiguous. It may be a theory about how men become morally entitled to goods and services (by making things or acquiring them by fair trade) or it may be a theory about how, in fact, things come to have and change values. If the former, it is a set of moral injunctions and if the latter it is a set of predictions. The instructions cannot be mistaken in the way that the predictions can. An alternative or supplementary thesis is the claim that objects and services come to have a "value" because people want them and that their "market value" represents some relation between those wants (demand) and the responses to them (supply). This leads to endless refinements beginning, inevitably, with distinctions between those wants which are backed by ability to pay and those which are not effective demands, and progressing through analysis of the time intervals which relate wants and responses. But this account can be made ambiguous. It may be a claim that one *ought* to allow supply to meet demand and it may be a prediction that supply will meet demand.

Innis was aware of all this and much of his life work was devoted to an analysis which would, somehow or other, create an understanding about the process whereby goods and services come to have value and *also* have some genuine bearing on the moral question involved. Most of his writings, however, suggest very strongly that he would have found the rather traditional distinctions in the paragraphs above between moral claims and predictions rather unsubtle. To begin with, his concern with notions of time complicates the problem of prediction and, for what it is worth, we may notice that not many predictions are to be found in his writings. Indeed, one who would choose "Minerva's Owl" for the title of his presidential address to the Royal Society of

Canada and begin with the familiar phrase from Hegel—Minerva's Owl begins its flight only in the gathering dusk—can hardly be expected to view prediction with much equanimity. Prediction must have reference to a time-frame and one must believe that the time-frame will remain constant for the prediction to be true in any literal sense. But such frames are, for Innis, the central structures of value systems. Thus, to predict *is* to make a choice which has value connotations. It may not be easy to see that this is so but consider: The simple economic predictions involved in such notions as the addition of value through labour, the tendency of supply to meet certain kinds of demand, the likelihood that increased demand will increase the cost of borrowing all suppose a time in which there is a certain order to events, in which there is a certain openness to the future, and in which there are no cultural or political inhibitions placed on the flow of events. They are imaginary worlds in which certain values triumph because we choose a certain kind of social arrangement. The classical economists were occasionally confused by the fact that it seemed to them that the choice of non-interference was a different *kind* of choice than the choice represented by a decision to interfere in a social situation. Thus they thought the economic consequences of leaving things alone were natural laws of economics while the consequences of human interference were interventions which challenged nature. But any Hegelian would insist that, as Hegel said, "Negation is just as much Affirmation as Negation."[50] So much, then, for the value-neutrality of predictions and for the notion of social prediction itself.

What, then, of the moral injunctions? Surely, there is a measure of dialectical inversion between the two sides of the issue. To claim that you ought to value something because of the human effort which went into it is to claim, at least, that that effort *really* changed the situation and that, objectively, there is something there which is important and deserving of attention. Those are questions, in fact, which can be settled. How much sweat and skill went into this object and what, therefore, is a fair exchange for it? Similarly, with the supply and demand situation, to say that somebody really wants something (not just that he says he does, or that he bids for it on the open market) is to say that it has significance for him. And that is a claim which can be tested by reference to his biological nature or to the structure of his culture.

Thus, on the one side, we cannot get rid of values by switching to the cheap and seemingly neutral language of economic prediction. On

50 G. W. F. Hegel, *Science of Logic*, translated by W. H. Johnston and L. G. Struthers (London: George Allen & Unwin, 1966), vol. 1, p. 65. (First published in German, 1812-1816. First published in English in 1929.)

the other side, however, the admitted moral claims may well have an objectively investigative nature even if it is the case that they must remain for all possible kinds of natures partially indeterminate. There is not something perfectly value-neutral and there is not anything whose nature is to be, simply, indeterminate value.

Social science is possible but it will have to cope with values, it will have to deal with the particularities of culture, the generalities of biology, the limiting conditions of geography and demography, the mechanics of exchange, and the possibilities of coercion.

Through it all, we may yet be reasonable—even if being reasonable is mainly the confronting of our insights with the constraints which inhibit our ordinary actions.

FOURTEEN

FAITH AND REASON

The Catholic Philosophers

C ATHOLIC PHILOSOPHY in Canada is as old as the country itself. It arrived, after all, with Monseigneur de Laval[1] and the seminary at Quebec. In English Canada, too, though at most places and times Catholics have constituted a minority, the need to maintain an effective priesthood necessitated the creation of seminaries wherever there were substantial centres of population, and the teaching of philosophy, sometimes thought a luxury and even a dangerous one in Protestant circles, has always been regarded as essential in the Catholic tradition.

Indeed, the strength of philosophy in Canada from the beginning of the period which this book covers has owed much to that tradition. Philosophy departments in Canadian universities—at least in central Canada and in the Maritime Provinces—have usually been larger than those in American universities of comparable size and a good part of the reason is that Protestant institutions sought to defend their positions against a well-organized Catholic tradition of which they stood in genuine fear. It is worth noting that one of the reasons given for not closing Queen's university altogether in 1850 was that "the whole of the superior education of those large sections of country, of which Kingston is the natural capital, would be made over to a Roman Catholic Seminary."[2] The Presbyterian authors of these sentiments did not only keep their college open; they insisted that the best minds from Scotland must be enlisted to combat this threat. Thus did we get our Murrays and Watsons.

That negative influence was only a beginning. When the Baldwin Bill of 1849 established a secular university in Toronto, the Protestant colleges shunned affiliation with it. The mentors of the struggling Catholic St. Michael's College who served, for the most part, a less

---

1 Monseigneur de Laval, 1623-1708, founded the Seminary in Quebec out of which grew Laval University.

2 Laurence K. Shook, *Catholic Post-Secondary Education in English-Speaking Canada: A History* (Toronto and Buffalo: University of Toronto Press, 1971), p. 23.

affluent constituency and who could see no good reason for duplicating all the efforts of their Protestant rivals, immediately sought affiliation. The university resisted but it was obvious to everyone that it must eventually accede. Something like the contemporary plan, in which affiliated religious colleges teach religion, some philosophy (traditionally ethics at Toronto), and a limited number of other specialities, and leave the rest of the curriculum to a shared secular central university, would develop. The result of this was to bring the Catholic outlook with its emphasis on the matching of faith and reason into direct confrontation with all of the rival traditions. Not only were they compelled to build strong programmes in philosophy in self-defence, but the philosophers so employed were compelled to pay serious attention to an important historical tradition. The result has been a lasting one which shows itself in the strong focus Canadian institutions have given to the history of philosophy, in the continued ability to resist fads, and in the central concern of many Canadian philosophers with system building.

The Baldwin Bill did not bring all this about instantly. Prior to Confederation there was a rush of Catholic college charters (Regiopolis in Kingston, Ottawa College, St. Jerome's in Berlin [now Kitchener], and the Ursuline Academy at Chatham). Most of these institutions were struggling, and just managed to maintain the essentials of their seminary functions and the provision of some measure of intellectual background for their clerical and lay constituencies. The Toronto pattern of affiliated colleges spread, fairly slowly and unevenly, west across the prairies and eventually in the middle of this century to British Columbia. St. Jerome's finally became federated with the University of Waterloo only in recent years and the University of Ottawa remained, until recently, an essentially Catholic institution.

Nevertheless, the federal plan not only allowed struggling institutions to survive and gave impetus to philosophy as a device for making one's religious and cultural traditions intelligible; it also enabled institutions to concentrate their resources. The ultimate result of this was the development of St. Michael's College and its associated Pontifical Institute of Mediaeval Studies into a world centre of Catholic thought. Though those institutions are now rivalled by the University of Ottawa—whose English- and French-language philosophy programmes are by no means confined to Catholic thought—they represented in the 1930s and 1940s the most widely renowned intellectual endeavour in English Canada.

Writing about Catholic philosophy presents special problems. Though the philosophy taught in French Canada was, from the beginning, influenced by Cartesian ideas and, later, the ideas of Locke and others were influential on textbook writers there, virtually all of the philosophical activity amongst Catholic thinkers in English Canada dates from the period of the Thomist revival (beginning well before 1850) and the subsequent period of Thomist orthodoxy, ushered in by Leo XIII's *Aeterni Patris*.[3] That period ended, finally, only after the period with which this book is mainly concerned.

The result is that most of the philosophical writing is historical in kind and exegetical in nature and either consists of textbooks or of highly scholarly papers and monographs. To assess, for instance, the extent and nature of the Canadian contribution to Thomist scholarship would be to undertake a task which would require a degree of specialist knowledge which only a handful of experts on St. Thomas really possess. Even if one could enlist the aid of someone adequately qualified, it is by no means certain that the task could be completed. The Catholic Church, we need hardly remind ourselves, is an international organization which, at least until recently, was comparatively unhampered by linguistic problems since, to one degree or another, its scholars shared a facility in Latin. The result of this is that it is common for a Canadian Catholic philosopher to serve in a Catholic university in Rome and to write extensively in Latin. An example is Bernard Lonergan, whose main work, alas, belongs to the period after the one covered by this study.

While the leading figures of the Pontifical Institute and St. Michael's included names like Joseph Owens, Anton Pegis, Gerald Phelan, and Lawrence Lynch, who surely may reasonably be associated mainly with those institutions, they also include Etienne Gilson and Jacques Maritain, whose reputations were made elsewhere and whose associations are only peripherally with Canada.

The real influence of Catholic philosophy in English Canada does, as a matter of fact, stem largely from Gilson[4] and Maritain,[5] not so much in the literal detail of doctrines as in the general attitude which they disseminated. (Most obviously, the presence of men so universally

3   St. Thomas Aquinas, *The Summa Theologica of St. Thomas Aquinas*, Part I, QQ I-XXVI, literally translated by the Fathers of the English Dominican Province (London: Burns, Oates and Washbourne, 1920). See Encyclical Letter of Pope Leo XIII, pp. ix-xxxiii.

4   Etienne Gilson arrived from Paris in 1927 and spent most of the next thirty-five years at North American universities, especially the Pontifical Institute of Mediaeval Studies in Toronto.

5   Jacques Maritain arrived at the Institute in 1932-33, and lectured there until 1938. He continued to lecture there regularly during the forties and occasionally since then, maintaining a close relationship with the Institute.

acknowledged to be first-rate made it difficult to ignore the claims of Catholic philosophy to be taken seriously.)

What seems important and appropriate for this chapter, then, is to explain something of what those attitudes and influences have been and why they have been important for the development of Canadian thought. It is certainly part of the story of the development of concepts of reason in Canada and it is, as well, a continuing episode which must be understood if we are to understand the others. If it is more difficult to chronicle than the other episodes it is for the reasons we have already suggested, together with the fact that what is important here has to be stated obliquely. It is not, for instance, that Gilson believed such-and-such about St. Thomas or was engaged in this or that controversy as a result of his account of the concept of being which matters for *this* purpose (though they matter very much in the context of the scholastic controversies to which they belong). What matters, rather, is the way in which he went about his business, the way in which he opened Catholic thought to the influence of contemporary philosophy, the way he understood philosophical disputes. Similarly, it would be inappropriate here to pursue the details of Maritain's reading of Thomas' theory of the state, his particular way of supplementing the Thomistic arguments for the existence of God, or his theory of art. To hold that those doctrines were part of Canadian philosophy would be dubious, to explain them without writing a book about Thomist philosophy would be impossible, and to claim they were influential on other Canadian philosophers would be to claim for Maritain what it is difficult to claim for anyone. But we may well be concerned with the way in which certain of his ideas entered into a federation of ideas, with his methods and attitudes, with the general coming to maturity of Catholic thought as something which has become a permanent feature of Canadian culture.

In light of the background of European thought from the mid-nineteenth century onwards, it is not difficult to understand how this influence came to be important and even pervasive. The Thomist revival of the mid-nineteenth century had a number of causes, but the most important are probably these: The rise of history as a significant, independent, and ultimately "scientific" discipline posed a special threat to a religion which claimed to be historical, but relied upon assurances for that history which were very different from any which the "scientific" historian was likely to countenance. The development of evolutionary theory added to this threat by giving credence to the Heraclitean claim that everything is mutable. If everything changes (or evolves), why should anyone suppose that religious belief *had* remained static or that *if* it had, it ought to have? Finally, of course, the gradual movement of the concepts of a mechanistic physics toward the centre of the belief systems of intelligent men left open the possibility that religion would become divorced from reason. For exactly what it means to say that mechanistic concepts borrowed from physics tended toward the centre of the belief systems of thoughtful men is that the kinds of reasons which a physicist of the period would have accepted tended to become the characteristically successful reasons. Anything which deviated from the pattern gradually came under the heading of "unreason."

There were, as we have seen throughout this book, many ways of meeting the challenge. One might admit, as did a line of Protestant theologians from Kierkegaard to Barth, that religion and reason were divorced. There was, after all, historical precedent as far back as Tertullian for holding that Christians might rejoice in unreason. One might, as the fundamentalists did, simply challenge the claims of history, biology, and physics with the counter claims of the Bible. One might, as (to cite one of our own examples) James Beaven did, try to use reason much as the scientists themselves did in order to show that the claims of science are actually compatible with the claims of religion—in the process, no doubt, abandoning much of the more difficult material in one's theological texts. More daringly, one could, as the Hegelians did, try to show that scientific reason was one of the more specialized sub-species of reason, that there are others, and that religion and science may live together in peace within the context of an acceptable metaphysics. We have seen, however, that this process leads to a considerable transformation in our understanding of both science and religion. It may seem that these are the evident ways of being defiant or of coming to terms with new ideas and that the list we have just offered is much what one would expect.

To some degree analogues of all these possibilities were advanced within the Catholic Church. There emerged, as the years went by, proponents of the doctrine of progressive revelation who held that, indeed, faith did go on developing: biblical critics, who sought to distinguish the reliable from the dubious, devotees of faith as the master of reason, and even reformist metaphysicians. The largest concern seems to have been over the understanding of history itself. It is important for our purposes to emphasize that fact, because we have seen that philosophy in English Canada became increasingly historically oriented as time went on, as if history were quite unproblematic and one could pass easily from serious difficulties about philosophy to relatively easy tasks in the history of ideas. Despite the steady increase in historical orientation, it was not until well on in this century that philosophers in English Canada came to be seriously concerned with the philosophy of history at all. In the Catholic context, however, it seems fair to say that it was the problem of history which seemed most threatening and it was that which, finally, seems to have determined the course to be adopted.

There seem to be good reasons for this: The church, from the beginning, had coped with rival cosmologies, usually without embarrassment. Plato, Aristotle, the neo-Platonists, the variants of these theses posed by the Arab philosophers, all could be, and were, coped with in one way or another. The controversy over the arrangements of the heavens did, indeed, accompany the appearance of modern astronomy but it was a short-lived scuffle and, at that, had mainly to do with second-order claims. The offence of Descartes was not so much that he lent credence to the claims of the physicists and the astronomers as that he seemed to claim that reason could get along quite well without faith. Even the cosmology of Spinoza might have been acceptable but for his arrogant rationalism. There was nothing special in the claims of nineteenth-century physics which added much to what the church had to cope with. And as for biology, surely a church which had once been able to come to terms with the emanations of Plotinus (Did not Augustine even draw renewed faith from their contemplation?) could surely come to terms with the doctrine that there are mutable life forms. If, in the end, it sometimes chose not to, it was for quite different reasons to which we shall come in due course.

History, however, was another matter. Christianity seemed to depend upon the belief that certain events, the birth, life, and crucifixion of Jesus in particular, took place in real, human time. Though most other things had been challenged frequently from the time of the church fathers onwards, the historical record seldom was. The church, after all, could simply claim that each generation of authorities had received the record directly from its predecessors and that there was an unbroken chain which led back to Christ himself. Nor was there, until the end of the eighteenth century, a strong historical sense to the European mind. History became a major concern of European thinkers only in the period which produced first Vico, Kant, and then Herder, and came to play a major role in philosophical theorizing only with the philosophy of Hegel. True, throughout the eighteenth century and back into the seventeenth, there were continuous signs of what was to come. Spinoza questioned the authenticity of the Scripture, Berkeley once gave betting odds on its truth, the whole history of Protestantism with its emphasis on the biblical roots of Christianity led to examination and re-examination of the texts, controversy over translation, and the pitting of authority against counter-authority. But the problem of history itself settled only slowly into the European mind. Spinoza's reality was real *sub specie aeternitatis*—and not the appearances. Berkeley's metaphysic posited a continuous if not eternal relation between the divine mind and the individual spiritual substances. For that matter, the whole notion of a renaissance implied that classical learning was as relevant and viable in the modern world as in the ancient—that time was unimportant to human nature.

The first sign of real trouble was in the writings of Vico. Vico insisted on the mutability of human nature and on the relativity of language and culture and the constantly changing nature of both. That, in itself, was a central challenge to orthodoxy. If human nature changes constantly, how shall we all be saved by the same formulae? If language itself evolves, how can any text continue to be reliable? How shall we determine the culture which would give the "real" meaning to biblical texts? Vico charitably refrained from pressing these lessons home and, just as charitably, was ignored. Behind these surface doctrines, however, were more serious claims. Vico claimed that physics was a speculative science, that there was always a distance between theory and experience, that nothing was ever finally confirmed. But history, he said, was different. We *make* history. It consists of *our* acts. Therefore we have an immediate understanding of it. More than that, the past is itself a creation which we come to understand only through language. These claims, which were to usher in a variety of kinds of speculative philosophy of history, of historical relativism, and of historical scepticism, generally were left discreetly unread or uncommented upon until well into the eighteenth century. Taken seriously, however, such doctrines might well lead to the conclusion that Christianity was essentially a curious psychological artifact.

What led to such speculations? Vico had been dissatisfied with Descartes' attempt to rebut the scepticism of Sextus Empiricus, distressed by the de-humanizing effects of the new cosmologies, puzzled as one who professed jurisprudence for a living by the problems of the origin and reliability of the law. But these are particular circumstances which have to do with the effects of a renewed interest in classical culture, a growing uncertainty as to the sources of authority, a serious distress at the human condition in a period of temporal disorientation.

The Renaissance claim to the eternal validity of classical learning was, in itself, a claim to the effect that time is irrelevant. But it was not possible to make it without setting in train a hunt for the genuine as against the spurious classical culture. Such a search could not fail to rouse historical problems. The dispute between Galileo and the popes was about rival claims to authority—the authority of experience against the authority of the church. It was not, as we have suggested, his beliefs, but his certainty, his claim to authority, his preference for the telescope against the Book, which started the quarrel. The revival of classical culture was itself, however, a result of uncertainty about authority. The growing complexity of doctrine, the dubious moral models of some church leaders, and the new richness of popular culture contributed as much as the availability of classical languages to the view that one should attempt to find the original models. But pagan classicism was thus set against the church fathers—two authorities of the same time. The Protestant taste for biblical sources was hardly more than an attempt to decide between the authorities by going behind both of them to search for a genuine original. But that, too, was bound to raise problems about history.

When these questions began to become serious, the internal tensions in Christian doctrine were certain to be exposed. The church had generally allowed two different versions of the theological relevance of time to stand side by side. On one of them one might liken the world to a commando training course—a device for the preparation of high-grade minds, souls, or spirits. Filled with booby traps, it fitted the faithful for the vision of God and shifted the unfaithful into their proper sphere. As such, it needed to change little from the time of the creation to the time of the last judgment. The insistence that it was created in time (a mediaeval Christian stance taken firmly against the Arab followers of Aristotle) and would end in time was hardly more than a proforma necessity predicated upon the belief that the world must be finite in order to be truly dependent upon God for its existence and continuance. On the other version, the world was an arena of progressive development. Human kind was created with Adam, all men fell with Adam's sin, all were transformed and could be saved as a result of the intervention of Christ. The world had a story which had a purpose. It was accident that the world was created in time and would end in time. Each moment in it presumably met the demands of divine providence and the whole of it would become intelligible at the time of the last judgment.

The significant difference between the two views is that one has to do with individual salvation and the other has to do with the fall of man and the redemption of the world. On one view we are saved (if at all) one by one. On the other, we all fell together and we shall all find our proper places when and only when the whole divine business with the world is complete and time can be brought to an end.

In the post-mediaeval period, the question of human bonding had become acute and the issues which, in the high Middle Ages, had been largely absorbed into the theological outcomes of the philosophical debate over universals, tended to break out anew. There were upsurges of nominalism, attractive, perhaps, because men did not feel themselves effectively a part of communities. The conflict of authority now included the rival claims of church and state as well as the claims of state against the regional authority of the local nobility, and the question of the sense in which men were responsible for one another was, indeed, pressing. So long as the historical question, the question of the significance of doctrine in time, was dormant, the church could make use of whatever model of the world suited its needs most. Once the question of time was raised, it began to turn out that the existence of rival accounts of the past was threatening in the extreme. Kant, for instance, offered nothing as perilous as the theories of Vico. Yet, when he sought for a way to reconcile Divine Providence with the apparent badness of the world, he was compelled to find an answer in the notion that the plan of the world takes time to work out, that the unsocial sociability of man works toward human salvation only over a long time span. But this is to suggest (as indeed he does) that human nature cannot appear to us all at once but can be seen in its reality over time and that the meaning of history itself, consequently, can only be understood over a long span of time. The meaning of history, though, is the nature of Providence, and this would mean that doctrine could only be understood in terms of a progressive revelation. Should the church reject that doctrine would it not then be left with only the commando training course model of the universe—a model which can cope with problems of individual salvation but not with the fall of man and the redemption of the world? Much worse, of course, it was not just that the upholders of orthodoxy had to choose between one model and another but rather that they had to find some way of *showing* which model was right without admitting that there was a serious uncertainty to begin with.

In all this there developed room for any number of disputes, most of which are still with us. Predestination versus free will again become an issue as it became apparently necessary to ask whether or not Providence determined the whole of history. The dispute between communitarians and individualists took on religious, political, commercial, and philosophical significance.

By the opening of the nineteenth century, it had become clear that the crucial question was to be the question of history—the problem of the understanding of a world which actually develops in time, of a world in which what is true now was once false and will be false again. Hegel's claim that the *Absolute* could come to be in a process of development of great grandeur, complexity, and length was shortly followed by Darwin's claim that *we* could only come to be in a process of great grandeur, complexity, and length. For Christians, the challenge was a hard one. They could save the meaning of time, but only by denying the reliability of faith. If truth is emergent, what is to become of the faith of our fathers? Should they associate God with Hegel's Absolute they would, seemingly, be creating peace with science by moving God into the far future. Should they insist that God had nothing to do with such schemes, they could salvage their simplest forms of belief but at the cost, apparently, of making God irrelevant to an evolving world. To claim that the church is emergent is to escape from the burden of its past mistakes at the cost of admitting that reliability lies only in the future and the present is full of doubt.

Protestants, as we have suggested, met this challenge in a variety of ways, none of which could command more than a minority following. Catholics sought for a solution in their own past. The great philosophers since the Middle Ages had been Protestant—Locke, Berkeley, Hume, Leibniz, Kant, and Hegel, or Jewish—Spinoza, or (unreliably) Catholic—Descartes, Malebranche. The mediaeval period had reached its peak in a confrontation between the neo-Platonist Bonaventure and the Aristotelean Thomas Aquinas, moved through the refinements of Duns Scotus, and then entered into a period of niggling controversy which went from William of Ockham to Nicholas of Autrecourt (the mediaeval Hume). The choices, therefore, were not numerous and, as Gilson was later to claim, there was good reason to think that, if one wanted a real philosophical system, it was Aquinas or nothing.

But the Thomist revival seemed instinctively based on the probability that Thomas could be read as the doctor who could, if not cure the disease of the hour, at least bring it under control.

Thomas had originally made his fame in a context which was promising for the occasion. Faced with a new Arab view of the world, the science of its time, the church had had to come to terms with it and with its proponents. Bonaventure had in effect urged no quarter—the claims of the faith know no limit, no truth is to be understood independently of faith. Aquinas had urged a compromise, a distinction between the realm of reason and the realm of faith. His *Summa Contra Gentiles*[6] was addressed to those same Arabs and his vaster and even

6   St. Thomas Aquinas, *On the Truth of the Catholic Faith, Summa Contra Gentiles*, trans. with an Introduction by Anton C. Pegis (Garden City, N.Y.: Doubleday Image Books, 1955).

more impressive *Summa Theologica*[7] was addressed to young men in the Dominican order who would be trained to do intellectual battle with the new heresies amongst Christians and with the infidels who made them possible. In the debates between Thomas and the nominees of Bonaventure, it was generally thought that Aquinas had won handily.

But could Thomas handle the new challenge from the friends of time? Well, after all, the difference between his system and that of Aristotle—or at least between the system he recommended in the two Summae and that of Aristotle as Aristotle was understood by the Arabs—had to do with just that question. The Arabs supposed reason led to the view that the world was eternal. Thomas insisted that it was created at a moment of time and would end at another. The Arabs thought the world was static, Aquinas was prepared to concede that it changed in time according to a purpose of Providence. More importantly, Aquinas apparently was able to hold these things without in the least coming to the conclusion that the faith was historically suspect or being more embarrassed than Augustine had been about predestination or lapsing into the heresy of universalism.

Part of the advantage was secured simply by a strategic way of determining the respective spheres of faith and reason and part by the construction of a fairly elaborate metaphysic which permitted the optimal development of a number of strains of knowledge. The separation of faith and reason was made by insisting that (1) faith and reason cannot contradict each other, (2) not all elements of the faith can be demonstrated, and (3) when there is an apparent conflict which cannot be resolved by categorizing the element of faith as belonging to the sphere of the undemonstrable, one should assume that there has been a mistake of reasoning and begin over again with a different sort of reasoning. To make this work there had to be a variety of ways of acquiring the requisite knowledge.

Reason generally provided knowledge of the necessary and the possible. Experience provided knowledge of the contingently actual. But reason could not provide complete and adequate knowledge of the whole domain of the necessary. For reason proceeds from general principles and does not provide insights into what is, in principle, unique. Since no particular experience is a necessary ingredient in the life of any sentient creature, the unique and necessary cannot be known after the manner of the contingent, i.e., in experience, even though experience does give us knowledge of what is unique in our own lives.

7   St. Thomas Aquinas, *The Summa Theologica of St. Thomas Aquinas*, literally translated by the Fathers of the English Dominican Province (London: Burns, Oates and Washbourne, 1912-1937).

There is therefore a sphere which lies outside the grasp of knowledge but which, nonetheless, is crucial for human welfare. We may know from general principles, for instance, *that* God exists; but the nature of God necessarily transcends such general principles and the doctrine of the Trinity, for instance, could not be demonstrated. If true, it can only be grasped by faith. The appearance of God in history—the incarnation, the resurrection, the guidance of the church by Divine Providence—for the most part, similarly, belongs to the domain of faith. For it consists of unique particulars which compose events whose meaning could not be grasped either by reason or by the simple experience of them.

The effect of the Thomist position was this: For those who accepted it, the matters belonging to the sphere of reason became open for debate. Whether one was right or wrong in one's position about such matters depended, simply, on the strength of one's reasons. Where reason was combined with experience, authority was naturally vested in those with experience—those skilled in reasoning about such experiences and so on. But the faith was effectively sealed from such influences. Logically, no reason and no experience could refute the claims of its defenders. But this did not mean that the faith was open to anyone who wanted to make a claim to divine revelation. On the contrary, in the view of Thomas and his followers, it greatly increased the visible importance of the church.

How shall we decide which faith to follow? First of all, the answer has been given and in the only way that such answers could be given—uniquely, individually, from Jesus to his disciples, to the fathers of the church, to the councils of the church, and so on in unbroken succession. One cannot, really, even decide to believe. Only divine grace can achieve that for us. But insofar as reason bears on the matter at all, it can lead us in the direction of the right answer. Those who seek belief, or seek understanding through preserving faith, either will or will not all be inclined toward the same beliefs. If there is no true faith or if God does not intend us to have it, they will tend to come to many disparate conclusions. If there is such a faith and we are intended to have it, then those who are sincere and open to it will tend toward a common faith—assuming they can recognize it. Despite human frailty, numerous admitted mistakes, the confusions of language and culture, the uncertainties of time, those whom the church has identified through its councils and high offices have tended toward a common and persistent belief. That is not a proof and the fate of the church itself is in the hands of God who could, after all, reject its pretensions, but it forms a necessary check on private belief and fallibility. The consistent concern of the church over schism, heresy, plurality of belief, and the development of doctrine issues from the fact that the test only works so long as there is, if not a unanimity of believers, at least a clear doctrinal path across time.

In its own time, Thomism had severe competition from the continuing Augustinian tradition represented by Bonaventure, his Franciscan colleagues, and their successors. Thomas had offered a compromise and, like all compromises, it was viewed with suspicion. Technical grounds were found under which he could be condemned at Paris and at Oxford, but very likely the real concern continued to be that he had allowed reason a sphere immune to the faith. Secular knowledge meant secular authority and secular power. (The association of knowledge with wealth and power is no modern discovery: It was taken as axiomatic in the high Middle Ages that a monopoly of knowledge went with a monopoly of authority.) Bonaventure offered a programme in which reason and faith would run continuously and assuredly through all knowledge. For, he argued, given that God exists, it is clear that we cannot, no matter what, know anything unless He wills it. Thus one without faith lacks the state and condition of mind within which knowledge is, in any case, possible. On the other side, reason cannot be excluded from any claim which is to be taken seriously. Scripture comes to us in words, so do the writings of the fathers of the church. Words have meanings and Scripture is not immune to misunderstanding. But even the fathers, in seeking to explain doctrine, must make use of philosophical concepts and they and we must reason our way to a conclusion. Bonaventure, in short, is offering the third (and much the most traditional) answer to the faith/reason controversy: Faith and reason may be seen as competing co-claimants for the same territory, they may be seen as claimants to different territories, or they may be seen as non-competing co-claimants to the same territory in the sense that one is unintelligible without the other. Logically, there is at least a fourth possibility. It may be that there are two independent truths which are non-competing in the sense that, though they seem to occupy the same region, there is no logical connection between them. Dissidents who were known as Latin Averroists (not very fairly to the Arab philosopher Averroes) adopted, or were widely thought to have adopted, that position.

Whatever may be the philosophical situation, it ought to be admitted that, politically, Thomism offered the safest way out of the difficulties. The Augustinian position of Bonaventure was a two-edged sword and always had been. It exposed all claims to knowledge to the critique of faith but it also exposed all claims to faith to the critique of reason.

Augustine himself had associated God with truth and truth with the inner light—a position with which church authorities did not always come to terms readily or easily. The claim that faith and reason were competitors for the same prize would have put the faith at risk on a constant basis and, what is more, would have elevated the claims of humans to equal status with the claims of God. The Thomist position kept the faith intact, minimized conflict, and, certainly not least, made general sense. Given Thomas' model of knowledge and the modal distinctions between possibility and contingency, there did indeed appear to be a crucial realm in which belief could be sustained only by faith. Furthermore, most of Thomas' claims about particular Christian doctrines which fell into this classification seemed to fit the distinctions without undue strain.

Nevertheless, Thomism was just one of the options; it was a compromise, it was not without its presumptions and not without its own potential arrogance. If it ultimately gained a clear following, its following was never universal within the church and, though the late nineteenth-century *Aeterni Patris* of Leo XIII gave it official and preferred status, the claims made in that encyclical were not absolute. Thomas was commended to the faithful as the most likely guide to the truth.

The official return to Thomism cannot have been merely an attempt to respond to the crisis about time, history, and culture in the way that the church had responded to crises brought about by the Arab philosophers and the extensions of the scope of reason associated with the renewal of interest in Aristotle. Now the sides, in a sense, were reversed. The Arabs had worried the faithful with the claims of reason to trespass on matters which belonged only to God.

In his concern to preserve the divine options, Thomas appears as the partisan of uniqueness, of the claim that not everything can be reduced to principle, of the Christian distinction between the spirit and the letter, the law and the truth. Faith is preserved as a region in which the unique may be confronted, the mechanical overcome, the personal allowed to triumph.

In that sense, one might actually think of Thomas as in sympathy with the temper of the nineteenth-century concern with time, history, and uniqueness, and think of the church as offering to its assailants a hand of friendship. But, in fact, in Thomas' world, time is not important in the ways which it seemed to matter to the critics who posed the nineteenth-century threat.

In Thomas' philosophy, one does not, for instance (as one does in Hegel's philosophy), ask what time it is before one determines what one ought to do. True, Christianity—as understood by Thomists and others—*may* permit variable answers to some kinds of moral questions. (In a general way, it seems not to permit variable answers to questions of the form, Is it permissible to do x? for whether it is permissible or not depends on the relation between the essential nature of the act, human nature, and specific divine ordinances. It may and usually does permit variable answers to questions of the form, What should I do now? for it is accepted that each of us is unique and that Divine Providence has, therefore, unique intentions for us. The answer will, therefore, vary from person to person, from time to time in one person's life, and may well change with the successes and failures which we encounter as we move through the world. More surprisingly, however, it permits variable answers to such questions as, How ought I to respond to one who does x? That is, though we are all forbidden to commit adultery, we are not required to pass uniform or harsh judgments on one who does commit adultery. The New Testament, indeed, is laced with examples of interference by Jesus with those who are about to pass harsh judgments, cast stones, and so forth. This variation has to do, apparently, with the situation of the sinner and his judge vis-à-vis the prospective salvation of each of them—a sympathetic understanding of one's own and of the human condition is, it would seem, recommended as a reasonable precondition to the availability of salvation. Each of us stands, at every moment, in a unique relation to God and to his own salvation or damnation. The proper response to us and by us depends upon that relation. Judgment is, therefore, ultimately, left to God.)

Just how would Thomas confront the notion that faith ought to change with culture? Can one not argue that God might have said things to primitive desert tribesmen which He surely would not have said to sophisticated Parisians of the thirteenth or the twentieth centuries? Surely, too, the church must have acquired a thick overlay of rubbishy superstition which, from time to time, one ought to strip off. Even more likely, as our archeology, our linguistics, our ability to reconstruct ancient documents grow more sophisticated, we must expect to obtain better and more accurate knowledge of the Scriptures themselves, of the meaning of stories told within various cultures, of the line which ancient peoples would have drawn between imagination and reality.

No one can imagine Thomas as anything other than horrified at all these propositions—propositions which must seem eminently sensible to many of us and were coming to seem sensible to some of the church's critics and some of its friends in the middle of the nineteenth century. God would not tell half-truths, offer misleading claims, practise bait and switch like some bargain discount dealer. Thomas would admit that we never know whether we have grasped the full meaning of all the Scripture or even of the doctrines of the councils of the church. Human understanding may change, but faith does not. And it would be rash to suppose that God had allowed or encouraged the general muddle-headedness of the church fathers. Nor ought we to suppose that what seems to us superstition is superstition. The difficulty about that is that our views about superstition stem mostly from our views about the science of the day. Thomas, too, lived in a time of changing technology, of scientific re-conceptualization. But the faith lies in a region logically separate from these concerns and we must not mistake one for the other. He would admit, certainly, the church managers of any given time are given to all the usual sorts of human frailty and that it is quite possible that matters will be claimed for faith which are really the domain of science. But the development of historical understanding will not help us to spot those occasions. What will help us to spot them is the development of an adequate theology. Scientific and cultural sophistication will not necessarily make for a sound theology. Quite the reverse. Science had advanced and culture was more advanced in Thomas' time than in the time of the church fathers and the decline of the Roman Emperor, but theology faced serious problems and was in general need of renewal.

The third set of historical claims is more puzzling. Certainly the tools for reading Scripture, understanding ancient cultures, providing the content for meetings of the church councils do increase in sophistication, and learning about them is cumulative. The church has, at most times, encouraged the development of such knowledge and advocated that it be made use of.

It is just here that the Thomist claim lands in most difficulties with the nineteenth-century partisans of history. If faith is separated from reason and so from knowledge in the various ways in which we understand the secular claims to it, what are we to make of controversies about the meaning of Scripture? On one view, it is only by divine grace, in any case, that we can expect to understand Scripture. For the matters it alludes to are matters of faith, and faith we cannot generate for ourselves. That enables us to seek divine guidance as to how we should read it, but it also seems to render various important kinds of scholarship redundant and to cast doubts upon the work of honest, believing scholars. Why bother if only God can provide the answer? Indeed, is it not arrogant, sinful, wilful to approach Scripture as though one might decode it for oneself? But, then, no serious person will hold that the casual reader of the Bible or the proceedings of a church council is likely to do as well as the scholar. Perhaps God helps those who help themselves. The problem is that it seems increasingly likely that border skirmishes between faith and reason are not easily to be put down. In the late nineteenth century, more than one liberal churchman felt that *Aeterni Patris* was not really meant to bring about peace and harmony but to keep in check the growing body of biblical and associated scholarship.

Nor did it turn out that the ideas which had to be coped with could be neatly stacked and kept hygienically, each on its own side of the border. Knowledge on the Thomist scheme turned out to be expressible chiefly in the form of standard Aristotelean definitions: "Man is a rational animal" is a traditional form which states the sort of thing man is—an animal—and then states what distinguishes him from the others, his rationality. Such statements are atemporal, are true at all times, and seek to state the essential characteristics of things which define the places they ought to occupy in the system which is the world. It does not make sense to ask, Since *when* was a man a rational animal? and Will he always be a rational animal? There was a tendency, therefore, for parts of the science of biology, especially the non-taxonomic parts and particularly evolutionary theory, to collide with the Thomist view of secular knowledge. For here are not eternal truths, but time-dominant truths. But it was, after all, by giving secular knowledge special characteristics that the Thomist scheme succeeded in marking out the boundaries of faith and reason. If there came to be secular truths which have special, unique features associated with time, immediacy, and so forth, the boundary dispute would open again. Notice it was not in this case some element of the *faith* which collided with secular knowledge but a form given to secular knowledge which collided with another form given to secular knowledge. Scripture has it that God created great whales. It doesn't say how. It also doesn't say whether whales are a stage in a continuous process or a special and discrete thing. In fact, the trouble was not with biology. In all the sciences, workers were getting rid of the Aristotelean notion of essence, the neat Aristotelean classifications of things, the notion that the world forms an immutable system, and replacing them with notions of process, continuous change, statistical approximation, fields instead of forces. It is of little moment that all of these innovations may have been misguided. They all had some connection to the new notions of the importance of time, of relativity, of quantity rather than quality.

The reversion to Thomism bought time in the sense that it gave the church a standard to hang onto, a position from which to reflect. But it did not stop the new challenges created by the growing importance of the notion of time. Inevitably, also, when a large and powerful bureaucratic institution adopts a system of ideas, they become formalized. The Thomism of the late nineteenth- and early twentieth-century texts with its collections of neat and tidy formulae, its easy solutions to every problem, its quick rejections of every other philosophical system rather quickly became a bore. If it provided quick and easy ways to tell the faithful from the heretical, it also provided quick and easy ways of turning thought to matters other than philosophy.

It is to this situation that the church in English Canada had to turn itself, after World War I. The church in French Canada had become conservative—fearing that its small, faithful enclave would be over-run by the surrounding increasingly irreligious and commercial culture of industrial North America. The faith was to protect the minds of the faithful with an iron grille of safe ideas. Some churchmen worried even about philosophy.[8] In French Canada the tendency for Thomist thought to collide at numerous places with advancing ideas outside philosophy was certainly increased sharply by the form which the standard Thomist texts took. In English Canada, more moderate but hardly more imaginative (often American) texts were in general use. Canadian and American Catholic institutions traded off scholars and ideas. (Canadians were often active in the American Catholic Philosophical Association and similar, smaller bodies.)

Into this situation came a modest classicist, philosopher, and eventual rector of St. Michael's and president of the Pontifical Institute, Henry Carr.[9] Up to the end of the nineteenth century, the college had provided the philosophy necessary to meet the canonical requirements for those training in the priesthood—perhaps twelve hours a week. Between 1907 and 1911, Carr undertook the refashioning of the course and philosophy teaching expanded to as much as thirty-seven hours a week with a staff of as many as eight philosophers (nearly all of whom also taught something else) involved.

Carr was concerned to carry out not the letter but the spirit of *Aeterni Patris*. The additional teaching made possible much more hard examination of original texts and tough-minded review of real ideas rather than empty forms. Carr's ideal was at Louvain, that always pesky, usually original, almost never second-rate bastion of European Catholic thought. In pursuit of this idea, he brought Maurice DeWulf to Toronto at the beginning of 1919. DeWulf, the founder of Louvain's

8   See, for example, *L. A. Paquet, textes, choisis et présentés par Yvan Lamonde* (Montréal: Fides, 1972).

9   Henry Carr arrived at St. Michael's, Toronto, from Assumption College, Windsor, in 1904.

Revue Néo-scholastique and long-time professor at the Louvain Institute, began a new era. The same year Sir Bertram Windle,[10] newly resigned principal of University College, Cork, a man of many interests including astronomy, anthropology, and vitalist biology was persuaded to join St. Michael's philosophy department.

It is not on record that Carr frightened anyone, though his strategy must have been obvious and must at least have aroused curiosity and a little nervousness. DeWulf's public lectures were intended specifically to raise the question of the relation of mediaeval thought and culture to our thought and culture. (They were entitled "Civilization and Philosophy in the Heart of the Middle Ages.") DeWulf returned to Belgium that April but came back to lecture at St. Michael's in each of the next four years. Windle was concerned quite specifically to raise the question of the relation between science and a Christian cosmology—to urge that a secular understanding of biology would increase the likelihood of our belief in the church's view of the world. To do one of these is to raise questions of the relevance of time; to do the other is to raise again the bearing of secular knowledge and the faith and vice versa. To do both at once is to subject official Thomism to a substantial overhaul. There is no reason to think that Carr himself deviated to any extent at all from the most orthodox outlook on such questions and certainly none to believe that he sought to undermine the doctrine of *Aeterni Patris*. What he did seek was to stir honest thought, to avoid the substitution of formulae for serious answers, to make Catholic intellectual life adequate to the challenge of the time.

By 1922, there was an active philosophy club at St. Michael's and participants included not only the college's own staff but that of the other institutions of the University of Toronto as well. In 1925, Gerald Phelan—who was to have a profound influence both on the college and on the Mediaeval Institute—was recruited from Halifax where he was serving as a priest. Phelan was another Louvain graduate and this slant was strengthened in 1926 when Carr, who had completed his term as a superior of the college and returned to be head of the philosophy department, brought Léon Noel to teach there.

The department by then was strong enough to undertake a substantial graduate programme and was beginning to become an intellectual force, at least in the university. Its force began to extend well outside with the coming of Etienne Gilson in 1927. With that addition, the St. Michael's department, as strong as any ever has been in Canada, for the moment far outstripped any other department in a Catholic

10 See Sir Bertram C. A. Windle, *What is Life? A Study of Vitalism and Neo-vitalism* (London: Herder, 1908).

institution[11] and could only be compared to two or three departments in institutions of any kind. It is now rivalled in the Catholic world by Ottawa. But for most of the period which concerns us, the centre of Catholic philosophy was at St. Michael's.

The coming of Gilson was not only an event which brought a certain prestige to St. Michael's and to Catholic thought in Toronto, it was a deliberate acknowledgement that a re-thinking of at least some aspects of Thomist doctrine was in order. It was an event calculated to take the work Carr had long been doing onto a larger stage. Gilson's philosophical position, however, was very special. He was not merely the ranking world expert in the mediaeval philosophy of Europe and an established ornament to the University of Paris. He had also been strongly influenced by Henri Bergson and sought to make his attraction to Bergson consistent with his commitment to St. Thomas—which is to say, he sought to see how Thomism might actually be made to live up to the challenge of the times.

In his *The Philosopher and Theology*,[12] Gilson describes the frustrations he had felt with the traditional Thomist textbooks.

Let us pause a moment to consider what scholasticism is ... as it presented itself to my mind in the barren form in which it was taught at the Grand Séminaire of Paris ... the *Elementa Philosophiae Scholasticae* by Sébastien Reinstadler, published in 1904 by Herder in Freiburg (Breisgau) as well as in several other places, including St. Louis in the United States. ...

As a student I was familiar with other philosophical methods, but I could not open these volumes without being greatly surprised. It was not so much the doctrine that disturbed me. ... What really disturbed me was that these volumes, which claimed to give an account of *philosophy*—a point not to be forgotten—drew their inspiration from a source entirely foreign to those of other philosophies. True, the other philosophies contradicted one another often enough, but they were not based upon any a priori refusal to communicate among themselves. They rather believed in dialogue. On the contrary, in the scholastic philosophy of the schools, every main part of Reinstadler's manual concluded with a series of ringing refutations. It was a case of scholasticism against all comers.

... Reinstadler preferred to teach a body of Aristotelian tenets topped off by the master conclusions of Christian philosophy. Divided according to the traditions of Wolff rather than that of Aristotle and Saint Thomas, this manual refused to take the other philosophies into consideration. Not that

11 Shook, *Catholic Post-Secondary Education in English-Speaking Canada*, p. 249. Shook details the activities of Catholic institutions in eastern and western Canada. Philosophy was vigorously alive in most of them, but produced no major philosophers.

12 Etienne Gilson, *The Philosopher and Theology*, translated from the French by Cécile Gilson (New York: Random House, 1962).

Reinstadler refused to speak about them, nor was he incapable of understanding them. Far from it. His exposition of Kant was as good as could be reasonably expected from that type of book. But he made absolutely no effort to understand the motives behind these philosophies. Reinstadler never judged their answers in the light of the problems the philosophers had attempted to solve. For him the main point was to demonstrate that the philosophy of Kant was false.[13]

We have quoted Gilson at some length for two reasons: One is to show that the problem of the Catholic thinker was at least widespread and that Gilson started clearly aware of it. The other is to let him state in his own words a perhaps subtle point which is of great importance here. Gilson did not just go back to the texts of the Middle Ages in order to get a vision of St. Thomas and his contemporaries, richer and more useful than the ones which could be found in the by-then ossified manuals of philosophy. He was also developing an historical method which changed, in important ways, the significance of the philosophers of the Middle Ages—at least for him and, no doubt, for many of his readers, Catholic and otherwise. The insistence is not, now, in discovering whether a given philosopher has any given answers, right or wrong, to some question which one wants to ask for oneself but, rather, to determine whether or not the philosopher gave a reasonable account of himself given the questions which *he* wanted to ask. The philosopher's quest then becomes, largely, one of finding out what it is that motivated the philosopher himself and then in a give-and-take between rival philosophers one may gradually (if one is lucky) come to grasp the bearing of it all on the questions one is to ask for oneself. Thus one could not, *in one move*, determine intelligently what the response of the Christian philosopher ought to be to a given position or challenge. Since it is unlikely that St. Thomas faced exactly that challenge, it is correspondingly unlikely that there is, literally, a "Thomist" answer to a modern question, if by that one means an answer which one can formulate as a doctrine to be found in so many words in a text of St. Thomas.

To take such a position is to free oneself from the straight-jacket of the manuals, of a body of official thought, of a set of mechanical responses. In choosing to come again and again (apart from the years of World War II) to St. Michael's, Gilson was choosing to come to a place where, in general, he felt at home. Carr's persistently open policy, though surely not revolutionary or even radical, had created a climate in which such thought might flourish as well as it did in Paris. Gilson, determined, as always, to be fair, may have exaggerated the extent to

13 Ibid., pp. 46-48.

which the manual writers were unusual amongst philosophers. Would he have written, "Outside the restricted society of scholastics, very few practice this kind of philosophizing,"[14] had he not been protected at the Sorbonne and at St. Michael's from daily confrontation with two generations of analytic philosophers?

Apart from these outbursts of what he liked to call philosophical "bad manners,"[15] two things concerned Gilson in a way which was to give a specific direction to his philosophy. One was that he repeatedly noticed that intelligent and sensitive young philosophers and churchmen were being influenced by the work of Henri Bergson even though that influence usually led to serious difficulties for those who were closely associated with the church. The other was a growing tendency, sparked by men like Lucien Laberthonnière, to link the philosophy of St. Thomas with that of Aristotle and then to decry the opposition between Christian doctrine and Greek philosophy.

His own interest in Bergson and Bergson's writings inevitably led him to examine closely the question of the opposition, if any, between the thought of the then leading intellect of the French-speaking world and the real nature of "Christian philosophy." The quest on which he set out was necessarily complex, baffling, and, as he recounts the story himself, understandably tinged with emotional tension.

One might have thought, at first sight, that two philosophers could hardly be farther apart than Bergson and St. Thomas and still be within the western tradition. Bergson was essentially the philosopher of time and process: For him, reality was a flow, not a flow of anything for that would imply that substance was still a category prior to process, but simply a flow. He maintained that the intellect, which sought to freeze the world so as to extract information of practical value to the biological creature, distorted reality. The biologist paints the development of the lepidoptera from egg through larva and pupa to adult as though it passes through specific discrete stages in little jumps. In fact, Bergson said, he *knows* perfectly well that the process is continuous; he is aware that the knowledge he has is of dead or frozen moths. His intellectual activities probably do not even deceive him, for he is confronted all along with an immediate intuition of reality.

Yet this flow has a direction, a meaning. In *Creative Evolution*,[16] Bergson ascribed this movement to the *élan vital*. In his account of

14 Ibid., p. 48.
15 Ibid.
16 Henri Bergson, *Creative Evolution*, authorized translation by Arthur Mitchell of Harvard University, with a Foreword by Irwin Edman of Columbia University (New York: Random House, 1944), pp. 97ff.

human affairs in *Time and Free Will*,[17] he described an analogous reality which he named the "deeper self."

In the years just after the turn of the century, a generation of young Frenchmen and of young intellectuals around the world for that matter, found this heady stuff. To many of them, Bergson was demanding a release from official formulae, from dogma, from two thousand years of the accretions of the western intellect, and championing feeling, creativity, intuition, and freedom. No one was much surprised that the church did not find these new doctrines very appealing. Later, in *The Two Sources of Morality and Religion*,[18] Bergson modified his views in a way which, perhaps, orthodoxy might have found more attractive but that was a very long time after Bergson's first impact and long after Gilson's early wrestling with his doctrines.

Gilson recounts that he was at no time able to consider himself anything other than a Christian. "No one is born a Christian," he wrote, "but a man born in a Christian family soon becomes one without having been consulted."[19] There was never, therefore, a question in his mind of whether he should turn his back on Christian philosophy. But even though his philosophical reading suggested to him that he had a clear sense of what conflicted with Christian doctrine, he remained unconvinced that between Bergson and Christianity there was, necessarily, the kind of opposition which many others took to be obvious.

If he were right and they were wrong and if, nonetheless, the philosophical theology of Thomas Aquinas represented the central truths of Christian philosophy, it would seem to follow that a return to the texts of Aquinas himself would show some explanation for the mystery. At any rate, he might well expect to find out whether his general sense of the philosophical dimensions of Christianity was accurate and adequate.

He quite quickly became suspicious of the identification which the texts wanted to make between Aristotle and St. Thomas and he suspected that the crucial difference might have to do with what made St. Thomas a Christian and Aristotle a pagan, for he doubted that, in the literal sense, one could call St. Thomas or any of the major figures in the Middle Ages philosophers. They were theologians who sought to

17 Henri Bergson, *Time and Free Will*, authorized translation by F. L. Pogson (London: Allen & Unwin, 1913). Bergson's discussion of the "deeper self" is introduced in chapter 2, pp. 129-39. He refers to "the deeper strata of the self," p. 136.

18 Henri Bergson, *The Two Sources of Morality and Religion*, translated by Ashley Audra and Cloudesley Brereton with the assistance of W. Horsfall Carter (Garden City, N.Y.: Doubleday, 1935).

19 Gilson, *The Philosopher and Theology*, p. 8.

ask philosophical questions within the context of their theologies. The mark of Christian theology should, therefore, be clear upon them.

To make a long story simple and a subtle doctrine perhaps blunter than it ought to be, the centre of the problem turned out to be in the concepts of God developed, used, or deployed by Aristotle and St. Thomas. Aristotle's God is a fixity somehow beyond the reach of the world, the prime mover, the object of the world's desire. But St. Thomas repeatedly insists that God is "pure act."[20]

Gilson's work is invariably cautious, historically oriented, and replete with qualifications which make it difficult to know just how far he intended to go, at any given time, in making use of that doctrine. One may, however, look at it this way without (perhaps) doing too much violence to his intentions: Thomas came to Aristotle in the context of the intellectual excitement engendered essentially by the ideas of the Arab philosophers and confronted by the duty of a Christian to make the faith available to the infidel. To undertake to make Christianity compatible with Aristotle was to go as far as one reasonably could in accommodating the Arab intellectuals. So far as Thomas himself goes, it is easy to find a strong neo-Platonist direction in his early important work, *On Being and Essence*,[21] a work which seems less concerned with the confrontation of Arab thought than either of the Summae. And, despite their emphasis on Aristotelean doctrine and concerns, the Summae themselves contain a good many neo-Platonist passages. It is therefore, not always easy to tell what Thomas thinks is the best rendering available in the circumstances and what he thinks is reasonable to accept as the best rendering in any context. It may well be that it is his strategy to modify Aristotle as little as possible in order to make his case as effectively as possible to those whom he surmises to be Aristoteleans. If so, we should be careful to distinguish between those Aristotelean doctrines which he thinks permissible to a Christian and those Aristotelean doctrines about whose ultimate truth he is more or less satisfied— bearing in mind that, apart from the truths of the Christian faith, Aquinas supposes that all propositions are subject to error.

There does, however, seem clearly to be a place at which he draws the line and insists that Aristotle is to be modified and this has to do with the doctrine of God as "pure act." By "pure act" he evidently means that

20 St. Thomas Aquinas, *On Being and Essence*, trans. with an introduction by Armand Maurer, 2d ed. rev. (Toronto: Pontifical Institute of Mediaeval Studies, 1968), p. 53. Aquinas writes, "If we find some forms that can exist only in matter, this happens to them because they are far removed from the first principle, which is the primary and pure act." For further references see footnote by Maurer, p. 32, and the *Summa Theologica*.

21 See footnote 20 above.

which simply *is* and he reminds us that God, when He appeared to Moses in the burning bush, confined Himself to a simple declaration of being—"I am." Gilson takes Thomas to be asserting, at this point, a straightforward Christian doctrine and to be doing so for reasons which are theological rather than, or at least more than, philosophical. One could argue that the reasons were at least as much philosophical: Aristotle's problem, as Thomas conceives his schema at any rate, stems from the fact that Aristotle's world consists of matter, which is only the potentiality to take on form, and of form which is nothing except insofar as it *informs*. The difference between the possible and the actual is not in the matter or the form but in the act of being. It is this act of being which seems to have no place in Aristotle—at least if Aristotle is taken literally. It likely makes no difference whether one takes this to be Thomas' philosophical discovery or whether we take it to be the more or less natural and inevitable result of applying Christian theology to an Aristotelean framework. The pure act, however, is nothing like the distant Aristotelean prime mover or the teleological object of the world's desire, but something involved immediately in the world at every moment. It is conceptually distinct from every event in the world, never exhausted by any of the events of the world or all of them taken together, and yet inseparable from each. Such a notion thus preserves the traditional notion of a God who is both immanent and transcendent, both in and of the world and infinitely beyond it.

We now have a God who is very far from being a thing, a static state, a substance in the traditional sense, or whatever. Instead He is the animating force of the world. He is "being" as active, He becomes manifest over time in the particular and unique historical occasions of the world. All of this, needless to say, turns out to be much closer to Bergson than anyone had suspected. What is more, it may well turn out that it is that aspect of Thomas not immediately opposed to the intuitions of Bergson which is most important to Christians generally and, perhaps, to Thomas himself. The Aristotelean features of the Thomist system were an historical packaging. Were they more important to their own time than to ours?

Gilson, ever cautious, was not about to leap to rash conclusions. In a sense, Christianity flourished in the high Middle Ages in a way in which it does not now. ("In a sense," because it does not follow that a time in which nearly everyone is nominally a Christian is necessarily a time when more men are really Christians, more souls are saved, the cause of Providence best advanced.) Mediaeval Aristoteleanism was not merely attractive to Arab intellectuals. Arab intellectuals were worthy of concern in part because their ideas were attractive to mediaeval

Christians, or at least those of them attached to the great and burgeoning universities. In inquiring into the thought of the Middle Ages and its relation to the thought of our time, then, one must take account of this fact and of the relation of Aristotelean ethics, legal theory, and political theory to the prospects of a Christian life. For the most part, in his writings Gilson was much readier to listen to Bergson on the nature of being than to accept the popular readings of Bergson's doctrines in relation to freedom, creativity, and the individuality of value. He was not alone in that: Bergson puzzled over these secondary implications himself, as *The Two Sources of Morality and Religion* was eventually to show.

Furthermore, the mediaeval confrontation with the concept of being is a long adventure story, nothing so simple as the paragraphs above might seem to suggest, and Gilson faced them in basic studies on nearly all the great mediaeval thinkers and, finally, in the book which forms the nearest approach other than his autobiography to the exposition of his own philosophy, *Being and Some Philosophers*,[22] a work whose publication was finally entrusted to the Mediaeval Institute in Toronto.

Gilson's arrival in 1927 probably made certain that the plans for the creation of The Pontifical Institute of Mediaeval Studies would succeed and, in 1929, it was opened with Henry Carr as President and Gilson as Director of Studies.

Gilson made clear that his reason for accepting what amounted to a permanent post at St. Michael's was his desire to take part in the founding of the Mediaeval Institute. It was not a large undertaking and had as its staff Edmund McCorkell, an English professor, Henry Bellisle, an expert on the church fathers, Joseph Muckle, whose work centred on mediaeval Latin, Carr, and Gilson himself. Some associate faculty was recruited from St. Michael's and some, principally George Brett, from the University of Toronto. (Brett, by then Dean of Graduate Studies, brought official recognition and the practical commitment of the University of Toronto to the undertaking.)

Why was Gilson so enthusiastic? He had come to Toronto from Harvard; he had a permanent post at the University of Paris and certainly had no immediate need of money, encouragement, or whatever little prestige Toronto and St. Michael's could muster. His intellectual autobiography, *The Philosopher and Theology*, throws no direct light on the question. Apart from the material supplied by the publisher on the dust jacket of the English version of that book there is no mention of his adventures in Toronto. That work does show, however,

---

22 Etienne Gilson, *Being and Some Philosophers* (Toronto: Pontifical Institute of Mediaeval Studies, 1949).

that the controversies of Paris, particularly the controversies over Bergson and the doctrinal disputes amongst French Catholics themselves, cut rather deeper than the reader of any of Gilson's other books would have expected. There is a substantial bitterness mixed with the genuinely Christian humility of his prose and he writes:

> When a Frenchman complains in Rome that his country bears the brunt of ecclesiastical censure, the answer is always the same: Why do your countrymen spend so much time in denouncing one another? ... When a Catholic does not agree with another Catholic on any problem, the easiest way to outdo him is to get his position condemned as suspect and, if possible, as erroneous.[23]

Gilson had no intention of giving up altogether his French connections and went on from the Sorbonne to occupy the first Chair of History of Mediaeval Philosophy at the Collège de France. (The honour in national terms was great, but Gilson remarked wryly:

> One day he [Bergson] was entrusted by his colleagues with the thankless task of saying what the Collège de France had contributed to philosophy since the time of its foundation in the sixteenth century. This was not easy to do since, to be quite truthful about it, the only outstanding service the Collège ever rendered philosophy had been to appoint Bergson.[24])

But he may have felt that the parts of each year he spent in Toronto brought him into an intellectual world to which he had a quite different relation. Here he was not the brilliant but suspect Thomist with a weakness for Bergson, but simply the senior scholar in his field. Catholics in English Canada tended, on the whole, to fear less the lapse from orthodoxy than a failure to appreciate the importance of modern thought. They were suspected of being conservative, doctrinaire, English-speaking replicas of Monseigneur Paquet and they welcomed, understandably, someone whose claims to scholarship were impeccable and who seemed to be able to understand contemporary thought and to draw strength from it without finding it necessary to abandon the traditional positions of the Catholic philosopher.

With its small staff, its original tiny library of a few thousand books, its quarters a made-over private house, the Institute for Mediaeval Studies can hardly have appeared a very promising platform from which to undertake a major programme to influence thought in English Canada.

23 Gilson, *The Philosopher and Theology*, p. 57.
24 Ibid., p. 115.

Gilson, however, probably had no such grandiose ideas in mind. Rather, the reception he received in English Canada more likely convinced him that Toronto would provide an atmosphere in which important studies could be undertaken. The difficulty of writing in Paris and the advantage of working in Toronto (even though one had a mere $200,000 on which to build a major institution) had to do rather with the nature of background controversy. Even a mediaevalist in Paris at the time was suspected of or assumed to be working away to some end related to doctrinal controversy. In Toronto professed innocent intentions might be accepted as such and might, indeed, be just what they seemed to be.

The early publications of the Institute certainly bore out this hope. Anton Pegis' *St. Thomas and the Problem of the Soul in the Thirteenth Century,*[25] for instance, might have been a polemical work or might have been searched by rival disputants for signs of buried polemic. In fact, it achieved an open, careful objectivity. The edition of *Algazel's Metaphysics*[26] edited by J. T. Muckle in 1933 was typical of another kind of activity: the preparation of scholarly texts and translations which would make arguments more objective and cool-headed, make possible the collaboration of parts of the philosophical community whose main skills were not in ancient languages, and generally make mediaeval philosophy available to a larger public. Backing this was the Institute's journal, *Mediaeval Studies*, which has now long been a major force in the field.

Gilson, in short, succeeded in what he and Carr wanted: the creation of a cool-headed intelligent community of men who could be devout without being narrow-minded, faithful without being suspicious, tolerant without being soft-headed.

The philosophers who have been added over the years to the Institute and to St. Michael's—Jacques Maritain who was first a visitor in 1933, Joseph Owens and Lawrence Lynch who have been mainstays of the institutions for many of the post-war years, Anton Maurer who made basic contributions to Thomist scholarship—have sustained this tradition. In theology, St. Michael's was later to gain the reputation (through the work of men like Gregory Baum) for a kind of liberal reformism which has added something important to intellectual life in Toronto. But its philosophers, for the most part, have maintained the balanced openness which Gilson and Carr had in mind.

25 Anton Pegis, *St. Thomas and the Problem of the Soul in the Thirteenth Century* (Toronto: St. Michael's College, 1934).

26 al-Ghazzālī, *Algazel's Metaphysics: A Mediaeval Translation*, ed. J. T. Muckle (Toronto: St. Michael's College, 1933).

The Institute was not without its controversies. Its status in the university was, for a long time, rather ambiguous. The statutes of the university made no provision for the creation of graduate programmes by the affiliated colleges and the Institute's programmes were recognized through a set of complex but unofficial understandings. The papal charter which added to its title was not granted, finally, until 1939 and subsequently there were disputes, recorded by Professor Shook, between the Institute's management and the Basilian order which created and managed St. Michael's College. They led to Gerald Phelan's resignation of the presidency and his "exile" for several years in the United States at Notre Dame University in Indiana—where he promptly founded another Institute of Mediaeval Studies. In the end, however, he returned to Toronto and all of these controversies seem, in fact, to have been small in scale and finally unhurtful to the college or the Institute.

In time, therefore, the scholarship which Carr and Gilson founded had its effect. Though Henry Carr had to go himself to inaugurate effective teaching of mediaeval philosophy at the University of British Columbia in the years after World War II (and became embroiled in tragi-comic dispute as to whether or not he could wear his cassock in class), mediaeval thought became something to be reckoned with across Canada. Catholic philosophy, as well, came to be thought of throughout English Canada as something much more than the dogmatic summaries in the Thomist manuals. Gilson and Maritain received a hearing in the classroom. Indeed, the day was to come when Canadian scholars, defensive and self-denigrating about nearly everything else, said routinely to sceptical foreigners, "Well, we *do* have the Institute of Mediaeval Studies in Toronto, you know."

Perhaps the ultimate sign of that pride came in the nineteen-sixties when the University of Toronto decided that it should have its own Mediaeval Studies programme and its own Centre for those studies. The studies that Carr and Gilson started had ceased to be parochial.

Laurence Shook has noted, however, that the future may not be so clear. With, as he puts it, "a decline of interest in Thomism especially among the graduates of Catholic colleges,"[27] will the new stance of the church render mediaeval philosophy substantially less important and, if that happens, will there be no reason for there to be specifically Catholic philosophy?

27 Shook, *Catholic Post-Secondary Education in English-Speaking Canada*, p. 223.

FIFTEEN

THE IDEA OF REASON AND THE CANADIAN SITUATION

REASON IS A HUMAN capacity, essentially the capacity to order thought and experience intelligibly. Its scope needs to be seen in the activities it governs. There are no simple definitions. One can only seek to show it at work.

The creation of new meanings is dangerous and the preservation of old ones is difficult. There has always been a struggle to imprison reason in rules: The rules of formal logic govern the acceptable forms of propositions, the moves one is allowed to make from premise to secure conclusion, the conditions under which the expression of an assertion may be modified without altering its conventionally assigned truth values. Theories of meaning seek to establish the limits under which expressions are allowed to "count" as potentially true or false. All such attempts, however, are normative: They inhibit those forms of expression which are non-standard, eccentric, "crazy."

But since intelligibility is not given in such simple ways, reason invariably outfoxes all such attempts. Indeed, if it did not, it would not be possible to stand outside our logics and theories of meaning in order to assess them. Reason is thus also to be found in the literary forms which give shape to poetry or transform a picaresque into a novel, in our attempts to transform feeling into intelligible emotion and, above all, in the large-scale world pictures which form the backdrops to all our talk and action.

If, as we suggested at the beginning, culture is created by the process of assigning meaning to human acts and the unity of culture is created by the sharing of meaning, then the relation between culture and one's attitude to reason is crucial. Attitudes to reason usually appear most clearly in philosophical writings where the nature of the problems forces open declarations—though voluntary declarations such as those one finds in the literary criticism of Northrop Frye may be just as clear. The examination of the work of philosophers, therefore, provides an insight into culture. It is not, to be sure, the insight that one finds by doing social history, or the insight one finds in literary criticism, or the insight which comes from anthropological or sociological investigation. Yet inquiries into philosophical reason may provide clues to the nature of a culture, and those clues can be compared to those which are produced by other studies.

If one seeks to probe philosophical reason, what should one include? One might simply see what has turned up as a result of the sifting process which is a normal part of academic philosophy. But, in Canada, the academy has not generally (until very recently) admitted the work of Canadian philosophers as part of the normal, obligatory, or even optional list of subject matters for study. One did not hire professors to expound the work of Watson, Blewett, or Brett. Thus we do not have a body of sifted and carefully examined work. It may turn out that the philosophers examined in this book do not form a complete list of the major figures or that their work has not been done justice here; but it should at least be obvious that there has been important philosophy written in Canada. We thus do have *something* toward which to direct our analysis.

In absence of a reliable academic tradition, one must find another way to determine what ought to go into the analysis of philosophical reason. As suggested in the preface, we tried to include everyone who wrote substantially on a variety of philosophical topics and who lived and worked in Canada for an extended period of time. (One can rarely grasp a philosopher's use of reason from a single philosophical enterprise or from several rather narrowly oriented ones.) But do they represent the range of concerns to which one ought to direct one's attention? Have we found enough material to answer our own most basic questions?

One can look to see whether or not the study includes at least sample responses to the central issues: Reason must develop in response to changing views of the human condition necessitated by advances in science and in public awareness, to changing points of intersection between faith and reason, to occasions on which traditional systems of education meet new populations, to circumstances in which man's relation to nature becomes problematic, to occasions on which political activity requires re-articulation, and to circumstances in which public intellectual activity itself becomes open to question. If one does not have examples under each of these headings something has gone awry, and in each case if the diagnosis of reason and its relation to culture is accurate, the results ought to show some common features.

These inquiries could (and should) occupy other and different books and ought to go along with an account of the taxonomy of reason in its various guises. But it is interesting at the end of this rather modest inquiry to look very briefly at what has been turned up under these headings.

We included discussions of Bucke and Lighthall, for instance, really because, given the place they occupied in our history and in our national intellectual life, it would have been absurd not to. But it is important to see, now, why that is so.

Consider Bucke's case: The advance in medical science made it possible to treat the insane. The development of liberal societies and of notions of tolerance made it socially necessary to treat them. But someone had to think it out. That made it inevitable that the phenomena of madness should be assessed and given new meanings. The first necessity in such a project was to re-conceptualize human nature. One had to dispose of the thesis that there was a standard human nature from which individuals lapsed mainly through wilful action, want of self-control, failure of moral principle, or divine disfavour. What was needed, evidently, was a theory of human development combined with a richer account of the ways in which human beings might fail in the course of many transitions. Bucke's moral theory sought to explain behaviour by reference to physiology and his general theory of human development adopted an evolutionary model. That was ordinary enough in the last half of the nineteenth century. Less ordinary is Bucke's way of rejecting the social Darwinist notion that the survival of the fittest was the law of nature and that the weak and the unfit should be weeded out by a vigorous programme of competition. By postulating that the next development in evolution was a kind of consciousness whose characteristics appear to include an increase in compassion, a decrease in hate, and a general growth in the civilizing virtues, he neatly undercuts that whole scheme. Instead, we would expect an increase in the virtues of community. In re-working the ideas, Bucke gives weight to communitarian values and virtues which exhibit what we have suggested are the central values of the society in which he lived. It is surely in character that he did his work in a public institution and without the intervention of private wealth. It is also in character that in a society which valued tradition, he should have based his theory on a new analysis of human history—one which went back to Moses and went on through the major reference points which the community used as points of orientation for its normal expressions of value. Here again one finds reason used as a device for the extension of vision and not, primarily, as a device for the mounting of combative argument.

Lighthall worked, above all, at the unification of culture: He worked across the humanities as philosopher, historian, literary organizer, critic, and poet. He also sought to find a way of integrating the humanistic culture with a society increasingly founded on science and technology. Like Bucke, he used dominantly evolutionary themes to create a theory of human development within which scientific belief could be integrated with traditional value. Reason is used here to bring coherence to a body of beliefs and values which seemed increasingly divergent and to find a basis for a unified culture within which, once again, the individual could accept the community as the possessor of values which might transcend his own. The struggle is to get a coherent picture which will permit the liberal virtues of tolerance and diversity while combatting the individualist vices which arose from a deeply fragmented society. Lighthall sought to transform the meanings assigned to a great variety of events—to reverse the accepted view that the assault on aboriginal cultures represented a simple triumph for a higher civilization, to overturn the reading of biological evolution which made it a mechanical, essentially meaningless process involving nothing more than the reorganization of matter, to erode the individualist view that the universe knows no higher values than our personal, immediate satisfactions. He created a larger synthesis which he hoped would be seen to make more sense of each and all of the facts. Notice the way in which quite common early twentieth-century materials are transformed in a way which makes sense in a pluralistic society with a strong sense of tradition and a marked communitarian bias—in this case by Lighthall, a wealthy, successful lawyer facing the twin crises of new kinds of human knowledge and a marked tendency toward social fragmentation.

Bucke and Lighthall are also concerned with the relation between faith and reason: Both are struggling to make faith intelligible by using reason to create a new conceptual framework. Both end up by urging a new faith. The fact that they were driven to that expedient is, to a degree, a measure of the conceptual strain involved, and a measure, perhaps, of their failure to get imaginative reason to accord with their otherwise rather traditionalist inclinations. The faith/reason relation illustrates philosophical reason and its cultural setting in other more subtle contexts, however.

In the last chapter, for example, we dealt with a group of Catholic philosophers for whom the relation between faith and reason was central and for whom, again, the establishment of their position in a pluralistic society was a necessary feature. The relation is interesting. It would be absurd to think that Gilson and Maritain were primarily influenced by Canadian society or that they tailored their philosophy to our needs. But they were no doubt attracted to Toronto by a pluralistic situation which created a general atmosphere characterized by liberality and which, above all, created points of contact between their ideas and those of others. Gilson makes clear in his autobiography that he had felt his thought to be in collision with powerful forces in France. Liberation from that feeling (even if it was not based on fact) would certainly have had an effect on his subsequent work. In Gilson's writing, most interestingly, perhaps, reason is used to preserve tradition by creating a system of ideas within which traditional Thomistic notions were seen to have intelligible and surprising connections to a philosophy strongly associated with central issues of the twentieth century—that of Henri Bergson. In the process, Bergson's defence of the values of spirit and his attack on the materialist reading of science could be used to buttress the Thomistic defence of the same values. The performance was surely impressive. It may well, for instance, have convinced Bergson himself. The advantage of the Canadian setting was also obvious: First, to be located in a society within the confines of federated institutions like the University of Toronto was to be located in a milieu in which traffic with the ideas of those outside one's own pattern of beliefs was normal and expected, and made obvious what, in another setting, had seemed suspicious. Secondly, the philosophical environment was one in which reason was not seen primarily as a set of rules which could be used to outlaw one's opponent's position, but as a capacity which could be used to give new and alternative meanings to experience.

On the surface, at least, these attitudes in English Canada were markedly less conservative than those of Catholic philosophers in Quebec. Certainly, Maritain is more liberal, say, than Charles de Koninck, the Laval philosopher who was the most talked-about figure in Quebec philosophy in the inter-war years and in the period just after World War II. Louis Lachance, perhaps the most important philosopher writing in Montreal at the time, was more conservative, in *some* sense, than Gilson.

But the *detailed* study of the work of these Quebec philosophers is really only beginning—though the main parameters, as we noted in our preface, have been marked out by the studies of Roland Houde, Yvan Lamonde, and others. It is probable that there are surprises in store. De Koninck evidently believed that Maritain was altogether too much the child of the liberal, individualist enlightenment and that Maritain in the end slighted the community. Lachance was concerned with ideas of nationalism, culture, community, and individual, in ways which raised questions inherently more complex and perhaps more profound than those which animated Maritain. It is very likely to turn out that, though Gilson more closely expresses the surface values of the community of liberal Catholics in English Canada, Lachance and perhaps de Koninck were more closely involved in the deepest concerns which have always tended to unite all Canadians. It is increasingly hard for those educated in post-enlightenment individualist traditions to understand these concerns as they are expressed by de Koninck and Lachance, and many young Quebec intellectuals have tended to write off most of the philosophers of inter-war and post-war periods as simple-minded pedlars of Thomist clichés. As Quebeckers become more and more interested in their own past, it is likely that a measure of fundamental unity in Canadian philosophy will emerge.

One of the difficulties is that reason appears in complex disguises. But there is, for instance, a strong resemblance between central features of the political philosophies of Lachance and Watson: Both were concerned to combat excessive individualism while maintaining a strong sense of human rights and liberties; both were concerned to develop and defend a kind of nationalism which would be compatible with a world order; both saw human societies as something which must develop historically and cannot just be made to order as the social contract theorists have tended to suppose. Each used a metaphysical system—an all-encompassing world picture—as a central device. Within that picture the facts about men, communities, and history were seen to make sense in a way which suggested the conclusions being argued for. The way of making the orders intelligible depended upon the metaphysical structures and since the structures were different, it has not been obvious how close the political theories were.[1]

Watson and Lachance, however, were evidently responding to a situation which was clearer in Canada than in most parts of the world. Canada's position in history, geography, and trade created strong relations of dependence while the internal complexities of Canadian society prohibited assimilation into any of the adjoining cultures. For Lachance, a Quebec nationalist, the tension was particularly acute and much of his writing concerns the relations between nationalism and universal human history and between the individual and the community. But Charles de Koninck, a Belgian by birth, expressed in his contribution to the Tremblay commission a strong sense of those tensions and a clear response to them. Watson's philosophical federalism is not so different though Lachance would not have been so sanguine about the choice of the British Commonwealth as a model for

1   Leslie Armour, "Watson, Lachance and the Two Solitudes," a paper presented to the Canadian Philosophical Association, Saskatoon, June 1979. An extended version will appear in the forthcoming *The Idea of Canada* to be published by Steel Rail Publishing, Ottawa.

the solution of such problems. Here we see reason responding to the political situation in ways that clearly illustrate the central features of the culture though, of course, many central features—especially the choice of metaphysical models—are surely dictated by considerations which transcend the immediate Canadian culture.

Political structures are only one of the features of a culture, however, and one may often see it more clearly when the flags are not flying. Rupert Lodge, responding in Winnipeg to the inherent pluralism of prairie society, was confronting in his classrooms a situation utterly unlike that of the Oxford dons he left behind. Thus his philosophy, with its insistence on an irreducible plurality of world schemes, is characteristically unlike any which were produced in more homogeneous cultures during the nineteen-thirties and it is equally unlike the mainstream American philosophies of the period which (like the political theories of Dewey) recognized but sought to overcome that pluralism. Lodge is searching for the *limits* of reason in order to establish a truce between the combatant parties so that he can create, in an educational setting, a common heritage while preserving a cultural plurality.

John Macdonald, working seven hundred miles north-west, on the northern edge of the dense settlements, saw the challenge in a different focus: For him the problem was the maintenance of civilization, the preservation of social continuity. Against the Deweyite notion that the child might create his own educational world in response to biological and social needs, Macdonald insisted on the deliberate, articulate transmission of a coherent body of information and belief: Reason in his view could discern patterns in history and apply them to current experience, rendering experience intelligible and knowledge capable of deliberate transmission. The argument between Macdonald and Dewey is thus not only one between one who believes that societies develop and cannot be made by fiat and one who tends toward a much more constructionist view of society, but also between a man living in a settled community with well articulated culture and one living in Edmonton, a community with many recent immigrants, whose culture, always in the making, was always in peril. Dewey could afford to abandon articulate reason for a system which emphasized immediate response. Macdonald felt that he could not.

Reason was also called upon to respond to more basic challenges. Blewett witnessed the breaking of some of the thin prairie soils, saw first hand some of the pathetic confrontations of aboriginal societies and technology, lived in Massachusetts long enough to get a clear sense of the possibilities of still newer technologies. He could see that the fragile Canadian environment was headed for disaster unless the notion that nature is merely something to be used at our will could be eradicated. Again, he draws constantly on the whole of Canadian experience, personal, literary, political, which suggests that nature is neither public convenience nor romantic idol but something to be understood and worked with. How does reason cope with such a problem? Essentially, again, the device which Blewett uses is a metaphysical system. He wants to find a picture of the world in which the world is not a mere plaything of God's and not a mere machine. He wants to find a view of the world within which, once again, animal life comes to have a point beyond its possibilities for human food, clothing, and amusement. He struggles to adapt an Hegelian theory of development (but to tame and strip it of its dark, Germanic overtones). Blewett uses reason essentially to create an order in which the facts as he observes them can finally be made to make sense.

The details of such processes of reasoning come out frequently when even more basic challenges emerge. William Lyall, for instance, sees the great challenge of a highly abstract and formalized reason in the ultimate split between reason and emotion. He therefore seeks to examine in as much detail as he can muster the process in which reason becomes separated from emotion and concludes that the separation detaches man from reality. Had he lived to see a world in which men have used technologized reason to create devices capable of destroying everyone alive several times over, he would surely have felt vindicated. But the challenge he leaves for us is the challenge of finding, again, the relation between reason as a human activity and reason as a regulative device. The contention we have been making here, of course, is that an examination of the uses of philosophical reason in the Canadian context suggests that the connection is to be found in processes of assigning meanings. That that challenge is particularly strong in the Canadian environment where a conviction of the necessity of social continuity clashed continuously with the needs of a new environment goes without saying. We watched it at work in our study of the remarkable development of James Beaven's mind as he came to terms with democracy, Indians, and even Methodists and Americans. We saw it in the struggles of Paxton Young to create a secular morality from within which he could finally judge the controversies circumstances had created (first in Scotland and then, even more confusingly, in Canada) in his church.

Most impressively, one can see reason making those transitions in the philosophy of John Clark Murray as Murray moves from the philosophy of Sir William Hamilton to a developed idealism and as he pits his traditional view of society and social history against the need to understand the developing industrial community in Montreal. Again, the communitarian convictions, the opposition to a developing class structure, the insistence on an ultimate pluralism, play important parts in the development of his thought. We can watch the same processes at work in the development of the thought of Jacob Gould Schurman.

In the end, of course, reason was called upon to question the whole direction of intellectual activity. Brett was a friend of the sciences, a partisan of the new science of psychology, and yet almost everything he wrote is a call for a return to historical reason—to a reason which sees itself as a developing thing, which takes its meaning from history, and which sees science as another human activity in an historical context. Brett, in a sense, was ahead of his time. Because he saw the limitations of technology and of the kind of abstract reasoning which went into it, he was able to sense its prospective failures—though his complaints are gentle and his warnings polite. Brett uses other people's metaphysical schemes to show the limitations of reason as well as its development, though he resists any open, explicit scheme of his own.

Innis, by contrast, is in a full revolt against a massive historical movement which has its origins in the beginnings of "modern" thought, in the separation of fact and value in the seventeenth and eighteenth centuries, and in the notion that the most fundamental kind of knowledge is to be found in the direct introspection of the individual human mind. Here reason is, once again, not the application of formal rules to extract conclusion from premise—for the formal rules as we know them are part and parcel of the scheme which Innis wants to call into question—but the use of reason to create new patterms within which new meanings might be discerned.

Finally, therefore, we may begin to see why Canadian philosophy has tended to be ignored by those committed to the philosophical schemes which have been most popular in other western cultures in the period since World War I. The most popular (though by no means all) of those philosophies can be divided into two sorts: the "analytic" philosophy of the English-speaking world and the various forms of Kierkegaardian fideism, post-Husserlian phenomenology, and existentialism which have been popular in continental Europe. The first essentially saw reason as abstract, formal, rule-bound, and associated with science and technology. Its paradigms have been mathematics and physics. The tendency has been to regard questions which cannot be solved within those paradigms as essentially foolish or even meaningless. Even in the "soft" forms of analytic philosophy which date from the later Wittgenstein, the powers of reason have been largely confined to those realms while traditional philosophical questions have frequently been reduced to misunderstandings of the ordinary language. The alternative uses of reason have only recently become of central concern. The European response—apart from that of Husserl himself and of his more orthodox followers—has tended to centre on a revolt against technological and formal reason and to take the form, often enough, of a revolt against reason itself. However different the Canadian philosophers discussed here have been from one another, they have tended both to reject technological and formal reason as incomplete, misleading, and inadequate and to make use of reason in quite other guises. They have been the partisans of reason—but partisans who have held that reason cannot be confined to a straight-jacket, even one made in Vienna, Harvard, Cambridge, or the California Institute of Technology. Surely, they will now repay a little study.

AUTHOR AND TITLE
INDEX

WORKS REFERRED to in the text will be found in this index. Some long titles have been abbreviated. Bibliographical information will *usually* be found on the page indicated by the first entry. Titles include books, chapter titles, articles, unpublished manuscripts, archival notes, and theses. The nature of the item is described on the indicated pages. This index includes only works cited.[1] A complete bibliography of philosophy in Canada is in preparation by Professors Jack Stevenson and John Slater at the University of Toronto and Roland Houde at the University of Québec at Trois Rivières. The present authors have supplied to the project at Toronto the information at their disposal, and no attempt has been made to duplicate their work.

1   The following works are among those consulted but not cited in the text: Yvan Lamonde, *Philosophie et son enseignement au Québec, 1665-1920* (Montreal: Hurtubise, 1980); John Watson, *Christianity and Idealism: The Christian Ideal of Life in its Relations to the Greek and Jewish Ideals and to Modern Philosophy* (New York: Macmillan, 1896), *Kant and his English Critics: A Comparison of Critical and Empirical Philosophy* (Glasgow: James Maclehose, 1881), and *Philosophical Basis of Religion: A Series of Lectures* (Glasgow: J. Maclehose and Sons, 1907); and Clifford Williams, "The Epistemology of John Watson" (Ph.D. Thesis, University of Toronto, 1966), and "The Social Philosophy of Two Canadians: W. C. Keirstead and John Watson" (M.A. Thesis, University of Western Ontario, 1953).

TITLE INDEX

F ULL BIBLIOGRAPHICAL information will usually be found on the first pages cited. A few very long titles have been abbreviated for the index; full titles will be found in the citations. Periodicals are listed here by their titles.

523

GENERAL INDEX